THE TEACHINGS OF
Spencer W. Kimball

THE TEACHINGS OF
Spencer W. Kimball

Twelfth President
of
The Church of Jesus Christ
of Latter-day Saints

Edited by
Edward L. Kimball

Bookcraft
Salt Lake City, Utah

Library of Congress Catalog Card Number: 82-73497
ISBN 0-88494-472-1

3 4 5 6 7 8 9 10   89 88 87 86 85 84 83

Lithographed in the United States of America
PUBLISHERS PRESS
Salt Lake City, Utah

The editor received substantial assistance in the editorial process from Mary Kimball, Miles S. Kimball, and Spencer E. Kimball, who together spent hundreds of hours helping in the selection and organization of excerpts to be included in this work.

Contents

Righteous Living

The Church

Preface

A book of the teachings of Spencer W. Kimball could have any of several purposes. It could serve as a source of proof-texts, wherein President Kimball is cited for his support of teachings being put forward. It could serve as a coherent text on the gospel as perceived in its many facets by a single careful student of the scriptures and Church teachings. It could serve as a collection of memorable passages for inspirational reading. It could serve as a memorial to the apostolic career of the man, showing what he talked about and how he expressed himself.

This book is none of these and all of them. Multiple criteria have been used in determining which passages to include. A quotation might be included because it represents a significant viewpoint on Church doctrine, because it is a useful summary of even elementary propositions, because it provides an eloquent expression that might enhance others' speaking or uplift or move the reader, or because it reveals the interests and values of a remarkable man of God.

In his office at home President Kimball has several sets of black binders. One set contains his journals, which were the primary source for his biography, the book *Spencer W. Kimball,* published in 1977. Another set, occupying 4½ feet of shelf space, contains copies of most of his prepared sermons up to the time he became Church President, along with some "teaching" letters. That material, supplemented by some other writings and sermons which appeared in the various Church periodicals, constitutes the primary source for this volume. His secretary provided copies of unpublished addresses delivered after the last days of 1973, when he succeeded to the Presidency. Altogether, about seven hundred sources were reviewed in the preparation of this book—sermons, articles, books, and letters.

These sources do not exhaust the body of the teachings of Spencer W. Kimball, for he has given thousands of unrecorded talks at stake conferences, funeral services, firesides, and so on. The unavailability of those sources does not detract greatly from this collection, however, because enough extemporaneous talks at conferences and funeral services and dedications were recorded, transcribed, and then considered for inclusion in this collection to suggest that the fugitive material tended to be repetitious of other statements and less carefully formulated than those he prepared in more permanent form.

There are several things this book does not do. For instance, it does not indicate the frequency with which President Kimball has relied on the scriptures for authority and illustration, because most such passages have been omitted. Readers looking for scriptural authority will need to go to other sources, preferably to the scriptures themselves, which have been made highly accessible with the publication of the Topical Guide and the Index.

The excerpts used in this book similarly do not reflect the frequency with which he quoted others. In the selection of passages for inclusion, preference was given to *his* contributions to our understanding. His filing cabinets at home bulge with files of magazine clippings on subjects that interest him or of passages copied from books. A whole set of binders on his shelves are labeled "Sermon Seeds." His wide reading has not been for his entertainment, nor for learning alone, but for ideas he could use in his primary mission of teaching the gospel and persuading people to live righteously.

Nor of course can this collection carry the flavor and continuity of a complete book or sermon on a particular theme. Those who wish to see Spencer W. Kimball writing at length should read *The Miracle of Forgiveness.* Those who wish to read full sermons should read the conference reports. A selection of thirty-four edited sermons can be found in *Faith Precedes the Miracle. The Teachings of Spencer W. Kimball* quotes from them all and from still other talks and letters.

Certain omissions have been deliberately made. As an example, the ready availability of President Kimball's principal book, *The Miracle of Forgiveness,* led to relatively sparing use of passages from that source. Many personal anecdotes were omitted because they had already been embodied in his biography. With space at a premium, these gave way to other material.

In numerous meetings over the years, President Kimball has talked about the Apostasy and the Restoration. Relatively little space is devoted to those subjects in this book because his presentations to nonmembers of the Church on apostasy and restoration are relatively straightforward recitations of the standard Church viewpoints, sometimes eloquent, but offering little that is unique. Rather than focusing on conversion of nonmembers, he has sought to convert members. He is the preacher of righteousness to those who have already accepted the Latter-day Saint understanding of the gospel of Christ.

Sometimes an entire sermon did not lend itself to excerpting. Such sermons operated not so much to communicate information as to evoke a feeling. That does not mean they were not important as sermons, but only that they served a different purpose. For example, "Hidden Wedges" (66-03) teaches the dangers of procrastinating repentance. The sermon was effective enough to be printed separately in tens of thousands of copies, but it is really not quotable in excerpts. Others of the same sort are " 'Wisdom and Great Treasures' " (68-11) and "Glimpses of Heaven" (71-18), which both reflect the joys of righteous living. (The numbers following these titles and each quotation in the book refer to the sources listed in the back of the book; in the case of sermons, the first two digits indicate the year.)

The quantity of material included on any subject is not necessarily proportionate to its importance in the body of sermons, since in subjects frequently addressed there is much overlapping— surprisingly little exact repetition, but extensive restating of ideas. When there were several similar statements, usually only one has been included here, the one which was most complete, most succinct, or most eloquent. All statements had equal standing as candidates for inclusion regardless of when they were delivered, because the objective was not so much to provide a manual of authoritative pronouncements as to illustrate the ideas which Spencer W. Kimball has espoused over a long life of teaching.

In preparing this book the editor obtained or made copies of all the materials listed under Sources. One of his three assistants then read each of these and marked passages for possible inclusion, assigning each to one or another of 103 subject headings. The editor then read the sources again for the same purpose. The items were

xvi   *Preface*

then organized and headings provided. Compression of such a large body of material into a single volume required a very high degree of selectivity.

In the inclusions, omissions are indicated by ellipsis points, but a new sentence after ellipsis points starts with a capital even though an initial word or phrase, such as *But, And,* or *On the other hand,* has been omitted.

Naturally, some of what is said in the sermons is rhetorical over-statement. For example, one sermon says that deciding whom to marry "is perhaps the most vital of all the decisions" one makes, whereas such a decision surely ranks behind the decision to follow Christ. We should allow President Kimball to speak without his being held to the most literal possible interpretation. Just as scriptures can be wrested out of their original intent, so can President Kimball's statements. The only fair interpretation puts the particular passage in the context of his whole teachings, which show remarkable con-sistency in content and style.

It would be difficult to identify a statement with the appropriate period of his life, except perhaps by subject matter. His choice of that matter flowed in large degree from his Church assignments. From 1947 to 1973 he often talked about the Lamanites because of his long-time assignment as head of the Church Indian Committee. His assignments to work on the Missionary Committee and with moral problems during much of that period are also reflected in the emphasis on these subjects in his sermons. By contrast, he spoke relatively little about temple work or welfare principles while he was an Apostle. But when he became President of the Church his concerns broadened, so that since then he has often spoken of temple work and of welfare principles. One unchanging thing, however, is his expression of testimony about Christ and the importance of living the commandments generally.

In earlier years, he maintained voluminous correspondence with many people. His letters sometimes were lengthy, carefully reasoned tracts seeking to persuade—encouraging a disheartened missionary, following up on counseling with a homosexual, challenging a lax

Church member, pointing out the hazards of marrying outside the faith. Some of these letters he later used as the basis for sermons (see, for example, 71-19, 77-22, 77-31).

Some quotations date from the time when he was in a stake presidency (1924-1943); most come from talks given while he was a member of the Quorum of the Twelve (1943-1973); others come from sermons given as Church President (since 1973). From this and the source information the reader can generally distinguish the speaker's status at the time, if that seems significant.

Of the many people to whom thanks is due, special appreciation goes to D. Arthur Haycock for assistance in gathering the materials on which the book is based; he has served President Kimball as personal secretary with extraordinary dedication, often at great personal sacrifice. Special thanks go also to Evelyn Bee Madsen Kimball, who has been a valued sounding board and unfailingly patient during many months of intense work.

Most of all, appreciation is expressed to President Kimball himself as the originator of the material and for his approving its publication in this form. He has been pleased at the prospect of this volume and has frequently expressed interest in its progress.

While in quantity the book incorporates only a tiny faction of his speaking and writing, it contains the essence of that lifelong effort to teach the gospel of Jesus Christ. It is now offered to further that same objective.

Introduction

President Kimball's patriarchal blessing, which he has quoted on occasion for its indication that he had a special calling to serve the Lamanites, says more than just that. Note the several elements: "(1) You will preach the gospel to many people, (2) but more especially to the Lamanites, (3) for the Lord will bless you with the gift of the language and power to portray before that people the gospel in great plainness."

As to (1), the scope of his preaching effort, there is no leader of the Church, past or contemporary, who has preached to so many people. As to (2), he has reached out especially to the Lamanites, the North American Indians and all the peoples of Central and South America and Polynesia who share that heritage. As to (3), one cannot doubt that he has spoken with power and plainness both to Lamanites and to the rest of Israel.

In a letter to a relative (3/15/63) he expressed his own perception of his role as preacher: "I hope you know that I feel most humble in my position and I do not presume, or at least I think I do not presume. I do not claim to be a scholar [and] I do not claim to understand fully the scriptures nor the program. I feel a great obligation to motivate the people. I have no desire to entertain them. In all my sermons, my objective is to get people to doing things, the good things, the right things. Knowledge is of no value unless used. When I know the requirements of the Lord and see how far that we his people come from fully meeting those requirements, it gives me a great urge to do all in my power to help the people of his Church to measure up to all the requirements."

His perception shown in this letter is accurate on all counts. Through his sermons runs an obvious and genuine humility; he does not prate his own righteousness and does not speak dogmatically about scriptural interpretations. He makes no pretension to being a theologian. His emphasis is on doing, not just on knowing. He has always felt that ordinary efforts—his or anyone else's—are not good enough for the Lord's program.

He has always worried over his talks, especially those to be given at general conference and at Brigham Young University. For the conferences he has sometimes prepared two or three different sermons, searching for the right subject, and he might be unsure which he would use until the last moment. His concern at BYU has been how to approach what he feared might be a critical audience. For such a relatively sophisticated audience he wanted to put his message in the best possible form, so that its content would not be inappropriately discounted because of some weakness in presentation.

Though not considering himself a theologian, he has come to some conclusions which differ at least in emphasis from interpretations frequently taught in the Church. For example, in explaining the parable of the Prodigal Son he has stressed the superiority of the faithful son over the prodigal, while detracting nothing from the desirability of the prodigal's return nor the father's happiness at seeing the lost one found.

Again, he has concluded that when Christ said on the cross, "Father, forgive them; for they know not what they do," he was referring to the soldiers and not to the people and leaders who had cried, "His blood be on us, and on our children." The latter could not be forgiven when they were not repentant. (See MF 167, 280.) Christ in his charity had no personal wish for vindictiveness, but for the sinner to avoid the consequences of his act without repentance would go against the order of heaven. The immutable law is that men cannot be saved *in* their sins. Similarly he concluded that when Christ dealt with the woman taken in adultery he did not forgive her, but admonished her to go her way and repent so that she could be forgiven. (See MF 165.) And the thief on the cross received not forgiveness, but a promise of opportunity to hear the gospel and repent fully in the world of spirits. (See MF 166.) If the thief, who had acknowledged Christ, was not forgiven immediately, why should it be thought that those who had not acknowledged him but had wrought his death and denied his divinity would receive forgiveness without repentance?

At the other end of the spectrum he undertook to qualify Joseph Smith's assertion that an adulterer cannot enter the celestial kingdom, pointing out that if taken without qualification the statement would be inconsistent with the scriptures and the general tenor of the gospel. An adulterer, despite his grievous sin, can obtain forgiveness if truly repentant. (See MF 347-352.)

He has made a somewhat different point in an impassioned defense of Peter, whom he calls "my brother." In light of Peter's show of bravery in the Garden when Christ was taken and his boldness after the Crucifixion, President Kimball expressed doubt that Peter's denial of Christ was an act of cowardice. He suggested several other explanations, but concluded that in any event Peter's years of powerful ministry would eclipse any moment of weakness. (See 71-12.)

Spencer W. Kimball has been willing to tackle subjects which were either unpopular or called upon the people for substantial sacrifice: he expressed disapproval of hunting for sport, criticized delay of marriage and child-bearing, decried abortion except in extreme cases, called for every normal young man in the Church and many young women and older couples to serve a full-time mission, criticized the elevation of reason above faith, denounced war and the building up of arms, taught that homosexuals can change, condemned placing personal interest and convenience (including comfort, education, and money) ahead of the Lord's program, and declared that only men's lack of faith and diligence prevents the rapid filling of the whole earth with the "stone cut out of the mountain without hands."

In his frequent preaching against sin, President Kimball has persuasively made the case that sin is not just bad, it is foolish. It constitutes the worst in selfishness and shortsightedness. He has also asserted persistently the possibility of change and the capacity of men and women to become godlike. Man's responsibility in life is to do what he knows is right, without equivocation, knowing that God will bless all such righteous efforts.

If one had to compress the essence of a life's teaching into two dominant themes, these might be that keys to the heavens are in having faith on Jesus Christ and in taking charge of one's life.

Most of President Kimball's sermons would not be termed eloquent, though some surely are. He put content ahead of form and was often willing to repeat a point again and again to insure that the message could not be missed.

After becoming Church President he typically spoke five times at each general conference and at each area conference. As an Apostle he had usually spoken only once at each general conference (the great increase in frequency of major public addresses after he became President can easily be seen by examining the list of sources). Sermons as an Apostle usually were careful single-subject expositions. As President he often shifted to exhortation covering a wide range of subjects, probably because the President bears responsibility for all Church programs and wants to give guidance on a wide variety of issues. There is reason to fear, too, that speaking on a single subject might cause people to give undue emphasis to that, to the neglect of other matters of importance.

When he became Church President, President Kimball's speaking style also changed. It now contained less doctrinal development and less use of scripture, more use of personal anecdote and more direct admonition and exhortation. Despite his personal humility, he assumed a prophetic role, speaking with more direct authority.

In recent years his sermons, particularly at area conferences, have tended to fall into a pattern, with emphasis on temples, missionary work, and rearing families in righteousness. But in some instances he broke from the pattern. For example, in Bogotá in 1977 he delivered a strong statement about avoiding extreme political solutions, such as revolution. (See 77-22.) And in Lakeland, Florida, he delivered a jeremiad on the need for repentance in the world. (See 80-23.) These seem to indicate that in the midst of routine he responded to a special stimulus, whether it was a humanly perceived need for a particular message or a divine inspiration to that same end.

In regard to his own calling as prophet, President Kimball shows a wonderful blend of certitude and humility. He speaks boldly what he feels God would have him say, while he acknowledges that the great respect he receives attaches largely to his office and not to himself. He has made the suggestion that he was called as an Apostle and prophet because there were so many ordinary people in the Church who needed an ordinary prophet.

The reading of the whole body of this man's teaching is at once sobering and exhilarating. The tremendous effort it represents sobers anyone who has done enough writing to know the pain of composition. Spencer W. Kimball did this writing on top of a heavy load of conference visits, counseling people with problems, and administrative work of the Church.

In reading so extended a discussion of gospel topics by a single person, one feels enlightened not only about the gospel but also about the person's mode of thinking and his perspective. Finally one gains an exhilarating sense of how quickly the Lord's work could sweep forward toward its destined end if only large numbers of people had a fraction of the dedication of this man.

There is no doubt about the devotion, earnestness, power, or humility of Spencer W. Kimball. The study of his life's writings, coupled with knowledge of his personal qualities and close observation of the consistency between what he says and what he does, fortifies a testimony that he is a prophet of God, as worthy as any mortal to be the Lord's spokesman.

CHAPTER 1

The Godhead

God, the Eternal Father

God lives. God, our Heavenly Father—Elohim—lives. That is an absolute truth. All four billion of the children of men on the earth might be ignorant of him and his attributes and his powers, but he still lives. All the people on the earth might deny him and disbelieve, but he lives in spite of them. They may have their own opinions, but he still lives, and his form, powers, and attributes do not change according to men's opinions. In short, opinion alone has no power in the matter of an absolute truth. He still lives. And Jesus Christ is the Son of God, the Almighty, the Creator, the Master of the only true way of life—the gospel of Jesus Christ. The intellectual may rationalize him out of existence and the unbeliever may scoff, but Christ still lives and guides the destinies of his people. That is an absolute truth; there is no gainsaying.

The watchmaker in Switzerland, with materials at hand, made the watch that was found in the sand in a California desert. The people who found the watch had never been to Switzerland, nor seen the watchmaker, nor seen the watch made. The watchmaker still existed, no matter the extent of their ignorance or experience. If the watch had a tongue, it might even lie and say, "There is no watchmaker." That would not alter the truth.

If men are really humble, they will realize that they *discover,* but do not *create,* truth. (77-31)

Worship is in man's nature. Man is naturally a religious being. His heart instinctively seeks for God whether he reverences the sacred cow or prays to the sun or moon; whether he kneels before wood and stone images, or prays in secret to his Heavenly Father, he is satisfying an inborn urge. (63-04)

Without teaching or training, man inclines toward the infinite. It seems to be as integral a part of his nature as breathing or eating.

If the instinctively religious man is in darkness and cannot perceive and know the True and Living God, he will then select and elevate to godship such things as he considers supernatural and super powerful. The river overflows its banks causing loss of life and property and the savage will name it a god and worship and propitiate it with sacrifices. The mountain belches forth smoke, gases and rivers of molten lava and the native calls it god and throws into the seething, boiling volcano a beautiful maiden or an innocent child to appease the wrath of this god. Or he may fashion of wood or stone or marble or of precious metals a god before whom he will kneel and worship.

And so it is fundamental in the life of man to worship and to have a god on whom he may bestow adoration and to whom sacrifices may be offered. (63-03)

There is pathos in the present struggle of heralded theologians, shuffling their feet in the dark with sweat and toil, in their quest for something to satisfy their inborn needs of a God to worship, to admire, to love, to lean upon in perilous times. It is sad to see them groping their way through the darkness only to find nothing at the end of their trail. . . .

If all the theologians, the great thinkers, the philosophers, and the so-called Christian atheists in their intensive and continuous search were coming to a unity of faith or doctrine, then the world would sit up and take notice, but when their ideas run from mythology to personality, from reality to vagueness, how can one have much respect for their claims. (66-05)

Man can know God. It is not only a privilege to know God, it is a necessity if man wishes to gain highest blessings. "It is the first principle of the Gospel to know for a certainty the character of God...." (Joseph Smith.)

The Lord has promised to make himself and these mysteries known to all flesh on condition that they reach and search in humility and teachableness. (66-05)

Knowledge of God comes not by reason alone. As servants of the Lord, we proclaim to all the world that any man, every man may know of God, and participate in the great saving and exalting work of God. But that man must know that he cannot make automobiles with a physician's instruments; build Aswan dams with spoons. He cannot conquer the desert with a guitar; nor build Empire State buildings in chemical laboratories; nor can he create a God out of his imaginations. Our God, our Creator, lives and he must be disgusted at puny man's theological conclusions. (66-05)

Ignorance of some does not prove God unknowable. One theologian indicated it was impossible for man to find God or know God. This is like saying: "I have never climbed Mt. Ararat—no one can climb Ararat; or, I have never bathed in the clear warm waters of the Adriatic—there is no Adriatic Sea; or, I have never seen the wild life in Kreuger Park—there is no Kreuger Park; or, I have always had health—therefore, the pain which people claim must be a figment of their imaginations. I have never astronauted into space, therefore, no one can speed through space." How different then is it to say I have never heard nor seen God—therefore, no man has ever seen nor heard God nor walked with him. How presumptuous and arrogant for any man to say God is unapproachable, unknowable, unseeable, unhearable because that one himself has not prepared himself for the experience. (66-05)

Father and Son are distinct. We declare in all solemnity the reality of God the Eternal Father and his Son Jesus Christ, as like as any father and son, yet distinct individuals. On more than one occasion the Christ has made known that a knowledge and acquaintance with God is basic to exaltation. . . .

There are three Gods: the Eternal Father, Elohim, to whom we pray; Christ or Jehovah; and the Holy Ghost who testifies of the others and witnesses to us the truth of all things.

Many seem to delight in confusing the matter with their rationalizations and human calculations. The Father and the Son, in whose image we are created, separate and distinct beings, have identified themselves through the ages. (64-03)

Men need protection to see God. To know God, one must be aware of the person and attributes, power, and glory of God the Father and God the Christ. Moses declares he ". . . saw God face to face, and he talked with him." (Moses 1:2.) This experience of Moses is in harmony with the scripture which says:

"For no man has seen God at any time in the flesh, except quickened by the Spirit of God. Neither can any natural man abide the presence of God, neither after the carnal mind." (D&C 67:11-12.)

It must be obvious then that to endure the glory of the Father or of the glorified Christ, a mortal being must be translated or otherwise fortified. Moses, a prophet of God, held the protecting Holy Priesthood: ". . . and the glory of God was upon Moses; therefore Moses could endure his presence." (Moses 1:2.)

Deep shade or smoked glass can modify the withering heat and burning rays of the midday sun. There is a protective force which God brings into play when he exposes his human servants to the glories of his person and his works. . . .

It is significant to note that when the protection from such transcendent glory was relaxed, that Moses was left weak and near helpless.

The scripture says: "And the presence of God withdrew from Moses, that his glory was not upon Moses; and Moses was left unto himself. And . . . he fell unto the earth." (Moses 1:9.) Many hours elapsed before he could regain his natural strength. (64-03)

God is omniscient. There are no corners so dark, no deserts so uninhabited, no canyons so remote, no automobiles so hidden, no homes so tight and shut in but that the all-seeing One can penetrate and observe. The faithful have always known this. The doubters should take a sober look at the situation in the light of the electronic devices which have come into increasing use in the last few years and which are often delicate and tiny but so powerful as almost to annihilate man's personal privacy....

In the light of these modern marvels can anyone doubt that God hears prayers and discerns secret thoughts? A printer's camera can make a negative three feet square. What magnification! If human eyes and ears can so penetrate one's personal life, what may we expect from perfected men with perfected vision! (MF 110-11)

God is good. God is good, so good in fact that we can hardly conceive the depth and richness of his goodness. He is just, so just that we mortals cannot comprehend the fairness of his justice. I am sure that no mortal will ever fail to receive every blessing and glory which he merits. Mortal death cannot rob him. There will be a way, and every promise of God will be fulfilled. A virtuous, progressive, active young man will sacrifice no blessing to which he was entitled by his (to us) premature passing into eternity. We may not understand fully just how it will be accomplished, but we may know that it will be. Remember what the Lord himself said: "Eye hath not seen, nor ear heard, neither have entered into the heart of man, the things which God hath prepared for them that love him." (1 Corinthians 2:9.)

Can we not trust in the goodness of the Lord? Remember that he is the Father also of this son. He is the Parent of the living part, you of the tabernacle only. Will he not be infinitely more concerned with the welfare of this son than we mortals could ever be? Can we not know this: "His purposes fail not, neither are there any who can stay his hand"? (D&C 76:3.) There is no tragedy except in sin. Let us know therefore that life is eternal, and that God doeth all things well; and this righteous son, the offspring of God, was not born for a day, a decade, or a century, but for eternity. Only his own lack of righteousness could ever deprive him of any blessing promised by the Lord. Thy son liveth and continues to radiate life, not death; light, not darkness; commencement, not termination; assurance, not uncertainty; joy eternal, not sorrow; sweetness, not bitterness; youthful maturity, not senility; progress, not stoppage; sunshine, not clouds; clearness of vision, not confusion and dimness; fulfilment, not frustration; an open gate with light ahead, not barred windows with darkness beyond. (45-03)

The Lord Jesus Christ

Christ is central to the gospel and the Church. The gospel of Jesus Christ knows no borders nor bounds. At the center of it all stands Jesus Christ, the resurrected Son of our Heavenly Father. (77-27)

You mention that you feel that Christ is obscured by other things in our teachings. I think you again do not fully understand. May I explain it this way: I know a sect which teaches only one thing, namely, that all one needs do is to believe that Jesus is the Christ and he is saved. Naturally, with only one simple doctrine, they mention the name of Christ in their every sentence.

In the enlarged program which he has given us there are so many truths and doctrines, so far-reaching and all-inclusive, that as we discuss them in their broad aspects we share our time and attention between his person and his teachings which are legion. The Savior in his teachings gave whole sermons without mentioning his Father, then he would give the credit to his divine parent. This might have sometimes given rise to the feeling that we were not thinking of Christ's mission as basic. Of course it is. When we take away the foundation, the whole house falls. He is the chief cornerstone. He is the head of the kingdom—these are his followers—this his Church—these his doctrines and ordinances—these his commandments. You have likely never heard a sermon or a prayer or a testimony that was not given in the name of Jesus Christ our Redeemer. Many of my sermons are directed almost wholly to the life and ministry of the Lord and all of them to his teachings and commandments. We place him on a pedestal as no other group I know of. To us he is not only the Son of God, he is also a God and we are subject to him. And I am sure that no people in Christianity are so ready to sacrifice and consecrate their time, talents, money, and themselves to Christ and to his program on the earth. (1/9/48)

No matter how much we say of him, it is still too little.
He is not only the Carpenter, the Nazarene, the Galilean, but Jesus Christ, the God of this earth, the Son of God, but most importantly, our Savior, our Redeemer. (74-37)

As the living, verdant spring follows the dismal, deathlike winter, all nature proclaims the divinity of the risen Lord, that he was Creator, that he is the Savior of the world, that he is the very Son of God. (69-02)

I add my own testimony. I know that Jesus Christ is the Son of the living God and that he was crucified for the sins of the world.
He is my friend, my Savior, my Lord, my God. (78-29)

Men may know Christ. The ultimate and greatest of all knowledge, then, is to know God and his program for our exaltation. We may know him by sight, by sound, by feeling. While relatively few ever *do* really know him, everyone may know him, not only prophets—ancient and modern—but, as he said: "Every soul who forsaketh his sins and cometh unto me, and calleth on my name, and obeyeth my voice, and keepeth my commandments, shall see my face and know that I am." (D&C 93:1.)
If men qualify, they have this unalterable promise from their Redeemer. (68-11)

We are happy in our knowledge that the God of this universe is a God of revelation. Our Lord communicates his mind and will to his children on earth. If we seek it, he will reveal himself more and more and in greater and greater fulness, and we shall comprehend him as well as it is possible for mortal man to comprehend God. We cannot worship a being of our own creation or of the imaginations of our minds. We worship a being who lives, who has created, who communicates to us his character and his attributes and the greatness of his being. (73-05)

Christ is the creator. The Christ declared himself to be the Lord God Almighty, Christ the Lord, the beginning and the end, the Redeemer of the world, Jesus the Christ, the mighty one of Israel, the Creator, the Son of the living God, Jehovah.

The Father Elohim declares Jesus to be "Mine Only Begotten Son, the word of my power." And twice, at least, at the Jordan baptism and then on the Mount of Transfiguration, he declared:

"This is my beloved Son in whom I am well pleased" (see Mark 1:11; Luke 3:22), and stated that "the worlds were made by him: Men were made by him: All things were made by him, and through him and of him" (see Moses 1:33). (64-03)

Christ is Jehovah. Through childhood . . . I had the mistaken idea that the God of the scriptures was Elohim, the Father, and that all through the Old Testament we were reading of the Father when the prophets spoke of "God" or "The Lord." . . .

I was surprised and perhaps shocked a little when I learned that it was the Son, Jehovah, or his messengers who led Abraham from Ur to Palestine, to Egypt, and back to the land of Palestine. I did not realize that it was Jesus Christ, or Jehovah, who inspired the long line of prophets in their leadership of the people of God through those centuries.

I did not know that Jehovah, or the future Christ, was the God of the burning bush when Moses received his call to spectacular service. . . .

As I came to realize that this world was largely entrusted to Jehovah, I was still greatly inspired to know that Elohim, the Father, had never totally abandoned us here. It pleased me greatly to know that even though his responsibilities were nigh unlimited, that there were a few specific and most important times when the Father came on our earth. (74-08)

Christ chose to experience mortality's grief. Perhaps he could have died long years earlier and accomplished the first of the requirements: resurrection and immortality. But it seemed that he must live a long and dangerous life until he should have established firmly the way to perfection.

For more than three decades, he lived a life of hazard and jeopardy. From Herod's bloody debacle in the merciless murder of Bethlehem's infants to Herod's and Pilate's merciless giving him to the human wolves, Jesus was in constant danger. Even after his early death, it seemed that he could not conscientiously leave the earth until he had trained further his leaders. Forty days he remained to prepare the apostles in leadership and the people in sainthood. Perilously he lived from day to day with a price on his head, the final price paid being thirty pieces of silver. It seemed that not only human enemies would snarl his life but even his friends would desert him and even Satan and his cohorts would hound him ceaselessly. As it had been predicted, he was a "man of sorrows and acquainted with grief."

How could he effectively lead his people—how could he exemplify his commands unless he partook of the results of them? How could it ever be known if perfection is possible—how could one be persuaded to reach for it, did not some one prove it could be done? So he lived on the brink of tragedy day and night, all his life. (62-11)

Christ exemplifies all virtues. No one else, no matter how talented, how capable, how worthy, how righteous, has ever approached him in his excellence.

I challenge you to add one little thing to Jesus to make him better. You can't make him more just, more righteous, more honest, more loving, or more kind. Jesus stands on the horizon of human experience as the only one who cannot be improved. (74-36)

Jesus inspired art and motivates personal change. Jesus was not a painter, and yet he inspired Michelangelo and many other great painters. They painted Jesus and he was the inspiration for it. He was not an orator, and yet no man spake as this man spoke. He didn't wave his hands and shout in stentorian sounds, but he penetrated men's souls with his thoughts. His sayings have been hammered in marble, chiseled into imperishable stone and granite, wrought into enduring bronze tablets, written in stained glass windows of numberless churches, and fashioned in rich mosaics upon temple walls and set in arched domes of colossal cathedrals.

He was not a poet, but he inspired the greatest poems that have ever been written. He was not a musician so far as we know, but the greatest musical compositions have [been] centered around him by such men as Mozart and Schubert and Beethoven, Mendelssohn, and countless others. He was not an artist nor a sculptor nor a painter, and yet Rafael, Michelangelo, and countless other great artists received their inspiration from him.

He was not an architect, nor a contractor, nor a builder. He was only a Galilean carpenter, a maker of wooden plows and oxen yokes. But he inspired the noblest, most marvelous architecture known to man. He himself specialized in character engineering, to make men, human masterpieces. He took a Peter and made a Saint. He took a Saul and made a Paul. And he took you and me and he will make of us gods if we will comply and follow along. What a picture! So terrible and yet so sublime. So awesome and yet so grand. So painful and yet so productive.

At length, Jesus cried out as he was on Calvary and on the cross. He said, "It is finished." And when he died, the veil of the temple was rent in twain from the top to the bottom.

That was the Christ. That was the perfect person who is our example, who is our mold. We follow him. We do the things he said and did. We become self masters, masters of our every ambition, our every passion, our every thought, our every act. We become the master of our appetites of hunger and thirst. We become the masters in every field—not the slaves, the masters. And when we become the total masters as did he, then we will have become perfect and we will go and live with him, for the scripture says, "Blessed are the pure in heart: for they shall see God." (Matthew 5:8.) (64-04)

Christ was the greatest psychiatrist. My dear brother, is it possible that your greatest interest is to be the cross on which you shall crucify yourself? Will you let the very thing which could be one of your greatest media of service to your fellowmen be the monkey wrench which would clog your machinery for progress? Will you let your profession rob you of all that is eternally valuable? Can you, even with your unusual achievement, read the thoughts and intents of men? Could you read the mind of the rich young ruler and know exactly what his obstacle to progress was? Could you know that at the edge of the city Jerusalem would be found an unbroken colt tied, and could you know exactly what the owners would say when they were asked for its use? Could you unravel the life's story of a strange woman, surprising her with the statement that she had had five husbands and the man she now had was not her husband? Can any of your fellow scientists do this? Could you, seeing Nathaniel at a distance as a total stranger, know that in him was no guile? The Master Psychiatrist could and did. Could you or your associates heal the sick, the lame, the blind, and raise the dead? The Master Physician did. Could you or they create an earth, cause it to function so perfectly, and people it with a master creation in whom would be found the seeds of godhood? The Master Creator did. And if there is a greater psychiatrist, physician, creator, would we not do well to follow that Master? Can any of us create a spirit or place one in a body or return one to its abandoned body? Until we can, then, would we not do well to acknowledge our inferiority and accept as our guide and leader him who can do all these things and so perfectly? (7/30/53)

Christ was the greatest teacher. Jesus Christ was the greatest teacher who ever taught. He made known the greatest truths ever learned. He revealed the meaning of life, the way to success, and the secret of happiness. (67-13)

And all that he taught was focused on eternal life. He preached no telestial program. He was too busy to preach a terrestrial way of life. His whole message seems to have been focused on celestial life. It was his constant theme and he followed it explicitly. (67-14)

Christ taught without contention. As you know well, the gospel of Jesus Christ was accepted by a relatively small group even when its author taught it and promulgated it. When Christ came into Palestine he found many religions, and I suppose all of them had a measure of truth and certainly all of them had many good people as well as many hypocrites. The Lord accepted none of them. He brushed them all aside and practically ignored them. He developed his own program, which was planned before the foundation of the earth. He taught his true gospel, organized his own true church, and so far as he was concerned all the combined sophistries and philosophies of men could not change the truth and distort it into their decaying philosophies and religious beliefs. He made no effort to take the theories of the Pharisees or of the Sadducees or of the Essenes or any other group and change them or reform them or rebuild them. He left them where they were and spent all his energies in converting the people to his true program, which he himself had fashioned. (12/2/63)

Christ set the example for everyday goodness. I think of the Lord as he walked through Galilee and Palestine. I realize that he must have become tired and hungry and weary and thirsty, but he was ever patient. He was loving; he was kind. It seems that though it was necessary at times to rebuke people, he did what he told us in the modern revelations to do, he reproved then showed forth afterwards an increase of love toward him he had reproved (see D & C 121:43)— he had his arm around them, too. O how I love him for his tenderness—so forgiving, so kind.

I think of his kindness when proud and loving mothers so wanted their children to have a sight of the Master, to touch the hem of his garment, and they were pushed away—I think of that incident at the conclusion of nearly every session of conference as we go out the back door and people crowd around to just see and speak to Christ's modern prophet—and he said, "Suffer the little children to come unto me, and forbid them not: for of such is the kingdom of God." (Mark 10:14.)

Several have said no one ever saw him laugh; however, I can imagine the Lord Jesus Christ smiling as he looked upon his people in their devotion. . . .

I think he smiles when he looks upon this his prophet, President David O. McKay, who gives such inspired leadership to his people, who is so close to him, who hears his word, and who receives his revelations. I think the Lord Jesus Christ is smiling when he looks into the homes of this people and sees them on their knees in family prayer night and morning, the children participating also. I think he smiles when he sees young husbands and wives, and older ones, with deep affection for each other, who continue their courtship as our prophet has said, who continue to love each other with all their souls until the day they die and then accentuate it through eternity.

Oh, I love the Lord Jesus Christ. I hope that I can show to him and manifest my sincerity and devotion. I want to live close to him. (56-06)

To be like Christ! What an ambitious goal! What a lofty ideal! The Savior had a pleasing personality, he was kind, he was pleasant, he was understanding, he never went off on tangents, he was perfectly balanced. No eccentricities could be found in his life. Here was no ostentation and show, but he was real and humble and genuine. He made no play for popularity. He made no compromises to gain favor. He did the right thing always, regardless of how it might appeal to men. He drew all good people to him as a magnet.

"What manner of men ought ye to be?" The answer, "Even as I am," means that one must be forgiving, there must be no grudges, no hatreds, no bitterness. . . .

To be like him, then, one must resist evil. One must fortify one's self by keeping away from temptation, out of the devil's area. One must control desire, harness passion, bridle every urge, and keep away from the approach of error. Total cleanliness in thought and action is required if one is to be Christlike.

"What manner of men ought ye to be?" The answer, "Even as I

am," brings us to a realization that we must love our neighbor as ourselves. . . . [It] imposes itself upon us as a command to honor our parents, to be obedient to them, to love and cherish and sustain them, and to glorify them with rich and abundant lives. We remember how, even while on the cross suffering the mortal agonies, he remembered and provided for his mother.

"What manner of men ought ye to be?" he asked. And the answer, "Even as I am," brings us to our knees in prayer; for . . . he, the Son of God with the powers of creation and with control of life and death, went frequently "into a mountain apart to pray."

"What manner of men ought ye to be?" The answer, "Even as I am," reflects a studious life—a life of learning. And he says: "Search the scriptures; for in them ye think ye have eternal life: and they are they which testify of me." (John 5:39.)

"What manner of men ought ye to be?" The answer comes: "Even as I am." It means a life of courage. Jesus was bold in defense of the truth, even against great odds of numbers in the temple when he discussed the scriptures with the great and the mighty. He was courageous when he flailed the Pharisees and Sadducees, when he with uncompromising boldness lashed out against their wickedness, their hypocrisies, their deceitfulness. He, unarmed, unprotected, called them to repentance of their sins, convicted them of their weaknesses. He walked into the camps of his enemies fearlessly to do that which needed doing. He chastised the wicked but always had compassion for the righteous and the downtrodden and the humble. He attacked the sins of the times fearlessly. He urged mercy from creditor to debtor. He insisted on the payment of debts. He decried the divorce evil. He chastened the rich [man] who collected usury and who ground his heel upon the poor.

For a moment will you consider your heroes. Think of the individual who impresses you most as [having attained] perfection in chastity, cleanliness of mind and of heart and of body, in thought and in deed.

Now think of the one who is most unselfish, whose life is bound up in the lives of others, who thinks little of self and much of associates; one who has made sacrifices and has suffered and been deprived to give to others.

Now let pass in review one who is your ideal in kindliness, who forgives with all the heart, who carries no bitterness, no envy, no jealousy.

Now, who is the individual whom you admire the most as one who is obedient, tractable, and accountable, who is not servile but humble and free from arrogance and rebellion, who fears God and obeys his laws and commandments, who is devout yet not fanatic, who prays with most sincerity and who follows righteous teachings most completely.

And now consider the person whom you most admire who is alert of mind, who is keen of intellect, who is great in perception, whose wisdom and judgment are supreme, who knows much but is ever learning; and the individual who is most unselfish, who gives himself, his time, his talents generously for others, who gives and does not get.

And now, the one who exhibits the greatest degree of love—love for the Lord, love for his fellowmen, love for his associates, his family; the one who is gracious, personable, generous, loving; the ideal son, father, daughter, mother, and friend.

And now, my young friends, combine all these heroic people with all their monumental virtues into one composite figure and you still have an inferior to the Lord, Jesus Christ, who had all virtues at their best, than whom there is no peer except his Father, God. (54-05)

Christ conquered death. Man, created in the image of God, was placed on the earth to experience mortal life, an intermediate state between premortal life and immortality.

Our first parents, Adam and Eve, disobeyed God. By eating the forbidden fruit, they became mortal. Consequently, they and all of their descendants became subject to both mortal and spiritual death (mortal death, the separation of body and spirit; and spiritual death, the separation of the spirit from the presence of God and death as pertaining to the things of the spirit).

In order for Adam to regain his original state (to be in the presence of God), an atonement for this disobedience was necessary. In God's divine plan, provision was made for a redeemer to break the bonds of death and, through the resurrection, make possible the reunion of the spirits and bodies of all persons who had dwelt on earth.

Jesus of Nazareth was the one who, before the world was created, was chosen to come to earth to perform this service, to conquer mortal death. This voluntary action would atone for the fall of Adam and Eve and permit the spirit of man to recover his body, thereby reuniting body and spirit. (78-06)

He needed to die, that he might open the graves of all men as his own tomb was opened. Without the deep darkness of the crucifixion hour, there could have been no spring of coming from the grave. "For as in Adam all die, even so in Christ shall all be made alive." (1 Corinthians 15:22.) (75-13)

Never before was one resurrected on this earth. Never would any soul have been reunited in the Resurrection had not he, who was mortal and divine, broken the bands of death and opened the doors to eternal life. It was a voluntary thing. He had power to "give" his life, and he had power to "take it up again." Without it "this flesh must have laid down to rot and to crumble to its mother earth, to rise no more." (2 Nephi 9:7.) (58-03)

Being mortal and divine, and having suffered all things, he now became perfect. He had overcome temptations, he had restored the gospel, established his Church, and now suffered death to come upon him "to fulfill all righteousness" (Matthew 3:15), that he might inaugurate the wholly new program of the Resurrection, so mysterious and unexplainable to the people. (47-04)

Christ was both mortal and divine. The Resurrection must be brought to pass, not by a mortal, but by one who was son both of mortality and of divinity. Christ, from his mother Mary, had within him the seeds of death, but from his Father in Heaven, the power to die and to overcome death. With this combination of powers he gave his life—no one could have taken it from him—that all might live. (50-02)

The Resurrection was Christ's great miracle. Only a God could bring about this miracle of resurrection. As a teacher of righteousness, Jesus could inspire souls to goodness; as a prophet, he could foreshadow the future; as an intelligent leader of men, he could organize a church; and as a possessor and magnifier of the priesthood, he could heal the sick, give sight to the blind, even raise other dead; but only as a God could he raise himself from the tomb, overcome death permanently, and bring incorruption in place of corruption, and replace mortality with immortality.

. . . Ever since mortality came upon Adam, men had feared death, the one enemy which could never be conquered. Herbs and medicines, prayers and surgery, medicine-men and priests, sorcery and magic, all had been used for millenniums in an attempt to overcome or at least to postpone death—but, in spite of all the machinations and efforts of men in all the earth, up to this time they had failed; and the rich and poor, ignorant and educated, black, brown, red, or white, priest and people, all had gone down in death and gone back to mother earth.

But now came the miracle—the revolution, the unbelievable marvel which none could explain and which none could deny. For the body which these hosts had seen persecuted, tortured, and drained of its life's blood, and left dead upon the cross; the body from which all life had ebbed; the body which lay entombed those long hours in a small, closed and sealed, oxygenless room into the third day; the person who had suffered the fate of death like hundreds of millions before him was calmly walking in the garden, animated, fresh, alive!

No human hands had been at work to remove the sealed door nor to resuscitate nor restore. No magician nor sorcerer had invaded the precincts to work his cures; not even the priesthood, exercised by another, had been brought in use to heal, but the God who had purposefully and intentionally laid down his life had, by the power of his godhead, taken up his life again. The change had been wrought in the little sealed room without help or knowledge of the sorrowing individuals who would gladly have done anything to assist. Alone, by the power he possessed within himself, came the greatest miracle. The spirit which had been by him commended to his Father in Heaven from the cross, and which, according to his later reports, had been to the spirit world, had returned and, ignoring the impenetrable walls of the sepulcher, had entered the place, re-entered the body, had caused the stone door to be rolled away, and walked in life again, with his body changed to immortality, incorruptible—his every faculty keen and alert.

Unexplainable? Yes! And not understandable—but incontestable. More than 500 unimpeachable witnesses had contact with him. They walked with him, talked with him, ate with him, felt the flesh of his body and saw the wounds in his side and feet and hands; discussed with him the program which had been common to them, and him; and, by many infallible proofs knew and testified that he was risen, and that that last and most dreaded enemy, death, had been overcome. And they testified also that since he had opened the grave, many others had been likewise raised into immortality through the same program, and had likewise been identified and accepted in Jerusalem. And so, for forty days, the earth he had created was sanctified by his presence; his Church was perfected; his people were inspired with a fire that would never be extinguished; and then he ascended to his Father in Heaven.

And so we bear testimony that the being who created the earth and its contents, who made numerous appearances upon the earth prior to his birth in Bethlehem, Jesus Christ, the Son of God, is resurrected and immortal, and that this great boon of resurrection and immortality becomes now, through our Redeemer, the heritage of mankind. (47-04)

Mary's grief was overshadowed by Christ's triumph. One particular mother who poured out her soul to me was inclined to be bitter. She said: "Why would the Lord take my son from me? Why didn't the Lord answer my prayers and save him? I know my son has remained clean; why should he be taken?"

... With all my soul I prayed that the Father would help me to bring her comfort.

As I sat in meditation my mind went back to a little hill, far away on which were silhouetted against the deepening shadows of a black, tragic day, three crosses on which were human beings writhing in the agonies of death, and the central One cried out: "My God, my God, why hast thou forsaken me?" (Matthew 27:46.)

And I seem to see at the foot of the heavy cross the crouching figure of a mother torn in agony, saying: "Why should he die? So young, so pure, so able to teach the world a better way? Why, oh, why?"

Then I seem to see another more modern picture of a mother grief-stricken, watching the approaching caravan which was bringing two beloved sons home from a foul martyrdom in a jail some distance away, and I can almost hear her through her sobs: "Why should they be killed? Why should they be taken from the infant Church which needs them so much? Why must they die, so young, so pure, so strong?"

Then I realize that God does not take these lives. It is permitted because men have their free agency.

"Woe unto the world because of offences! for it must needs be that offences come; but woe to that man by whom the offence cometh!" (Matthew 18:7.)

Was there defeat in the crucifixion of Jesus the Christ? If so, all creation were doomed and man would have remained in sin. If so, the crucifixion would not have taken place until a later date—until his hour had come. His life was not taken from him—he gave his life. . . .

He was taken from his mother, though it broke her heart. His prayer, perhaps the most sincere and worthy ever uttered, was not answered as she would have had it. His was the perfect life, clean, guileless, divine, and yet he passed. His mother was devout as also were some of his people, yet his life ebbed. He was young and had not had time to establish himself in life. His first thirty years were spent in preparation; his next three years in originating and developing his program, and now when he could have turned over to his followers much of the detail of the work, and could have perhaps enjoyed family and other associations, he was crucified. Why? There was a definite reason. Being divine and mortal, he had a work to do which could not be done in mortality, which required his transfer to other spheres of activity. Was his work frustrated? It did leave a sorrowing mother. There were brethren who were numbed. There were perhaps many loved ones who doubted and questioned. But in his death, and in his resurrection, came a boon to mankind that only this Son of God could bring. Would we have had it different? Would we have saved his life, if we could, now that we know that he through this very circumstance brought redemption to the world? Would his agonized mother today have it otherwise as she looks back on the entire program? Would the apostles on whom the burden of the kingdom fell have it otherwise? (45-03)

Christ wanted to avoid martyrdom if possible. Jesus Christ was the very Son of God the Eternal Father, and as such had supernatural powers not possessed by us, his wholly mortal brothers and sisters on the earth. It was within his power to die or to continue to live. Most people, given that choice, would continue to live. But a great principle was at stake. It was a monumental choice to make. He loved life. He wanted to live. He had his sweet mother, his brothers and sisters and friends. His work had been prospering—thousands had heard his message gladly and had accepted his gospel. His Church was young but showed signs of growth and permanence. That he wanted very much to live is evidenced by his recorded prayer to his Father when in Gethsemane he cried out in the agony of his soul: "O my Father, if it be possible, let this cup pass from me . . . ." (Matthew 8:39.)

The cup assigned to him to drain was his death by martyrdom, for the sins of the world. It would seem that the Savior would have been most happy had it been possible for an atonement for the people to have been effected in some other way so that he could have lived on in peace and joy. Having received no favorable reply to his pleading, he cried again and again: "O my Father, if this cup may not pass away from me, except I drink it, thy will be done." (Matthew 26:42.) (50-02)

Christ submitted to the crucifixion. What dignity, mastery, control, when he the perfect, the sinless, the Son of God should be weighed. He, the Holy One, the Good, the Prince of Life, the Just, was on one side of the scales, and the murderer and seditionist and insurrectionist Barrabas was on the other side of the scales, and Barrabas won—he won his liberty and the Christ was crucified, yet not a word of condemnation to the magistrate who made the unjust decision. The people called for Barrabas and, concerning him, they cried, "Give us Barrabas," and of the Christ, they cried, "Crucify him. Crucify him and his blood be upon us and our children." Yet no show of bitterness nor venom nor condemnation. Only calm tranquillity. This is Divine Dignity, Power, Control, Restraint. Barrabas for Christ! Barrabas instead of Christ! Barrabas released, Christ crucified. The worst and the best; the just and the unjust; the Holy One crucified, the degenerate malefactor released. Yet no revenge, no name-calling, no condemnation. No lightning struck them though it could have done. No earthquake, though a severe one could have come. No angels with protective weapons, though legions were ready. No escape, though he could have been translated and moved from their power. He stood and suffered in mind and body. "Bless them that curse you," he had taught.

A further test came. Though pronounced innocent, Pilate had him scourged. Men unworthy to lick the dust from his shoes were ordered to lash him, the pure and the Holy One, the Son of God. One word from his lips and all his enemies would have fallen to the earth, helpless. All would have perished, all could have been as dust or ashes. Yet, in tranquillity, he suffered. . . .

His hour had come—alone, drained, feverish, dying, he called out. He was alone among crowds of people. Alone he was with eager angels waiting to comfort him—alone with his Father in deepest sympathy but helpless to bring comfort because that Son must walk alone the bloody, tortuous path. *"My God, my God, why hast thou forsaken me?"* Hast thou also forsaken me? He had been alone in the garden—he had prayed for the strength to drink the bitter cup. How could he be perfect, how could he be a God if help he received, if he received comfort? He *must* be alone. He was alone. (62-11)

Christ's atonement gives man hope. We have a hope in Christ here and now. He died for our sins. Because of him and his gospel, our sins are washed away in the waters of baptism; sin and iniquity are burned out of our souls as though by fire; and we become clean, have clear consciences, and gain that peace which passeth understanding. (See Philippians 4:7.)

But today is just a grain of sand in the Sahara of eternity. We have also a hope in Christ for the eternity that lies ahead; otherwise, as Paul said, we would be "of all men most miserable." (1 Corinthians 15:19.) (78-29)

Not so important to know upon which great stone the Master leaned in agonizing decision-prayers in the Garden of Gethsemane, as to know that he did in that area conclude to accept voluntarily crucifixion for our sakes. Not so needful to know on which hill his cross was planted nor in what tomb his body lay nor in which garden he met Mary, but that he did hang in voluntary physical and mental agony; that his lifeless, bloodless body did lie in the tomb into the third day as prophesied, and above all that he did emerge a resurrected perfected one—the first fruits of all men in resurrection and the author of the gospel which could give eternal life to obedient man.

Not so important to know where he was born and died and resurrected but to know for a certainty that the Eternal, Living Father came to approve his Son in his baptism and later in his ministry, that the Son of God broke the bands of death and established the exaltation, the way of life, and that we may grow like him in knowledge and perfected eternal life. (61-01)

The Holy Ghost

The Holy Ghost is a personage who leads into truth. The Holy

Ghost is a personage of spirit and comes into our lives to lead us in the paths of righteousness. Each person on whom authoritative hands have been placed will receive the Holy Ghost. He will lead us unto all truth. And so we are a blessed people with all these special blessings. If one does not receive the great gift of the Holy Ghost, then it is his fault, that he hasn't been spiritual enough or close enough to Heavenly Father. (75-43)

The Holy Ghost is a revelator, teacher, comforter. The Holy Ghost is a revelator. Every worthy soul is entitled to a revelation, and it comes through the Holy Ghost. In Moroni's farewell to the Lamanites, he says: "And by the power of the Holy Ghost ye may know the truth of all things." (Moroni 10:5.)

He is a reminder and will bring to our remembrance the things which we have learned and which we need in the time thereof. He is an inspirer and will put words in our mouths, enlighten our understandings and direct our thoughts. He is a testifier and will bear record to us of the divinity of the Father and the Son and of their missions and of the program which they have given us. He is a teacher and will increase our knowledge. He is a companion and will walk with us, inspiring us all along the way, guiding our footsteps, impeaching our weaknesses, strengthening our resolves, and revealing to us righteous aims and purposes. (55-02)

The Holy Ghost is a sure witness, not to be denied. The depth and durability of impressions made by "spirit speaking to spirit" perhaps explains the Lord's statement to Thomas after his resurrection: "Thomas, because thou hast seen me, thou hast believed: blessed are they that have not seen, and yet have believed." (John 20:29.) Here was the reference to the surer witness. The eyes can be deceived, as can the other physical senses, but the testimony of the Holy Ghost is certain.

The sin against the Holy Ghost requires such knowledge that it is manifestly impossible for the rank and file to commit such a sin. Comparatively few Church members will commit murder wherein they shed innocent blood, and we hope only few will deny the Holy Ghost. (MF 122)

CHAPTER 2

The Plan of Salvation

The Eternal Perspective

Truth is eternal. A truth is not proved by experimentation or logic but is merely demonstrated. *Truth* is defined as things as they were, as they are and as they ever will be. We do not create truth, we merely rediscover it for ourselves, it having been in existence always. (63-04)

Truth is stronger than the sword. No man apologizes for doing right. Right is the master of the universe. (66-11)

The gospel is true beyond all questioning. There may be parts of it we do not yet know and fully understand, but we shall never be able to prove it untrue for it includes all truth, known and unknown, developed and undeveloped. (72-02)

Truth comes from God. All true knowledge is of God. There is but one world; it is a spiritual one encased in the physical, and when the end approaches, it will be found that all the teachings of the secular world which are found to be exact and absolute will fade into the spiritual, for God is not the father of the mind and the body only. (63-04)

Life is unending. We are eternal beings. We have no way of comprehending how long we dwelt in the presence of God as his spirit children. We are here in mortality for a moment of testing and trial. Then we will come forth in the resurrection, receive an inheritance in whatever kingdom we deserve, and go on living the commandments to all eternity.... The life that is to be is forever. It will have no end. Men will rise from the grave and not die after. Life is eternal, unending; never after the resurrection will the children of our Father taste death. (78-29)

Awareness of eternity affects our decisions. The more clearly we see eternity, the more obvious it becomes that the Lord's work in which we are engaged is one vast and grand work with striking similarities on each side of the veil....

If we live in such a way that the considerations of eternity press upon us, we will make better decisions. (77-01)

Man's Origin and Potential

God has given man knowledge of his plan. If we then accept the truth of the existence of God and his parentage then there immediately devolves upon us a responsibility to him and his children, our fellowmen. If he organized and planned the world, is it not most likely that he has made a perfect plan by which we might become closer to him and by which we might progress?

God has given us a plan. He has sent us all to earth to obtain bodies and to gain experience and growth. He anticipated the fall of Adam and Eve and the consequent change in their mortal condition and provided his Son Jesus Christ to redeem man from the effects of the fall and to show to man a perfect example of right living so that man, too, might improve and become more godly. (63-03)

Men and women in the image of heavenly parents. God made man in his own image and certainly he made woman in the image of his wife-partner. (72-02)

You [women] are daughters of God. You are precious. You are made in the image of our heavenly Mother. (72-08)

Man can become like God. In each of us is the potentiality to
become a god—pure, holy, influential, true and independent of all
these earth forces. We learn from the scriptures that each of us has an
eternal existence, that we were in the beginning with God. And
understanding this gives to us a unique sense of man's dignity. (78-37)

I would emphasize that the teachings of Christ that we should become perfect were not mere rhetoric. He meant literally that it is the
right of mankind to become like the Father and like the Son, having
overcome human weaknesses and developed attributes of divinity.

[Even though] many individuals do not fully use the capacity that
is in them, [that] does nothing to negate the truth that they have the
power to become Christlike. It is the man and woman who use the
power who prove its existence; neglect cannot prove its absence.
(78-27)

Now, when man has been created in the image of God and in his
likeness, then limitations are for man nonexistent except as man
limits himself. And, when each person gets this dignified concept,
then he has begun to find himself. (63-04)

Mortal man has not become what he may become. Perhaps
there is something else that we will learn as we perfect our bodies and
our spirits in the times to come. You and I—what helpless creatures
are we! Such limited power we have, and how little can we control the
wind and the waves and the storms! We remember the numerous
scriptures which, concentrated in a single line, were stated by a
former prophet, Lorenzo Snow: "As man now is, God once was; as
God now is, man may be." This is a power available to us as we
reach perfection and receive the experience and power to create, to
organize, to control native elements. How limited we are now! We
have no power to force the grass to grow, the plants to emerge, the
seeds to develop. (77-25)

How great is man! and yet how puny! Great he is as compared to
all other created things. For did not the Lord, after creating him, give

him dominion over all living plants and creatures? But it is not the flesh and bones, but the intangible, invisible (to us) part of man which enables him to subjugate the forces of nature to his will. He tills the land, produces food; and sails the seas conquering that vast and powerful element; he invented speech and writing and recorded and perpetuated his thoughts. He carved marble and painted pictures. He tunneled the Alps and spoke around the world. He built cities, made laws, and organized schools; he has accumulated the knowledge of the centuries which has enabled him to continue to find aids with which to conquer the forces of the universe.

This soul of man! Though it controls and organizes and programs and does so many mighty things, yet science tells us that without the spirit about all that is left is a quantity of water, fat enough to make about seven bars of soap, sulphur enough to rid one dog of fleas, iron enough for a large nail, magnesium for one dose, lime enough to whitewash a chicken coop, phosphorous sufficient to tip some 2200 matches, potassium enough to explode a toy cannon, sugar to fill a shaker, and little more. But with a spirit directing mental processes and physical maneuvers man is "little lower than the angels" and is "crowned . . . with glory and honour." (Psalm 8:5.)

And yet man in his vanity and impudence has taken unto himself the glory of all his accomplishments, set himself up as God and, as has been said, has even "created God in his (man's) own image." It is as if the Boulder Dam should say: "I am powerful. I hold back great quantities of water. Parched land becomes fertile and productive because of me. There were no builders. I am the great cause and responsible to no power." (46-03)

Becoming godlike requires conscious change. We are not like the animal which can change little and lives largely by instinct. Being the real offspring of God, we can, if we are normal, fashion our own lives and make them productive, beautiful, godlike. (71-07)

Man alone, of all creatures of earth, can change his thought pattern and become the architect of his destiny. (MF 114)

Man can transform himself and he must. Man has in himself the seeds of godhood, which can germinate and grow and develop. As the acorn becomes the oak, the mortal man becomes a god. It is within his power to lift himself by his very bootstraps from the plane on which he finds himself to the plane on which he should be. It may be a long, hard lift with many obstacles, but it is a real possibility. (74-27)

Each of us is a son or daughter of God, and has a responsibility to measure up to, finally returning to him with a perfected Christlike life of self-mastery. (60-04)

My brothers and sisters, we're away from home. We're off to school. Our lessons will not be easy. The way we react to them, the way we conquer and accomplish and live will determine our rewards, and they will be permanent and eternal. (74-39)

The gospel of Christ guides to perfection. The gospel is a program, a way of life, the plan of personal salvation, and is based upon personal responsibility. It is developed for man, the offspring of God. Man is a god in embryo and has in him the seeds of godhood, and he can, if he will, rise to great heights. He can lift himself by his own bootstraps as no other creature can do. He was created not to fail and degenerate but to rise to perfection like his Lord Jesus Christ. (64-05)

So it is up to us as to what we shall do with our lives, whether we shall be neglectful, or perfect our lives. You say we can't be perfect? The Lord said we could. He said: "Be ye therefore perfect, even as your Father which is in heaven is perfect." (Matthew 5:48.) And it is repeated several times in the scriptures: "Blessed are the pure in heart, for they shall see God." (Matthew 5:8.) No one will ever see God who is not pure in heart. The celestial world can only be entered by unlocking the doors with the proper keys—the first key being baptism by immersion for the remission of sins and then the reception of the Holy Ghost follows, by those in authority to give it. Then we must continue with our church and temple work, serving others, loving the Lord with all our heart, might, mind, and strength, and loving our fellowmen more than ourselves. (48-04)

Perfection is a long, hard journey with many pitfalls. It's not attainable overnight. Eternal vigilance is the price of victory. Eternal vigilance is required in the subduing of enemies and in becoming the master of oneself. It cannot be accomplished in little spurts and disconnected efforts. There must be constant and valiant, purposeful living—righteous living. The glory of the Lord can be had only through correct and worthy marriage and living a clean, worthy life. (74-27)

Laying Foundations of Earth Life

A plan was presented in the great council. Before this earth was created the Lord made a blueprint, as any great contractor will do before constructing. He drew up the plans, wrote the specifications, and presented them. He outlined it and we were associated with him. This was probably when, according to the scientist, this earth was just a nebulous mass in space. Our Father called us all together as explained in the scripture, and plans were perfected now for forming an earth. In his own words: "And there stood one among them that was like unto God, and he said unto those who were with him: We will go down, for there is space there, and we will take of these materials, and we will make an earth whereon these may dwell; And we will prove them herewith, to see if they will do all things whatsoever the Lord their God shall command them." (Abraham 3:24-25.) That assemblage included us all. The gods would make land, water, and atmosphere and then the animal kingdom, and give dominion over it all to man. That was the plan. He gave it all to man that man might grow and develop and perfect himself and become godlike. "And the Lord God formed man of the dust of the ground, and breathed into his nostrils the breath of life; and man became a living soul." (Genesis 2:7.) And that wasn't by accident, either, nor by chance. God was the Master-worker, and he created us and brought us into existence. The Psalmist in addressing the Lord said, "What is man, that thou art mindful of him? and the son of man, that thou visitest him? For thou hast made him a little lower than the angels, and hast crowned him with glory and honour." (Psalm 8:4-5.)

Man is the masterpiece—in all the creations of God nothing even approaches him. The animals were given instincts. They can seize food, escape from enemies, hide from danger, sleep and rest, but they have practically none of the faculties given to this god-man, to this god in embryo.

Instinct is like a single note of a flute, beautiful but limited, whereas the human brain contains all the notes of all the instruments in the orchestra. Man can coordinate these tones to give the world beautiful symphonies. (48-04)

Long before this world was created, all of the spirits of the men and women who were assigned to this earth lived in a spiritual existence. And one day a great conference was held, ... there were billions of spirits attending. And He who presided at this meeting said to all of us who were assembled: "We will go down because there are materials out in space, and we will take of these materials and will make an earth—not an earth out of nothing, but an earth out of materials already in existence. We will organize them and we will make it especially for these souls to enjoy. We will give it deep soil and big rivers, forests and plains. We will put on it everything that a man could possibly desire. And then we will let each one of you go down to the earth, in your turn, and we will see if you will do all the things that we command you. Now the world is for you, and everything that is in it. I want you to be happy and have every necessity and luxury, and all I ask is that ... you will do certain things that I specify. I don't want your worship for myself. I want you to worship me because it will draw you closer to me. I don't want your tithing but I shall turn it right back to your own good. I will ask you to pray, not because I want praise, but because it will be a development of your soul. I will ask you to keep your lives clean, not to satisfy my ego, but for your good, and every law I give you shall be for your good entirely. Now, when you go down to the earth I expect you to follow these rules and live the commandments strictly." (55-11)

Life is for growth. We understood well before we came to this vale of tears that there would be sorrows, disappointments, hard work, blood, sweat, and tears; but in spite of all, we looked down and saw this earth being made ready for us, and we said in effect, Yes, Father, in spite of all those things I can see great blessings that could come to me as one of thy sons or daughters; in taking a body I can see that I will eventually become immortal like thee, that I might overcome the effects of sin and be perfected, and so I am anxious to go to the earth at the first opportunity. And so we came. There is a purpose in the building of this earth and in the creation of man, that he might have a place in which to live, to perfect himself, that he might become perfect and...raise himself, with the help of his Father, to godhood. (48-04)

Each one of you has it within the realm of his possibility to develop a kingdom over which you will preside as its king and god. You will need to develop yourself and grow in ability and power and worthiness, to govern such a world with all of its people. You are sent to this earth not merely to have a good time or to satisfy urges or passions or desires. You are sent to this earth, not to ride merry-go-rounds, airplanes, automobiles, and have what the world calls "fun."

You are sent to this world with a very serious purpose. You are sent to school, for that matter, to begin as a human infant and grow to unbelievable proportions in wisdom, judgment, knowledge, and power. (76-59)

Now, this mortal life is the time to prepare to meet God, which is our first responsibility. Having already obtained our bodies, which become the permanent tabernacle for our spirits through the eternities, now we are to train our bodies, our minds, and our spirits. Preeminent, then, is our using this life to perfect ourselves, to subjugate the flesh, subject the body to the spirit, to overcome all weaknesses, to govern self so that one may give leadership to others, and to perform all necessary ordinances. Secondly comes the preparation for the subduing of the earth and the elements. In Genesis we read: "And God said, . . . Be fruitful, and multiply, and replenish the earth, and subdue it: and have dominion." (Genesis 1:28.)

To subdue self is not only the more important but the more difficult. Many men have power over certain natural forces who cannot control their own desires, urges, passions. (62-01)

God desires man's success. The gospel of Jesus Christ is the eternal plan of salvation. It is the plan devised and announced by God, the Eternal Father, for the salvation of all who will believe and obey. (78-29)

God has taken these intelligences and given to them spirit bodies and given them instructions and training. Then he proceeded to create a world for them and sent them as spirits to obtain a mortal body, for which he made preparation. And when they were upon the earth, he gave them instructions on how to go about developing and conducting their lives to make them perfect, so they could return to their Father in heaven after their transitions. (77-25)

The Lord has never asked us to do anything which would not redound to our good. He is not selfish and [for] his offspring has no selfish plans. His great work is to see that man becomes like him, in knowledge, service, accomplishment, and righteousness. (71-13)

It is the destiny of the spirits of men to come to this earth and travel a journey of indeterminate length. They travel sometimes dangerously, sometimes safely, sometimes sadly, sometimes happily. Always the road is marked by divine purpose. (MF 1)

Opposition of Satan

Satan's plan rejected. Long before you were born a program was developed by your creators. There was rebellion in the ranks. The proposed program called for total controls by each individual of his personal life, including restraints, sacrifices, and self-mastery. The rebellion with its warring elements and conflicts was of such proportion that our civil war of rebellion, and even our World War II are insignificant as to number of people involved in the conflicting armies and the principles fought for. Had the rebels won that great war you and I would have been in a totally different position. Ours would have been a life under force. You could make no decisions. You would *have* to comply. Every determination would be made for you regardless of your will. Under compulsion you would do the bidding of your dictator leader in whose image the Khrushchevs, Hitlers, Napoleons, and Alexanders were but poor and ineffectual novices in comparison. Your life would be cut out for you and you *would* fit into the mold made for you.

But thank God that there were enough sane and sagacious souls on the side of truth and wisdom and the rebellious souls were vanquished as to the eternal and ultimate program. The principal personalities in this great drama were a Father Elohim, perfect in wisdom, judgment, and person, and two sons, Lucifer and Jehovah. (12/19/59)

Satan can be resisted. You know the evil one has opposed us all the way from before the beginning. He has promised himself that he is going to disturb every person in this earth and try to get him to do evil. But remember that the evil one is a spirit only. He has no body. Therefore, every one of you is stronger than Satan. If you will exercise your brain, your morals, your teachings, you can be superior to him. (76-13)

Satan continues efforts to influence man. There are two forces working with every individual constantly. One is the power of darkness with intentions to enslave and destroy. When Lucifer was expelled from the realms of God, "he became Satan, yea, even the devil, the father of all lies, to deceive and to blind men, and to lead them captive at his will, even as many as would not hearken unto my voice." (Moses 4:4.)

The other influence is the Spirit of the Lord, striving to lift and inspire and build and save.

Satan boasted he would *buy* his helpers, and he has devised and concocted every plan imaginable to deceive and fetter man. He is clever. He is experienced. He is brainy. He seeks to nullify all the works of the Savior. He is the arch deceiver. (67-13)

Satan tempted both Christ and Moses. There is another power in this world forceful and vicious. In the wilderness of Judaea, on the temple's pinnacles and on the high mountain, a momentous contest took place between two brothers, Jehovah and Lucifer, sons of Elohim. When physically weak from fasting, Christ was tempted by Lucifer: "If thou be the Son of God, command this stone that it be made bread." (Luke 4:3.)

On the temple's pinnacles, the Evil One taunted again, suggesting the unwarranted use of power. [Christ responded:] "Thou shalt not tempt the Lord thy God." (Luke 4:12.)

On a high mountain the devil tantalized the Christ, offering kingdoms, thrones, powers, dominions, satisfactions of urges, desires, passions, the glory of wealth, ease, comfort—all to possess on condition that he worship Lucifer.

The Lord in his mortality was tempted but resisted: "Get thee hence, Satan:..." (Matthew 4:10) he said....Satan, also a son of God, had rebelled and had been cast out of heaven and not permitted an earthly body as had his brother Jehovah. Much depended upon the outcome of this spectacular duel.

And again, could the mastermind, Lucifer, control and dominate this Prophet Moses who had learned much directly from his Lord? "Moses, son of man, worship me," the devil tempted, with promise of worlds and luxuries and power. But, he courageously:

"...looked upon Satan and said, Who art thou? For behold I am a son of God, in the similitude of his Only Begotten." (Moses 1:13.) And Moses knew well his role and was prepared for this mastermind:

"...where is thy glory, that I should worship thee?

"For behold, I could not look upon God, except his glory should come upon me, and I were transfigured before him. But I can look upon thee in the natural man. Is it not so, surely?" he taunted. (Moses 1:13-14.) (64-03)

Satan is a personal being. In these days of sophistication and error men depersonalize not only God but the devil. Under this concept Satan is a myth, useful for keeping people straight in less enlightened days but outmoded in our educated age. Nothing is further from reality. Satan is very much a personal, individual spirit being, but without a mortal body. His desires to seal each of us his are no less ardent in wickedness than our Father's are in righteousness to attract us to his own eternal kingdom....

Yes, the devil is decidedly a person. He is also clever and trained. With thousands of years of experience behind him he has become superbly efficient and increasingly determined. (MF 21)

Satan says, "There is no devil." The powerful Lucifer has his day. He whispers into every man's ears. Some reject his enticing offers, others yield. Satan whispers, "This is no sin. You are no transgressor. I am no devil. There is no evil one. There is no black. All is white." (67-13)

Obtaining a Body

Soul is body animated by spirit. Man is a dual being. There is the body and the spirit. Together they compose the soul of man. Each is dependent on the other for completeness. The spirit is the life, the body the tabernacle. The spirit may live independent of the body, but without the spirit, the body becomes as the clod, subject to early dissolution. This mystery is most striking as one goes through the harrowing experience of death. One moment there is life, movement, vocal expression, reasoning, memory. In an instant, there lies the same flesh and bones, but without feeling, movement, thought, or power. It is wholly inanimate as a rock, as soil. "For as the body without the spirit is dead, so faith without works is dead also." (James 2:26.)

Man is a soul, the combination of that mortal matter called the body, and that immortal matter called spirit. The former is created of the elements of a mortal earth and when inhabited by the organized eternal spirit matter, is the soul of man. . . .

In accordance with the plan of God the Creator, our earthly parents in partnership with him have provided the earthly tabernacle, and at the proper moment, the Lord has provided and sent to that tabernacle the spirit body to give it life, understanding, power. (46-03)

The body has great importance. All of us, even the child who dies in infancy, have received a body, which is an absolute necessity toward maximum growth and development. For the body, though disintegrated in death, will eventually be literally resurrected and our eternities will be spent in a body; but it will be one of flesh and bone and spirit, the corruptible blood being replaced by a finer substance giving life to the body. And thus, in this resurrected state, free from limitations of space and gravity and other forces to which we are subject here, our bodies, like that of the resurrected Redeemer, will be free to do much that the mortal body cannot do. (58-13)

We have responsibility for body. When we take precautions to protect ourselves from hazards, accidents, death, we are thinking not only of saving ourselves from suffering, from pain, from expense, but to preserve our bodies for their eternal destiny.

The body goes through many changes. Cells divide and growth follows. We grow from pudgy infancy, through fast-growing childhood, through gangling youth to full maturity, and finally into the shrinking, furrowing, stiffening old age.

A soul can continue to develop mentally and spiritually through these changes, but the body reaches a summit from which it traverses a declining path. The body resurrected will be neither the unbalanced body of immature youth, nor the creaking, wrinkling one of many years, but when it is restored and resurrected it will undoubtedly return in the bloom of its greatest mortal perfection.

Some sectarian peoples minimize the body and look forward to freedom from it. Some flail and beat and torture the body, but the gospel of Jesus Christ magnifies the importance of the body and the dignity of man. This body will come forth in the resurrection. It will be free from all imperfections and scars and infirmities which came to it in mortality which were not self-inflicted. Would we have a right to expect a perfect body if we carelessly or intentionally damaged it?

We shall have our resurrected, perfected bodies through the eternities. They were given to us—we had little to do with getting them.

It then becomes our duty to protect them from hazards, from mutilation or disfigurement. We should treat them well, building them with proper foods, proper rest, proper exercise and keep them strong, robust, beautiful, and undamaged and live on and on till called home by our Lord. (00-04)

Death

All must expect to die. Death is a part of life. People must die. There can never be total victory over disease and death until the end of time. Much headway has been made, and mortality tables are encouraging; more infants survive, more mothers go through childbirth successfully, and more people, generally, live to a riper age than in centuries past. We are grateful to all those hard-working scientists who have contributed to this great accomplishment. But die we must; otherwise there could be no resurrection, and without that there could be no immortality and further development. (PKSO 81)

Man may shorten life. I am positive in my mind that the Lord has planned our destiny.

We can shorten our lives, but I think we cannot lengthen them very much. Sometime we'll understand fully, and when we see back from the vantage point of the future, we shall be satisfied with many of the happenings of this life which seemed so difficult for us to comprehend. (55-15)

Death is critical only for sinful. Yes, men die—all men die. Millions have died unheard, unsung, unknown. The question is, when they die have they fulfilled the measure of their mortal creation? Certainly it is not so much that men die, or when they die, but that they do not die in their sins. (80-54)

"Those that die in me shall not taste of death." (D&C 42:46.) I think that means they are not going into the other world feeling resentment and reticence. After they get past a certain point they go with happiness, peace and contentment. (61-02)

Death is no tragedy. Why should a young mother die? Why should her eight children be left motherless? Why did not the Lord heal her of her malady?

A young man died in the mission field, and people critically questioned: "Why did not the Lord protect this youth while he was doing proselyting work?"

I wish I could answer these questions fully. Sometime we'll understand and be reconciled.

The following conclusions are my own, and I take full responsibility for them.

... Could the Lord have prevented these tragedies? The answer is yes. The Lord is omnipotent, with all power to control our lives, save us pain, prevent all accidents, drive all planes and cars, feed us, protect us, save us from labor, effort, sickness, even from death. But is that what you want? Would you shield your children from effort, from disappointments, temptations, sorrows, suffering?

The basic gospel law is free agency. To force us to be careful or righteous would be to nullify that fundamental law, and growth would be impossible.

Should we be protected always from hardship, pain, suffering, sacrifice, or labor? Should the Lord protect the righteous? Should he immediately punish the wicked? If growth comes from fun and ease and aimless irresponsibility, then why should we ever exert ourselves to work or learn or overcome? If success is measured by the years we live, then early death is failure and tragedy. If earth life is the ultimate, how can we justify death, even in old age? If we look at mortality as a complete existence, then pain, sorrow, failure, and short life could be a calamity. But if we look upon life as an eternal thing stretching far into the pre-earth past and on into the eternal post-death future, then all happenings may be put in proper perspective.

Is there not wisdom in his giving us trials that we might rise above them, responsibilities that we might achieve, work to harden our muscles, sorrows to try our souls? Are we not permitted temptations to test our strength, sickness that we might learn patience, death that we might be immortalized and glorified?

. . . If mortality be the perfect state, then death would be a frustration, but the gospel teaches us there is no tragedy in death, but *only* in sin.

We know so little. *Our* judgment is so limited. We judge the Lord often with less wisdom than does our youngest child weigh our decisions. (55-15)

The meaning of death has not changed. Though the present conflict is crowding the gates of eternity, though the War God, taking the place of the Angel of Death, rides wantonly through the earth, bringing early death to millions long before their allotted time, though death comes home to us, yet the *meaning* of death does not change.

To friends it brings distress and sorrow, to relatives anguish and grief, to closest dear ones, desolation.

Though death is more common during war, death's meaning is the same. To the unbeliever it is the end of all, associations terminated, relationships ended, memories soon to fade into nothingness.

But to those who have knowledge and faith in the promise of the gospel of Jesus Christ, death's meaning is also the same as formerly: a change of condition into a wider, serener sphere of action; it means the beginning of eternal life, a never-ending existence. It means the continuation of family life, the reuniting of family groups, the perpetuation of friendships, relationships, and associations. (43-01)

Paul, approaching his death, said, "For I am in a strait betwixt two, having a desire to depart, and to be with Christ; which is far

better: Nevertheless to abide in the flesh is more needful for you."
(Philippians 1:23-24.)

Sometimes we think of death as a great calamity, but death is a
blessing; it never comes when we want it or how we want it, but...
Paul wasn't thinking of it as a calamity.

...I once went to the top of a mountain which I had never
climbed before. And from those heights I saw a beautiful valley I had
never seen before. I gasped at the beauty of the scene. The far-
reaching valley in the distance, and the mountains beyond. I saw the
homes shimmering in the sun and the metal barns reflecting the light.
I saw the clumps of trees and orchards and groves and vineyards. I
saw the farms that raise alfalfa, grain, and cotton and I gasped at the
sheer beauty of them. I imagine that it might be just a little taste of
what one might see after emerging through the veil.... "Eye hath not
seen, nor ear heard, neither have entered into the heart of man, the
things which God hath prepared for them that love him." (1 Corinthians 2:9.) (61-02)

While in the city of Honolulu, we stayed in a room which was enclosed in glass on three sides. The light in the room illumined it and
we could see the shining glass, the beautiful furniture, ceiling, floor,
walls, the vases and other ornaments, everything in the room only.
Our vision was limited to the small room and its contents. And then
we turned out the lights and went to the window and through that
window, which before had been the end of our vision, now we could
see clearly over the housetops, over the trees, to the thoroughfares
beneath with their many street lights, studded with the lights of automobiles, and beyond that we could see the seashore and the great
hotels and Waikiki Beach, the Punchbowl and Old Diamond Head
with their craters, and the great ocean with its ships carrying the
commerce of the world.

Life, again, is like eternity. Here we are limited in our visions.
With our eyes we can see but a few miles. With our ears we can hear
but a few years. We are encased, enclosed, as it were, in a room, but
when our light goes out of this life, then we see beyond mortal
limitations....

The walls go down, time ends and distance fades and vanishes as we go into eternity . . . and we immediately emerge into a great world in which there are no earthly limitations comparable to ours as to time, distance, or speed. (46-01)

Tears at the death of a righteous person are for ourselves. I am sure that the thousands of our Latter-day Saint mothers, who like Mary, the mother of the Lord, today stand grieving helplessly at the foot of a heavy cross, shall come in time to see clearly and may even bless the day when their clean, talented, stalwart sons went forward into other spheres.

In death do we grieve for the one who passes on, or is it self-pity? To doubt the wisdom and justice of the passing of a loved one is to place a limitation on the term of life. It is to say that it is more important to continue to live here than to go into other fields. Do we grieve when our son is graduated from the local high school and is sent away from home to a university of higher learning? Do we grieve inconsolably when our son is called away from our daily embrace to distant lands to preach the gospel? To continue to grieve without faith and understanding and trust when a son goes into another world is to question the long-range program of God, life eternal with all its opportunities and blessings. (45-03)

The days of waiting will seem long until they are spent. Then looking back they will seem as momentary. (71-07)

Death does not change character. Have you ever realized that there is no magic in death, that ceasing to breathe does not make angels of careless people, does not make believers of disbelievers, does not bring faith where there was skepticism? (74-21)

You will arise about the way you die. You will not change very much. You cannot repent on the Word of Wisdom violation in the spirit world because you have no body which you must change. You can hardly change its urges and desires and its pleadings and pullings in the spirit world. This is the time to put your lives in order. (57-02)

Funeral speakers are apt to distort. The practice of speakers wiping out every fault and magnifying every seeming virtue of faithless persons as soon as they are dead, leaves the false impression that the acceptance of the gospel and complete obedience to its standards while in this life are not important. Extravagant statements, promises, or assurances, unless clearly dictated by the Spirit, should not be made at funerals.... Maybe we can change a pattern. The things that are said at funerals sometimes are absurd and ridiculous. The deceased have been promised celestial life and eternal life and first resurrection and immediate entrance into the Lord's arms and all this, numerous times in my experience, when it was a travesty and an abomination. Lacking sincerity and understanding, it did no good and some harm. (62-08)

The spirit world is near. As we approach this sacred hour when we will dedicate a new temple in a year or two or three, we expect that there are unseen visitors here, as one of the Brethren suggested. I expect that every one of the presidents of the Church, all twelve of us, have been dreaming glorious dreams about a temple in Tokyo. This world is not so far from the world of those who have passed on. We feel certain that they are permitted to visit the earth at times, and I think that Joseph Smith, Brigham Young, and all of the presidents, including Heber J. Grant, are surely not far from us this day. (75-34)

I have had few dreams which had meaning. Of the thousands through the years, most have passed out of mind with the dawn, but this was different. I stood in the room with other people around me, then I saw him. Father was a handsome person, tall, with dark piercing eyes and a commanding appearance. And there he was, not as a vague apparition, but so real and so like himself. I called out "Oh! Father, Father, it is so good to see you." He had a radiant smile such as he had had in life. It warmed me. I was pulsating with gladness. I could not understand why others could not see him, he was so clear and distinct and pleasing. "Oh, my beloved father!" Then he seemed to be moving away. He had been only an arm's length from me. He faded out of the picture and was gone. I awakened and lay reliving the dream or vision again and again. I did not want it to pass from my memory. I went to my desk and wrote it in my journal and went back to bed, lying quietly in the darkness musing, reliving the hallowed experience. So vivid it was that I felt sure it had some meaning. I am not sure for what purpose it was given to me. Many times in years gone by I have wondered if either my father or mother would some day come to me; I knew they must be proud of the position given me and the honor which had come to them. And, so, I have been grateful through the year [since the dream] for that sweet moment. If it did nothing more for me than to more completely connect mortality with the life beyond, it served a good purpose. As I have contemplated these months the exquisite joy which came to me in a reunion with my earthly father, I came to anticipate with infinitely greater happiness the possible meeting of my Lord and Savior and our Eternal Father. And there began to bear in upon me the feeling expressed in the song I have sung so many times, "O grave, where is thy victory? O death, where is thy sting?"

Somehow after this, the future, whatever it was, did not look so bleak and nebulous. There settled down over me a comfort and a peace which, except in a few weak moments, has never left me. (57-04)

The spirit world though foreign to many mortals is not [more] strange, perhaps, then the miraculous physical world of 1946 would be to Washington or Luther or Columbus. (46-03)

Resurrection of the Body

Christ rose from the dead. Oh, my friends, how can one doubt the resurrection of the dead? Men are sentenced in our courts upon the testimony of one or two. But here were hundreds of witnesses who saw and heard and felt. Their testimony was not of an apparition, but of a series of appearances, numerous and real. These manifestations of the Risen Lord were not in the dark or in great excitement, but in calm, sacred moments, in house and field and on the mountain top; at the table; in the worship assemblies; on the sea; at morning, noon, and night; in homes and gardens and temples. . . .

Verily he lives! He came forth from the tomb that first Easter morning—tangible, personal, immortal. (56-04)

As in Adam all die, so in Christ shall all be made alive. Adam and Eve transgressed a law and were responsible for a change that came to all their posterity, that of mortality. Could it have been the different food which made the change? Somehow blood, the life-giving element in our bodies, replaced the finer substance which coursed through their bodies before. They and we became mortal, subject to illness, pains, and even the physical dissolution called death. But the spirit, which is supreme in the dual man, transcends the body. It does not decompose but proceeds to the spirit world for further experience, with the assurance that after sufficient preparation there, a reunion will take place where the spirit will be housed eternally in a remodeled body of flesh and bones. This time the union will never be dissolved, since there will be no blood to disintegrate and cause trouble. A finer substance will give life to the body and will render it immortal.

This resurrection referred to is the work of Jesus Christ, the Savior, who, because he was both mortal (the son of Mary) and divine (the Son of God), was able to overcome the powers governing the flesh. He actually gave his life and literally took it up again as the "first fruits," to be followed by every soul that has ever lived. Being a god, he gave his life. No one could take it from him. He had developed, through his perfection in overcoming all things, the power to take up his life again. Death was his last enemy, and he overcame even that and established the resurrection. This is an absolute truth. All the theorists in the world cannot disprove it. It is a fact. (77-23)

The resurrected body is regenerated. As Jesus' spirit left his body hanging on the cross and later lying in the tomb, so shall our spirits eventually leave our bodies lying lifeless. As Jesus preached to spirits in the spirit world in his spiritual state, so shall our spirits continue active and expand and develop. As Jesus appeared in the garden a resurrected soul, so shall each of us come forth a perfect immortal with every organ perfect, every limb intact, with every injury or deformity restored and put right; with the infirmities of mortality replaced with strength and vigor and power and beauty of virile maturity.

The meaning of death has not changed. It releases a spirit for growth and development and places a body in the repair shop of Mother Earth, there to be recast, remolded into a perfect body, an immortal glorious temple, clean, whole, perfected, and ready for its occupant for eternity. (43-01)

I am confident that when we come back with our body again, there will be no aches or pains. There will be no wrinkles or deformities. I am sure that if we can imagine ourselves at our very best, physically, mentally, spiritually, that is the way we will come back—perhaps not as a child or youth, perhaps in sweet and glorious maturity, but not in age or infirmity or distress or pain or aches. (55-05)

The Resurrection is central to our religion. Applying the teachings of Jesus Christ here and now can make this life richer and more abundant, but ultimately true Christianity focuses on man's opportunity to triumph over all his enemies, including death.

Jesus of Nazareth came into the world to bring to pass the Atonement, which gives to all men everywhere immortality through the gift of the resurrection. Thus Jesus' teachings can clearly help us to live a righteous life and to be happier here, but his great sacrifice guarantees to us immortality and the extension of our individual identity and life beyond the grave. (77-37)

The Righteous Judgment

Judgment is sure. Of two very important things we may be absolutely certain—that it is not vain to serve the Lord, and that the day of judgment will come to all, the righteous and the unrighteous.

The time of reckoning is as sure as is the passage of time and the coming of eternity. All who live shall eventually stand before the bar of God to be judged according to their works. Their final assignments will constitute rewards and punishments according to the kinds of lives they lived on earth. (MF 301)

The judgment is based on works. After a period of time there will be a literal resurrection, when this live and conscious spirit will return to the earth to take up its reconstructed and resurrected body, raised in the bloom of its greatest earthly perfection; and the soul, composed of the resurrected body and the eternal spirit, will be ready for its next experience and every soul will come before the great judge to receive its final assignment for the eternity. Every soul that has been born will also be redeemed in the flesh and come forth in the resurrection before his maker for judgment "to be judged out of the records according to their works" of life. (58-13)

God's judgment will be just. The judges at the gate will know for certain the formula, the records, the spirit, the true deserts. The Book of Life (see Revelation 20:12) will show the earthly activities of all of us, and the book of the angels will give the entire story of every man and what he did in the light and in the shadows, in the open and in the corners, all that is said in the secret places and from the housetops, all that was thought and expressed, whether good or bad. There will be no escape. The honest judge will give full value to all for their good works and will not overlook the other. (73-06)

God is just. I know that every man will enjoy every blessing which he has earned and I know that every man will receive no blessing through mercy as that word is often connotated. Justice will be tempered with mercy but not replaced by it. I am positive that no man will ever be judged without opportunity, blessed beyond his deserts, nor punished for something for which he was not responsible. (6/15/63)

Earthly inequities will be adjusted. This life, this narrow sphere we call mortality, does not, within the short space of time we are allowed here, give to all of us perfect justice, perfect health, or perfect opportunities. Perfect justice, however, will come eventually through a divine plan, as will the perfection of all other conditions and blessings—to those who have lived to merit them. (77-37)

On the earth there are many apparent injustices, when man must judge man and when uncontrollable situations seem to bring undeserved disaster, but in the judgment of God there will be no injustice and no soul will receive any blessing, reward, or glory which he has not earned, and no soul will be punished through deprivation or otherwise for anything of which he was not guilty. (58-13)

In God's house are many mansions. The age-old concept of heaven and hell is erroneous. It is not true that there is but one dividing line between heaven and hell and that all who barely fail to reach heaven will be doomed to a fire and brimstone hell, and conversely untrue, that all who are just a little better than the condemned ones will go to a common heaven, there equally to play harps or to sing praises eternally. This is a false concept. The scriptures have made it clear that every soul will pay penalties for evil deeds and receive rewards for good deeds and all will be judged according to their works. They will not be put into two categories but in as many as there are individuals who have different degrees of accomplishment and performance, and this is just. Think for one moment how unjust it would be to put all law-breakers—the murderer, adulterer, thief, and car-parking violator—in the same penitentiary with the same punishments, deprivations, and the same period to serve; how unjust to put in the same world [of] development and happiness and glory the person who has merely confessed the name of Christ with all those who not only confessed it but lived his every commandment and perfected their lives and became godlike in all their attributes. God is just. (58-13)

There are three degrees of glory. Then shall all men stand before the bar of the great Jehovah to be judged according to the deeds done in the flesh.

Those who have lived after the manner of the world shall go to a telestial kingdom whose glory is as the stars.

Those who have been decent and upright and who have lived respectable and good lives will go to a terrestrial kingdom whose glory is as the moon.

Those who have believed in Christ, who have forsaken the world, who have taken the Holy Spirit for their guide and been willing to lay their all on the altar, those who have kept the commandments of God—they shall go to a celestial kingdom whose glory is as the sun. (78-29)

Lukewarm Saints get terrestrial glory. The terrestrial kingdom will not be enjoyed by the very wicked, for they shall obtain only the telestial. Neither will the terrestrial be given to the valiant, the faithful, the perfected, for they will go into the celestial kingdom prepared for those who live the celestial laws. But into the terrestrial will go those who do not measure up to the celestial. Speaking of one category of terrestrial people, the Lord says: "These are they who are not valiant in the testimony of Jesus; wherefore, they obtain not the crown over the kingdom of our God." (D&C 76:79.) The "unvaliant" Latter-day Saint will find himself there.

It is true that repentance is always worthwhile. But spirit world repentance cannot recompense for that which could and should have been done on earth. (MF 315)

Procrastination leads to loss of exaltation. One of the most serious human defects in all ages is procrastination, an unwillingness to accept personal responsibilities *now.* Men came to earth consciously to obtain their schooling, their training and development, and to perfect themselves, but many have allowed themselves to be diverted and have become merely "hewers of wood and drawers of water," addicts to mental and spiritual indolence and to the pursuit of worldly pleasure.

There are even many members of the Church who are lax and careless and who continually procrastinate. They live the gospel casually but not devoutly. They have complied with some requirements but are not valiant. They do no major crime but merely fail to do the things required—things like paying tithing, living the Word of Wisdom, having family prayers, fasting, attending meetings, serving. . . .

One Church member of my acquaintance said, as she drank her coffee: "The Lord knows my heart is right and that I have good intentions, and that I will someday get the strength to quit." But will one receive eternal life on the basis of his good intentions? . . .

It is true that many Latter-day Saints, having been baptized and confirmed members of the Church, and some even having received their endowments and having been married and sealed in the holy temple, have felt that they were thus guaranteed the blessings of exaltation and eternal life. But this is not so. There are two basic requirements every soul must fulfill or he cannot attain to the great blessings offered. He *must* receive the ordinances and he *must* be faithful, overcoming his weaknesses. Hence, not all who claim to be Latter-day Saints will be exalted. (MF 7-9)

Exaltation in the Celestial Kingdom

"Salvation" is not "exaltation." Everything we do is with one goal, and that is to make ourselves perfect so that we may be like the Lord and able to have eternal life. The world doesn't know what eternal life is. They talk about being "saved."

There is a great difference between exaltation and merely being saved. All will be saved from the grave. No question about it, if they are good and righteous people, they will be saved in some glory. Whether they are Catholics or Protestants or Jews or Gentiles, they will be saved from spiritual death. But to be "saved" is not good enough. One needs to be exalted to attain the great blessings. (64-04)

Surely there are good people—wonderful people in all of them [other churches]; there are many people in leadership in those organizations who are sincere and devoted. That is not the thought we wish to convey. Many good people are deceived. The Lord restored his kingdom in these days, with all its gifts and powers and blessings. Any church that you know of may possibly be able to take you for a long ride, and bring you some degree of peace and happiness and blessing, and they can carry you to the veil and there they drop you. The Church of Jesus Christ picks you up on this side of the veil and, if you live its commandments, carries you right through the veil as though it weren't there and on through the eternities to exaltation. The word *salvation* has many connotations. Every soul will be saved in some kingdom who is not a criminal. In every church there are those who will be saved.

One man said the other day, the only thing he didn't like about the Mormon Church was that it claims to be the only one through which a man could be saved. I said, "Oh no, we make no such claim. We say that every good religionist and every good man who is not a religionist will be saved but there are degrees of salvation, same as there are degrees of education. Do you claim that everybody who goes through the college door will receive a Ph.D.? Do you think they should? Or do you think that everybody who enrolls in the college course, one or more or hundreds, should receive credits for the hours he spends, the time he gives, the efforts he expends, the things he learns and can teach or pass on to others?" (57-03)

Ordinances are required for exaltation. Clearly, attaining eternal life is not a matter of goodness only. That is one of the two important elements, but one must practice righteousness *and* receive the ordinances. People who do not bring their lives into harmony with God's laws and who do not receive the necessary ordinances either in this life or (if that is impossible) in the next, have thus deprived themselves, and will remain separate and single in the eternities. There they will have no spouses, no children. (MF 245)

No progression between kingdoms. After a person has been assigned to his place in the kingdom, either in the telestial, the terrestrial, or the celestial, or to his exaltation, he will never advance from his assigned glory to another glory. That is eternal! That is why we must make our decisions early in life and why it is imperative that such decisions be right. (MF 243-44)

"Immortality" is not "eternal life." If we are true and faithful, we shall rise, not alone in immortality but unto eternal life. Immortality is to live forever in an assigned kingdom. Eternal life is to gain exaltation in the highest heaven and live in the family unit. (78-29)

Men require priesthood for exaltation. No man will ever reach godhood who does not hold the priesthood. You have to be a member of the higher priesthood—an elder, seventy, or high priest—and today is the day to get it and magnify it. (80-13)

Righteousness and ordinances are required. Can you conceive of the vastness of the program? Can you begin to understand it? But remember this: exaltation is available only to *righteous* members of the Church of Jesus Christ; only to those who accept the gospel; only to those who have their endowments; only to those who have been through the holy temple of God and have been sealed for eternity and who then continue to live righteously throughout their lives. (51-02)

Those without eternal marriage may be angels. Now, the angels will be the people who did not go to the temple, who did not have their work done in the temple. And if there are some of us who make no effort to cement these ties, we may be angels for the rest of eternity. But if we do all in our power and seal our wives or husbands to us . . . then we may become gods and pass by the angels in heaven. (75-39)

Some might say, "Well, I'd be satisfied to just become an angel," but you would not. One never would be satisfied just to be a ministering angel to wait upon other people when he could be the king himself. (76-59)

Exaltation requires diligence. Why will only a few reach exaltation in the celestial kingdom? Not because it was not available to them, not because they did not know of its availability, not because the testimony was not given to them, but because they would not put forth the effort to pattern their lives and make them like the Savior's life and establish them so well that there would be no deviation until the end. (57-02)

Exaltation is within the reach of all men. You have the great powers of thinking and the ability to plan and organize and love. All these powers that were given to you were given for the purpose that you someday might become like your Father in Heaven. That is the possibility, and if you do not become that, it is your fault totally. (76-39)

You could be the queen of Holland, the czar of Russia, or the emperor of Japan. You could be any great person in this world, but you would be a pygmy compared to what you can be in this Church. Every one of you can be a queen who will not lose her crown when she dies, a king who will not lose his sceptre when he dies. Every one of you! Not just the smartest of you, but *every one* of you can become a queen or a king and have princes and princesses of your own. It all depends on what you do. (75-18)

Exaltation is a glorious extension of this life. If you can think of the greatest real joys that have ever come to you in this life, then think of the next life as a projection of this one with all the purposeful things multiplied, enlarged, and even more desirable. All in these associations of our lives here have brought to you development and joy and growth and happiness. Now, when life ends, we shall return to a situation patterned after our life here, only less limited, more glorious, more increased joys. (74-05)

Exaltation is to be like God. Now, the sealing for eternity gives to you eternal leadership. The man will have the authority of the priesthood, and if he keeps his life in order he will become a god. Now, that's hard to understand, isn't it? But that's the way it is. You see, we have a Father in Heaven and we have a mother in heaven. And so we have a spiritual father and mother as we have a material father and mother on the earth. The Lord created this earth for us and made it a beautiful place to live. He promised us that if we would live the right way we could come back to him and be like him. (75-05)

After death we continue to learn. Exaltation means godhood, creatorship. "As man now is, God once was; as God now is, man may be." (Eliza R. Snow Smith, *Biography of Lorenzo Snow* [Salt Lake City: Deseret News Co., 1884], p. 46.) This is in the future. It is obvious that before one can take of the materials in existence and develop them into a world like our own, he must be master of geology, zoology, physiology, psychology, and all the others. It is obvious, also, that no soul can in his short mortal life acquire all this knowledge and master all these sciences, but he can make a beginning and with the foundation of spiritual life and controls and mastery, and with the authorities and powers received through the gospel of Christ, he is in a position to begin this almost limitless study of the secular. (62-01)

It must be very difficult to reach out into the great universe and bring to one's self the priesthood, which is the power to create, and . . . to make something out of nothing. Of course, we do not do that. We take one element, and we transform it and organize it into another. . . . You look out there in the starry night and you see the sky is filled with stars. There are in the universe numerous bits or quantities of materials—gases and other elements—which brought together in the proper way can create an earth and can eventually produce fruit trees, and grain fields, and forests.

All of that is possible, and you are the men the Lord has chosen to do this work. Now it will take a long while, of course, for us to learn enough to be able to do that, but we're on our way. Every week we learn more about the priesthood. Every week we learn better how to handle it. The time will come when we will not only create with our wives the mortal tabernacles which our earthly children occupy, but we will be able to expand our efforts and extend them and go out into the great eternities. And we will be able to produce great families of spirit children who in turn may return to that planet which you will have organized and will have made habitable. And those children will be permitted to go to those planets or earths, and there they will receive mortal bodies to have their schooling process so that eventually they also can return to their Heavenly Father. (75-06)

Faith

Faith Must Come First

Faith precedes the miracle. In faith we plant the seed, and soon we see the miracle of the blossoming. Men have often misunderstood and have reversed the process. They would have the harvest before the planting, the reward before the service, the miracle before the faith. Even the most demanding labor unions would hardly ask the wages before the labor. But many of us would have the vigor without the observance of the health laws, prosperity through the opened windows of heaven without the payment of our tithes. We would have the close communion with our Father without fasting and praying; we would have rain in due season and peace in the land without observing the Sabbath and keeping the other commandments of the Lord. We would pluck the rose before planting the roots; we would harvest the grain before sowing and cultivating. . . .

It takes faith—unseeing faith—for young people to proceed immediately with their family responsibilities in the face of financial uncertainties. It takes faith for the young woman to bear her family instead of accepting employment, especially when schooling for the young husband is to be finished. It takes faith to observe the Sabbath when "time and a half" can be had working, when sales can be made, when merchandise can be sold. It takes a great faith to pay tithes when funds are scarce and demands are great. It takes faith to fast and have family prayers and to observe the Word of Wisdom. It takes faith to do home teaching, stake missionary work, and other service, when sacrifice is required. It takes faith to fill foreign missions. But know this—that all these are of the planting, while faithful devout families, spiritual security, peace, and eternal life are the harvests.

Remember that Abraham, Moses, Elijah, and others could not see clearly the end from the beginning. They also walked by faith and without sight.

Remember again that no gates were open; Laban was not drunk; and no earthly hope was justified at the moment Nephi exercised his faith and set out finally to get the plates.

Remember that there were no clouds in the sky nor any hygrometer in his hand when Elijah promised an immediate break in the long-extended drouth. Though Joshua may have witnessed the miracle of the Red Sea, yet he could not by mortal means perceive that the flooding Jordan would back up for the exact time needed for the crossing, and then flow again on its way to the Dead Sea.

Remember that there were no clouds in the sky, no evidence of rain, and no precedent for the deluge when Noah builded the ark according to commandment. There was no ram in the thicket when Isaac and his father left for Moriah for the sacrifice. Remember there were no towns and cities, no farms and gardens, no homes and storehouses, no blossoming desert in Utah when the persecuted pioneers crossed the plains.

And remember that there were no heavenly beings in Palmyra, on the Susquehanna, or on Cumorah when the soul-hungry Joseph slipped quietly into the grove, knelt in prayer on the river bank, and climbed the slopes of the sacred hill.

But know this, that just as undaunted faith has stopped the mouths of lions, made ineffective fiery flames, opened dry corridors through rivers and seas, protected against deluge and drouth, and brought heavenly manifestations at the instance of prophets, so in each of our lives faith can heal the sick, bring comfort to those who mourn, strengthen resolve against temptation, relieve from the bondage of harmful habits, lend the strength to repent and change our lives, and lead to a sure knowledge of the divinity of Jesus Christ. Indomitable faith can help us live the commandments with a willing heart and thereby bring blessings unnumbered, with peace, perfection, and exaltation in the kingdom of God. (FPM 11-12)

Faith precedes knowledge. Faith must come first, then follows knowledge. Faith, then the miracle. Jesus said: "If any man will do the will of the Father, he shall *know*..." (See John 7:17.) Call it blind faith if you like, but it *is* faith. It is not the product of reason. The gospel will be found to be reasonable, but we do not take it because of reason. Logic is the father of hundreds of sects; it is the mother of the great apostasy. Revelation is the rock and the Lord has given us the key above. By faith, do the will of the Father, and the knowledge follows. (5/31/48)

Adam was a man of God with a great faith, and he continued to offer sacrifices unto the Lord because it had been commanded, even though he did not fully understand why, and even though it meant a considerable financial sacrifice to him. Why did he offer sacrifices—because it was a commandment of his Heavenly Father. He had been told to perform this act by one whom he knew to be his God. He had absolute faith and confidence that blessings would come through such obedience, and he did not hesitate. After he had lived the law, then came the understanding, for the miracle follows the faith rather than faith the miracle. The angel explained to him that it was to keep him in constant memory of the coming of the Christ who would save the world, and exalt those of the people who would live the commandments. (51-08)

Obtaining Faith

Anyone can obtain testimony for a price. A testimony is a personal revelation—one of the important gifts—and may be enjoyed by every soul who will pay the price. (59-07)

In experiences of mortality we sometimes suffer from optical illusions; we hear noises that do not exist; we experience nocturnal adventures quite unreal, and distorted; but in the spiritual realm one can have positive certainty, for the Lord has repeated numerous times the definite promise here expressed: "If any man will do his will, he shall *know* of the doctrine, whether it be of God, or whether I speak of myself." (John 7:17; italics added.)

In courts of law the witness is asked to take an oath that the information he is about to give is "the truth, the whole truth, and nothing but the truth," and the statements made are called his "testimony." In spiritual matters, we may likewise have a testimony. This sureness of the spiritual is unique and pertains to the realness of a personal God; the continued active life of the Christ, separate from but like his Father; the divinity of the restoration of the organization and doctrines of God's church on the earth and the power of the divine, authoritative priesthood given to men, through revelations from God. These can be known as surely as that the sun shines, by every responsible person, and to fail to attain this knowledge is to admit that one has not paid the price. Like academic degrees it is obtained by intense strivings. That soul who is clean through repentance and the ordinances receives it if he desires and reaches for it, investigates conscientiously, studies, and prays faithfully.

A sure knowledge of the spiritual is an open door to rewards attainable and joys unspeakable. To ignore the testimony is to grope in caves of impenetrable darkness; to creep along in fog over hazardous highways. That person is to be pitied who may still be walking in darkness at noonday, who is tripping over obstacles which can be removed, and who dwells in the dim flickering candlelight of insecurity and skepticism. The testimony is the electric light illuminating the cavern; the wind and sun dissipating the fog; the power equipment removing boulders from the road. It is the mansion on the hill replacing the shack in the marshes; the harvester shelving the sickle and cradle; the tractor, train, automobile, and plane displacing the ox team. It is the rich, nourishing kernels of corn instead of the husks in the trough. It is much more than all else, for "this is life eternal, that they might know thee the only true God, and Jesus Christ, whom thou hast sent." (John 17:3.) (58-04)

Faith requires willingness to believe. The gospel is true or it is not.

The Lord lives or he is dead. The Church is divine or it is not. We must make up our minds and let our hearts whisper the correct answer to us. (71-13)

But why, we plead, must a student pride himself in vain glory upon his own unfettered thinking, which leads him to disbelieve and miss the sweetness and solemnity of yielding to the spiritual life which impels to good works. Why, we say, must one wait until the night of death to see the star through hope and faith. Why cannot young hearts surrender themselves to a life of faith and works, and combine the spiritual life with the mental and physical to give a well-balanced life and link mortality and immortality into a golden chain that will fill their lives with bliss and peace and accomplishment and eternal progression through eternities? (46-03)

Every individual that has been born in this world may have a testimony or a direct revelation from God, and when he gets this testimony, it will have come from God and not from study alone. Study is an important element, of course, but there must be associated with study, prayer and reaching, and then this revelation comes. And when you individually know that Jesus was not only a great philosopher but that he was verily the Son of God, that he came into the world in the way that we claim that he did, and that he went out of the world for the purpose that we claim he did—when you know that positively, and know that Joseph was a prophet of God and that this is the divine church established by Jesus Christ, then you've had a revelation. (57-01)

Faith does not depend on miracles. The Lord made it clear that faith was not developed by miracles. John said: "But though he [Jesus] had done so many miracles before them, yet they believed not on him." (John 12:37.)

In our own modern times we have eloquent evidence of this. Sidney Rigdon did not retain his membership in the kingdom even though he had, with Joseph Smith, witnessed marvelous signs. (52-06)

Faith is based on past experience. It is not blind obedience, even without total understanding, to follow a Father who has proved himself. (66-07)

How like Saul are many in Israel today. . . .

He will serve in a Church position, for here is activity which he likes and honor which he craves, or contribute to a chapel where his donation will be known, but rationalization is easy as to tithepaying which he finds so difficult. He cannot afford it—sickness or death has laid a heavy hand—he is not sure it is always distributed as he would have it done, and who knows anyway of his failure? . . .

Saul was like that. He could do the expedient things but could find alibis as to the things which countered his own desires.

To obey! To hearken! What a difficult requirement! Often we hear: "Nobody can tell me what clothes to wear, what I shall eat or drink. No one can outline my Sabbaths, appropriate my earnings, nor in any way limit my personal freedoms! I do as I please! I give no *blind obedience*!"

Blind obedience! How little they understand! The Lord said through Joseph Smith: "Whatever God requires is right, no matter what it is, although we may not see the reason thereof until long after the events transpire." (*Scrapbook of Mormon Literature,* vol. 2, p. 173.)

When men obey commands of a creator, it is not blind obedience. How different is the cowering of a subject to his totalitarian monarch and the dignified, willing obedience one gives to his God. The dictator is ambitious, selfish, and has ulterior motives. God's every command is righteous, every directive purposeful, and all for the good of the governed. The first may be blind obedience, but the latter is certainly faith obedience.

The patriarch Abraham, sorely tried, obeyed faithfully when commanded by the Lord to offer his son Isaac upon the altar. Blind obedience? No. He knew that God would require nothing of him which was not for his ultimate good. How that good could be accomplished he did not understand. He knew that he had been promised that through the seed of the miracle son Isaac should all the multitude of nations be blessed, and God having promised, it would be fulfilled. . . .

It was not blind faith when the patriarch Noah built an ark some forty-two centuries ago or when the prophet Nephi built a boat about twenty-five centuries ago. . . . Here was no blind obedience. Each knew the goodness of God and that he had purpose in his strange commands. And so each with eyes wide open, with absolute freedom of choice, built by faith. Noah's family was saved from physical drowning and spiritual decadence, and Nephi's people were saved likewise. . . .

Is it blind obedience when the student pays his tuition, reads his text assignments, attends classes, and thus qualifies for his eventual degrees? Perhaps he himself might set different and easier standards for graduation, but he obeys every requirement of the catalog whether or not he understands its total implication.

Is it blind obedience when one regards the sign "High Voltage —Keep Away," or is it the obedience of faith in the judgment of experts who know the hazard?

Is it blind obedience when the air traveler fastens his seat belt as that sign flashes, or is it confidence in the experience and wisdom of those who know more of hazards and dangers?

Is it blind obedience when the little child gleefully jumps from the table into the strong arms of its smiling father, or is this implicit trust in a loving parent who feels sure of his catch and who loves the child better than life itself?

Is it blind obedience when an afflicted one takes vile-tasting medicine prescribed by his physician or yields his own precious body to the scalpel of the surgeon, or is this the obedience of faith in one in whom confidence may safely be imposed?

Is it blind obedience when the pilot guides his ship between the buoys which mark the reefs and thus keeps his vessel in deep water, or is it confidence in the integrity of those who have set up protective devices?

Is it then blind obedience when we with our limited vision, elementary knowledge, selfish desires, ulterior motives, and carnal urges, accept and follow the guidance and obey the commands of our loving Father who begot us, created a world for us, loves us, and has planned a constructive program for us, wholly without ulterior motive, whose greatest joy and glory is to "bring to pass the immortality and eternal life" of all his children?

Blind obedience it might be when no agency exists, when there is regimentation, but in all of the commands of the Lord given through his servants, there is total agency free of compulsion. Some remonstrate that agency is lacking where penalties are imposed and condemnations threatened—to be damned for rejecting the gospel seems harsh to some and to take away free agency. This is not true, for the decision is ours—we may accept or reject, comply or ignore.

In all of our life activities it is the same—we may attend college or stay away from the campus; we may apply ourselves to our studies or waste our time; we may fulfill all requirements or ignore them. The decision is ours; the agency is free.

We may take the medicine or secretly pour it down the drain; we may yield our bodies to the surgeon's knife or refuse his service; we may follow paths or get lost in the jungle; but we cannot avoid the penalties of disobedience to law. . . .

So also did the man born blind move toward wholeness of sight, yet he obeyed the voice of authority. Questioned by the skeptical Pharisees as to his unparalleled sight recovery, he stoutly maintained, "He put clay upon mine eyes, and I washed, and do see. . . . He is a prophet." (John 9:15, 17.)

A simple little formula it was. A little spittle, a little clay, a simple anointing, a simple command, and an act of faith obedience; and darkness was replaced with light. "Lord, I believe," he said as he worshiped in gratitude. . . .

Is there healing in mere clay to make eyes see? Is there medicinal value in the spittle to cure infirmities? Are there curative properties in the waters of Siloam to open eyes of congenital blind? The answer is obvious. The miracle was conceived in the womb of faith and born and matured in the act of obedience.

And so we render intelligent, constructive obedience when we voluntarily, humbly, and happily obey the commands of our Lord. (54-06)

Faith is a principle of daily life. One may enjoy the benefits of the miracles in the physical world without a complete knowledge of the underlying principles involved. He may turn darkness into light by pushing a button and read in the darkest night. He need not be able to develop the electricity, nor to have the knowledge to wire the home. But he must have the faith sufficient to secure lamps and faith to turn the switch. He then may receive the light. He may have but a primary scientific knowledge, but his enjoyment of the light can be as complete as for the engineer who built the power plant or those who supplied the wire or fixtures. He may turn a dial and enjoy sweet music from afar without being able to fashion a radio or understand fully its workings, but the blessing will never be his unless he connects his set with the power, and turns the dial correctly. In like manner, one may receive spiritual blessings and manifestations, by establishing contact turning the dial. Faith manifested by prayer and works is that key.

"If any man will do his will, he shall *know* of the doctrine. (John 7:17.) The turning on of the radio can bring to us at once, music, sermon, news in our physical world. A humble prayer on bended knees, followed by the other works, is the invisible switch to tune us with the infinite and bring to us programs of knowledge, inspiration, and faith.

Few people have seen the powerhouse which provides the light and power for their cities, businesses, and homes, nor the engineer who operates it, yet with faith in "the things of man" they accept the proposition that they do exist. A comparatively few people have seen the Father, yet there are those who have, and who have told us of his goodness and mercy. Among them was the youthful prophet of the latter days. With little knowledge of the physical, and certainly limited knowledge of the spiritual world, Joseph Smith turned the key in the lock and opened the door into the heavens. Providing as a medium his clean body and unfettered and unbiased mind, he turned the switch in accordance with instructions. It turned on the light by which he could see clearly through the mists, and spiritual darkness was dissipated. (46-03)

Must we not admit that the apparent differences, then, between the spiritual and the physical worlds are the result of our own limitations and in our own powers? Must we always hear or see to believe? "Oh ye of little faith!" What about the great mysteries of our own decade? Can you see an atom? And yet do you deny its existence or power after Hiroshima? (46-03)

Testimony is obtained by earnest seeking. Now, it is a good question which has been asked by millions since Joseph Smith phrased it: How am I to know which of all, if any, of the organizations is authentic, divine, and recognized by the Lord?

He has given the key. You may *know.* You need not be in doubt. Follow the prescribed procedures, and you may have an absolute knowledge that these things are absolute truths. The necessary procedure is: study, think, pray, and do. Revelation is the key. God will make it known to you once you have capitulated and have become humble and receptive. Having dropped all pride of your mental stature, having acknowledged before God your confusion, having subjected your egotism, and having surrendered yourself to the teaching of the Holy Spirit, you are ready to begin to learn. With preconceived religious notions stubbornly held, one is not teachable. The Lord has promised repeatedly that he will give you a knowledge of spiritual things when you have placed yourself in a proper frame of mind. He has counseled us to seek, ask, and search diligently. These innumerable promises are epitomized by Moroni in the following: "And by the power of the Holy Ghost ye may know the truth of all things." (Moroni 10:5.) What a promise! How extravagant! How wonderful!

May I repeat, the time will come when there will be a surrender of every person who has ever lived on this earth, who is now living, or who ever will live on this earth; and it will be an unforced surrender, an unconditional surrender. When will it be for you? Today? In twenty years? Two hundred years? Two thousand or a million? When? Again, to you, John, I say, it is not *if* you will capitulate to

the great truth; it is *when,* for I know that you cannot indefinitely
resist the power and pressure of truth. Why not now? Much time has
been lost. The years ahead can be far more glorious for you than any
years in the past.

How foolish would be the enslaved Israelite who was born in
slavery and had never known anything but slavery to say to himself,
"This is life. There is nothing better than this. Here I get my belly full
daily and a fair space in which to sleep." How shortsighted he would
be to prefer such status when he is told that across the sea and across
the desert a promised land awaits where he can be free and well-fed,
be master of his own destinies, and have leisure, culture, growth, and
all one's heart could rightfully desire. What does it matter? What is
the difference between light and darkness—growing and shrivel-
ing—a giant and a pygmy—freedom and slavery—eternity and the
one day—life and death? (77-31)

Reach for truth and hold it as each particle comes to you. You
may know as numerous of your fellow members know. If your life is
clean and your inclinations and desires are constructive you may
know as Peter knew, as many of us know. Many in former days and
in latter days have given their lives for their faith. You can know so
surely that this is the divine truth that you also would give your life,
your profession, or your all or any part of it for your testimony. If
you do not receive this assurance, this testimony, it is *your* fault. The
Lord is most anxious to give it to you through the Holy Ghost when
you have really humbled yourself and paid the price in reaching, fasting, praying, studying, pondering, and cleansing and purging. You
have spent years of intense study to gain your professional knowledge. Half as much devotion to your spiritual knowledge with the
other requisites would have made your faith invincible, and you
would not now be floundering. You will never resolve your conflicts
unless you let the gospel be first. You cannot give it up. You already
know too much to abandon it without serious repercussions. You will
never forget the sweet experiences which have come to you in your
spiritual ministrations. You will never forget, even in eternities, the
testimonies you have heard, the warnings you have received. Even at

the bar of God you will remember the earnest pleadings, the exhortations, and the testimony of your humble brother who pleads with you now. (7/30/53)

It should be kept in mind that God cannot be found through research alone, nor his gospel understood and appreciated by study only, for no one may know the Father or the Son but "he to whom the Son will reveal him." (Luke 10:22.) The skeptic will some day either in time or eternity learn to his sorrow that his egotism has robbed him of much joy and growth, and that, as has been decreed by the Lord, the things of God cannot be understood by the spirit of man; that man cannot by himself find out God or his program; that no amount of research nor rationalizing will bring a testimony, but it must come through the heart when compliance with the program has made the person eligible to receive that reward. The Savior could have taken highly trained minds from the temple porches for the chief builders of his kingdom, but he went to the seashore to get humble fishermen. He wanted men who would not depend upon their own intellects *only* to ferret out the truths, but unbiased men to whom he might reveal his new program, men who were trusting and sincere and willing to serve. He tested Peter on one occasion by asking him to identify him, and with power and sure of his grounds the first apostle declared: "Thou art the Christ, the Son of the living God." (Matthew 16:16.) Surely the Redeemer must have been pleased, and he then revealed the source of Peter's knowledge by saying: "Blessed art thou, Simon Bar-jona: for flesh and blood hath not revealed it unto thee, but my Father which is in heaven." (Matthew 16:17.)...

To acquire a testimony, then, one must be in tune with the Spirit of the Lord, keep his commandments, and be sincere. Because one does not receive this positive assurance is no reason why another cannot. To say that another person cannot see the light because you fail to comprehend it is to place unwarranted limitations on another's power. To say that no one can know of the doctrine because you do not is like saying that there is no germ or virus because it is not visible to you, and is to deny the word of God. (44-07)

Skepticism cannot refute spiritual knowledge. I have met many young people in my work and have tried to have an understanding heart and to sympathize with them in their honest doubts and worries and conflicts. Of the many who have come to me, I have found two groups: those who, though they see through the mist darkly, are honest in their wonder and questioning and are willing to accept the light when it is proffered; and those others who, full of egotism, boasting in their expanding minds, take glory and pride in throwing to the winds sacred beliefs, the faith of their parents, and the spiritual realities—who will not believe till they have thrust their fingers in the prints of the nails and the wound made by the spear.

I believe agnosticism is a disease of youth and adulthood to which most are exposed and many suffer, but like other maladies, recovery is quite sure if known remedies are used. And a sure restorative is given by John; when he said: "If any man will do his will, he shall know of the doctrine, whether it be of God, or whether I speak of myself." (John 7:17.)

There are those who have questioned the existence of God, of the spirit world, and of spiritual manifestations because they have been unable to perceive them by use of their five senses. They have seen no God, therefore he does not exist. They have felt no presence of spiritual forces, and their conclusion is that such are nonexistent. They have heard no voice, consequently, there could be no such sound. They go so far as to say that because *they* have seen no light and heard no voice, that no one has, and that there is no light and no voice.

There are those who, in a laboratory, will follow in the minutest detail the rules of combining chemicals to get a certain result, but, strange to say, the same student will deviate far from the rules in spiritual matters, taking liberties with the same, and yet denounce religion when results are not obtained.

And yet the program is infallible, and can be followed to a successful conclusion by anyone willing to pay the price—"do his will." It is not an easy thing to do. There must be belief and faith, the living of a clean life and prayer that will keep the communication channel open. There must be sacrifice and service and love. And when all requirements are met, the promise is given to all: "Ye shall *know* of the doctrine."

The story is told of a lad flying a kite on a windy day in March. His long cord had permitted the kite to fly so high that it was hidden in the low overhanging clouds. A gentleman, seeing him straining at the cord, asked what he was doing. "I'm flying my kite," said the boy. "But I can see no kite," replied the man. "How can you know that there is a kite in the air when you cannot see it?" And as the boy braced himself in the wind, he said, "You may not be able to see the kite, but I know it is there for I can feel the pull on the cord." . . . And those who will keep and follow requirements will know also of the existence of God and his power, by the pull and the feel. (46-03)

The testifier may be unable to prove his assertion or demonstrate his sureness by any physical senses. He may never have seen, heard, nor touched a deity, nor have seen nor heard anyone who had; yet, with a total conviction amounting to an absolute knowledge, he bears witness that he knows. (59-07)

Testimony may come imperceptibly. He who has a testimony does not know exactly of what it is made, or where it came from. He cannot measure it. He cannot weigh it. He cannot count it. He can only feel it. That is the testimony, and it is like a breeze or the dew. We were in Upper Galilee the other day, and there you have the dews from heaven that the Lord talked about. Even though there had been no clouds in the sky, there were a million little sparkling diamonds on the little blades of grass. . . . Nobody knew when it came. It was just there. . . .

It is a warm day. You stand perspiring in the warmth and all at once there is a little cooling wind or breeze. You feel it, a pleasant cooling sensation. You do not know from where it comes, but all at once you are cooled and refreshed and that is like the Spirit when a man is born again. "The wind bloweth where it listeth, and thou hearest the sound thereof, but canst not tell whence it cometh, and whither it goeth: so is every one that is born of the Spirit." (John 3:8.) (62-02)

Faith and Works

Both faith and works are needed for exaltation. There can be no real and true Christianity, even with good works, unless we are deeply and personally committed to the reality of Jesus Christ as the Only Begotten Son of the Father, who bought us, who purchased us in the great act of atonement. (79-02)

On highway signs and from sectarian pulpits, we are told: "For by grace are ye saved through faith; and that not of yourselves: it is the gift of God: Not of works, lest any man should boast." (Ephesians 2:8-9.) . . . This above verse, together with other isolated ones taken out of context, are interpreted by many to mean that personal religious activity and works are unnecessary and that all men need do is to believe in the name of Christ. . . .

This misconception of those who eliminate or deemphasize works arises in large measure from a lack of understanding.

When the resurrected Lord vacated his tomb after his crucifixion, a transcendently important thing happened. He gave a priceless gift to all men. He opened the door and made possible this redemption that every man would enjoy reunion of body and spirit. To this redemption, all men everywhere are heir, independent of their works, and it comes to the rebellious as well as to the saint; to the unbeliever as well as the believer.

When Adam intentionally and wisely partook of the forbidden fruit in the Garden of Eden, he brought upon all of us, his descendants, two deaths—the physical or "mortal death," and the spiritual death or the banishment from the presence of the Lord.

From this physical death man was saved . . . by the *grace* of our Savior, Jesus Christ, and not by our works. The resurrection then is salvation from the grave. . . .

To attend elementary school is one thing, and to receive a Ph.D. is another. To pour a foundation is one thing, and to complete the structure and make it usable is another. And so, to be merely saved in resurrected state is quite a different thing than to be exalted with eternal life. . . .

Numerous people may be saved in lower kingdoms who will never see God, but all who are exalted will have that glorious privilege.

The Lord said: "Blessed are the pure in heart: for they shall see God." (Matthew 5:8.) He spoke of performance—reaching perfection of life.

When he gave the memorable Sermon on the Mount, he was speaking of belief plus works of righteousness. He said: "Not every one that saith unto me, Lord, Lord, shall enter into the kingdom of heaven; but he that *doeth* the will of my Father which is in heaven." (Matthew 7:21.)

To receive so great a reward by merely believing is unthinkable. We pay a price for everything commensurate with its value. Paul points out throughout his epistles that to enjoy the greater blessings of eternal life there was much work to do.

To the Corinthian saints, he explained that after the resurrection, there were three heavens or degrees of glory—the telestial, terrestrial, and celestial. In modern revelation, Joseph Smith amplifies these truths. All good people of every nation will be saved in one of these kingdoms, but neither Paul nor Peter nor modern prophets, nor the Lord himself, has ever promised celestial life or eternal life to any soul who does not live celestial laws.

Some religionists claim that the murderer dying on the gallows can go immediately to God if he has made confession of belief in Christ. This is unthinkable and untrue. To think that the criminal hanging beside the Lord on Calvary would receive the same reward as the martyr Stephen is unreasonable and untrue. . . .

If one wishes to be forgiven of his sins and reach the celestial kingdom and have associations with the Father and his Son, [he must] repent and serve and do the proper works. . . .

Now, from the second death we are saved by the atoning blood of Jesus Christ and this conditionally. As Adam made himself mortal, he also moved himself out of the presence of God, thus bringing spiritual death penalties upon all his posterity. All men were halted in their progression. But in the meridian of time came the Son of God, born of an immortal father and a mortal mother, and as he climbed crucifixion's hill, he carried that Adamic penalty, and as the nails through his hands and feet, and the spear in his side, drained from his body all of his precious blood in this, his voluntary sacrifice, he neutralized and paid for all the Adamic sins.

Now, John said all folks have personal sins also. Here is the area of cooperation between the Lord and man, for even the Savior cannot save men *in* their sins. He will redeem them *from* their sins, but then only through repentance.

Paul told the Romans that Christ "will render to every man according to his deeds: To them who by patient continuance in well doing seek for glory and honour and immortality, eternal life." (Romans 2:6-7.)

There is no doubt. Intellectual assent will no more exalt mortal men than it will the evil spirits. The acknowledgment and confession of the divinity of Christ in itself is insufficient to bring the great eternal gift of exaltation.

And John the Revelator made it clear that, at the bar of God, men will be judged according to their works.

The truth in the matter is understandable to all who will search and read and pray and open their hearts. (67-04)

Christ's sacrifice is fully effective only for the repentant. He suffered and died for us, yet if we do not repent, all his anguish and pain on our account are futile. (MF 145)

The Lord is merciful, but mercy cannot rob justice. His mercy extended to us when he died for us. His justice prevails when he judges us and give us the blessings which we have duly earned. (64-06)

Some people not of our Church like to quote ... the following words of Paul: "For by grace are ye saved through faith; and that not of yourselves: it is the gift of God: Not of works, lest any man should boast." (Ephesians 2:8-9.)

One of the most fallacious doctrines originated by Satan and propounded by man is that man is saved alone by the grace of God; that belief in Jesus Christ alone is all that is needed for salvation.... One passage in the Book of Mormon, written perhaps with the same intent as Paul's statement above—to stress and induce appreciation for the gracious gift of salvation offered on condition of obedience—is particularly enlightening: "For we labor diligently to write, to persuade our children, and also our brethren, to believe in Christ, and to be reconciled to God; for we know that it is by grace that we are saved, *after all we can do.*" (2 Nephi 25:23; italics added.)

And the Lord further emphasized the fact: "And no unclean thing can enter into his kingdom; therefore nothing entereth into his rest save it be those who have washed their garments in my blood, because of their faith, and the repentance of all their sins, and their faithfulness unto the end." (3 Nephi 27:19.)

... However good a person's works, he could not be saved had Jesus not died for his and everyone else's sins. And however powerful the saving grace of Christ, it brings exaltation to no man who does not comply with the works of the gospel.

Of course we need to understand terms. If by the word *salvation* is meant the mere salvation or redemption from the grave, the "grace of God" is sufficient. But if the term *salvation* means returning to the presence of God with eternal progression, eternal increase, and eventual godhood, for this one certainly must have the"grace of God," as it is generally defined, plus personal purity, overcoming of evil, and the good "works" made so important in the exhortations of the Savior and his prophets and apostles.

Few, if any, have understood these matters better than the Apostle Paul, who would have been surprised that any other construction should be put upon his words. Throughout his writings he stresses the importance of deeds of righteousness. (MF 206-8)

Faith is the power behind good works. The exercising of faith is a willingness to accept without total regular proof and to move forward and perform works. "Faith without works is dead" (James 2:26), and a dead faith will not lead one to move forward to adjust a life or to serve valiantly. A real faith pushes one forward to constructive and beneficial acts as though he knew in absoluteness. The Prophet Alma gave the near perfect address on faith in the thirty-second chapter of

Alma. He gives us: "Faith is not to have a perfect knowledge of things; therefore if ye have faith ye hope for things which are not seen, which are true." (Alma 32:21.)

Faith is the planting of seeds, the taking of steps. Faith is the child, and when nourished and fed, grows into maturity and becomes adult in deep assurance and perfect knowledge.

Without faith, it is impossible to please him.

And therefore, when one has the conviction, he recognizes his imperfections; sets about to overcome them; is immersed in water by proper authority; and thereafter, by the imposition of hands, receives the glorious blessing, the companionship of the Holy Ghost. These are the basic principles and ordinances of the gospel of Jesus Christ. (55-02)

Herein lies the genius of the gospel of Jesus Christ, perceived by only the spiritual eye. Under the gospel's beneficent laws, everyone—rich or poor, learned or unlearned—is encouraged first to perceive with the eye of faith and then, through effort, to express that faith in a higher, nobler life. (76-34)

The Fruits of Faith

Faith motivates self-improvement. When we have love for God and mankind and a testimony, then we are moved to improve ourselves. (74-13)

Faith brings security. For forty years the children of Israel wandered about in the parched desert, not permitted to enter into the promised land—this because of their unbelief. Why must modern men stagger hungering and thirsting in the parched and arid deserts of unbelief and doubt and cynicism, when just over the mountain range of spiritual surrender lies the rich, lush valley—the promised land where is contentment, peace, joy and eternal growth and life? (46-03)

Security is not born of inexhaustible wealth but of unquenchable faith. And generally that kind of faith is born and nurtured in the home and in childhood. (73-02)

Faith in God involves emotional closeness. Above all, I hope you will teach them faith in the living God and in his Only Begotten Son—not a superficial, intellectual kind of acceptance, but a deep spiritual inner feeling of dependence and closeness; not a fear composed of panic and terror, but a fear of the Lord composed mostly of intense love and admiration and awesome nearness in a relationship of parent and offspring—father and son—father and daughter. (66-07)

Faith leads to eternal life. Our faith is tried, and we must live by faith, because there are many things we do not fully understand. "We glory in tribulations," Paul tells us, "knowing that tribulation worketh patience; And patience, experience; and experience, hope." (Romans 5:3-4.) And we might go on and say hope worketh belief and belief develops into faith and faith into knowledge and knowledge into eternal life. (48-04)

Knowledge of God is the greatest treasure. Of all treasures of knowledge, the most vital is the knowledge of God: his existence, powers, love, and promises. (68-11)

Sometimes an individual stands alone in a family as a witness for Christ. God bless him who stands faithful and true, even alone. (74-26)

One may see God in this life. Men who know God and love him and live his commandments and obey his true ordinances may yet in this life, or the life to come, see his face and know that he lives and will commune with them. (64-03)

I have learned that where there is a prayerful heart, a hungering after righteousness, a forsaking of sins, and obedience to the commandments of God, the Lord pours out more and more light until one finally has power to pierce the heavenly veil and to know more than man knows. Such a person has a priceless promise that one day he will see the Lord's face and know that he is (see D&C 93:1). (79-17)

The Lord Jesus Christ... said, "Blessed are the pure in heart: for they shall see God." (Matthew 5:8.) Sometimes we say, "Oh, that isn't possible." But the Savior does not deal with idle words. He says that any perfected being can see the Lord the Father.

Now, there are many approaches toward this experience. There are dreams and visions and actual sight. The Prophet Joseph Smith saw the Father and the Son and heard their voices, and he knew as no one else in the whole world knew at that time the personality of God the Father and Jesus Christ the Son. We may know by the Holy Ghost and have a testimony of these things. But every one of you here tonight can perfect your lives so that you may see God....

We will not seek to see our Heavenly Father to satisfy our curiosity, but only to have the great satisfaction of knowing that he is our Father....

I would like to tell you the experience of one of the apostles, Orson F. Whitney, who has long been dead....

"Then came a marvelous manifestation, and admonition from a higher source, one impossible to ignore. It was a dream, or a vision in a dream, as I lay upon my bed in the little town of Columbia, Lancaster County, Pennsylvania. I seemed to be in the Garden of Gethsemane, a witness of the Savior's agony. I saw Him as plainly as I have seen anyone....

"All at once the circumstances seemed to change, the scene remaining just the same. Instead of before, it was after the crucifixion, and the Savior, with the three Apostles, now stood together in a group at my left. They were about to depart and ascend to heaven." Then Brother Whitney says this, "I could endure it no longer. I ran from behind the tree, fell at His feet, clasped Him around the knees, and begged Him to take me with Him.

"I shall never forget the kind and gentle manner in which He stooped, raised me up, and embraced me. It was so vivid, so real. I felt the very warmth of His body, as He held me in His arms and said in tenderest tones: 'No, my son; these have finished their work; they can go with me; but you must stay and finish yours.' Still I clung to Him. Gazing up into His face—for He was taller than I—I besought Him fervently: 'Well, promise me that I will come to you at the last.' Smiling sweetly, He said: 'That will depend entirely upon yourself.' I awoke with a sob in my throat, and it was morning. . . .

"But from that hour, all was changed. I never was the same man again." (Bryant S. Hinckley, *The Faith of Our Pioneer Fathers* [Salt Lake City: Bookcraft, Inc., 1956], pp. 211-13.) (77-14)

The Growth of Faith

Faith is not static. I think many people, if not most people, have times of greater faith and other times of lesser faith. We live in valleys and on hills. Our prayers seem to reach out to our Heavenly Father sometimes and sometimes we pray with less faith and less response. (2/14/58)

Even to the religionist there may come a day of doubt and misgivings, but with patience most will plod through this period of adjustment and emerge from the darkness strengthened and reassured in the faith. (63-03)

A positive attitude engenders faith. There are two kinds of people I have run into in my experience: those who build their house upon the sands of doubt, skepticism, free thinking, private interpretation, and rationalizing. Their houses may look good in the glistening sand when all is calm and no strain is placed upon the house, but when the rains of doubt descend, and the floods of adversity come, and the winds of temptation blow and beat upon the house, there is nothing solid to hold it up and great is the fall thereof.

But there are those who build their houses on the rock of faith and hope, and though the rains and winds and storms do their worst, the building stands.

Can one ever be supremely happy in the philosophy of destruction? To be an iconoclast might satisfy one's egotism, but it could hardly do for one what a constructive life of faith would do. Mere knowledge is not saving. (46-03)

Faith grows through church activity. Generally one's faith begins to waver when he is inactive and critical. Few, if any, will ever seriously question the divinity of the work of God if they remain virtuous, active, loyal, and enthusiastic in service to God and fellowmen through church work. (00-06)

Faith grows through spiritual experience. Man cannot discover God or his ways by mere mental processes. One must be governed by the laws which control the realm into which he is delving. To become a plumber, one must study the laws which govern plumbing. He must know stresses and strains, temperatures at which pipes will freeze, laws which govern steam, hot water, expansion, contraction, and so forth.

Any intelligent man may learn what he wants to learn. He may acquire knowledge in any field, though it requires much thought and effort. It takes more than a decade to get a high school diploma; it takes an additional four years for most people to get a college degree; it takes nearly a quarter-century to become a great physician. Why, oh, why do people think they can fathom the most complex spiritual depths without the necessary experimental and laboratory work accompanied by compliance with the laws that govern it?

You must go to the spiritual laboratory, use the facilities available there, and comply with the governing rules. Then you may know of these truths just as surely, or more surely, than the scientist knows the metals, or the acids, or other elements. (77-31)

Faithlessness

Faith seems difficult. Few men have ever knowingly and deliberately chosen to reject God and his blessings. Rather, we learn from the scriptures that because the exercise of faith has always appeared to be more difficult than relying on things more immediately at hand, carnal man has tended to transfer his trust in God to material things. Therefore, in all ages when men have fallen under the power of Satan and lost the faith, they have put in its place a hope in the "arm of flesh" and in "gods of silver, and gold, of brass, iron, wood, and stone, which see not, nor hear, nor know" (Daniel 5:23)—that is, in idols. This I find to be a dominant theme in the Old Testament. Whatever thing a man sets his heart and his trust in most is his god; and if his god doesn't also happen to be the true and living God of Israel, that man is laboring in idolatry. (76-29)

Do not be puzzled if sometimes there are those in the world who mock how you live and what you believe, saying it is all false, but who, deep inside themselves, are really afraid that what you believe is really true. (79-02)

Faith must be tested. Some become bitter when oft-repeated prayers seem unanswered. Some lose faith and turn sour when solemn administrations by holy men seem to be ignored and no restoration seems to come from repeated prayer circles. But if all the sick were healed, if all the righteous were protected and the wicked destroyed, the whole program of the Father would be annulled and the basic principle of the gospel, free agency, would be ended. . . .

If pain and sorrow and total punishment immediately followed the doing of evil, no soul would repeat a misdeed. If joy and peace and rewards were instantaneously given the doer of good, there could be no evil—all would do good and not because of the rightness of doing good. There would be no test of strength, no development of character, no growth of powers, no free agency. . . . There would also be an absence of joy, success, resurrection, eternal life, and godhood. (55-15)

Faithlessness is a sign of spiritual immaturity. There are some who seem to feel they are "superior" and more intellectual if they do not bind themselves down with church and creed. And some pride themselves that they have reached a point where they can discard God and do without him. All this, of course, is but a symptom of immaturity and a lack of understanding, rather than being the evidence of wisdom and sagacity. To call religion a superstition is stone-throwing in glass houses, and the smart mind will spend its energy groping for the basic truths of true religion instead of dismantling or belittling it. As one matures and grows in knowledge, he may come to know the truth of things at which he scoffs when he had but a smattering of knowledge.

There is so much to learn and so few years in which to learn it; how futile for one to build up images which some day must crumble. Ultimately all will acknowledge the existence of God and bow the knee to him—then, what wastefulness to build up concepts which must be discarded. Great men are not scoffers; only little folk disclaim God. (63-04)

Teaching that destroys faith is a serious offense. He had attended a class in his ward and had heard a discussion on the mysteries. Subjects were debated on which there was little recorded revelation and on which there were conflicting opinions, and he had heard criticism of Church leaders, of Church policies, and of Church doctrines, and he wondered! He had read a book, the author of which was one of rich endowments, of much learning, and of considerable prestige. The things which our youth had always accepted were ridiculed. Logic was used; rationalizing was done; corrupt writers of a bygone day were quoted; the supernatural was explained away; the revelations were said to be man's wisdom; prophets were demoted to the status of laymen; and even Gods were dethroned and made a creation of man. All this in strict denial and total destruction of the basic things which had always been his life—and he continued to wonder. He had gone to school when the war was over, under his G.I. Bill of Rights. Here he had been further confused. There was no personal God, he was told, but God was a figment of the imagination, a creation of intellectual man. And God, being a creation of man, could not help him, but man was alone to work out his own destiny. He was led to believe that religion was for only the simple and gullible. . . .

The great objective of all our work is to build character and increase faith in the lives of those whom we serve. If one cannot accept and teach the program of the Church in an orthodox way without reservations, *he should not teach.* It would be the part of honor to resign his position. Not only would he be dishonest and deceitful, but he is also actually under condemnation, for the Savior said that it were better that a millstone were hanged about his neck and he be cast into the sea than that he should lead astray doctrinally or betray the cause or give offense, destroying the faith of one of "these little ones" who believes in him. And remember that this means not only the small children, it includes even adults who believe and trust in God.

Man is like the volcano which in a few weeks can devastate the countryside, wreck cities, and smother human lives. And the human destructionist can likewise inject into other human lives in a short time the doubt and skepticism which can mean total loss of faith. It may take centuries for the other forces of nature to pulverize the lava around a volcano so that it may eventually again give life to plants and animals, and just as surely the damage to faith of an individual done by an iconoclast, whether deliberate or not, may take years or ages of rebuilding, if it is ever fully restored....

Far better to take from a man his flocks or herds, his lands or wealth, even his sight or limbs, than to be responsible for the loss of his faith. (48-02)

As truly as one sows the wind and reaps the whirlwind, so also shall they who sow disbelief and doubt, reap unhappiness and despair. (46-03)

CHAPTER 4

Repentance, Baptism, and the Gift of the Holy Ghost

Importance of Repentance

Righteousness is knowledge in action. It is not so much what we know, as what we do. The devil knew all, and yet lost all. Knowledge itself is not the end. Knowledge applied, of course, can bring us the testimony and the wisdom and can bring us to our goal—exaltation. (62-08)

This is the day of repentance. I weary of discussing too much the matter of the moral situation in our world. But I read in the Doctrine and Covenants where the Lord said, "Say nothing but repentance unto this generation; keep my commandments and assist to bring forth my work, according to my commandments." (D&C 6:9.)

Then he said, "And how great is his joy in the soul that repenteth!" (D&C 18:13.)...

And so today...is the day of repentance—a day for people to take stock of their situations and to change their lives where that is necessary. (75-15)

Repentance is for all. But when most of us think of repentance we tend to narrow our vision and view it as good only for our husbands, our wives, our parents, our children, our neighbors, our friends, the world—anyone and everyone except ourselves. Similarly there is a prevalent, perhaps subconscious, feeling that the Lord designed repentance only for those who commit murder or adultery or theft or other heinous crimes. This is of course not so. If we are humble and desirous of living the gospel we will come to think of repentance as applying to everything we do in life, whether it be spiritual or temporal in nature. Repentance is for every soul who has not yet reached perfection. (MF 32-33)

And so, repentance must be as universal as is sin. (49-07)

Repentance is hard but brings forgiveness. No one can ever be forgiven of any transgression until there is repentance, and one has not repented until he has bared his soul and admitted his intentions and weaknesses without excuses, or rationalizations. When one admits that his sin is as *big* as it really *is,* then he is ready to begin his repentance; and any other elements of repentance are of reduced value, until the conviction is established totally. Then repentance may mature and forgiveness eventually come.

The way of the transgressor is hard and tough and long and thorny. But the Lord has promised that for all those sins and errors outside of the named unpardonable sins, there is forgiveness. But sometimes it takes longer to climb back up the steep hill than it did to skid down it. And it is often much more difficult.

When a total self-conviction is stirred to a new life, and prayers have been multiplied, and fasting, through humility, intensified, and weeping has been sanctified, repentance then begins to grow and eventually forgiveness may come....

But to those who have broken the law ... and who have complied as above, there is the promise of forgiveness; and the Lord charges the leaders of his Church that when they have totally repented, "Thou shalt forgive them."

"Behold, he who has repented of his sins, the same is forgiven, and I, the Lord, remember them no more. By this ye may know if a man repenteth of his sins—behold, he will confess them and forsake them." (D & C 58:42-43.) (65-02)

When people know right from wrong and find themselves in the broad way to destruction, they have two ways to go. They may repent and cleanse themselves and obtain eventual peace and joy, or they may rationalize and excuse themselves and try the "escape" road. Those who follow the latter road sometimes so completely rationalize that they become calloused and lose the desire to repent, until the Spirit of God ceases to strive with them. Those who choose to meet the issue, and transform their lives, find it the harder road at first but the more desirable one in the end. (64-05)

One never solves problems by trying to escape from them. If you have stumps in the field, you dig them out and then you can make straight furrows. To plow around them is evasive, and only the escapist does that. (0/0/56)

Hope is indeed the great incentive to repentance, for without it no one would make the difficult, extended effort required—especially when the sin is a major one. (MF 340)

Procrastination of Repentance

Repentance becomes harder if delayed. While repentance is possible at any stage in the process of sin it is certainly easier in the early stages. Sinful habits may be compared to a river which flows slowly and placidly at first, then gains speed as it nears the falls over the precipice. Where it is slow and quiet, one can cross it in a rowboat with relative ease. As the stream flows faster it becomes more difficult to cross, but this is still possible. As the water nears the falls, it become almost a superhuman effort to row across without being swept mercilessly over the falls. The rowboat and its passenger have little chance when the speeding stream prepares to take its leap to the gorge below. But even now, with much external help, one might still be saved from destruction. Likewise, in the stream of sin, it is relatively easy to repent at first, but as the sin becomes more and more entrenched the overcoming becomes increasingly difficult.

If one ignores the roar of the falls below he is doomed; if he will not listen to the warnings given him, he is sucked into the swift current to destruction. (MF 168-69)

Sin becomes a habit. Sin is intensely habit-forming and sometimes moves men to the tragic point of no return. Without repentance there can be no forgiveness, and without forgiveness all the blessings of eternity hang in jeopardy. As the transgressor moves deeper and deeper in his sin, and the error is entrenched more deeply and the will to change is weakened, it becomes increasingly nearer hopeless and he skids down and down until either he does not want to climb back up or he has lost the power to do so. (MF 118)

Too often we find many excuses of our own calculation, and usually the delay in repentance encourages the continuation of the sin. You remember . . . that it is better to have a fence around the edge of the cliff than an ambulance at the base down in the valley. (74-09)

Repentance is for this life. Repentance is inseparable from time. No one can repent on the cross, nor in prison, nor in custody. One must have the opportunity of committing wrong in order to be really repentant. The man in handcuffs, the prisoner in the penitentiary, the man as he drowns, or as he dies—such a man certainly cannot repent totally. He can wish to do it, he may intend to change his life, he may determine that he will, but that is only the beginning.

That is why we should not wait for the life beyond but should abandon evil habits and weaknesses while in the flesh on the earth. . . .

Clearly it is difficult to repent in the spirit world of sins involving physical habits and actions. There one has spirit and mind but not the physical power to overcome a physical habit. (MF 167-68)

Procrastination steals opportunity. And then I think: Procrastination—thou wretched thief of time and opportunity!

When will men stand true to their one-time inspired yearnings?

Let those take care who postpone the clearing of bad habits and of constructively doing what they ought. "Some day I'll join the Church," says one. "I'll cease my drinking soon," says another. "One day I'll smoke no more," others pledge. "Some day we'll be ready for our temple sealings," promise a delayed-action husband and wife. "Some day, when they apologize, I'll forgive those who injured me," small souls say. "Some day I'll get my debts paid." "We'll get around soon to having our family prayers, and next week we'll start our home evenings." "We shall start paying tithing from our next paycheck." Tomorrow—yes, tomorrow. (66-03)

Process of Repentance

Steps of repentance. Repentance is a kind and merciful law. It is so far-reaching and all-inclusive. It has many elements and includes a sorrow for sin, a confession of sin, an abandonment of sin, a restitution for sin, and then the living of the commandments of the Lord, and this includes the forgiveness of others, even the forgiving of those who sin against us. (49-07)

To every forgiveness there is a condition. The plaster must be as wide as the sore. The fasting, the prayers, the humility must be equal to or greater than the sin. There must be a broken heart and a contrite spirit. There must be "sackcloth and ashes." There must be tears and genuine change of heart. There must be conviction of the sin, abandonment of the evil, confession of the error to properly constituted authorities of the Lord. There must be restitution and a confirmed, determined change of pace, direction, and destination. Conditions must be controlled and companionship corrected or changed. There must be a washing of robes to get them white and there must be a new consecration and devotion to the living of all of the laws of God. In short, there must be an overcoming of self, of sin, and of the world. (MF 353)

Repentance seems to fall into five steps:
1. *Sorrow for sin.* To be sorry for our sin we must know some-

thing of its serious implications. When fully convicted, we condition our minds to follow such processes as will rid us of the effects of the sin. We are sorry. We are willing to make amends, pay penalties, to suffer even to excommunication if necessary.

2. *Abandonment of sin.* It is best when one discontinues his error because of his realization of the gravity of his sin and when he is willing to comply with the laws of God....

The discontinuance must be a permanent one. True repentance does not permit repetition....

3. *Confession of sin.* The confession of sin is an important element in repentance. Many offenders have seemed to feel that a few prayers to the Lord were sufficient. They have thus justified themselves in hiding their sins.

Especially grave errors such as sexual sins shall be confessed to the bishop as well as to the Lord. There are two remissions which one might wish to have. First, the forgiveness from the Lord, and second, the forgiveness of the Lord's church through its leaders. As soon as one has an inner conviction of his sins, he should go to the Lord in "mighty prayer" as did Enos and never cease his supplications until he shall, like Enos, receive the assurance that his sins have been forgiven by the Lord. It is unthinkable that God absolves serious sins upon a few requests. He is likely to wait until there has been long, sustained repentance as evidenced by a willingness to comply with all his other requirements....

The bishop claims no authority to absolve sins, but he does share the burden, waive penalties, relieve tension and strain; and he may assure a continuance of activity. He will keep the whole matter most confidential.

4. *Restitution for sin.* When one is humble in sorrow, has unconditionally abandoned the evil, and confessed to those assigned by the Lord, he should next restore insofar as possible that which was damaged. If he burglarized, he should return to the rightful owner that which was stolen. Perhaps one reason murder is unforgivable is that having taken a life, the murderer cannot restore it. Restitution in full is not possible. Also, having robbed one of virtue, it is impossible to give it back.

However, the truly repentant soul will usually find things which can be done to restore to some extent. The true spirit of repentance demands this.

A pleading sinner must also forgive all people of all offenses committed against himself. The Lord is under no obligation to forgive us unless our hearts are fully purged of all hate, bitterness, and accusations against all others.

5. *Do the will of the Father.* . . . (80-53)

Sorrow for Sin

Conscience stirs up a desire to repent. How wonderful that God should endow us with this sensitive yet strong guide we call a conscience! Someone has aptly remarked that "conscience is a celestial spark which God has put into every man for the purpose of saving his soul." Certainly it is the instrument which awakens the soul to consciousness of sin, spurs a person to make up his mind to adjust, to convict himself of the transgression without soft-pedaling or minimizing the error, to be willing to face facts, meet the issue, and pay necessary penalties—and until the person is in this frame of mind he has not begun to repent. To be sorry is an approach, to abandon the act of error is a beginning, but until one's conscience has been sufficiently stirred to cause him to move in the matter, so long as there are excuses and rationalizations, one has hardly begun his approach to forgiveness. (MF 152)

God's spirit encourages repentance. God's Spirit continues with the honest in heart to strengthen, to help, and to save, but the Spirit of God ceases to strive with the man who excuses himself in wrongdoing. (74-20)

There must be sorrow for sin. True repentance must come to each individual. It cannot be accomplished by proxy. One can neither buy nor borrow nor traffic in it. There is no royal road to repentance: whether he be a president's son or a king's daughter, an emperor's prince or a lowly peasant, he must himself repent and his repentance must be personal and individual and humble. . . .

There must be a consciousness of guilt. It cannot be brushed aside. It must be acknowledged and not rationalized away. It must be given its full importance. If it is 10,000 talents, it must not be rated at 100 pence; if it is a mile long, it must not be rated a rod or a yard; if it is a ton transgression, it must not be rated a pound. . . .

There must be a pricking of conscience, perhaps sleepless hours, eyes that are wet, for Alma says: "None but the truly penitent are saved." (Alma 42:24.)

Remorse and deep sorrow then are preliminary to repentance.

There must not be rationalization to cover and hide. Alma, the great authority on this subject, we quote again: "Do not *endeavor to excuse yourself* in the least point because of your sins, by denying the justice of God; but do you let the justice of God, and his mercy, and his long-suffering have full sway in your heart; and let it bring you down to the dust in humility." (Alma 42:30; italics added.)

This is important: do let yourself be troubled; let the tears flow; let your heart be chastened. Do not endeavor to excuse yourself in the least point because of your sin. Let the justice of God have full sway in your heart so that it will bring you to the dust in humility.

There should be the element of shame. . . .

Rationalizing is the enemy to repentance. Someone has said, "Rationalizing is the bringing of ideals down to the level of one's conduct, while repentance is the bringing of one's conduct up to the level of his ideals."

The searing of one's conscience is certainly inimical to repentance, and to justify and rationalize is not the highway to repentance. . . .

Very frequently people think they have repented and are worthy of forgiveness when all they have done is to express sorrow or regret at the unfortunate happening, but their repentance is barely started. Until they have begun to make changes in their lives, transformation in their habits, and to add new thoughts to their minds, to be sorry is only a bare beginning. (74-10)

One is not repentant until he bares his soul and admits his actions without excuses or rationalizations, until he has really and truly suffered. Suffering is a very important part of repentance. One has not begun to repent until he has suffered intensely for his sins. (76-46)

In the revelation relating to the new and everlasting covenant, the Lord emphasizes the seriousness of certain transgressions by saying that even though the offenders may be redeemed and finally be exalted, "they shall be . . . delivered unto the buffetings of Satan unto the day of redemption, saith the Lord God." (D&C 132:26.)

Just what constitutes the "buffetings of Satan" no one knows except those who experience them, but I have seen many people who have been buffeted in life after they have come to themselves and realized to some degree the horror of their acts. If their sufferings were not the "buffetings of Satan," they must be a near approach to them. Certainly they reflect great sorrow, anguish of soul, shame, remorse, and physical and mental suffering. Perhaps this condition approaches the sufferings of which the Lord spoke when he said: "But if they would not repent they must suffer even as I; Which suffering caused myself, even God, the greatest of all, to tremble because of pain, and to bleed at every pore, and to suffer both body and spirit." (D&C 19:17-18.) (MF 356)

Repentance involves deep humility. The recognition of guilt should give one a sense of humility, of a "broken heart and a contrite spirit," and bring him to the proverbial "sackcloth and ashes" attitude. This does not mean that one must be servile and self-effacing to the destructive point, but rather one must have an honest desire to right the wrong.

Whatever our predispositions when influenced by the pride of our hearts, the person convinced of his sin and suffering godly sorrow for it in humility is reduced—or rather in this case elevated—to tears. Thus he expresses anguish for his folly and for the grief it has brought to the innocent. Those who have not been through the experience may not comprehend this reaction, but the spiritual writers with their deep insight understood that there is a healing balm in tears for the humble soul who is reaching toward God. Jeremiah wrote: "Oh that my head were waters, and mine eyes a fountain of tears, that I might weep day and night." (Jeremiah 9:1.) The Psalmist cried in his anguish: "I am weary with my groaning; all the night make I my bed to swim; I water my couch with my tears." (Psalm 6:6.) And again he pleaded: "Turn thee unto me, and have mercy upon me; for I am desolate and afflicted." (Psalm 25:16.) (MF 159-60)

Godly sorrow is not coerced. The felon in the penitentiary, coming to realize the high price he must pay for his folly, may wish he had not committed the crime. That is not repentance. . . .

The truly repentant man is sorry before he is apprehended. He is sorry even if his secret is never known. He desires to make voluntary amends. The culprit has not "godly sorrow" who must be found out by being reported or by chains of circumstances which finally bring the offense to light. The thief is not repentant who continues in grave offenses until he is caught. Repentance of the godly type means that one comes to recognize the sin and voluntarily and without pressure from outside sources begins his transformation. (MF 153)

Abandonment of Sin

Repentance requires change, not just expression of regret. This connection between effort and the repentance which attracts the Lord's forgiveness is often not understood. In my childhood, Sunday School lessons were given to us on the eighth chapter of John wherein we learned of the woman thrown at the feet of the Redeemer for judgment. My sweet Sunday School teacher lauded the Lord for having forgiven the woman. . . . This example has been used numerous times to show how easily one can be forgiven for gross sin.

But did the Lord forgive the woman? Could he forgive her? . . . His command to her was, "Go, and sin no more." He was directing the sinful woman to go her way, *abandon her evil life, commit no more sin, transform her life.* He was saying, Go, woman, and start your repentance; and he was indicating to her the beginning step—to *abandon her transgressions.* . . . Even Christ cannot forgive one in sin. The woman had neither time nor opportunity to repent totally. When her preparation and repentance were complete she could hope for forgiveness, but not before then. . . .

Another mistaken idea is that the thief on the cross was forgiven of his sins when the dying Christ answered: "Today shalt thou be with me in paradise." (Luke 23:43.) . . .

All the Lord's statement promised the thief was that both of them would soon be in the spirit world. The thief's show of repentance on the cross was all to his advantage, but his few words did not nullify a life of sin. The world should know that since the Lord himself cannot save men *in* their sins, no man on earth can administer any sacrament which will do that impossible thing. Hence the mere display of death-bed faith or repentance is not sufficient.

When the Lord, in his dying moments, turned to the Father and requested, "Father, forgive them; for they know not what they do" (Luke 23:34), he was referring to the soldiers who crucified him. They acted under the mandate of a sovereign nation. It was the Jews who were guilty of the Lord's death. Again, how could he forgive them, or how could his Father forgive them, when they were not repentant? (MF 68, 165-67)

One must change the conditions that led to sin. In abandoning sin one cannot merely wish for better conditions. He must make them. He may need to come to hate the spotted garments and loathe the sin. He must be certain not only that he has abandoned the sin but that he has changed the situations surrounding the sin. He should avoid the places and conditions and circumstances where the sin occurred, for these could most readily breed it again. He must abandon the people with whom the sin was committed. He may not hate the persons involved but he must avoid them and everything associated with the sin. He must dispose of all letters, trinkets, and things which will remind him of the "old days" and the "old times." He must forget addresses, telephone numbers, people, places, and situations from the sinful past, and build a new life. He must eliminate anything which would stir the old memories.

Does this mean that the man who has quit smoking or drinking or had sex pollutions find life empty for a time? The things which engaged him and caught his fancy and occupied his thoughts are gone, and better substitutions have not yet filled the void. This is Satan's opportunity.... Victory in the fight to abandon sin depends on constant vigilance.... Satan will not readily let go. Rather, he will probably send a host of new temptations to weaken the resolve of the repentant one. (MF 171-72, 86)

Now, my beloved brother, in the kindest, most understanding way, I ask you to change your life. I urge you to move away from your companions who may continue to fortify you in the rationalizations of destruction. You are vulnerable here to the attack of the destroyer. You are somewhat removed from the influence and enticings of the righteous influences and activities. Get off to yourself. Perhaps you could rent a room with a good Latter-day Saint family where you would see the contrasts. Fight your battle on neutral ground, at least, so that the righteous workers may have an equal break at least. (2/28/66)

Do not be discouraged by setbacks. Whenever there is a failure, get on your knees and make new pledges to your Father after having asked his forgiveness. You may feel, "What is the use?" when you may have failed many times and prayed many times, but you will eventually conquer. (9/6/57)

Confession of Sin

Admitting errors is painful but necessary. It is with you as though you were in mid-ocean swimming for your life. With the great confidence in your own power to swim to shore, you ignore the lifeline that is being thrown to you....

One day, I came home from school to find one of the horses tangled in the wire fence, bleeding profusely. He had been struggling to extricate himself and had cut deep gashes in his shoulder and legs. I shall never forget that day. As I remember it, the larger gash was about six inches long and so deep that a heavy piece of flesh and hide hung down, leaving an ugly bleeding wound. What could I do? There was no veterinary in the town, my father was away, the neighbor men were at work, and perhaps none of the boys in the area could do any better than I could do and time was of the essence, and so I faced the task, with the help of my sister, realizing that at best, I might do a clumsy job, but there was no alternative. I must try.

I washed the wound with hot soapy water, spread over the gash some of the common liniment we always had for our animals, and, with a large needle and common thread, I began to sew it together. When I pushed the needle through his sensitive flesh and skin, he jumped back and struck at me with his front feet and bit me on the arm. I had some mixed emotions at this juncture as I nursed my own wound. Here I was trying so hard to relieve him and this was the thanks I received. I realized he did not fully comprehend what I was trying so earnestly to do for him.

Now, I put a noose on his lower lip with a stick in it and twisted his lip so that his attention was turned to his lip agony while I could sew up the gash and get the wound fixed so it could heal itself. I had my little sister hold the noose tight. In and out, I pushed the needle through the quivering flesh until the edges of the wound were tied tight together.

Even after I had released the noose and the wound was firmly sewed together, I was still sure that this horse never knew nor fully realized what I had done for him. If he remembered me at all, it was probably as the one who had pricked his tender flesh with needles and severely pinched his lip in a noose.

The wound healed. There was always an ugly scar on the shoulder but the horse lived to give much service on the little farm.

You are "kicking against the pricks," my friend. You are swimming alone in a turbulent sea when you could have a raft or a rescue boat. You have done nothing yet of which you could not be forgiven, for the Lord is merciful and compassionate, but the day can come when all rescue boats will sail on to shore without you and it can be a wide, desolate sea. I am praying that I might say the right thing that would stir you to save yourself.

I am sure you are proud and it will take much courage to admit your errors and to accept assistance. My door will be open when you come. (2/0/00)

If there is any young person who has had misfortune to break the commandments of the Lord, let him or her seek an interview with the bishop on a very confidential basis. Generally having discussed the whole matter with the parents, let such a person confide in total truth to the bishop who has been named by your Heavenly Father through processes to be your common judge. It isn't a matter of just another man. He's the bishop; he has the responsibility, and you have the privilege of going to the bishop for a confidential interview.

We teach our bishops that they shall keep very sacred and confidential the things that are revealed to them in these interviews. In some very serious and continued problems of immorality, there is sometimes disciplinary action, but the bishop is entitled to the revelations of the Lord to make that judgment, and he can be a great blessing to his members. (74-09)

Confession is not only the revealing of errors to proper authorities, but the sharing of burdens to lighten them. One lifts at least part of his burden and places it on other shoulders which are able and willing to help carry the load. . . . Confession brings peace. How often have people departed from my office relieved and lighter of heart than for a long time! Their burdens were lighter, having been shared. They were free. The truth had made them free. (MF 187)

God requires proper confession. The Lord has planned an orderly process in this matter. It is the true way even though there have been distortions and spurious programs advanced. Some have complained at the need for confessing one's sins to Church authorities, stating that this is like the practices of other churches. In many areas in Church service, there are the genuine and the spurious. But the fact

that there is priestcraft is no reason for discarding the true priesthood; because there is a distorted form of baptism is no reason for
renouncing the true gateway to the Church; because there are presumptuous, spurious claims and practices is no reason for the Church
to forfeit the true and correct. . . .

While the major sins . . . call for confession to the proper Church
authorities, clearly such confession is neither necessary nor desirable
for all sins. Those of lesser gravity but which have offended others—
marital differences, minor fits of anger, disagreements and such—
should instead be confessed to the person or persons hurt and the
matter should be cleared between the persons involved, normally
without a reference to a Church authority. And if one confesses his
sins, there is an obligation on the part of the Church membership to
accept and forgive, to eradicate from their hearts the memory of the
transgression or ill feelings. (MF 184-85)

Perhaps confession is one of the hardest of all the obstacles for
the repenting sinner to negotiate. His shame often restrains him from
making known his guilt and acknowledging his error. Sometimes his
assumed lack of confidence in mortals to whom he should confess his
sin justifies in his mind his keeping the secret locked in his own heart.

Notwithstanding the difficulty the repenting sinner may experience, the requirement remains. . . . The confession of his major sins to
a proper Church authority is one of those requirements made by the
Lord. These sins include adultery, fornication, other sexual transgressions, and other sins of comparable seriousness. This procedure
of confession assures proper controls and protection for the Church
and its people and sets the feet of the transgressor on the path of true
repentance.

Many offenders in their shame and pride have satisfied their consciences, temporarily at least, with a few silent prayers to the Lord
and rationalized that this was sufficient confession of their sins. "But
I have confessed my sin to my Heavenly Father," they will insist,
"and that is all that is necessary." This is not true where a major sin
is involved. Then two sets of forgiveness are required to bring peace

to the transgressor—one from the proper authorities of the Lord's church, and one from the Lord himself. . . .

From the Lord's word to modern Israel—"confessing thy sins unto thy brethren, and before the Lord" (D&C 59:12)—it is plain that there are two confessions to make: one to the Lord and the other to "the brethren," meaning the proper ecclesiastical officers. . . . Thus one must not compromise or equivocate—he must make a clean, full confession. When the apples in a barrel rot, it is not enough to throw away half of the spoiled apples from the barrel and replace them with fresh apples on top. . . .

The voluntary confession is infinitely more acceptable in the sight of the Lord than is forced admission, lacking humility, wrung from an individual by questioning when guilt is evident. . . .

Unfortunately, many have to be brought to the involuntary or forced admission of sin. This comes when circumstances and information point to the guilt of the person who is seeking to hide his sin. It often precedes his final admission, and has led through the path of lies, then excuses after his lies have collapsed. This course heaps further sins upon him. . . .

Even making the admission upon confrontation is better than continuing to lie and evade the truth. In fact, many of those forced sooner or later to admit their sins do come to a full, sincere repentance and a humble desire to receive forgiveness. . . . We can hide nothing from God. True, it is possible sometimes, by lying and evasion and half-truth, to conceal the truth from God's servants on earth, but to what purpose? It will be impossible to lie to God on judgment day, so the unrepented sins will certainly be revealed then. Far better to confess them and forsake them now, and be rid of their burden!

How can one lie to the Lord or to his servants, especially when he may come to know that the Lord's servants may discern his lie? Section 1 of the Doctrine and Covenants reads: "And the rebellious shall be pierced with much sorrow; for their iniquities shall be spoken upon the housetops, and their secret acts shall be revealed." (D&C 1:3.) . . .

Those who lie to Church leaders forget or ignore an important rule and truth the Lord has set down: that when he has called men to high places in his kingdom and has placed on them the mantle of authority, a lie to them is tantamount to a lie to the Lord; a half-truth to his officials is like a half-truth to the Lord; a rebellion against his servants is comparable with a rebellion against the Lord; and any infraction against the Brethren who hold the gospel keys is a thought or an act against the Lord. (MF 178-85)

Missionaries should not parade old sins. As I have met with many groups of missionaries throughout the mission, I find a tendency for missionaries to tell their faults to their companions, their friends, and sometimes in public. There is not place in the mission field to publicize your weaknesses. When you have something that is disturbing you, you should go to your mission president. To him you may unburden yourself, confess your sins and your weaknesses. You may tell him your hopes and aspirations, but there is no reason why you should tell every companion the fact that you might have smoked a few cigarettes in your life before you came, or that you had taken the name of the Lord in vain, or any other of your weaknesses. We go forward on the assumption that you are worthy to do this work. If there is something of major importance in your life that had not been adjusted before your coming into the mission field, then certainly you should make those adjustments through your president. Don't tell the saints. That does not do anyone any good. It does not mean you are being hypocritical. You had some weaknesses, you repented, and those weaknesses are no longer a part of your life, and you are living in conformity with the program of the Church. (47-11)

Public acknowledgment of sin is proper. Long years ago in nearly every testimony meeting we had people who arose and said to their brothers and sisters, substantially, this: "I confess before you my weaknesses and imperfections and ask your assistance, your help, your tolerance, your understanding, and I pray the Lord will forgive me." We do not hear it so much anymore. The Lord so instructed us that we might seek forgiveness of our sins by having confessed them humbly, acknowledging them before the people and the Lord.

The Lord inspired his ancient prophet to say: "He that covereth his sins shall not prosper: but whoso confesseth and forsaketh them shall have mercy." (Proverbs 28:13.) (49-07)

Church Courts and Restitution

Penalties aid repentance. Much has been written in scripture of that part of true repentance that is confession. It is wholly proper for the transgressor to go to the bishop or stake or mission president and to confess voluntarily the transgressions he has committed. He should be frank and offer the information and answer honestly all the questions propounded to him by that authority. This brings humility and takes courage: The Church's authority will in confidence hear his story and suggest recovery plans and impose the penalties.

In transgressions of lesser magnitude he may place the person on probation, or in the more serious ones he may disfellowship or excommunicate. If he feels that the transgression is minimal and deserves forgiveness, he may grant a waiver of penalties that we sometimes call forgiveness and permit that person to continue his activity in the Church, and he will likely say to that person, "Because the sin was minimal and your repentance seems to be sincere, I feel the Lord would have me forgive you for the Church." But one should remember that that forgiveness is conditional, and if repeated, the original sins return. . . .

The true confession is not only a matter of making known certain developments, but it is a matter of getting peace, which seemingly can come in no other way.

Frequently people talk about time: How long before they can be forgiven? How soon may they go to the temple?

Repentance is timeless. The evidence of repentance is transformation. We certainly must keep our values straight and our evaluations intact.

Certainly we must realize that penalties for sin are not a sadistic desire on the part of the Lord, and that is why when people get deep in immorality or other comparable sins, there must be action by courts with proper jurisdiction. Many people cannot repent until they have suffered much. They cannot direct their thoughts into new, clean channels. They cannot control their acts. They cannot plan their future properly until they have lost values that they did not seem to fully appreciate. Therefore, the Lord has prescribed excommunication, disfellowshipment, or probation, and this is in line with Alma's statement that there could be no repentance without suffering, and many people cannot suffer, having not come to a realization of their sin and a consciousness of their guilt.

One form of punishment is deprivation, and so if one is not permitted to partake of the sacrament or to use his priesthood or to go to the temple or to preach or pray in any of the meetings, it constitutes a degree of embarrassment and deprivation and punishment. In fact, the principal punishment that the Church can deal is deprivation from privileges. . . .

If no penalties are assessed, if no punishment is required, if no deprivation is expected, then what would induce the average transgressor to change his ways? (74-10)

Church penalties for sin involve deprivations—the withholding of temple privileges, priesthood advancements, Church positions and other opportunities for service and growth. Such deprivations result from errors which are not always punishable by serious measures but which render the perpetrator unworthy to give leadership and receive high honors and blessings in God's kingdom. These are all retardations in our eternal progress which a person brings on himself. (MF 326)

Bishops should act decisively. Today is the day. When something develops that is ugly and nasty, you had better get busy and don't be afraid of any situation. The Lord is on your side and you must remember that numerous people are saved by excommunication. They are not *lost* by excommunication. They are *saved* through excommunication—when it's necessary, of course, only when it's necessary. But don't give a little ruling that one will be disfellowshipped when he ought to be excommunicated, because he will come back. Nearly all of them do come back because they come to realize they had committed sins and they have to pay the penalties. When they have paid the penalties and have repented of their sins, they can come back and life then has meaning to them. (74-19)

The former presidents of the Church have all been quoted over and over and over that we must not forgive so easily. Now, that sounds bad in some way, doesn't it? We must be forgiving as far as we are concerned, but as far as the Church is concerned, we have got to be extremely careful, and I am speaking to you bishops particularly now. You have no right to say, "Well, alright, John. I can see the tears in your eyes. You can be free of it." You had better be pretty careful. You had better be sure that they are repentant and that they have changed their lives. We must remember that repentance is more than just saying, "I am sorry." It is more than tears in one's eyes. It is more than a half a dozen prayers. Repentance means suffering. If a person hasn't suffered, he hasn't repented. I don't care how many times he says he has. If he hasn't suffered, he hasn't repented. He has got to go through a change in his system whereby he suffers and then forgiveness is a possibility. Nobody can be forgiven unless there is adequate repentance. You bishops remember that, will you! . . . The Savior can do almost anything in the world, but he can't forgive somebody who hasn't repented.

There has got to be "that much" repentance before "that much" sin can be forgiven. Just as sure as you live. No bishop has got a right to just sit there in back of his desk and say, "Well, Linda, I can see that you are sorry that you did this. You are all forgiven and are clean in every way." She isn't, because the Lord has made a rule and has given us a law, and he can't break it himself, can he? He wouldn't be God if he would just ignore all his own rules. Now, if you will remember that, brethren, that it is very important, let them show their repentance. Let them prove their repentance, for a person who continues to go back to the same evil is not repentant at the first. There has to be a total abandonment as well as tears and prayers and service. And that we must watch very, very carefully. (74-33)

Disfellowshipment and excommunication are serious matters. If careful consideration indicates the necessity, action for disfellowship-

ment is taken and this denies the blessings of Church activity and
participation, though it does not deprive the sinner of membership or
priesthood. When such action is taken, it remains for the repentant
one to continue in his efforts to be faithful and prove himself worthy
to do all that he would normally be permitted to do. When this is
done sufficiently, to the satisfaction of the Church court which
imposed the penalty, generally the hand of fellowship may be restored and full activity and participation be permitted the erring
one. . . .

The scriptures speak of Church members being "cast out" or
"cut off," or having their names "blotted out." This means excommunication. This dread action means the total severance of the individual from the Church. The person who is excommunicated loses his
membership in the Church and all attendant blessings. As an excommunicant, he is in a worse situation than he was before he joined the
Church. He has lost the Holy Ghost, his priesthood, his endowments,
his sealings, his privileges, and his claim upon eternal life. This is
about the saddest thing which could happen to an individual. Better
that he suffer poverty, persecution, sickness, and even death. A true
Latter-day Saint would far prefer to see a loved one in his bier than
excommunicated from the Church. If the one cut off did not have
this feeling of desolateness and barrenness and extreme loss, it would
be evidence that he did not understand the meaning of excommunication.

An excommunicant has no Church privileges. He may not . . .
partake of the sacrament, serve in Church positions, offer public
prayers, or speak in meetings; he may not pay tithing except under
certain conditions as determined by the bishop. . . .

There is a possibility of an excommunicant returning to the blessings of the Church with full membership, and this can only be done
through baptism following satisfactory repentance. The way is hard
and rough and, without the help of the Holy Ghost to whisper and
plead and warn and encourage, one's climb is infinitely harder than if
he were to repent before he loses the Holy Ghost, his membership,
and the fellowship of the saints. The time is usually long, very long,
as those who have fought their way back will attest. Any who have

been finally restored would give the same advice: Repent first—do not permit yourself to be excommunicated if there is a possible way to save yourself from that dire calamity. (MF 328-30)

Waiving of Church sanctions is not absolution. When the bishop or stake president terminates the deprivation of a transgressor and permits him to continue in his Church services and opportunities, he is waiving penalties and, in a sense, forgiving for the Church. In such cases, I have always told the individuals, "You must also seek and secure from the God of heaven a final repentance, and only he can absolve." (12/16/64)

Although there are many ecclesiastical officers in the Church whose positions entitle and require them to be judges, the authority of those positions does not necessarily qualify them to forgive or remit sins. Those who can do that are extremely few in this world.

The bishop, and others in comparable positions, can forgive in the sense of waiving the penalties. In our loose connotation we sometimes call this forgiveness, but it is not forgiveness in the sense of "wiping out" or absolution. . . .

Let it be said in emphasis that even the First Presidency and the apostles do not make a practice of absolving sins. . . . It is the Lord, however, who forgives sins. (MF 332-33)

We must help the transgressor return. While we cannot tolerate sin and we exercise Church discipline against those who do sin, we must help the transgressor, with love and understanding, to work his or her way back to full fellowship in the Church. Let us help each toward the blessing of a lasting repentance, a resolute turning away from error. (77-34)

Repentance requires restitution where possible. The sinner should make restitution. It is obvious that the murderer cannot give back a life he has taken; the libertine cannot restore the virtue he has violated; the gossip may be unable to nullify and overcome the evils done by a loose tongue; but, so far as is possible, one must restore and make good the damage done. (49-07)

"A broken heart and a contrite spirit" will usually find ways to restore to some extent. The true spirit of repentance demands that he who injures shall do everything in his power to right the wrong. (MF 195)

Forgiving Others and Keeping Commandments

Repentance requires forgiving others. The pleading sinner, desiring to make restitution for his acts, must also forgive others of all offenses committed against him. The Lord will not forgive us unless our hearts are fully purged of all hate, bitterness, and accusation against our fellowmen. (MF 200)

A man who had confessed infidelity was forgiven by his wife, who saw much in him to commend and believed in his total repentance. To him, I said: "Brother Blank, you should from this day forward be the best husband a woman ever had. You should be willing to forgive her little eccentricities, overlook her weaknesses, for she has forgiven you the ten-thousand-talent sin and you can afford to forgive numerous little hundred-pence errors." (MF 195)

"For if ye forgive men their trespasses, your heavenly Father will also forgive you: But if ye forgive not men their trespasses, neither will your Father forgive your trespasses." (Matthew 6:14-15.)
Hard to do? Of course. The Lord never promised an easy road, nor a simple gospel, nor low standards, nor a low norm. The price is high, but the goods attained are worth all they cost. The Lord himself turned the other cheek; he suffered himself to be buffeted and beaten without remonstrance; he suffered every indignity and yet spoke no word of condemnation. And his question to all of us is: "Therefore, what manner of men ought ye to be?" And his answer to us is: "Even as I am." (3 Nephi 27:27.) (77-35)

To obtain forgiveness of our sins we must forgive. Read the scriptures given us on that point: "And be ye kind one to another, tenderhearted, forgiving one another, even as God for Christ's sake hath forgiven you." (Ephesians 4:32.)

To you who will not forgive there comes great condemnation, probably even greater than that to him who gave the offense. . . .

Why does the Lord ask you to love your enemies and to return good for evil? That *you* might have the benefit of it. It does not injure him so much when you hate a person, especially if he is far removed and does not come in contact with you, but the hate and the bitterness canker your unforgiving heart.

"Lord, how oft shall my brother sin against me, and I forgive him?" And the Lord said: "I say not unto thee, Until seven times: but, Until seventy times seven." (Matthew 18:21-22.) . . . When they have repented and come on their knees to ask forgiveness, most of us can forgive, but the Lord has required that we shall even forgive if they do not repent nor ask forgiveness of us.

It must be very clear to us, then, that we must still forgive without retaliation or vengeance, for the Lord will do for us such as is necessary. "Vengeance is mine; I will repay, saith the Lord." (Romans 12:19.) Bitterness injures the one who carries it, it hardens and shrivels and cankers. . . .

Another impressive example of unholy judging comes to us in the Lord's parable of the unmerciful servant who owed to his lord ten thousand talents, but being unable to pay, his lord commanded him to be sold, and his wife and children and all that he had, and payment to be made. The servant fell down and begged for a moratorium. When the compassionate lord had loosed him and forgiven his debt, this conscienceless person straightway found one of his fellow-servants who owed him an hundred pence. Taking him by the throat he demanded payment in full, and upon failure of the debtor, cast him into prison. When the lord heard of this rank injustice, he chastised the unmerciful servant. . . .

According to my Bible, the Roman penny is an eighth of an ounce of silver, while the talent is 750 ounces. This would mean that the talent was equivalent to 6000 pence, and ten thousand talents would be to one hundred pence, as 600,000 is to one. The unmerciful servant then, was forgiven 600,000 units, but would not forgive a single one.

I met a woman once, demanding and critical. She accused her stake president of harshness and would have displaced him if she could. She had committed adultery, and yet with her comparative debt of sixty million pence, she had the temerity to criticize her leader with a hundred pence debt. I also knew a young man who complained at his bishop and took offense at the leader's inefficiency and his grammatical errors, yet he himself had in his life sins comparable to the talents and had the effrontery to accuse his bishop of weaknesses comparable only to the pence. (49-07)

Forgiving involves forgetting. "I, the Lord, will forgive whom I will forgive, but of you it is required to forgive all men." (D&C 64:10.)...

The lesson stands for us today. Many people, when brought to a reconciliation with others, say that they forgive, but they continue to hold malice, continue to suspect the other party, continue to disbelieve the other's sincerity....

I may add that unless a person forgives his brother his trespasses *with all his heart* he is unfit to partake of the sacrament....

Some people not only cannot or will not forgive and forget the transgressions of others, but go to the other extreme of hounding the alleged transgressor. Many letters and calls have come to me from individuals who are determined to take the sword of justice in their own hands and presume to see that a transgressor is punished....

To such who would take the law into their own hands, we read again the positive declaration of the Lord: "There remaineth in him the greater sin." (D&C 64:9.) The revelation continues: "And ye ought to say in your hearts—let God judge between me and thee, and reward thee according to thy deeds." (D&C 64:11.) When known transgressions have been duly reported to the proper ecclesiastical officers of the Church, the individual may rest the case and leave the responsibility with the Church officers. If those officers tolerate sin in the ranks, it is an awesome responsibility for them and they will be held accountable....

The spirit of revenge, of retaliation, of bearing a grudge, is entirely foreign to the gospel of the gentle, forgiving Jesus Christ....

The Lord can judge men by their thoughts as well as by what they say and do, for he knows even the intents of their hearts; but this is not true of humans. We hear what people say, we see what they do, but being unable to discern what they think or intend, we often judge wrongfully if we try to fathom the meaning and motives behind their actions and place on them our own interpretation. (MF 262-68)

Repentance requires keeping all the commandments. One of the requisites for repentance is the living of the commandments of the Lord. Perhaps few people realize that as an important element; though one may have abandoned a particular sin and even confessed it to his bishop, yet he is not repentant if he has not developed a life of action and service and righteousness, which the Lord has indicated to be very necessary: "He that repents and does the commandments of the Lord shall be forgiven." (D&C 1:32.) ...

True repentance incorporates within it a washing, a purging, a changing of attitudes, a reappraising, a strengthening toward self-mastery. It is not a simple matter for one to transform his life overnight, nor to change attitudes in a moment, nor to rid himself in a hurry of unworthy companions. (74-10)

Repentance is a lifelong task. Since all of us sin in greater or lesser degree, we are all in need of constant repentance, of continually raising our sights and our performance. One can hardly do the commandments of the Lord in a day, a week, a month, or a year. This is an effort which must be extended through the remainder of one's years. To accomplish it every soul should develop the same spirit of devotion and dedication to the work of the Lord as the bishop or the Relief Society president enjoy. Most often theirs is near total devotion. (MF 202)

We are all sinners. We all need to repent. We all need to change our lives and to make them more righteous, and become valiant as the children of Enoch were valiant, so that we may receive the blessings which are promised to us and which we are striving for.

Many of us have not yet surrendered, or if it has been a surrender it has been a conditional surrender, with many reservations. (51-03)

The Fruits of Repentance

Repentance brings the miracle of forgiveness. When we think of miracles, most of us think of healings under the power of the priesthood. But there is another, even greater miracle—the miracle of forgiveness....

The essence of the miracle of forgiveness is that it brings peace to the previously anxious, restless, frustrated, perhaps tormented soul. In a world of turmoil and contention this is indeed a priceless gift. (MF 362-63)

I am grateful for the Lord's longsuffering. He seems to get so little in return for his investment in us. However, the principle of repentance—of rising again whenever we fall, brushing ourselves off, and setting off again on that upward trail—is the basis for our hope. It is through repentance that the Lord Jesus Christ can work his healing miracle, infusing us with strength when we are weak, health when we are sick, hope when we are downhearted, love when we feel empty, and understanding when we search for truth. (79-17)

God forgives even ugly sins. Sometimes a guilt consciousness overpowers a person with such a heaviness that when a repentant one looks back and sees the ugliness, the loathsomeness of the transgression, he is almost overwhelmed and wonders, "Can the Lord ever forgive me? Can I ever forgive myself?" But when one reaches the depths of despondency and feels the hopelessness of his position, and when he cries out to God for mercy in helplessness but in faith, there comes a still, small, but penetrating voice whispering to his soul, "Thy sins are forgiven thee." (MF 344)

Even adultery is forgivable. In the matter of sexual sin many have ... been deeply worried by their interpretation of a statement by the Prophet Joseph Smith...: "If a man commit adultery, he cannot receive the celestial kingdom of God. Even if he is saved in any kingdom, it cannot be the celestial kingdom." (DHC 6:81.)...

If the above quotation were taken literally, it would seem difficult to reconcile it with other scriptures and with the practices and policies of the Church. Is it possible that the Prophet just did not take time to elaborate on the matter at that time, or that in recording it he did not double check the implications? Or was it properly recorded when he gave it?

The same Joseph Smith who gave us that quotation also gave us many scriptures which state that there is forgiveness; and other holy scriptures attest that repentance can bring forgiveness if that repentance is sufficiently "all-out" and total....

Joseph Smith added the significant words "who receive me and repent," which are italicized in the following passage: "All manner of sin and blasphemy shall be forgiven unto men *who receive me and repent;* but the blasphemy against the Holy Ghost, it shall not be forgiven unto men." (Joseph Smith Translation, Matthew 12:26.)

Going back to the Prophet's original statement, had he inserted in it the three words I believe it implies—"and remains unrepentant" —this statement would fit perfectly in the program as given in the numerous scriptures, many of which came through the Prophet himself....

Perhaps Paul's comment to the Corinthians shows a like situation. "Be not deceived: neither fornicators, nor idolaters, nor adulterers, nor effeminate, nor abusers of themselves with mankind, Nor thieves, nor covetous, nor drunkards, nor revilers, nor extortioners, shall inherit the kingdom of God." (1 Corinthians 6:9-10.)...

But Paul's next thought is comforting as well as clarifying: "And such were some of you: but ye are washed, but ye are sanctified, but ye are justified in the name of the Lord Jesus, and by the Spirit of our God." (1 Corinthians 6:11.)

This is the great secret. Some of those who inherit the kingdom may have committed such grievous sins but are no longer in those categories. They are *no longer unclean,* having been washed, sanctified and justified. Paul's hearers had been in those despicable categories, but having now received the gospel with its purifying, trans-forming powers they were changed. (MF 347-52)

Repentance brings peace. Numerous others who have walked critical, lonely, thorny paths in abject misery, have finally accepted correction, acknowledged errors, cleansed their hearts of bitterness, and have come again to peace, that coveted peace which is so con-spicuous in its absence. And the frustrations of criticism, bitterness, and the resultant estrangements have given place to warmth and light and peace. And all those who have come into the warmth of the love of the Lord Jesus Christ and his program, could shout with the Prophet Joseph Smith:

> Let your hearts rejoice, and be exceedingly glad. . . .
> And let the sun, moon, and the morning stars sing together, and let all the sons of God shout for joy! And let the eternal creations declare his name forever and ever! And again I say, how glorious is the voice we hear from heaven, proclaiming in our ears, glory, and salvation, and honor, and immortality, and eternal life; kingdoms, principalities, and powers! (D&C 128:22-23.) (55-06)

God forgets sins after repentance. One day in the temple in Salt Lake City, as I walked down the long hall preparing to go into one of the rooms to perform a marriage for a young couple, a woman fol-lowed me . . . and with great agitation she said, "Elder Kimball, do you remember me?" Her eyes were searching and her ears were seek-ing to hear if I remembered her. I was abashed. For the life of me I could not make the connection. I was much embarrassed. I finally said, "I am sorry, but I cannot remember you." Instead of disap-pointment, there was great joy that came to her face. She was relieved. She said, "Oh, I am so grateful you can't remember me. With my husband I spent all night with you one time, while you were trying to change our lives. We had committed sin, and we were struggling to get rid of it. You labored all night to help me to clear it. We have repented, and we have changed our lives totally. I am glad you don't remember me, because if you, one of the apostles, cannot remember me, maybe the Savior cannot remember my sins." (76-47)

Resistance to sin is better than repentance. Another error into which some transgressors fall, because of the availability of God's forgiveness, is the illusion that they are somehow stronger for having committed sin and then lived through the period of repentance. This simply is not true. That man who resists temptation and lives without sin is far better off than the man who has fallen, no matter how repentant the latter may be. The reformed transgressor, it is true, may be more understanding of one who falls into the same sin, and to that extent perhaps more helpful in the latter's regeneration. But his sin and repentance have certainly not made him stronger than the consistently righteous person. (MF 357)

The faithful son is more blessed than the prodigal. In the impressive parable of the prodigal son the Lord taught us a remarkable lesson. This squanderer lived but for today. He spent his life in riotous living. He disregarded the commandments of God. His inheritance was expendable, and he spent it. He was never to enjoy it again, as it was irretrievably gone. No quantity of tears or regrets or remorse could bring it back. Even though his father forgave him and dined him and clothed him and kissed him, he could not give back to the profligate son that which had been dissipated. But the other brother, who had been faithful, loyal, righteous and constant, retained his inheritance, and the father reassured him: "All that I have is thine." ...

When I was a child in Sunday School my teacher impressed upon me the contemptibility of the older son in his anger and complaining, while she immortalized the adulterous prodigal who was presumed to have expressed repentance. But let no reader compare grumbling and peevishness with the degrading sins of immorality and consorting with harlots in riotous living. (MF 307, 309)

Baptism follows repentance. Repentance is preliminary to and a necessary forerunner of the baptism of the water and of the Spirit. Repentance contemplates a transformation of life. (55-02)

Baptism

Baptism is essential. Jesus Christ . . . traveled to the River Jordan to be baptized by immersion by his cousin John, called the Baptist. By participating in this symbolic ordinance, he demonstrated to all that baptism is the door into this church. From heaven, his Father acknowledged the important occasion, saying, "This is my beloved Son, in whom I am well pleased." (Matthew 3:17.) (78-06)

To be baptized is to enter into a covenant of commission. But to fail to be baptized when one is convinced the work is divine is a sin of omission, and penalties will be assessed for failure to meet this requirement. Tens of thousands of people having heard the gospel have failed to be baptized, giving trivial excuses. This is a most serious sin. The Lord told Nicodemus that he and others would not even see the kingdom of God if they rejected the required baptism. (MF 94)

To gain eternal life there must be a rebirth, a transformation, and an unburdening self of pride, weaknesses, and prejudice. You must begin as a little child, clean, teachable. . . . He expects you to divest yourself of every foreign thought, act, and inclination, and accept him and live his plan. And the "rest," which is exaltation, will be your glory. . . .

Can you envision the cleanliness as one emerges from the watery grave, washed, and the freedom and joy and glory of it? (58-04)

Everyone must be baptized, he must receive the Holy Ghost, and when he is baptized and confirmed, he is a member of the kingdom of God upon the earth, which has its counterpart in heaven and is the kingdom of heaven.

He said to authorized servants, "Go ye into all the world and preach the gospel. He that believeth and is baptized shall be saved and he that believeth not shall be damned." And what did he mean by being damned? He didn't mean to go to the physical, everlasting, burning fires. He meant they would be stopped in their progress.

They would be held to the area where their work had been done, telestial or terrestrial. They will be saved in those kingdoms. They will be damned in those kingdoms. Doesn't matter which way they use it. It means they will be relegated to the area wherein they have earned their reward. And baptism, he has said over and over, is an absolute, and no one can have the kingdom without the baptism. That is one of the works. That is one of the first of all the principles and ordinances. That is a celestial law, and no one will go into the celestial kingdom without it. They can belong to any other organization and go into the terrestrial and telestial kingdom. (57-03)

Parents must prepare children for baptism. The scripture says that parents shall teach their children to pray and walk uprightly before the Lord. And if they haven't taught their children the law of baptism and confirmation, and to do right by the time they are eight years of age, then the sin will be upon the heads of the parents. (D&C 68:25-28.) Now, that does not say parents start to teach the child at eight. It should have been done by the time the child is eight years of age. By then the child should have received many of the concepts that will be an important part of his life. So you will already have had your child taught and trained in honesty, uprightness, integrity, and cleanliness; in the love of the Lord and his fellowmen; and in all the things that a grown person should know. He should know much of it before he is eight. Then, when he is eight, he is clean, he is sweet, he is free from immorality or sins of any kind; and the father leads him to the baptismal font, perhaps, or baptizes him himself. My father baptized me. I baptized all my children, with the permission of the bishop, who has the responsibility, of course. We don't go and do it ourselves without authority. (76-35)

Others prepare children of inactive parents. We can baptize nearly every child that becomes eight years of age. There is a feeling among many people that we shouldn't baptize a child from an inactive home. We baptize him when he is eight, of course with the consent of his parents, and sometimes we have to labor on that. Then we go forward with the Sunday School, the Primary, our home teaching program, and with home evenings and every effort to keep that child growing up in the Church. That's our responsibility. (70-03)

Baptism is a covenant with God. All members have been baptized by immersion in water and have received the Holy Ghost by the laying on of hands by properly authorized men who hold the holy priesthood. We all have been received by baptism into The Church of Jesus Christ when we have humbled ourselves before God, have desired to be baptized, have come forth with broken hearts and contrite spirits, and when we have witnessed before the Church that we are truly repentant of our sins and are willing to take upon us the name of Jesus Christ, having a determination to serve him to the end and thus manifest by our works that we have received the Spirit of Christ unto the remission of our sins. (75-13)

Detractors in the Church breach baptismal covenants. Paul fiercely denounced those who "served the creature more than the Creator," the "haters of God." There were in those days, as today and among our own people, groups who deny "the Lord that bought them" with his own blood, and yet claim membership in his Church and in their hypocrisy and egotism pretend allegiance. There are those who receive the benefits of the Church while not only failing to make any contributions to it but actually being destructive of it and its standards. Those hypocritical unbelievers use their powers to destroy rather than to build up. (MF 58)

Remembering covenants prevents apostasy. That is the real purpose of the sacrament, to keep us from forgetting, to help us to remember. I suppose there would never be an apostate, there would never be a crime, if people remembered, really remembered, the things they had covenanted at the water's edge or at the sacrament table and in the temple. I suppose that is the reason the Lord asked Adam to offer sacrifices, for no other reason than that he and his posterity would remember—remember the basic things that they had been taught. I guess we as humans are prone to forget. It is easy to forget. Our sorrows, our joys, our concerns, our great problems seem to wane to some extent as time goes on, and there are many lessons that we learn which have a tendency to slip from us. The Nephites forgot. They forgot the days when they felt good.

I remember a young Navaho boy returning from his mission who was supported largely by a seventies quorum in the Bonneville Stake. I happened to be present the day he made his report and as tears rolled down his face, he said, "Oh, if I could only remember always just how I feel now." (67-03)

The Gift of the Holy Ghost

All men have the benefit of conscience. You must realize that you have something like the compass, like the Liahona, in your own system. Every child is given it. When he is eight years of age, he knows good from evil, if his parents have been teaching him well. If he ignores the Liahona that he has in his own makeup, he eventually may not have it whispering to him. But if we will remember that everyone of us has the thing that will direct him aright, our ship will not get on the wrong course and suffering will not happen and bows will not break and families will not cry for food—if we listen to the dictates of our own Liahona, which we call the conscience. (76-56)

You folks have all been born with the Spirit of Christ. All of you and all of your friends have been given this opportunity, have had a conscience, and the conscience explains to people why things are not wrong or that they are wrong. (76-20)

Those who are baptized receive the gift of the Holy Ghost. The Holy Ghost, a personage of spirit, a member of the Godhead, comes temporarily and on special occasions to some, but is given to all the children of men when they have fully complied with the program provided by the Savior of the world. When the hands of proper authority in due process are laid upon the head, the Holy Ghost is received by every worthy soul who has been properly baptized into the kingdom. (55-02)

The Holy Ghost makes right and wrong clear. You know what is right and what is wrong. You have all received the Holy Ghost following your baptism. You need no one to brand the act or thought as wrong or right. You know by the Spirit. (74-32)

The Holy Ghost influences intangibly. Little can we feel, see or smell, or identify with our five senses the little breeze that comes up each day and cools our warmed countenance . . . but we know there has been a breeze. We have felt its cooling influence. And so is the Spirit when it comes to us in the holy ordinances of God's program. I think of the dawn. The night is dark, and suddenly it begins to grey, then it becomes lighter, and finally in its glory like the sun. That is the way the Spirit moves us. It is not tangible, it is hard to catalogue, but here comes the spirit birth after the water birth. (55-13)

The gift of the Holy Ghost grows with worthiness. If you are baptized when you are eight years old, of course you are a child, and there is much you would not be expected to know. But the Holy Ghost comes to you as you grow and learn and make yourselves worthy. It comes a little at a time as you merit it. And as your life is in harmony, you gradually receive the Holy Ghost in a great measure. (75-40)

Follow promptings of the Holy Ghost. There is only one safe and sure way for man to act. The Lord has given him free choice and has given him, gratis, the information which is the best choice to make and what will be the results of either choice made. The Lord has never condemned nor permitted destruction to any people until he has warned them. Warning is as universal as the need for warning. One cannot say he did not know better. Ignorance is no excuse in the law. Every normal person may have a sure way of knowing what is right and what is wrong. He may learn the gospel and receive the Holy Spirit, which will always guide him as to right and wrong. In addition to this, he has the leaders of the Lord's church. And the only sure, safe way is to follow that leadership—follow the Holy Spirit within you and follow the prophets, dead and living. (68-08)

CHAPTER 5

Spiritual Development

Importance of Prayer

We are commanded to pray. Inherent in the "thou shalt not" is the inference "thou shalt." It is not enough not to worship the manmade creations, but it is incumbent upon man to bow down in humility to our Father in Heaven and serve him. It is not enough not to curse and blaspheme the name of Deity and think of him irreverently, but man must call upon his name frequently in personal, family, and public prayers in reverence and adoration. We should speak often of him and his program. We should read of him and his works. (MF 98)

Spirituality comes with prayer. Prayer is the passport to spiritual power. (73-02)

Some have said, "Why pray when our Father in Heaven already knows what we need and want?" We all enjoy doing for those who are appreciative. Even the Lord wishes us to voice our thoughts. The value comes to us. As we address his holy name, we become calm and quiet and attune ourselves to spiritual things. (38-01)

Prayer provides solace. The Lord has not promised us freedom from adversity and affliction. Instead, he has given us the avenue of communication known as prayer, whereby we might humble ourselves and seek his help and divine guidance. (82-02)

Family Prayer

Prayer knits families together. Our Father in Heaven has given us the blessing of prayer to help us succeed in our all-important activities of home and life. I know that if we pray fervently and righteously, individually and as a family, when we arise in the morning and when we retire at night, and around our tables at mealtime, we will not only knit together as loved ones but we will grow spiritually. We have so much need for our Heavenly Father's help as we seek to learn gospel truths and then live them, and as we seek his help in the decisions of our lives. It is especially in our family circles where our children can learn how to talk to Heavenly Father by listening to their parents. They can learn about heartfelt and honest prayer from such experiences. (82-01)

In the family prayer there is even more than the supplication and prayer of gratitude. It is a forward step toward family unity and family solidarity. It builds family consciousness and establishes a spirit of family interdependence. Here is a moment of the rushed day with blatant radios hushed, lights low, and all minds and hearts turned to each other and to the infinite; a moment when the world is shut out and heaven enclosed within. (46-02)

Universal family prayer could change the nations. O my beloved hearers, what a world it would be if a million families in this church were to be on their knees like this every night and morning! And what a world it would be if nearly a hundred million families in this great land and other hundreds in other lands were praying for their sons and daughters twice daily! And what a world this would be if a billion families through the world were in home evenings and church activity and were on their physical knees pouring out their souls for their children, their families, their leaders, their governments!

This kind of family life could bring us back toward the translation experience of righteous Enoch. The millennium would be ushered in. (73-02)

Prayer protects families. Let us all revive our individual and family prayers. Prayer is an armor of protection against temptation and I promise you that if you will teach your children to pray, fervently and full of faith, many of your problems are solved before they begin. (38-01)

Family prayer is neglected. There is another thing in the lives of these youngsters that you can do in regard to prayer. I am shocked week after week, as I reorganize or organize stakes and interview the prominent people in various communities, to find the large number of them who do not have their family prayers night and morning. Men of the stature of stake presidencies, high councils, bishoprics, and so on, seem to get by with having only one prayer a day and sometimes not that regularly and they seem to justify themselves. You can be instrumental in changing that pattern, I am sure. It cannot be done in a day because your youth have no controls in their homes, but they will be marrying before very long. Teach them to pray the Church way. Have them say their own individual prayers, of course, and use whatever influence they might have in their own homes to get family prayer started every night and morning and so plan their own family lives after their marriage. (62-08)

Family prayer helps establish values. The children will learn to honor and revere the Lord's anointed leaders as they are taught to pray for their local and general authorities; they will love the Lord as they pray for his work; they will love their fellowmen as they pray for the sick, the mourners, the distressed. They will anticipate with gladness their own missions as they pray for the missionaries out preaching the gospel. (46-02)

When we kneel in family prayer, our children at our side on their knees are learning habits that will stay with them all through their lives. If we do not take time for prayers, what we are actually saying to our children is, "Well, it isn't very important, anyway. We won't worry about it. If we can do it conveniently, we will have our prayer, but if the school bell rings and the bus is coming and employment is calling—well, prayer isn't very important and we will do it when it is convenient." Unless planned for, it never seems to be convenient. On the other hand, what a joyous thing it is to establish such customs and habits in the home that when parents visit their children in the latter's homes after they are married they just naturally kneel with them in the usual, established manner of prayer! (MF 253)

Let me tell you about the little Indian child who came into the home of a white family in the West here for the year, to go to school. The little child came in very timidly, and the day passed on, and finally it came time for the evening meal. When they came to the table, the foster father and mother took hold of their chairs, as to pull them out and sit in them, and then they happened to notice that down at her chair was a little Indian girl kneeling. They must have made a very quick decision. It must have been a rather difficult one to make, a decision that meant that they either had to explain to this little girl that they did not have family prayers, or they had to break a custom of their lifetime, and so two people who had never before been on their knees, knelt down with the little Indian girl in the first family prayer of their married life. (55-04)

Father or mother should initiate family prayer. If the father is home, he takes charge, and calls on one of the family to pray. If father is not there, the mother is in charge. If both are gone, the oldest child is in charge, and every night and every morning, the family is on their knees in prayer to the Lord. (62-05)

Each should lead in prayer. It is not proper that the father should do all the praying. As called upon by him, the mother, and each child should participate. Even in preschool days, many little ones will be able to take part if a simple little prayer is taught them. "We learn to do by doing." One cannot learn to pray by merely listening, but must be given experience. (46-02)

When and How to Pray

Prayers should suit the occasion. Prayers are of many kinds. The prayers in public should always be appropriate to the occasion. A dedication prayer may be longer but an invocation much shorter. It should request the needed things for that particular occasion. The benediction can be still shorter—a prayer of thanks and dismissal. The anointing with oil is a short and specific part of an ordinance and should not overlap the sealing which follows and which may be extended as is appropriate in calling down blessings on the recipient. The blessing on the food need not be long, but should express gratitude for and blessings requested on the food. It should not be repetitious of a family prayer that has just been given.

The family group prayer should be in length and composition appropriate to the need. A prayer of a single couple would be different from one for a family of grown children or for one of small children. Certainly, it should not be long when little children are involved, or they may lose interest and tire of prayer and come to dislike it. When the children pray, it is not likely they will pray overlong. The Lord's Prayer, given as a sample, is only about thirty seconds and certainly one can do much thanking and requesting in one or two or three minutes, though there are obviously times when it might be appropriate to commune longer. (FPM 201)

Use "Thee" in prayer. The presidency of the Church are quite anxious that everybody address the Lord with the pronouns "thee" and "thou" and "thine" and "thy." Youth may feel that "you" and "yours" are a little more intimate and affectionate. Will you do what you can to change this pattern? It is largely in your hands. (62-08)

Avoid wordy prayers. How often do we hear people who wax eloquent in their prayers to the extent of preaching a complete sermon?

The hearers tire and the effect is lost, and I sometimes wonder if perhaps the dial of the heavenly radio is not turned off when long and wordy prayers are sent heavenward. I feel sure that there is too much to do in heaven for the Lord and his servants to sit indefinitely listening to verbose praises and requests, for as we are told in Matthew, he knows, before we ask, our needs and desires. (See Matthew 6:8.) (38-01)

Pray in thanksgiving. In many countries, the homes are barren and the cupboards bare—no books, no radios, no pictures, no furniture, no fire—while we are housed adequately, clothed warmly, fed extravagantly. Did we show our thanks by the proper devotion on our knees last night and this morning and tomorrow morning?

Ingratitude, thou sinful habit!

Around the world are millions groping in the dark, fettered through superstition and fear and insecurity. Here we live in the light with joy and love and abundance and hope.

Behind the Iron Curtain, the Bamboo Curtain, the Cuban Curtain—behind all the walls and all the curtains of oppression and dictatorship, behind the walls of force and slavery, live millions of our brothers and sisters in fear while we live in liberty and privilege. Do we appreciate that and do we express our gratitude in solemn thanksgiving? (75-45)

Prayers are often self-centered. Even in our prayers, our words are mostly *gimme*—"Father, *make* us strong, *give* us health, *make* us righteous"—when we should be thanking him mostly and asking only for help in our doing these things for ourselves. (58-07)

For whom and what should we pray? For whom and what should we pray? We should express gratitude for past blessings. Paul says to Timothy: "I exhort therefore, that, first of all, supplications, prayers, intercessions, and giving of thanks, be made for all men." (1 Timothy 2:1.) . . .

Paul asked that we pray "for kings, and for all that are in authority." (1 Timothy 2:2.) This will help develop loyalty to community leaders and concern for the Lord's influence on them.

We pray for the poor and needy, and at the same time remember our obligation to do something for them. "If a brother or sister be naked, and destitute of daily food, And one of you say unto them, Depart in peace, be ye warmed and filled; notwithstanding ye give them not those things which are needful to the body; what doth it profit?" (James 2:15-16.)

If we pray we are more likely to pay our fast offerings, contribute to the welfare program, and pay our tithing, for out of these tithes and offerings comes much of the assistance to the poor and needy.

We pray for the missionaries. Children who have petitioned to "bless the missionaries" are most likely to be desirous of filling missions and of being worthy for such service.

We pray for our enemies. This will soften our hearts, and perhaps theirs, and we may better seek good in them. And this prayer should not be confined to national enemies but should extend to neighbors, members of the family, and all with whom we have differences....

We pray for righteousness but do not expect the Lord to *make* us good. He will help us to perfect ourselves, and as we pray for controls and exercise those controls, we grow toward perfection.

We pray for the Church leaders. If children all their days in their turn at family prayers and in their secret prayers remember before the Lord the leaders of the Church, they are quite unlikely to ever fall into apostasy....

The children who pray for the brethren will grow up loving them, speaking well of them, honoring and emulating them. Those who daily hear the leaders of the Church spoken of in prayer in deep affection will more likely believe the sermons and admonitions they will hear.

When boys speak to the Lord concerning their bishop, they are likely to take very seriously the interviews with the bishop in which priesthood advancements and mission and temple blessings are being discussed. And girls too will have a healthy respect for all church proceedings as they pray for the leaders of the Church....

We pray for our own family members, their incomings and out-goings, their travels, their work, and all pertaining to them. When children pray audibly for their brothers and sisters, it is likely that quarreling and conflicts and jarrings will be lessened.

We pray for enlightenment, then go to with all our might and our books and our thoughts and righteousness to get the inspiration. We ask for judgment, then use all our powers to act wisely and develop wisdom. We pray for success in our work and then study hard and strive with all our might to help answer our prayers. When we pray for health we must live the laws of health and do all in our power to keep our bodies well and vigorous. We pray for protection and then take reasonable precaution to avoid danger. There must be works with faith. How foolish it would be to ask the Lord to *give* us knowledge, but how wise to ask the Lord's help to acquire knowledge, to study constructively, to think clearly, and to retain things that we have learned. How stupid to ask the Lord to protect us if we unnecessarily drive at excessive speeds, or if we eat or drink destructive elements or try foolhardy stunts.

We pray for forgiveness. . . .

We pray for everything that is needed and dignified and proper. I heard a boy about fourteen years of age in family prayer imploring the Lord to protect the family sheep upon the hill. It was snowing and bitterly cold. I heard a family pray for rain when a severe drought was on and conditions were desperate. I heard a young girl praying for help in her examinations that were coming up that day.

Our petitions are also for the sick and afflicted. The Lord will hear our sincere prayers. He may not always heal them, but he may give them peace or courage or strength to bear up. We do not forget in our prayers the folks who need blessings almost more than the physically imperfect—the frustrated and confused people, the tempted, the sinful, the disturbed.

Our prayers are for our children's welfare. Sometimes as children grow up, there comes into their lives a rebellious attitude in spite of all that we can say and do. Alma found his admonitions futile with his sons and he prayed for them, and his prayers were mighty ones. Sometimes that is about all there is left for parents to do. The prayer of a righteous man availeth much, says the scripture, and so it did in this case. . . .

No mother would carelessly send her little children forth to school on a wintry morning without warm clothes to protect against the snow and rain and cold. But there are numerous fathers and mothers who send their children to school without the protective covering available to them through prayer—a protection against exposure to unknown hazards, evil people, and base temptations. (FPM 202-7)

Pray "Thy will be done." Perhaps there are those who demand rather than request. There may be those who pray for certain blessings without any question in their minds as to the value of those things to them. Perhaps they are disappointed and even shaken in their faith if their prayer is not granted. Remember that our prayers are often as inconsistent and inappropriate to our Father in Heaven as are the demands of our little children upon us. What earthly parent would give to a little one a bottle of poison with which to play, even though the child might ask and demand and cry for it? Or who of you would turn a four- or six-year-old child loose with a powerful automobile, in spite of the fact that he insisted and pleaded for it? And yet we sometimes ask for just such impossible things, just such dangerous things, and the Lord in his mercy withholds them. Let us pray with the attitude always of the crucified One, "nevertheless not my will, but thine, be done." (Luke 22:42.) (38-01)

Praying for Inspiration

Be willing to accept negative answers. Unequally yoked? Which direction the children? Will they follow father or mother or neither? What do you want them to do? Are you thinking of your children? Do you care? Or, are you concerned only with what you think and feel as of today? Do you want guidance? Have you prayed to the Lord for inspiration? Do you want to do right or do you want to do what you want to do whether or not it is right? Do you want to do what is best for you in the long run or what seems more desirable for the moment? Have you prayed? How much have you prayed? How did you pray? Have you prayed as did the Savior of the world in Gethsemane or did you ask for what you want regardless of its being proper? Do you say in your prayers: "Thy will be done"? Did you say, "Heavenly Father, if you will inspire and impress me with the right, I will do that right"? Or, did you pray, "Give me what I want or I will take it anyway"? Did you say: "Father in Heaven, I love you, I believe in you, I know you are omniscient. I am honest. I am sincerely desirous of doing right. I know you can see the end from the beginning. You can see the future. You can discern if under this situation I present, I will have peace or turmoil, happiness or sorrow, success or failure. Tell me, please, loved Heavenly Father, and I promise to do what you tell me to do." Have you prayed that way? Don't you think it might be wise? Are you courageous enough to pray that prayer? Or, are you afraid that he might not see eye to eye with you? Are you willing to take your own judgment and throw his to the winds? Well, what about it? Are you omniscient? Can you see the future? Are you more clever than God? Can you guess what tomorrow has for you? Do you love yourself? Do you worship yourself, your mind, your judgment? Do you want to be happy forever or for life, or do you want to satisfy only the demands of today? (5/0/00)

Prayers are not always answered as we wish them to be. Even the Redeemer's prayer in Gethsemane was answered in the negative. He prayed that the bitter cup of sorrow, pain, and mortal life termination could pass, but the answer was a "no" answer.

Can each youth keep an unbiased mind in prayer as did the Lord and have the personal strength to accept the verdict even though it counters desire? (54-05)

Prayer is not just words but communication. If one rises from his knees having merely said words, he should fall back on his knees and remain there until he has established communication with the Lord who is very anxious to bless, but having given man his free agency, will not force himself upon that man. (5/4/70)

After openhearted prayer, listen. Difficult as it seems, I have found when praying, other than in private and secret, that it is better to be concerned with communicating tenderly and honestly with

God, rather than worrying over what the listeners may be thinking. The echoing of "amen" by the listeners is evidence of their accord and approval. Of course, the setting of prayers needs to be taken into account. This is one reason why public prayers, or even family prayers, cannot be the whole of our praying.

Some things are best prayed over only in private, where time and confidentiality are not considerations. If in these special moments of prayer we hold back from the Lord, it may mean that some blessings may be withheld from us. After all, we pray as petitioners before an all-wise Heavenly Father, so why should we ever think to hold back feelings or thoughts which bear upon our needs and our blessings? We hope that our people will have very bounteous prayers.

It would not hurt us, either, if we paused at the end of our prayers to do some intense listening—even for a moment or two—always praying, as the Savior did, "not my will, but thine, be done." (Luke 22:42.) (79-20)

In our prayers, there must be no glossing over, no hypocrisy, since there can here be no deception. The Lord knows our true condition. Do we tell the Lord how good we are, or how weak? We stand naked before him. Do we offer our supplications in modesty, sincerity, and with a "broken heart and a contrite spirit," or like the Pharisee who prided himself on how well he adhered to the law of Moses? Do we offer a few trite words and worn-out phrases, or do we talk intimately to the Lord for as long as the occasion requires? Do we pray occasionally when we should be praying regularly, often, constantly? Do we pay the price to get answers to our prayers? Do we ask for things absurd and not for our good? The Lord promised:

> Draw near unto me and I will draw near unto you; seek me diligently and ye shall find me; ask, and ye shall receive; knock, and it shall be opened unto you.
>
> Whatsoever ye ask the Father in my name it shall be given unto you, that is expedient for you;
>
> And if ye ask anything that is not expedient for you, it shall turn unto your condemnation. (D&C 88:63-65.)

When we pray, do we just speak, or do we also listen? Our Savior

... stands and knocks. If we do not listen, he will not sup with us nor give answer to our prayers. We must learn how to listen, grasp, interpret, understand. The Lord stands knocking. He never retreats. But he will never force himself upon us. If our distance from him increases, it is we who have moved and not the Lord. And should we ever fail to get an answer to our prayers, we must look into our own lives for a reason. (FPM 207-8)

Pray with fervor. The supplication of Enos is written with a pen of anguish and on the paper of faith and with a willingness to totally prostrate himself that he might receive forgiveness. His words are mighty and definitive. He could have said merely, "I want information, Lord." But he said, "My soul hungered." He could have merely prayed unto the Lord like too many pray, but in his eagerness for forgiveness, he said, "I kneeled down before my Maker, and I cried unto him in mighty prayer and supplication for mine own soul." (Enos 1:4.) (75-04)

Acknowledge dependence. Man never stands alone unless his own desires are independence and egotism and selfishness. . . . The realness and closeness and degree of communication depends upon us, his children. If we find our own paths, calculate our own best movements, continue independent of him, then of course we are estranged to that extent. Or on the other hand, our Lord is as close as we draw him to us by our righteousness and belief and faith. (73-05)

Prayer brings guidance. The blessing of revelation is one that all should seek for. Righteous men and women find that they have the spirit of revelation to direct their families and to aid them in their other responsibilities. But, like Abraham, we must seek to qualify for such revelation by setting our lives in order and by becoming acquainted with the Lord through frequent and regular conversations with him. (75-21)

Prayer provides assurance God lives. He had abandoned his Lord. I said, "How often do you pray?" "Well, not so very often."

"Why don't you pray?" "I am not sure anymore." "Why aren't you sure anymore?" Because you have cut all the communication lines. You have lost his address. You do not have his telephone number even, and you do not have any address. The communication lines have been severed. How do you expect to know whether he is living or dead? If you went for two years without ever hearing from your parents and they were in the opposite end of the world, how would you know if they were alive or dead? How do you know if God is dead or alive if you have lost communication? Now, you get on your knees, my boy. If you want to be happy, get on your knees and crawl on your knees to the city of happiness. Only there is peace. (66-12)

Apparently, the "thinkers" spend years in their spiritual conflicts when hours on knees in prayer and contemplation could bring them a true knowledge. . . . Arrogant, egotistical man with his limitations in thought, experience, knowledge, trying to deal independently with the existence and life of his Creator, with the being of his Lord. . . .

Why will these belabored souls clumsily stagger in the dark with shuffling feet, and reaching hands for something they yearn for but do not recognize nor grasp? (66-05)

The Command to Study the Scriptures

Scriptures are man's spiritual memory. In a very real sense, special records, such as the holy scriptures, are the spiritual memory of mankind. (80-25)

Scripture study is commanded. The Lord is not trifling with us when he gives us these things, for "unto whomsoever much is given, of him shall be much required." (Luke 12:48.) Access to these things means responsibility for them. We must study the scriptures according to the Lord's commandment (see 3 Nephi 23:1-5). . . .

One cannot receive eternal life without becoming a "doer of the word" (see James 1:22) and being valiant in obedience to the Lord's commandments. And one cannot become a "doer of the word"

without first becoming a "hearer." And to become a "hearer" is not
simply to stand idly by and wait for chance bits of information; it is
to seek out and study and pray and comprehend. . . .

The Lord's teachings have always been to those who have "eyes
to see" and "ears to hear." The voice is clear and unmistakable, and
against those who neglect so great an opportunity the witness is sure.

So I ask all to begin now to study the scriptures in earnest, if you
have not already done so. And perhaps the easiest and most effective
way to do this is to participate in the study program of the Church.

In the adult curriculum of the Church, the Melchizedek Priesthood quorums and the Sunday School Gospel Doctrine classes study
the standard works in rotation. Over a period of eight years the Old
Testament, the Pearl of Great Price, the New Testament, the Book of
Mormon, and the Doctrine and Covenants are all studied thoroughly. (76-51)

Neglecting the scriptures contributes to loss of spirituality. At a
distant stake conference one Sunday I was approached after the
meeting by a young man whose face was familiar. He identified himself as a returned missionary whom I had met out in the world a few
years ago. He said he had not attended the conference but came at its
conclusion wanting to see me again. Our greetings were pleasant and
revived some choice memories. I asked him about himself. He was in
college, still single, and fairly miserable. I asked him about his service
in the Church and the light in his eyes went out and a dull, disappointed face fashioned itself as he said, "I am not very active in the
Church now. I don't feel the same as I used to feel in the mission
field. What I used to think was a testimony has become something of
disillusionment. If there is a God I am not sure anymore. I must have
been mistaken in my zeal and joy."

I looked him through and through and asked him some questions. . . .

The answers came as expected. He had turned loose his hold on
the iron rod. He associated largely with unbelievers. He read, in
addition to his college texts, works by atheists, apostates, and Bible
critics. He had ceased to pray to his Heavenly Father. His communication poles were burned; his lines sagging.

I asked him now, "How many times since your mission have you read the New Testament?"

"Not any time," was the answer.

"How many times have you read the Book of Mormon through?"

The answer, "None."

"How many chapters of scripture have you read? How many verses?"

Not one single time had he opened the sacred books. He had been reading negative and critical and faith-destroying things and wondered why he could never smile. He never prayed anymore yet wondered why he felt so abandoned and so alone in a tough world. For a long time he had not partaken of the sacrament of the Lord's Supper and wondered why his spirit was dead.

Not a penny of tithing had he paid and wondered why the windows of heaven seemed closed and locked and barred. (72-05)

Scripture study is a family responsibility. Scripture study as individuals and as a family is most fundamental to learning the gospel. Daily reading of the scriptures and discussing them together has long been suggested as a powerful tool against ignorance and the temptations of Satan. This practice will produce great happiness and will help family members love the Lord and his goodness. . . . Home is where we become experts and scholars in gospel righteousness. (82-01)

Men and women have equal duty to study scriptures. Study the scriptures. Thus you may gain strength through the understanding of eternal things. You young women need this close relationship with the mind and will of our Eternal Father. We want our sisters to be scholars of the scriptures as well as our men.

You need an acquaintanceship with his eternal truths for your own well-being, and for the purposes of teaching your own children and all others who come within your influence. (78-24)

Youth need literacy in scriptures. Gospel, doctrine, or organization illiteracy should never be found among our youth. Proper scriptures can be learned well and permanently by children; doctrines can be taught and absorbed by youth. (73-03)

Children should own scriptures. "You shall teach one another the doctrine of the kingdom." (D&C 88:77.) This would imply careful, regular, and systematic study of the standard works of the Church. Herein will be found the material for a lifetime of profitable study. One could not possibly, in mortality, learn all about the way of life, consequently these books should be in every home, available for constant reference and reading. Splendid it would be if gifts to children in their early years were book-gifts. How fine if every child could have the New Testament even in early years, and, a little later, his own triple combination of the three books and also his own Bible. (63-06)

With diligence one can read all the scriptures. From infancy I had enjoyed the simplified and pictured Bible stories, but the original Bible seemed so interminable in length, so difficult of understanding that I had avoided it until a challenge came to me from Sister Susa Young Gates. She was the speaker at the MIA meeting of stake conference and gave a discourse on the value of reading the Bible. In conclusion she asked for a showing of hands of all who had read it through. The hands that were raised out of that large congregation were so few and so timid! It seemed that some of them were trying to explain: "We haven't read it through but we have done much studying of parts of it." I was shocked into an unalterable determination to read the great book.

As soon as I reached home after the meeting I began with the first verse of Genesis and continued faithfully every day with the reading. Most of the reading was done in my attic bedroom which I occupied alone. I burned considerable midnight oil and read long hours when I was thought to be asleep.

Approximately a year later I reached the last verse in Revelation. (43-03)

It was formidable, but I knew if others did it that I could do it.

I found that there were certain parts [of the Bible] that were hard for a fourteen-year-old boy to understand. There were some pages that were not especially interesting to me, but when I had read the 66 books and 1,189 chapters and 1,519 pages, I had a glowing satisfaction that I had made a goal and that I had achieved it.

Now, I am not telling you this story to boast; I am merely using this as an example to say that if I could do it by coal-oil light, you can do it by electric light. I have always been glad I read the Bible from cover to cover. (74-04)

Memorize basic scriptures. When I was nine years old, I milked nine cows each day at my home in Thatcher, Arizona. I thought, "What a waste of time, to sit on a three-legged stool. Maybe there is something else I could do while I am milking." So I sang the songs of Zion until I knew all the well-known hymns that are generally sung. Then I said, "Well, I have got to have something more!"

So I got a copy of the Articles of Faith and put it on the ground right beside me and I went through them, over and over again, a thousand times. Then I got a copy of the Ten Commandments. I typed them up on cards and took them out with me where I milked and repeated them over and over until I knew them by heart.

Then, as I got a little closer to my mission, I typed scriptures that I thought would be helpful to me and I learned them . . . so that when I went on my mission I would be prepared for it. If every Latter-day Saint would do this, I think it would be a wonderful thing. (75-18)

Profiting from the Scriptures

Scriptures provide vicarious experience. Few of the billions of earth can walk with God as did Adam and Abraham and Moses, yet, in the world in which we live, the scriptures are available to nearly every soul, and, through them, men can become intimately acquainted with their Heavenly Father, his Son Jesus Christ, and with conditions and opportunities and expectations of life eternal. (63-06)

Scriptures illustrate good and evil. We learn the lessons of life more readily and surely if we see the results of wickedness and righteousness in the lives of others. To know the patriarchs and prophets of ages past and their faithfulness under stress and temptation and persecution strengthens the resolves of youth. To come to know Job well and intimately is to learn to keep faith through the greatest of adversities. To know well the strength of Joseph in the luxury of ancient Egypt when he was tempted by a voluptuous woman, and to see this clean young man resist all the powers of darkness embodied in this one seductive person, certainly should fortify the intimate reader against such sin. To see the forbearance and fortitude of Paul when he was giving his life to his ministry is to give courage to those who feel they have been injured and tried. He was beaten many times, imprisoned frequently for the cause, stoned near to death, shipwrecked three times, robbed, nearly drowned, the victim of false and disloyal brethren. While starving, choking, freezing, poorly clothed, Paul was yet consistent in his service. He never wavered once after the testimony came to him following his supernatural experience. To see the growth of Peter with the gospel as the catalyst moving him from a lowly fisherman—uncultured, unlearned, and ignorant, as they rated him—blossoming out into a great organizer, prophet, leader, theologian, teacher. Thus youth will take courage and know that nothing can stop their progress but themselves and their weaknesses.

When one follows the devious paths of Saul from a tender of asses to king of Israel and prophet, and then through arrogance and pride and hostilities and ignoring his Lord and the prophet to watch this madman slip down from his high place to the tent of Endor's witch, and then to see him in defeat in battle, rejected of the prophet to ignominy and devastation; and then to see his decapitated head placed upon the wall for all his enemies to gloat over and spit at—this will surely teach vital lessons to youth. He climbed from peasant to king and prophet and then slid back to witchcraft. What a lesson on pride and arrogance!

Our children may learn the lessons of life through the perseverance and personal strength of Nephi; the godliness of the three Nephites; the faith of Abraham; the power of Moses; the deception and perfidy of Ananias; the courage even to death of the unresisting Ammonites; the unassailable faith of the Lamanite mothers transmitted down through their sons, so powerful that it saved Helaman's striplings. Not a single one came to his death in that war.

All through the scriptures every weakness and strength of man has been portrayed, and rewards and punishments have been recorded. One would surely be blind who could not learn to live life properly by such reading. The Lord said, "Search the scriptures; for in them ye think ye have eternal life: and they are they which testify of me." (John 5:39.) And it was this same Lord and master in whose life we find every quality of goodness: godliness, strength, controls, perfection. And how can students study this great story without capturing some of it in their lives? (66-07)

Book of Mormon is vital scripture. I am constrained to speak to you of it today. It is a story of courage, faith, and fortitude, of perseverance, sacrifice, and superhuman accomplishments, of intrigue, of revenge, of disaster, of war, murder, and rapine, of idolatry, and of cannibalism, of miracles, visions, and manifestations, of prophecies and their fulfillment.

I found in it life at its best and at its worst, in ever-changing patterns. I hardly recovered from one great crisis until another engulfed me. . . .

It is a fast-moving story of total life, of opposing ideologies, of monarchies and judgeships and mobocracies. Its scenes carry the reader across oceans and continents. It promises to tell of the "last days of God," but instead records the "last days of populous peoples" and the triumph of God. Class distinction is there with its ugliness, race prejudice with its hatefulness, multiplicity of creeds with their bitter conflicts. . . .

It is the word of God. It is a powerful second witness of Christ. And, certainly, all true believers who love the Redeemer will welcome additional evidence of his divinity.

This inspiring book was never tampered with by unauthorized translators or biased theologians but comes to the world pure and directly from the historians and abridgers. The book is not on trial— its readers are.

Here is a scripture as old as creation and as new and vibrant as tomorrow, bridging time and eternity; it is a book of revelations and is a companion to the Bible brought from Europe by immigrants and agrees in surprising harmony with that Bible in tradition, history, doctrine, and prophecy; and the two were written simultaneously on two hemispheres under diverse conditions. It records the very words people would say when this hidden record should be presented to them:

"A Bible! A Bible! We have got a Bible, and there cannot be any more Bible." ...

The book of which I speak is the keystone of true religion, the ladder by which one may get near to God by abiding its precepts. It has been named, "The most correct of any book on earth."

My beloved friends, I give to you the Book of Mormon. May you read it prayerfully, study it carefully, and receive for yourselves the testimony of its divinity. (63-02)

Remember in the book of Moroni 10:4-5 the promise is given that on certain conditions God "will manifest the truth of it unto you, by the power of the Holy Ghost. And by the power of the Holy Ghost ye may know the truth of all things." Such a testimony is not promised to anyone who reads the book with a critical attitude nor one who reads it to satisfy curiosity nor to one who resists it, but definitely it will come to everyone who has fully surrendered himself with an open mind and heart. And when this testimony comes to readers it is quite unlikely that it will come by flourish of trumpets or by hand-writing on the wall or by audible voice, but by a burning of hearts in bosoms, and he that will receive it will know it and appreciate it, but if there is resistance it will not come. (3/6/47)

We overestimate our scriptural knowledge. I ask us all to honestly evaluate our performance in scripture study. It is a common thing to have a few passages of scripture at our disposal, floating in our minds, as it were, and thus to have the illusion that we know a great deal about the gospel. In this sense, having a little knowledge can be a problem indeed. I am convinced that each of us, at some time in our lives, must discover the scriptures for ourselves—and not just discover them once, but rediscover them again and again. (76-51)

Scripture study deepens understanding. The years have taught me that if we will energetically pursue this worthy personal goal in a determined and conscientious manner, we shall indeed find answers to our problems and peace in our hearts. We shall experience the Holy Ghost broadening our understanding, find new insights, witness an unfolding pattern of all scripture; and the doctrines of the Lord shall come to have more meaning to us than we ever thought possible. As a consequence, we shall have greater wisdom with which to guide ourselves and our families, so that we may serve as a light and source of strength to our nonmember friends with whom we have an obligation to share the gospel. (75-35)

Scripture study increases love and testimony. I find that all I need to do to increase my love for my Maker and the gospel and the Church and my brethren is to read the scriptures. I have spent many hours in the scriptures during the last few days. I prescribe that for people who are in trouble. I cannot see how anyone can read the scriptures and not develop a testimony of their divinity and of the divinity of the work of the Lord, who is the spokesman in the scriptures. (66-08)

I find that when I get casual in my relationships with divinity and when it seems that no divine ear is listening and no divine voice is speaking, that I am far, far away. If I immerse myself in the scriptures the distance narrows and the spirituality returns. I find myself loving more intensely those whom I must love with all my heart and mind and strength, and loving them more, I find it easier to abide their counsel. (66-07)

Modern revelations help understanding of Bible. Ever since Luther revolted against the Catholic church and the Bible came to be reading matter for the laymen, people in reading the Bible [have been] earnestly and eagerly trying to find the total truth. It has been impossible for anyone [by this means alone] to find the whole truth, and numerous scriptures in the Bible, and particularly in the New Testament, have new rich meaning after one understands the revelations of modern days. (11/2/62)

Words of modern prophets deserve study. No father, no son, no mother, no daughter should get so busy that he or she does not have time to study the scriptures and the words of modern prophets. None of us should get so busy that we crowd out contemplation and praying. (76-26)

Writings of commentators are not doctrine. Now, I am sure it was quite a surprise to you when I indicated that the writings of all the good members of the Church were not scripture and could not necessarily be depended upon, and that their writings, numerous of which there are, were their own concepts. I did not want to deprecate their splendid efforts, for on the whole the commentaries written by many people are excellent, but the student of the gospel must be able to cull the material and to take that which fits into the total big program, and to discard anything else which appears to be speculative on the part of the writer of the commentary. (11/2/62)

Misunderstanding may result from differences in terminology. Many of the misunderstandings and differences of opinion in scriptural considerations result from a lack of definition of words and terminology, far more than in difference of opinion. For instance, there is quite a different color to the statement that the Lord goes around killing people than if it is stated that the Lord permits the wicked to slay the wicked, and the wicked to slay themselves because he had previously given them their free agency. (11/2/62)

Understanding requires desire and patience. One's faith can be strengthened by a program involving several elements—by reading the scriptures with a happy frame of mind and desire to absorb additional truth. This reading needs to be done with a constructive attitude—a reaching for truth and a ready acceptance of it. As one reads something which does not for the moment seem to have meaning he can put that item on the shelf and move forward with the reading. In most instances the additional information gained and faith developed seem to provide the background so that the un-understandable item falls naturally into place. If anything seems to counter previous concepts, one can read and study and ponder and pray and *wait* and usually a clarification comes. To increase testimony one must want very much to do so. (2/14/58)

Testimony Bearing

Those who can must bear testimony. When I was a small boy, I was taught the habit of going to sacrament meetings. Mother always took me with her. Those warm afternoons I soon became drowsy and leaned over on her lap to sleep. I may not have learned much from the sermons, but I learned the habit of "going to meeting." The habit stayed with me through my life. And even from those early years in the testimony meetings, I often came home distressed by the expressions of critical people who took issue with those who had borne their testimonies with such fervor and sureness. "Why does Sister Blank say she knows that Jesus is the Christ? How can she know? Why does Brother Doe declare with such definiteness that Joseph Smith was a prophet of God and that this is the Church and kingdom of God? I doubt if they know any more about it than I do." Speaking to those who fear him and delight to serve him in righteousness unto the end, [the Lord] says:

> And to them will I reveal all mysteries, yea, all the hidden mysteries of my kingdom from days of old, and for ages to come, will I make known unto them the good pleasure of my will concerning all things pertaining to my kingdom. Yea, even the wonders of eternity shall they know, and things to come will I show them. (D&C 76:7-8.)

To hold his testimony one must bear it often and live worthy of it. The Lord declared his displeasure in the failure of his people to bear testimony.

Destructive criticism of the officers of the Church or its doctrines is sure to weaken and bring an eventual end to one's testimony if persisted in. (44-07)

On the first Sabbath of the month it is expected that you shall come to your meeting fasting. As in other meetings each should take active part in the praying and singing and in the spirit of the meeting. In addition, the privilege is here granted for the members to bear testimony, with a "broken heart and a contrite spirit," with thanksgiving and a cheerful heart, confessing to the Lord and the brethren their imperfections, and worshipping with the brethren and sisters. The meeting belongs to the people. Even the bishop must not deprive them of this opportunity. The spirit should not be curbed, nor premature closing cut too short this service. Members should not permit the time to be wasted, for it is displeasing to the Lord. (48-03)

As a vital link in the conversion process, we should bear our testimonies that the gospel is true; our testimonies may well be the spark that ignites the conversion process. Consequently, we have a double responsibility: we must testify of the things we know, feel, and have felt, and we must live so the Holy Ghost can be with us and convey our words in power to the heart of the investigator. (77-32)

Testimony bearing is not preaching. Do not exhort each other; that is not a testimony. Do not tell others how to live. Just tell how you feel inside. That is the testimony. The moment you begin preaching to others, your testimony ended. Just tell us how you feel, what your mind and heart and every fiber of your body tells you. (62-02)

Children can express feelings. We have critics who say it is silly to have little children bear their testimonies and that they cannot know it is true. Undoubtedly their knowledge is limited. But they can have feelings, and testimonies are feelings, not merely the accumulation of facts. Testimonies come from the heart. (62-02)

Testimony is not static but can come in surges. I have been carrying with me your letter of a month ago, hoping to get a chance to answer it. I realize that it must be discouraging to meet so much languor and passiveness. It is far more stimulating to the missionary to receive active and bitter opposition; however, I hope you will not permit yourself to get discouraged. The evil one is very anxious to discourage the missionary. He will do his best to convince you that "It is of no use," but remember the comfort and consolation offered in the eighteenth section of the Doctrine and Covenants.

I hope you will permit my comment on your statement, "I told one fellow we contacted once and talked with a long while, that I know of the truthfulness of what I told him, and said that the Holy Ghost had borne witness of it to me, I felt—and when I thought about it later I was a little concerned that I should do such a thing when I didn't later feel that way, so I've carefully avoided bearing my testimony to anyone beyond the point of saying, 'I firmly believe, etc.' "

Now, I think I know exactly how you felt, for I went through the same experience in my mission. I wanted to be very honest with myself and with the program and with the Lord. For a time I couched my words carefully to try to build up others without actually committing myself to a positive, unequivocal statement that I *knew*. I felt a little sensitive about it too, for when I was in tune and doing my duty and had the Spirit, I really wanted to say that which I really felt, that I did know, but I was reticent. When I approached a positive declaration it frightened me, and yet when I was wholly in tune and spiritually inspired, I wanted to so testify. I thought I was being honest, very honest, but finally decided that I was fooling myself as I became better acquainted with the program of the Lord.

I remembered that Heber C. Kimball stood in the Tabernacle when the Saints' clothing was threadbare and little chance to get more, and by the time it came from the East by freight in wagons over the great desert the cost was almost prohibitive, and yet in the face of all that, Grandfather stood and when warmed up with the Spirit, prophesied that clothes and commodities would soon be sold in the streets of Salt Lake cheaper than in New York City. And when he sat down and the spirit of prophecy left him he almost gasped: "I guess I have missed it that time!" How could it ever come to pass?! But as you know the heavily laden wagons of the forty-niners rushing to the gold fields of California became impatient to reach their destination and disposed of their surplus clothes and commodities at any price they would bring, thus fulfilling the prophecy which was so hopeless of fulfillment (looking at it with human vision) but which was uttered under the revelations of the Lord.

Many of the brethren with whom I have labored have testified that they had felt impelled to utter promises in sealing the anointing that made them actually shiver after the blessing was over. The blessing was fulfilled and the impossible happened. While they were under the influence of the spirit of inspiration or revelation they felt it, but after they cooled off they trembled for fear they had been too lavish in their promises.

Many times I have had similar experiences even in the old days at Safford, but especially since I have done so much blessing here. Many times after I have ordained or set apart people I have had the stake president or bishop whisper to me: "You must have been inspired, for you gave that man the very blessing which was most appropriate. It could not have met his particular needs better if you had known him all your life instead of being a total stranger to him."

I have promised life in some cases (though I am generally very conservative); I have promised missionaries and servicemen a safe return; and I have literally trembled in my shoes afterward when I realized what a responsibility I was under, but long ago I have come to the conclusion that I shall speak what I seem inspired to say, having asked the Lord for that inspiration, and any effort on my part to curb the Spirit would be rank folly and unappreciativeness and unresponsiveness to the moving of the Spirit. I have come to realize that the Lord does not expect to reveal to us generally in actual daylight vision as he did to Joseph Smith in the grove. Sometimes it will come in open vision, sometimes in dreams, sometimes in whisperings, but generally his revelations will come about as he explained to Oliver Cowdery. Oliver had not kept himself in tune and the power of translation through revelation was taken from him. "Behold, you have not understood; you have supposed that I would give it unto you, when you took no thought save it was to ask me. But, behold, I say unto you, that you must study it out in your mind; then you must ask me if it be right, and if it is right I will cause that your bosom shall burn within you; therefore, you shall feel that it is right, but if it be not right, you shall have no such feelings, but you shall have a stupor of thought." (D&C 9:7-9.) . . .

Undoubtedly the day you testified to your investigator that you *knew* it was true, the Lord was trying so hard to reveal this truth to you through the power of the Holy Ghost. While you were in the spirit and in tune and defending the holy program, you felt it deeply, but after you were "out of the spirit" and began to reason with yourself and check yourself and question yourself, you wanted to back out.

I have no question in my mind of your testimony. I am sure that you (like I did) have countless golden threads of testimony all through your being only waiting for the hand of the Master Weaver to assemble and weave them into a tapestry of exquisite and perfect design.

Now, my son, take my advice and "quench not the Spirit," but whenever the Spirit whispers, follow its holy promptings. Keep in tune spiritually and listen for the promptings and when you are impressed speak out boldly your impressions. The Lord will magnify your testimony and touch hearts. (3/6/47)

I know it is true. Because those few words have been said a billion times by millions of people does not make it trite. It will never be worn out. I feel sorry for people who try to couch it in other words, because where are no words like "I know." There are no words which express the deep feelings which can come from the human heart like "I know." (62-02)

Testimony must be nourished. If you still have your testimony, treasure it, and build it. It wanes and nearly expires when you are breaking all the laws, for "whom we serve, we love," and "whom we disobey, we hate." You may think you have dispossessed yourself of your faith but it will revive and grow into a flame if you get on your knees and fan it back to life. (0/0/66)

What are you going to do with your testimony? Are you going to keep it sharpened like the knife with which our mothers cut the meat?

Are you going to let it get dull and rusty? . . . It is a little like a rose. Just keep the rain off it; just keep the irrigation water off it for a little while and what happens to your rose? It dies. Your testimony dies. Your love dies. Everything has to be fed. You feed your body three times a day. The Lord says to keep your testimony, to keep your spirit alive, you have to feed it every day. That is why he says morning, noon, and night. That is why he says pray every night and morning. That is why he says pray continually so that you keep that line open. (66-12)

Loss of testimony is a great tragedy. The darkest day in all a man's life or eternity is not when he is physically injured or suffers untimely death, but that day when the fire for lack of proper fuel dies down and flickers and sputters and goes out. I repeat—the saddest hour of any man's eternity is when his rationalizations put out his fires and leave them but embers. (2/28/66)

The ghastly pictures of starving humanity in Europe reveal the emaciated limb, the bloated stomachs, and the pinched faces of those poor unfortunates who suffer for the food which will nourish and build up the body. No less tragic is the sight of those still more unfortunate ones even among us, who have starved themselves for the spirit food which would make them wholesome, virile, and strong spiritually and with a living faith. Far worse I say, for the former is mortal homicide, the latter spiritual suicide; in the one the victim was brought to that condition through no fault of his own; in the latter it is a self-inflicted curse. (46-03)

Testimony of martyrs carries special weight. Joseph Smith sealed his testimony with his blood. He could have saved his life. . . . He loved life. He loved his wife and family and friends. He wasn't anxious to go over into eternity. He wanted to live a normal and natural life. He either had to give up his testimony—to recant—or he had to give up his life. He wasn't willing to give up his testimony. He said, "Who am I to deny that I have had heavenly manifestations— that the Lord has appeared before me?"

And so he went calmly, knowing that his life would be taken. He said, "I go as a lamb to the slaughter"; and he went up to Carthage, knowing that the mob was gathering there and knowing they had bullets in their guns. He went calmly and passed on. He said, as he passed on, "Lord, forgive them, for they know not what they do"—almost what Stephen had said when he stood in the pit where others had been stoned. . . .

The great testimonies must be sealed by blood, it seems. Jesus sealed his testimony with his blood. Stephen did. Joseph Smith has now sealed his testimony with blood and died as a young man to say unto all the world that the plates from which the Book of Mormon came forth were found on a hill near Palmyra in the state of New York. And thus, through understanding of this book and the Holy Bible, the gospel of Jesus Christ, through administration of his angels, was again restored to the earth. (44-02)

We testify of truth. Eternal life is our goal. It can be reached only by following the path our Lord has marked out for us.

I know this is true and right. I love our Heavenly Father and I love his Son, and I am proud to be even a weak vessel to push forward their great eternal work. I testify to all this humbly, sincerely, in the name of Jesus Christ. Amen. (74-12)

Brethren and sisters, I want to add to these testimonies of these prophets my testimony that I know that He lives. And I know that we may see him, and that we may be with him, and that we may enjoy his presence always if we will live the commandments of the Lord and do the things which we have been commanded by him to do and reminded by the Brethren to do. (74-05)

And now may I write what I cannot speak, that through the silent hours I have had a chance to weigh, and ponder, and evaluate, and through all these experiences my vision has been expanded, my love deepened, my determinations to grow more like our Savior increased and my knowledge fortified that mortality is but one important incident in life, that the plan of salvation and exaltation is a positive reality, that our Lord speaks constantly from the heavens, that this is his work, that we are his unprofitable servants and that the rewards are sure. That is the way it is. That I know. (57-04)

Knowing full well that before long, in the natural course of events, I must stand before the Lord and give an accounting of my words, I now add my personal and solemn testimony that God, the Eternal Father, and the risen Lord, Jesus Christ, appeared to the boy Joseph Smith. I testify that the Book of Mormon is a translation of an ancient record of nations who once lived in this western hemisphere, where they prospered and became mighty when they kept the commandments of God, but who were largely destroyed through terrible civil wars when they forgot God. This book bears testimony of the living reality of the Lord Jesus Christ as the Savior and Redeemer of mankind.

I testify that the holy priesthood, both Aaronic and Melchizedek, with authority to act in the name of God, was restored to the earth by John the Baptist, and Peter, James, and John; that other keys and authority were subsequently restored; and that the power and authority of those various divine bestowals are among us today. Of these things I bear solemn witness to all within the sound of my voice. I promise in the name of the Lord that all who give heed to our message, and accept and live the gospel, will grow in faith and understanding. They will have an added measure of peace in their lives and in their homes and by the power of the Holy Ghost will speak similar words of testimony and truth. I do this and leave my blessing upon you in the name of Jesus Christ. Amen. (80-05)

Fasting

Fasting is a commandment. Likewise, failing to fast is a sin. In the fifty-eighth chapter of Isaiah, rich promises are made by the Lord to those who fast and assist the needy. Freedom from frustrations, freedom from thralldom, and the blessing of peace are promised. Inspiration and spiritual guidance will come with righteousness and closeness to our Heavenly Father. To omit to do this righteous act of fasting would deprive us of these blessings. (MF 98)

Fasting brings spiritual blessings. The law of the fast is another test. If we merely go without food to supply welfare funds, it is much of the letter, but in real fasting, for spiritual blessings, come self-mastery and increased spirituality. (51-08)

On a full stomach it's easy to talk about fasting. The test comes, of course, when a grumbling stomach demands food. (57-02)

Fast with purpose. We must ever remind ourselves and all members of the Church to keep the law of the fast. We often have our individual reasons for fasting. But I hope members won't hesitate to fast to help us lengthen our stride in our missionary effort, to open the way for the gospel to go to the nations where it is not now permitted. It's good for us to fast as well as to pray over specific things and over specific objectives. (76-24)

Do not force children to fast. Many parents leave it up to the child to make his mind up when he will begin to fast. . . . Because his older brothers and sisters fast, he will want to as soon as he can. He should not be forced to do it but should be taught and trained and educated to do it. It's amazing how much your little children know about life. (75-34)

Generous fast offering develops unselfishness. We wish to remind all the Saints of the blessings that come from observing the regular fast and contributing as generous a fast offering as we can. . . .

This principle of promise, when lived in the spirit thereof, greatly blesses both giver and receiver. Upon practicing the law of the fast, one finds a personal wellspring of power to overcome self-indulgence and selfishness. (78-05)

If we give a generous fast offering, we shall increase our own prosperity both spiritually and temporally. (77-33)

Sometimes we have been a bit penurious and figured that we had for breakfast one egg and that cost so many cents and then we give that to the Lord. I think that when we are affluent, as many of us are, that we ought to be very, very generous. . . .

I think we should . . . give, instead of the amount saved by our two meals of fasting, perhaps much, much more—ten times more when we are in a position to do it. (74-00)

Collecting fast offerings is an important responsibility. I thought it was a great honor to be a deacon. My father was always considerate of my responsibilities and always permitted me to take the buggy and horse to gather fast offerings. My responsibility included that part of the town in which I lived, but it was quite a long walk to the homes, and a sack of flour or a bottle of fruit or vegetables or bread became quite heavy as it accumulated. So the buggy was very comfortable and functional. We have changed to cash in later days, but it was commodities in my day. It was a very great honor to do this service for my Heavenly Father: and though times have changed, when money is given generally instead of commodities, it is still a great honor to perform this service. (75-14)

CHAPTER 6

Righteousness and Perfection

The Principle of Righteousness

Righteousness is a matter of individual choice. In these days
directly ahead of you is the decisive decision. Are you going to yield
to the easy urge to follow the crowd, or are you going to raise your
head above the crowd and let them follow you? Are you going to slip
off into mediocrity, or are you going to rise to the heights which your
Heavenly Father set for you? You could stand above the crowd and
become a leader among your people so that some day they would call
your name blessed, or you can follow the usual demands and urges
and desires and lose yourself in the herd of millions of folks who do
not rise to their potential. The decision is yours and yours only. No
one else can fashion and order your life. We, your real friends, can
suggest and encourage and help you, but you are now in these
months and this year or two setting the bounds and the limitations on
your life. (2/20/58)

Righteousness and ordinances complement one another. Now, in
addition to the ordinances there must be righteousness. Neither will
exalt alone. They complement each other. There must be a faith in
God that will cause men to cleanse their lives, to forget themselves in
the service of their fellowmen, and to overcome all weaknesses of the
flesh; a faith that will bring about a repentance which is total,

continuing, and which will bring them to baptism, the priesthood, and temple ordinances; for man is carnal and devilish to begin with, and is naturally more like the beasts than like the Creator.

With the ordinances completed, he now faces the even more difficult part—that of becoming the perfected being, the master of himself. He must not only avoid adultery but must protect himself against every thought or act which could lead to such a terrible sin. Man must not only be free from revenge and retaliation but must "turn the other cheek," "go the second mile," "give the cloak and coat also." Man must not only love his friends but he must even more than tolerate his enemies and those who do him injustice; he must pray for them and actually love them. This is the way to perfection. Man must not only be above burglary or theft but must be honest in thought and deed in all the numerous areas where rationalization permits dishonesty in every common walk of life, in padding reports, in chiseling on time or money or labor, and every shady or questionable practice. Man must not only cease from his worship of things of wood and stone and metal but he must actively worship in true fashion the living God. This is the strait and narrow way. (62-01)

Righteousness requires action. People tend often to measure their righteousness by the absence of wrong acts in their lives, as if passivity were the end of being. But God has created "things to act and things to be acted upon" (2 Nephi 2:14), and man is in the former category. He does not fill the measure of his creation unless he *acts,* and that in righteousness. "Therefore to him that knoweth to do good, and doeth it not," warns James, "to him it is sin." (James 4:17.)

To be passive is deadening; to stop doing is to die. Here then is a close parallel with physical life. If one fails to eat and drink, his body becomes emaciated and dies. Likewise, if he fails to nourish his spirit and mind, his spirit shrivels and his mind darkens. (MF 91-93)

One cannot avoid responsibility with impunity. I have known people who would not be baptized and confirmed and who would not receive the priesthood because of the grave responsibility they would assume by accepting. Clearly one will not escape condemnation by refusing to accept the responsibility. (MF 124)

[There] are Church members who are steeped in lethargy. They neither drink nor commit the sexual sins. They do not gamble nor rob nor kill. They are good citizens and splendid neighbors, but spiritually speaking they seem to be in a long, deep sleep. They are doing nothing seriously wrong except in their failures to do the right things to earn their exaltation. To such people as this, the words of Lehi might well apply: "O that ye would awake; awake from a deep sleep, yea, even from the sleep of hell, and shake off the awful chains by which ye are bound, which are the chains which bind the children of men, that they are carried away captive down to the eternal gulf of misery and woe." (2 Nephi 1:13.) (MF 211-12)

God expects us to use our talents. Likewise, the Church member who has the attitude of leaving it to others will have much to answer for. There are many who say: "My wife does the Church work!" Others say, "I'm just not the religious kind," as though it does not take effort for most people to serve and do their duty. But God has endowed us with talents and time, with latent abilities and with opportunities to use and develop them in his service. He therefore expects much of us, his privileged children. The parable of the talents is a brilliant summary of the many scriptural passages outlining promises for the diligent and penalties for the slothful. (MF 100)

We must endure to the end. Having received the necessary saving ordinances—baptism, the gift of the Holy Ghost, temple ordinances and sealings—one must live the covenants made. He must endure in faith. No matter how brilliant was the service rendered by the bishop or stake president or other person, if he falters later in his life and fails to live righteously "to the end," the good works he did all stand in jeopardy. In fact, one who serves and then falls away may be in the category spoken of by Peter, "the dog turning to his vomit or the sow returning to her wallowing in the mire." (See 2 Peter 2:22.) (MF 121)

The commandments date from the beginning. Moses came down from the quaking, smoking Mount Sinai and brought to the wandering children of Israel the Ten Commandments, fundamental rules for the conduct of life. These commandments were, however, not new. They had been known to Adam and his posterity, who had been commanded to live them from the beginning, and were merely reiterated by the Lord to Moses. (75-13)

The gospel defines the abundant life. The Church of Jesus Christ has gone forward with its policy of progress and development. Its teachings are designed by God to give to men an abundant life in this world, and eternal life in the world to come. It teaches that men should be honest and upright, and that they should love their fellowmen next to God. It teaches a single moral standard by which men and women everywhere should adhere to the high standard of chastity. "Immorality is next to murder," is a statement frequently made by its leaders. Good members of the Church abstain from the use of liquor and tobacco, tea and coffee, and endeavor to live a healthful life by carefully following this standard. (47-05)

Mercy cannot rob justice. The Lord's program is unchangeable. His laws are immutable. They will not be modified. Your opinions or mine do not made any difference and do not alter the laws. Many of the world think that eventually the Lord will be merciful and give to them *unearned* blessings. Mercy cannot rob justice. College professors will not give you a doctorate degree for a few weeks of cursory work in the university, nor can the Lord be merciful at the expense of justice. In this program, which is infinitely greater, we will each receive what we merit. Do not take any chances whatever. (76-59)

God's law must be obeyed. We have come far in material progress in this century, but the sins of the ancients increasingly afflict the hearts of men today. Can we not learn by the experiences of others? Must we also defile our bodies, corrupt our souls, and reap destruction as have peoples and nations before us?

God will not be mocked. His laws are immutable. True repentance is rewarded by forgiveness, but sin brings the sting of death. (77-34)

Temptation and Sin

Satan tempts us at our weak points. The adversary is so smart and subtle that he takes every man in his own game. The man whose weakness is money will be led inch by inch and yard by yard and mile by mile into that area where his wants can be satisfied. If one's ambition is power, the evil one knows exactly how to build him up to that point. If one's weakness is sex, Satan in his erudition and experience and brilliance knows a thousand reasons why sex may be liberated to run rampant and express itself and satisfy itself. Lucifer is real. He is subtle. He is convincing. He is powerful. (2/28/66)

Having been reared on the farm, I know that when the pigs got out, I looked first for the holes through which they had previously escaped. When the cow was out of the field looking for greener pastures elsewhere, I knew where to look first for the place of her escape. It was most likely to be the place where she had jumped the fence before, or where the fence had been broken. Likewise, the devil knows where to tempt, where to put in his telling blows. He finds the vulnerable spot. Where one was weak before, he will be most easily tempted again. (MF 171)

The adversary is subtle; he is cunning, he knows that he cannot induce good men and women immediately to do major evils so he moves slyly, whispering half-truths until he has his intended victims following him, and finally he clamps his chains upon them and fetters them tight, and then he laughs at their discomfiture and their misery. (67-09)

And the Savior said that the very elect would be deceived by Lucifer if it were possible. He will use his logic to confuse and his rationalizations to destroy. He will shade meanings, open doors an inch at a time, and lead from purest white through all the shades of gray to the darkest black. (80-53)

Satan appeals to desire for the easy and pleasant. "Then cometh Jesus with them unto a place called Gethsemane, and saith unto the disciples, Sit ye here, while I go and pray over yonder.... And he went a little farther, and fell on his face and prayed, saying, O my Father, if it be possible, let this cup to pass from me: nevertheless not as I will, but as thou wilt." This was a trying circumstance. Life he could hold, or life he could give....

"And he cometh unto the disciples, and findeth them asleep, and saith unto Peter, What, could ye not watch with me one hour?" (See Matthew 26:38-40.)

That brings to my thought, am I asleep; are you asleep? Are you taking for granted all of the joys and blessings of this world without thinking of the eternities that are to come beyond? Are we asleep? Are we his disciples called by him to serve and to teach and to train, and are we asleep? That question always reaches into my heart. "Watch and pray, that ye enter not into temptation: the spirit indeed is willing, but the flesh is weak." (Matthew 26:41.) We all have flesh, that flesh which tempts us to yield to the things that are easy, that are satisfying for the moment, that give us pleasure. (76-28)

Sin has great attraction. Whoever said that sin was not fun? Whoever claimed that Lucifer was not handsome, persuasive, easy, friendly? Whoever said that sin was unattractive, undesirable, or nauseating in its acceptance?

Transgression wears elegant gowns and sparkling apparel. It is highly perfumed, has attractive features, a soft voice. It is found in educated circles and sophisticated groups. It provides sweet and comfortable luxuries. Sin is easy and has a big company of bedfellows. It promises immunity from restrictions, temporary freedoms. It can momentarily satisfy hunger, thirst, desire, urges, passions, wants, without immediately paying the price. But, it begins tiny and grows to monumental proportions. It grows drop by drop, inch by inch. (76-29)

The attractiveness of sin is a lie. Have you seen a real mirage in the distance with lakes and trees and dwellings and castles and water, but as the thirsty traveler moves on and on and on through it, he finds it but an illusion, and when he has gone too far to return he stumbles choking in the desert deception. That is like life—wealth and pride, wit and physical charm, popularity and flattery are the shadows of the nothingness that can bring us only disappointment and frustration. (1/5/60)

Sin is slavery. Carnal pleasures are fleeting and frothy and they always bring their retribution sooner or later. In the breaking of every law of God there is the breaking down of the divine elements of the man. Each command we obey sends us another rung up the ladder to perfected manhood and toward godhood; and every law disobeyed is a sliding toward the bottom where man merges into the brute world. Only he who obeys law is free. Serfdom comes to him who defies law. "The truth shall make you free" (John 8:32) was another of the incontrovertible truths authored by the Master. He truly is free who is master of situations, habits, passions, urges, and desires. If one must yield to appetite or passion and follow its demands, he is truly the servant of a dictator. (56-02)

Sin limits progress. Since the beginning there has been in the world a wide range of sins. Many of them involve harm to others, but every sin is against ourselves and God, for sins limit our progress, curtail our development, and estrange us from good people, good influences, and from our Lord. (80-53)

The scriptures say that "God is not the God of the dead, but of the living." (Matthew 22:32.)
There are no dead except those who have chosen to be dead as to the law, dead as to the benefits, dead as to the blessings, dead as to the eternal nature of the gift. (74-21)

Faith helps us withstand temptation. Temptations are great. Satan tells us that black is white. He lies to us; therefore, we must be prepared to make a bold stand before Satan, who is without flesh and blood, and against principalities and powers and the rulers of darkness. We need the whole armor of God that we may withstand. We must quench the fiery darts of the wicked with the shield of truth. (75-46)

Temptation is like Goliath. Now, my young brothers, remember that every David has a Goliath to defeat, and every Goliath can be defeated. He may not be a bully who fights with fists or sword or gun. He may not even be flesh and blood. He may not be nine feet tall; he may not be armor-protected, but every boy has his Goliaths. And every boy has access to the brook with its smooth stones.

You will meet Goliaths who threaten you. Whether your Goliath is a town bully or is the temptation to steal or to destroy or the temptation to rob or the desire to curse and swear; if your Goliath is the desire to wantonly destroy or the temptation to lust and to sin, or the urge to avoid activity, whatever is your Goliath, he can be slain. But remember, to be the victor, one must follow the path that David followed:

"David behaved himself wisely in all his ways; and the Lord was with him." (1 Samuel 18:14.) (74-32)

Sin produces suffering. Disobedience is certain to call down upon us the wrath of God. But the Lord doesn't punish us. . . . The chain smoker is not beaten by the Lord, but his own foolishness causes him to die; he may die of lung cancer. The heavy drinker will be upset that his body and equilibrium and his bodily organs finally refuse to act normally. The murderer is almost certain to finally get caught and land in jail. The unrestrained gormandizing individual may get so heavy that his heart cannot carry the load, and his extra weight disturbs him, and he drops dead in his climb up the stairs. The drunken driver is almost sure to kill himself eventually, in addition to a number of innocent people. And so it is with permissive living. Every thought that one permits through his mind leaves its trace. Thoughts are things. Our lives are governed a great deal by our thoughts. (76-20)

There are many causes for human suffering—including war, disease, and poverty—and the suffering that proceeds from each of these is very real, but I would not be true to my trust if I did not say that the most persistent cause of human suffering, that suffering which causes the deepest pain, is sin—the violation of the commandments given to us by God. There cannot be, for instance, a rich and full life unless we practice total chastity before marriage and total fidelity after. There cannot be a sense of wholeness and integrity if we lie, steal, or cheat. There cannot be sweetness in our lives if we are filled with envy or covetousness. Our lives cannot really be abundant if we do not honor our parents. If any of us wish to have more precise prescriptions for ourselves in terms of what we can do to have more abundant lives, all we usually need to do is to consult our conscience. (77-37)

Every soul must stand trial and pay the uttermost farthing in one way or another. Escape from the consequences of acts of free agency is an impossibility. No one, however clever, bypasses the "due reward of our deeds." There are dark, deep corners, locked rooms, isolated spots, but no act, good or bad; no thought, ugly or beautiful, ever escapes being seen or heard. Every one will make the imprint on the individual and be recorded, to be met and paid for. Hence, one only deceives himself to think he is "getting by" with anything improper. (68-06)

Sin brings unhappiness, righteousness brings joy. There is frustration in frantic criticism; there is concern in doubt; there is torment in faithlessness; there is mean conscience in error; there is misery in apostasy. (66-11)

You have done the very things to breed unhappiness. You have been planting weed seeds all this time. Do you want to be happy? There is only one path to happiness and it isn't like the road to Rome we hear so much about—that any road will lead to Rome. Happiness is a city where peace prevails, but you will never find it by going devious ways. (66-12)

Sin never brought happiness. Carelessness does not bring happiness. Casualness does not bring happiness—only devotion and consecration. (66-12)

Rewards of Righteousness

Righteousness brings joy. "Men are that they might have joy" (2 Nephi 2:25), and true joy and real happiness come through righteousness, for there is no compatibility between happiness and evil, and no one yet has ever found happiness from evil. The kind of life which brings happiness, brings also growth and development and leads toward perfection. Perfection is our goal, for with perfection comes exaltation and eternal life. (54-05)

Righteousness brings clear conscience. Live righteously that your memory will give you roses in December. Live gloriously as though you would live forever—you will. May the Lord be with you and inspire and guide you . . . that your vision may be undimmed as you walk steadily toward the sunkist heights on which your ambitious eyes are fixed today, and that the peace which passeth understanding may come to you eternally. (44-04)

Righteousness brings religious expertise. Experience in one field does not automatically create expertise in another field. Expertise in religion comes from personal righteousness and from revelation. (77-31)

Righteousness brings discernment. How comforting it is to know that on judgment day we shall be treated fairly and justly and in the light of the total, true picture and the discernment of the Judge!

A similar power of discernment and perception comes to men as they become perfect and the impediments which obstruct spiritual vision are dissolved. (MF 110-12)

Righteousness of descendants brings honor to parents. Could the thousands of our pioneers have voice this morning, I am sure that they would ask for no shrine, no monuments to their name, no words of praise, but this thing would they ask: that we, their posterity, should consecrate our lives, our fortunes, our energies, and ourselves to the work of the Lord, the cause for which they gave so much.

Their fondest wish would be that we carry on, living the gospel, remembering that our example is most telling. Many people among us hear our professions and, in some cases at least, find us not living up to our standards. They judge the Church and the gospel by the way we live.

May each of us assume personally the responsibility of honoring the memories of our noble ancestors by living as they wished us to live, and by fulfilling the hopes they had for us. (44-06)

Righteousness creates heaven on earth. Heaven is a place, it is true, but heaven is also a condition. We make those conditions— we live our lives clean, worthy, true, and faithful, and heaven is ours. We are true to our trust, to our companions, to our children, the Church, and our Lord, and being true and loyal and clean and worthy, we will constantly be in a heavenly atmosphere, or in heaven. (49-04)

Righteousness brings peace to the heart. Peace is the fruit of righteousness. It cannot be bought with money, and cannot be traded nor bartered. It must be earned. The wealthy often spend much of their gains in a bid for peace, only to find that it is not for sale. But the poorest as well as the richest may have it in abundance if the total price is paid. Those who abide the laws and live the Christlike life may have peace and other kindred blessings, principal among which are exaltation and eternal life. They include also blessings for this life. (MF 363-64)

The law-abiding citizen does not fear the policeman, does not hide at the sound of a siren. The righteous need have no fear of death. He who follows strictly the Lord's commands, keeping himself unspotted from the sins of the world, lies down at night in calm tranquillity; his dreams are sweet, his conscience at rest. A great peace settles over him as he sleeps or wakes. Strength is given him to meet difficulties, fortitude in the face of adversity, calmness in the wake of misfortune and in his life total peace which knoweth no understanding. Life with religion is life with real purpose. (56-02)

Peace means the absence of hostilities, whether they be battles with gun and saber and bomb, or battles with sin and weakness or other inward conflict. Peace means an absence of discord, of moral conflict, of agitating passions and fears. . . .

Tranquillity of soul, joy, and peace are the fruits of right living, nearness to and a dependence upon God, and an assurance of acceptability of one's life and a conviction of the completeness and divinity of the program.

Peace is when you can turn a corner without apprehension and look in the eye those you meet; it is the supremacy over fear, not fearlessness, but the courage to go forward in spite of fear; it is the hearing of the telephone bell without a start; the opening of your door to the police without a quiver; the receiving of a telegram without a tremble.

Peace is when the fracture is knit; when the chasm is bridged; when the villagers come home at night from their fields knowing where they will sleep; when the grain is stored in the barn; the folded linen is piled in the drawer and the fruit is canned and stored in the cupboard. . . .

Peace is like standing on a solid rock high above the water after having stood on melting sands lapped by treacherous tides. . . .

Peace is when destruction ceases and production begins; when maneuver fields are turned by the plow and barracks reconstructed into homes. And when hunger is history, education increased, and every man goes home at night to his family unafraid. (44-04)

Righteousness brings peace to the world. The Lord gave us the formula, simple and plain. He says: "I will give you peace in the land, and ye shall lie down and none shall make you afraid." (Leviticus 26:6.) No cold wars and no hot wars.

All we have to do is to live up to the commandments of God, and we can destroy all the munitions. And there is no nation under the sun, today, or yesterday, or tomorrow that can touch us. Is that fanciful? Is that wishful thinking? Not if you believe in God. If you know that God lives, and that Jesus is Christ, and that they have the world and everything within their power, it is not fanciful. (55-09)

Righteousness prepares us for celestial happiness. And when we are asked why we are such a happy people, our answer is: "Because we have everything—life with all its opportunities, death without fear, eternal life with endless growth and development." (74-30)

When one realizes the vastness, the richness, the glory of it all, which is the Lord's promise to bestow to all the faithful, it is worth whatever it costs to be patient, have faith, sacrifice, to endure sweat and tears. The blessings of eternity are ours because the Lord has promised them, if we will live all of his commandments. (78-15)

Free Agency

Men have free agency. Men have free agency, as the Lord has made clear. They may do right or wrong but they cannot escape the responsibility of answering for their errors if they are normal individuals. (64-05)

We may pick up our life where we consciously find it and lift it to a plane where our intelligent ponderings would have us take it. There is high purpose in our being. Man is not merely an animal. It was never intended that he should be controlled by passion, hunger, fear, and other urges. Rather was it expected that he would reach high, overcoming through harnessing all such urges. Man has thinking processes, the power to make conscious decisions, the ability to harness and bridle and control. He has his free agency in all his determinations and must accept the responsibility resulting from the exercise of such agency. (56-02)

Man is not free to determine truth. You probably think you have found a new freedom: to think wholly for yourself, to make wholly your own determinations, to criticize and decide for yourself what is right and wrong. That was decided eternities ago. Right and wrong are not to be determined by you or me. Those elements were decided for us before our birth. We have the free agency to do the right or do the wrong, but who are we to alter those changeless things? We can scoff at sacred things, express our own little opinions, but remember that millions of men and women with keener minds than ours, with more erudite training than yours and mine, have said things and done things more startling, more ugly, more skeptical than you or I could think of. Millions have gone down the path you are entering. They have all come to grief or will ultimately. Shall the violin say to Tony Stradivarius, "You did not make me"? Shall the created thing question the creator? . . .

Now, because the Redeemer, Jehovah, won the great war in heaven, you have been given your choice. Christ would never force the children of men to be righteous. He would call, persuade, and direct aright, but has left us to make our own decisions. You, my boy, may do as you please. You may criticize any or everything; you may destroy all that is holy; you may develop iconoclastic attitudes; you may cut your mission; you may discard your garments and laugh at them; you may abandon right and proper concepts received in your score of years through good training; you may drink or smoke; you may neutralize all your proper development of the past; you may commit any sin or transgression and sexual sin, including fornication, adultery, and its numerous manifestations; you may commit armed robbery and even take life in murder or suicide; but my beloved young brother, believe this absolute and unchangeable truth: *You cannot avoid the responsibility of your acts!* Think that through clearly. Do not fool yourself. Your own life is too precious! The lives of your posterity are too priceless! You will receive the rewards of right thinking, righteous doing, conforming attitudes; and wholly beyond your own controls, you will pay penalties—not that God will punish you but that you, yourself, will bring down upon yourself the judgments. (12/19/59)

We make our own destiny. Your own life, our own lives, are precious ones. We can satisfy ourselves with mediocrity. We can be common, ordinary, dull, colorless, or we can so channel our lives to be clean, vibrant, progressive, colorful, and rich.

We can soil our records, defile our souls, trample underfoot virtue, honor, and goodness, or we can command respect and admiration of our associates and the love of the Lord. . . .

Your destiny is in your hands and your all-important decisions are before you. (72-04)

Wanted! Youth who will maturely carve their own destinies from the hard marble of life with the chisels of courage and mallets of determination and undeviating purpose. (60-02)

Regardless of your present age, you are building your life; it will be cheap and shoddy or it will be valuable and beautiful; it will be full of constructive activities or it can be destructive; it can be full of joy and happiness, or it can be full of misery. It all depends upon you and your attitudes, for your altitude, or the height you climb, is dependent upon your attitude or your response to situations. (74-32)

Difficult circumstances do not relieve us of responsibility. No one should deny the importance of circumstances, yet in the final analysis the most important thing is how we react to the circumstances.

I have seen poverty produce quite different results in people; some it embitters, so that in their self-pity they simply give up and abandon the future; others it challenges, so that in their determination to succeed in spite of obstacles they grow into capable, powerful people. Even if they never escape from economic stress, they develop inner resources that we associate with progress toward a Christlike character.

It is a tenet of my faith that every normal person has the capacity, with God's help, to meet the challenge of whatever circumstances may confront him. One of the most comforting scriptures carries the message that God will not leave us helpless—ever.

"God is faithful, who will not suffer you to be tempted above that ye are able; but will with the temptation also make a way to escape, that ye may be able to bear it." (1 Corinthians 10:13.) (71-05)

Righteousness grows like a crop. Youth is the springtime of life —the time of the sowing of the seed, of careful planning, of wise organizing; for, as you sow, so shall you also reap. Soon will come middle life, the summer when tender sprouted plants are nourished and some replanting may be done when the stand is not good. Then comes the fall or time of harvest of the crops so planted and cultivated. No amount of cultivating, watering, or hoeing can make grow seeds which were never planted, nor seeds which did not fall on good soil. Therefore, look to your ideals! See that the roots of good seeds are firmly imbedded in rich soil. . . .

May you keep your personal ambitions secondary to your pursuit of high purpose and let your task literally glow with the noble end to which it is fully dedicated. May you be sensitive to the pulse beats of humanity's heart, and may you rise above the drudgery of life to glory in its spiritual universe and to hand down to your posterity and associates a spiritual heritage. (63-05)

Conscience warns but does not govern. Conscience tells the individual when he is entering forbidden worlds, and it continues to prick until silenced by the will or by sin's repetition. (80-53)

When the Lord said, "My spirit shall not always strive with man . . ." this was not because the Spirit is unwilling to strive but because he is made so unwelcome. He is willing to come to the rescue of anyone who really wants to be helped, who will yield to assistance. But when a person pushes the Spirit away and ignores and puts out the "unwelcome sign," eventually the Spirit of the Lord ceases to strive. He does not move away from the individual; it is the person who moves away from the Lord. (71-19)

Keep the door closed to temptation. It is extremely difficult, if not impossible, for the devil to enter a door that is closed. He seems to have no keys for locked doors. But if a door is slightly ajar, he gets his toe in, and soon this is followed by his foot, then by his leg and his body and his head, and finally he is in all the way.

The importance of not accommodating temptation in the least degree is underlined by the Savior's example. Did not he recognize the danger when he was on the mountain with his fallen brother, Lucifer, being sorely tempted by that master tempter? He could have opened the door and flirted with danger by saying, "All right, Satan, I'll listen to your proposition. I need not succumb, I need not yield, I need not accept—but I'll listen."

Christ did not so rationalize. He positively and promptly closed the discussion, and commanded: "Get thee hence, Satan," meaning, likely, "Get out of my sight—get out of my presence—I will not listen—I will have nothing to do with you." Then, we read, "the devil leaveth him."

This is our proper pattern, if we would prevent sin rather than be faced with the much more difficult task of curing it. As I study the story of the Redeemer and his temptations, I am certain he spent his energies fortifying himself against temptation rather than battling with it to conquer it. (MF 215-17)

We are responsible for our thoughts. What goes on in our minds is not really private, in a sense, because it affects our behavior and our attitudes toward others and toward life. (74-20)

Make plans. Failure to plan brings barrenness and sterility. Fate brushes man with its wings, but we make our own fate largely. (70-09)

To travel listlessly is just futile. One should have a destination and a goal to reach. One should determine what he wants out of life and then bend every effort toward reaching that goal. He must realize that life is more than meat and drink and fun and fortune. However, it is often easy for us as young people to follow the line of least resistance and, like the Nephites and Lamanites on the eve of the last battle, to be found to be "even as chaff is driven before the wind, or as a vessel is tossed about upon the waves, without sail or anchor, or without anything wherewith to steer her." (Mormon 5:18.) (74-27)

Make one-time decisions to do right. I have mentioned at this
pulpit before some determinations made early in my life, which decisions were such a help to me because I did not have to remake those
decisions perpetually. We can push some things away from us once
and have done with them . . . without having to brood and redecide a
hundred times what it is we will do and what we will not do.

Indecision and discouragement are climates in which the adversary loves to function, for he can inflict so many casualties among
mankind in those settings. My young brothers, if you have not done
so yet, decide to decide! (76-26)

One of the basic tasks for each individual is the making of decisions. A dozen times a day we come to a fork in the road and must
decide which way we will go. Some alternatives are long and hard,
but they take us in the right direction toward our ultimate goal;
others are short, wide, and pleasant, but they go off in the wrong
direction. It is important to get our ultimate objectives clearly in mind
so that we do not become distracted at each fork in the road by the
irrelevant questions: Which is the easier or more pleasant way? or,
Which way are others going?

Right decisions are easiest to make when we make them well in
advance, having ultimate objectives in mind; this saves a lot of
anguish at the fork, when we're tired and sorely tempted.

When I was young, I made up my mind unalterably that I would
never taste tea, coffee, tobacco, or liquor. I found that this rigid
determination saved me many times throughout my varied experiences. There were many occasions when I could have sipped or
touched or sampled, but the unalterable determination firmly established gave me good reason and good strength to resist.

The time to decide on a mission is long before it becomes a matter
of choosing between a mission and an athletic scholarship. The time
to decide on temple marriage is before one has become attached to a
boyfriend or girl friend who does not share that objective. The time
to decide on a policy of strict honesty is before the store clerk gives
you too much change. The time to decide against using drugs is
before a friend you like teases you for being afraid or pious. The time

to decide that we will settle for nothing less than an opportunity to live eternally with our Father is now, so that every choice we make will be affected by our determination to let nothing interfere with attaining that ultimate goal.

Some people feel that decisions are really out of our hands, that we merely respond to circumstances without choice, like a rudderless ship that drifts at the mercy of the wind and waves. And I agree that there can come a time when we no longer have control over our destinies, but I believe that this is only after the cumulation of our own past decisions has left us helpless.

In the beginning, each of us is a bundle of potential that can be developed and shaped by what we choose to do. In youth there is still great malleability. We can choose what we will become. As the years go by, we find our past choices have narrowed the alternatives still open to us and we have less and less control over our future. (71-05)

Attainment of Perfection

Perfection is an attainable goal. He said, "Be ye therefore perfect, even as your Father which is in heaven is perfect." (Matthew 5:48.) Now, that is an attainable goal. We will not be exalted, we shall not reach our destination, unless we are perfect, and now is the best time in the world to start toward perfection. I have little patience with persons who say, "Oh, nobody is perfect," the implication being: "so why try?" Of course no one is wholly perfect, but we find some who are a long way up the ladder. (58-10)

The gospel has perfection as its standard. The norm of "olden time" was the highest standard which could be expected of the children of Israel as they were emerging from the degeneracy and limitations of four centuries of serfdom with long working hours to leave them little else to think about but bread and sleep and sex. But the new law [was] suited to superior beings, with centuries of growing, expanding freedoms; and with a people now enjoying the full light of liberty and truth, no such low mean standard could be acceptable. The law was a schoolmaster to bring us to higher things; the gospel [is] a new norm to bring us to God in his majesty, honor and glory, we to enjoy with him immeasurable blessings. (60-01)

And how to work toward perfection in our lives? It is not a one-time decision to be made, but a process to be pursued, slowly and laboriously through a lifetime. We build from simple building blocks, adding refinements as the building rises towards the heavens.

In the time of Moses, the Lord led his people out of Egypt. They had been slaves for four hundred years. They wandered in the desert struggling for identity and direction. Through Moses the word of the Lord came down from the mountain. The commandments which the Lord gave to his people set minimum standards of conduct. By obedience to those principles they would rise above their former condition. These commandments are, said Paul, "our schoolmaster to bring us unto Christ, that we might be justified by faith." (Galatians 3:24.)

Our living by the letter of the law of the Ten Commandments is only the beginning of perfection. Jesus taught his followers the sanctity of the Ten Commandments, but pointed out repeatedly that there was more to do yet. . . . As the Lord asked him [the rich young man] to take on a more difficult task after he had mastered the lesser ones, so as we gain strength from keeping the simpler commandments the Lord will ask us to undertake greater tasks with this new strength.

Latter-day Saints are widely known among their neighbors as good people. But sometimes they are best known for their negative goodness. They do not drink, they do not smoke, they do not steal, they do not break the sabbath. How wonderful that is, when so many in the world do and break those particular commandments. But how much more glorious it would be if we could be known for far more in our lives. (78-22)

Christ is our pattern of righteousness. I urge you sons and daughters of God, who are in the image of your creator, to put your minds in the image of his, and to discipline and mold your spirits after the pattern of the Only Begotten. If you will do so, the Lord has promised that joys will follow eternally, and you need never fear having cheated yourself of what might have been. (72-03)

The cultivation of Christlike qualities is a demanding and relentless task—it is not for the seasonal worker or for those who will not stretch themselves, again and again. (78-24)

How difficult it must have been for him who could wither a fig tree with a single command, to restrain himself from cursing his enemies. Rather, he did pray for them. The spectre of death preceded him, sat with him, walked with him, and followed him.

To retaliate and fight back is human, but to accept indignities, as did the Lord, is divine. He was possibly anticipating the time when he himself would be tested, when he would permit himself to be kissed by a known traitor, yet not resist, when he would be captured by a vicious mob, yet not permit his loyal apostle Peter to defend him, though that worthy was apparently willing to die, fighting for him.

With twelve legions of angels at his command, he would yield himself and his armed, courageous apostles by his side. He would accept this manhandling and these humiliating indignities without retaliation. Had he not said, "Love your enemies"? (62-11)

Perfection is achieved by abolishing weakness. A famous sculptor once said that there was nothing in [his] art except just cutting away the marble that he didn't want there. And so there's nothing to attaining perfection either, except removing all the obstacles and the obstructions which pollute it. (75-01)

Patience in suffering cleanses the soul. I'm grateful that my priesthood power is limited and used as the Lord sees fit to use it. I don't want to heal all the sick—for sickness sometimes is a great blessing. People become angels through sickness.

Have you ever seen someone who has been helpless for so long that he has divested himself of every envy and jealousy and ugliness in his whole life, and who has perfected his life? I have. Have you seen mothers who have struggled with, perhaps, unfortunate children for years and years, and have become saints through it? Have you seen people who have calamity like the woman in my childhood who came home after a party and found seven children in ashes, her children, whom she had locked in her home. I am glad that we don't have to make those decisions. No pain suffered by man or woman upon the earth will be without its compensating effects if it be suffered in resignation and if it be met with patience. (61-02)

Being human, we would expel from our lives, sorrow, distress, physical pain, and mental anguish and assure ourselves of continual ease and comfort. But if we closed the doors upon such, we might be evicting our greatest friends and benefactors. Suffering can make saints of people as they learn patience, long-suffering, and self-mastery. The sufferings of our Savior were part of his education. (55-15)

The way to perfection is through obedience. Therefore, to each person is given a pattern—obedience through suffering, and perfection through obedience. Let each person learn obedience of faith in all things and thus exemplify the attributes of the Master. (72-04)

I believe it was from this very pulpit that my grandfather presented a sermon in which he said, "The test, the test, the *test* is coming." Well, the test is here. The test has always been here. We came into the world as a test. All the way down the line there are adjustments to make. There are sins to overcome. There is much to learn. There are weaknesses above which we must rise. We must gain self-mastery, become righteous, and attain unto perfection. (51-08)

We must take initiative. It is easy for us to fit into the old established programs, to do the things that we are required to do, to put in a certain number of hours, to sing so many times and pray so many times, but you remember the Lord said it is a slothful servant that waits to be commanded in all things. (55-04)

Self-Mastery

Perfection is attained by self-mastery. Perfection is a long, hard journey with many pitfalls. It is not attainable overnight. Eternal vigilance is the price of victory. Eternal vigilance is required in the subduing of enemies and in becoming master of oneself. It cannot be accomplished in little spurts and disconnected efforts. There must be constant and valiant, purposeful living—righteous living. The glory of the Lord can be had only through correct and worthy marriage and living a clean, worthy life. . . .

There are those today who say that man is the result of his environment and cannot rise above it. Those who justify mediocrity, failure, and even weakness and criminality are certainly misguided. Surely the environmental conditions found in childhood and youth are an influence of power. But the fact remains that every normal soul has its free agency and the power to row against the current and to lift himself to new planes of activity and thought and development. Man can transform himself. Man must transform himself.

Abraham did. He came out of an idol-worshiping family; yet he headed a dispensation of worshipers of the true and living God. Moses was born to poverty and slavery, was reared in luxury and court honors, and had great opportunities. He came to the heights which man can attain and walked and talked with God. Saul of Tarsus was born and reared and trained, but he completely transformed himself and became an apostle of God. Saul, the king of Israel, came of humble birth, but when Samuel had dealt with him and anointed him and trained him, he became another person. God gave him another heart and turned him into another man.

. . . Self-mastery, then, is the key, and every person should study his own life, his own desires and wants and cravings, and bring them under control. . . .

As we have stated before, the way to perfection seems to be a changing of one's life—to substitute the good for the evil in every case. Changes can come best if we take one item at a time. For instance, it is not difficult to be perfect in tithe paying, for if one pays one-tenth of his income annually, he is perfect in that respect. It is not difficult to become perfect in avoiding a swearing habit, for if one locks his mouth against all words of cursing, he is en route to perfection in that matter. (74-27)

Asceticism is distortion of true principle. You ask if asceticism is a virtue. No. Not as asceticism. But I am sure that most of the vices and errors of the world are distortions of truths. As I see it, asceticism is but a terrible extreme and distortion of the truth: Thou shalt know and control thyself. The Lord fasted forty days and nights. Was that not a lesson in self-control, self-discipline? Did not he gain moral strength by his fast? We have drink appetites, eating appetites, flesh appetites. They are all good. Without such appetites we would soon choke or starve or the race would peter out. It is the control of them which makes us gods in embryo. God gave us sex and prescribed uses and times and seasons and proprieties. We came on this earth to prove ourselves. It is in the disciplining and controlling of ourselves that we approach perfection. (5/31/48)

Conquest of self is more important than conquest of nature. Since you came into the world, there have been many changes in transportation, communication, entertainment, in merchandising, education, advertising and on and on. The country people move to the city and the city people crowd closer together into apartments which rise higher and higher in the air, and rural life gives way to urban life which builds toward the megalopolis. Improved tools have brought prosperity and wealth to many. Fewer people till the soil yet our tables in our own land are heaped higher than ever with the bounties of the earth.

But, basic things have not changed since Adam. Men still have the same inherent goodnesses and weaknesses. Passions, urges, desires, wants are unchanged. Sin has not changed. Right has not changed. God has not changed. . . .

Folks are born into greater luxury and, after a prolonged life, are buried in greater splendor, but the birthing and the living and the dying processes are still much the same.

We still have the same basic desires and urges and rebellions, jealousies and selfishness. There are still delinquencies to curb, and characters to build, and ideals to foster. There is still sin to overcome and faith to build and preparation to be made for the life which is unending.

Business is bigger, industry more varied, and leaders are commanding more men—but even industrial giants have not learned much better to command themselves, and they still give way to temper, emotions, appetites, and passions. The same great human urges properly controlled and directed could make them world leaders and exalted men.

Accordingly, the world's business is not only to explore the moon and fly to planets, and to conquer air and space; it is not only to feed the starving world, bridge the barriers and subdue the earth and develop peace among nations, but it is to master self and help the millions of others to overcome and perfect themselves. . . .

The real solution to problems is so simple that it is usually ignored.

When the young generation taking over the important posts in the nation, state and local, are courageous, fear no pressures, yield to no corruption; when professional and political men dare to do right under all circumstances; when our children are taught by fearless, selfless teachers; when industry is developed by men of virtue and integrity, problems *will* be solved. . . .

There is yet an earth to subdue, forces to control, nature to be harnessed, original elements to be made to serve mankind. There are wildernesses yet to conquer, and there are deserts yet to bloom. And there are also deserts in men's hearts and wildernesses in men's souls. . . .

But when man has conquered himself, the world will be at peace and the problems of mankind solved. . . .

Let us not be misunderstood. The physical worlds must be conquered and we must be about the business of it, but when we shall, like our Savior, have become the total master of ourselves then next the elements may yield to our persuasion. The Christ caused the waves to be still, water to turn into wine, disease to give way—*after* he had conquered himself. (63-05)

When Satan is bound in a single home—when Satan is bound in a single life—the Millennium has already begun in that home, in that life. (68-05)

Substitute habits, change environment. Change comes by substituting new habits for old. You mold your character and future by thoughts and actions.

You can change by changing your environment. Let go of lower things, and reach for higher. Surround yourself with the best in books, music, art, and people. (74-13)

Righteousness requires practice. Consider these boys and girls who sang; I was proud of every one of them. They did so well! Well, now, every time they do it they can do it better. It takes practice, and so we practice prayer, we practice paying our tithes, we practice doing all the things the Lord has commanded. Eventually it gets easier to do it, and we get so that we can do it so much better! (60-07)

Steadfastness and Diligence

Each generation must establish its own righteousness. It is not enough for us to be the seed of a great man—we must rise to greatness in our own right. And the Lord himself said to such as prided themselves on their heritage, "If ye were Abraham's children, ye would do the works of Abraham." (John 8:39.)

My cousins, if we are sons and daughters of Heber C. Kimball in more than name, we shall do the works which he did, fight the battles he fought, espouse the cause to which he gave his life, and live the kind of righteous life to which he directed his great energies. Let us honor the memory of our illustrious grandfather by more than words, let us bring real honor to his name by a rededication of our lives and interests and possessions and talents to the service of our fellowmen and to our God with a devotion which tries to equal or surpass that of our forebear. That is what he would most want of us, as it is what we would most want of our children. (79-08)

Each day is a new task. Each of us has a definite niche to fill. Let us not try to escape our work or shirk our responsibility. Let us ask ourselves each morning, "What is my work today?" We do not know where the influence of today will end. Today is, for all we know, the opportunity and occasion of our lives. Let us lay hold on happiness today; for know this, if you are not happy today, you may never be happy. Today is given you to be patient, unselfish, purposeful, strong, and eager to work mightily. (39-01)

Diligence in daily tasks develops character. The great calamity, as I see it, is when you or I with so much potential grow very little. That is the calamity—when I could be so much and I am so little; when I am satisfied with mediocrity in proselyting, in dentistry, in teaching, in whatever I am going to do with my life; when I am satisfied with this, oh, that is a sad, sad day because it has an everlasting and eternal influence upon me. (66-12)

Diligence brings joy. We are not here for the fun of it. We are here for the joy of it, and we want to go forward and do our work as we should do it. (76-09)

Resist procrastination. In my office at home in Salt Lake City, I have a little sign and it says, "Do it!" (78-16)

I suppose if I have learned anything in life, it is that we are to keep moving, keep trying—as long as we breathe! If we do, we will be surprised at how much more can still be done. (80-06)

There are many examples of Abraham's obedience to the Lord's will. In Genesis we learn that God commanded Abraham to circumcise every male in his household. Upon receiving that commandment, Abraham did not say, "Yes, I will obey the Lord, but first I must

move my sheep to another pasture, and mend my tents. I should be
able to obey by the end of the week, or by the first of next week, at
the latest." But instead of so procrastinating his obedience, Abraham
went out and complied "in the selfsame day." (Genesis 17:26.)

A similar, but even more impressive, example is Abraham's obedience to God's command that he sacrifice his only son, Isaac.
Abraham could have put this abhorrent task aside or even chosen to
ignore the commandment entirely, but instead he arose early the next
morning and began the journey to the appointed place.

How often do Church members arise early in the morning to do
the will of the Lord? How often do we say, "Yes, I will have home
evening with my family, but the children are so young now; I will
start when they are older"? How often do we say, "Yes, I will obey
the commandment to store food and to help others, but just now I
have neither the time nor the money to spare; I will obey later"? Oh,
foolish people! While we procrastinate, the harvest will be over and
we will not be saved. Now is the time to follow Abraham's example;
now is the time to repent; now is the time for prompt obedience to
God's will. (75-21)

Let us "lengthen our stride." So much depends upon our willingness to make up our minds, collectively and individually, that present
levels of performance are not acceptable, either to ourselves or to the
Lord. In saying that, I am not calling for flashy, temporary differences in our performance levels, but a quiet resolve on the part of
General Authorities, Regional Representatives of the Twelve, stake
mission presidents, bishops, mission presidents, and branch presidents to do a better job, to lengthen our stride. (74-29)

When I think of the concept of "lengthening our stride," I, of
course, apply it to myself as well as urging it upon the Church. The
"lengthening of our stride" suggests urgency instead of hesitancy,
"now," instead of tomorrow; it suggests not only an acceleration,
but efficiency. It suggests, too, that the whole body of the Church
move forward in unison with a quickened pace and pulse, doing our

duty with all our heart, instead of halfheartedly. It means, therefore, mobilizing and stretching all our muscles and drawing on all our resources. It suggests also that we stride with pride and with a sense of anticipation as we meet the challenges facing the kingdom. Out of all this will come a momentum that will be sobering and exhilarating at the same time.

Brothers and sisters, we cannot improve on the doctrines or the basic organization of the Church. The Church is perfect in organization and the doctrines are God-given. But we can improve on ourselves, and we can improve the way in which we do our individual duties, the way we keep in step with the progress. We are not suggesting in the "lengthening of our stride" that we try to move faster than we are able, or than would be wise, but rather a mobilization of our potential in order to move the kingdom forward for the more rapid and deeper benefit of our fellowmen everywhere.

The idea of "lengthening our stride" or "stretching our muscles" or "reaching our highest" has an interesting scriptural base. The second verse in the fifty-fourth chapter of Isaiah proclaims: "Enlarge the place of thy tent, and let them stretch forth the curtains of thine habitations: spare not, lengthen thy cords, and strengthen thy stakes."

Jesus, significantly, during his visit to the Nephites, quoted the same passage with only minor changes. (75-25)

Loyalty is a great virtue. And teachers, will you lead them to be loyal? Loyalty is the stuff of which great characters are made. Without loyalty to persons and causes and God, one is barren and desolate and fruitless. The Prophet Joseph said of Brigham and Heber once, "They are the only men of all the brethren who have never kicked up their heels against me." (66-07)

Those who try hard will be forgiven frailties. Accept the reality that personal improvement on the part of each priesthood holder is expected by our Father in Heaven. We should be growing and we should be developing constantly. If we do, others will sense the

seriousness of our discipleship and can then more easily forgive us
our frailties which we sometimes show in the way in which we lead
and manage. (76-26)

God gives us tasks within our capacities. We need not feel overwhelmed by our tasks, for God never gives us anything to do unless
he gives us the power of accomplishment. But he always gives us beginnings closest to our home. (74-26)

Church progress stems from individual efforts. Now, my brothers
and sisters, it seems clear to me—indeed, this impression weighs
upon me—that the Church is at a point in its growth and maturity
when we are at last ready to move forward in a major way. Some decisions have been made and others are pending which will clear the
way, organizationally. But the basic decisions needed for us to move
forward, as a people, must be made by the individual members of the
Church. The major strides which must be made by the Church will
follow upon the major strides to be made by us as individuals.

We have paused on some plateaus long enough. Let us resume
our journey forward and upward. Let us quietly put an end to our
reluctance to reach out to others—whether in our own families,
wards, or neighborhoods. We have been diverted, at times, from
fundamentals on which we must now focus in order to move forward
as a person or as a people.

Seemingly small efforts in the life of each member could do so
much to move the Church forward as never before. Think, brothers
and sisters, what would happen if each active family were to bring
another family or individual into the Church before next April
conference. . . .

Think of the blessings here and on the other side of the veil if each
holder of a temple recommend were to do just one more endowment
this next year! And how would our nonmember neighbors and
friends feel if we were each to do just one more quiet act of Christian
service for them before October conference—regardless of whether
or not they are interested in the Church!

Imagine how much richer our family life would be if our spouses and children were to receive a few more minutes of individual attention each month! (79-06)

God magnifies the efforts of the diligent. I find that sometimes when I have skimped on my time and my efforts, I feel a loss of the intensity of the Spirit.

But, when I do not limit my time or efforts, and lose myself in ... [others'] needs, I find myself somewhat in the position mentioned by the Prophet Joseph, who said, "... Great things shall be accomplished by you from this hour; and you shall begin to feel the whisperings of the Spirit of God; and the work of God shall begin to break forth from this time; and you shall be endowed with power from on high." (DHC 2:182.) (71-02)

From Caleb's example we learn very important lessons. Just as Caleb had to struggle and remain true and faithful to gain his inheritance, so we must remember that, while the Lord has promised us a place in his kingdom, we must ever strive constantly and faithfully so as to be worthy to receive the reward.

Caleb concluded his moving declaration with a request and a challenge with which my heart finds full sympathy. The Anakims, the giants, were still inhabiting the promised land, and they had to be overcome. Said Caleb, now at eighty-five years, "Give me this mountain." (Joshua 14:12.)

This is my feeling for the work at this moment. There are great challenges ahead of us, giant opportunities to be met. I welcome that exciting prospect and feel to say to the Lord, humbly, "Give me this mountain," give me these challenges.

Humbly, I give this pledge to the Lord and to you, my beloved brothers and sisters, fellow workers in this sacred cause of Christ: I will go forward, with faith in the God of Israel, knowing that he will guide and direct us, and lead us finally to the accomplishment of his purposes and to our promised land and our promised blessings....

I will "wholly follow the Lord my God" to the fullest extent of my energy and my ability.

Earnestly and fervently I urge that each of you make this same pledge and effort—every priesthood leader, every woman in Israel, each young man, each young woman, every boy and girl. (79-22)

A united group has great influence. I come to realize more and more, as my experience broadens, the vast influence and power that a small minority may wield in this world, in politics, in religion, in social activities, everywhere you go. A small group, united in purpose, with definite goals, may greatly influence the great majorities. (52-05)

Pioneers exemplified great determination and sacrifice. They had the persistence of ocean tides, which led them on; the strength of virgin forests, which braced their minds; the quiet of prairie vastness, which stilled their souls; the majesty of mountains[, which] gave them inspiration. These indomitable spirits faced the unknown with eyes upward, and footsteps forward. There are men in this world who are made of adobe with a thin veneer carrying a high polish; but these men of the pioneer companies were of granite through and through. They did not shrink at difficult situations.... They went forth to conquer, and conquer they must and would, and did. (44-06)

Let us not lose the "Winter Quarters" habit of starting crops to be harvested by those who follow. Let us be pioneers (for our people yet to be born) by planting the wheat of our witness, that those who follow us may eat of the bread of belief in time of famine elsewhere in the world! (76-26)

Lamanites show great devotion. The converted Lamanite is devout. Few ever apostatize. Some lose their way as they partake of the worldliness about them, but generally the children of Lehi of the twentieth century have inherited that grace and ability to believe like their ancestors of the long ago. We read in Helaman 6:36: "And thus we see that the Lord began to pour out his Spirit upon the Lamanites, because of their easiness and willingness to believe in his words."...

A meeting was called for all the membership of the Mexican branches in a certain district.... When the meeting and the usual handshaking were over and these humble people still remained, I asked the president why they tarried when it was getting late.

The answer amazed and humbled me. "The last bus ran at 8 p.m. There will be no more buses until morning. These devout people are waiting for us all to go home so they may huddle in their blankets on the chapel benches until morning when they will catch an early bus to take them back to their home area." Disembarking, they then would have long but happy miles to trudge back to their work for the new day. (53-02)

Sacrifice brings forth blessings. Sacrifice brings forth the blessings of heaven. And when we get away from sacrifice in all of our Church work, in our service and in the organizations and the subsidiaries, I tell you, when we get away from the sacrifice, we have slipped a cog....

Sacrifices for a just cause make character. (74-29)

The witness of a martyr lives on. Another day dawns—a new dispensation; the heavens are opened. The Father and the Son bear witness again to earth. Other heavenly visitors restore priceless blessings to men, and another martyr gives his precious life to testify to a faithless, skeptical, and unbelieving world that a personal God lives; that Jesus his Son is the Redeemer; and that truth is again restored. The details of the life of Joseph Smith are familiar to us. He announced at once his glorious vision of the Father and the Son and was immediately oppressed and persecuted. Modern scribes and Pharisees have published libelous books and articles by the hundreds, imprisoned him some forty odd times, tarred and feathered him, shot at him, and done everything in their power to destroy him. In spite of their every effort to take his life, he survived through more than a score of years of bitter and violent persecution to fill his mission until his hour should come.

Twenty-four years of hell he suffered, but also twenty-four years of ecstasy he enjoyed in converse with God and other immortals! His mission was accomplished—heaven and earth were linked again; the Church was organized; Brigham Young and other great leaders were trained to carry on; and he had conferred upon the heads of the Twelve every key and power belonging to the apostleship which he himself held, and he had said to them: "I have laid the foundations and you must build thereon, for upon your shoulders the kingdom rests."

And his hour had come to seal with his blood his testimony, so often borne to multitudes of friends and foes.

Someone has said, "Anyone can found a religion," and Talleyrand answered: "Yes. If he is willing to die for it." And the martyr is willing to do exactly that. But the powers of earth and hell cannot take him till "the hour is come." . . .

Into the pattern of martyrdom comes the voluntary phase. In every instance the martyr could have saved his life by renouncing his program. . . .

The Savior has said: "I lay down my life for the sheep. . . . No man taketh it from me, but I lay it down of myself. I have power to lay it down and I have power to take it again." (John 10:15, 18.) . . .

Joseph Smith did not want to die. He had so much to live for, with his family, his friends, with his interest in the expanding kingdom, and he was still a young man, but though he hoped and prayed that the cup could pass, he knew it was inevitable. He said: "I am going like a lamb to the slaughter." . . .

And a slaughter it was! The shots rang out! And freely flowed the blood of martyrs, for Hyrum, his older brother, had chosen to remain with him. This precious blood soaked into the earth, sealing an undying and unanswerable testimony which continued to ring in minds and hearts. . . .

In the final hours of the life of the martyr comes a calm serenity that baffles all human explanations. It is an unanswerable challenge to those who would rationalize and explain away.

Abinadi faced his enemies triumphantly: "[They] durst not lay their hands on him, for the Spirit of the Lord was upon him; and his face shone with exceeding luster, even as Moses' did while in the mount of Sinai, while speaking with the Lord." (Mosiah 13:5.) . . .

And as the death sentence fell upon Stephen, "all that sat in the council, looking stedfastly on him, saw his face as it had been the face of an angel." (Acts 6:15.) . . .

Paul said later: "For where a testament is, there must also of necessity be the death of the testator. For a testament is of force after men are dead: otherwise it is of no strength at all while the testator liveth. Whereupon neither the first testament was dedicated without blood." (Hebrews 9:16-18.)

But they had borne witness; truth was established; blood had been spilled; and the testimony would stand eternally against those who rejected the truth and were the villains in the tragedies.

But martyrs do not die. They live on and on. When the Savior said, "It is finished," he referred to his mortal experience, for his crucifixion marked but a milepost in his ever-expanding power. Hundreds of millions have been influenced for good by this perfect life and martyr's death. He had said himself: "And whoso layeth down his life in my cause, for my name's sake, shall find it again." (D&C 98:13.) His work continues to spread to this day.

The blood of martyrs is the seed of the Church. Stephen *dead* is greater than Stephen *alive*. His sermons continue to inspire his readers. . . .

Men do not give their lives to perpetuate falsehoods. Martyrdom dissipates all question as to the sincerity of the martyr. Personalities do not survive the ages. They rise like a shooting star, shine brilliantly for a moment, and disappear from view, but a martyr for a living cause, like the sun—shines on forever. Great characters, students, businessmen, scientists, followed the youthful prophet to his death. They were not deceived. They lost him in martyrdom but inspired with the divinity of the cause went forward without hesitancy. Thousands gave lives they could have saved, in Missouri, Illinois, and crossing the plains, and today a great people hailed for their education, practicality, and virtue, stand to bear witness that the martyrdom of Joseph Smith, like that of the martyrs before him, is another of the infallible proofs of the divinity of the gospel of Jesus Christ, restored in its fulness through that humble prophet. (46-04)

Martyrdom is still possible. Would you think it a glorious privilege to die for the Church? Someday some of us might. Martyrs are promised eternal life. (62-02)

Truth stirs opposition. We are continually being tried and tested as individuals and as a church. There are more trials yet to come, but be not discouraged nor dismayed. Always remember that if this were not the Lord's work, the adversary would not pay any attention to us. If this Church were merely a church of men and women, teaching only the doctrines of men, we would encounter little or no criticism or resistance—but because this is the Church of him whose name it bears, we must not be surprised when criticisms or difficulties arise. With faith and good works, the truth will prevail. This is his work. There is none other like it. Let us, therefore, press forward, lengthening our stride and rejoicing in our blessings and opportunities. (81-03)

Do not falter nor be distressed when others misrepresent us, sometimes deliberately and sometimes in ignorance. This has been the lot of the Lord's people from the beginning, and it will be no different in our time. (80-03)

Live in such a way that if the enemies of the Church choose to speak critically of you, they must do so falsely. Never be a cause of any embarrassment to the Church. (80-02)

Those who rest lose. While the bridegroom tarried they all slumbered and slept. In the Church there are a great number of people who are slumbering and sleeping when they ought to be awake and doing their duties. They are resting on their oars. They plan to go "tomorrow" to get oil for their lamps. Tomorrow they are going to be active! ...

I was on a train one day going to the Northwest, and the conductor who took my ticket said, "Oh, you're Brother Kimball." I said, "Yes. You must be a member of the Church." He said, "Well, I am." And I said, "What ward and stake do you live in?" He said, "I hardly know." And I asked him why, and his answer was: "Well, when I came home from my mission I lived in Sanpete County. They loaded me so heavily with Church positions and obligations that when we moved to Salt Lake I said to my wife, "We're going to rest one year before we take any position of responsibility." I said, "How long ago was that?" "Nine years," was the answer. Nine years of inactivity, waiting to live. . . .

These ten virgins were members of the Church. The bridegroom was the Lord Jesus Christ. These belonged, the wise *and* the foolish. (57-02)

Those not valiant will be disappointed. As I read the seventy-sixth section of the Doctrine and Covenants, the great vision given to the Prophet Joseph Smith, I remember that the Lord says to that terrestrial degree of glory may go those who are not valiant in the testimony, which means that many of us who have received baptism by proper authority, many who have received other ordinances, even temple blessings, will not reach the celestial kingdom of glory unless we live the commandments and are valiant.

There are many people in this Church today who think they live, but they are dead to the spiritual things. And I believe even many who are making pretenses of being active are also spiritually dead. Their service is much of the letter and less of the spirit. (51-03)

Resistance to right affects one's family. A *goad* is defined as a spear or a sharp pointed stick used to sting or prick. The burro who kicks the sharp instrument with which he is being prodded is kicking at the pricks. His retaliation does little damage to the sharp stick or to him who wields it but brings distress to the foot that kicks it.

I well remember in my youth a neighbor who moved about for some days on crutches. He was evasive when asked the cause of his misfortune, but an ear witness told me, as he chuckled: "John stubbed his toe on a chair in the night and in his quick, fierce anger, he kicked the chair and broke his toe." The rocking chair rocked on and on, and perhaps smiled at the stupidity of man. . . .

There is the man who, to satisfy his own egotism, took a stand against the authorities of the Church. He followed the usual pattern, not apostasy at first, only superiority of knowledge and mild criticism. He loved the brethren, he said, but they failed to see and interpret as he would like. He would still love the Church, he maintained, but his criticism grew and developed into ever-widening circles. He was right, he assured himself; he could not yield in good conscience; he had his pride. His children did not accept his philosophy wholly, but their confidence was shaken. In their frustration, they married out of the Church, and he lost them. He later realized his folly and returned to humbleness, but so very late. He had lost his children. . . . "The fathers have eaten sour grapes, and the children's teeth are set on edge." (Ezekiel 18:2.)

There is the man who resisted release from positions in the Church. He knew positions were temporary trusts, but he criticized the presiding leader who had released him, complaining that proper recognition had not been given; the time had not been propitious; it had been a reflection upon his effectiveness. He bitterly built up a case for himself, absented himself from his meetings, and justified himself in his resultant estrangement. His children partook of his frustrations and his children's children. In later life he "came to himself," and on the brink of the grave made an about-face. His family would not effect the transformation which now he would give his life to have them make. How selfish! Haughty pride induces eating sour grapes, and innocent ones have their teeth set on edge. "It is hard for thee to kick against the pricks." (55-06)

Loss of membership in the Church is the ultimate tragedy. As I looked over the congregation I saw this man. I had never seen him before. I said to myself "That is the man. He will come up after the meeting and we will have a visit about his problems." And sure enough, as soon as the people had gone, there he was and he was weeping. He had held a high place in the Church, but he had been excommunicated for cause, the one cause for which we often excommunicate people and he was weeping. He said, "Brother Kimball, how long will I have to wait? How long before I can be baptized in the kingdom? Brother Kimball, my children are growing up. They were up to my knees when I committed the sin. Now they are deacon age. I can't ordain them and they say every week, 'Daddy, why don't you take the bread and water? Daddy, why don't you go to priesthood meeting?' " And he wept.

I wish the members of the Church who have ever given a thought to taking their names off the record or those who are even casual could have been in the corner somewhere and heard him and heard many of the people who have begged for the privilege to come back into the Church. It's hard. You can't get out of the Church like that and you can't get into the Church like that. The easiest time to get into the Church is the first time you are converted. You can, in a few weeks, learn enough about the gospel and get a testimony of the gospel with correct living and proper repentance, to get baptized in the kingdom, but once excommunicated from the Church, it may take years and years before you can even be rebaptized and years again before the priesthood can be restored to you again. It is sad. This woman thought she could do it by just writing a note. You are not cut off easily. One doesn't go to the ward clerk and say, "Strike my name off." No ward clerk will ever rub off anyone's name. No ward clerk has the authority. The keys of sealing and loosing are only in the Presidency of the Church, the total keys, but he has delegated them on down to the bishop. He can release them and excommunicate them under certain circumstances and the stake president can excommunicate any member of the stake, but it isn't an easy process. One is summoned to a meeting and there they are given a chance to answer for their fellowship, and give reason why they should not be excommunicated. They are labored with over and over and finally, if they are still rebellious, their secret acts are made known, they are excommunicated from the Church. They may sigh a sigh of relief that they won't be bothered about it anymore but the day will come when they will know it was the saddest hour of their entire life and they will look back from someplace and see, of all the sad days of all their lives, that was the saddest hour when they didn't fight for their membership, the most precious thing in the kingdom. (57-03)

CHAPTER 7

Respect for Life, Truth, and the Holy Name

Respect for Life

Man is responsible to foster life. It is not enough to refrain from killing. We are rather under the obligation to respect life and to foster it. Far from killing, we must be generous in helping others to have the necessities of life. We must find ways to help them to have a more abundant life, satisfying life, beyond mere existence. And when these have been accomplished, we seek to foster the life of the mind and the spirit. And what we do for others we do for ourselves as well. We refrain from taking harmful substances into our bodies. And then we go on to seek good health and a strong sense of physical well-being. Finally, we promote the satisfaction of the senses by the pursuit of beauty, with its capacity to refine and ennoble the spirit. (78-22)

Love life. I remember the author [Robert Louis] Stevenson, and his zest for life and his great battle to continue it. He spent much of his life in bed trying to recover from illnesses which would destroy him....Some of his work was done in bed when he could not even speak for fear of a lung hemorrhage....

Stevenson had much that most people need. He loved life. He proved that even with a sickly body, one can have a healthy outlook on life.

In my work I find many people who have lost it, who have neither the courage to keep that life nor to give it up. And in their letters and interviews, they talk about ending their lives. (73-04)

Suicide

Shortening life is sin. This temple of God is the body that the Lord has given us. It has been given to us to last a long time. It is a terrible criminal act for a person to go out and shorten his life by suicide or by any other method if it is intentional, by shortening it with the things that will create an early death. That isn't the way the Lord arranged it. He intended that men should live to the age of a tree. . . . (76-20)

Suicide affects others. Your life doesn't belong to you totally. Your life belongs to your family and to your children, to your posterity. You have no right to throw away your life. Suicide is a terrible crime, yet it is followed and meditated by many people. (75-28)

Mentally ill suicides are not fully responsible. To take a life that we could not give is a sin. To commit suicide is a sin if one is normal in his thinking. We should avoid becoming disturbed in our minds or thinking about it. The terrible sin of suicide is tragic, and it is far more prevalent than we would like to admit. So if the party is mentally well, he has the responsibility to keep himself well and his thinking clear. (75-03)

Suicide is no escape. Suicide can only add another great crime to those already committed. It cannot alleviate any distress but can double or treble or quadruple it. It does not postpone the day of retribution nor of sorrow very long, for one plunges immediately from time into eternity, from mortality into the spirit world, and he goes with all his faculties, his mentality, his attitudes, his weaknesses, and his strengths. (12/16/64)

Avoid considering suicide. A minister acquaintance of mine, whom I knew rather well, was found by his wife hanging in the attic from the rafters. His thoughts had taken his life. He had become morose and despondent for two or more years. Certainly he had not come to suicide in a moment, for he had been a happy, pleasant person as I had known him. It must have been a long decline, ever steeper, controllable by him at first and perhaps out of hand as he neared the end of the trail. No one in his "right mind," and especially if he has an understanding of the gospel, will permit himself to arrive at this "point of no return." (MF 106)

Homicide

Murder hurts the killer. "Thou shalt not kill." Again, this command is for our good, for Cain suffered far more than did Abel, and murder is far more serious to him who commits it than to him who suffers from it. (11/2/62)

Premeditated murder is a heinous sin. Perhaps one reason murder is so heinous is that man cannot restore life. Man's mortal life is given him in which to repent and prepare himself for eternity, and should one of his fellowmen terminate his life and thus limit his progress by making his repentance impossible it is a ghastly deed, a tremendous responsibility for which the murderer may not be able to atone in his lifetime.

Of course, the laws both of the land and of God recognize a greater difference between murder or wilful slaughter and manslaughter which was not premeditated. (MF 129)

Abortion

Abortion is a serious sin. There is such a close relationship between the taking of a life and the taking of an embryonic child, between murder and abortion, that we would hope that mortal men would not presume to take the frightening responsibility. . . .

Abortion is a calamity, and if the gospel came into play in the lives of men and women, an abortion would be rare indeed, if at all. If men and women are living the gospel of Jesus Christ, which is the cure for all ills, there would be no illegitimate conceptions, and this would erase from the abortion docket the great majority of the abortions. However, weak, selfish women now require abortions, even in many cases where there is not the illegitimate conception. (71-17)

Abortion calls for Church discipline. Much is being said in the press and in the pulpit concerning abortion. This Church of Jesus Christ opposes abortion and counsels all members *not* to submit to nor participate in any abortion, in any way, for convenience or to hide sins.

Abortion must be considered one of the most revolting and sinful practices in this day, when we are witnessing a frightening evidence of permissiveness leading to sexual immorality. We take the solemn view that any tampering with the fountains of life is serious, morally, mentally, psychologically, physically.

Members of the Church guilty of being parties to the sin of abortion must be subjected to the disciplinary action of the councils of the Church, as circumstances warrant. We remember the reiteration of the Ten Commandments given by the Lord in our own time, when he said, "Thou shalt not steal; neither commit adultery, nor kill, nor do anything like unto it." (D&C 59:6.) We see some similarities. (75-13)

Abortion is permissible only in exceptional situations. Abortion, the taking of life, is one of the most grievous of sins. We have repeatedly affirmed the position of the Church in unalterably opposing all abortions, except in . . . rare instances . . . and when competent medical counsel indicates that a mother's health would otherwise be seriously jeopardized. (76-54)

Those encouraging abortion share guilt. It is almost inconceivable that an abortion would ever be committed to save face or embarrassment, to save trouble or inconvenience, or to escape responsibility. How could one submit to such an operation or be party in any way by financing or encouraging? (74-12)

Certainly the women who yield to this ugly sin, . . . and those who assist them, should remember that retribution is *sure*. (74-30)

Easy abortion is related to licentiousness. When abortions are permitted and encouraged even as a means of population limitation, it is the voice of the underworld encouraging sex without license or controls. (72-02)

Treatment of Animals

Animals are created for man's respectful use. Everything that has been created is for us. They are all means. There is no end in the cow, there is no end in the monkey, nor end in any other creation of the Lord. All of them were made for us. (55-04)

Be kind to animals. I had a father who was infuriated if he saw a man beating a balky horse, or kicking his dog, or starving his other animals.

Wise Solomon said, "A righteous man regardeth the life of his beast." (Proverbs 12:10.) (76-54)

Killing for sport is reprehensible. I remember many times singing with a loud voice:

> Don't kill the little birds,
> That sing on bush and tree,
> All thro' the summer days,
> Their sweetest melody.
> Don't shoot the little birds!
> The earth is God's estate,
> And he provideth food
> For small as well as great.
> (*Deseret Songs*, 1909, no. 163.)

I had a sling and I had a flipper. I made them myself, and they worked very well. It was my duty to walk the cows to pasture a mile away from home. There were large cottonwood trees lining the road, and I remember that it was quite a temptation to shoot the little birds "that sing on bush and tree," because I was a pretty good shot and I could hit a post at fifty yards' distance or I could hit the trunk of a tree. But I think perhaps because I sang nearly every Sunday, "Don't Kill the Little Birds," I was restrained. . . .

This made a real impression on me, so I could see no great fun in having a beautiful little bird fall at my feet. (78-07)

We do not kill. We are even careful about killing animals, unless we need them for food. When I was a little boy . . . I would see boys there with a flipper flipping the birds up in the trees. . . . Isn't that a terrible thing, to take life just for the fun of it? (77-09)

Now, I also would like to add some of my feelings concerning the unnecessary shedding of blood and destruction of life. I think that every soul should be impressed by the sentiments that have been expressed here by the prophets.

And not less with reference to the killing of innocent birds is the wildlife of our country that live upon the vermin that are indeed enemies to the farmer and to mankind. It is not only wicked to destroy them, it is a shame, in my opinion. I think that this principle should extend not only to the bird life but to the life of all animals. . . .

President Joseph F. Smith said, "I do not believe any man should kill animals or birds unless he needs them for food, and then he should not kill innocent little birds that are not intended for food for man. I think it is wicked for men to thirst in their souls to kill almost everything which possesses animal life. It is wrong, and I have been surprised at prominent men whom I have seen whose very souls seemed to be athirst for the shedding of animal blood." (*Gospel Doctrine,* 5th ed., Salt Lake City: Deseret Book, 1939, pp. 265-66.) . . .

It is quite a different matter when a pioneer crossing the plains would kill a buffalo to bring food to his children and his family. There were also those vicious men who would kill buffalo only for their tongues and skins, permitting the life to be sacrificed and the food also to be wasted.

When asked how he governed so many people, the Prophet

Joseph Smith said, "I teach them correct principles, and they govern themselves."

We look to the Prophet Joseph Smith for proper teaching. He said once: "I exhorted the brethren not to kill the serpent, bird, or an animal of any kind during our journey unless it became necessary in order to preserve ourselves from hunger." (DHC 2:71-72.) (78-28)

Honesty and Integrity

Integrity is a key virtue. Integrity is one of the cornerstones of character.... Integrity is a state or quality of being complete, undivided, or unbroken. It is wholeness and unimpaired. It is purity and moral soundness. It is unadulterated genuineness and deep sincerity. It is courage, a human virtue of incalculable value. It is honesty, uprightness, and righteousness. Take these away and there is left but an empty shell....

Integrity in individuals and corporate bodies is not to ask, "What will others think of me, and my practices?" but, "What do I think of myself if I do this or fail to do that?" Is it proper? Is it right? Would the Master approve? ...

Integrity in man should bring inner peace, sureness of purpose, and security in action. Lack of it brings the reverse: disunity, fear, sorrow, unsureness. (70-08)

Integrity (which includes the willingness and ability to live by our beliefs and commitments) is one of the foundation stones of good character, and without good character one cannot hope to enjoy the presence of God here or in the eternities....

If there is a chink in your integrity, that is where the devil concentrates his attack. (79-17)

Honor is like the precious stone, the price of which is greatly depressed by a single flaw. (65-11)

If everyone were clothed in integrity, if every heart were just, frank, and kindly, the other virtues would be well nigh useless since their chief purpose is to make us bear with patience the injustices of our fellows. (75-20)

Honesty can be taught but not legislated. "There ought to be a law," many say when corruption raises its ugly head, and our answer is that there are laws—numerous laws which are not enforced; but our further answer is that you cannot legislate goodness and honor and honesty. There must be a return to consciousness of those values. (58-07)

Parents can develop respect for others' property and rights in their growing children by example and precept. Parents who require their youngsters to apologize and make good and return—perhaps even double or triple—that which they have taken, broken, or destroyed—those children will be honorable citizens and will bring honor and glory to their parents. Those parents who themselves respect law and order and observe all the rules can, by that pattern and by their expression of approval or disapproval, discipline and protect their children against disorder and rebellion. Inner disciplines are substituting for the outer ones as the outer ones become habitual and effective. As one is obedient to his own sound principles, it is far more important and gratifying than obedience to others'. (78-03)

Can anyone truthfuly claim that he did not know stealing was wrong? Possessiveness seems to be a basic impulse in humans, but while a child may want other children's toys he soon comes to know that they are not his. Small thefts grow into larger ones unless the desire is curbed. Parents who "cover up" for their children, excuse them and pay for their misappropriations, miss an important opportunity to teach a lesson and they thereby do untold damage to their offspring. If the child is required to return the coin or the pencil or the fruit with an appropriate apology, it is likely that his tendencies to steal will be curbed. But if he is lionized and made a little hero, if his misappropriation is made a joke, he is likely to continue in ever-increasing thefts. Most burglars and hold-up men would not have become so if they had been disciplined early. (MF 50)

Temple-goers should be honest in secular pursuits. We speak often of other standards of the Church and possibly overlook some basic qualities. We ask the candidates for temple recommends about chastity, the Word of Wisdom, and tithing. We should include such questions as: Are you honest in your dealings? Do you bear a good reputation among Saints and nonmembers for paying obligations? Do you live within your means? Do you only borrow what you have reasonable chance to repay? Do you oppress the employee? Do you give an honest day's work for your wages? Do you keep your word? (58-07)

Members should not take unfair advantage of Church programs. The consciences of many seem seared as they are willing to not only "soak the rich" but get from the Church all possible. Most people receiving welfare aid are honorable, but occasionally one is found who will defraud the Church. Sometimes wards are wont to get everything possible from the Church on new construction rather than assume their full load. Some mission areas resist stakehood until they can get all their units housed because in the mission the Church pays 70 percent while in the stake it pays only 50 percent. (58-07)

In this institution students and faculty commit themselves explicitly to abide by a code of conduct which includes both living by the moral precepts of the gospel and conforming to a dress and grooming code. Some purport to accept the moral standards as important and denigrate the other as trivial and as intruding on their freedom of choice. These people fundamentally misperceive the question, which is not whether the dress or grooming code is wise, but whether they should consider themselves bound by a promise. It is not that such a code is forced upon anyone; there is free choice to come here or to go to some other institution which makes no such demands. Indeed, other schools, often supported by tax monies, may be less costly to attend, may have equally high academic standards, and will probably have associated with them a Church-sponsored institute of religion—a program which provides for wholesome social life and gospel study without binding the students to abide by BYU standards. There is no disgrace in making that choice; it is a wholly legitimate option. But once having elected to come here and to participate in this community with its special calling to represent the Church and its highest standards, you must not compromise your integrity by promising what you will not do. By taking covenants lightly, you will wound your eternal self.

I use the word *covenant* deliberately; it is a word with sacred connotations and I mean to use it with all its special spiritual force. Self-justification is easy and rationalization seductive, but the Lord explains in modern revelation that "when we undertake to cover our sins, or to gratify our pride, our vain ambition . . . the heavens withdraw themselves; the Spirit of the Lord is grieved; and . . . he is left unto himself, to kick against the pricks." (D&C 121:37-38.) Of course we can choose; the free agency is ours, but we cannot escape the consequences of our choice. (79-17)

Honor requires preventing dishonesty of others. We approve [dishonesty] tacitly, by our silence. Sometimes we get very negligent and want not to bother anybody or cause anyone any trouble, or we have not the "courage of the commonplace" to report it. Is it being a "stool pigeon" to report lawbreaking? I think not. The normal righteous have rights. . . . They have a right to peace. The others are subnormal and have no right to steal or pilfer or to do anything disturbing the safety and peace of the great decent majority. A strongly expressed public opinion can make it most unpleasant for the dishonest one. (58-10)

Be meticulously honest in business. Good business [is] profitable to the buyer and profitable to the seller. I believe that the agent is entitled to his commissions only when he has by the sale benefited the buyer. . . .

Perhaps the real test of one's business would be if he can pray for guidance in developing it and ask the blessings of the Lord upon his completed service. (66-06)

Shun dishonest business practices. In every walk of life there are chances for the stories of dishonesty. Professional people are said to be charging prohibitive prices for service: "All that the law will allow." Colored water sold as a costly prescription, a few cents' worth of drugs for many dollars, poor material in the hidden places in building construction, improper billing, "cutting in" by clerks, so-called borrowing without consent by one entrusted with money. There is the workman who steals time, the employer who oppresses and takes advantage of his employees, the missionary who soldiers on the job, the speeder, the merchant selling inferior goods at marked-up prices, the constant close-out sales intended to misrepresent and deceive, the mark-up of prices in order to show remarkable sales values, the adjusted scales and measures, raising rents because of house shortage not because of increased costs of maintenance or interest rates. (58-07)

Be honest in employment and indebtedness. Perhaps the birth and tremendous growth of labor unions is the result of the over-bearing employer who underpaid and overworked his employees into the state of rebellion, bringing into being an antagonist hard to reckon with....

There is sometimes a lack of honor in office and business—the employee who does less than he has agreed to do; the one who cuts time, who comes late and leaves early, who visits and wastes precious time, who uses long noon hours and overstays the so-called coffee break....

He is dishonest who buys more than he can reasonably expect to pay for. This is defrauding. He has little honor who fails to pay his honest debts. It would seem to me that every luxury one enjoys at the expense of a creditor is not wholly honest.... It is not always dishonorable to be in debt, but certainly it is to ignore debts....

Bankruptcies are common and numerous today. I hope bankruptcy proceedings are not intended to free men of their honest obligations. They may serve well to give the debtor a breathing period and an opportunity to make back the money but he should pay his honest obligations even though the law might have protected him against them. (65-11)

Pay customs duties. One basic field of integrity is in the crossing of national boundaries without paying proper customs dues. Sometimes people rationalize. There are those who would hesitate to take from a neighbor or steal from a merchant but have so completely geared their thinking that it has come to be all right with them to avoid customs and fail to make proper report of purchases. We decry this and urge our people to be honest in every field and in all that they do. We decry any exception to this rule and hope that our people will be punctiliously honorable and honest in all these customs obligations and other dealings also. (75-47)

Speeding is dishonest. Another area in which numerous people show a lack of total honesty and integrity is on the highway. Is it dishonest to break speed limits? What are we doing to our children and others when we not only exceed limits but boast about it? Perhaps there are few of us who do not exhibit this fault, but is it right because many break the law? How light the right foot becomes suddenly as we see a police car following us or hear a siren.

Why should we need inspectors, policemen, game wardens? Should it not be enough that the rules be published? Why must grown men be watched and checked? (58-07)

Vandalism is abhorrent. When I lived in Arizona as a boy, nearly all the farmers had melon patches, and some of the farmers raised them for the market. Sometimes some boys would gang up and in the darkness of the night, go to one of these melon patches, and with their jackknives go through the patch and slash all the melons they could reach. They did not want the melons to eat, merely an ugly, destructive urge to destroy. This I never could understand, and I could never understand setting fire to things or breaking windows or tearing rugs or any of the mean tricks that were destructive in nature. (74-32)

Avoid all varieties of dishonesty. To all thieveries and dishonest acts the Lord says, "Thou shalt not steal." Four short common words he used. Perhaps he wearied of the long list he could have made of ways to steal, misrepresent, and take advantage, and he covered all methods of taking that which does not properly belong to one by saying, "Thou shalt not steal." (76-54)

Dishonesty is destructive to character. The theft of pennies or dollars or commodities may impoverish little the one from whom the goods are taken, but it is a shrivelling, dwarfing process to the one who steals. (58-07)

Practically all dishonesty owes its existence and growth to this inward distortion we call "self-justification." It is the first, the worst and the most insidious and damaging form of cheating—to cheat oneself. (67-02)

Clean house of petty dishonesties. Since the Lord said, "Be ye therefore perfect, even as your Father which is in heaven is perfect" (Matthew 5:48), it would be well if all of us would take frequent inventory to see if hidden away under the rugs and in the corners of our lives there might be some vestige of hypocrisy and ugliness or error... small eccentricities and dishonestness. Are there any cobwebs in ceilings and corners which we think will not be noticed? Are we trying to cover up the small pettiness and the small gratifications we secretly allow ourselves—rationalizing the while that they are insignificant and inconsequential? Are there areas in our thoughts and actions and attitudes which we would like to hide from those we respect most?... "The rebellious shall be pierced with much sorrow; for their iniquities shall be spoken upon the housetops, and their secret acts shall be revealed." (D&C 1:3.) (67-02)

Profanity

Profanity insults God. In the hospital one day I was wheeled out of the operating room by an attendant who stumbled, and there issued from his angry lips vicious cursing with a combination of the names of the Savior. Even half-conscious, I recoiled and implored: "Please! Please! That is my Lord whose names you revile." There was a deathly silence, then a subdued voice whispered: "I am sorry."

Recently I saw a drama enacted on the stage of a San Francisco theater. The play had enjoyed a long continuous run in New York. It was widely heralded. But the actors, unworthy to unloose the latchets of the Lord's sandals, were blaspheming his sacred name in their common, vulgar talk. They repeated words of a playwright, words profaning the holy name of their Creator. The people laughed and applauded, and as I thought of the writer, the players, and the audience, the feeling came over me that all were party to the crime....

On the stage, on the telephone, sensitive ears and eyes are outraged daily by the unwarranted and blasphemous use of the names of the Lord our God. In the club, on the farm, in social circles, in business, and in every walk of life the names of the Redeemer are used presumptuously and sinfully....

Why do they take in their unholy lips and run through their sacrilegious pens the names of their own Creator, the holy names of their Redeemer? Why do they ignore his positive command, "And ye shall not swear by my name falsely, neither shalt thou profane the name of thy God: I am the Lord." (Leviticus 19:12.)...

Let us rededicate ourselves to reverential attitudes, toward an expression of gratitude to our Lord for his incomparable sacrifice. (53-03)

Profanity displays poverty of language. We note the increasing coarseness of language and understand how Lot must have felt when he was, according to Peter, "vexed with the filthy conversation of the wicked." (2 Peter 2:7.) We wonder why those of coarse and profane conversation, even if they refuse obedience to God's will, are so stunted mentally that they let their capacity to communicate grow more and more narrow. Language is like music; we rejoice in beauty, range, and quality in both, and we are demeaned by the repetition of a few sour notes. (78-08)

The Lord's name should be used with care. The Lord has said, "I am the Almighty." "I am Jesus Christ." "I am Jehovah." He is the one we worship. We sing about him in nearly every song. We pray about him in all our prayers. We talk about him in all our meetings.

We love him, and we adore him. And we promise and rededicate ourselves over and over and over that we will from this moment forth live
nearer to him and to his promises and to the blessings which he has
given us. (75-48)

Declare allegiance to Christ. It is not enough to refrain from
profanity or blasphemy. We need to make important in our lives the
name of the Lord Jesus Christ. In the waters of baptism we take
upon us the name of Christ. And as we partake of the sacrament of
the Lord's Supper, we renew that commitment. While we do not use
the Lord's name lightly, we should not leave our friends and our
neighbors or our children in any doubt where we stand. Sometimes
we have been accused in this church of leaving Christ out of the
program, and I always say, you never hear a sermon, you never hear
a prayer, you never realize anything in an LDS service but that was
accompanied and done in the name of Jesus Christ.

One person said to his friend, "I knew you were a Mormon and
that you spent a great deal of your time at church services with all
kinds of activities, but I was surprised to learn just recently that you
are a Christian."

Let there be no doubt of it in our lives and where our allegiance
lies. (78-22)

CHAPTER 8

Measurable Commandments— The Word of Wisdom, Tithing, the Sabbath

The Word of Wisdom

The Word of Wisdom is a commandment. In 1851 President Brigham Young gave to this Church the Word of Wisdom as a final and definite commandment. From the time it was given to the Prophet Joseph until 1851 it was considered as a matter of preference or suggestions to the people, a word of advice and counsel. From 1851 until this day it is a commandment to all the members of the Church of Jesus Christ. (57-01)

The Lord gave in a sacred revelation in 1833 what we have more recently learned through research: "Hot drinks are not for the body." This is tea and coffee. "Tobacco is not for the body . . . and is not good for man. . . . Wine or strong drink . . . is not good, neither meet in the sight of your Father." (See D&C 89:5-9.) . . .

The Lord knew when these things were discovered that constant smoking could lead to cancer; that constant drinking could lead to many accidents and diseases.

It is now a command to all his members, and as we see some members using these prohibited things, we wonder how they reconcile such activities with the statement of the Lord Jesus Christ when he said: "And why call ye me, Lord, Lord, and do not the things which I say?" (Luke 6:46.) (75-13)

Wisdom goes beyond the letter of the law. Generally when we speak of the Word of Wisdom, we are talking about tea, coffee, tobacco, and liquor, and all of the fringe things even though they might be detrimental are not included in the technical interpretation of the Word of Wisdom. I never drink any of the cola drinks and my personal hope would be that no one would. However, they are not included in the Word of Wisdom in its technical application. I quote from a letter from the secretary to the First Presidency, "But the spirit of the Word of Wisdom would be violated by the drinking or eating of anything that contained a habit-forming drug." With reference to the cola drinks, the Church has never officially taken any attitude on this matter . . . but I personally do not put them in the class as with the tea and coffee because the Lord specifically mentioned them [the hot drinks]. . . .

I might say also that strychnine and sleeping pills and opium and heroin are not mentioned in the Word of Wisdom and yet I would discourage them with all my power. . . .

Regarding the eating of meat, the Church leaves that also to the discretion of the individual. What would be required by one person might be too much for another. It would seem to me that a man engaged in very heavy, physical manual labor would require more meat than one sitting at a desk.

If one's physical condition required an extra supply of meat, I would not worry about the breaking of the Word of Wisdom, in that matter especially, if this was on doctor's orders or if they felt that this was the thing to do. (10/19/62)

There may be other things which are destructive to the body, but since the Lord through his prophets has specifically mentioned certain items, then these we must refrain from using. Should the Lord later include in the Word of Wisdom any other things which are difficult, we will also obey them. (51-08)

Word of Wisdom is a spiritual test. The Lord has insisted upon our refraining from the use of liquor, tobacco, and tea and coffee. I am sure that such abstinence will increase the length of our lives and increase the vigor of our lives. But I am sure that a deeper value comes from the observance of the Word of Wisdom than the mere length of life, for after all we must finally all pass away. The time will come when our bodies and spirits are separated, and our bodies will be laid in Mother Earth to go through the regular process, and though we do wish to continue our mortal existence as long as we can consistently, I am confident that there are greater blessings which will come to us than the strictly physical.

When I refrain from the use of these forbidden things, I am obeying my Heavenly Father, and whether or not I understand the purpose, I will still receive the blessing. The Lord has promised to all of us who obey his commandments and live his statutes that all that he has is ours. The living of the Word of Wisdom is a test. Perhaps he chose to make a part of this test those things which would be universally used and would take character and courage and strength to leave alone. It was given as a principle and "adapted to the capacity of the weak and the weakest of all saints, who are or can be called saints." (D&C 89:3.) If one obeys the Word of Wisdom only because of the physical, perhaps it is of the letter. But if he can stand the test and prove himself, that he will obey the commands of God, then it is of the spirit, and he will reap rich blessings. (51-08)

Abstinence demonstrates self-mastery. All the difficulty is not wrapped up in the sin itself, but the sin is evidence of weakness of the flesh. When one smokes, it is not the tobacco that does him the great harm but the breakdown of the moral fibre of the individual. If I drink, the poison of the liquor is secondary to my becoming slave instead of master. (9/6/57)

"Thou shalt not use tea, coffee, tobacco or liquor." Again, it is we who profit by keeping the forbidden things from our lives. True it is that there are numerous other things that could also damage our bodies and shorten our lives, but generally, if one can live in the world and yet be not of the world, if he can mingle with society and drink not with them nor smoke with them, if he can go to banquets and be perhaps the only one who has the courage to forego the tea or coffee, that individual has proved his obedience, has proved his supremacy in self-discipline and has put some of the enemies under his feet. To be in a position to smell the aroma of coffee or smell the smoke of a cigarette or see the sparkling liquor in a goblet in front of one and to resist is an indication that he has made progress. To be able to take from his purse one-tenth of all that he has earned and turn it over to leaders to redispense is a test of faith. To fast is self-mastery. To bear one's testimony is a control of one's emotions and feelings. To be unselfish totally, always thinking of others before one's self, is a great step toward self-mastery. To forgive one who is mean and offensive is the act of one near to perfection, and especially if the offender is not repentant. (11/2/62)

Personal integrity requires conformity. Sometimes it is easier to explain what integrity is by showing what it is not. I stepped into the Hotel Utah coffee shop in Salt Lake City to buy some hard rolls, and as I placed my order with the waitress, a middle-aged woman I knew was sitting at the counter with a cup of coffee at her plate. I am sure she saw me, though she tried not to show it. I could see her physical discomfort as she turned her face from me at a right angle, and there it remained until I had made my purchase and had gone to the cash register. She had her free agency—she could drink coffee if she wanted to, but what a wallop her character had taken, because she was unwilling to face a friend! How she shriveled! At the waters of baptism, in sacrament meetings, and in the temple, she had promised that she would have a broken heart and contrite spirit, repent of all her sins, take upon herself the name of Jesus Christ and serve him unto the end, manifesting it by her works.

Probably she was certain that I had not seen or recognized her, but the ten stories of the building above her were not enough to keep the angels in heaven from photographing her movements and recording her thoughts of deception. It was a petty thing, but for her it was withering—a weak, mean, cheap, little tricky thing that sent her honor skidding down the incline toward bankruptcy of self-esteem. (FPM 241-42)

Conformity requires only one decision. I remember that, without being pressured by anyone, I made up my mind while still a little boy that I would never break the Word of Wisdom. I knew where it was written and I knew in a general way what the Lord had said, and I knew that when the Lord said it, it was pleasing unto him for men to abstain from all these destructive elements, and that the thing I wanted to do was to please my Heavenly Father. And so I made up my mind firmly and solidly that I would never touch those harmful things. Having made up my mind fully and unequivocally, I found it not too difficult to keep the promise to myself and to my Heavenly Father.

I remember once in later years when I was district governor of the Rotary Clubs of Arizona that I went to Nice, France, to the international convention. As a part of that celebration there was a sumptuous banquet for the district governors, and the large building was set for an elegant meal. When we came to our places, I noted that at every place there were seven goblets, along with numerous items of silverware and dishes; and everything was the best that Europe could furnish.

As the meal got underway, an army of waiters came to wait on us, seven waiters at each place, and they poured wine and liquor. Seven glass goblets were filled at every plate. The drinks were colorful. I was a long way from home; I knew many of the district governors; they knew me. But they probably did not know my religion nor of my stand on the Word of Wisdom. At any rate, the evil one seemed to whisper to me, "This is your chance. You are thousands of miles from home. There is no one here to watch you. No one will ever know if you drink the contents of those goblets. This is your chance!" And then a sweeter spirit seemed to whisper, "You have a covenant with yourself; you promised yourself you would never do it; and with your Heavenly Father you made a covenant, and you have gone these years without breaking it, and you would be stupid to break this covenant after all these years." Suffice it to say that when I got up from the table an hour later, the seven goblets were still full.... (74-04)

If every boy and girl would make up his or her mind, "I will not yield," then no matter what the temptation is: "I made up my mind. That's settled."...Then see what a lot of time and worthiness we have saved. (74-24)

Alcohol

Use of alcohol is a curse. Drinking curses all whom it touches—the seller and the buyer and the consumer. It brings deprivation and sorrow to numerous innocent ones. It is associated with graft, immorality, gambling, fraud, gangsterism, and most other vices. In its wake come wasted money, deprived families, deteriorated bodies, reduced minds, numerous accidents. It has everything against it, nothing for it, yet states sell it and receive revenue from it, and it has become an accepted "normal" part of modern life. (MF 55)

One of Satan's sharpest tools is alcohol, for it blinds and deafens, numbs and manacles, impoverishes and maims, and kills unfortunate victims.

Liquor has been used to neutralize the inhibitions and dull the senses of many a young woman so that her virtue might be more easily taken. (67-13)

Sale of liquor is selfish enterprise. While deceitful men produce and sell alcoholic drinks the whole world over, to the amount of millions of gallons and for millions in gains and profits, the truth of the Lord's words is coming home today in the terms of poverty; broken health; broken homes; broken hearts; industrial distress through loss of efficiency, lower production, and absenteeism; and carnage on the world's highways, caused partly through the determination to exceed the speed limits on the highways. (77-34)

The liquor fight is an eternal battle and moves from scene to scene and sin to sin.

There are numerous people who profit financially—some politicians, manufacturers, wholesalers, deliverers, dispensers, and the underworld. Added to that army are the rationalizers who demand their liquor, regardless of harm to others. Do they pray over their work?

"The liquor traffic is sacrilege, for it seeks profit from the damnation of human souls." (Harry Emerson Fosdick.)

Arguments are specious, but to the gullible, unsuspecting, righteous, busy people, they are made to seem plausible. The tax argument, the employment one, the school lunch program, the freedom to do as one pleases—all are like sieves with many holes. There is just enough truth in them to deceive. Satan deals in half truths. (67-13)

They know that there are many good people who would not accept the whole parcel, so they feed it to them an ounce at a time. And they seem to be able to give convincing arguments that it is not so bad. The inch-by-inch process takes its toll—with liquor it starts through controls only in package; then the liquor can be carried into the restaurant and consumed there. And then to legalize it to be served at tables and now they would sell it in little bottles. Then would come any and all bottles regardless of size. And then would come liquor by the drink. And the tavern and the old-time saloon would rule and Babylon and Rome would return. We are gullible people and we accept this medicine from their very smart mouths. Many of us would pitch a seller out on his head if he tried to sell the whole package, but we will buy the deadening potion little by little, being deceived by the powers of darkness from high places. (66-07)

Alcohol is a crutch for the inadequate. People need help who feel that a party cannot be held, a celebration enjoyed, without liquor. What a sad admission that a party must have liquor for people to have a good time. How barren must some guests be if they must be inebriated! (67-13)

Tobacco and Drugs

Tobacco is a devil's tool. A cigarette seems to some such a little thing. But it too is... another of the devil's traps.... It takes a person away from his best friends, places him in undesirable company. It robs him of the spirit of truth—the gospel and the wholesome influences of proper friends, family, and the Church. It is habit-forming and estranges one from his best interests. (68-05)

A noxious weed becomes a favorite pastime and an uncontrollable habit, and fortunes are wasted and people die of cancer and offense is given to many, and spiritual opportunities are missed. (71-17)

Any drug dependency is undesirable. We hope our people will eliminate from their lives all kinds of drugs so far as possible. (74-30)

Even sleeping pills, tranquilizers, and such which were thought to be harmless have sometimes brought injury and death; these might well be limited or avoided and, if used at all, taken only under the strict supervision of a reputable physician. (MF 57)

Tithing

Tithing is a tenth of income. Inquiries are received at the office of the First Presidency from time to time from officers and members of the Church asking for information as to what is considered a proper tithe.

We have uniformly replied that the simplest statement we know of is the statement of the Lord himself, namely, that the members of the Church should pay "one-tenth of all their interest annually" which is understood to mean income (see D&C 119:4.) (80-34)

The salaried man complained: "My neighbor has a farm. His family lives upon it. *We* buy our living from a store with cash. *They* kill a beef, a pork, and feed themselves from their deep freeze. Their garden loads the table with vegetables; the field feeds the cows that furnish milk products; their farm grows wheat for the poultry and for the table; and the hens furnish meat and eggs. Do you pay tithes on your farm land production?"

The answer is: "Of course, you pay if you are true to your commitments. No honest man would rob his Lord of tithes and offerings." (68-03)

Pay tithing as money is earned. If a person has no income, then he is exempt, and that is just as honorable as being a full tithe payer, if we are sure we are exempt, if we are sure that we had no income. But I'm sure that most of us [even students] have some income in the summer or after hours, or Saturdays, or sometimes. We are not concerned whether it is cents or dollars or hundreds or thousands; we are concerned with the fact that . . . you're a full tithe payer. . . . The time to pay your tithes is every week, or every month, or every time an income is in your hands. . . .

We frequently have people say, "Oh, we believe in tithing, but the tenth of December we had a serious accident that took all of our reserves, and therefore we couldn't pay our tithing at the end of the year." If they had been paying their tithing every time they had an income of a few dollars or more, then they might not have had the accident; at any rate, they would have had their tithing paid. (57-02)

Tithes do good throughout the world. "Faith without works is dead," says James. Properly, all contribute labor and services and funds. Everyone, regardless of size or age, who earns small or larger amounts pays his tithing—the just and equitable law of sacrifice and bounty. It not only tests the faith of the payer and assures him limitless blessings, but fills a reservoir with funds from which amounts may be drawn by the proper authorities for many useful purposes, each again requiring cooperative action. A chapel is needed in South Africa, and to the smaller amount subscribed by the local members, there comes from the tithing reservoir the larger amount to pay for the edifice. In Chicago or Macon or Tucson or Missoula, or in any other of the thousands of branches and wards, the accumulated funds from the reservoir come to bring blessings which otherwise would be out of reach for the individual community. A temple is needed in Europe for the tens of thousands who cannot travel nor emigrate to the United States, and a channel is opened and cooperative funds flow to build, equip, and administer a temple there.

A school is required for young Mexicans, otherwise deprived, and the reservoir is tapped, and buildings are constructed, teachers employed and youth trained.

A fertile field for proselyting develops in a foreign country, and another faucet is turned, and wealth is drawn to buy property, establish a mission home, and pay return fares for the numerous missionaries who also, in a great cooperative effort, proselyte and bring thousands into the Church yearly.

And numerous Church projects are made possible by mass effort which would not be possible to each individual.

Thus from the widow in Ogden, the little child in Finland, the young Lamanite convert in Guatemala, the rich man of New York, the newsboy in Seattle, the blind woman of New Zealand come the funds in pennies and *pesos, francs,* and *marks* for the numerous progressive and productive projects of a great organization involving a million and a half people—all by cooperation of effort. (57-05)

Tithing is to be handled by the Church. "A woman lost a valuable ring and claimed the $2000 in insurance which the insurance company duly paid. A year later, she found the ring and wrote to the insurance company stating that as she had found the ring, she did not think it fair that she should keep the money. Accordingly, she was sending it as a donation to the funds of the Boy Scouts." Sometimes, we are very generous with other people's money.

And this is especially true of the Lord's money. We have known men who diverted their tithing for building funds, welfare assessments, to help the poor, to assist their hardup family members. To be tolerant with them, perhaps we could say they did not understand that the tenth of their income never was, never is, and never will be their own, that it belongs to the Lord from the beginning, and that to dispense it for any other purpose is dishonesty and fraudulent mishandling of funds. (65-11)

Tithe paying is a free decision. The law of tithing, like all other laws, is voluntary and optional. There are many members in the Church who do not pay tithing. There are also many who have become inactive because it is hard to live the gospel fully, and the world has many other allurements. There is no compulsion in one going to meetings or to praying or to having home evening, or to living the law of the Sabbath or any of the other laws of the Ten Commandments or the other scores of commandments, but the Lord seems to know what will make people supremely happy, and he has outlined a program which will develop and give growth to the people. (10/8/69)

If you would ask this congregation, each one in private, and say, "Would you like to have your money back?" I would guess that not one single person in this audience would say, "Yes, I would like to have it back, please." They would say, "No, I *gave* it! I gave it from my heart and from my pocket. I love the program and I want it to be a contribution." (76-58)

Tithe paying is for our benefit. It is my candid opinion that the Lord does not need the tithes we pay. Certainly he puts them to beneficial use, in the erection of chapels, temples, in missionary work, in educational endeavors, but the Lord could find other ways and means to finance his program without the tithes. It is you and I who are blessed when we pay the tithes. We have obeyed a principle; we have mastered our desires; we have obeyed a commandment without necessarily knowing fully why. (51-08)

Tithe paying brings feelings of satisfaction. It is the uncompensated things we do from a spirit of unselfishness which bring us uplift and satisfaction and growth. Little exultation is experienced when one pays his taxes, for he here has no choice; but when one pays his tithing with a grateful heart for the privilege and no one knows but himself and the bishop, and no acclaim or publicity or worldly renown is given him, he is compensated in the feeling that he has "measured up"—that he has kept faith with his faith. (10/29/47)

Tithe paying involves a covenant. There is the covenant of tithing. The windows of heaven are to be opened to us if we fulfill our part

...of the agreement. It is a solemn obligation given us. We may easily cheat here and few will know it since our bishops keep sacredly in confidence this matter. We cheat the Lord by not meeting this tithing obligation, but he and his Church can get along without the relatively small amount any one of us should pay, but we cheat ourselves. (58-07)

Tithing is a commandment. The Lord herein makes clear that tithing is his law and is required of all his followers. It is our honor and privilege, our safety and promise, our great blessing to live this law of God. To fail to meet this obligation in full is to deny ourselves the promises and is to omit a weighty matter. It is a transgression, not an inconsequential oversight.

Yes, it may take great faith to pay tithes when funds are scarce and demands are great. But we remember the promise from the Father to Malachi. We also remember the Lord's promise in our day: "I, the Lord, am bound when ye do what I say; but when ye do not what I say, ye have no promise." (D&C 82:10.) (81-01)

The poor have special need to tithe. There are people who say they cannot afford to pay tithing, because their incomes are small. They are the people who need the blessings of the Lord! No one is ever too poor to pay tithing, and the Lord has promised that he will open the windows of heaven when we are obedient to his law. He can give us better salaries, he can give us more judgment in the spending of our money. He can give us better health, he can give us greater understanding so that we can get better positions. He can help us so that we can do the things we want to do. However, if we like luxuries or even necessities more than we like obedience, we will miss the blessings which he would like to give us. (62-05)

One woman went to her bishop and wanted to pay a little tithing that she owed. The bishop said, "No, you keep it. You can't afford to pay tithing. You need every cent that you make." But this woman said, "Bishop, you have no right to deprive me of the blessing that I will receive if I pay tithing." (47-10)

Encourage children to tithe. Now, I know that you do not have very big incomes, but remember it does not matter how little you make, you pay your tithing. Give the children a chance to learn tithing. If one of the little boys or girls earns only fifty cents in a whole year, he goes to the branch president and pays one nickel for tithing and that is just as good as the man who pays $10,000. The Lord is not looking at the amount; all he is looking at is the percentage. (60-07)

Let children see parents pay tithing. So, wouldn't it be wonderful if every father in Zion would take his children with him to pay his tithing and let them see him give the bishop the amount of money that represents sacrifice to him, so that the children also would feel the need of it. (77-30)

The tithing principle is a solution for poverty. The cure to poverty lies in Isaiah fifty-eighth chapter and in Malachi third chapter: "Bring ye all the tithes into the storehouse, that there may be meat in mine house."

I hear voices asking in insolence and wonder and disbelief: "How can a scripture solve poverty and want?" Then I quote further: "And prove me now herewith, saith the Lord of hosts, if I will not open you the windows of heaven, and pour you out a blessing, that there shall not be room enough to receive it." (Malachi 3:10.)

Ah! That is what we need across the tracks, in India and Pakistan, in our big cities, in disadvantaged countries—to have the heavens open.

Apparently earth has not provided the answer; now shall we try heaven? The Lord has promised to open the windows of heaven.

To hear the population explosion experts talk and write—those people who think themselves so wise—they would depopulate the earth so that the few left would roll in luxury rather than that all the Lord's children could come to earth and have a body and mortality and the good things of the earth. . . .

I was in Lima. A number of men of the press from the big newspapers circled me in the mission home. Most of their questions were respectable ones, intelligent ones and satisfactory ones. And when most of them had made their notes and departed seemingly satisfied, one young upstart remained to question me. His questions now centered around polygamy, racism, poverty, and war. I tried to answer meaningfully and respectfully his insinuating questions....

He disdainfully asked why the "Mormon" church had not cured this world of poverty. Then I turned on him and said something like this:

Sir! What is this you ask? Do you know where poverty is born, where it resides, where it is nourished? I have traveled over your country considerably from coastline to highest mountain tops. I have been upon your dreaded Huascaran. I have been in your museums of gold and your cathedrals of grandeur. I have seen your mountain folk barely existing on primitive fare in squalid shacks, with limited food, with an absence of luxury. In your big city I see your mansions and palaces, but I also see your numerous homes of pasteboard, and tin cans, and store cartons, and the emaciated bodies of your Indians from inland and upland. I have seen your cathedrals with altars of gold and silver and your beggars on the cold floors of such edifices, with their skinny arms extended and their bony hands cupped and raised to those who come to see or to worship. And you ask *me* about poverty. I have been through the Andes Mountains and wept for the Indians who are still persecuted and deprived and burdened and ignored. They are carrying their burdens on their backs, their commodities to market on their backs, their purchases on their backs. And when they come to your cities, I see them snubbed and ignored and unaccepted. Four hundred years you have had them. Four centuries they have been just poor deprived Indians. For many generations they have been humans merely subsisting. For four hundred years, as the children of Israel were, they have been in veritable slavery. With their unrelenting poverty are many generations of ignorance and superstition, hunger and pestilence and convulsions of nature. And you talk to *me* of poverty and deprivation and suffering and want.

Four hundred years you have had them. Have their morals improved, their superstitions decreased, their culture enriched? Have their ideals heightened? Their ambitions stirred? Their production increased? Their faith enlarged? What have you done for them? How much better off are they today, in the Andes, than when you came four centuries ago? . . .

I would have you come to the headquarters of Mormonism, which you snipe at. I think you will not see a single beggar in Salt Lake City, none starving, and few, if any, unclothed and unhoused. There are no slums as you know slums.

He gathered up his papers and pencils. (71-17)

Observing the Sabbath

The Sabbath is for rest and righteous activities. In Hebrew the term *Sabbath* means "rest." It contemplates quiet tranquillity, peace of mind and spirit. It is a day to get rid of selfish interests and absorbing activities.

The Sabbath day is given throughout the generations of man for a perpetual covenant. It is a sign between the Lord and his children forever. It is a day in which to worship and to express our gratitude and appreciation to the Lord. It is a day on which to surrender every worldly interest and to praise the Lord humbly, for humility is the beginning of exaltation. It is a day not for affliction and burden but for rest and righteous enjoyment. It is a day not for lavish banqueting, but a day of simple meals and spiritual feasting; not a day of abstinence from food, except fast day, but a day when maid and mistress might be relieved from the preparation. It is a day graciously given us by our Heavenly Father. It is a day when animals may be turned out to graze and rest; when the plow may be stored in the barn and other machinery cooled down; a day when employer and employee, master and servant may be free from plowing, digging, toiling. It is a day when the office may be locked and business postponed, and troubles forgotten; a day when man may be temporarily released from that first injunction, "In the sweat of thy face shalt thou eat bread, till thou return unto the ground." (Genesis 3:19.) It is a day when bodies may rest, minds relax, and spirits grow. It is a day when songs may be sung, prayers offered, sermons preached, and testimonies borne, and when man may climb high, almost annihilating time, space, and distance between himself and his Creator.

The Sabbath is a day on which to take inventory—to analyze our weaknesses, to confess our sins to our associates and our Lord. It is a day on which to fast in "sackcloth and ashes." It is a day on which to read good books, a day to contemplate and ponder, a day to study lessons for priesthood and auxiliary organizations, a day to study the scriptures and to prepare sermons, a day to nap and rest and relax, a day to visit the sick, a day to preach the gospel, a day to proselyte, a day to visit quietly with the family and get acquainted with our children, a day for proper courting, a day to do good, a day to drink at the fountain of knowledge and of instruction, a day to seek for-giveness of our sins, a day for the enrichment of our spirit and our soul, a day to restore us to our spiritual stature, a day to partake of the emblems of his sacrifice and atonement, a day to contemplate the glories of the gospel and of the eternal realms, a day to climb high on the upward path toward our Heavenly Father.

The question may be asked: Can one observe the Sabbath without attending his meetings and doing full service in his spiritual responsi-bilities? The sick and the afflicted might have excuse, but the well and firm people should fill the day with constructive spiritual service. It is not enough to do nothing. One is not justified in substituting home reading for sacrament meetings.

The Savior said that the Sabbath was for man and not man for the Sabbath. The Sabbath is for man to obey and in which to find profit but not to break or desecrate. The Savior repeatedly insists upon the hallowing of the Sabbath day. He recognized the fact that livestock must be loosed from the stall and taken to water and fed and that other chores must be done. He recognized also that the ox might get into the mire or the ass fall into the pit; but neither in the letter nor in the spirit did he ever approve the use of the Sabbath for ordinary and regular work or for amusements and play. He healed the sick on the Sabbath, preached in the synagogues on this day, but he gave the Sabbath not for amusement and labor but for rest to the mind and body, change and relaxation from heavy service, and leisure for works of mercy. The observance of the Sabbath is a part of the new covenant. (64-01)

We encourage a thoughtful and prayerful review of the suggestions the Brethren have felt to approve for your consideration in planning Sabbath, home evening, and other weekly activities in our homes:

"As we plan our Sunday activities, we may want to set aside time for our family to be together, for personal study and meditation, and for service to others. We might want to read the scriptures, conference reports, and Church publications; study the lives and teachings of the prophets; prepare Church lessons and other Church assignments; write in journals; pray and meditate; write to or visit relatives and friends; write to missionaries; enjoy uplifting music; have family gospel instruction; hold family council meetings; build husband-wife relationships; read with a child; do genealogical research, including the four-generation program and family or personal histories; sing Church hymns; read uplifting literature; develop our appreciation for the cultural arts; plan family home evening study and activities; plan other family activities; friendship nonmembers; fellowship neighbors; visit the sick, the aged, and the lonely; hold interviews with family members...." (82-01)

God encourages man to seek the spirit of the Sabbath. To many, Sabbath breaking is a matter of little moment, but to our Heavenly Father it is one of the principal commandments. It is a test to "see if we will do all things" commanded....

In the early days of Israel specific injunctions were given, and the death penalty was imposed for violation. Perhaps this was the only way that these former slaves could be taught the law of obedience and be brought to an understanding of the commandments of the Lord. Rabbis and priests made mockery of the commands by carrying them to unwarranted extremes in which a knot could not be tied nor loosed; a fire could not be kindled nor extinguished; a broken bone could not be set; a dead body could not be moved from wreckage; a bed could not be moved; sticks could not be gathered. And it was against these excesses that the Savior lashed rather than the Sabbath day itself, for he who instituted the Sabbath had greatest respect for it. . . .

It would appear that the reason the Sabbath day is so hard to live for so many people is that it is still written on tablets of stone rather than being written in their hearts. . . .

In the days of weak Israel it seemed necessary for the Lord to specify the many things which people must not do on the Sabbath, but in our own day it would seem that he recognized the intelligence of his people, and assumed that they would catch the total spirit of worship and of the Sabbath observance when he said to them: "Thou shalt offer a sacrifice unto the Lord thy God in righteousness, even that of a broken heart and a contrite spirit." (D&C 59:8.)

And then he gave us the first and great commandment: "Thou shalt love the Lord thy God with all thy heart, and with all thy soul, and with all thy mind." (Matthew 22:37.)

It is unthinkable that one who loves the Lord with all his heart and with all his soul and who with a broken heart and contrite spirit recognizes the limitless gifts which the Lord had given him would fail to spend one day in seven in gratitude and thankfulness, and carrying forward the good works of the Lord. The observance of the Sabbath is an indication of the measure of our love for our Heavenly Father.

In the U.S. the second Sunday of May is set apart to honor our mothers; the Fourth of July to memorialize our independence; everywhere family members have their birthdays. How thoughtless and inconsiderate would one be thought who would ignore loved ones' birthdays or who would pay no attention to Mother's Day. How disloyal for one to forget the birthday of the nation or to ignore election day. And yet, one day in seven has been set apart to remember the Lord, as the Sabbath day—a day for rest, for doing good, for service, for spiritual regeneration, for worship of God. Greedy business fills its store windows with Mother's and Father's Day cards, with Halloween wares and valentines, with birthday remembrances, and with Christmas gifts, but how often does it lend its windows to the encouragement of Sabbath honoring? (64-01)

Sabbath Meetings

Saints worship together. It seems the Lord's idea of a full and abundant Sabbath is the worship and the learning of him and partaking of his sacrament. He would have us fill the day with useful and spiritual activities. He would have us do these things with thanksgiving and cheerful hearts and countenances, and not with much laughter. He would have our men and boys attend their priesthood meeting . . . [having] prepared their lessons and with a glad heart. He would have his people attend the Sunday School and there learn his plan of salvation. He would have his people attend the sacrament meeting to sing with the Saints and to pray in spirit with him who is mouth, and to partake of the sacrament emblems, repledging total allegiance, unconditional surrender, undeviating works, a constant remembrance of him, his program, his sacrifice. He would have us proselyte, visit the homebound, read the scriptures. When one shall have taken care of his religious duties in spirit as well as by the letter and shall have filled in the interims with these constructive activities, there will be little temptation to falter.

People frequently wonder where to draw the line: what is worthy and what is unworthy to do upon the Sabbath. But if one loves the Lord with all his heart, might, mind, and strength; if one can put away selfishness and curb desire; if one can measure each Sabbath activity by the yardstick of worshipfulness; if one is honest with his Lord and with himself; if one offers a "broken heart and a contrite spirit," it is quite unlikely that there will be Sabbath breaking in that person's life.

It is a happy satisfaction to find many people who are willing to adjust their affairs so that they may worship the Lord on the Sabbath. In a certain cattle-feeding area many men excused themselves from their Sunday responsibilities, saying the cattle must be fed, but one resourceful man among them fed his cattle on Saturday in one pasture for Saturday and in another pasture for Sunday. The next morning he unlocked the gate and drove the cattle onto the Sunday feed ground and went with his family to his Sabbath devotions. (64-01)

A man of my acquaintance remained home each Sabbath and justified himself by saying that he could benefit more by reading a good book at home than by attending the sacrament meeting and listening to a poor sermon. But the home, sacred as it should be, is not the house of prayer. In it no sacrament is administered; in it is not found the fellowship with members, nor the confession of sins to the brethren. The mountains may be termed the temples of God and the forests and streams his handiwork, but only in the meetinghouse, or house of prayer, can be fulfilled all the requirements of the Lord. And so he has impressed upon us that: "It is expedient that the church meet together often to partake of bread and wine in the remembrance of the Lord Jesus." (D&C 20:75.) (45-02)

But we do not go to Sabbath meetings to be entertained or even simply to be instructed. We go to worship the Lord. It is an individual responsibility, and regardless of what is said from the pulpit, if one wishes to worship the Lord in spirit and in truth, he may do so by attending his meetings, partaking of the sacrament, and contemplating the beauties of the gospel. If the service is a failure to you, you have failed. No one can worship for you; you must do your own waiting upon the Lord. (FPM 271)

The Savior emphasized that the tangible bread and water of the Sacrament were to remind us continually of the sacrifice he made for us and for renewal of our covenants of righteousness. The Sabbath day, one in seven, is set apart that we may be reminded of our spiritual duties and, on Easter Sunday once a year, that we may remember the resurrection of the Lord....

This far-reaching event calls for solemnity and sacred rejoicing. So grateful were they at the announcement "He is risen" that the two Marys ran to bring word to the disciples with fear and great joy, and as they met him they fell to his feet to worship him.

But we celebrate it in a worldly manner, in thoughtless disregard of the bitter cup of voluntary, purposeful death he suffered and the revolutionary thing he did. The disciples were overjoyed on that first resurrection day.

On the anniversary of it, we go skiing, riding, picnicking to satisfy our urge for fun, even breaking the Sabbath and forgetting our debt—forgetting that bitter cup which was drained in vain, and showing that the pains on Calvary were of no value, and displaying that the voluntary death was without effect—unless we take advantage of our opportunities and experience repentance and righteous living. (58-03)

Attend sacrament meetings. Who should attend sacrament meetings? The commandment was addressed through the Prophet to those "whose feet stand upon the land of Zion," the membership of his church. The requirement is not confined to adults but includes young and old alike. Much is being said these days about family solidarity. What could parents do to better help in solidifying the family than for the entire family, large and small, to go in a body to the meetinghouse to the sacrament meetings? There the children will learn the habit of regular attendance, will be kept from breaking the Sabbath, and even though very young, will absorb of the teachings and testimonies, and of the spirit there. Stake and ward and quorum leaders should be exemplary in this respect to the people. (45-02)

The consolidated meeting schedule was implemented largely in order to provide several more Sabbath hours for families. Therefore, take time to be together as families to converse with one another, to study the scriptures, to visit friends, relatives, and the sick and lonely. This is also an excellent time to work on your journals and genealogy.

Do not neglect those among us who do not now have the blessings of living in traditional families. These are special souls who often have special needs. Do not let them become isolated from you or the activities of your ward or your branch. (81-04)

And again, the Lord says: "Thou shalt go to the house of prayer and offer up thy sacraments upon my holy day." (D&C 59:9.) "The sacrament" is the ordinance of partaking of the bread and water. But *sacrament,* in its wider sense, "stands for any sacred rite or ceremony whereby we affirm our allegiance to our divine Lord." It could be in the form of songs, prayers, praise, testimonies, partaking of the sacrament, study, contemplation of the word of the Lord. (64-01)

Reverence

The chapel is a place of reverence. To Latter-day Saints the chapel is not a recess or a cell in a cathedral, not a place with altars of gold and precious stones. It is a place without ostentation or show, without statues and mostly without pictures, decorated simply and plainly, clean and light and worshipful. It is a place where the people are seated comfortably, in true brotherhood, where lessons are taught, choirs sing, members pray and preach, and where all gain knowledge and inspiration—and where old and young receive the sacrament. Here habits of thought and action are conceived and introduced into lives, and here faith is born, rekindled, and sanctified.

The chapel is not dedicated to pharisaical piety where are found long faces, stiff formalities, or cold and barren silences, yet reverence for holy places, sacred purposes, and divine personages should always be found there.

Since men are naked before their Father in Heaven, honesty with self and with him is important. Reverence is not furthered by shows of eloquence, display of scholarliness, parades of stylish hats and clothing. Many devout women prefer to do their worshipping without hats and many people save their costly adornments and jewelry for festive social occasions. Here is a place of refinement, simplicity, humility, brotherliness....

A great person is reverent. He will be deferential in a house of worship even though he be the only soul therein. No congregation was assembled when the Lord commanded Moses: "Put off thy shoes from off thy feet, for the place whereon thou standest is holy ground!" Presiding officers should plan so carefully that no whispering would be heard or seen on the stand. Parents should train and discipline their children and sit with them (except where class groups are supervised). Ushers should be trained to quietly care for seating with a minimum of disturbance. Attenders should arrive early, do their friendly greeting in subdued tones, slow their step, find seats toward the front, and sit in quiet contemplative mood. All should participate as fully as possible—singing with the singers, praying with him who prays, partaking of the sacrament with a grateful heart and a reconsecration to covenants previously made. An opportunity is given to follow sympathetically lessons that are taught, the sermons that are preached and the testimonies that are borne, judging not by eloquence but by sincerity. Here is a chance to drink deeply from fountain heads, for the humblest teacher or speaker will contribute thought which can be developed. As we quietly enter the door of the chapel we may leave behind us outside all criticisms, worries, and cares—all occupational, political, social, and recreational plans—and calmly give ourselves to contemplation and to worship. We may bathe in the spiritual atmosphere. We may devote ourselves to learning, repenting, forgiving, testifying, appreciating, and loving. (00-02)

Parents should teach reverence in chapels. Are we a reverent people? Do our actions in the home and at church show reverence for our Creator?

Sometimes we wonder. We attend sacrament meetings and conferences where children wander unrestrained in the aisles. During the service, we notice adults talking with their neighbors, people dozing, and young people gathering in the foyers. We see families coming late and filing noisily to their seats, and groups engaged in loud conversation in the chapel after the meeting.

Our thoughts turn to investigators, friends, and those whose testimonies are fragile and developing. Are our meetings the powerful missionary tools they can be, where the Spirit of the Lord reigns and penetrates hearts? Or to sense the Spirit must we first block out many needless distractions? . . .

As with the other principles of the gospel, reverence leads to increased joy.

We must remember that reverence is not a somber, temporary behavior that we adopt on Sunday. True reverence involves happiness, as well as love, respect, gratitude, and godly fear. It is a virtue that should be part of our way of life. In fact, Latter-day Saints should be the most reverent people in all the earth. . . .

Where, then, does reverence begin, and how can we develop it?

The home is the key to reverence, as it is to every other godlike virtue.

Let me emphasize the importance of teaching children to pray. It is during personal and family prayers that little ones learn to bow their heads, fold their arms, and close their eyes while our Father in Heaven is being addressed. Behavior learned at home determines behavior in Church meetings. A child who has learned to pray at home soon understands that he must be quiet and still during prayers in worship services. . . .

The last-minute rush to gather the children, dress, and hurry to meetings is destructive to reverence.

When families fall into this pattern they are frequently late to church, there are often cross words and hurt feelings, and the children are often upset and restless during the service. How much more reverent is the family that prepares well ahead of time for meetings, that arrives at the chapel well before the meeting begins, and that sits together to listen to the prelude music and put worldly concerns out of their minds. . . .

Often, before and after meetings, members of the Church cluster in the chapel to exchange greetings. Some seeming irreverence is due innocently to the fact that we are a friendly people and that the Sabbath is a convenient time to visit, to fellowship, and to meet new people. Parents should set an example for their families by doing their visiting in the foyers or other areas outside of the chapel before or after meetings. After a meeting, parents can help to carry the spirit of the service into the home by discussing at home a thought, a musical number, or some other positive aspect of the meeting with their children. . . .

True reverence is a vital quality, but one that is fast disappearing in the world as the forces of evil broaden their influences. We cannot fully comprehend the power for good we can wield if the millions of members of Christ's true church will serve as models of reverent behavior. We cannot imagine the additional numbers of lives we could touch. Perhaps even more important, we cannot foresee the great spiritual impact on our own families if we become the reverent people we know we should be. (76-01)

The Sacrament

The sacrament of the Lord's Supper should be taken worthily. The letter killeth, but the spirit giveth life. Do we take the bread and the water in remembrance of the body, the flesh, and the blood of our Lord Jesus Christ, or do we just take bread and water? (51-07)

And every time we take the bread and water, there should be a reconsecration, a rededication. When we are not living the commandments, when we are in transgression, when we have angers and hatreds and bitterness, we should consider seriously if we should take the sacrament. Yesterday I saw a mother-in-law and a daughter-in-law both take the bread and water, yet there was confessed irreconcilable animosity between them. Remember, it is what we do, not wholly what we know, that will save us in the kingdom. The sacrament is so sacred, and yet we find very few people who refrain from taking it—I guess because it is embarrassing not to do so. Yet we fear that many times unworthy people partake of the sacrament. The Lord says, "Nevertheless, if any have trespassed, let him not partake until he makes reconciliation." (D&C 46:4.) (62-08)

We expect you leaders to be an example in everything, that you will attend to every meeting, that you will come worthy to partake of the sacrament, having cleared up all difficulties with your friends and other members, and even though you are wholly right and the other party is wholly wrong, the revelations say that you must go and conciliate yourself with your neighbor so that every Sabbath day you may partake of the bread and water with a clear conscience. (47-10)

Let us not be like the Church member who partakes of the sacrament in the morning, then defiles the Sabbath that afternoon by cleaning the house or by watching television or by choosing an afternoon of sleep over an afternoon of service. (75-21)

Children and visitors may participate in the sacrament. Long, long ago, there were some of the wards who refused to permit anyone other than a member of the Church to partake of the sacrament, with the thought that they were taking it unworthily. There are those who feel, as you have indicated, that little children should not partake of it. And, there are those who partake of it whenever it is passed regardless of how unworthy they may be but to save themselves embarrassment, I suppose. . . .

The sacrament is to serve us in somewhat the same manner as the sacrifice did from Adam to Christ. . . . Both the sacrifice in the old days and the sacrament in our day are to keep us reminded of our covenants, that we will remember the sacrifice, that we are willing to take upon us the name of Christ, and that we will remember him and keep his commandments.

The Lord, himself, said, "And now behold, this is the commandment which I give unto you, that ye shall not suffer any one knowingly to partake of my flesh and blood unworthily, when ye shall minister it. . . . Therefore if ye know that a man is unworthy to eat and drink of my flesh and blood ye shall forbid him." (3 Nephi 18:28-29.) Apparently, he is not speaking of little children but of men who are accountable and responsible and who would defile themselves or the program and unworthily partake. Even in this case, he would not have the man cast out unless he was vicious. . . .

The sacrament is for the Saints, for those who have actually made covenants at the waters of baptism primarily, but there is no evidence that I find where the Lord would ever exclude the children who were rapidly moving toward baptism and who were learning and being taught to worship the Lord and be ready for the covenants as their age and development would permit. . . .

If a person, not a member of the Church, is in the congregation, we do not forbid him partaking of it, but would properly advise that the sacrament is for the renewing of covenants. And, since he has not made the true covenant of baptism or temple covenant, he is exempt. However, his partaking of the sacrament if he is clean and worthy and devout would not bring upon him any condemnation as it would for those who have made solemn covenants and then have ignored or defied them. (5/2/63)

Breach of Sabbath

Unnecessary Sabbath work produces tainted money. I wonder if many of us are not hasting to be rich. Are we making compromises in order to accumulate? I wonder if money earned upon the Sabbath, when it is unnecessary Sabbath earning, might not also be unclean money. I realize that some people must work on the Sabbath; and when they do, if they are compelled, that is, of course, a different situation. But men and women who will deliberately use the Sabbath day to develop business propositions, to increase their holdings, to increase their income, I fear for them. I think the Lord was speaking to them when he said: "Woe unto them that call evil good." (Isaiah 5:20.) Sometimes we salve our consciences by saying that the more we get the more we can give to the worthy causes, but that, of course, is a subterfuge. There are people who work on the Sabbath, not through compulsion but because the income is attractive, and others who work voluntarily to get the "time and a half" that Sabbath work gives them.

In a stake recently I interviewed a man for an important position in the stake reorganization. And I said to him, "What is your occupation?" And he said, "I operate a service station." And I asked, "Do you operate on the Sabbath?" His answer was, "No, I do not." "Well, how can you get along? Most service station operators seem to think they must open on the Sabbath." "I get along well," he said. "The Lord is good to me." "Do you not have stiff competition?" I asked. "Yes, indeed," he replied. "Across the street is a man who keeps open all day Sunday." "And you never open?" I asked. "No, sir," he said, "and I am grateful, and the Lord is kind, and I have sufficient for my needs."

I was in another stake, also in a reorganization program, and another brother was considered for one of the highest positions; and when we asked him of his occupation, he said he was a grocer by trade. "Well, most of the stores keep open on the Sabbath. Do you?" "We lock our store on Sunday," he said. "But how can you compete with these people who are open seven days a week?" "We compete. At least we get along very well," was his reply. "But would not the Sabbath be your biggest day?" "Yes," he answered, "we would probably sell twice as much on the Sabbath as we would on an average day, but we get along without it, and the Lord has been kind; he has been gracious; he has been good." "What do you sell in this store?" I asked him. He said, "Groceries and miscellaneous merchandise." "Your competitors sell other things including forbidden things, do they not?" I asked. "Yes, but we have felt it was not right," he said. "We lose trade, of course. People leave our store and go to the other store and buy many dollars' worth of groceries where they can get a few cans of beer or some wine, but we do not sell it." And I could not refrain from saying, "God bless you, my faithful brother. The Lord will not be unmindful of these seeming sacrifices. Your dollars are clean. They will surely not hinder you in finding your way into the kingdom of God."

The Savior knew that the ox gets in the mire on the Sabbath, but he knew also that no ox deliberately goes into the mire every week.

In my extensive travels I find many faithful people who forego the Sabbath day profits and those which come from the handling of the forbidden things. I have found cattle communities where the stockmen never carry on their roundup on the Sabbath; fruit stands along the roadside which are open night and day, but which close on Sunday even in the short fruit season; drugstores and confectionery businesses which earn their money on the six weekdays; eating houses and wayside stands, closed on the Lord's day. And there are many other people who might rationalize and justify themselves in Sunday profit taking but who take satisfaction and joy in refraining. And every time I see good folk who are willing to forego these profits, I rejoice and feel within my heart to bless them for their steadfastness, their courage, and their faith. . . .

I know that men will never suffer, ultimately, for any seeming financial sacrifices that might be made, for he has commanded us to live his laws and then has challenged us: "Prove me now herewith, saith the Lord of hosts, if I will not open you the windows of heaven, and pour you out a blessing, that there shall not be room enough to receive it." (Malachi 3:10.) (53-06)

It is true that some people must work on the Sabbath. And, in fact, some of the work that is truly necessary—caring for the sick, for example—may actually serve to hallow the Sabbath. However, in such activities our motives are a most important consideration. (78-01)

It is conceded that many good folk are compelled to labor on Sunday. Their alternatives are to work or lose their employment. But frequently those whose shift work occupies part of the day excuse themselves from Sabbath activities using their work as an alibi. Shift workers seldom work more hours a day than other folk, and if they are determined, such people can usually find ample time to render service and to hallow the Sabbath in the hours that remain. . . .

Can the employer rest easy in his pew at church while his employees make profits for his bank account on the Sabbath? Can the parents fully enjoy their meetings having hired baby-sitters to watch their children, who also should attend Sabbath meetings? (64-01)

Studying on the Sabbath should be minimal. I hope students will use the Sabbath for studying only as an emergency. . . . I believe that generally, with careful organization of time through the week, most studying can be done on weekdays, leaving the Sabbath for worship. . . . There might be times when one would feel forced to study, when he might feel that it was an ox in the mire. I am expressing only my personal opinions on this matter, but since we are talking to students, it would be my hope that your studying could be done in the season thereof and not as a cramming process just before you go on Monday mornings. (57-02)

Recreation violates the Sabbath. While attending one of the conferences last fall, one of my first down state, I was housed in a hotel, and early Sunday morning I was awakened by considerable noise in the halls and the lobby of the hotel, and when I came down I found that the lobby and the cafe near it were filled with men with colored shirts and caps and with hunting regalia. Their guns were clean and shining. They were all en route to the mountains and the canyons to get their deer. When the conference day was ended and evening found us on our way home, many were the cars that we passed with a deer on the running board or on the bumper.

Another Sabbath I drove through an agricultural area, and was distressed to find there were mowing machines and balers and perspiring men engaged in harvesting the crops.

Still another Sabbath I drove through Main Street of one of our larger towns, and I was dismayed to find lines of people standing and waiting their turns to get into the picture shows.

Still another time when large numbers of people with hiking breeches and slacks were driving to mountain retreats with picnic lunches to enjoy the beauteous Sabbath in the canyons.

And the word of the Lord continued to resound in my consciousness: "In the days of their peace they esteemed lightly of my counsel; but in the day of their trouble, of necessity they feel after me."

I wondered if we must be brought low with adversity before we will serve the Lord.

There came ringing again in my ears the solemn command brought down from the thundering of Mount Sinai: "Remember the sabbath day, to keep it holy." So far as I know, that commandment has never been rescinded nor modified. To hunt and fish on the Lord's day is not keeping it holy. To plant or cultivate or harvest crops on the Sabbath is not keeping holy the Lord's day. To go into the canyons for picnics, to attend games or rodeos, or races, or shows, or other amusements on that day is not to keep it in holy remembrance.

Our Savior said: "Whosoever therefore shall break one of these least commandments, and shall teach men so, he shall be called the least in the kingdom of heaven." (Matthew 5:19.)

Strange as it may seem, some of our brethren, faithful in all other respects, seem to justify themselves in missing their sacrament meetings, and their stake conferences, in order to beat all the other hunters into the wildlife area when the season opens. The Church favors legitimate recreation, and urges its people to organize picnic parties and to enjoy the great outdoors for the fellowship that it offers, but with six other days in the week, the Sabbath certainly need not be desecrated. . . . I think it isn't so much a matter of giving up things; it is a matter of shifting times and choosing seasons. (44-03)

Sabbath-breakers too are those who buy commodities or entertainment on the Sabbath, thus encouraging pleasure palaces and business establishments to remain open—which they otherwise would not do. (MF 46)

CHAPTER 9

The Second Mile

Kindness, helpfulness, love, concern, and generosity—this list of virtues is endless, and it is the development of these traits which the Lord asks of us, after we have first firmly committed ourselves to upholding the simpler, more basic commandments. (78-22)

Humility

Humility is not weakness but strength. A lone man, armed only with a cord whip, drove money-changers from the temple. Confronted by reprobates who presented an adulteress for stoning, he put them all to flight. He upbraided the thousands of inhabitants of Chorazin, Bethsaida and Capernaum without a guard to protect him. Almost alone among his accusers, he chided and condemned them. One can be bold and meek at the same time. One can be courageous and humble. . . . If the Lord was meek and lowly and humble, then to become humble one must do what he did in boldly denouncing evil, bravely advancing righteous works, courageously meeting every problem, becoming the master of himself and the situations about him and being near oblivious to personal credit.

Humility is not pretentious, presumptuous, nor proud. It is not weak, vacillating, nor servile. . . .

Humble and *meek* properly suggest virtues, not weaknesses. They suggest a consistent mildness of temper and an absence of wrath and passion. Humility suggests no affectation, no bombastic actions. It is not turgid nor grandiloquent. It is not servile submissiveness. It is not cowed nor frightened. No shadow or the shaking of a leaf terrorizes it.

How does one get humble? To me, one must constantly be reminded of his dependence. On whom dependent? On the Lord. How remind one's self? By real, constant, worshipful, grateful prayer. . . .

Humility is teachableness—an ability to realize that all virtues and abilities are not concentrated in one's self. . . .

Humility is gracious, quiet, serene—not pompous, spectacular, nor histrionic. It is subdued, kindly, and understanding—not crude, blatant, loud, or ugly. Humility is not just a man or a woman but a perfect gentleman and a gentlelady. It never struts nor swaggers. Its faithful, quiet works will be the badge of its own accomplishments. It never sets itself in the center of the stage, leaving all others in supporting roles. Humility is never accusing nor contentious. It is not boastful. . . .

When one becomes conscious of his great humility, he has already lost it. When one begins boasting of his humility, it has already become pride—the antithesis of humility.

Humility is repentant and seeks not to justify its follies. It is forgiving others in the realization that there may be errors of the same kind or worse chalked up against itself. . . .

It is not self-abasement—the hiding in the corner, the devaluation of everything one does or thinks or says; but it is the doing of one's best in every case and leaving of one's acts, expressions, and accomplishments to largely speak for themselves. (63-01)

Humility develops through prayer and study. Somebody asked me this morning, "How do you keep humble? Sometimes I am humble and sometimes I am unhumble." How do you keep humble? I think there is a formula that will never fail. First, you evaluate yourself. What am I? I am the circle. I am the hole in the doughnut. I would be nothing without the Lord. My breath, my brains, my hearing, my sight, my locomotion, my everything depends upon the Lord. That is the first step and then we pray, and pray often, and we will not get up from our knees until we have communicated. The line may be down; we may have let it fall to pieces, but I will not get up from my knees until I have established communication—if it is twenty minutes, if it is all night like Enos. . . . If it takes all day long, you stay on your knees until your unhumbleness has dissipated, until you feel the humble spirit and realize, "I could die this minute if it were not for the Lord's good grace. I am dependent upon him—totally dependent upon him," and then you read the scriptures. Could you read these scriptures . . . and not be lifted and inspired? Can you read about the prophets—David O. McKay—and not feel weak and small in comparison? Well, you can create humility, and humility has to be fed, too, in the same way, with the right kind of vitamins. And when you have success, you do not glory in it for you, you glory in it for the Lord. (66-12)

Those able in one area profess general expertise. Many voices, loud and harsh, come from among educators, business and professional men, sociologists, psychologists, authors, movie actors, legislators, judges, and others, even some of the clergy, who, because they have learned a little about something, seem to think they know all about everything.

This egotism and pride is prompted by the cunning father of lies. (71-06)

Children should be taught humility. Teach our children and youth to be humble even in their righteousness. Never may they become "holier than thou" or speak their own goodness or outstanding qualities. (66-07)

Take no honor for healings. I have been impressed at the number of times the Lord said, "Go thy way and tell no man." And I have been led many times in my blessings—when I felt there was going to be special healing, and that they were such people as would go out and shout it from the housetops—to say, "And when you are healed, tell no man who laid his hands upon your head." I think that takes away from me the temptation to want to be spectacular, or to want praise, or to want credit, and from them the urge to publish a sacred, intimate miracle. That relieves me. It leaves me more humble and I am sure then I am in a better position to call down the blessings of the Lord again. Remember when Moses, after long service, said in effect to his people, "How long must I bring you water and food. How long must I do it." The moment he himself began to be an important element in the performance of the Lord's blessing, he lost his place and was denied entrance into the promised land. As important as he was, Moses was only the mouthpiece of the Lord. . . .

I have heard men say, "I have the gift of healing. I would like to give you a blessing." That seems to me to be wholly out of line, and I can imagine that it would not be long until the Lord would take away his gift of healing when he was so eager to take the credit and honor for it. (62-08)

General Authorities are honored as representatives. This time between stake conferences, I visited some areas that had never been touched by a General Authority out in the outskirts, way down in southern Chile and in little cities up in northern Argentina. To see these people come long distances at great expense to be there to greet us, I felt tremendously humble, like bowing my head . . . and then I recognized again that I am but a symbol to them. They did not know me. They had never seen me. They came not to see me. They came to see the apostle and their reverence and their interest was to the Church, to its leadership, to the program, and I was but a symbol, and it makes me humble indeed. (66-13)

Tolerance

Tolerance is ability to see another's viewpoint. The most lovable quality any human being can possess is tolerance. It is the vision that enables one to see things from another's viewpoint. It is the generosity that concedes to others the right to their own opinions and peculiarities. It is the bigness that enables us to let people be happy in their own way instead of our way. (43-01)

Tolerance for others' beliefs has increased. I express my thankfulness that in the passing years the spirit of tolerance for the beliefs of others has increased throughout our broad land. The right to worship according to the dictates of an honest conscience is one of the principles for which our nation is fighting today. I am sure the blessings of heaven attend this tremendously important endeavor. (44-01)

Fanaticism is destructive. They who get off on tangents and ride hobby horses to death are they who become fanatic. Let them understand that they must be tolerant of others' faults but never accept as justifiable their own. Let them be kind and gracious, friendly and personable, and let them work with worldly people as the need is found, but never to be of the world or accept its low standards or choose to play with worldly people. One can protect himself against the overwhelming evil influences while obligated to work with evil ones, but it is near impossible to protect oneself from degenerate practices of those with whom we play. (66-07)

Avoid undue concern about others. When you do not worry or concern yourself too much with what other people do and believe and say, there will come to you a new freedom. (11/2/62)

Intolerance is not Christlike. We do wish that there would be no racial prejudice among people, but the fact that a person is a member of the Church is no indication that he is going to accept a Christlike view until he becomes Christlike. Often our own people snub and belittle our Mexican members. We do not uphold them in this and would that they would treat them as brothers should be treated. (4/0/00)

Feelings of superiority are unfounded. Now then, who are you and who am I that will distinguish between an Indian child and a white child? Who are we that we are so preferred in the kingdom of heaven? What have we done that we are entitled to so many blessings? What did you individually do that made you superior to your other darker brothers and sisters? Was it something you did?

Well, maybe it was because you were fortunate enough to be born in Latter-day Saint homes, homes that were full of faith, to people who were in a country where there was freedom and opportunity, and so we all come here today well dressed, well fed, housed comfortably, have all the luxuries of life, and yet, are we any better than those who have been deprived? And who are we to differentiate? (49-02)

If the Indians had all that was rightfully theirs they would not be where they are and we would not be where we are. Remember that.

We are here through the grace of God, and do not forget it. The Lord gave us to share an inheritance with the Indians in this glorious land which is choice above all other lands in all the world. But it is ours only on the condition, as I see it, that we do our part in seeing that these people come into the Church.

What the Lamanite needs is opportunity. The only difference between us and the Indian is opportunity. Give them an opportunity, sisters, so that they, too, can enjoy the blessings that you do.

And take this message back to your people in the stakes, that they leave off their racial prejudice. Racial prejudice is of the devil. Racial prejudice is of ignorance. There is no place for it in the gospel of Jesus Christ. (49-06)

Intolerance by Church members is despicable. A special problem exists with respect to blacks because they may not now [1972] receive the priesthood. Some members of the Church would justify their own un-Christian discrimination against blacks because of that rule with respect to the priesthood, but while this restriction has been imposed by the Lord, it is not for us to add burdens upon the shoulders of our black brethren. They who have received Christ in faith through authoritative baptism are heirs to the celestial kingdom along with men of all other races. And those who remain faithful to the end may expect that God may finally grant them all blessings they have merited through their righteousness. Such matters are in the Lord's hands. It is for us to extend our love to all. . . .

The fastest-growing component of Church membership, however, is not black or white, but brown—the Lamanite people of the

Americas. There is a sorry history of oppression of them by white men, and ... members of the Church are not immune to the disease of intolerance. Yet it is particularly ironic that Church members who profess to believe the Book of Mormon would hiss and spurn a people to whom such spectacular promises are made by the Lord. Though intolerance is abhorrent anywhere, it is doubly offensive to the Lord when it is directed to those of Israel. . . .

What a monster prejudice is! It means prejudging. How many of us are guilty of it? Often we think ourselves free of its destructive force, but we need only to test ourselves. Our expressions, our voice tones, our movements, our thoughts betray us. We are often so willing that others make the contacts, do the proselyting, have the associations. Until we project ouselves into the very situation, we little realize our bias and our prejudice.

Why will we, the prospered, the blessed, hiss? When, oh when, will we cease to spurn? When will we who think we are free of bias purge from our souls the sometimes unconscious prejudice we possess? When will we end our making game of these different from ourselves? When will we cease throwing our pennies disdainfully to them at the gate? When will we follow the example of the Savior?

We who take pride in our own ancestry sometimes forget the great heritage that belongs to men and groups whom we take lightly. A prime example is the long list of heroes from whom the Indians are descended. (FPM 295-301)

Peoples take turns suffering discrimination. Our redskin brothers are today called unclean and common, but formerly it was we, the Gentile nations, who were the outcasts. Yesterday it was "an unlawful thing for a man that is a Jew to keep company or come unto one of another nation." (Acts 10:28.) Today we revile the Jew and his brother-Israelite, the Indian. "What fools we mortals be!"

Yesterday the super-race consciousness was so solidly rooted that it was necessary for the Lord to send a vision to his chiefest apostle before the gospel could go to the Gentile nations. . . .

There were superior peoples in the days of these Lehites who were intolerant, and Jacob called them to repentance with boldness:

Wherefore, a commandment I give unto you, which is the word of God, that ye revile no more against them because of the darkness of their skins; neither shall ye revile against them because of their filthiness; but ye shall remember your own filthiness, and remember that their filthiness came because of their fathers. (Jacob 3:9.)

Again he warned: "I fear that unless ye shall repent of your sins that their skins will be whiter than yours, when ye shall be brought before the throne of God." (Jacob 3:8.) . . .

See what God hath wrought! He has blessed, honored, and preserved this race. He has . . . ministered to them; miracles have been countless among them; two centuries of continuous righteousness was lived by them; supreme faith was manifested by them; martyrs burned and bled among them; the flesh and the world were overcome by them. Peace of long duration was enjoyed by them and the Son of Man visited them.

Yesterday we of the Gentile nations were the common and unclean—today we so call the Indian. Yesterday we were the persecuted; today we are the persecutors. . . . Yesterday we were they who went from Jerusalem to Jericho; today we are the priest and the Levite who passed "by on the other side."

But to these children of the prophets, God has made lavish promises. Today is the brighter day—the day of the Lamanite. . . .

They shall become fair, clean, and worthy. They shall become physically sound, mentally alert, economically secure. They shall plant and harvest and build and inhabit. They shall take their rightful place as peers with us in industry, in business and professions. They shall know their history and believe the truth; they shall know and worship the true and living God. "For the eternal purposes of the Lord shall roll on, until all his promises shall be fulfilled." (Mormon 8:22.)

May God help us to recognize our duty toward these our brothers and sisters, and help us show our love for him by our devotion to the work of bringing all blessings which we enjoy to these our kinsmen. (49-03)

Condescension must be replaced by brotherhood. My young brothers and sisters, in conclusion, I plead with you to accept the

Lamanite as your brother. I ask not for your tolerance—your cold, calculating tolerance; your haughty, contemptible tolerance; your scornful, arrogant tolerance; your pitying, coin-tossing tolerance. I ask you to give them what they want and need and deserve: opportunity and your fraternal brotherliness and your understanding; your warm and glowing fellowship; your unstinted and beautiful love; your enthusiastic and affectionate brotherhood. (53-05)

Forgiving

Love your enemies. Brothers and sisters, pray for the critics of the Church; love your enemies. Keep the faith and stay on the straight and narrow path. Use wisdom and judgment in what you say and do, so that we do not give cause to others to hold the Church or its people in disrepute. Do not be surprised or dismayed if trials and challenges come upon us. This work, which Satan seeks in vain to tear down, is that which God has placed on earth to lift mankind up! (80-03)

Refusal to forgive is the greater sin. I was struggling with a community problem in a small ward...where two prominent men, leaders of the people, were deadlocked in a long and unrelenting feud. Some misunderstanding between them had driven them far apart with enmity. As the days, weeks, and months passed, the breach became wider. The families of each conflicting party began to take up the issue and finally nearly all the people of the ward were involved. Rumors spread and differences were aired and gossip became tongues of fire until the little community was divided by a deep gulf. I was sent to clear up the matter. After a long stake conference, lasting most of two days, I arrived at the frustrated community about six p.m., Sunday night, and immediately went into session with the principal combatants.

How we struggled! How I pleaded and warned and begged and urged! Nothing seemed to be moving them. Each antagonist was so sure that he was right and justified that it was impossible to budge them.

The hours were passing—it was now long after midnight, and despair seemed to enshroud the place; the atmosphere was still one of ill temper and ugliness. Stubborn resistance would not give way. Then it happened. I aimlessly opened my Doctrine and Covenants again and there before me it was. I had read it many times in past years and it had had no special meaning then. But tonight it was the very answer. It was an appeal and an imploring and a threat and seemed to be coming direct from the Lord. I read from the seventh verse on, but the quarreling participants yielded not an inch until I came to the ninth verse. Then I saw them flinch, startled, wondering. Could that be right? The Lord was saying to us—to all of us—"Wherefore, I say unto you, that ye ought to forgive one another."

This was an obligation. They had heard it before. They had said it in repeating the Lord's Prayer. But now: "... for he that forgiveth not his brother his trespasses standeth condemned before the Lord ..." (D&C 64:7-9.)

In their hearts, they may have been saying: "Well, I might forgive if he repents and asks forgiveness, but he must make the first move." Then the full impact of the last line seemed to strike them: "For there remaineth in him the greater sin."

What? Does that mean I must forgive even if my antagonist remains cold and indifferent and mean? There is no mistaking it.

A common error is the idea that the offender must apologize and humble himself to the dust before forgiveness is required. Certainly, the one who does the injury should totally make his adjustment, but as for the offended one, he must forgive the offender regardless of the attitude of the other. Sometimes men get satisfactions from seeing the other party on his knees and grovelling in the dust, but that is not the gospel way.

Shocked, the two men sat up, listened, pondered a minute, then began to yield. This scripture added to all the others read brought them to their knees. Two a.m. and two bitter adversaries were shaking hands, smiling and forgiving and asking forgiveness. Two men were in a meaningful embrace. This hour was holy. Old grievances were forgiven and forgotten, and enemies became friends again. No reference was ever made again to the differences. The skeletons were buried, the closet of dry bones was locked and the key was thrown away, and peace was restored. (MF 281-82)

The offended person should take the initiative. It frequently happens that offenses are committed when the offender is not aware of it. Something he has said or done is misconstrued or misunderstood. The offended one treasures in his heart the offense, adding to it such other things as might give fuel to the fire and justify his conclusions. Perhaps this is one of the reasons why the Lord requires that the offended one should make the overtures toward peace....

Do we follow that command or do we sulk in our bitterness, waiting for our offender to learn of it and to kneel to us in remorse? (49-07)

Marriage partners must be quick to forgive. If we will sue for peace, taking the initiative in settling differences—if we forgive and forget with all our hearts—if we can cleanse our own souls of sin, bitterness, and guilt before we cast a stone or accusation at others—if we forgive all real or fancied offenses before we ask forgiveness for our own sins—if we pay our own debts, large or small, before we press our debtors—if we manage to clear our own eyes of the blinding beams before we magnify the motes in the eyes of others—what a glorious world this would be! Divorce would be reduced to a minimum; courts would be freed from disgusting routines; family life would be heavenly; the building of the kingdom would go forward at an accelerated pace; and the peace which passeth understanding would bring to us all a joy and happiness which has hardly "entered into the heart of man." (49-07)

Taking offense at Church leaders hurts only us. There are many other ways we can cheat ourselves too. We may get angry with our parents, or a teacher, or the bishop, and dwarf ourselves into nameless anonymity as we shrivel and shrink under the venom and poison of bitterness and hatred. While the hated one goes on about his business, little realizing the suffering of the hater, the latter cheats himself.

... To terminate activity in the Church just to spite leaders or to give vent to wounded feelings is to cheat ourselves. (72-03)

We must learn to control temper. If you permit your anger to rise every time you are crossed, as you indicate in your letter, you are sure to be unhappy much of the time. We came on the earth to learn to control ourselves, to test ourselves, to see if we could do *all* things whatsoever the Lord commanded us. (Abraham 3:25.) We did not come on earth to love ourselves, to appease our tempers, to satisfy our desires, lusts, longings. We came to subjugate the flesh—to make our minds and bodies do the things which the spirit knows are best in the long run. (2/2/51)

Love

God gives power to forgive and to love. If there be misunderstandings, clear them up, forgive and forget, don't let old grievances change your souls and affect them, and destroy your love and lives. Put your houses in order. Love one another and love your neighbors, your friends, the people who live near you, as the Lord gives this power to you. (80-24)

God is the prime object of our love. It is not enough for us to acknowledge the Lord as supreme and refrain from worshipping idols; we should love the Lord with all our heart, might, mind, and strength. We should honor him and follow him into the work of eternal life. What joy he has in the righteousness of his children! (78-22)

Love of material things is idolatry. Idolatry is among the most serious of sins. There are unfortunately millions today who prostrate themselves before the images of gold and silver and wood and stone and clay. But the idolatry we are most concerned with here is the conscious worshipping of still other gods. Some are of metal and plush and chrome, of wood and stone and fabrics. They are not in the image of God or of man, but are developed to give man comfort and enjoyment, to satisfy his wants, ambitions, passions, and desires. Some are in no physical form at all, but are intangible.

Many seem to "worship" on an elemental basis—they live to eat and drink.

Modern idols or false gods can take such forms as clothes, homes, businesses, machines, automobiles, pleasure boats, and numerous other material deflectors from the path of godhood.

Intangible things make just as ready gods. Degrees and letters and titles can become idols.

Many people build and furnish a home and buy the automobile first—then they find they "cannot afford" to pay tithing. Whom do they worship?

Young married couples who postpone parenthood until their degrees are attained might be shocked if their expressed preference were labeled idolatry.

Many worship the hunt, the fishing trip, the vacation, the week-end picnics and outings.

Still another image men worship is that of power and prestige. Many will trample underfoot the spiritual and often the ethical values in their climb to success. These gods of power, wealth, and influence are most demanding and are quite as real as the golden calves of the children of Israel in the wilderness. (MF 40-42)

God's love is our pattern. We know also that God is perfect in his love for each and all of us as his spirit children. When we know these truths, my sisters and associates in this divine cause, it should help us greatly as we all experience much less than perfect love and perfect justice in the world. If, in the short term, we are sometimes dealt with insensitively and thoughtlessly by others, by imperfect men and women, it may still cause us pain, but such pain and disappointment are not the whole of life. The ways of the world will not prevail, for the ways of God will triumph. (79-19)

Love must be coupled with discipline. There are times when virtues are developed best, when two moral forces appear to pull in opposite directions. For example, Jesus lived and taught the virtues of love and kindness and patience. He also taught the virtues of firmness and resolution and persistence and courageous indignation. These two sets of virtues seem to clash with each other . . . love and indignation, yet both are necessary. If there were but one, love without discipline, love without deep conviction of right and wrong, without courage to fight the wrong, such love becomes sentimentalism. Conversely, the virtues of righteous indignation without love can be harsh and cruel. (76-37)

Love is unselfish. For many years I saw a strong man carry his tiny, emaciated, arthritic wife to meetings and wherever she could go. There could be no sexual expression. Here was selfless indication of affection. I think that is pure love. I saw a kindly woman wait on her husband for many years as he deteriorated with muscular dystrophy. She waited on him hand and foot, night and day, when all he could do was to blink his eyes in thanks. I believe that was love.

I knew a woman who carried her little, handicapped daughter until the child was too heavy to carry, and then pushed her in a wheelchair for the following years until her death. The deprived child could never express appreciation. It seems to me that that was love. Another mother visited regularly her son who was in the penitentiary. She could receive nothing from him. She gave much, all she had. (65-02)

Giving love is greater than giving money. We must be generous, the very antithesis of the thief's ultimate selfishness. When money is needed, we give money. But often what is needed more is love and the time and caring which money cannot buy; when that is true, even generosity with our money is not enough. (78-22)

One can learn to be loving. If one patterns his life in the mold of love—if he consciously and determinedly directs his thoughts, controls his acts, and tries to feel and constantly express his love, he becomes a person of love, for "As he thinketh in his heart, so is he." (Proverbs 23:7.) . . .

To be good one must *will* to be good, fashion his life in the pattern of goodness, and refuse to deviate therefrom. (54-05)

Love involves giving of oneself, as Christ did. Christmastime is a glorious time of happy friendliness and unselfish sacrifice; a time of increased hospitality, devotion, and love; a time of the subduing of selfish impulses; a time of renewing friendships, cementing loosening ties, and the swelling of the heart. It transcends the individual, the family, the community, the nation; it approaches the universal, crosses borders, and touches many nations of the earth. Our caroling voices sing the sweet songs of Christmas reminiscent somewhat of the host of heavenly angelic voices in the long ago, praising God and saying: "Glory to God in the highest, and on earth peace, good will toward men."

We set up the evergreen tree with its gleaming, brightly colored lights; we hang wreaths and bells; and we light candles—all to remind us of that wondrous gift, the coming of our Lord into the world of mortality.

We send Christmas cards to numerous friends and relatives, pulling back into happy memories the loved ones who have moved out of our immediate association. Like the wise men who opened their treasury and presented to Jesus gifts of gold and frankincense and myrrh, we present to our loved ones things to eat and wear and enjoy.

Though we make an effort to follow the pattern of gift giving, sometimes our program becomes an exchange—gift given for gift expected. Never did the Savior give in expectation. I know of no case in his life in which there was an exchange. He was always the giver, seldom the recipient. Never did he give shoes, hose, or a vehicle; never did he give perfume, a shirt, or a fur wrap. His gifts were of such a nature that the recipient could hardly exchange or return the value. His gifts were rare ones: eyes to the blind, ears to the deaf, and legs to the lame; cleanliness to the unclean, wholeness to the infirm, and breath to the lifeless. His gifts were opportunity to the downtrodden, freedom to the oppressed, light in the darkness, forgiveness to the repentant, hope to the despairing. His friends gave him shelter, food, and love. He gave them of himself, his love, his service, his life. The wise men brought him gold and frankincense. He gave them and all their fellow mortals resurrection, salvation, and eternal life. We should strive to give as he gave. To give of oneself is a holy gift. (78-44)

Good feelings at Christmas approach the ideal. Christmas comes once a year to reveal to us the beautiful and near approach man can make to the divine, to the ideal, to the Christlike life.

Once a year on this day we raise the flag of truce. All men are friends. We are our "brother's keeper." It comes so clearly to us that all mean well, that their greetings are sincere. We lift high the open hand of fellowship. There is no race, no color, no rich or poor, no bond or free. Christmas comes to remind us of the fatherhood of God and the brotherhood of man. It comes to show us the real progress we would make, could all our days be unselfish, friendly, helpful, and clear of bitterness and strife. (34-01)

Believers share love as a family. Love one another. I look forward to reunion one day with my parents—a loving mother whom I lost seventy-three years ago, and a faithful father by whose deathbed I sat fifty-five years ago. I have often felt their continuing concern for my welfare, and I know from my own experience how sweet the love of family can be. But I am also grateful for the larger family of which you are all part: my brothers and sisters in Christ. I love you, in all of your variety and in spite of your human failings, and I know that the Lord loves you more—much more—than is in our mortal capacity to love. (79-17)

Love ignores rejection. But where there are special challenges, we fail only if we fail to keep trying. Let our love of each member of our family be unconditional. (82-01)

Love requires no schedule. How long has it been since you took your children, whatever their size, in your arms and told them that you love them and are glad that they can be yours forever? How long has it been since you husbands or wives purchased an inexpensive gift as a surprise for your spouse for no other reason than just to please? How long has it been since you brought home a rose or baked a pie with a heart carved in the crust or did some other thing to make life more aglow with warmth and affection? (74-31)

Love in marriage transcends sex. Your love, like a flower, must be nourished. There will come a great love and interdependence between you, for your love is a divine one. It is deep, all-inclusive, most comprehensive. It is not like that association of the world which is misnamed love, but which is mostly physical attraction. When marriage is based on this only, the parties soon tire of each other. There is a break and a divorce, and a new, fresher physical attraction comes with another marriage, which in turn may last only until it too becomes stale. The love of which the Lord speaks is not only physical attraction, but also faith, confidence, understanding, and partner-ship. It is devotion and companionship, parenthood, common ideals and standards. It is cleanliness of life and sacrifice and unselfishness. This kind of love never tires nor wanes. It lives on through sickness and sorrow, through prosperity and privation, through accomplish-ment and disappointment, through time and eternity. John and Mary, this is the love that I feel you are bringing to each other, but even this richer, more abundant love will wilt and die if it is not given food, so you must live and treat each other in a manner that your love will grow. Today it is a demonstrative love, but in the tomorrows of ten, thirty, fifty years it will be a far greater and more intensified love, grown quieter and more dignified with the years of sacrifice, suffering, joys, and consecration to each other, to your family, and to the kingdom of God.

For your love to ripen so gloriously, there must be an increase of confidence and understanding, a frequent and sincere expression of appreciation of each other. There must be a forgetting of self and a constant concern for the other. There must be a focusing of interests and hopes and objectives into a single channel. (49-01)

Love includes generosity. In one of the stakes of Zion lives a family who also believe in a birthday for Jesus. It was on the sixth of April, 1955, and as they gave to me a crisp fifty-dollar bill, they said, "Today is the Lord's birthday. We always give gifts to our family members on their birthdays. We should like to give a gift to the Savior. Will you place this money where it will please the Redeemer most."

Two days later, Sister Kimball and I were on our way to Europe for a six-month's tour of all the missions. . . . There were numerous opportunities to present the gift, for the majority of the Saints over there could use extra funds. But we waited.

Toward the end of the mission tour we met a sweet little woman in Germany. . . . It was nearing the time of the temple dedication at Bern, Switzerland. I said to this sweet woman, "Are you going to the temple dedication?" I saw the disappointment in her eyes as she said how she would like to go but how impossible it was because of lack of finances. "Here is the place for the gift," was the thought which rooted itself in my mind. I quietly checked with the mission president as to her worthiness and the appropriateness of her going to the temple. . . .

Another year rolls around. Again it is the sixth of April. The birthday family comes again. This time it is a hundred dollars. They have been pleased with the happiness their last gift had brought. . . .

"Verily I say unto you, Inasmuch as ye have done it unto one of the least of these my brethren, ye have done it unto me." (Matthew 25:40.) (56-14)

Service

Helping others live the gospel is service. One has hardly proved his life abundant until he has built up a crumbling wall, paid off a heavy debt, enticed a disbeliever to his knees, filled an empty stomach, influenced a soul to wash in the blood of the lamb, turned fear and frustration into peace and sureness, led one to be "born again."

One is measuring up to his opportunity potential when he has saved a crumbling marriage, transformed the weak into the strong, changed a civil to a proper temple marriage, brought enemies from the cesspool of hate to the garden of love, made a child trust and love him, changed a scoffer into a worshiper, melted a stony heart into one of flesh and muscle. (67-15)

Christ's life is the epitome of service. Give yourselves away. That's the life of the Savior of this world. He gave himself away when he personally went to the house of Peter and blessed his mother-in-law "who was sick of a fever." He gave himself away when he stood on the mount and preached for hours "the way of salvation" to the multitude.

He gave himself away when he walked long, dusty, tortuous miles to Bethany to bring comfort and even life back to Lazarus, and to Mary and Martha, the sisters who were grieving. He gave himself away when he healed the sick and opened the blind eyes and cleared the stopped hearing and gave strength to the sick.

He gave much of himself in every blessing. When the woman reached forth to touch the hem of his garment, he felt the power had gone out of him. He gave that power and part of himself willingly, and after three years of spectacular ministry, he voluntarily walked back into the trap set for him, announced his approaching fate, walked out of Gethsemane into the hands of mobsters and to the courts of politicians and to the cross and gave himself for all mankind. (74-39)

Giving a life of service is to find life. A striking personality and good character is achieved by practice, not merely by thinking it. Just as a pianist masters the intricacies of music through hours and weeks of practice, so mastery of life is achieved by the ceaseless practice of mechanics which make up the art of living. Daily unselfish service to others is one of the rudimentary mechanics of the successful life. "For whosoever will save his life," the Galilean said, "shall lose it, and whosoever will lose his life for my sake shall find it." (Matthew 16:25.) What a strange paradox this! And yet one needs only to analyze it to be convinced of its truth. I know a man whose every thought through three quarters of a century had been for and of himself. Everything desired and everything that happened was interpreted in terms of the big "I" and the little "u." He had sought to keep his life for himself, and to gather all the good things of life for his own development and enjoyment. Strangely enough, trying to keep his life for himself, and he has shrunk, has lost his friends, and his own people shun him as a bore.

And now, as life is ebbing out gradually, he finds himself standing alone, forsaken, bitter, unloved, and unsung; and with self-pity, he can still think of only one person, himself. He has sought to save for himself his time, talents, and his means. He has lost the abundant life.

On the other hand, I know another man who has never given thought to himself. His every desire was for the protection and pleasure of those about him. No task was too great, no sacrifice too much for him to make for his fellowmen. His means brought relief from physical suffering; his kind work and thoughtfulness brought comfort and cheer and courage. Wherever people were in distress, he was on hand, cheering the discouraged, burying the dead, comforting the bereaved, and proving himself a friend in need. His time, his means, and his energies were lavished upon those needing assistance. Having given himself freely, by that same act he has added to his mental, physical, and moral stature until today he stands in his declining years a power for good, an example and an inspiration to many. He has developed and grown until he is everywhere acclaimed, loved, and appreciated. He has given life and in a real way has truly found the abundant life. (39-01)

Only when you lift a burden, God will lift your burden. Divine paradox this! The man who staggers and falls because his burden is too great can lighten that burden by taking on the weight of another's burden. You get by giving, but your part of giving must be given first. (35-01)

Rich and poor can serve equally. The rich man may far outstrip his less fortunate neighbor in giving huge sums of money for charity, but when it comes to giving one's self, they are on a common level, for each can give freely of himself, but each has only one single self to give. (39-01)

Mundane service can be of great value. God does notice us, and he watches over us. But it is usually through another mortal that he meets our needs. Therefore, it is vital that we serve each other in the kingdom....

So often, our acts of service consist of simple encouragement or of giving mundane help with mundane tasks—but what glorious consequences can flow from mundane acts and from small but deliberate deeds! (74-13)

Opportunities for service grow. May I assure you of the everlasting significance of your personal life. And even though at times the range of your life may seem to be very small, there can be greatness in the quality of your life....

There must be an assembling in you of those basic qualities of goodness which will permit the Lord to do his own sculpturing on your soul. Use, therefore, the talents that you have. Use the opportunities for service around you. Use the chances for learning that are yours, sifting as always the wheat from the chaff. Learn to be effective first in the small human universe that is your own family if you would prepare yourselves to be effective in contributing to the larger human family. (79-02)

Service is a means of expressing thanks. Every boy should want to serve, to go on a mission. There is only one way you can pay the debt you owe your parents and the Lord and that is to give service. The Lord has given you life. He has given you everything you have. You didn't earn it and you didn't buy it. Your parents sowed the seed that you might descend and become a son of God or a daughter of God. So, when you think, "What could I do to repay?" I don't think you could give money, because it goes up and down and deteriorates. You could say, "I'm going to give You my life, all my years, all my effort." (75-18)

Missionary service blesses many lives. The missionary work of the Church is a panorama of more than a century of service and privations and hardships and sacrifices. The closer one is to the program, the more completely one can understand and appreciate it. When my grandfather Heber C. Kimball left for his mission, he and Brigham Young left their families destitute and ill and they themselves needed help to get into the carriage which took them from their homes. As they started off they raised themselves to their elbows and waved back to their weeping wives and children. Thousands of people came into the Church as a result of those missions, and tens of thousands have been benefited indirectly and are now enjoying the blessings of the gospel because of those sacrifices. To one who did not understand, such devotion and sacrifice on the part of those men would have been considered foolhardy and silly. But to the Young and Kimball families it was a mark of great faith. And to the thousands who will, through the eternities, call the names of those missionaries blessed, the privations and sacrifice were not wasted. (4/24/50)

Compassionate service makes women more godlike. And finally, perhaps the most essential godlike quality: compassion and love—compassion shown forth in service to others, unselfishness, that ultimate expression of concern for others we call love. Relief Society indeed provides women with special opportunities to express their feelings of charity, benevolence, and love. There are other avenues of service—the community and particularly the home. Wherever women are true to their feminine natures and magnify their opportunities for loving service, they are learning to become more like God. (76-23)

Difficult service produces growth. Let us not shrink from the next steps in our spiritual growth, brothers and sisters, by holding back, or sidestepping our fresh opportunities for service to our families and our fellowmen.

Let us trust the Lord and take the next steps in our individual lives. He has promised us that he will be our tender tutor, measuring what we are ready for: "And ye cannot bear all things now; nevertheless, be of good cheer, for I will lead you along." (D&C 78:18.)

He will not ask us to bear more than we can bear nor thrust upon us that for which we are not yet ready. But likewise, we must not tarry too long when we are ready to move on. (79-06)

Sometimes the solution is not to change our circumstance, but to change our attitude about that circumstance; difficulties are often opportunities for service. (74-13)

Service builds testimony. The most vital thing we can do is to express our testimonies through service, which will, in turn, produce spiritual growth, greater commitment, and a greater capacity to keep the commandments. (74-13)

Service puts problems in perspective. I have learned that it is by serving that we learn how to serve. When we are engaged in the service of our fellowmen, not only do our deeds assist them, but we put our own problems in a fresher perspective. When we concern ourselves more with others, there is less time to be concerned with ourselves. In the midst of the miracle of serving, there is the promise of Jesus, that by losing ourselves, we find ourselves.

Not only do we "find" ourselves in terms of acknowledging guidance in our lives, but the more we serve our fellowmen in appropriate ways, the more substance there is to our souls. (74-13)

Service alleviates loneliness. We offer some suggestions which may lead toward an alleviation of the aloneness and the loneliness of the singles.

There are many things one can do to make his life abundant. . . .

I am thinking of a young woman who had a serious accident and all the rest of her life, probably forty years or more, was spent in a wheelchair, but even then she used her mind and her education and her talents to do one of the very few things she could do in that condition and that was to give book reviews. . . .

The girl of the wheelchair continued to support her mother and sister and herself and always with a smile. She never married. Conditions did not seem to be favorable, but I am as certain of this as I am of anything, that she will receive all the blessings the Lord has in store for his faithful, providing that she has measured up and does the things that are necessary.

I am thinking of the numerous hospital ladies who go to the sickrooms to perform many services without pay, but the compensation they get is a full realization that they are serving and contributing and making lives brighter.

I am thinking of many women and men who have passed the years of employment but who continue to fill their lives full of good service, working through the Church and social agencies to bring blessings to the unfortunate.

I am thinking of the missionary work, and there are numerous people in the retired group who do and could give much of their energies and time in a selfless proselyting effort to bring souls unto Christ, the greatest service. There may be some limitation on the foreign, "away from home" missionary work, but almost no limit to the missionary service that could be performed in one's own community with one's own neighbors in one's own time.

There is a work to be done by the homebound and those who are not so vigorously strong. We believe in the work for the dead. There are numerous people who could learn the processes of genealogical work and become a blessing to themselves and their posterity. It takes energy and some little cost, but it's richly rewarding.

There are numerous good men and women who have been retired, and I would urge that they never accept total retirement but merely a change of interest. There are personal histories to write, journals to bring up to date of the self and of parents and grandparents that could be preserved for posterity.

In our own neighborhood there are sick people, in your neighborhood the same, some older ones who anticipate death but are having a long struggle to get there. Again an opportunity for many people to spread sunshine and to bring consolation and comfort.

In the long years and when I worked in the bank, I decided I could be a more profitable employee if I could type. I therefore bought a little typewriter book and came to the bank half an hour early every morning and trained my fingers, and this alone has saved me thousands of hours in these years and perhaps a little more efficiency.

I have seen at commencement exercises of the colleges many mothers and grandmothers who march in the line of graduates with cap and gown to receive that honor they had missed in their youth but were now making their lives more full and more complete.

In saying all this I wonder how anyone could go on living without growing.

I think of the printing press and the countless books and magazines that are available and especially the scriptures, and I yearn for time to reach this material that is found in them. I have well over a thousand books in my own little home library, and I look at them wishing that I had time to read and study them. . . .

Most people can sing. Someone has said that 95 percent of all women can sing and 80 or maybe 90 percent of all men. So here is an opportunity. Join the ward choir and sing.

Perhaps you could take a loaf of bread or a covered dish to someone in need. Uncompensated service is one answer, one good answer to overcome loneliness. (74-39)

Serve people, not organizations. Too often in the past, organizational lines in the Church have become walls that have kept us from reaching out to individuals as completely as we should. We will also find that as we become less concerned with getting organizational or individual credit, we will become more concerned with serving the one whom we are charged to reach. We will also find ourselves becoming less concerned with our organizational identity and more concerned with our true and ultimate identity as a son or daughter of our Father in Heaven, and helping others to achieve the same sense of belonging. (74-13)

Take initiative. None of us should become so busy in our formal Church assignments that there is no room left for quiet Christian service to our neighbors. (76-08)

It is easy for us to fit into the old established programs, to do the things that we are required to do, to put in a certain number of hours, to sing so many times and pray so many times, but you remember the Lord said it is a slothful servant that waits to be commanded in all things. (55-04)

"Verily I say, men should be anxiously engaged in a good cause, and do many things of their own free will, and bring to pass much righteousness." (D&C 58:27.)

All men have been given special powers and within certain limitations should develop those powers, give vent to their own imaginations, and not become rubber stamps. They should develop their own talents and abilities and capacities to their limit and use them to build up the kingdom. (67-15)

Education provides the means to serve others. And so, as young people in this great church of our Lord Jesus Christ, great opportunities are yours. You are not going to be satisfied, I am sure, with merely preparing to make a living, important as that is, but it must be secondary to the great and important thing of helping the Lord to bring to pass the immortality and eternal life of man, unselfish service. I would hope that you who are training to be teachers would not be learning to teach for the compensation that would come each month, but that you might inspire people throughout your lifetime, that you might build faith and build character in many. I would hope that you who are following other fields of endeavor, that your education and your employment would be a means to an end and not the end in and of itself. . . . Do great things for the glory of God and for the benefit of mankind. (47-01)

Be discriminating in the causes you serve. Some observers might wonder why we concern ourselves with such simple things as service to others in our communities when the world is in turmoil over wars and other dramatic problems. Yet, one of the advantages of the gospel of Jesus Christ is that it gives us perspective about the people on this planet, including ourselves. Most of us have little influence on world affairs. If we can make a contribution to peace on a large scale, we should do so; but our first task is to regulate our own lives properly and to care for our families and our neighbors before we go too far afield.

There is no end of potential causes to which you can devote your time and talents and treasure. Be careful to select good causes. There are many of these causes to which you can give yourself fully and freely and which will produce much joy and happiness for you and for those you serve. There are other causes, from time to time, that may seem more fashionable and that may produce the applause of the world, but these are often selfish in nature. These latter causes tend to arise out of what the scriptures call "the commandments of men" rather than the commandments of God. Such causes have some virtues and some usefulness, but they are not as important as those causes which grow out of keeping the commandments of God to bless the lives of the widows and orphans, the sick and the sorrowing, and to love our neighbors as ourselves. (PKSO 40-41)

Friendship

Fellowship new converts. In a survey made by Elder Benson . . . 46 percent of those who fell away from the Church did so in their first three months after baptism. They were not fellowshipped and were not made a part of the whole body. (67-11)

When we baptize somebody it is a crime to let them just slide slowly back out of the Church and out of the gospel because of a lack of fellowship. Fellowshipping is an important responsibility. We should be able to fellowship everybody that comes in. That is the reason we want the members to do the missionary work as well as to get help from the missionaries. We want the people, the high priests, the seventies, and the elders to go out and do this work because they are still the neighbors after the person is baptized. They can still fellowship them; they can still call for them and take them to priesthood meeting; they can still encourage them and help them in their home evenings and so on. (76-35)

It is imperative that those who are baptized as converts immediately be assigned home teachers who will fellowship them in a very personal and concerned manner. These home teachers, working with their priesthood officers, should see that each mature convert is given some challenging activity as well as an opportunity and encouragement to increase his knowledge of the gospel. He should be assisted in establishing social relationships with the members of the Church so that he will not feel alone as he begins his life as an active Latter-day Saint. (77-35)

Integration of converts is Christian service. The Church will always be a church filled with converts. Whether the place be Salt Lake City or Sao Paulo, Los Angeles or London, Tokyo or Turino, Italy, it is the Lord's plan that there be converts among us, brothers and sisters newly brought into the fold of Christ through the efforts of their loving friends and neighbors. Let us fellowship and love each other in the true spirit of the gospel. . . .

It is an inspiration and joy to see this same spirit at work throughout the Church, to see the Saints embrace and help and assist and pray for those who daily enter the kingdom of our Lord. Continue to reach out to each other—and the many more who will enter the Church. Welcome them and love and fellowship them.

Sadly, there have been occasional incidents where some among us have not done so, accounts of some who have rejected those whom the Lord has accepted by baptism. If the Lord was "not ashamed to call them brethren" (Hebrews 2:11), let us, therefore, as with Peter at the temple gates, take our brothers and sisters by the hand and lift them up into our circles of concern and love. (75-35)

Befriending foreigners is missionary work. Let us fellowship the students as well as other people from all nations as they come to our lands, so that we, above all other people, treat them as brothers and sisters in true friendship, whether or not they are interested in the gospel to start with. None of our Father in Heaven's children is foreign to him, and this is his work. In the light of the gospel they are "no more strangers and foreigners." (Ephesians 2:19.) (78-25)

Missionaries should continue contact. Missionaries, keep warm your missionary friendships. You met and labored with some of the choicest people in the Church and in the world while you served in the field. They are still valuable contacts. Do not let such friendships fade. You have a powerful influence still on those missionary companions. Continue to bear testimony to them by your words and your lives.

Don't forget the Saints who have befriended and fed and encouraged you in the mission field. An occasional contact by letter or visit will stimulate them and yourself. Your continued testimony will add to their enthusiasm.

Remember the investigators. Perhaps a few more letters of encouragement and direction and testimony to them might bring them into the Church. Your influence, even though absent, might be greater than that of some new missionary. (45-01)

Minority converts deserve special care. We hope all of our people will be loving and kind and helpful to all of the minority people who come into the Church. (76-54)

Lonely and bereaved members need attention. Be mindful always of the members of your flock who are sad, lonely, bereaved, or bereft. There are always some among us who need our special care and attention. We must never forget or overlook them. "Pure religion and undefiled before God and the Father is this, To visit the fatherless and widows in their affliction." (James 1:27.) (80-33)

Members belong to a worldwide family. If I happened to move ... into a ward that has a new building just paid for, you wouldn't expect me to buy an interest in it, would you? You would say, "Brother Kimball, come on, you belong to us. We are all part of the same family and the building belongs to you."

The moment your certificate of membership arrives, you own just as much as anybody in the whole world, regardless of how much they paid, because they are your brothers and sisters and we're all one great big family.

When we begin to think of the people who have made the contribution to build the building, we must not forget the greatest contributors are your unseen brothers and sisters far across the sea. (59-04)

Church organizations are superior to social fraternities. The Lord has a fraternity—a glorious one. Everybody who has received the priesthood belongs to that fraternity. And then he breaks us up into little groups—in the quorum, in the ward, in the stake. That is the best fraternity in the world—the only one that is worthy of very much of our attention. And sororities—well, the Lord has never spoken about sororities, but we have some good organizations which he set apart for us. And so, we will want to be careful about any other organizations which could divert us from the path in the slightest or blind us to our objectives. (65-01)

Be friendly to strangers. In Salt Lake as I go down the street, I say hello to everybody, a stranger or otherwise. I know that they do not know me, but I like to say hello and I think they appreciate it. I notice their faces light up with a smile and I believe that if all the people in our great city of Salt Lake would do that, the whole world would begin to say it is the "Friendly City." You can do a tremendous thing here. We get so absorbed, we do not always speak to our friends. Speak to them, even strangers, you are not going to give offense. ...Go out of your way to be friendly to the Indian, Mexican, the Oriental, and all the minority groups with whom you come in contact. (58-10)

I can remember when . . . those few girls who were very popular nearly danced their heels off. Whereas, the poor little girls who were wallflowers never got a chance. There was one man, I remember well, that stimulated my admiration. Every strange girl who came to the dance he would go dance with. The rest of us, I guess I was as bad as any of them, danced with our friends. Well, he danced with those girls who didn't get to dance. I admired him. (58-10)

Value friends. Friendships are not on the bargain counter; love is not on the market. Peace of mind, joy, and happiness cannot be purchased with money or worldly goods. (39-01)

Impoverished is the life fenced in with few friends. (60-02)

The group urge is normal to the younger set, and homemade recreational and social activities of the crowd are proper and can be broadening as well as entertaining. Safety, physical and moral, is increased in the multiplicity of friends. (60-02)

Always keep good company. Never waste an hour with anyone who doesn't lift you up and encourage you. (76-49)

Perceptions are affected by character. The story is told of a man who moved to a new place and desired to make investigation before settling down. He met one old-timer in the new town and asked him: "What kind of people live in this town?" The wise man asked, "What kind of people lived in the city from which you came?" The newcomer brightened up and said: "They were wonderful people, happy, kind, friendly. They were good citizens, good neighbors, good Christians." And the wise old-timer said: "That is the kind of people you will find in this city and every city you live in."
Another man, a different type, moving to the same city, asked the same wise old-timer the same question: "What kind of people live in this town?" And the answer from the wise one was: "What kind of people lived in the town you came from?" The fellow said: "They were unpleasant people there. That is the reason I am moving. They are unkind, unsocial, gossips, poor neighbors, vicious." And the answer from the wise one was: "You will find that same kind of people in our town." (12/30/58)

Speak no ill of others. Slander, backbiting, evil speaking, faultfinding are all destructive termites that destroy the home. Quarreling and swearing are also evils that sometimes affect the home. (76-27)

Lies and gossip which harm reputations are scattered about by the four winds like the seeds of a ripe dandelion held aloft by a child. Neither the seeds nor the gossip can ever be gathered in. The degree and extent of the harm done by the gossip is inestimable. (MF 54)

CHAPTER 10

Chastity and Dating

God's Law of Chastity

God requires chastity. We stand for a life of cleanliness. From childhood through youth and to the grave, we proclaim the wickedness of sexual life of any kind before marriage, and we proclaim that everyone in marriage should hold himself or herself to the covenants that were made.

In other words, as we have frequently said, there should be total chastity of men and women before marriage and total fidelity in marriage. The fact that so-called sex revolutionists would change the order and change the status is repugnant to us. We abhor, with all our power, pornography, permissiveness, and the so-called freedom of the sexes, and we fear that those who have supported, taught, and encouraged the permissiveness that brings about this immoral behavior will someday come to a sad reckoning with him who has established the standards. (75-47)

All sex activity outside marriage is sin. The early apostles and prophets mention numerous sins that were reprehensible to them. Many of them were sexual sins—adultery, being without natural affection, lustfulness, infidelity, incontinence, filthy communications, impurity, inordinate affection, fornication. They included all sexual relations outside marriage—petting, sex perversion, masturbation, and preoccupation with sex in one's thoughts and talking. Included are every hidden and secret sin and all unholy and impure thoughts and practices. One of the worst of these is incest. (80-53)

Church stand on chastity is unchanging. That the Church's stand on morality may be understood, we declare firmly and unalterably, it is not an outworn garment, faded, old-fashioned, and threadbare. God is the same yesterday, today, and forever, and his covenants and doctrines are immutable; and when the sun grows cold and the stars no longer shine, the law of chastity will still be basic in God's world and in the Lord's church. Old values are upheld by the Church not because they are old, but rather because through the ages they have proved right. It will always be the rule....

The world may countenance premarital sex experiences, but the Lord and his church condemn in no uncertain terms any and every sex relationship outside of marriage. (80-53)

Wholesome family life with children was set up as the perfect way, thousands of years ago. If all the world should devise some other sort of relationship, it would be wrong even if the voting were 3½ billion to one. (68-06)

Seriousness of Sexual Sin

Chastity is of great value. Chastity and virtue are "most dear and precious above all things" (Moroni 9:9), more valuable than rubies or diamonds, than herds and flocks, than gold and silver, or than automobiles and land. But, sadly, in many cases they are on sale at the cheapest shops and at the cheapest prices. (79-20)

Even mortal life itself, when placed upon the balance scales, weighs less [than chastity]. (60-04)

All unchastity will one day be disclosed. There comes a time when the fornicator, like the murderer, wishes he could hide—hide from all the world, from all the ghosts, and especially his own, but there is no place to hide. There are dark corners and hidden spots and closed cars in which the transgression can be committed, but to totally conceal it is impossible. There is no night so dark, no room so tightly locked, no canyon so closed in, no desert so totally uninhabited that one can find a place to hide from his sins, from himself, or from the Lord. Eventually, one must face the great Maker. (76-46)

Unchastity is moral filthiness. It is not the soil of earth or the grease on a person's hands that defile him; nor is it the fingernails "edged in black," the accumulated perspiration from honest toil, or the body odor resulting from heavy work. One may bathe hourly, perfume oneself often, have hair shampooed frequently, have fingernails manicured daily, and be a master at soft-spoken utterances, and still be as filthy as hell's cesspools. What defiles is sin, and especially sexual sin. . . .

To a young man seeking help who had allowed himself to indulge heavily in fornication but was not quite repentant, I wrote:

"Your sin is the most serious thing you could have done in your youth this side of murder. . . . Your last experience in immorality was far more obnoxious than the first. You had been to the temple and had made solemn vows of chastity before God and holy angels. You made covenant that you would never have such ungodly relations. You had already done it and then did it again with that solemn promise on your lips." (MF 62)

Some fail to understand the gravity of unchastity. I hope their values will not be mixed and distorted like the man who stole the coal but would not drink a cup of coffee, or like the young girl recently who was pregnant, but so distorted was her view that her emphasis was on temple marriage at all costs and no thought of preparation for it. She would not marry the father of her unborn child because temple marriage was not available to her at this time. Fornication was of lesser moment to her but she had definitely settled on her temple marriage. The spirit giveth life—the word killeth. (66-07)

The World's Acceptance of Immorality

Society has accepted immorality as normal. In the latter times some shall depart from the faith, said Paul. (See 1 Timothy 4:1.) These are the latter times. We are the Latter-day Saints. These are the days when some shall depart from the faith. . . . I think it's not just so much the disbelieving apostate, but more likely this permissiveness. They would give heed to the seducing spirits and doctrines of devils. It seems that the devil has a way of making very attractive the things that he proposes to mankind. (76-20)

Your time covers a period when magazine and book writers and public speakers tear down the old monuments of trust and faith and honor, leaving the debris at the feet of new idols, attractive to many, made of brightly colored sand, decorated with tinsel and fool's gold—when rainbows are stolen colors, put together by hired specialists, and pots of gold at the ends of the improvised rainbows are filled with gold-colored froth and scum. (68-06)

Again we see history repeating itself. When we see the pornography, the adulterous practices, homosexuality gone rampant, the looseness and permissiveness of an apparently increasing proportion of the people, we say the days of Satan have returned and history seems to repeat itself.

When we see the depravity of numerous people of our own society in their determination to force upon people vulgar presentations, filthy communications, unnatural practices, we wonder, has Satan reached forth with his wicked, evil hand to pull into his forces the people of this earth? Do we not have enough good people left to stamp out the evil which threatens our world? Why do we continue to compromise with evil and why do we continue to tolerate sin? (75-15)

Once the carnal in man is no longer checked by the restraints of family life and by real religion, there comes an avalanche of appetites which gathers momentum that is truly frightening. As one jars loose and begins to roll downhill, still another breaks loose, whether it is an increase in homosexuality, corruption, drugs, or abortion. Each began as an appetite that needed to be checked but which went unchecked. Thus misery achieves a ghastly momentum. (78-08)

Today we have a so-called new morality wherein the sexual revolution turns itself loose and "everything goes." We now have liberty becoming license and libertinism moral decay. . . .

When a nation will send its young, vigorous sons to a faraway country without their families and take no steps to prevent their impregnating the native girls, leaving a quarter million or more such fatherless children who are accepted neither by their Oriental relatives nor their new Caucasian relatives, certainly life is complex and a world rotting. Abortions are numerous now. "Beget and destroy" seems to be the slogan.

What could the gospel do for this? There would be no unwanted babies, no fatherless children, no mothers who feel burdened, no children who grow up spurned by all.

We talk of pollution with oil slicks, of cans and bottles, of waste papers everywhere, of indestructible plastic, old car bodies, or pesticides and smoke, and industrial wastes; but pollution is not only in the realm of the physical. The more serious pollution is in the spiritual and mental phases of our lives. There is lewdness and licentiousness; there is pornography and V.D.; there is pollution growing everywhere in men's minds and their souls are contaminated.

Thou shalt not commit adultery. Thou shalt not commit fornication. Thou shalt not commit sexual perversions. Thou shalt not be guilty of petting nor do anything like unto it. When a generation lives for sex and translates every message into that language, what can be expected of its people?

The importance and necessity of virtue, real virtue, total virtue, is as old as the inhabited world. If we had the record we would probably find that Cain was promiscuous, for seldom do great crimes travel in single file. (71-17)

The world teaches that sexual license is desirable. There are many other "physicians" in the colleges, on the streets, in business places among us who have worsened the patients. They have laughed at the conventions; they have proclaimed a gospel of error; they have advanced the hellish doctrine that sexual promiscuity is not only allowable but beneficial and normal and proper.

Numerous times have I interviewed young men who have been told by people in whom they had confidence that masturbation was normal and natural and necessary. Numerous times have I visited with young people who have been advised to greatly limit their children. More than a few times have I been advised by frustrated people that they have been advised to seek promiscuous sexual life to cure their maladies. (64-05)

Many errors are induced by society's approval. The subject of chastity is hard to preach about. In nearly every group in meetings, firesides, etc., there is a mixed group, both sexes and youth of different degrees of mentality, training, and experience. To clear the thinking of one youth would put ideas into another mind. I think we should clarify the thinking for the people, but it must be done with great care. If we think and talk sex too much, harm can come from it; and if it is too little, harm may come, so it is hard to know just how far to go. These interviews with singles are most satisfactory. If every youth would voluntarily come to someone in whom he had confidence and discuss boldly and frankly these matters, much good could come. Many missionaries have enthusiastically thanked me after an interview in which I have tried to properly and decently and understandingly discuss with them the dangers and possible damages which can come from masturbation, petting, and especially "heavy petting," and the sin of unchastity. Many young men have seemed a bit surprised that the Church could not wink at the former two. They told me that at the university the doctor and the physical education instructors had spoken of the thing as a necessary thing or as a habit, universal and without harm. Several prospective missionaries have said, after our interview: "Thanks, Brother Kimball. I am so glad you spoke to me of these things. I didn't know. I can wholly give it up and shall do so. I didn't know the Church considered it immoral."

Again, may I sum up by saying that many of the things done are not immoral in and of themselves, but it is the thinking and attitudes and feelings associated with those things. (5/31/48)

The Emptiness of Immorality

"New morality" leads to enslavement. The so-called "new morality" is but the old immorality in a new setting, except perhaps less restrained, less inhibited. Freedom of sex, freedom to drink and smoke, and freedom to rebel and march—all come into the picture. Such evils as glue sniffing and LSD are taking their toll, and narcotics are introduced by dope pushers to unsuspecting youth. Mugging, brutality, and many other aberrations—all come in turn supposedly to relieve boredom as new "kicks." All these and more fasten themselves like a leech upon unprotected folks, later to become the tyrannical master. The simple experiment becomes a complex habit; the embryo becomes a giant; the little innovation becomes a dictator; and the person becomes the slave with a ring in his nose. The so-called freedom becomes abject slavery. (67-06)

One girl said, "Chastity is outdated because in these enlightened days, people are freer."

Yes: Free to commit sin; free to break laws. Free to contract V.D. Free to shorten life; free to deny God; free to be free of all real freedoms.

We see our world sinking into depths of corruption. Every sin mentioned by Paul is now rampant in our society. (71-06)

Unchastity is ultimately futile. Sexual life outside of marriage, whether it be heterosexual or homosexual, is as a dream of the night that fades when the sun rises. It is as chaff that is discarded when the germ of the grain is taken. It is as the froth that accumulates on pounding waters. (73-06)

Sexual encounters outside of legalized marriage render the individual a *thing* to be used, a *thing* to be exploited, and make him or her exchangeable, exploitable, expendable, and throw-awayable.

And when we come before the great Judge at the bar of justice, shall we stand before him as a *thing* or as a person, as a depraved body of flesh and carnal acts, or as a son or daughter of God standing straight and tall and worthy?

To be unwilling to accept responsibility is cowardly, disloyal. Marriage is for time and eternity. Fornication and all other deviations are for today, for the hour, for the "now." Marriage gives life. Fornication leads to death. Premarital sex promises what it cannot possibly produce nor deliver. Rejection is often the fruit as it moves its participants down the long highway of repeated encounters.

Proper sex functions bring posterity, responsibility, and peace; but premarital sex encounters bring pain, loss of self-esteem, and spiritual death, unless there is a total, continuing repentance.

We live in a sterile age, or so it seems—an age when young people turn to sex to escape loneliness, frustration, insecurity, and lack of interest. "What can we do?" the youth complain. They are little interested in reading, or in family associations, youth socials, or the community dance. They must have something more exciting. (65-02)

There is no compatibility between light and darkness. Unchastity is darkness. It is ugly, bitter, destructive, and consuming. It neutralizes good. It darkens minds. It produces spiritual amnesia. It comes in many ugly forms and has many distasteful names. It is born in the mind and is given expression with directed body members. It is a tyrant, demanding and uncompromising and unreasonable, tending toward monopoly. It is like creeping paralysis, slipping up in the darkness, getting hold with its tentacles, and clings on so tenaciously that it takes a prince with a sharp sword to cut it loose. (78-10)

Paul speaks of "lovers of pleasure more than lovers of God." (2 Timothy 3:4.) Does that not describe the wanton sex permissiveness of our own day? The Spirit of the Lord and sin do not mix; and when unrepented-of transgression persists in one's life, the Spirit of the Lord must exit, for they do not go together. (78-09)

The problem of youth is to keep all urges and desires and passions properly harnessed and properly bridled. Nothing wrong with passion. The race would die out if it weren't for passion. But they must be controlled. (56-10)

Sex involvement outside of marriage locks the doors to temples, and thus bars the way to eternal life. (78-09)

Excommunication hangs over the head of the adulterer on a very tiny thread, like Damocles' sword. The sin is forgivable providing the repentance is sufficiently comprehensive. "But if he doeth it again, he shall not be forgiven, but shall be cast out." (D&C 42:26.) (MF 72-73)

Immorality brings generally a deep sense of guilt. These unresolved guilt complexes are the stuff from which mental breakdowns come, the building blocks of suicide, the fabric of distorted personalities, the wounds that scar or decapitate individuals or families. (76-46)

Those who seem to flout the institution of marriage, and who regard chastity before marriage with fidelity after as old-fashioned, seem determined to establish a new fashion on their own and impose it upon others. Can they not see the gross selfishness that will lead finally to deep loneliness? Can they not see that, pushed by pleasure, they will become more and more distant from joy? Can they not see that their kind of fulfillment will produce a hollowness and an emptiness from which no fleeting pleasure can finally rescue them? The law of the harvest has not been repealed. (78-08)

Uncontrolled passion can burn one into spiritual ashes. (60-04)

Sexual activities entail responsibilities. The principle of restitution is brought into focus where two unmarried young people have entered into sin by which both lives are damaged, and especially if virtue has been taken. In such circumstances serious consideration should be given to marriage which will hold the sin in one family. Why should they not marry when by their iniquitous act they have plunged themselves into an adult role?

This is especially true if pregnancy results from the sin. In this situation it is the girl who suffers most. She must not have an abortion, for that would add serious sin to serious sin. She carries most of the burdens, while the boy often goes penalty-free. The girl must go through the uncomfortable nine months with its distress, deprivations, limitations and embarrassments, and then the pain and expense of delivery and the difficult life afterward. It is a cowardly boy who would not propose marriage, pay the costs, share the deprivations and embarrassment. Yet many young men have walked away and abandoned the girl to all the devastating payments for the sin of them both. Parents frequently excuse the son on one pretext or another, and leave the girl to suffer for the sins of them both. Sometimes, parents of the boy curiously feel magnanimous when they offer to pay the actual financial costs of the delivery, not taking into account that the financial is a one-time experience, while the girl has the problems throughout her life, and they are heavy burdens.

To buy the girl off or abandon her to her lifelong problem is not courageous, nor fair, nor right. The time will come when every individual will pay full price, and perhaps with interest, every obligation incurred, even though it was hidden or covered at the time.

The young girl who sins should realize that all the sorrows, inconvenience, and suffering she goes through incident to the carrying and bearing of a child does not fully constitute forgiveness for her sin. She must repent and make her proper adjustment. Let the boy realize too that none of the suffering of the girl minimizes his guilt, but rather magnifies it. For many reasons he may not be prepared to settle down to family life, but he has by his immoral act projected himself into adulthood and has brought upon himself responsibilities which he will do well to accept and discharge as honorably as he can. Like the girl, he needs to find his way to total repentance, and the road leads through acceptance of responsibility, not away from it. (MF 196-97)

Homosexuality

Homosexual conduct is serious sin. The unholy transgression of homosexuality is either rapidly growing or tolerance is giving it wider publicity. If one has such desires and tendencies, he overcomes them the same as if he had the urge toward petting or fornication or adultery. The Lord condemns and forbids this practice with a vigor equal to his condemnation of adultery and other such sex acts. And the Church will excommunicate as readily any unrepentant addict.

Again, contrary to the belief and statement of many people, this sin, like fornication, is overcomable and forgivable, but again, only upon a deep and abiding repentance, which means total abandonment and complete transformation of thought and act. The fact that some governments and some churches and numerous corrupted individuals have tried to reduce such behavior from criminal offense to personal privilege does not change the nature nor the seriousness of the practice. Good men, wise men, God-fearing men everywhere still denounce the practice as being unworthy of sons of God; and Christ's church denounces it and condemns it so long as men have bodies which can be defiled. (80-53)

Homosexuality is an ugly sin.

There is today a strong clamor to make such practices legal by passing legislation. Some would also legislate to legalize prostitution. They have legalized abortion, seeking to remove from this heinous crime the stigma of sin.

We do not hesitate to tell the world that the cure for these evils is not in surrender. (77-34)

Homosexual relationships are dead-end. What would this man do for you, or these men, should you suddenly fall victim to a dread disease, an incurable disease? Suppose your body shriveled; suppose you could no longer satisfy or get satisfaction sexually; suppose you could no longer be "used." How long would the alleged friendship or friendly ties last? (12/20/65)

The homosexual life tends to be a furtive, shifty, concealed life. This abnormal involvement with a person of one's own sex can be only barren and desolate, having for its purpose only temporary physical satisfaction. There is no future in it but only a stirring moment and a dead past. There can be no posterity, no family life, no permanent association, and, of course, nothing that can give eternal joy. It is lonely because it is wrong and because it is selfish. The Lord has given us a program of family life and has planned that the young man and the young woman will be attracted to each other, carry forward a courtship which is clean and free from carnal thoughts and acts, and result in a sweet marriage and where that God-given sex can be used with proper intents and safeguards to draw two people permanently close together as they bring their family into the world and create a heavenly unit on earth of parents and children wherein selflessness can be the rule and tremendous development and faith and accomplishment can be a reality. (5/4/70)

Homosexual practices are enslaving. These practices are somewhat like the use of drugs, alcoholism, or other vicious habits which eventually take over control of the person and make him slave and put fetters on his wrists and rings in his nose and chains on his feet. No man is free when manacled with such fetters. These sins are forgivable and can be overcome if there is adequate restraint and repentance. There are those who tell you there is no cure and thus weaken your resolves and add to your frustration. They *can* be cured. They *can* be eventually forgiven. Your problem *can* be solved.

There are two forces working with every individual—one is the spirit of evil, the powers of darkness with a desire to enslave and destroy.

The other influence is the Spirit of the Lord striving to lift and inspire and build and save. If one lives all of the commandments of the Lord, then he has the power to withstand the temptations of the devil. If he yields to the evil one, then he gets weaker and weaker until he is unable to cope with the strength of the powers that afflict him.

Now, let us assure you that you are not permanently trapped in this unholy practice if you will exert yourself. Though it is like an octopus with numerous tentacles to drag you to your tragedy, the sin is curable and you may totally recover from its tentacles. One of Satan's strongest weapons is to make the victim believe the practice incurable regardless of one's effort. Lucifer is the "father of all lies."

Satan tells his victims that it is a natural way of life; that it is normal; that perverts are a different kind of people born "that way" and that they cannot change. This is a base lie. All normal people have sex urges and if they control such urges, they grow strong and masterful. If they yield to their carnal desires and urges, they get weaker until their sins get beyond control. (71-19)

Homosexual tendencies can be controlled. "God made me that way," some say, as they rationalize and excuse themselves for their perversions. "I can't help it," they add. This is blasphemy. Is man not made in the image of God, and does he think God to be "that way"? Man is responsible for his own sins. It is possible that he may rationalize and excuse himself until the groove is so deep he cannot get out without great difficulty, but this he can do. Temptations come to all people. The difference between the reprobate and the worthy person is generally that one yielded and the other resisted. It is true that one's background may make the decision and accomplishment easier or more difficult, but if one is mentally alert, he can still control his future. That is the gospel message—personal responsibility. (80-53)

Certainly it can be overcome, for there are numerous happy people who were once involved in its clutches and who have since completely transformed their lives. Therefore to those who say that this practice or any other evil is incurable, I respond: "How can you say the door cannot be opened until your knuckles are bloody, till your head is bruised, till your muscles are sore? It can be done." (MF 82)

A homosexual can change himself. I firmly believe that no one can cure a deeply entrenched pervert except himself. The Lord will help, his servants will help, and kind friends will help, but the major effort must come from the individual who has the weakness. . . .

The first thing after one has mentally repented and is determined to restore himself is to abandon every person, thing, place, or situation which could return him to his problem. . . .

In the great majority of the cases brought to our attention, prayer has been neglected or abandoned. The person has either ceased to pray or has permitted his prayers to stray from actual communication down to a wordy repeating of familiar phrases. He has generally hestitated to fervently ask for forgiveness when he perhaps intends to return to his perfidy or has not fully made up his mind that he has terminated it. One then should return to his Lord, remembering that the Lord is always there, anxious to enter the life of his sons and daughters on the earth. . . .

He should develop new associations of honorable, strong, spiritual people who will lift him rather than downgrade him. The Lord has given us the Church, and while the people therein are not perfect, the spiritual average and the moral average certainly is much higher.

As one begins to repent and climb out of the pit, he comes to have a great sense of unworthiness as indicated above. This sense can do wonders in helping him to repent if he will not let it go to the other extreme to destroy him. . . .

Your faith can be increased, your testimony developed, and your power to overcome greatly increased by the reading of the scriptures. Organize a program and set apart a time every day to read the scriptures along with your prayers. (5/4/70)

The continued contact seems to be helpful. To have the man return to report success in his efforts or even partial failure is helpful, and to these continuing visits credit may be given for recoveries. Many find that since they will be making reports, an additional strength comes from that realization and they control themselves and their thoughts a day at a time, a week at a time, and soon the months have passed and thoughts are controlled and actions are above reproach. (64-05)

Transsexual operations are travesty. Then we're appalled to find an ever-increasing number of women who want to be sexually men and many young men who wish to be sexually women. What a travesty! I tell you that, as surely as they live, such people will regret having made overtures toward the changing of their sex. Do they know better than God what is right and best for them? (74-27)

Some people are ignorant or vicious and apparently attempting to destroy the concept of masculinity and femininity. More and more girls dress, groom, and act like men. More and more men dress, groom, and act like women. The high purposes of life are damaged and destroyed by the growing unisex theory. God made man in his own image, male and female made he them. With relatively few accidents of nature, we are born male or female. The Lord knew best. Certainly, men and women who would change their sex status will answer to their Maker. (74-30)

Heterosexual Misconduct

Cohabitation without marriage flouts God's law. I read of the common practice of the associations of men and women not marriage partners; and they are claiming long and loudly that marriage is no longer necessary. And apparently almost without shame do they live together in a sexual partnership without marriage. Has God changed his laws? Or has puny, irresponsible, presumptuous man dared to change the laws of God? Was sin yesterday? Did the devil reign in the hearts of men only in the faraway past? (75-15)

Fornication results from lust, not love. Across the desk from me sat a handsome nineteen-year-old boy and a beautiful, shy, but charming eighteen-year-old girl. They appeared embarrassed, apprehensive, near-terrified. He was defensive and bordering on belligerency and rebellion. They admitted they had broken the moral code and thus gone contrary to some standards, but they quoted magazines and papers and speakers approving premarital sex and emphasizing that sex was a fulfillment of human existence. . . . Had it not been fairly well established, then, in their world, that sex before marriage was not so wrong? Did there not need to be a trial period? How else could they know if they would be compatible for marriage?

Finally, the boy said, "Yes, we yielded to each other, but we do not think it was wrong because we *love* each other." I thought I had misunderstood him. Since the world began there have been countless immoralities, but to hear them justified by a Latter-day Saint youth shocked me. He repeated, "No, it is not wrong, because we *love* each other." . . .

The Savior said that if it were possible the very elect would be deceived by Lucifer. He uses his logic to confuse and his rationalizations to destroy. He will shade meanings, open doors an inch at a time, and lead from purest white through all the shades of gray to the darkest black.

This young couple looked up rather startled when I postulated firmly, "No, my beloved young people, you did not *love* each other. Rather, you *lusted* for each other." . . . The beautiful and holy word of *love* they had defiled until it had degenerated to become a bedfellow with lust, its antithesis. As far back as Isaiah, deceivers and rationalizers were condemned: "Woe unto them that call evil good, and good evil; that put darkness for light, and light for darkness; that put bitter for sweet, and sweet for bitter!" (Isaiah 5:20.) (65-02)

If one really loves another, one would rather die for that person than to injure him. At the hour of sin, pure love is pushed out of one door while lust sneaks in the other. Affection has then been replaced with desire of the flesh and uncontrolled passion. Accepted has been the doctrine which the devil is so eager to establish, that illicit sex relations are justified. When the unmarried yield to lust, that is called fornication. When married fall into this same sin, that is called adultery.

In order to live with themselves, people who transgress must follow one path or the other of two alternatives. The one is to sear the conscience or to dull the sensitivity with mental tranquilizers so that the transgressing may be continued. The other is to permit remorse to lead to total sorrow, repentance, and eventual forgiveness. (76-46)

Lust becomes idolatry. We fear that never in the history of the world have there ever been so many more people bowing to the god of lust than there were bowing to golden calves and the images of wood and stone and metal. This idolatry, so closely associated with the destruction of mind and body, could inundate the world. (75-13)

"Necking" and "petting" are wrong. Instead of remaining in the field of simple expressions of affection, some have turned themselves loose to fondling, often called "necking," with its intimate contacts and its passionate kissing. Necking is the younger member of this unholy family. Its bigger sister is called "petting." When the intimacies have reached this stage, they are surely the sins condemned by the Savior.

"Ye have heard that it was said by them of old time, Thou shalt not commit adultery:

"But I say unto you, That whosoever looketh on a woman to lust after her hath committed adultery with her already in his heart." (Matthew 5:27-28.)

Who would say that he or she who pets has not become lustful, has not become passionate? (80-53)

Among the most common sexual sins our young people commit are necking and petting. Not only do these improper relations often lead to fornication, pregnancy, and abortions, but in and of themselves they are pernicious evils, and it is often difficult for youth to distinguish where one ends and another begins. They awaken lust and stir evil thoughts and sex desires. They are but parts of the whole family of related sins and indiscretions. . . .

Too often, young people dismiss their petting with a shrug of their shoulders as a *little* indiscretion, while admitting that fornication is a base transgression. Too many of them are shocked, or feign to be, when told that what they have done in the name of petting was in reality fornication. The dividing line is a thin, blurry one. . . . The devil knows how to destroy our young girls and boys. He may not be able to tempt a person to murder or to commit adultery immediately, but he knows that if he can get a boy and a girl to sit in the car late enough after the dance, or to park long enough in the dark at the end of the lane, the best boy and the best girl will finally succumb and fall. He knows that all have a limit to their resistance. . . .

Almost like twins, "petting"—and especially "heavy petting" —and fornication are alike. Also like twins, the one precedes the other, but most of the same characteristics are there. The same passions are aroused and, with but slight difference, similar body contacts are made. And from it are likely to come the same frustrations, sorrows, anguish, and remorse. (MF 65-67)

Kissing has been prostituted and has degenerated to develop and express lust instead of affection, honor, and admiration. To kiss in casual dating is asking for trouble. What do kisses mean when given out like pretzels and robbed of sacredness? What is miscalled the "soul kiss" is an abomination and stirs passions to the eventual loss of virtue. Even if timely courtship justifies the kiss it should be a clean, decent, sexless one like the kiss between mother and son, or father and daughter.

If the "soul kiss" with its passion were eliminated from dating there would be an immediate upswing in chastity and honor, with fewer illegitimate babies, fewer unwed mothers, fewer forced marriages, fewer unhappy people.

With the absence of the "soul kiss" necking would be greatly reduced. The younger sister of petting, it should be totally eliminated. Both are abominations in their own right. (60-04)

Small indiscretions lead to serious immorality. Immorality does not begin in adultery or perversion. It begins with little indiscretions like sex thoughts, sex discussions, passionate kissing, petting, and such, growing with every exercise. The small indiscretion seems powerless compared to the sturdy body, the strong mind, the sweet spirit of youth who give way to the first temptation. But soon the strong has become weak, the master the slave, spiritual growth curtailed. But if the first unrighteous act is never given root, the tree will grow to beautiful maturity and the youthful life will grow toward God, our Father. (80-53)

Solitary Vices

Thoughts largely determine immorality of acts. Holding hands would generally not be immoral, but it would depend on whether or not one's mind ran rampant. An embrace may not be immoral, but if the closeness of the body awakens immoral desires, then that is another thing. "As [a man] thinketh...so is he." (Proverbs 23:7.) "Unto the pure all things are pure: but unto them that are defiled and unbelieving is nothing pure." (Titus 1:15.) One must keep the thoughts clean....Two people could embrace, kiss, dance, look, and I can conceive of one of them being immoral and the other innocent of sin. (5/31/48)

Masturbation is disapproved weakness. Masturbation, a rather common indiscretion, is not approved of the Lord nor of his church, regardless of what may have been said by others whose "norms" are lower. Latter-day Saints are urged to avoid this practice. Anyone fettered by this weakness should abandon the habit before he goes on a mission or receives the holy priesthood or goes in the temple for his blessings. (80-53)

Thus prophets anciently and today condemn masturbation. It induces feelings of guilt and shame. It is detrimental to spirituality. It indicates slavery to the flesh, not that mastery of it and the growth toward godhood which is the object of our mortal life....

While we should not regard this weakness as the heinous sin which some other sexual practices are, it is of itself bad enough to require sincere repentance. What is more, it too often leads to grievous sin, even to that sin against nature, homosexuality. For, done in private, it evolves often into mutual masturbation—practiced with another person of the same sex—and thence into total homosexuality. (MF 77-78)

Pornography pollutes the mind. The stench of obscenity and vulgarity reaches and offends the heavens. It putrifies all it touches. (66-07)

Each person must keep himself clean and free from lusts. He must shun ugly, polluted thoughts and acts as he would an enemy. Pornography and erotic stories and pictures are worse than polluted food. Shun them. The body has power to rid itself of sickening food. That person who entertains filthy stories or pornographic pictures and literature records them in his marvelous human computer, the brain, which can't forget this filth. Once recorded, it will always remain there, subject to recall—filthy images. (74-27)

Reject pornography. I remember when the calendar man always came to my business place to sell calendars. The first time he came he put out all over the big table there pictures of nude girls and ugly things. And I said, "No, not that. I don't like that or want anything like that. Have you got a beautiful building or a beautiful scene? Have you got something that would suit a family or something like that? If yes, we will buy one of them. But not any of those." Well, in all the years that we were in business, he never did show another picture like that. He learned his lesson immediately. And they will. They know whether men are yielding or easily influenced this way. I think that is the answer. None of us, I guess, are quite totally perfect. Perhaps there are thoughts that come into our minds. But that is the time to kill them and crush them and to put your heel on them and turn it to crush the thought that good could come from an adulterous thought. (74-33)

Assess television entertainment. Be concerned about the types of programs your family is watching on television or hearing on radio. There is so much today that is unsavory and degrading, so much that gives the impression that the old sins of Sodom and Gomorrah are the "in thing" to do today. (78-07)

Fight pornography. We hope that our parents and leaders will not tolerate pornography. It is really garbage, but today is peddled as normal and satisfactory food. Many writers seem to take delight in polluting the atmosphere with it. Seemingly, it cannot be stopped by legislation. There is a link between pornography and the low, sexual drives and perversions.... We pray with our Lord that we may be kept from being in the world. It is sad that decent people are thrown into a filthy area of mental and spiritual pollution. We call upon all of our people to do all in their power to offset this ugly revolution.

It is ridiculous to imply that pornography has no effect. (74-30)

We need to constantly guard against immorality, pornography, and sexual permissiveness that would destroy the purity of the family members, young and old.... What must we do? We must be constantly alert to their evil presence in our homes and destroy them as we would the germs and filth of disease. We must hunt them from the closets of our minds, freeing ourselves of such worldliness, quenching the embers of wickedness before they become destructive flames. How do we do this? ...

There is only one sure way and that is through the gospel of the Lord Jesus Christ and being obedient to its profound and inspired teachings. Surely we must be made to realize that the purchase price of a family hearth free of such evil influences is the keeping of the commandments of God. (79-03)

We abhor pornography that seems to be flooding the land. Legislation makes an effort to curb it, but the best way to stop it is to have men and women, with their families, build barriers against it. We ask you, "Do you good people of your community want this ugly vice to corrupt your families and your neighbors?" (75-13)

Should people be free to infect society with obscene pictures and vulgar articles and flaunt corruption before children and others? Why should a few be granted freedom from restraint when many are fettered by the ugliness to which they are exposed? (66-11)

Important as it is, building stronger homes is not enough in the fight against rising permissiveness. We therefore urge Church members as citizens to lift their voices, to join others in unceasingly combatting, in their communities and beyond, the inroads of pornography and the general flaunting of permissiveness. (77-34)

And so we say to you: Teach your children to avoid smut as the plague it is. As citizens, join in the fight against obscenity in your communities. Do not be lulled into inaction by the pornographic profiteers who say that to remove obscenity is to deny people the rights of free choice. Do not let them masquerade licentiousness as liberty.

Precious souls are at stake—souls that are near and dear to each of us.

Sins spawned by pornography unfortunately perpetuate other serious transgressions, including abortion. (76-54)

Obscenity will disappear when there is no demand. Obscenity will not be stamped out until men and women recoil at the mere suggestion of it. Vulgarity will not cease until we the people feel ourselves outraged at the sexy stories and lewd suggestions. Vulgar stories and lewd jokes will never cease to be told until there is no laugh to encourage and no ear to listen and no lips to repeat. (66-07)

Proper Dating Patterns

Dress modestly. You girls go and find the modest clothes and wear them, make them as beautiful as you can and be attractive and make up to your boyfriends in bright intellect and sweet spirit and attractive demeanor that which some girls can only do with their bodies. It is a pretty weak girl if she has only her body to attract somebody. (56-10)

Any young woman who conducts herself so as to be attractive spiritually, mentally, and physically, but will not by word, nor dress, nor act stir or stimulate to physical reactions, she is a jewel. (76-46)

Stylish clothes can be modest. You can always be in style and still be modest. I have never seen a style yet in my many years that one couldn't follow and still be modest. . . .

Our girls . . . don't need to be backwoods, neither do they need to dress like a harlot. There is a nice medium place where everybody can dress well. When dresses are long, you can wear them long; and when they are flaring, you can wear them flaring; and when they are short, you can wear them short; but you don't need to outdo everybody in getting them short. . . .

If you want to stay in the realm of modest womanhood, you keep your body covered and no decent man will ever think less of you for it and every good, honorable man who would think of marrying you would love you more for it. . . .

There is no time when a Latter-day Saint woman should wear a strapless gown. They are not righteous nor approved. (56-10)

Modesty is for men, also. Now just a word to the boys. Sometimes we have young men, they swim scantily clad, of course, when they are in the water, that's all right. Sometimes they play games, basketball, for instance, with very, very little on them. Maybe that's all right on the basketball floor, but certainly it is immodest for them to go around dating before and after the game in those kinds of clothes. It is just as bad for a man to be undressed as it is for a woman to be undressed and that, I am sure, is the gospel of Christ. We have only one standard of morality, only one standard of decency, only one standard of modesty, and I hope our men will remember that. There is no reason why a man should go around half dressed either before the people. (56-10)

Extreme styles betray character weakness. Our young people should know also that it is hard for them to hide their upbringing, their inner thoughts, their weaknesses. There is nothing criminal about grammatical errors or careless speech or even slang. But such do reveal the character of the user and reflect upon his home life. It may be an unwarranted and weak demand for attention which one feels powerless to stir otherwise. The chewing of gum in public certainly gives no suggestion of culture or refinement and certainly will not build confidence in or esteem for the one who indulges. Inappropriate clothes, extreme makeup, fantastic hairdos, gum chewing, slang, ugly speech, bad table manners, and other such irregularities brand the individual at once as weak, uncouth, cheap or careless, and thoughtless, and his family is judged by his weaknesses. . . .

Boys seldom criticize a girl for using too little makeup. Sometimes they say, "She's a nice girl, but I wish she'd dress up, and she uses too much makeup." To be overdressed, to be gaudily dressed, to be dressed to look sexy, to be overdecorated is bad taste, to say the least. The young woman is smart who can don just enough powder and lipstick to convince the fellows it isn't makeup at all, but the "real you."

Perhaps there is no transgression in painted eyelids or dangling earrings or fancy hairdos, but surely all these eccentricities and extremes betray character. Her life is open like a book, and people read it. There may be no harm in the style itself, but it may indicate some weakness, some insecurity, some unsureness.

Young men should keep their faces shaved, their hair combed, their haircuts reasonably conservative, their nails cleaned. Overtight, suggestive pants brand young men as vulgar. Young people can be smart and personable, dignified and attractive by finding an area somewhere less than the extremes and still in good style....

There may be nothing wrong with an extreme crew cut or a beard or for one to cover his forehead "Beatle" style and let the hair grow long all around, but he is opening his book for the world to read, and employers and other thoughtful people may bypass the eccentric and the extremist in his distortion and abnormalities to find those who are stylish in moderation and who are dignified, for here is an indication of depth and width and strength. (65-10)

Good company supports high morals. Oh, if our young people could learn this basic lesson to always keep good company, never to be found with those who tend to lower their standards! Let every youth select associates who will keep him on tiptoe, trying to reach the heights. Let him never choose associates who encourage him to relax in carelessness. (65-02)

Early dating increases temptation. A vicious, destructive, social pattern of early steady dating must be changed....

It is my considered feeling, having had some experience in interviewing youth, that the change of this one pattern of social activities of our youth would immediately eliminate a majority of the sins of our young folks; would preclude numerous early, forced marriages; would greatly reduce school dropouts; and would be most influential in bringing a great majority of our young men and women to the holy marriage altar at the temple—clean, sweet, full of faith to become the worthy parents of the next generation. (65-10)

I would add a suggestion for avoiding undue temptation. Young men and women, not yet ready for marriage, should be friends with many others, but they should not engage in courting. Immaturity makes them susceptible to temptation. We want them to grow up clean, with a life plan for missions, then wholesome courting and eternal marriage in the holy temple. It is timing that is vital. The sexual relationship that is wrong before marriage is right and beautiful as part of the union encouraged by God. Friendship, not courtship, should be the relationship of teenagers. (PKSO 9)

The monster of sin can raise its ugly heads anywhere and corrupt people can always find a place for planned licentiousness, but a car unwisely used can carry unsuspecting youth to unfrequented places where a combination of darkness, leisure, and temptation may trip even innocent ones who may naively have created situations where unsuspected, unplanned tragedies may occur.

The privacy of the car made easy the passionate intimacies which crept upon them stealthily as a snake slithers through the grass. They intended no evil.

At lane ends, in canyon defiles, desert wastes, and quiet streets at late hours—these are places where people discuss little of art, music, or doctrines, but think of baser things, talk in lower veins, and when talk wears thin there are things to do, the doing of which bring dust of ashes where roses should be blooming. (60-03)

In high school days it is natural and normal for the young man's fancy to turn to young women, and young girls to turn their eyes toward handsome young men.

But the need of the hour is for control. One's wants and urges and passions need the controls of bridle and harness. There are yet many years ahead for serious courtship and marriage.

Early dating—especially early steady dating—brings numerous problems—much heartache and numerous disasters. The early date ofttimes develops into the steady date; the steady date frequently brings on early marriages, of which there are hundreds of thousands with sixteen- and seventeen-year-old brides; early marriages often end in disillusionment, frustration, and divorce with broken homes and scarred lives. Far more high school marriages end in divorces than marriages of more mature young people.

Dating and especially steady dating in the early teens is most hazardous. It distorts the whole picture of life. It deprives the youth of worthwhile and rich experiences; it limits friendships; it reduces the acquaintance which can be so valuable in selecting a partner for time and eternity.

Steady dating is the source of much evil. The casual relationship grows rapidly into intimacies, develops heavy temptations, and stirs passions far beyond the ability of most young people to cope with. Nearly 40 percent of our unwed mothers are between fifteen and nineteen years of age. Even our finest young people will find difficulty in withstanding for a long period the temptations of the intimate, frequent association. And the best young men and women may be overwhelmed and led down the path of the sins of necking, petting, fornication, and other detestable and loathsome perversions and practices.

To speed up the physical process of maturity by early steady dating is like forcing a rose from a bud or eating fruit before it is ripe. The mother who thinks it "cute" to permit her little girl makeup, high heels, fancy hairdos is asking for trouble. Those parents who permit or encourage early social activities are unwittingly begging for sorrows and heartbreaks.

Mothers often fear spinsterhood for their teenage daughters who are not immediately overpopular. Their every push is likely to bring them sorrows and tears. (65-10)

Youth should emphasize group social activities. The urge for group activity is normal to the younger set, when they are not prematurely and immaturely stimulated in other ways, and the recreational and social activities of the crowd can be wholesome and entertaining. Physical and moral safety is increased in the multiplicity of friends. Group homemade recreation activities can be not only great fun but most beneficial. Firesides may create friendships, and inspire the spirit and train the mind. Group picnics can discipline youth in gentle manners and fellowship and extend circles of intimate friends.

Sports can develop the body in strength and endurance. They can train the spirit to meet difficulties and defeats and successes, teach selflessness and understanding, and develop good sportsmanship and tolerance in participant and spectator. Drama can develop talent, teach patience, and foster fellowship and friendliness. Group music activities have similar effects, and also can soften and mellow the spirit and satisfy the aesthetic needs.

The properly conducted dancing party can be a blessing. It provides opportunity to spend a pleasant evening with many people to the accompaniment of music. It can create and develop friendships which will be treasured in later years. Alternatively it can become a restricting experience.

Well-ordered dances provide favorable places, pleasing times, and auspicious circumstances in which to meet new people and to enlarge circles of friends. They can be an open door to happiness. In an evening of pleasurable dancing and conversation, one can become acquainted with many splendid young folk, every one of whom has admirable traits and may be superior to any one companion in at least some qualities. Here partners can begin to appraise and evaluate, noting qualities, attainments, and superiorities by comparison and contrast. Such perceptive friendships can be the basis for wise, selective, occasional dating for those of sufficient age and maturity, this to be followed later in proper timing by steady dating, and later by proper courtship which culminates in a happy, never-ending marriage.

On the other hand, for a youth to dance all evening with one partner, which we might call "monopolistic" dancing, is not only antisocial but it circumscribes one's legitimate pleasures and opportunities. Also it can encourage improper intimacies by its exclusiveness. Dancing with dates, single or steady, should presuppose the exchange of partners, which we could call "multiple" dancing. (MF 221-22)

CHAPTER 11

Marriage

The Commandment to Marry

Marriage is of God. It is the normal thing to marry. It was arranged by God in the beginning, long before this world's mountains were ever formed. Remember: "Neither is the man without the woman, neither the woman without the man." (1 Corinthians 11:11.) . . . Every person should *want* to be married. There are some who might not be able to. But every person should want to be married because that is what God in heaven planned for us. (76-59)

Marriage is ordained of God. It is not merely a social custom. Without proper and successful marriage, one will never be exalted. (76-59)

Civil marriage is an earthly contract, completed in the death of either party. Eternal celestial marriage is a sacred covenant between man and woman, consecrated in the holy temple by servants of God who hold authoritative keys. It bridges death; it includes both time and eternity. (74-27)

Man is complete only with marriage. "And I, God, said unto mine Only Begotten, which was with me from the beginning: Let us make man [not a separate man, but a complete man, which is husband and wife] in our image, after our likeness; and it was so."

(Moses 2:26.) Such a marriage extends beyond the grave. What a beautiful partnership! Adam and Eve were married for eternity by the Lord. All peoples should call for this kind of marriage. (75-46)

Marriage is part of a normal life sequence. Missionaries should begin to think marriage when they return from their missions, to begin to get acquainted with many young women so that they will have a better basis for selection of a life's companion, and when the times comes, they should marry in the holy temple and have their families, and complete their education, establish themselves in a profitable and rewarding occupation, and give themselves to their families, the gospel, and the Church. (73-06)

Marriage should not defer to education. For a young man to get his mission two years and then four to six to eight years of university training, the way must look long and forbidding. When the times demand highly trained people; when keen competition requires extended education; when ambition and desire push one toward multiple degrees; when family and friends expect great accomplishment; when the wealth and renown of those who have become highly trained loom haughtily up before the beginner, it must indeed take a stout heart to let wisdom and propriety rule.

This often brings a rather natural, but not always justified, delay and postponement of marriage and there seems to be an increasing number who abandon the idea of marriage....

There will be many excuses, of course: "I could not support a wife and go to college." "I could not have children and maintain myself in school." "I thought it would be proper to wait a few years for my marriage and my children." What the Lord will say to these excuses we can only imagine. We are sure he will at least say, "You have not placed first things first." (68-05)

Those who choose not to marry deprive themselves. There are some men who fail to marry through their own choice. They deprive themselves. There may be many women who also deprive themselves of blessings. There are others who have never married because they had no opportunity. We know, of course, that the Lord will make ample provision and that no one will ever be condemned for something he or she could not help. This is the Lord's program. (75-24)

Some might say, "Well, I'd be satisfied to just become an angel," but you would not. One never would be satisfied just to be a ministering angel to wait upon other people when he could be the king himself. (76-59)

He knew he was commanded to find a wife and marry her and make her happy. He knew it was his duty to become the father of children and provide a rich, full life for them as they grew up. He knew all this, yet postponed his responsibility....

I shall feel sorry for this young man when the day comes that he faces the Great Judge at the throne and when the Lord asks this boy: "Where is your wife?" All of his excuses which he gave to his fellows on earth will seem very light and senseless when he answers the Judge. "I was very busy," or "I felt I should get my education first," or "I did not find the right girl"—such answers will be hollow and of little avail. (74-21)

Advice to Unmarried Women

Righteous unmarried will be deprived of no blessing. The message of the Lord through all his days was love—love for the aged, love for the child, love for the intermediate group, and though he does not promise us all sunshine and no rain, all ease and no pain, he does promise us that much of what we do can be turned into pleasant days and pleasant times.

I am aware of some who seemingly have not been successful in total fulfillment. Some have been on missions; they have completed their education, kept their grooming right, and yet have passed the period of their greatest opportunity, have increased in age, and while still attractive and desirable and efficient, find themselves alone and lonely.

To the large group of young women in this category, we can only say, you are making a great contribution to the world as you serve your families and the Church and world. You must remember that the Lord loves you and the Church loves you. We have no control over the heartbeats or the affections of men, but pray that you may find total fulfillment. And in the meantime, we promise you that insofar as your eternity is concerned, that no soul will be deprived of rich, eternal blessings for anything which that person could not help, that eternity is a long time, and that the Lord never fails in his promises and that every righteous woman will receive eventually all to which she is entitled which she has not forfeited through any fault of her own. (74-39)

Meanwhile, one does not need to be married or a mother in order to keep the first and second great commandments—those of loving God and our fellowmen—on which Jesus said hang all the law and all the prophets. (79-19)

Unmarried women should take no offense at emphasis on family. Now, the General Authorities are very much aware of the fact that many of our sisters are widows. Others have become divorced. Still others have never had the privilege of temple marriage. We want all such sisters to understand that when we speak of family life, it is not done to make them feel sad or unappreciated. The leaders of the Church have said often, and clearly, that women in such circumstances include some of the most noble spirits of our Father in Heaven. Those who make the best of what life has given to them will be rewarded for all that they have done in the service of our Heavenly Father and their fellowman.

Those of you who do not now experience the traditional women's role, not by choice, but for reasons beyond control, can still do so much to help others. Your talents and time must not be misused simply because all of the preferred ways of sharing and giving are not open to you presently.

We have no choice, dear sisters, but to continue to hold up the ideal of the Latter-day Saint family. The fact that some do not now have the privilege of living in such a family is not reason enough to stop talking about it. We do discuss family life with sensitivity, however, realizing that many sisters do not presently have the privilege of belonging or contributing to such a family. But we cannot set aside this standard, because so many other things depend upon it.

Young women should plan and prepare for marriage and the bearing and rearing of children. It is your divine right and the avenue to the greatest and most supreme happiness. You should also make choices looking forward to productive use of your time once the children are grown and gone from under your wing. You should seek for ways to bless the lives of all with whom you associate. You should know the truth of all things. You should be prepared to help build the kingdom of God.

You may answer that finding a husband is not within the power of a young woman. The man has the choice. To the extent that that is true, remember that what the Lord expects of each of his daughters is that she seek out those opportunities and make those choices which will keep her worthy of living again with him. Then she will be prepared for marriage.

There is a great and grand principle involved here. Just as those who do not hear the gospel in this life, but who would have received it with all their hearts had they heard it, will be given the fulness of the gospel blessings in the next world—so, too, the women of the Church who do not in this life have the privileges and blessings of a temple marriage, through no fault of their own, who would have responded if they had an appropriate opportunity—will receive all those blessings in the world to come. We desire all you sisters to know how much we love and appreciate you. We respect you for your valiant and devoted service, and have many opportunities to observe how dedicated you are! (78-24)

Make yourself attractive as a marriage partner. How nice and easy would it be if we had a magic wand! But we haven't. You might take a careful inventory of your habits, your speech, your appearance, your weight, if it is heavier than most people appreciate, and your eccentricities, if you have them. Take each item and analyze it.

What do you like in others? What personality traits please you in others? Are your dresses too short, too long, too revealing, too old-fashioned? Does your weight drive off possible suitors? Do you laugh raucously? Are you too selfish? Are you interested only in your own interests or do you project yourself into the lives of others? Do you have annoying mannerisms, such as "A penny for your thoughts"? Do you repeat old stories till they are threadbare? Are you too anxious or too disinterested? Can you make some sacrifices to be acceptable? Are you dull or are you too exuberant? Are you flashy or are you disinteresting? What do you do to make yourself desirable? Do you overdo or underdo? Too much makeup or too little? Scrupulously clean both physically and morally? Are you in the right place or have you pegged yourself? One young girl was getting into the twenties and without opportunity. I urged her to move from the home which she shared with several older girls, leave the office as steno, and go to college where she would meet people of the right age. Time passed. I happened one day to be on that campus sometime later and here she came to me, bubbling like a fresh new breeze, with a bright ribbon tying her hair and an optimistic and happy personality. A few months later I was invited to a temple marriage. It may not always work that well.

What are your eccentricities, if any? I think nearly all people have some. If so, then go to work. Classify them, weigh them, corral them, and eliminate one at a time until you are a very normal person.

These suggestions apply to some extent to the men, and also to the older women. It is not likely that anyone will propose to you out of a sense of duty. You must do something about it. (74-13)

Importance of Temple Marriage

Temple marriage overshadows civil ceremony. Down in South America, one must be married by designated local authorities, but that means little. It is like acquiring some clothes to be baptized in. It is not the baptism. I mean because of some legal technicalities in some countries, a local man, a judge or a minister, has to marry a couple. We cannot help that. We tolerate it. It is not the real marriage, really. Then we come to the temple and are sealed for eternity. (65-01)

Temple marriage perpetuates loving relationships. The greatest joys of true married life can be continued. The most beautiful relationships of parents and children can be made permanent. The holy association of families can be never-ending if husband and wife have been sealed in the holy bond of eternal matrimony. Their joys and progress will never end, but this will never fall into place of its own accord. . . .

God has restored the knowledge of temples and their purposes. On the earth this day are holy structures built to this special work of the Lord, and each is the house of the Lord. In these temples, by duly constituted authority, are men who can seal husbands and wives and their children for all eternity. This is a fact even though it is unknown to many. . . .

It is inconceivable that otherwise intelligent, astute, and highly educated people should ignore or willfully disregard this great privilege. The doors can be unlocked. The gap can be bridged. And men can walk safely, securely to never-ending happiness, making their marriages timeless and eternal. (74-27)

Any of you would go around the world for the sealing ordinance if you knew its importance, if you realized how great it is. No distance, no shortage of funds, no situation would ever keep you from being married in the holy temple of the Lord. (76-59)

Temple marriages are less likely to result in divorce. For marriages performed outside the temples, the threat of divorce is much greater. In a study of our own groups, we found that there was only one divorce in every 16 marriages of those who were sealed in the temple, while there was one divorce in every 5.7 marriages of those who were not. . . .

Not only the ordinance itself, but also the preparation for the ordinance and the deep appreciation of it achieve this end. The righteousness of your life, the feeling of responsibility in preparation for temple marriage, as well as the sacred sealing ordinance, combine to solemnize marriage vows, make holy family relationships, and cement ties, resulting in continuous and blissful marriage. (76-59)

Only temple marriage survives death. I remember we had in our community in Arizona a good man who passed away. He and his lovely wife had resisted the teachings of the Church. And the wife, when he died, said, "I know that we will be associated as husband and wife through eternity." But she could say that a thousand times and it would still not come true because they were not humble enough to accept the law of marriage. They may receive other blessings, but not exaltation. That is reserved for those who are faithful and who obey the commandments. (75-30)

Since we know well that mortal death does not terminate our existence, since we know that we live on and on, how devastating to realize that marriage and family life, so sweet and happy in so many homes, will end with death because we fail to follow God's instructions or because we reject his word when we understand it.

It is clear in the Lord's announcement that righteous men and women will receive the due rewards of their deeds. They will not be damned in the commonly accepted terminology but will suffer many limitations and deprivations and fail to reach the highest kingdom, if they do not comply. They become ministering servants to those who complied with all laws and lived all commandments. (74-27)

Marriage to unbelievers precludes temple marriage. Over the years many times women have come to me in tears. How they would love to train their children in the Church, in the gospel of Jesus Christ! But they were unable to do so. How they would like to accept positions of responsibility in the Church! How they would like to pay their tithing! How they would love to go to the temple and do the work for the dead, to do work for themselves, to be sealed for eternity, and to have their own flesh and blood, their children, sealed to them for eternity!

But the doors are locked! They themselves have locked them, and the doors have often rusted on their hinges. Someone did not teach these individuals sufficiently, or they did not study the scriptures and they did not understand, or they ignored the warnings which came to them. They married out of the Church. Perhaps he was a good man. Maybe he was handsome. He may have been cultured and well trained; but he did not have the qualification that he needed most and which they overlooked. He did not have membership in the kingdom; he did not have the priesthood, the ordinances, and the righteousness that would carry them to exaltation.

No implication is here made that all members of the Church are worthy and that all nonmembers are unworthy, but eternal marriage cannot be had outside of the temple, and nonmembers are not permitted to go into the temple. Of course, they can become members if they are interested enough and prove that interest.

Without common faith, trouble lies ahead. When two people marry who have different standards, different approaches, and different backgrounds, it is a very difficult thing. There are exceptions, but the rule is a harsh and unhappy one. Religious differences imply wider areas of conflict. Church loyalties clash, and family loyalties clash.

Paul said: "Be ye not unequally yoked together with unbelievers: for what fellowship hath righteousness with unrighteousness? and what communion hath light with darkness?" (2 Corinthians 6:14.) Perhaps Paul wanted them to see that religious differences are fundamental differences. . . .

Yes, a small minority are finally baptized. Some good men and women have joined the Church after the interfaith marriage and have remained most devout and active. God bless them! We are proud of them and grateful for them. These are our blessed minority.

Others who do not join the Church are still kind, considerate, and cooperative, and permit the other spouse to worship and serve according to the Church pattern. God bless them also!

Many others join the Church ostensibly for the marriage, then fail to live the commandments. Many of them are later divorced. Others, though not divorced, continue to have friction, particularly in religious matters in the home.

The majority, however, do not join the Church. Surveys have indicated that only one of seven finally join the Church—the odds are against the others. And nearly half of those who marry out of the Church become inactive. As parents give up their religion, an increasing number of their children are brought up without any religion.

So you are taking a desperate chance if you say, "Well, maybe he will join after we are married. We will go ahead and try it and see." It is a pretty serious thing to take a chance on.

Frequently young people think, "Oh, that doesn't matter. We'll get along all right. We'll adjust ourselves. My spouse will permit me to do as I please or I will make adjustments. We'll both live and worship according to our own pattern." This is not broad-mindedness, but even if it were, to be broad-minded with the Lord's eternal program is somewhat like being generous with other people's money. (76-59)

Certainly you would not want to bring deprivation to your children, would you, even if there were no spiritual elements in this? The religious phase in your family life is most deep-seated, and young people do not always realize this fact until it is too late. They are trying to satisfy their immediate desires rather than to complete a proper pattern—a total program. They have not stopped to think that they are going to have children some day and that children are frustrated in unhappy and broken homes, and live unnatural lives in homes where there is no religious training and where the religious thoughts of parents conflict. (51-02)

Do not take the chance of dating nonmembers, or members who are untrained and faithless. A girl may say, "Oh, I do not intend to marry this person. It is just a 'fun' date." But one cannot afford to take a chance on falling in love with someone who may never accept the gospel. . . .

In isolated instances a lovely young woman might be so far removed geographically from other Church members that she would either have to marry out of the Church or stay unmarried. Some might feel justified in such circumstances in making an exception to the rule and marrying a nonmember but, justification or not, it is important to recognize that the hazards in such a marriage would remain. To minimize the dangers the girl should by all means make sure that she marries a man who is honorable and good, so that even if he cannot at present be brought to accept the gospel there is a fair chance of his being converted later. (MF 241-42)

Encouragement for temple marriage should start early. It seems to me it would be a fine thing if every set of parents would have in every bedroom in their house a picture of the temple so the boy or girl from the time he is an infant could look at the picture every day and it becomes a part of his life. When he reaches the age that he needs to make this very important decision, it will have already been made. (76-59)

The Marriage Decision

Choosing a marriage partner is a vital decision. The greatest single factor affecting what you are going to be tomorrow, your activity, your attitudes, your eventual destiny . . . is the one decision you make that moonlit night when you ask that individual to be your companion for life. That's the most important decision of your entire life! It isn't where you are going to school, or what lessons you are going to study, or what your major is, or how you are going to make your living. These, though important, are incidental and nothing compared with the important decision that you make when you ask someone to be your companion for eternity. (59-01)

Spouses should be chosen prayerfully. The question "whom shall I marry?" is an important one to ask, for the proper answer to this question brings a proper answer to many others. If you marry the proper "whom" and if you marry in the proper "where," then you will have an infinitely better chance of happiness throughout all eternity.

Therefore, the decision is not made on the spur of the moment. It is something you plan all your life. Certainly the most careful planning and thinking and praying and fasting should be done to be sure that of all decisions, this one is not wrong.

In true marriage there must be a union of minds as well as of hearts. Emotions must not wholly determine decisions, but the mind and the heart, strengthened by fasting and prayer and serious consideration, will give one a maximum chance of marital happiness. (76-59)

Cultural differences pose dangers for marriage. When I said you must teach your people to overcome their prejudices and accept the Indians, I did not mean that you would encourage intermarriage. I mean that they should be brothers, to worship together and to work together and to play together; but we must discourage intermarriage, not because it is sin. I would like to make this very emphatic. A couple has not committed sin if an Indian boy and a white girl are married, or vice versa. It isn't a transgression like the transgressions of which many are guilty. But it is not expedient. Marriage statistics and our general experience convince us that marriage is not easy. It is difficult when all factors are favorable. The divorces increase constantly, even where the spouses have the same general background of race, religion, finances, education, and otherwise. (58-08)

The interrace marriage problem is not one of inferiority or superiority. It may be that your son is better educated and may be superior in his culture, and yet it may be on the other hand that she is superior to him. It is a matter of backgrounds. The difficulties and hazards of marriage are greatly increased where backgrounds are different. For a wealthy person to marry a pauper promises difficulties. For an ignoramus to marry one with a doctor's degree promises difficulties, heartaches, misunderstandings, and broken marriages.

When one considers marriage, it should be an unselfish thing, but there is not much selflessness when two people of different races plan marriage. They must be thinking selfishly of themselves. They certainly are not considering the problems that will beset each other and that will beset their children. . . .

If your son thinks he loves this girl, he would not want to inflict upon her loneliness and unhappiness; and if he thinks that his affection for her will solve all her problems, he should do some more mature thinking.

We are unanimous, all of the Brethren, in feeling and recommending that Indians marry Indians, and Mexicans marry Mexicans; the Chinese marry Chinese and the Japanese marry Japanese; that the Caucasians marry the Caucasians, and the Arabs marry Arabs. (0/0/59)

Choose a spouse who will motivate growth. You [missionaries] go home and find a person that will stimulate you, one that will keep you on your toes, that will make you be bigger than you are—never anyone that will let you relax. I would never be in the Council of the Twelve today if I had married some of the girls that I have known. Sister Kimball kept me growing and never let me be satisfied with mediocrity. . . .

Go all over the Church if you need to, to find the girl that is better than you are. The first time if she measures up, invite her again. If she measures up again, you are old enough to go steady! (59-01)

Choose a spouse who will encourage righteousness. He takes time enough to find the girl who has all those great qualities that makes her wanted the most. Not just a pretty face, not just a beautiful form, but the girl who will help him when life begins to get difficult, when there are questions to be answered and decisions to be made. He wants to have a girl who will help him to pay tithing, help him to get to priesthood meeting on time, help him to rear their children. He will be a man to help her to properly discipline the children who come along, and be a real father, be a real husband. That is what honorable and righteous girls want. They are not interested in the fun things so much anymore. They are mature. After marriage and after the children come, there are many things to get their attention, like how many children; how to make a good living; how to make things work; how to do many things in the community in which one lives. (74-16)

Returned missionaries are good marriage candidates. As the young women begin their steady dating, it could properly be with the more worthy, the more personable, the more delightful returning missionaries who can worthily take them to temple marriage and a happy future. Every Latter-day Saint girl who grows up wholesome, sweet, clean, and personable is entitled to the best and should be satisfied with no less; and generally, every normal, young Latter-day Saint boy from infancy should dream of a mission to meet his obligation to the world and to the Lord. Accordingly, with this grand experience in the future, most young men will not get too serious in their romance until after their missions. (65-10)

Building a Good Marriage

Newlyweds should establish independence. Couples do well to immediately find their own home, separate and apart from that of the in-laws on either side. The home may be very modest and unpretentious, but still it is an independent domicile. Your married life should become independent of her folks and his folks. You love them more than ever; you cherish their counsels; you appreciate their association; but you live your own lives, being governed by your decisions, by your own prayerful considerations after you have received the counsel from those who should give it. (76-52)

Now, John and Mary, being human, you may some day have differences of opinion resulting even in little quarrels. Neither of you will be so unfaithful to the other as to go back to your parents or friends and discuss with them your little differences. That would be gross disloyalty. Your intimate life is your own and must not be shared with or confided in others. You will not go back to your people for sympathy but will thresh out your own difficulties. (49-01)

Happiness in marriage requires continued effort. Two people coming from different backgrounds soon learn after the ceremony is performed that stark reality must be faced. There is no longer a life of fantasy or of make-believe; we must come out of the clouds and put our feet firmly on the earth. Responsibility must be assumed and new duties must be accepted. Some personal freedoms must be relinquished and many adjustments, unselfish adjustments, must be made.

One comes to realize very soon after the marriage that the spouse has weaknesses not previously revealed nor discovered. The virtues which were constantly magnified during courtship now grow relatively smaller, and the weaknesses which seemed so small and insignificant during courtship now grow to sizeable proportions. The hour has come for understanding hearts, for self-appraisal, and for good common sense, reasoning, and planning. The habits of years now show themselves; the spouse may be stingy or prodigal, lazy or industrious, devout or irreligious, may be kind and cooperative or petulant and cross, demanding or giving, egotistical or self-effacing. The in-law problem comes closer into focus and the relationships of the spouses to them are again magnified.

Often there is an unwillingness to settle down and to assume the heavy responsibilities that immediately are there. Economy is reluctant to replace lavish living, and the young people seem often too eager "to keep up with the Joneses." There is often an unwillingness to make the financial adjustments necessary. Young wives are often demanding that all the luxuries formerly enjoyed in the prosperous homes of their successful fathers be continued in their own homes. Some of them are quite willing to help earn that lavish living by continuing employment after marriage. They consequently leave the home where their duty lies to pursue professional or business pursuits, thus establishing an economy that becomes stabilized so that it becomes very difficult to yield toward the normal family life. . . .

While marriage is difficult, and discordant and frustrated marriages are common, yet real, lasting happiness is possible, and marriage can be more an exultant ecstasy than the human mind can conceive. This is within the reach of every couple, every person. "Soulmates" are fiction and an illusion; and while every young man and young woman will seek with all diligence and prayerfulness to find a mate with whom life can be most compatible and beautiful, yet it is certain that almost any good man and any good woman can have happiness and a successful marriage if both are willing to pay the price.

The formula is simple; the ingredients are few, though there are many amplifications of each.

First, there must be the proper approach toward marriage, which contemplates the selection of a spouse who reaches as nearly as possible the pinnacle of perfection in all the matters which are of importance to the individuals. And then those two parties must come to the altar in the temple realizing that they must work hard toward this successful joint living.

Second, there must be a great unselfishness, forgetting self and directing all of the family life and all pertaining thereunto to the good of the family, subjugating self.

Third, there must be continued courting and expressions of affection, kindness, and consideration to keep love alive and growing.

Fourth, there must be a complete living of the commandments of the Lord as defined in the gospel of Jesus Christ.

With these ingredients properly mixed and continually kept functioning, it is quite impossible for unhappiness to come, misunderstandings to continue, or breaks to occur. Divorce attorneys would need to transfer to other fields and divorce courts would be padlocked.

Two individuals approaching the marriage altar must realize that to attain the happy marriage which they hope for, they must know that marriage is not a legal cover-all; but it means sacrifice, sharing, and even a reduction of some personal liberties. It means long, hard economizing. It means children who bring with them financial burdens, service burdens, care and worry burdens; but it also means the deepest and sweetest emotions of all.

Before marriage, each individual is quite free to go and come as he pleases, to organize and plan his life as it seems best, to make all decisions with self as the central point. Sweethearts should realize before they take the vows that each must accept literally and fully that the good of the little new family must always be superior to the good of either spouse. Each party must eliminate the "I" and the "my" and substitute therefor "we" and "our." Every decision must take into consideration that there are two or more affected by it. As she approaches major decisions now, the wife will be concerned as to the effect they will have upon the parents, the children, the home, and their spiritual lives. His choice of occupation, his social life, his friends, his every interest must now be considered in the light that he is only a part of a family, that the totalness of the group must be considered. (76-52)

I am convinced that almost any two good people can get along together and be reasonably happy together if both are totally cooperative, unselfish, and willing to work together. I realize that sometimes there are personality clashes which make the difficulty greater.

Many young people labor and live under false notions, feeling that a marriage contract, and especially if it is a temple marriage, solves all the problems; and many people further think that marriage is a sort of perpetual motion program. Once set in motion by a marriage ceremony, it will never run down. I want to tell you that there are no marriages that can ever be happy ones unless two people work at it.

When problems affect a couple the easy thing is to stand on one's pride and quarrel, yielding not an inch, and to permit those differences to continue to get bigger and more cankerous until each party seeks comfort from friends, relatives, and finally a dissolution of the marriage. The hard thing, when problems arise, is to swallow pride, eat humble pie, analyze the situation, accept the blame that is properly due and then grit one's teeth, clench one's fists, and develop the courage to say, "I'm sorry." (1/5/60)

Maintaining a Sound Relationship

Marriage requires unselfishness and loyalty. In a properly charted Latter-day Saint marriage, one must be conscious of the need to

forget self and love one's companion more than self. There will not
be postponement of parenthood, but a desire for children as the Lord
intended, and without limiting the family as the world does. The
children will be wanted and loved. There will be fidelity and confidence; eyes will never wander and thoughts will never stray toward
extramarital romance. In a very literal sense, husband and wife will
keep themselves for each other only, in mind and body and spirit.
(MF 250)

It is not enough to refrain from adultery. We need to make the
marriage relationship sacred, to sacrifice and work to maintain the
warmth and respect which we felt during courtship. God intended for
marriage to be eternal, sealed by the power of the priesthood in the
temples of the Lord. Daily acts of courtesy and kindness, conscientiously planned for, are part of what the Lord expects. (78-22)

The scriptures remind us that "Women have claim on their
husbands for their maintenance, until their husbands are taken."
(D&C 83:2.) Women also have a claim on their husbands for respect,
fidelity, and thoughtfulness, for in that subtle, sweet relationship that
should obtain between men and women, there is partnership with the
priesthood. (78-06)

The love of which the Lord speaks is not only physical attraction,
but also faith, confidence, understanding, and partnership. It is
devotion and companionship, parenthood, common ideals, and standards. It is cleanliness of life and sacrifice and unselfishness. This
kind of love never tires nor wanes. It lives on through sickness and
sorrow, through prosperity and privation, through accomplishment
and disappointment, through time and eternity. (49-01)

Marriage requires fresh effort. There are many marriages where
the spouses have permitted their marriage to grow stale and weak and
cheap. There are many spouses who have fallen from the throne of
adoration and worship and are in the low state of mere joint occu-

pancy in the home, joint sitters at the table, joint possessors of certain things which cannot be easily divided. These people are on the path that leads to trouble. These people will do well to reevaluate, to renew their courting, to express their affection, to acknowledge kindness, and to increase their consideration, so their marriage again can become beautiful, sweet, and growing. (76-59)

Spirituality enhances marriage. If two people love the Lord more than their own lives and then love each other more than their own lives, working together in total harmony with the gospel program as their basic structure, they are sure to have this great happiness. When a husband and wife go together frequently to the holy temple, kneel in prayer together in their home with their family, go hand in hand to their religious meetings, keep their lives wholly chaste, mentally and physically, so that their whole thoughts and desires and love are all centered in one being, their companion, and both are working together for the upbuilding of the kingdom of God, then happiness is at its pinnacle. (76-52)

Spouses of nonmembers must be patient. I can understand quite fully the problems that have arisen in your family life because of your conversion to the gospel of Jesus Christ sometimes called "Mormonism." It always has been so and sadly the future will continue to see it so. . . .

It would be our hope that, instead of bringing a chasm between your husband and you, the gospel could be the welding link that could bring you close together and finally into an unalterable, unterminating relationship with your precious children.

The Lord knew that it would not be easy for people to receive him and to accept his total truth. He knew full well that there would be numerous problems and misunderstandings between relatives and friends. . . .

It seems to me that your position would be to become the perfect wife and the perfect mother and make your husband love you so intensively that he would never give thought to the possibility of losing you for eternity, and that you would so thoroughly and properly rear your children so that their father would never entertain the thought of a possible loss of them.

As he studies the gospel, he must certainly come to a realization that the marriage of himself and you was a temporary matter and that the minister or other person who performed the ceremony made no claim that the marriage could last beyond death. Certainly, he will come to realize that death could come at any time and separate two people who are devoted to each other and love each other very much.

In my experience of many years, I have seen many unbelieving spouses finally brought into the Church in great happiness in the cases where there was long-suffering and deep understanding and much patience. (12/2/63)

The ideal spouse is constant. While one is young and well and strong and beautiful or handsome and attractive, he or she can (for the moment) almost name the price and write the ticket; but the time comes when these temporary things have had their day; when wrinkles come and aching joints; when hair is thin and bodies bulge; when nerves are frayed and tempers are taut; when wealth is dissipated; when man needs something firm and solid to hold to. There comes a time when those who flattered us and those whose wit and charm deceived us may leave us to our fate. Those are times when we want friends, good friends, common friends, loved ones, tied with immortal bonds—people who will nurse our illnesses, tolerate our eccentricities, and love us with pure, undefiled affection. Then we need an unspoiled companion who will not count our wrinkles, remember our stupidities nor remember our weaknesses; then is when we need a loving companion with whom we have suffered and wept and prayed and worshipped; one with whom we have suffered sorrow and disappointments, one who loves us for what we are or intend to be rather than what we appear to be in our gilded shell. (1/5/60)

Responsibility to spouse supersedes even children. The Lord says in definite terms: "Thou shalt love thy wife with all thy heart, and shall cleave unto her and none else." (D&C 42:22.)

The words *none else* eliminate everyone and everything. The spouse then becomes preeminent in the life of the husband or wife, and neither social life nor occupational life nor political life nor any other interest nor person nor thing shall ever take precedence over the companion spouse. We sometimes find women who absorb and hover over the children at the expense of the husband, sometimes even estranging them from him. This is in direct violation of the command: *None else.* (MF 251)

Sex in Marriage

Sex is for procreation and expression of love. It is the destiny of men and women to join together to make eternal family units. In the context of lawful marriage, the intimacy of sexual relations is right and divinely approved. There is nothing unholy or degrading about sexuality in itself, for by that means men and women join in a process of creation and in an expression of love. (PKSO 2)

The union of the sexes, husband and wife (and only husband and wife), was for the principal purpose of bringing children into the world. Sex experiences were never intended by the Lord to be a mere plaything or merely to satisfy passions and lusts. We know of no directive from the Lord that proper sex experience between husbands and wives need be limited totally to the procreation effort, but we find much evidence from Adam until now that no provision was ever made by the Lord for indiscriminate sex. (75-24)

Sexual relations in marriage are not unrestrained. Even though sex can be an important and satisfactory part of married life, we must remember that life is not designed just for sex. Even marriage does not make proper certain extremes in sexual indulgence. To the Ephesian saints Paul begged for propriety in marriage: "So ought men to love their wives as their own bodies. He that loveth his wife loveth himself." (Ephesians 5:28.) And perhaps the Lord's condemnation included secret sexual sins in marriage, when he said: "And those who are not pure, and have said they were pure, shall be destroyed, saith the Lord God." (D&C 132:52.) (MF 73)

If it is unnatural, you just don't do it. That is all, and all the family life should be kept clean and worthy and on a very high plane. There are some people who have said that behind the bedroom doors anything goes. That is not true and the Lord would not condone it. (78-33)

Divorce

Divorces often occur over sex, money, and child discipline. If you study the divorces, as we have had to do in these past years, you will find there are one, two, three, four reasons. Generally sex is the first. They did not get along sexually. They may not say that in the court. They may not even tell that to their attorneys, but that is the reason. ...Husband and wife...are authorized, in fact they are commanded, to have proper sex when they are properly married for time and eternity. That does not mean that we need to go to great extremes. That does not mean that a woman is the servant of her husband. It does not mean that any man has a right to demand sex anytime that he might want it. He should be reasonable and understanding and it should be a general program between the two, so they understand and everybody is happy about it....

Then of course finances come next—husbands who insist on being the financial manager and controlling everything....

The rearing of our children, that is important. Husbands take that all into their own hands. He tells the child what he cannot do and what he can do. That is another matter where parents should work together always. If the father says, "No, you can't," then the child can go to the mother and she says, "Yes, you can do it. It's all right," why, you have just destroyed the whole program. So if a husband and wife work together, the husband will always say, "Well, what did your mother say?" and the mother will say, "What did your daddy say? Well, that is what I say.'' It is always the same. Even if it is wrong, it is the same. If it is wrong you can go into the bedroom and lock the door and work it out later, but you do not do that before your children. . . .

It all comes back to one word, doesn't it: Selfishness. (74-33)

Divorces often result from disloyalty. Those who claim their love is dead should return home with all their loyalty, fidelity, honor, cleanliness—and the love which has become embers will flare up with scintillating flame again. If love wanes or dies, it is often infidelity of thought or act which gave the lethal potion. I plead with all people, young and old, bound by marriage vows and covenants to make that marriage holy, keep it fresh, express affection meaningfully and sincerely and often. Thus will one avoid the pitfalls which destroy marriages. (MF 251)

Every divorce is the result of selfishness on the part of one or the other or both parties to a marriage contract. Someone is thinking of self-comforts, conveniences, freedoms, luxuries, or ease. (76-52)

Nothing justifies infidelity. A husband and wife were quarreling and had reached such a degree of incompatibility that they had flung at each other the threat of divorce and had already seen attorneys. Both of them, embittered at each other, had found companionship with other parties. This was sin. No matter how bitter were their differences, neither had any right to begin courting or looking about for friends. And any dating or such association by wedded folk outside the marriage is iniquitous. Even though they proceeded with the divorce suit, to be moral and honorable they must wait until the divorce is final before either is justified in developing new romances. . . .

Nothing justifies evil. Two wrongs do not make one right. Spouses are sometimes inconsiderate, unkind, and difficult, and they must share the blame for broken homes, but this never justifies the other spouse's covetousness and unfaithfulness and infidelity. (62-09)

Divorce is an evil. Divorce is not a cure for difficulty, but is merely an escape, and a weak one.... The divorce itself does not constitute the entire evil, but the very acceptance of divorce as a cure is also a serious sin of this generation. Because a program or a pattern is universally accepted is not evidence that it is right. Marriage never was easy. It may never be. It brings with it sacrifice, sharing and a demand for great selflessness. (76-52)

Divorce selfishly hurts children. Certainly, selfishness is near its greatest peak when innocent children must suffer for the sins of their parents. Almost like a broken record come from divorcees that it is better to have them grow up in a single-parent home than a fighting home. The answer to that specious argument is: there need be no battling parents in fighting homes. (74-12)

Discourage divorce. Bishops, never encourage your members to get a divorce. Encourage them to be reconciled, to adjust their lives, their own personal lives generally. (76-26)

Most couples surmount problems. Perhaps you have thought that your home was the one home that was frustrated. You should know that most couples have their problems, that many couples master their problems, instead of permitting the problems to crush them. I think that most wives have shed bitter tears, and most husbands have lain sleepless hours over misunderstandings, but thanks be to the Lord that great numbers of these people have solved their difficulties. Partners stay in business together for years and years. They may be as different as fish and fowl, but because there is a great reason for their understanding of each other, they overlook each others' weaknesses, strengthen themselves, and work together. They seldom ever break up a partnership where they would both lose seriously by doing so. A celestial marriage is far more to fight for and to live for and adjust for, than any amount of money that two partners might have between them. (6/19/51)

Justifiable divorces are rare. I know there are many who feel that they have been justified, and there may have been some who were justified. We are not talking to them or of them. We are talking of the great majority that could have been salvaged, could have been saved if we had tried and tried hard enough. (74-39)

Relationship Between Men and Women

Marriage is a full partnership. When we speak of marriage as a partnership, let us speak of marriage as a *full* partnership. We do not want our LDS women to be *silent* partners or *limited* partners in that eternal assignment! Please be a *contributing* and *full* partner. (78-24)

In some places in the world, there are men who do not recognize their wives with full righteousness. The man and the wife are equals; one has to be in authority, and that is the man. That does not mean that he is superior. (77-13)

Men and women are complementary. I have mentioned only a few of the special blessings God gives his daughters in helping them to become like him. His sons have their own special opportunities. And in his wisdom and mercy, our Father made men and women dependent on each other for the full flowering of their potential. Because their natures are somewhat different, they can complement each other; because they are in many ways alike, they can understand each other. Let neither envy the other for their differences; let both discern what is superficial and what is beautifully basic in those differences, and act accordingly. And may the brotherhood of the priesthood and the sisterhood of the Relief Society be a blessing in the lives of all the members of this great Church, as we help each other along the path to perfection. (76-23)

We had full equality as his spirit children. We have equality as recipients of God's perfected love for each of us.... Within those great assurances, however, our roles and assignments differ. These are eternal differences—with women being given many tremendous responsibilities of motherhood and sisterhood and men being given the tremendous responsibilities of fatherhood and the priesthood—

but the man is not without the woman nor the woman without the man in the Lord (see 1 Corinthians 11:11). Both a righteous man and a righteous woman are a blessing to all those their lives touch.

Remember, in the world before we came here, faithful women were given certain assignments while faithful men were foreordained to certain priesthood tasks. While we do not now remember the particulars, this does not alter the glorious reality of what we once agreed to. (79-19)

The husband presides in marriage. In the beginning when God created man and the woman, he said to the woman, "Thy desire shall be to thy husband, and he shall rule [but I like the word *preside*] over thee." (Genesis 3:16.) (75-24)

The husband rules only by persuasion. "No power or influence . . . ought to be maintained by virtue of the priesthood." (D&C 121:41.)

We have heard of men who have said to their wives, "I hold the priesthood and you've got to do what I say." Such a man should be tried for his membership. Certainly he should not be honored in his priesthood. We rule in love and understanding. (75-11)

The wife follows the husband only as he follows Christ. No woman has ever been asked by the Church authorities to follow her husband into an evil pit. She is to follow him as he follows and obeys the Savior of the world, but in deciding this, she should always be sure she is fair. (75-46)

The husband is head of the family only insofar as he sacrifices for them. One of the most provocative and profound statements in holy writ is that of Paul wherein he directs husbands and wives in their duty to each other and to family. First, he commands the women:

"Wives, submit yourselves unto your own husbands, as unto the Lord.

"For the husband is the head of the wife, even as Christ is the head of the church: and he is the saviour of the body.

"Therefore as the church is subject unto Christ, so let the wives be to their own husbands in every thing." (Ephesians 5:22-24.)

This is no idle jest, no facetious matter. Much is said in those few words.

Paul says, "as unto the Lord."

A woman would have no fears of being imposed upon nor of any dictatorial measures nor of any improper demands if the husband is self-sacrificing and worthy. Certainly no sane woman would hesitate to give submission to her own really righteous husband in everything. We are sometimes shocked to see the wife take over the leadership, naming the one to pray, the place to be, the things to do.

Husbands are commanded: "Love your wives, even as Christ also loved the church, and gave himself for it." (Ephesians 5:25.)

Here is the answer: Christ loved the Church and its people so much that he voluntarily endured persecution for them, stoically withstood pain and physical abuse for them, and finally gave his precious life for them.

When the husband is ready to treat his household in that manner, not only the wife, but also all the family will respond to his leadership.

Certainly, if fathers are to be respected, they must merit respect; if they are to be loved, they must be consistent, lovable, understanding, and kind, and must honor their priesthood. (65-07)

Men often give women inadequate respect. I sometimes think our own Latter-day Saint women are "needy" just because some of us are not as thoughtful and considerate of them as we should be. Our pantries can be filled with food and yet our sisters can be starved for affection and recognition. (78-28)

Our sisters do not wish to be indulged or to be treated condescendingly; they desire to be respected and revered as our sisters and our equals. I mention all these things, my brethren, not because the doctrines or the teachings of the Church regarding women are in any doubt, but because in some situations our behavior is of doubtful quality. (79-21)

The Seductiveness of Two Incomes

Normally, the husband is the breadwinner. We believe that the place of the woman is in the home, as a general rule. We realize that some women may need to be employed when their children are grown, or when there have been problems in their home and the breadwinner has been taken from them. The most sacred privileges that a women could have are in the home, to be a partner with God in the creation of children. (73-11)

The Lord said women have claim upon their husbands for their maintenance until their husbands be taken (see D&C 83:2). Women are to take care of the family—the Lord has so stated—to be an assistant to the husband, to work with him, but not to earn the living, except in unusual circumstances. Men ought to be men indeed and earn the living under normal circumstances. (78-14)

When both spouses work, tensions result. Through both spouses working, competition rather than cooperation enters into the family. Two weary workers return home with taut nerves, individual pride, [and] increased independence, and then misunderstandings arise. Little frictions pyramid into monumental ones. Frequently spouses sinfully turn to new and old romances and finally the seeming inevitable break comes through a divorce with its heartaches, bitterness, and disillusionments, and always ugly scars. (76-59)

From such homes come many conflicts, marital problems, and divorces, and delinquent children. Few people in trouble ever ascribe their marital conflicts to these first causes, but blame each other for the problems which were born and nurtured in strained environments. Certainly the harmonious relationship of father and mother and the emotional climate prevailing between parents give soundness and security to children. (63-07)

Pursuit of luxury prejudices children. Too many mothers work away from home to furnish sweaters and music lessons and trips and fun for their children. Too many women spend their time in socializing, in politicking, in public services when they should be home to teach and train and receive and love their children into security. (62-10)

Rationalization can make convenience into necessity. Some women, because of circumstances beyond their control, must work. We understand that. We understand further that as families are raised, the talents God has given you and blessed you with can often be put to effective use in additional service to mankind. Do not, however, make the mistake of being drawn off into secondary tasks which will cause the neglect of your eternal assignments such as giving birth to and rearing the spirit children of our Father in Heaven. Pray carefully over all your decisions. (79-19)

Let every working mother honestly weigh the matter and be sure the Lord approves before she rushes her babies off to the nursery, her children off to school, her husband off to work, and herself off to her employment. Let her be certain that she is not rationalizing herself away from her children merely to provide for them greater material things. Let her analyze well before she permits her precious ones to come home to an empty house where their plaintive cry, "Mother," finds no loving answer. (63-07)

Magnifying Womanhood

Women's roles require development of many skills. We delight and marvel in the appropriate development and expressions of our sisters' many talents. Surely the Church's educational effort in behalf of its women is a sermon in itself.

Perhaps more than any other people of like size, we are deeply committed to the development of the skills and talents of our sisters, for we believe our educational program is not simply education for this world, but involves an education for all eternity.

The Church of Jesus Christ of Latter-day Saints has sponsored the advancement of women from its very outset. It was the Prophet Joseph Smith who set forth the ideals for womanhood. He advocated liberally for women in the purest sense of the word, and he gave them liberty to fully express themselves as mothers, as nurses to the sick, as proponents of high community ideals, and as protectors of good morals. (78-06)

Every girl, and I say every girl, should prepare herself for marriage and for domestic responsibilities. You are not reading that in the magazines today, but it's true nevertheless. She should be encouraged to be proud to prepare for true womanly service. She should become skilled in things that are useful and enriching to her family life. She should develop her talents, strengthen her knowledge and testimony of the gospel, and be eager to serve others. Some girls may be called on full-time missions, and all will have the opportunity to be highly useful in the kingdom of God if they prepare themselves.... We want our women to be well educated, for children may not recover from the ignorance of their mothers. (75-45)

Mary, you are to become a career woman in the greatest career on earth—that of homemaker, wife, and mother. And so, if you have failed to prepare for motherhood and homemaking when you could, you may make up somewhat by devoting yourself to those subjects now. In your spare time you could now study child psychology and child discipline, the fundamentals of nursing, the art of teaching, particularly how to tell stories and teach children; and you will want to get all the theory as well as the practice now in cooking, sewing, budgeting, and buying. John's limited income will spread far if you can learn to buy efficiently and cook expertly so that there will never be waste. And his small compensation can go far if you learn to make your own clothes and those for the children and utilize scraps and pick up bargains. And if you learn the rudiments of nursing, you may be able to save much in doctor and hospital costs by recognizing symptoms and treating minor afflictions, and you may also have the satisfaction of even saving the lives of your own precious family by your being able to do practical nursing. And so your economies will largely make up for the loss of your own income. (49-01)

Women should be students of scripture. We want our homes to be blessed with sister scriptorians—whether you are single or married, young or old, widowed or living in a family.

Regardless of your particular circumstances, as you become more and more familiar with the truths of the scriptures, you will be more and more effective in keeping the second great commandment, to love your neighbor as yourself. Become scholars of the scriptures—not to put others down, but to lift them up! After all, who has any greater need to "treasure up" the truths of the gospel (on which they may call in their moments of need) than do women and mothers who do so much nurturing and teaching? (79-19)

Women should be well-read. It is true of all of us that, as we progress spiritually, our sense of belonging, identity, and self-worth increases. Let us create a climate in which we encourage the sisters of the Church to have a program of personal improvement. It ought to be a practical and realistic program, which is determined personally and not imposed upon them. Yet it ought to cause them to reach for new levels of achievement. We are not asking for something spectacular, but rather for the women of the Church to find real self-fulfillment through wise self-development in the pursuit of righteous and worthy endeavors.

We should be as concerned with the woman's capacity to communicate as we are to have her sew and preserve food. Good women are articulate as well as affectionate. One skill or one attribute need not be developed at the expense of another. Symmetry in our spiritual development is much to be desired. We are as anxious for women to be wise in the management of their time as we are for women to be wise stewards of the family's storehouse of food.

We know that women who have deep appreciation for the past will be concerned about shaping a righteous future. We desire women to develop social refinements because these are very real dimensions of keeping the second great commandment—to love one's neighbor as oneself. We know that women who will improve their relationships with the Father in Heaven will also improve their relationships with their neighbors.

The women of God in all ages have been able to reflect with awe upon the handiwork of God in the heavens without neglecting the practical skills needed not only to survive on this planet but to live an abundant life. There is more of a connection than many realize between the order and purpose of the universe and the order and harmony which exists in a happy and good family. (78-24)

Mothers use leadership skills in family. Women have unique opportunities to grow in leadership skills. Do you think of leadership as telling others what to do, or as making all the decisions? Not so. Leadership is the ability to encourage the best efforts of others in working toward a desirable goal. Who has more significant opportunities to lead than a mother who guides her children toward perfection, or the wife who daily counsels with her husband that they may grow together? The tremendous contribution in leadership made by women in the auxiliaries of the Church and in their communities is likewise beyond measure. (76-23)

Mothers' prayers are powerful. A mother may pray with her children and call down the Lord's blessings upon them. She does not act by virtue of priesthood conferred upon her, but by virtue of her God-given responsibility to govern her household in righteousness. (74-31)

Righteous women will cause major Church growth. Finally, my dear sisters, may I suggest to you something that has not been said before or at least in quite this way. Much of the major growth that is coming to the Church in the last days will come because many of the good women of the world (in whom there is often such an inner sense of spirituality) will be drawn to the Church in large numbers. This will happen to the degree that the women of the Church reflect righteousness and articulateness in their lives and to the degree that the women of the Church are seen as distinct and different—in happy ways—from the women of the world.

Among the real heroines in the world who will come into the Church are women who are more concerned with being righteous than with being selfish. These real heroines have true humility, which places a higher value on integrity than on visibility. Remember, it is as wrong to do things just to be seen of women as it is to do things to be seen of men. Great women and men are always more anxious to serve than to have dominion. (79-19)

CHAPTER 12

Family Relationships

Childbearing

God established families. The Lord organized the whole program in the beginning with a father who procreates, provides, and loves and directs, and a mother who conceives and bears and nurtures and feeds and trains. The Lord could have organized it otherwise but chose to have a unit with responsibility and purposeful associations where children train and discipline each other and come to love, honor, and appreciate each other. The family is the great plan of life as conceived and organized by our Father in Heaven.

To any thoughtful person it must be obvious that intimate association without marriage is sin; that children without parenthood and family life is tragedy; that society without basic family life is without foundation and will disintegrate into nothingness and oblivion. (73-02)

We must share the gift of life. John and Mary, tomorrow when I repeat the phrases which will bind you for eternity, I shall say the same impressive words which the Lord said to that handsome youth and his lovely bride in the Garden of Eden: "Be fruitful, and multiply, and replenish the earth." (Genesis 1:28.) The Lord does not waste words. He meant what he said. You did not come on earth just to "eat, drink, and be merry." You came knowing full well your responsibilities. You came to get for yourself a mortal body which could become perfected and immortalized, and you understood that you were to act in partnership with God in providing bodies for other spirits equally anxious to come to the earth for righteous purposes. And so you will not postpone parenthood. There will be rationalists who will name to you numerous reasons for postponement. Of course, it will be harder to get your college degrees or your financial starts with a family, but strength like yours will be undaunted in the face of difficult obstacles. Have your family as the Lord intended. Of course it is expensive, but you will find a way, and besides, it is often those children who grow up with responsibility and hardships who carry on the world and its work. And, John and Mary, do not limit your family as the world does. . . .

Don't think you will love the later ones less or have fewer material things for them. Perhaps, like Jacob, you might love the eleventh one most. Young folk, have your family, love them, sacrifice for them, teach them righteousness, and you will be blessed and happy all the days of your eternal lives. (49-01)

Have large families regardless of social norms. In America and elsewhere in the world, the family limitation program is gaining much strength. Latter-day Saints do not believe in this. We believe in following the admonition of the Lord in having large families and rearing them righteously. We hope that our Latter-day Saints will not trade children for accommodation and luxury.

When you go to the temple for sealing, you will note that the Lord continues to command his people to live this commandment. It is not easy. It is much easier to limit the family to one or two, but great blessings come to those who struggle through the years with the small children. When they have reared them righteously, they will have crowns throughout eternity. The time will come when those men and women who have neglected their duties because they wanted luxuries will be very jealous of the joys and happiness of those who sacrificed in the early years of marriage. Certainly we do not just wish to bring children in the world and turn them loose to go wild. We must rear them in righteousness. Generally, you will find that the people that come from the large families are generally the best trained and the most faithful. (62-04)

Motherhood and fatherhood are primary. Now, it is wise for every young woman to be grateful for her womanhood and her privilege to create, with her husband and the Eternal God as her partners. To be a mother, to be a wife of a good man—what a great joy! While she is waiting for that holy, sacred hour, let her be happy and content to develop her mind and accumulate knowledge and prepare herself emotionally and spiritually for the happy times.

For the young man, his education is important, his mission vital; but his proper marriage and his proper life to be a righteous father and to properly provide for and give leadership to a family—that is wonderful, a wonderful role in life to play. (74-27)

Motherhood is a noble work. Motherhood is a holy calling, a sacred dedication for carrying out the Lord's work, a consecration and devotion to the rearing and fostering, the nurturing of body, mind, and spirit of those who kept their first estate and who came to this earth for their second estate to learn and be tested and to work toward godhood. . . .

Mothers have a sacred role. They are partners with God, as well as with their own husbands, first in giving birth to the Lord's spirit children, and then in rearing those children so they will serve the Lord and keep his commandments. Could there be a more sacred trust than to be a trustee for honorable, well-born, well-developed children? . . .

So our beloved mother Eve began the human race with gladness, wanting children, glad for the joy that they would bring to her, willing to assume the problems connected with a family, but also the joys. (75-46)

To be a righteous woman during the winding-up scenes on this earth, before the Second Coming of our Savior, is an especially noble calling. The righteous woman's strength and influence today can be tenfold what it might be in more tranquil times. She has been placed here to help to enrich, to protect, and to guard the home—which is society's basic and most noble institution. Other institutions in society may falter and even fail, but the righteous woman can help to save the home, which may be the last and only sanctuary some mortals know in the midst of storm and strife. (78-06)

I wish to say without equivocation that a woman will find no greater satisfaction and joy and peace and make no greater contribution to mankind than in being a wise and worthy woman and raising good children. (78-14)

When we sing that doctrinal hymn and anthem of affection, "O My Father," we get a sense of the ultimate in maternal modesty, of the restrained, queenly elegance of our heavenly mother, and knowing how profoundly our mortal mothers have shaped us here, do we suppose her influence on us as individuals to be less if we live so as to return there? . . .

God has placed women at the very headwaters of the human stream. So much of what our men and our institutions seek to do downstream in the lives of erring individuals is done to compensate for early failures. Likewise, so much of life's later rejoicing is a reflection of a woman's work well done at the headwaters of the home. (78-06)

Come home, wives, to your children, born and unborn. Wrap the motherly cloak about you and, unembarrassed, help in a major role to create bodies for the immortal souls who anxiously wait.

When you have fully complemented your husband in home life and borne the children, growing up full of faith, integrity, responsibility, and goodness, then you have achieved, your accomplishments supreme, without peer, and you will be the envy through time and eternity of your sisters who have spent themselves in selfish pursuits. (77-39)

Technology frees time for better child rearing. Today's women, especially in the United States and some other countries, have ease, comfort, leisure, conveniences, and time, such as no other women in history have had.

What has she done with her new-found liberties and freedoms and opportunities and time? Has she perfected her own life? Is she more dutiful and faithful to her reduced home duties than was her great-grandmother with her multiplicity of arduous ones? Is today's woman a better wife to her husband? Is the modern, electrically driven home of today a happier haven of refuge than the four walls of the last centuries? Is she today a better, more congenial neighbor than yesterday's woman? Does she have more children now that she has more time, better facilities, and more help? Does she train her children better than her ancestors did? Does she herself have more faith and piety than the women of old? And does she better instill into her children the faith which will make gods of them?

God bless the women, the wonderful women of every time and age and place, who establish first in their lives their Lord, his work, and their families. (58-01)

Women who are deliberately childless will regret it. I am not sorry for women who sacrifice their lives for children. I am not sorry for those women who have many children. But I am sorry . . . for women who come to the Judgment Day who have never assumed the responsibility of rearing children, who have been afraid of pain, resistant to sacrifice. They are the ones whose hearts will be heavy. . . .

I know there are many women who could not have children— God bless them! (54-03)

Childbearing should not be delayed for convenience. After marriage young wives should be occupied in bearing and rearing children. I know of no scriptures or authorities which authorize young wives to delay their families or to go to work to put their husbands through college. Young married couples can make their way and reach their educational heights, if they are determined. (74-21)

Supreme happiness in marriage is governed considerably by a

primary factor—that of the bearing and rearing of children. Too many young people set their minds, determining they will not marry or have children until they are more secure, until the military service period is over; until the college degree is secured; until the occupation is more well-defined; until the debts are paid; or until it is more convenient. They have forgotten that the first commandment is to "be fruitful, and multiply, and replenish the earth, and subdue it." (Genesis 1:28.) And so brides continue their employment and husbands encourage it, and contraceptives are used to prevent conception. Relatives and friends and even mothers sometimes encourage birth control for their young newlyweds. But the excuses are many, mostly weak. The wife is not robust; the family budget will not feed extra mouths; or the expense of the doctor, hospital, and other incidentals is too great; it will disturb social life; it would prevent two salaries; and so abnormal living prevents the birth of children. The Church cannot approve nor condone the measures which so greatly limit the family....

How do you suppose that the Lord would look upon a man and a woman whose marriage seems to be largely for the purpose of living together and sex gratification without the responsibilities of marriage? How do you think that the Lord looks upon those who use the contraceptives because in their selfish life it is not the convenient moment to bear children? How do you feel the Lord looks upon those who would trade flesh-and-blood children for pianos or television or furniture or an automobile, and is this not actually the case when people will buy these luxuries and yet cannot afford to have their children? Are there not numerous people who first buy the luxury article and then find they cannot pay the doctor or a hospital bill incident to childbirth? How do you think the Lord feels about women who forego the pleasures and glories of motherhood that they might retain their figures, that their social life might not be affected, that they might avoid the deprivations, pains, and agonies of childbearing and birthing? How do you think the Lord feels as he views healthy parents who could have children but who deliberately close the doors by operation or by contraceptives, close the doors upon spirits eager to enter into mortal bodies? (77-39)

Not everyone can have children. We realize, of course, there are some women who cannot have children, some men who cannot reproduce. The Lord will take care of all that if we have done everything in our power, if we have done what we could to make ourselves normal and productive and to follow the commandments of the Lord. (74-39)

Few couples need remain childless. Men and women who have been unable to have children should build their faith. Many a barren woman like Sarah has had children through special blessings of the Lord. She was blessed in having a son—a son to a barren woman.

Sometimes operations or adjustments or hormones may make parenthood possible. Frequently fears and frictions and tenseness are causes for barrenness and sterility. Such people should do everything in their power to put themselves in a position to have their babies. Adoption of parentless children brings joy to many hearts. Few, if any, parents need be childless through their years. (77-39)

Mother's health should be considered. In family life, men must and should be considerate of their wives, not only in the bearing of children, but in caring for them through childhood. The mother's health must be conserved, and the husband's consideration for his wife is his first duty, and self-control a dominant factor in all their relationships. (76-54)

Sterilization as a medical measure is a serious personal responsibility. On . . . sterilization or other surgery to prevent conception . . . the Church has felt that it was the individual responsibility of the couple; and while the Church leaves it to the individual to determine whether the ill health of the mother is sufficient to warrant the surgery which would make pregnancy impossible, yet it is a definite personal responsibility. In your case, since the surgery has already been completed, it cannot be undone, so it must be accepted as a fact and life can go on. Both parents should give themselves totally and fully to the rearing of their six children which they now have in a loving home with ideal surroundings. (12/16/64)

Sterilization to avoid the inconvenience of children is sinful. We marry for eternity. We are serious about this. We become parents and bring wanted children into the world and rear and train them to righteousness.

We are aghast at the reports of young people going to surgery to limit their families and the reputed number of parents who encourage this vasectomy. Remember that the coming of the Lord approaches, and some difficult-to-answer questions will be asked by a divine Judge who will be hard to satisfy with silly explanations and rationalizations. He will judge justly, you may be sure. (74-30)

Sterilization and tying of tubes and such are sins, and except under special circumstances it cannot be approved. (72-02)

The world can provide for growing population. Many people, some of them innocently caught up in the whirlpool of delusion errors, are worrying about the earth failing to provide for the on-coming generations. They take such means to influence the thinking of the people and repeat it so often that many of us were gullible and accepted it. We tend to believe what the world says. We often do not even ask what the Lord's program is. (72-02)

Training Children Spiritually

Children have destiny equal to our own. We do not rear children just to please our vanity. We bring children into the world to become kings and queens, and priests and priestesses for our Lord. (75-09)

Many people in the Church do not have the right concept of a child. They think that he is a personality to play with, to dress, to enjoy, to have, to hold. They never think seriously about the tremendous responsibility of developing that little spirit without earthly knowledge into a fit subject for the kingdom of God. (59-03)

Parents must rear children in righteousness. The family is the basic unit of the kingdom of God on earth. The Church can be no healthier than its families. No government can long endure without strong families. (78-07)

It is the duty of parents to so teach by example and precept that the child will fill the measure of his creation and find his way back to the glories of exaltation. Wise parents will see to it that their teaching is orthodox, character-building, and faith-promoting. (46-02)

It is the responsibility of the parents to teach their children. The Sunday School, the Primary, the MIA and other organizations of the Church play a secondary role. . . .

The Lord . . . gave us this law: when the child is eight years of age, he should have been trained—not that he should *begin* to be trained, as many of our parents surmise. (59-03)

Our Heavenly Father placed the responsibility upon parents to see that their children are well fed, well groomed and clothed, well trained, and well taught. Most parents protect their children with shelter—they tend and care for their diseases, provide clothes for their safety and their comfort, and supply food for their health and growth. But what do they do for their souls?

On a cold winter day most children set out for school warmly clothed. The soles of their shoes are thick, and they wear boots over them. They wear heavy coats, with scarves around their necks and mittens on their hands—all to protect them from the inclemency of the weather. But are these same children protected against the mistaken ideologies and ideas of other youth and the temptations of the day?

The skin diver wears a heavy rubber suit to protect his body from the cold, but are children protected by prayer and family unity and spiritual training to shield them from the cold, dark world in which they eat and drink and sleep and play?

The outdoor worker is protected against the elements by proper apparel, but how often are children fully protected by a life of family devotion, family love and respect, family understanding, proper training and discipline? (78-03)

Parents must not neglect spiritual training. How many parents there are who carefully supervise the training of their children in manners, recreation, and music, but leave the immature mind to grow up in a spiritual vacuum! I have heard them say: "I am going to leave Johnny free to choose his own religious thought." Isn't it likely that Johnny will leave his religious activity unpracticed the same as his music lesson without urging from his parents? (56-01)

Parents must first teach of Christ. We can see that not all activities we could engage in are of equal weight, even though they may appropriately be a part of a spiritually balanced family unity development program. Some concerns have higher priorities. We remember the words of Nephi as he counseled: "And we talk of Christ, we rejoice in Christ, we preach of Christ, we prophesy of Christ . . . that our children may know to what source they may look." (2 Nephi 25:26.) What inner strength would be in every person if he knew that the Master and His teachings were indeed his great source of guidance, his great source of correct example, his great source of help! That is our prime goal in all our teaching in the home. (82-01)

Parents build reservoirs of faith. I realized that there should be reservoirs of knowledge to meet the future needs; reservoirs of courage to overcome the floods of fear that put uncertainty in lives; storage of physical strength to help us meet the frequent contaminations and contagions; reservoirs of goodness; reservoirs of stamina; reservoirs of faith. Yes, reservoirs of faith so that when the world presses in upon us, we stand firm and strong; when the temptations of a decaying world about us draw on our energies, sap our spiritual vitality, and seek to pull us down to the level of the worldly world, we need a storage of faith that can carry youth through the tantalizing teens and through the problems of later years. Faith to carry us over the dull, the difficult, the terrifying moments, disappointments, disillusionments, and years of adversity, want, confusion, and frustration.

And who are to build these reservoirs? Is this not the reason that
God gave to every child two parents?

Who else but the forebears would clear the forests, plow the land,
carve out the futures? Who else would set up the businesses, dig the
canals, survey the territory? Who else would plant the orchards, start
the vineyards, erect the homes?

In his omniscience, our God gave to every child a father and
mother to pioneer the way. And so it is those parents who sired them
and bore them who are expected to lay foundations and to hold the
hands through the tender years to build the barns and tanks and bins
and reservoirs. . . .

Every family is urged to engage in regular night and morning
family prayers and to devote at least one evening a week at home in
the sweet family togetherness undisturbed by the world or any of its
allurements. They will plan to turn off the TV and radio, leave the
telephone unanswered, cancel all calls or appointments, and spend a
warm, homey evening together.

While one objective is reached by merely being together, yet the
additional and greater value can come from the lessons of life. The
father will teach the children. Here they can learn integrity, honor,
dependableness, sacrifice, and faith in God. Life's experiences and
the scriptures are the basis of the teaching and this, wrapped up in
filial and parental love, makes an impact nothing else can make.
Thus, reservoirs of righteousness are filled to carry children through
the dark days of temptation and desire, of drought and skepticism.
As they grow up, the children cooperate in building this storage for
themselves and the family. . . .

I like to compare the home evening, family prayer, and other
associated activities of the Church for the saving of the family, when
they are conscientiously carried out, with an umbrella. If the
umbrella is not opened up, it is little more than a cane and can give
little protection from the storms of nature. Likewise, God-given plans
are of little value unless they are used.

The umbrella spread out makes the silken material taut. When the
rain falls, it runs off; when the snow falls, it slides off; when the hail
comes, it bounces off; when the wind blows, it is diverted around the

umbrella. And in like manner, this spiritual umbrella wards off the foes of ignorance, superstition, skepticism, apostasy, immorality, and other forms of godlessness. (69-08)

Parental training often brings rebellious children back. The icebergs spawned by the Greenland ice sheet follow a highly predictable course. As the silent Labrador Current ceaselessly moves to the south through Baffin Bay and Davis Strait, it takes with it these mountainous icebergs, even against the force of the winds and the waves and the tides. Currents have much more power to control their course than the surface winds. . . .

The current of our life, as defined and developed in the lives of a family by the righteous teaching of parents, will often control the direction children will go, in spite of the waves and winds of numerous adverse influences of the world of error. . . .

I have sometimes seen children of good families rebel, resist, stray, sin, and even actually fight God. In this they bring sorrow to their parents, who have done their best to set in movement a current and to teach and live as examples. But I have repeatedly seen many of these same children, after years of wandering, mellow, realize what they have been missing, repent, and make great contribution to the spiritual life of their community. The reason I believe this can take place is that, despite all the adverse winds to which these people have been subjected, they have been influenced still more, and much more than they realized, by the current of life in the homes in which they were reared. When, in later years, they feel a longing to recreate in their own families the same atmosphere they enjoyed as children, they are likely to turn to the faith that gave meaning to their parents' lives.

There is no guarantee, of course, that righteous parents will succeed always in holding their children, and certainly they may lose them if they do not do all in their power. The children have their free agency.

But if we as parents fail to influence our families and set them on the "strait and narrow way," then certainly the waves, the winds of temptation and evil will carry the posterity away from the

path.... What we do know is that righteous parents who strive to
develop wholesome influences for their children will be held blame-
less at the last day, and that they will succeed in saving most of their
children, if not all. (74-31)

Parents' Obligations Toward Children

Parental care cannot be delegated. We have often said, "This
divine service of motherhood can be rendered only by mothers." It
may not be passed to others. Nurses cannot do it; public nurseries
cannot do it. Hired help cannot do it; kind relatives cannot do it.
Only by mother, aided as much as may be by a loving father, brothers
and sisters, and other relatives, can the full needed measure of
watchful care be given. (75-46)

Presence of parent offers security. At a distant conference, my
plane brought me to the city many hours early. The stake president
met me at the airport and took me to his home and, having important
work to do, excused himself and returned to his work. With the
freedom of the house, I spread my papers on the kitchen table and
began my work. His wife was upstairs sewing. In midafternoon, there
came an abrupt entry from the front door, and a little fellow came
running in, surprised to see me, but we became friends. Then he ran
through the rooms calling, "Mother," and she answered from
upstairs, "What is it, darling?" and his answer was, "Oh, nothing."
He went out to play.

A little later another voice came in the front door calling,
"Mother, Mother." He put his schoolbooks on the table and
explored the house until the reassuring answer came from upstairs
again, "Here I am, darling," and the second one was satisfied and
said, "OK" and went to play. Another half hour and the door
opened again and a young teenager moved in, dropped her books,
and called, "Mother." And the answer from upstairs, "Yes,
darling," seemed to satisfy, and the young girl became acquainted
with me, then began practicing her music lesson. None of the three
had gone upstairs.

Still another voice later called, "Mother," as she unloaded her high school books. And, again the sweet answer, "I am up here sewing, darling," seemed to reassure her. We became acquainted, and she tripped up the stairs to tell her mother the happenings of the day in a sweet mother-daughter relationship. Home! Mother! Security! Just to know Mother was home. All was well. . . .

A child needs a mother available more than all the things which money can buy. (63-07)

Responsibility for training children cannot be shifted to agencies. There seems to be a growing tendency to shift this responsibility from the home to outside influences such as the school and the church, and, of greater concern, to various child-care agencies and institutions. Important as these outward influences may be, they never can adequately take the place of the influence of the mother and the father. Constant training, constant vigilance, companionship, and being watchmen of our own children are necessary in order to keep our homes intact and to bless our children in the Lord's own way. (79-03)

Can it be arrested? Can we turn the tide and bring back decency and order out of chaos?

The answer is yes—a positive, stentorian *yes.* But the solution is not easy. If it could be solved with money, people would tax themselves to curb it. If penal or correctional institutions would suffice, a great building program would be initiated. If additional social workers could prevail, universities would add courses in social work. If courts and judges, attorneys and policemen, prisons and penitentiaries could stop the onrush of delinquency, such institutions would be dotted over all the land. But such means only salve it over temporarily, effecting no permanent cure.

However, the Lord has given us a plan, within our capacity to follow, but ignored by the masses because it requires that sacrifice and dedication that men are reluctant to give. (74-23)

Fathers have great responsibility for child rearing. We hope the fathers will take a more definite interest in the rearing of their children. It isn't enough for a father to provide just for the means. (76-38)

Some men think it is not manly to do anything in the home. But truly it is manly if a father takes care of his children and snuggles them close to him. (76-47)

The father must help the mother in rearing the children. It is said that when the child is two or three years old is the best time for the father to express a great influence with him. The father and mother together should rear their children. The father does not leave it to the mother only. The child gets its general attitudes from the father early in life. (76-49)

When you are judged by the great Judge, he will say, "Where are your sons? Where are your daughters? And why aren't they here in this family relationship?" Some of us try to make a lot of excuses, but I think the Judge will say, "I am not here to listen to excuses. I am here to check on your sons and daughters to see if they have been properly fathered." (76-39)

Fathers must merit respect. Certainly, if fathers are to be respected, they must merit respect—if they are to be loved, they must be consistent, lovable, understanding, and kind—and they must honor their priesthood. They must see themselves as fortunate trustees of precious spirit children whom God has entrusted to their care.

What a great incentive a mother has to honor and build up her worthy husband in the esteem of the offspring when she knows that this contributes to the well-adjusted lives of her children. And what a great incentive the father has for rising to his tallest spiritual stature to merit the love and respect of all members of the family.

And so we plead with you fathers to return to your little kingdoms and, with kindness, justice, proper discipline, and love, to inspire your family. We appeal to mothers to help create that happy family relationship. We desire that our people strengthen their families according to the pattern set by Abraham. We need to prepare all within our homes to serve beyond our homes, as calls and opportunities come to provide leaven for the world that wants for what we have. (75-45)

Fathers can give blessings. We hope you fathers will give blessings to your own children when they leave home to go to school, on missions, or wherever they may go. That is the privilege of the father. (75-04)

At one time a young man asked me for a blessing. "Wouldn't you like your father to give you this blessing?" I asked. "You are going a long way from home under difficult circumstances." He replied, "I don't think my father would want to give it to me." I said, "Oh, I am sure he would if he thought you desired it." A little later I found his father and asked, "Wouldn't you like to give your boy a blessing?" The father answered, "Oh, I don't think the boy would want me to. He would like you to." I said, "No, I think he would like you to do it." (The proper father-son relationship had never been fully developed.) The father said that he wouldn't know how, and I said that I would help him. So a little later, before the evening was over, we found ourselves in a back room, the boy sitting in a chair, the father's hands and mine upon his head. Somewhat haltingly and with just a little help the father gave his son a beautiful blessing, and they went into each other's arms and a beautiful father-son relationship was developed. (62-08)

Men are to bless families with the priesthood. True wives understand that their husbands hold the priesthood and that it has virtue within it—the power to bless, the power to heal, the power to counsel. Every father should rise to his tallest stature as he governs his family, his wife, and his children. (75-09)

A family may dedicate a home that is paid for. I was just wondering—how many of you folks have *your* homes dedicated as this one will be today? I remember when my youngest son came home from his mission. We had moved from Arizona, had purchased a new home, had moved into it, and were quite comfortable, and we called all the family together and invited this youngest son who had just filled his mission to offer the dedicatory prayer on our home. So we feel that that home is blessed, and it has a special significance. It belongs to the Lord, and we have the opportunity of using it. Of course, that means we have to pay for our homes, and that is something else, isn't it? In this day of great financing, where you can get any amount of money at any time, on any thing, almost, it is quite a temptation to live in a house that belongs to the bank, or the government, or somebody else.

When I was a little boy, I remember from my infancy that the Presidency and the Council of the Twelve, when they came to our stake, they would say, "Own your own home. Build your own home, and dedicate your own home." (76-58)

Teaching Children to Do Right

Children deserve love and discipline. Great, overwhelming, natural love, as taught by the Church in its total program, should be the blessing of the child from conception to its death. (71-17)

There are not enough good homes. Children still come to some homes where they will be abused, not loved, and not taught the truth.

We are greatly concerned with the fact that the press continues to report many cases of child abuse. We are much concerned that there would be a single parent that would inflict damages on a child. The Lord loved little children, and he said:

"Suffer little children, and forbid them not, to come unto me: for of such is the kingdom of heaven." (Matthew 19:14.) . . .

Let no Latter-day Saint parent ever be guilty of the heinous crime of abusing one of Christ's little ones! (78-06)

Discipline is probably one of the most important elements in which a mother and father can lead and guide and direct their children. It certainly would be well for parents to understand the rule given to the priesthood in section 121. Setting limits to what a child can do means to that child that you love him and respect him. If you permit the child to do all the things he would like to do without any limits, that means to him that you do not care much about him. (76-18)

Involve children in family activities. If there is to be a contribution to the building fund or the Red Cross, or a Saturday morning spent helping the elders quorum paint a widow's house, make sure the children are aware of it, and if it is feasible, let them have a share in the decision making and in the implementation of the decision. All the family could attend the baptism, confirmation, and ordination of a member of the family. All of the family could root for a son who is on the ball team. All meet regularly in home evening, at mealtime, at prayer time. Perhaps all of the family could pay tithing together, and each learns by precept and example the beautiful principle. . . .

In this inspired program the parents, and especially the father, will teach the children. And it is available to the people of the world regardless to what church they may belong. It provides a formal meeting and a planned program and consistent teaching of the gospel of Christ with participation in the reading of the scriptures and in the program by the children and parents. Each child has his own scriptures. The organizational teachings may complement the home teaching. (65-07)

Teach by establishing good family patterns. How do you teach your children tithing? Do you give many words trying to explain what the law is, or do they learn tithing like I learned it? When I was a little boy about four years old, my father had gone to work on Monday morning and my mother took my brothers and sisters and myself to see the bishop. (You see, my mother had eleven children). There were about four or five that were not in school, so Monday morning we started out on the road with two buckets of eggs. I was like many other little boys, I could ask many questions, and I said: "Where are we going, Ma?" and she said, "We are going to the bishop's," and I said, "Why are we going to the bishop's?" "These are tithing eggs," she said. Then I said, "Ma, what is tithing?" And then she explained, "Every time we take ten eggs out of the nest, we put one in a special bucket. The other nine we take to the store to buy clothes and food with and so these eggs in this special bucket keep increasing until we have a bucket full. And then every week we take them to the bishop and he gives us a receipt showing that we have paid our tithing."

Then, when I was a little bigger boy, I used to put up hay. I would drive the horses that were hitched to the wagon and tramp the hay down and my older brothers pitched it on the wagon, and when we had gone to the field in the morning, my father would say, "Now, boys, this is the tenth load this morning. This belongs to the Lord. You go up into the upper part where the hay is the best and get a big load and then take it over to the big barn in which the bishop keeps the Church hay." In that way I learned how to pay tithing, so it isn't hard for me to obey this law. (52-07)

The child will carry into his own life much that he sees in his family home life. If he sees his parents going to the temple frequently, he will begin to plan a temple life. If he is taught to pray for the missionaries, he will gradually gravitate toward the missionary program. Now, this is very simple, but it is the way of life. And we promise you that your children will bring you honor and glory as you give them proper example and training. (75-41)

The home should be a place where reliance on the Lord is a matter of common experience, not reserved for special occasions. One way of establishing that is by regular, earnest prayer. It is not enough just to pray. It is essential that we really speak to the Lord, having faith that he will reveal to us as parents what we need to know and do for the welfare of our families. It has been said of some men that when they prayed, a child was likely to open his eyes to see if the Lord were really there, so personal and direct was the petition. (74-31)

Teach children about sex. The home is the teaching situation [for sex education]. Every father should talk to his son, every mother to her daughter. Then it would leave them totally without excuse should they ignore the counsel they have received. (74-30)

Children must be taught that sex is not for ordinary conversation. It is not for regular thought consumption, and parents must teach their children that sex must be inseparably linked through proper marriage. (62-10)

Discourage premature sophistication. Mothers are not kind to little ladies to permit or encourage for them high heels or makeup or tight, short, grown-up dresses, or bold and eccentric hairdos. (65-10)

Teach children honesty. A parent who understates the age of the child to avoid adult prices in shows and planes and trains and buses is forcefully teaching the child to be dishonest. He will not forget these lessons. Some parents permit the child to break the law as to fire-crackers, the use of guns, fishing and hunting without license. The children are permitted to drive without a license or to falsify their ages. Those who take little things without accounting for them, such as fruit from the neighbor's yard, a pen from a desk, a package of gum from the help-yourself shelf, all are being taught silently that little thefts and dishonesties are not so bad. Cheating in school examinations has reached an alarming state, say the school officials.

We may be bucking a strong tide, but we must teach our children that sin is sin. (66-07)

Guide children's reading. Happy is the family whose members have learned to make good books their companions. The need of guidance by parents, teachers, and Church organizations is apparent, that the minds of children be properly stirred and fed. One is literally what he thinks, and his thinking is greatly influenced by what he reads. (63-06)

Children participate in family council. Concerning the governing of our families, we have been correctly taught that the family council is the most basic council of the Church. Under the direction of the father and mother, who should also counsel together, family councils may discuss family matters, discuss family finances, make plans, and support and strengthen family members. The Brethren have stated that "an atmosphere of listening, honest communication, and respect for the opinions and feelings of others is vital to the success of these meetings." ("Our Family," p. 6.) (82-01)

Church Programs and the Family

Family home evening is a basic program. We must not forget this home evening every Monday night. I say *every* Monday evening. We don't have other meetings, we don't go to shows, we don't go to ball games, we don't go to anything, because Monday has been set apart by the Lord and his people to hold the home evening. That is where we are going to save our nations. That is where we are going to have peace on earth, and it can come only through the family as the sacred unit that can be depended upon. So we have the home evening, and there we don't just have fun, we don't just have refreshments, and we don't just sit around and talk and play games. We have something serious in every home evening. The father is the head of every home, and even though the mother may be just as brilliant or more so, the father has been set apart by the Lord to look after his family. He can preside at that home evening and have a glorious program with all the members of the family taking part. We expect him to do it. Even though he might feel a little inferior sometimes, he holds the home evening. (76-35)

Include gospel instruction. Merely going to a show or a party together, or fishing, only half satisfies the real need, but to stay home and teach the children the gospel, the scriptures, and love for each other and love for their parents is most important.

We have recommended that so far as possible all the children have their own scriptures and learn to use them. (77-34)

Making home evening important communicates family values. The gospel has been a family affair. By committing ourselves to having the regular and inspirational family home evening and by carefully planning the content of that evening, we are sending a signal to our children which they will remember forevermore. When thus we give our children of our own time, we are giving of our presence, a gift that is always noticed.

The *Home Evening Manual* is replete with good suggestions, but it should never replace inspired parental development with regard to what should be done in a particular evening to meet particular needs. If we will feed our families from the gospel garden at home, then what they get from Church meetings can be a rich supplement, but not their only diet. (78-06)

Single adults should join forces. We are mindful that many of our members live alone or with family members who do not share fully their commitment to gospel principles. We encourage them to join together in special home evening groups and to participate in local single adult activities to accomplish these same objectives, always striving to strengthen their family ties with parents, brothers and sisters, and other relatives. (78-04)

Family home evening provides important training. Immorality, drug addiction, general moral and spiritual deterioration seem to be increasing, and the world is in turmoil. But the Lord has offered an old program in new dress, and it gives promise to return the world to sane living, to true family life, to family interdependence. It is to return the father to his rightful place at the head of the family, to bring mother home from social life and employment, the children from near-total fun and frolic. The home teaching program with its crowning activity, the family home evening, will neutralize the ill effects if people will only apply the remedy.

I wonder what this world would be like if every father and mother gathered their children around them at least once a week, explained the gospel, and bore fervent testimonies to them. How could immorality continue and infidelity break families and delinquency spawn? Divorce would reduce and such courts would close. Most ills of life are due to failure of parents to teach their children and the failure of posterity to obey.

Of course, there are a few disobedient souls regardless of training and teaching, but the great majority of children would respond
to such parental guidance. (65-07)

Many years ago we went to one of the Iron Curtain countries
when we were touring the world.

We attended a series of meetings at which many people were in
attendance. My first questions to these faithful Saints were these:
"How do you get along with your children? Are they taught about
God in their school?"

They said, "No. The teachers teach them that there is no God
and teach them many other things that are opposed to what we
believe."

Then I asked, "If every day the children receive that kind of
training, how do you keep them faithful to the Church?"

One of the brethren said, "We're holding our children. They
still go on missions, they still believe in God, they still pray, and
they still do all of the things that are required of good Latter-day
Saint boys and girls. We, as parents, provide good homes for them
and continue to teach and train them righteously. Therefore, what
they hear in the daytime from a godless schoolteacher makes no
difference to them. It just runs off like water on a duck's back."

When children go off to school or to play with their friends,
parents cannot be totally sure of what they are learning. But if
parents take time at home each evening to explain the gospel program to their children, it will offset the negative things they may
get during the day. (78-03)

Children grow in the gospel. Every child reaching the age of
eight should have been paying tithing for some time. Every child in
Zion should reach baptismal age having gone to sacrament meeting regularly with his parents. Every child should reach the age of
accountability having had the privilege of private prayers, prayers
at mother's knees, and family prayers in which he himself would
participate. Every child should grow to eight years knowing much
about the organization of the Church....

Our children must be converted to the gospel as every person has to be converted. When they reach eight years of age, they have borne their testimonies many times. They begin in a very childlike manner, just thanking the Lord for their fathers and their mothers. (59-03)

Church organization is to support families. Members should achieve personal and family preparedness, assisting and strengthening their own family members and others temporally and spiritually in the Lord's way. They should prepare for and obtain temple blessings for themselves and their kindred dead. They should share the gospel by example, by being a friend, bearing a testimony, serving missions, preparing sons for missions, and by supporting Church missionary efforts. Each member should develop talents, read good literature, be engaged in quality cultural pursuits, and become informed and participate appropriately in local and national civic affairs.

You will observe that all of these functions can best be accomplished through a strong home environment. (78-04)

Responsibility to Parents and Other Relatives

Adult children should care for aged parents. The other day we heard a story in our council meeting that I saw raise the ire of the Brethren. It was all righteous ire because of the things that had happened. A father who had been very careful in his investments and in his service had saved hundreds of thousands of dollars for his sweet little wife who had helped him to gather it. But unfortunately he died first and was laid away. His wife became a little older, and somewhat senile. She was put in a rest home. The money went to the children's bank accounts, and she went on suffering. Maybe she didn't fully understand all the suffering that came to her; but maybe she did. With inadequate clothes and with inadequate treatment and training, the poor woman is still living in a rest home. As far as we know her children *never* see her. . . .

This is very important, and I hope you will not forget it, you bishops. In your wards, remind your people that they should take care of their fathers and mothers, no matter if they do become senile, no matter if they do become difficult to handle. They should be taken care of; that is a part of the program of the Lord established when he first organized this world. (76-55)

Honor parents by righteous living. It is not enough to honor our parents in some narrow way. If we truly honor them, we will seek to emulate their best characteristics and to fulfill their highest aspirations for us. No gift purchased from a store can begin to match in value to parents some simple, sincere words of appreciation. Nothing we could give them would be more prized than righteous living for each youngster. Even where parents have not great strength of testimony, they will take pride in the strength and conviction of their children, if the relationship between them is a tolerant, loving, supporting one. (78-22)

Our grandfather Heber C. Kimball was unwavering in his devotion to the Lord and in his determination to keep the commandments. We are rightly proud to be his children, but that great heritage is a challenge to us to measure up. None of us now living knew Grandfather, but we shall meet him, perhaps sooner than we expect. What a pleasure that will be, especially if we can report that we have brought honor to the family name! (77-28)

Building relationships with relatives. Analysts of our modern time point out that in a fast-changing world, people suffer a kind of shock from losing a sense of continuity. The very mobility of our society means that our children are often moved from place to place and lose close contact with the extended family of grandparents, uncles, aunts, cousins, and longtime neighbors. It is important for us also to cultivate in our own family a sense that we belong together eternally, that whatever changes outside our home, there are fundamental aspects of our relationship which will never change. We ought to encourage our children to know their relatives. We need to talk of them, make effort to correspond with them, visit them, join family organizations, etc. (74-31)

Develop family organizations. We have asked the families of the Church to organize themselves to perform most effectively their sacred responsibilities, including temple and genealogical work. We have counseled that Latter-day Saints not only establish family organizations, but that they hold reunions and plan meetings to further secure the family ties. (77-29)

Keep journals and family records. Let us then continue on in this important work of recording the things we do, the things we say, the things we think, to be in accordance with the instructions of the Lord. For those of you who may not have already started your books of remembrance and your records, we would suggest that this very day you begin to write your records quite fully and completely. We hope that you will do this, our brothers and sisters, for this is what the Lord has commanded. (79-20)

Family home evenings are a most appropriate time and place to engage in such activities [as compiling family histories] and especially to train young children in the art of writing about their lives. (78-27)

Keeping journals reminds us of blessings. Those who keep a book of remembrance are more likely to keep the Lord in remembrance in their daily lives. Journals are a way of counting our blessings and of leaving an inventory of these blessings for our posterity. (78-08)

Personal history is a teaching tool. We renew our appeal for the keeping of individual histories and accounts of sacred experiences in our lives—answered prayers, inspiration from the Lord, administrations in our behalf, a record of the special times and events of our lives. From these records you can also appropriately draw as you relay faith-promoting stories in your family circles and discussions. Stories of inspiration from our own lives and those of our forebears as well as stories from our scriptures and our history are powerful teaching tools. I promise you that if you will keep your journals and records they will indeed be a source of great inspiration to you, each other, your children, your grandchildren, and others throughout the generations. (82-01)

Keep an honest, interesting journal. Again, how happy we are as we find our grandparents' journals and follow them through their trials and joys and gain for our own lives much from the experiences and faith and courage of our ancestors.

Accordingly, we urge our young people to begin today to write and keep records of all the important things in their own lives and also the lives of their antecedents in the event that their parents should fail to record all the important incidents in their own lives. Your own private journal should record the way you face up to challenges that beset you. Do not suppose life changes so much that your experiences will not be interesting to your posterity. Experiences of work, relations with people, and an awareness of the rightness and wrongness of actions will always be relevant. . . .

No one is commonplace, and I doubt if you can ever read a biography from which you cannot learn something from the difficulties overcome and the struggles made to succeed. These are the measuring rods for the progress of humanity.

As we read the stories of great men, we discover that they did not become famous overnight nor were they born professionals or skilled craftsmen. The story of how they became what they are may be helpful to us all.

Your own journal, like most others, will tell of problems as old as the world and how you dealt with them.

Your journal should contain your true self rather than a picture of you when you are "made up" for a public performance. There is a temptation to paint one's virtues in rich color and whitewash the vices, but there is also the opposite pitfall of accentuating the negative. Personally I have little respect for anyone who delves into the ugly phases of the life he is portraying, whether it be his own or another's. The truth should be told, but we should not emphasize the negative. Even a long life full of inspiring experiences can be brought to the dust by one ugly story. Why dwell on that one ugly truth about someone whose life has been largely circumspect?

The good biographer will not depend on passion but on good sense. He will weed out the irrelevant and seek the strong, novel, and interesting. Perhaps we might gain some help from reading *Plutarch's Lives* where he grouped forty-six lives in pairs, a Greek and a Roman in each pair. He tried to epitomize the most celebrated parts of their stories rather than to insist upon every slightest detail of them.

Your journal is your autobiography, so it should be kept carefully. You are unique, and there may be incidents in your experience that are more noble and praiseworthy in their way than those recorded in any other life. There may be a flash of illumination here and a story of faithfulness there; you should truthfully record your real self and not what other people may see in you.

Your story should be written now while it is fresh and while the true details are available.

A journal is the literature of superiority. Each individual can become superior in his own humble life.

What could you do better for your children and your children's children than to record the story of your life, your triumphs over adversity, your recovery after a fall, your progress when all seemed black, your rejoicing when you had finally achieved?

Some of what you write may be humdrum dates and places, but there will also be rich passages that will be quoted by your posterity.

Get a notebook, my young folks, a journal that will last through all time, and maybe the angels may quote from it for eternity. Begin today and write in it your goings and comings, your deepest thoughts, your achievements and your failures, your associations and your triumphs, your impressions and your testimonies. Remember, the Savior chastised those who failed to record important events. (75-52)

CHAPTER 13

Economics and Welfare Principles

Wealth

Wealth does not guarantee happiness. The abundant life, of course, has little to do with the acquisition of material things, though there are many wonderful individuals who have been blessed materially and who use their wealth to help their fellowmen—and this is most commendable. The abundant life noted in the scriptures is the spiritual sum that is arrived at by the multiplying of our service to others and by investing our talents in service to God and to man. (77-37)

If you can, just live on a little farm and get out and plow and raise your crops and think of your family and wish and pray for them as you plow and plant and harvest. I have a farm too, and I would still be on it if I hadn't been called away from it. I didn't need it for my living; I worked in town. I had a business, but it was good to get back to the things God created. I hope you will appreciate this place—the circular valley with water, mountains, birds, pure air—and really live. Sometimes we get wrong notions, we think we have to be in a luxurious house, in a large city, with a new car in order to be happy. Happiness isn't there. Happiness isn't in a new car, it isn't in a new and luxurious apartment. Happiness isn't in banks and stocks. Happiness is where you make it, it's up to you. It comes from within, it doesn't come from things. (49-04)

What honor is there in being the richest man in the cemetery? (00-03)

Man can be miserable under the best government and happy under the worst; he can be joyous without luxuries and almost without necessities and may be discontented and in misery surrounded with wealth and its attendant comforts, if he is without hope and without a satisfied soul. (63-03)

We live in a corrupt world where most of the things we *think* we want can be purchased with money or obtained through political power, but we also live in a wonderfully good world where the things which really bring us unbounded joy may still be had in rich abundance if we are willing to pay the price, and that price is expressed not in money but in effort. (39-01)

This nation thought it had found the abundant life in 1929 when luxury came alike to the lowly and the well-to-do, greater luxury than that enjoyed by early kings and emperors. We were driving our unpaid-for autos over heavily bonded highways, en route to the bank to make the monthly installment payments on the radio, the refrigerator, the vacuum cleaner, on Father's new golf clubs and on Mother's new gown. Luxury-mad, we were borrowing from and bonding the generations yet unborn that we might have an abundance of the things which gave comfort, pleasure, and ease. Did this increase our joy? Not at all. This was a poor substitute for the abundant life. Crime increased, divorces were more usual, homes were broken up. Finally, the end came to this orgy of spending. The Depression followed, and with it came temporary heartaches, disappointment, and despair, but after the smoke had cleared away, we found attendance at church services increased, friendships assumed new value, fellowship of interests was the rule, and men began to appreciate each other and again live a fuller life. For again rang down through the centuries the words of Divinity: "For a man's life consisteth not in the abundance of the things which he possesseth.... The life is more than meat, and the body is more than raiment ... but seek ye first the kingdom of God and its righteousness, and all other things will be added unto you.'' (See Luke 12:15-31.)

Having lost their expensive cars, or unable to purchase gasoline for them, groups remained at home and found real joy in family associations and in teaching the children the way of life. Short of means to lavish on expensive and showy parties, neighbors were content to visit in true friendship. Without means to sustain the club or social group, men and women again found good books interesting and companionable. And life again took on a new meaning. (39-01)

Luxuries do not make character. Most of the apostles come from humble homes, where they could not have all the luxuries that life could offer. Luxuries do make comfort. They do not make character. (62-04)

Too much prosperity is dangerous. I often pray that the Lord will bless the people with prosperity, but not too much, so that we will need to sacrifice and to find priorities. (75-08)

Bless all people, our Father, that they may prosper, but not more than their faith can stand. . . . We pray that they may not be surfeited with flocks and herds and acres and barns and wealth which would bring them to worship these false gods. (74-35)

As ease and leisure and the fruits of prosperity and wealth increase, we often note a decided decrease in power, courage and strength and character. (39-01)

It is hard to satisfy us. The more we have, the more we want. . . .
Why another farm, another herd of sheep, another bunch of cattle, another ranch? Why another hotel, another cafe, another store, another shop? Why another plant, another office, another service, another business? Why another of anything if one has that already which provides the necessities and reasonable luxuries? Why continue to expand and increase holdings, especially when those

increased responsibilities draw one's interests away from proper family and spiritual commitments, and from those things to which the Lord would have us give precedence in our lives? Why must we always be expanding to the point where our interests are divided and our attentions and thoughts are upon the things of the world? Certainly when one's temporal possessions become great, it is very difficult for one to give proper attention to the spiritual things. (53-06)

Striving for wealth can corrupt. I suppose every graduate dreams of the things a successful life will give him. I knew one such person who set aside his cap and gown with such a burning ambition. Success in terms of wealth, prestige, position, public acclaim was like the sun blinding him to all else. The fire must be kept burning at all costs, and one by one the real values were placed on the altar. His tithing went for dues in the clubs which would get him in the right groups. Church fellowship was pushed aside for social clubs for prestige.... Inch by inch,... faith gave way to the flames of... ambition.... [He] did become successful in a worldly sense, but... like a shadow it vanished when death came to this man and left his widow and children with home, cars, luxuries, money, memories but devoid of faith and eternal values. (63-05)

There are many ways to succeed. A few reach the pinnacle of professional or social or financial success through devious, even evil means. Others may be more virtuous, but still show a lack of sensitivity to loved ones, friends, and colleagues as they climb to the top.

Those who combine honor, integrity, devotion, and sensitivity to family and friends are rare indeed. (80-26)

Gambling is seeking wealth without work. We hope faithful Latter-day Saints will not use the playing cards which are used for gambling, either with or without the gambling. As for the gambling, in connection with horse racing or games or sports, we firmly discourage such things. (74-30)

From the beginning we have been advised against gambling of

every sort. The deterioration and damage comes to the person, whether he wins or loses, to get something for nothing, something without effort, something without paying the full price. (75-13)

Profiting from others' weaknesses displeases God. Clean money is that compensation received for a full day's honest work. It is that reasonable pay for faithful service. It is that fair profit from the sale of goods, commodities, or service. It is that income received from transactions where all parties profit.

Filthy lucre is blood money; that which is obtained through theft and robbery. It is that obtained through gambling or the operation of gambling establishments. Filthy lucre is that had through sin or sinful operations and that which comes from the handling of liquor, beer, narcotics, and those other many things which are displeasing in the sight of the Lord. Filthy lucre is that money which comes from bribery, and from exploitation.

Compromise money is filthy, graft money is unclean, profit and commissions on the sale of worthless goods, contaminated as is the money gained from other deceptions, excessive pricing, oppression to the poor, and compensation which is not fully earned. I feel strongly that men who accept wages or salary and do not give commensurate time, energy, devotion, and service are receiving money that is not clean. Certainly those who deal in the forbidden are recipients of filthy lucre. (53-06)

Love of riches is covetousness. The Lord said, "A rich man shall hardly enter into the kingdom of heaven." (Matthew 19:23.) . . . *Riches* is a relative term. Perhaps few people ever concede that they are rich, the wants and desires of man are so limitless. We may say that he is rich whose accumulations are sufficiently great to blind him to his spiritual and moral obligations and to render him slave instead of master.

Why should it be so hard for rich men to enter the kingdom? Wealth should give a man independence, time and opportunity to serve others and worship his God. It should give him a chance to alleviate suffering, teach righteousness and further all good works.

But frequently it seems to accentuate selfishness, encourage aloofness, create class distinction, and it too often blinds its possessor to the opportunity of uncompensated service to those who cannot reward him. . . .

[The rich young man's] sins were of omission and not so much of commission. In spite of his statement, he broke the tenth commandment, for the Lord indicates, "Thou shalt not covet"—not even our own properties. The Redeemer with perfect vision read the thoughts and desires of the inquirer. He knew that the trial of his faith was not murder, adultery, theft, or bearing false witness, but in giving up his "things of the world." Jesus knew where his first love and first loyalty were and knew further that the barrier of wealth must be removed before this young man could be cleansed and purified. Like the camel he must unload his burden and get on his knees in humility and in complete surrender before the treasures of eternity were made available to him. (49-05)

Saints must keep the covenant of consecration. The Lord has blessed us as a people with a prosperity unequaled in times past. The resources that have been placed in our power are good, and necessary to our work here on the earth. But I am afraid that many of us have been surfeited with flocks and herds and acres and barns and wealth and have begun to worship them as false gods, and they have power over us. Do we have more of these good things than our faith can stand? Many people spend most of their time working in the service of a self-image that includes sufficient money, stocks, bonds, investment portfolios, property, credit cards, furnishings, automobiles, and the like to *guarantee* carnal security throughout, it is hoped, a long and happy life. Forgotten is the fact that our assignment is to use these many resources in our families and quorums to build up the kingdom of God—to further the missionary effort and the genealogical and temple work; to raise our children up as fruitful servants unto the Lord; to bless others in every way, that they may also be fruitful. Instead, we expend these blessings on our own desires, and as Moroni said, "Ye adorn yourselves with that which hath no life, and yet suffer the hungry, and the needy, and the naked,

and the sick and the afflicted to pass by you, and notice them not.''
(Mormon 8:39.)

As the Lord himself said in our day, ''They seek not the Lord to
establish his righteousness, but every man walketh in his own way,
and after the image of his own god, whose image is in the likeness of
the world, and *whose substance is that of an idol,* which waxeth old
and shall perish in Babylon, even Babylon the great, which shall
fall.'' (D&C 1:16; italics added.) (76-29)

Wealth is not sinful in itself. I am not against wealth, and I like to
see people enjoy the blessings of this earth. Wealth ethically acquired
and properly used is not evil—it is good. It is the love of it, the
coveting of it, the lust for it, the compromises made for it which are
evil. (66-06)

But must one be poor to inherit eternal life? There is no such
ultimatum. The Lord delights to give us all. He created the earth for
us and gave to us as stewards all that it affords. ''The fulness of the
earth is yours,'' he said, but this fabulous gift came upon condition
that we unreservedly obey his commands. The Lord indicts those
who seek not earnestly the riches of eternity, but whose eyes are full
of greediness. . . .

Perhaps the sin is not in ''things'' but in our attitude toward and
worship of ''things.'' Unless an acquisitive person can positively
accumulate and hold wealth while still giving full allegiance to God
and his program—unless the rich man can keep the Sabbath, keep his
mind and body and spirit uncontaminated, and give unstinted service
to his fellowmen through God's appointed way—unless the affluent
man has total control and can hold all his possessions in trust, subject
to the call of the Lord through his authorized servants, then that
man, for the good of his soul, should certainly ''go and sell that thou
hast and give to the poor, . . . and come and follow me.'' (Matthew
19:21.)

''For where your treasure is, there will your heart be also.''
(Matthew 6:21.) (49-05)

Neither employer nor employee should make unreasonable demands. Farm hands, domestic help, and unprotected people are often oppressed, when economic circumstances place them in the position where they must accept what is offered or remain unemployed. And we sometimes justify ourselves in underpaying and even boast about it. . . .

And then there are those of us who require excessive compensation for services and who fail to give "value received" and who give no loyalty with their insufficient and inefficient service. . . .

The Lord knows that we need food, clothes, shelter, and other things. He expects us to earn our living. He commands us to give the necessities to our families. He permits, perhaps, that we may have reasonable luxuries, but not with unclean money. (53-06)

Work

God commands work. We believe in work. We remember the fourth of the Ten Commandments says, "Six days shalt thou labour, and do all thy work" (Exodus 20:9), and we are not sure that the rapidly decreasing work week is beneficial to mankind. We think the Lord knew what he was talking about. It would seem that we are play-conscious, travel-conscious, and our economy seems to be providing for the traveling public and the gaming public and the drinking public. (74-30)

Work has spiritual dimensions. Work is a spiritual necessity as well as an economic necessity. Our pioneer forebears understood this. (81-02)

Use time productively. Waste is unjustified, and especially the waste of time—limited as that commodity is in our days of probation. One must live, not only exist; he must do, not merely be; he must grow, not just vegetate. (MF 92)

Success requires diligent effort. Success is not like manna that falls every working day alike on the worker and the shiftless, on the resourceful one and the careless one. Success is reserved for those who work at it, those not afraid of the midnight oil. (66-06)

Work is one of the essentials to success. Remember Edison's favorite maxim, "Genius is 1 percent inspiration and 99 percent perspiration." The person who depends on his brilliance to carry him through, will be found by the wayside while the plodder will, like the tortoise of the fable, pass him by. . . . Those tremendously useful men, those powerful and invincible men, Marconi, Edison, Orville Wright, Burbank, who sit wrapped in purple robes of creative genius, are simply men who are capable of striking reiterated blows. They are men who reached success because they subjected themselves to the fierce fires of intellectual and physical endeavor. Men never ascend to eminence by a single leap or by growth overnight. Longfellow gave us this: "The heights by great men reached and kept were not attained by sudden flight, but they, while their companions slept, were toiling upward in the night." (32-01)

Work within limits of strength. We are concerned about those who are straining every muscle and resource. Be wise now that the immediate catastrophe [the breaking of the Teton Dam] has partly and largely passed. Pace yourselves. Delegate. Share. Rest. Plan. Work only normal days. Eat normally so that you can keep your strength for the problems that beset you. (76-31)

Teach children to work. It is right to work. Every man and woman and child should work. Even little children should learn how to share, to help do the housework and the yardwork, to plant gardens, to plant trees, to pick fruit, and to do everything that needs to be done, because that makes strong characters out of them and builds their faith and character.

We want you parents to create work for your children. Insist on them learning their lessons in school. Do not let them play all the time. There is a time for play, there is a time to work, and there is a time to study. Be sure your children grow up like you know they ought to grow. You know what happens to people who coast along—they just get in a boat and have no oars nor sails nor engine. They float down the river and the current just carries them down gradually until they come down into the swamps. (60-07)

Are we glamorizing out-of-home activities for our children when they should be home helping or off to work themselves? ...

The idle generation! Hours each day and nothing to do. Saturdays and nothing to do. Three long months of school vacation and nothing to do. No one has found a truer adage than: "The idle brain is the devil's workshop." ...

If a few million of the working mothers who need not work were to go home to their families, there might be employment for men now unemployed and part and full-time work for youth who ought to help in family finances and who need occupation for their abundant energy.

How many children today contribute toward the family living? Parents permit the youth to idle away their time.

"What can we do?" they ask again.

Do the shopping, work in the hospital, help the neighbors and the church custodian, wash dishes, vacuum the floors, make the beds, get the meals, learn to sew.

Read good books, repair the furniture, make something needed in the home, clean the house, press your clothes, rake the leaves, shovel the snow, peddle papers, do "baby-sitting" free for neighbor mothers who must work, become an apprentice. . . .

Lawmakers in their overeagerness to protect the child have legislated until the pendulum has swung to the other extreme. But no law prohibits most work suggested above, and parents can make work. (63-07)

I remember some years ago, a young man and his wife and little children moved to our Arizona community. As we got acquainted with them, he told me of the rigorous youth he had spent as he grew up. He'd had to get up at five and six o'clock in the morning and go out and deliver papers. He'd had to work on the farm, and he'd had to do many things that were still rankling in his soul. Then he concluded with this statement: "*My* boys are never going to have to do that." And we saw his boys grow up and you couldn't get them to do anything. They left off their Church activity and nothing seemed very important to them.

"Thou shalt not be idle," the Lord said. (D&C 42:42.) Idleness is of the devil, and we are not kind to our children when we become affluent and take from them their labors, their opportunities to serve and to be trained and to do things for themselves and for others. (76-55)

As a boy I saw how all, young and old, worked and worked hard. We knew that we were taming the Arizona desert. But had I been wiser then, I would have realized that we were taming ourselves, too. Honest toil in subduing sagebrush, taming deserts, channeling rivers, helps to take the wildness out of man's environment but also out of him. The disdain for work among some today may merely signal the return of harshness and wildness—perhaps not to our landscape but to some people. The dignity and self-esteem that honest work produces are essential to happiness. It is so easy for leisure to turn into laziness. (78-08)

Working develops the capacity to work. One of the numerous rewards in girding ourselves to do hard things is in the creation of a capacity for doing of the still harder things. (67-11)

The Welfare Program

Zion must be built up by the pure. For many years we have been taught that one important end result of our labors, hopes, and aspirations in this work is the building of a Latter-day Zion, a Zion characterized by love, harmony, and peace—a Zion in which the Lord's children are as one....

Unfortunately we live in a world that largely rejects the values of Zion. Babylon has not and never will comprehend Zion....

Zion can be built up only among those who are the pure in heart, not a people torn by covetousness or greed, but a pure and selfless people. Not a people who are pure in appearance, rather a people who are pure in heart. Zion is to be in the world and not of the world, not dulled by a sense of carnal security, nor paralyzed by materialism. No, Zion is not things of the lower, but of the higher order, things that exalt the mind and sanctify the heart.

Zion is "every man seeking the interest of his neighbor, and doing all things with an eye single to the glory of God." (D&C 82:19.) As I understand these matters, Zion can be established only by those who are pure in heart, and who labor for Zion, for "the laborer in Zion shall labor for Zion; for if they labor for money they shall perish." (2 Nephi 26:31.) (78-05)

Selflessness can bring Zion. May I suggest three fundamental things we must do if we are to "bring again Zion," three things for which we who labor for Zion must commit ourselves.

First, we must eliminate the individual tendency to selfishness that snares the soul, shrinks the heart, and darkens the mind. . . .

It is incumbent upon us to put away selfishness in our families, our business and professional pursuits, and our Church affairs. I am disturbed when I hear of stakes or wards having difficulty dividing equity in welfare projects or making equitable storehouse commodity production assignments. These things should not be. Let us resolve today to overcome any such tendencies.

Second, we must cooperate completely and work in harmony one with the other. There must be unanimity in our decisions and unity in our actions. After pleading with the Saints to "let every man esteem his brother as himself" (D&C 38:24), the Lord concludes his instructions on cooperation to a conference of the membership in these powerful words: Behold, . . . if ye are not one ye are not mine." (D&C 38:27.)

If the Spirit of the Lord is to magnify our labors, then this spirit of oneness and cooperation must be the prevailing spirit in all that we do. . . . There are few activities in the Church that require more

cooperation and concerted effort than welfare services. Whether it is
rallying to find employment for a displaced quorum member, toiling
on a production project, serving as a lead worker at a Deseret
Industries, or accepting foster children in the home, it is cooperation
and mutual concern that determines the overall success of the storehouse resource system.

Third, we must lay on the altar and sacrifice whatever is required
by the Lord. We begin by offering a "broken heart and a contrite
spirit." We follow this by giving our best effort in our assigned fields
of labor and callings. We learn our duty and execute it fully. Finally
we consecrate our time, talents, and means as called upon by our file
leaders and as prompted by the whisperings of the Spirit. In the
Church, as in the welfare system also, we can give expression to every
ability, every righteous desire, every thoughtful impulse.... and in
the end, we learn it was no sacrifice at all. (78-05)

Church Welfare Program bears many fruits. Welfare Services is
the full program the Lord has provided us—provident living, personal and family preparedness, home and visiting teaching, producing and distributing goods to the poor, rehabilitating members with
especially difficult needs or handicaps, securing jobs for the
unemployed, restoring emotionally disturbed souls to full activity in
the Church and society, with all of us consecrating our lives to the
building up of the kingdom of God on earth....

I feel it timely to talk about the fruit of our welfare labors....

The fruits experienced by the individual include dignity, self-
respect, strengthened testimony, selflessness, and increased personal
spirituality....

The primary fruit of welfare service is achieved in the lives of individuals. Only when achieved individually can it have its intended
influence on family units and the whole body of the Church. Just as
each individual's testimony adds to the strength of the Church, so
also does the individual labor of each member comprise the power of
unified welfare services.

At the family level, the fruits of our welfare work are many. They
include peace, love, harmony, solidarity, and contentment.

A true Latter-day Saint family is a haven against the storms and struggles of life....

When we practice the precepts, doctrines, and programs of welfare services, the fruit of our labors is the building of Zion. (78-26)

Church Welfare Program is the gospel in action. While often seen as temporal in nature, clearly we must understand that this work is spiritual at heart! It is people-centered and God-inspired....

As we travel and visit the people throughout the world, we recognize the great temporal needs of our people. And as we long to help them, we realize the vital importance of their learning this great lesson: that the highest achievement of spirituality comes as we conquer the flesh. We build character as we encourage people to care for their own needs.

As givers gain control of their desires and properly see other needs in light of their own wants, then the powers of the gospel are released in their lives. They learn that by living the great law of consecration they insure not only temporal salvation but also spiritual sanctification.

And as a recipient receives with thanksgiving, he rejoices in knowing that in its purest form—in the true Zion—one may partake of both temporal and spiritual salvation. Then they are motivated to become self-sustaining and able to share with others....

When viewed in this light, we can see that Welfare Services is not a program, but the essence of the gospel. *It is the gospel in action.* It is the crowning principle of a Christian life.

So as to better visualize this process and firmly fix the specific principles that undergird this work, may I rehearse to you what I believe are its foundational truths.

First is *love*. The measure of our love for our fellowman and, in a large sense, the measure of our love for the Lord, is what we do for one another and for the poor and the distressed....

Second is *service*. To serve is to abase oneself, to succor those in need of succor, and to impart of one's "substance to the poor and the needy, feeding the hungry, and suffering all manner of afflictions, for Christ's sake." (Alma 4:13.)...

Third is *work*. Work brings happiness, self-esteem, and prosperity. It is the means of all accomplishment; it is the opposite of idleness. . . .

Fourth is *self-reliance*. The Church and its members are commanded by the Lord to be self-reliant and independent.

The responsibility for each person's social, emotional, spiritual, physical, or economic well-being rests first upon himself, second upon his family, and third upon the Church if he is a faithful member thereof.

No true Latter-day Saint, while physically or emotionally able, will voluntarily shift the burden of his own or his family's well-being to someone else. So long as he can, under the inspiration of the Lord and with his own labors, he will supply himself and his family with the spiritual and temporal necessities of life.

Fifth is *consecration,* which encompasses sacrifice. Consecration is the giving of one's own time, talents, and means to care for those in need—whether spiritually or temporally—and in building the Lord's kingdom. In Welfare Services, members consecrate as they labor on production projects, donate materials to Deseret Industries, share their professional talents, give a generous fast offering, and respond to ward and quorum service projects. They consecrate their time in their home or visiting teaching. We consecrate when we give of ourselves.

Sixth is *stewardship*. In the Church a stewardship is a sacred spiritual or temporal trust for which there is accountability. Because all things belong to the Lord, we are stewards over our bodies, minds, families, and properties. (77-33)

Help nonmembers in disaster. Amid all the confusion and disorder [after the Teton Dam disaster], let us be orderly and courteous. Make no distinction between member and nonmember. We have heard inspiring reports of the Christian brotherhood in action. Preserve these good feelings in the challenging weeks ahead. Do not let jealousy or rivalry creep in. Act as the Savior himself would act in the weeks and months of future rebuilding. (76-31)

Church enemies should emulate our efforts. I wish our enemies could have seen this program this morning and seen the wide variety of help and assistance and succor that could be given to the people of this world.

We are doing a great service; and it would please us if they would go and do likewise rather than criticize our efforts. (75-50)

Cooperation is the strength of communities. Few parents could offer to build for their own little families a school building and employ a competent teacher to train their children. So a contribution is made from all the people, and public-minded citizens administer the funds and build and employ instruction and get the children taught.

No man could teach well all the things young people should learn. So one teaches mathematics; another, languages; another, engineering; another, medicine.

No man could be expert in building roads, auditing accounts, administering the healing arts, directing an army, and legislating. Each has his talents which he develops to the last degree, and society gets the benefit of expert service from many sources in every line.

A meeting place is necessary, and all members cooperate in building it. (57-05)

Let us remember the covenants we have made to bear one another's burdens and to succor each according to his need. (78-05)

Care for the elderly and reticent. We hear reports from time to time of older men and women who, in the sunset of their lives, are neglected by their families and their neighbors. Those who are both poor and old often suffer doubly. We hope family members, quorums, Relief Society officers, bishops, and others, using the Lord's own way, will make certain that they are not inadvertently neglecting such needy people. The ways the world has of helping the poor are not often the Lord's way. We must render help in the Lord's way, *but let us do it!* . . .

Be certain that we are proceeding appropriately to learn of such instances where people need help of one kind or another. Please don't assume that such individuals will always make their needs known. Often those who need help most are the last to make it known.

The ones about whom I am particularly speaking are those who will suffer in silence because they are proud or because they do not know what to do. Surely sensitive home teachers, visiting teachers, quorum leaders, and bishops can be more effective in both ascertaining and responding to the needs of these individuals. . . .

I do not worry about members of the Church being unresponsive when they learn of the needy as much as I worry about our being unaware of such needs. (78-25)

Welfare recipients should work. We urge the people to do something constructive by way of reciprocating for that which they receive. We urge our bishops to be wise in their providing help, neither stingy nor overgenerous, and that the people who need the temporary assistance will be honest and fair and wise. (74-30)

First, may I remind bishops of the vital need to provide recipients of welfare assistance with the opportunity for work or service that thereby they may maintain their dignity and independence and continue to enjoy the Holy Spirit as they benefit from Church Welfare Services' self-help efforts. We cannot be too often reminded that Church welfare assistance is spiritual at heart and that these spiritual roots would wither if we ever permitted anything like the philosophy of the dole to enter into our welfare services' ministrations. Everyone assisted can do something. Let us follow the order of the Church in this regard and insure that all who receive give of themselves in return. (78-05)

Thrift and Self-Reliance

Strive for economic independence. My thoughts went back to old Israel, who, becoming hungry, went south to Egypt and found corn. That corn tasted so good to them that they continued eating the corn of another people. Eventually they accepted the grain and the security it symbolized in full payment for their liberty. Chains and abject slavery came to them and to their children and their children's children. Their suffering accelerated in intensity until a great Moses, under God, came to emancipate them. Thank the Lord for a deliverer! But how much nobler if people could accept the advice of God's leaders before the bondage comes! . . .

Our pioneers came across the plains and developed a great commonwealth here by their toil and industry, frugality, savings. They were independent of all agencies except the Lord and their own hands and efforts, but many of their descendants have embraced, against counsel, the destructive philosophy that involved and well-nigh destroyed the ancients. (50-03)

The Lord's way builds individual self-esteem and develops and heals the dignity of the individual, whereas the world's way depresses the individual's view of himself and causes deep resentment.

The Lord's way causes the individual to hasten his efforts to become economically independent again, even though he may have temporary need, because of special conditions, for help and assistance. The world's way deepens the individual's dependency on welfare programs and tends to make him demand more rather than encouraging him to return to economic independence.

The Lord's way helps our members get a testimony for themselves about the gospel of work. For work is important to human happiness as well as productivity. The world's way, however, places greater and greater emphasis on leisure and upon the avoidance of work. . . .

Do what you can to make our projects economically viable, so that we don't rationalize that the welfare project is good simply because it gets men together. Even though it is good for the priesthood to labor side by side, we can have the brotherhood of labor and the economic efficiency too. (76-24)

Free agency requires self-reliance. No amount of philosophizing, excuses, or rationalizing will ever change the fundamental need for self-reliance. . . . With this agency we can rise to glory or fall to condemnation. . . . The principle of self-reliance stands behind the Church's emphasis on personal and family preparedness. (78-05)

With regard to all phases of our lives, I believe that men should help themselves. They should plow and plant and cultivate and harvest and not expect their faith to bring them bread. (74-20)

God could have set up a kingdom in which there would never have been oppression, hunger, nakedness, war, or sorrow, or illness, or death, but he chose to do it this way, to give men their free agency, and then to teach them to do right. (77-39)

The gospel helps people help themselves. I tell you there is more than meets the eye—the gospel develops ambition, gives hope, establishes purpose in lives so that men do their best. We do not reach the rich, the affluent to bring them into the Church. Many, many of the converts are very poor people, but the training in the Church and the self-help and the community endeavor brings them to their independence.

As I said before, it isn't the bread and beer that one puts in a belly, it is the purpose, interest, high adventure, the eternal insight, that goes into the mind and develops the spirit which is eternal.

Take an ordinary ghetto—I'll say a hundred thousand people —and give them food and things go in reverse. Give them all they want [and it] kills their ambition and increases their dependence. Build homes for them and they are soon wrecked, but teach them truth and give them the gospel and ambition is born, pride is nurtured, independence replaces slothfulness and men learn how to build their own homes and to furnish them and paint them, and then to build for others. (10/14/70)

Be thrifty. How well I remember my boyhood years in Arizona. Our living came from the soil. There was little money and seldom enough to go around. Going without and making do was our way of life. We learned to share: we shared the work; we shared joys and sorrows; we shared our food and our means. We had genuine concern for one another. Our daily prayers reminded us how dependent we are upon the Lord. We prayed and worked continually for our daily bread. (81-02)

We are also concerned with the great waste from our homes and stores and restaurants and otherwise. After the usual banquet, enough is carried out in the garbage to feed numerous mouths that have been drooling for a bite to eat in less-favored countries. Many are starving, and we throw away much and waste much. (74-30)

Budget carefully. For two people to work out their marriage together, they need a carefully worked out budget, made by both husband and wife, and then careful adherence to the same. Many marriages are defeated in the marketplace when unscheduled purchases are made. (75-47)

In 1830, in Doctrine and Covenants 19:35, the Lord gave a revelation to Martin Harris: "Pay the debt thou hast contracted with the printer. Release thyself from bondage." . . .

We talked to you last conference about a carefully planned budget for every family. Such will save many family quarrels and much misunderstanding.

"And why call ye me, Lord, Lord, and do not the things which I say?" (Luke 6:46.) (76-25)

Save for time of need. You must not spend all you make. Money must be put aside for missions and for schooling for your children. They can assume responsibilities and take little jobs whereby they can also help to raise these funds and instead of spending those little accumulations, they will save them for these great purposes. It may mean that the parents of today will go without many things that they would like, but tomorrow will come the harvest. (47-09)

I am not howling calamity, but I fear that a great majority of our young people, never having known calamity, depression, hunger, homelessness, joblessness, cannot conceive of such situations ever coming again. There are thousands of young families in this city who could not stand without suffering a three-months period without the threat of their home being foreclosed, their car repossessed, their electric and home equipment being taken back and themselves being reduced to unbelievable rations in the necessities.

The great difficulty is that when difficult times come, those who in normal times could lend assistance are also under the wheel of the grinding mill. It may be impossible to anticipate and prepare for the eventualities of depression, war, invasion, bombing, but we can go a long way. What I have seen with my own eyes makes me afraid not to do what I can to protect against the calamities. I went through two bank failures, two wars, major ones, loss of a job when jobs were scarce, but there has never been a time since our marriage that we did not have a few bonds or a savings account or some liquid assets on which to lean.

You have what you think adequate insurance, but are you prepared for and protected against death, illness, a long-continuing, crippling illness of the breadwinner? How long can you go if the income stops? What are your reserves? How long could you make your many payments on home, car, implements, appliances? How long could you carry armloads of groceries from a cash store?

The first reaction is: We just cannot do it. We can hardly get by using every cent of income monthly. The answer is eloquent. If you can hardly get by when you are earning increasingly, well employed, well, productive, young, then how can you meet emergencies with employment curtailed, illness and other unlooked-for problems arising? (1/0/00)

Insurance is worthwhile. I believe in insurance, ... because it levels off prosperity and poverty, excess and insufficiency, surplus and want. (66-06)

Insurance is a cooperative program which in reality "shares the wealth" on a wise and impartial basis. It takes the voluntary premiums from the healthy and the fortunate to give the benefits to the unfortunate in time of trouble. (70-08)

My father-in-law was a great character. When we talked about insurance, he said, "I am already insured. When I pay my tithing, I expect the Lord will protect me."...

But we also believe that the Lord helps those who help themselves and that men should do all in their power to protect themselves and avoid many misfortunes which could come to them. (74-20)

Living beyond one's means courts disaster. Analysts claim that hard times could come again. And we wonder what our people will do who have been spending their all and more. If employment and income should reduce, what then? Are you living beyond your means? Do you owe what you cannot pay if times became perilous? Are your shock absorbers in condition to take a shock? (74-30)

I had an experience once with a man whose wife was leaving him, taking their three little girls. He lost his position, his membership in the Church was in jeopardy, and he was deeply in debt and being "hounded" (as he called it) by collectors. Suicide was in his mind. I told him I would help him if he would cooperate. With reluctance he gave me a list of his long past due accounts. The collectors were threatening. There were payments on the house, car, furniture, clothes, gasoline, and tires. He owed the grocer, the barber, the music store, the drugstore, and the utility companies. I found him a job but it would pay only eighty dollars a month. He got himself a modest room with an electric plate. He was to fry his own eggs and eat a simple supper and buy one wholesome meal a day without desserts. He was to store the car in a yard and walk to work and church. Then we budgeted.

First there was eight dollars for tithing, for how could he ever expect to have the blessings of the Lord without showing his faith? Twenty-five dollars was to go to one creditor, fifteen dollars to another, five dollars or three dollars or fifty cents to another in proportion to the size of the accounts. At my insistence he went to these creditors and explained his helplessness, his income from this temporary job, and what he could do by way of liquidating the due amount. To his surprise all those whom he thought were tough and mean agreed to his plan. On each payday we allocated the funds. He met smiling faces, kindly people eager to assist one who was really trying. The money was not his. It belonged to his creditors to whom he had promised it. He thought I was tough when I cut out his shine money and told him to buy a box of shoe polish and shine his shoes like I did mine. He was surprised when I insisted on newspaper money going to his creditors. "Where you work, they take the newspaper. You can take the day-old copy home with you after it is discarded." He was a good sport, cooperative, and his countenance shone as he began to see himself coming out of the hole and becoming master of the situation. A few months went by and the smaller accounts were cleared away and larger payments were made to the larger ones. His walking to work and church and eating only wholesome foods gave him new vigor; his visit to the bishop every week brought him a new association pleasant to him; his feeling of triumph of being master of his destiny gave him a lighter step. He found a better job with twice the income. The creditors smiled as the payments increased. Not until all old accounts were squared did he move to a better apartment, and put gas in his car. (58-07)

Family and Personal Preparedness

Maintain a year's supply. The Lord has urged that his people save for the rainy days, prepare for the difficult times, and put away for emergencies, a year's supply or more of bare necessities so that when comes the flood, the earthquake, the famine, the hurricane, the storms of life, our families can be sustained through the dark days. How many of us have complied with this? We strive with the Lord, finding many excuses: We do not have room for storage. The food spoils. We do not have the funds to do it. We do not like these common foods. It is not needed—there will always be someone to help in trouble. The government will come to the rescue. And some intend to obey but procrastinate. (71-13)

We encourage families to have on hand this year's supply; and we say it over and over and over and repeat over and over the scripture of the Lord where he says, "Why call ye me, Lord, Lord, and do not the things which I say?" (Luke 6:46.) How empty it is as they put their spirituality, so-called, into action and call him by his important names, but fail to do the things which he says. (76-24)

As we become more affluent and our bank accounts enlarge, there comes a feeling of security, and we feel sometimes that we do not need the supply that has been suggested by the Brethren. It lies there and deteriorates, we say. And suppose it does? We can re-establish it. We must remember that conditions could change and a year's supply of basic commodities could be very much appreciated by us or others. So we would do well to listen to what we have been told and to follow it explicitly.

There are some countries which prohibit savings or surpluses. We do not understand it, but it is true. And we honor, obey, and sustain the laws of the country which is ours. (See Article of Faith 12.) Where it is permitted, though, which is most of the world, we should listen to the counsel of the Brethren and to the Lord. (76-24)

Do all of you people have a year's supply of the basic commodities? Be sure that you consider it very seriously. We realize that there may be some situations where it may be difficult, but we want you to keep it in mind. When distress or disaster comes to any of our people, we must be ready to help each other. The Church has storage in many places, and as a Church it can do a great deal to help many people. (76-50)

Plant gardens. Many have done much to beautify their homes and their yards. Many others have followed the counsel to have their own gardens wherever it is possible so that we do not lose contact with the soil and so that we can have the security of being able to provide at least some of our food and necessities.

Grow all the food that you possibly can on your own property, if water is available; berry bushes, grapevines, and fruit trees are most desirable. Plant them if your climate is right for their growth. Grow vegetables and eat those grown in your own yard. Even those residing in apartments or condominiums can generally grow a little food in pots and planters. (78-06)

We deal with many things which are thought to be not so spiritual; but all things are spiritual with the Lord, and he expects us to listen, and to obey, and to follow the commandments. (77-24)

Gardens promote independence. Should evil times come, many might wish they had filled all their fruit bottles and cultivated a garden in their backyards and planted a few fruit trees and berry bushes and provided for their own commodity needs.

The Lord planned that we would be independent of every creature, but we note even many farmers buy their milk from dairies and homeowners buy their garden vegetables from the store. And should the trucks fail to fill the shelves of the stores, many would go hungry. (74-30)

Gardens can provide savings and pleasure. We are highly pleased with the response to the planting of gardens. It is health-building, both from the raising of crops and the eating of them. It is delightful to see so many gardens all over the land, and reports come in from numerous families and individuals who have obtained much saving and pleasure in the planting of gardens. We hope this will be a permanent experience of our people, that they will raise much of what they use on their table. (77-34)

Gardening teaches children. I hope that we understand that, while having a garden, for instance, is often useful in reducing food costs and making available delicious fresh fruits and vegetables, it does much more than this. Who can gauge the value of that special chat between daughter and Dad as they weed or water the garden? How do we evaluate the good that comes from the obvious lessons of planting, cultivating, and the eternal law of the harvest? And how do we measure the family togetherness and cooperating that must accompany successful canning? Yes, we are laying up resources in store, but perhaps the greater good is contained in the lessons of life we learn as we live providently and extend to our children their pioneer heritage. (77-33)

Gardening brings us close to nature. Even if the tomato you eat is a two-dollar tomato, it will bring satisfaction anyway and remind us all of the law of the harvest, which is relentless in life. We do reap what we sow. Even if the plot of soil you cultivate, plant, and harvest is a small one, it brings human nature closer to nature as was the case in the beginning with our first parents. (78-08)

Gardening promotes neighborliness. Another commendable thing about gardening is the exchange of products by neighbors and the fostering of fellowship and neighborliness. (76-25)

Develop sewing skills. Whenever possible, produce your nonfood necessities of life. Improve your sewing skills; sew and mend clothing for your family. All the girls want to learn to type, they all want to go to an office. They don't seem to want to sew anymore, and to plant and protect and renew the things that they use. Develop handicraft skills as the sisters have told us, and make or build needed items. (76-24)

Clean up dilapidated properties. The Lord . . . created for us this beautiful world and gave command to our father Adam to till the ground and to dress the land and to make it habitable. That command continues to us.

We recommend to all people that there be no undue pollution, that the land be taken care of and kept clean, productive, and beautiful. He gave to us the herbs and the good things which come of the earth for food and raiment and houses and barns and orchards and gardens and vineyards, each in the season thereof, and all of this is given for the benefit and use of man, both to please the eye and to gladden the heart; for food and for raiment, for taste and for smell, to strengthen the body and to enliven the soul. And it pleased God that he had given all these things unto man; for unto this end were they made to be used, with judgment.

We are concerned when we see numerous front and side and back yards that have gone to weeds, where ditch banks are cluttered and trash and refuse accumulate. It grieves us when we see broken fences, falling barns, leaning and unpainted sheds, hanging gates, and unpainted property. And we ask our people again to take stock of their own dwellings and properties.

There is a story that President Brigham Young, having urged the people of certain communities to properly dress and clean their premises, refused to go back to them to preach to them, saying something like this: "You didn't listen to me when I urged you to fix up your premises. The same doors are off their hinges; the same barns are still unpainted; the same fences are partly fallen." (75-13)

We look forward to the day when, in all of our communities, urban and rural, there would be a universal, continued movement to clean and repair and paint barns and sheds, build sidewalks, clean ditch banks, and make our properties a thing of beauty to behold. (74-30)

Maintain physical fitness. After the Crucifixion, when the Savior was upon this continent with the Nephites and Lamanites, he said to them after days of teaching them the gospel, "Therefore, what manner of men ought ye to be?" And the answer which he himself gave was, "Even as I am." (3 Nephi 27:27.) "I, the Savior, even as I am, ye must be also. Ye must perfect your lives." He was not talking of the physical totally, and yet, that is a part of the program—that we will perfect our physical bodies. We will make them just as attractive as possible. We will keep them as healthy as possible. We will keep them in the best condition so far as we can. And so, we will make them like our Lord's. But, the most important thing is to gear our minds and our spirits so they will be like the Savior's. (64-04)

I have known many students in various schools of higher learning who have been fanatically zealous in their schoolwork. They have felt that they had no time for their physical development, and when it was called to their attention they said, "I am strong. I must push on and get through my studies and become established. I'll take care of the physical afterward." But graduation finds them still with the same attitude, and then they say, "I must get established in life, in my business or profession. After that I'll find time to do the things that are necessary for my body." But the years go on, and when they reach the point where they are able to afford the time to play golf and to go on vacations and to take it a bit easier and develop themselves with a balanced program, then they have perhaps lost some of their health until it isn't possible, and they have perhaps lost the desire to get that kind of development for their bodies. (47-01)

Personal appearance affects conduct. Some of you will recall in almost every general conference I have encouraged our Latter-day Saints to mend their fences, to fix up and paint up, or else tear down their old barns, to trim their hedges and repair their garages.

For all that we believe about gardens and grassland, about painting barns and cleaning ditches, we say anew and more vigorously to all of you: trim your hair appropriately. Wear modest, clean clothing. Your clothing doesn't need to be new and [it] should have some fashion of course, but [it] should be clean, modest, and neat. Be dignified in your outward manner and in your inward morality. Take pride in your principles. Tear down, as it were, any of the old sheds of the past. Repent of old transgressions and start this school year with clean hands and a pure heart, reflected by good grooming, acceptable apparel, and personal integrity. (78-23)

Shakespeare had Polonius truly say, "The apparel oft proclaims the man." (*Hamlet,* act 1, sc. 3.) We are affected by our own outward appearances; we tend to fill roles. If we are in our Sunday best, we have little inclination for roughhousing; if we dress for work, we are drawn to work; if we dress immodestly, we are tempted to act immodestly; if we dress like the opposite sex, we tend to lose our sexual identity or some of the graces that distinguish the eternal mission of our sex.

Now, I hope not to be misunderstood: I am *not* saying that you should judge one another by appearance, for that would be folly and worse; I am saying that there is a relationship between how we dress and groom ourselves and how we are inclined to feel and act. By seriously urging full conformity with the [BYU dress] standards, we must not drive a wedge between brothers and sisters; for there are some who have not heard or do not understand. These are not to be rejected or condemned as evil, but rather loved the more that we may patiently bring them to understand the danger to themselves and the disservice to the institutions to which they owe loyalty, if they depart from their commitments. We hope that the disregard we sometimes see is mere thoughtlessness and is not deliberate. (79-17)

Dress suggests our values. How far, we wonder, will men and women go to pay ovations to the god of style? Will men wear rings in their noses when style dictates? Will young people still fall prey to their god of style, which they worship? "Everybody does it."

Tell me: Is it not true that the dress, the grooming, paints an immediate picture and classifies a person? The famous Jerry Rubin says:

> Young kids identify short hair with authority, discipline, unhappiness, boredom, hatred of life and long hair with just "letting go." Wherever we go, our hair tells people where we stand on Vietnam, lawless campus destructions, and drugs. We're living TV commercials for the revolution. Long hair is the beginning of our liberation from sexual oppression.

What group do you wish to follow and with which group do you wish to identify? (74-27)

Some young people have prided themselves in wearing the most tattered, soiled, and grubby attire. If we dress in a shabby or sloppy manner, we tend to think and act the same way. I am positive that personal grooming and cleanliness, as well as the clothes we wear, can be tremendous factors in the standards we set and follow on the pathway to immortality and eternal life. (78-23)

CHAPTER 14

Learning

The Pursuit of Knowledge

The Church encourages growth in knowledge. The Church from the beginning has been committed to the principle that "the glory of God is intelligence." (D&C 93:36.) We therefore encourage our people to study and prepare to render service with their minds and with their hands.

Some are inclined toward formal university training, and some are inclined more toward the practical vocational training. We feel that our people should receive that kind of training which is most consistent with their interests and talents. Whether it be in the professions, the arts, or the vocations; whether it be university or vocational training, we applaud and encourage it. (77-34)

Parents should sacrifice for their children's education. Now, when I was a little boy in Southern Arizona our Latter-day Saints were the pioneers. They were struggling to get their feet planted in the soil—to establish themselves. They were largely employed by others, often at pitifully low levels of income. They were the post-hole diggers, the hewers of wood and the drawers of water. They were the farm hands, the mill workers, domestic servants in the homes, the railroad section hands. Now, I would not have you think that such work was dishonorable, nor unholy, nor improper, but it is limiting. But in my short life I have seen this people through education and thrift rise to new planes and become the leaders in the communities and hold high places in government, business, professional, social, and political affairs. I have seen them become the landowners and many of them become independent and financially secure, as well as faithful spiritually. . . .

If you will accomplish all these things that I have pointed out, and which I see as your potential, you must make the sacrifices and see that your children go to school, not through the grades alone, but through high school and through the colleges, where they will receive their degrees and go on to take their place in the world. I know that it is hard. I realize that many of you feel you are having difficulty getting by on your income. But "where there is a will there is a way," and if you parents will begin to sacrifice and insist upon your children getting these advantages, tomorrow they will be leaders in the world.

A hundred years ago our parents came into Utah and nearly starved for years, but the first thing they did was build schoolhouses and put schoolteachers in them and send their children to school. The parents deprived themselves of luxuries, fine clothes, and even almost went without enough to eat in order to keep their children in the schools. (47-09)

Be diligent students. Be serious about your studies. This is a university. Your minds need to be filled and stretched and trained. Adequate social opportunities are available, and these are important in terms of balance in your life, but do not subordinate your studies to the fleeting things of the moment.

Again, I urge you to work hard while you are here. The information, attitudes, and training you receive here will permit you to serve hundreds of others during the balance of your lives. So, in a very real sense, those who are not here today to speak for themselves need to be spoken for—by way of urging you to be true to your trust in this privileged learning adventure that carries with it special duties and obligations. Do not join the parade of pleasure seekers; it is too large already! Do not seek selfish fulfillment, for it will leave you desolate. (80-27)

Reinforce good teaching with praise. Before you leave this college campus, remember to give deserved and specific praise to the members of the faculty and the staff here for what they have done for you. Part of the process of renewal for this dedicated faculty of men and women is to have students validate, verbally as well as behaviorally, the fact that what the teachers have done for them does matter. Deserved praise is never wasted. (74-11)

Education is for everyone. You can set your goals, young women, to make you reach and strain. Keep striving for them. Be prayerful and humble in seeking wisdom and knowledge. You are in the time of your life for studying and preparing. Learn all you can. Growth comes from setting your goals high and reaching for the stars. (78-24)

Tens and hundreds of thousands of men have finished their education after their marriage and their wives are a great help to them. (76-59)

Education is the continuing and expanding process of learning which carries on long after the classrooms close behind you. (39-01)

Read in spare time. Numerous leisure hours have been made available to men. It is noticeable that many use these extra hours for fun and pleasure. Certainly an increased part of it could profitably be used for gaining knowledge and culture through the reading of good books.

Numerous people fail to take advantage of these opportunities. Many people spend hours in planes with only cursory glancing at mazagines, and in the train or bus, time is spent "sitting and thinking," and in many cases, "just sitting," when there could be such a constructive program of reading. People in beauty parlors, professional offices, waiting rooms, and elsewhere waste precious hours thumbing through outdated magazines when much valuable reading could be done in these islands of time. . . . Even in the beginning there was the written word, for Adam and Eve were conscious of the need for the development of the mind, "And by them their children were taught to read and write, having a language which was pure and undefiled." (Moses 6:6.) (63-06)

There is available a wide selection of books which will give development to the aesthetic and the cultural. Music, drama, poetry, fiction, and other cultural fields are available to everyone. The contributions come to us from great minds and great hearts and great sufferers and great thinkers.

In addition to all the serious study there should be time for just plain reading for pleasure. Here one needs assistance to select that which is pleasurable in a worthwhile way. There are countless works of fiction which help us to understand ourselves and others better, and to get real pleasure in the learning. (63-06)

Read scriptures more than commentaries. In the reading habits of men there should be a generous part directed to the spiritual:

> that you shall teach one another the doctrine of the kingdom . . . and . . . more perfectly in theory, in principle, in doctrine, in the law of the gospel, in all things that pertain unto the kingdom of God, that are expedient for you to understand. (D&C 88:77-78.)

This would imply careful, regular, and systematic study of the standard works of the Church. Herein will be found the material for a lifetime of profitable study. . . .

Here are the pictures of people who lived and met all the exigencies of life and overcame meanness, jealousies, envies, hatreds, and became pure of heart and clean of hands. Here are pictures of the winds of disobedience and rebellion and uncleanness and the whirlwinds that enveloped them. Here are men who approached perfection under trials and difficulties, like Job, and who emerged superior beings. Here are the biographies of the prophets and of leaders and of the Lord himself, giving example and direction so that men can, by following those examples, be perfected, happy, full of joy, and with eternity their goal and expectation. . . .

Among the "best books" to be read are the numerous commentaries of the leaders of the Church, too numerous to list, but which are stimulating and clarifying and written to give a better understanding of the plan. *The Articles of Faith* is a type of gospel explanation book. . . .

It must be remembered that all books published by Church authors are not official Church publications, and the reader must be discriminating and selective. But all these numerous books have much of value in them for the discriminating student. In all the commentaries, good as they may be, it must be remembered that none takes the place of the original source material. (63-06)

Education prepares one for service. Learning that includes familiarization with facts must not occur in isolation from concern over our fellowmen. It must occur in the context of a commitment to serve them and to reach out to them. (75-51)

Knowledge of languages facilitates Church work. In much of the world children are being taught English. Not that English is any more sacred than German or French or Spanish, but the Church has its headquarters in an English-speaking land and the great majority of the people of the Church speak English. So it is our hope that just as rapidly as people can learn the language, they will do so. It will facilitate their activity in the community. It will make it a little easier for them to get and hold employment. We do not ask that any people give up their own language. In fact, it is a very pleasing thing to be bilingual or trilingual. (65-04)

Knowledge of family-life skills is practical training. I heard an address from a college president in which he said that about 92 percent of all the young women in that college were preparing for careers. They were preparing to be stenographers, secretaries, teachers. . . . Though about 90 percent or more of the young women would eventually be presiding over homes and bearing children, very few were preparing for their life's work. . . .

They needed, really, courses in foods, clothing, home decoration; they needed training in psychology and child training; they needed physical education and nurse training to keep them fit, and special training to make them efficient in the bearing and teaching of children. (46-05)

Women may well need job skills. Young women may do well to finish their college work, for some day there is a possibility of widowhood and the financial problems of supporting a family. (65-10)

Literacy offers pleasure. We speak of literacy and education in terms of being prepared for a better occupation, but we cannot underestimate the present pleasure of our reading in the scriptures, Church magazines, and good books of every kind. (77-33)

Balancing Secular and Spiritual Concerns in Education

Promote excellence. We can do much in excellence and, at the same time, emphasize the large-scale participation of our students, whether it be in athletics or in academic events. We can bless many and give many experience, while, at the same time, we are developing the few select souls who can take us to new heights of attainment. (75-51)

Choosing student "royalty" appeals to vanity. I shall look forward to the day when we have no queen contests, or the most eligible man contests. I think it is a difficult thing for a king and queen to live normal lives. Such flattering honors give undue emphasis and are superficial. It isn't good for any girl to be named a queen. It is not good for any man to be named the finest. I hope we can start out something new and original, more wholesome. (58-10)

Secular knowledge has eternal significance. We believe in and encourage education, but not for education's sake alone. We educate ourselves in the secular field and in the spiritual field so we may one day create worlds, people and govern them. (68-05)

We understand, as few people do, that education is a part of being about our Father's business and that the scriptures contain the master concepts for mankind. (75-51)

Religious training should be part of education. Great knowledge and true facts can never disturb one's spiritual equilibrium, but half-truths and distorted notions can upset one who is not well founded.

It is quite understandable how budding intellectuals could become unbalanced when most receive many times as much secular study as religious training and when many receive no spiritual. It is our feeling that every student in every church should have religious training to balance the secular. (63-04)

Education involves character development. Character is not what people say of you, but what you really are. The character and personality of the teacher are the greatest influences in the school. And what an opportunity for the teacher to develop that character in her pupils! . . .

Some of the subjects in the curriculum properly interpreted and supplemented by experience, story, and pointing the way will give to the pupil the desire to do right, an eagerness to find the truth, a love of the beautiful, reverence for the Creator of all good things. He will be taught humility, the spirit of service, responsibility, honesty, reliability, law observance, and temperance. These will make for a really solid foundation for life. Without them all the mental training in the world is wasted. (30-01)

The moral dimension keeps learning from becoming selfish. Many in the secular world are often adrift and anchorless. Only an education which educates for eternity has the wholeness which humans need. When we separate learning from divine moral truth it quickly deteriorates into a restless, roving search for meaning and often drifts into a sensual selfishness. (74-06)

Education is the imparting or acquisition of knowledge, skill, or development of character. In its truest sense, it is not the amassing of cold facts, but the rounded development of the body, mind, and the soul of man. . . . True education prepares one for "making a life," not merely the "making of a living."

"Knowledge is power," is a proverb of old. But power to destroy as well as to construct and build comes from the possession of knowledge. . . . It was not an untutored nor an ignorant world that battled long agonizing years on the shell-cratered no-man's-land; but on the contrary, it was the so-called civilized and so-called educated world that shot the deadly missiles, sank the defenseless in the briny deeps, bombed the cities, and tortured and maimed the millions of the flower of the nations. But were they really educated in the true sense of the word? They had the power of knowledge, but lacked the development of the moral and spiritual side, the lack of which permitted them to use their knowledge toward the destruction of mankind, instead of the further teaching of the peoples of the universe, making them prosperous, happy, and contented. (32-01)

My dear young people, you are here to learn, not only history and chemistry but character and faith, and to solidify your lives, to develop a standard of performance from which you would never be diverted in your lives.

One might be smart and clever; one might be full of wit and humor; one might be dextrous in performance, but if he has not honor and integrity, he has little or nothing. (65-11)

Secular knowledge may lead to pride. As we attain knowledge, we stand in danger, for many people who attain such knowledge have "stumbled, because of the greatness of their stumbling block." They stumbled because of the "pride of their eyes" and they "preach up unto themselves their own wisdom and their own learning, that they may get gain and grind upon the face of the poor." (2 Nephi 26:20.) (74-11)

God must often use the unlettered. The Lord seems never to have placed a premium on ignorance and yet he has, in many cases, found his better-trained people unresponsive to the spiritual, and has had to use spiritual giants with less training to carry on his work. Peter was said to be ignorant and unlearned, while Nicodemus was, as the Savior said, a master, a trained one, an educated man. And while Nicodemus would in his aging process gradually lose his prestige, his strength, and go to the grave a man of letters without eternal knowledge, Peter would go to his reputed crucifixion the greatest man in all the world, perhaps still lacking considerably in secular knowledge (which he would later acquire), but being preeminent in the greater, more important knowledge of the eternities and God and his creations and their destinies. (67-10)

Academic achievement is not the measure of personal worth. You may have been judged by your grades in these past years, but the time has come for most of you when other weights and measures will be used. For there have been many persons whose grades were not to be boasted of, but who lived full and colorful lives and were known throughout their days as people who accomplish and whose success stories have been repeated through the ages.

I remember in my school days a particular family and all through the grades and high school and even into college, people almost gasped at the brilliance of these people, only to find them in a later generation unknown except in their immediate neighborhood, unsuccessful, ne'er-do-well folks, and some of them were dying in a drunkard's grave. (74-11)

Spiritual knowledge is even more important than secular. Knowledge is not merely the equations of algebra, the theorems of geometry, or the miracles of space. It is hidden treasures of knowledge as recorded in Hebrews, by which "the worlds were framed by the word of God" (Hebrews 11:3); by which Enoch was translated that he should not see death; by which Noah, with a knowledge no other human had, built an ark on dry land and saved a race by taking seed through the flood.

The treasures of both secular and spiritual knowledge are hidden ones—but hidden from those who do not properly search and strive to find them.... Spiritual knowledge is not available merely for the asking; even prayers are not enough. It takes persistence and dedication of one's life. The knowledge of things in secular life are of time and are limited; the knowledge of the infinite truths are of time and eternity.

Of all treasures of knowledge, the most vital is the knowledge of God: his existence, powers, love, and promises. (68-11)

Spiritual learning takes precedence. The secular without the foundation of the spiritual is but like the foam upon the milk, the fleeting shadow.

Do not be deceived! One need not choose between the two . . . for there is opportunity to get both simultaneously; but can you see that the seminary courses should be given even preferential attention over the high school subjects; the institute over the college course; the study of the scriptures ahead of the study of the man-written texts; the association with the Church more important than clubs, fraternities, and sororities; the payment of tithing more important than paying tuitions and fees?

Can you see that the ordinances of the temple are more important than the Ph.D. or any and all other academic degrees? . . .

The Lord emphasized: "Seek ye *first* the kingdom of God, and his righteousness, and all these things shall be added unto you." (Matthew 6:33.)

If we spend our mortal days in accumulating secular knowledge to the exclusion of the spiritual then we are in a dead-end street, for this is the time for man to prepare to meet God; this is the time for faith to be built, for baptism to be effected, for the Holy Ghost to be received, for the ordinances to be performed. Contemporary with this program can come the secular knowledge, for even in the spirit world after death our spirits can go on learning the more secular things to help us create worlds and become their masters. . . .

A highly trained scientist who is also a perfected man may eventually create a world and people it, but a dissolute, unrepentant, unbelieving one will never be such a creator even in eternities.

Secular knowledge, important as it may be, can never save a soul nor open the celestial kingdom nor create a world nor make a man a god, but it can be most helpful to that man who, placing first things first, has found the way to eternal life and who can now bring into play all knowledge to be his tool and servant. (62-01)

Our training must not only teach us how to build dams and store water to dampen parched earth to make the desert blossom as the rose and feed starving humanity, but it must prepare us to dam our carnal inclinations and desires with self-denial, creating reservoirs to be filled with spirituality.

We must study not only to cultivate fertile acres, plant seeds therein, and nurture them on to harvests, but we must plant in the hearts of men seeds of cleanliness and righteous living and faith and hope and peace.

We must not only know how to kill weeds and noxious plants which befoul our crops, but learn to eradicate from the souls of men the noxious theories and manmade sophistries which would cloud issues and bring heartache and distress to men.

We must not only be trained to inoculate and vaccinate and immunize against disease, set broken limbs, and cure illnesses, but we must be trained to clarify minds, heal broken hearts, and create homes where sunshine will make an environment in which mental and spiritual health may be nurtured. . . .

Our schooling must not only teach us how to bridge the Niagara River gorge, or the Golden Gate, but must teach us how to bridge the deep gaps of misunderstanding and hate and discord in the world. (46-05)

No conflict exists between the gospel and any truth. In your pursuit of truth, remember that while some truths matter more than others, all true principles are a part of the gospel of Jesus Christ. There is no true principle that we need to fear. . . .

However, there is a lot in the world that attempts to pass itself off as truth when it is not. A good education will help you to distinguish between sense and nonsense. As you also receive real literacy in things spiritual, you will have added discernment with which to weigh and test ideas and assertions as you make decisions and judgments.

In addition to being serious about your scholarship, do not be unduly fearful about conditions in the world. Be noticing. Be aware. But be of good cheer, and also be about your Father's business. The Lord has promised us, again and again, that he will watch over his people and lead them along. (80-27)

Man only rediscovers old truths. Columbus confirmed to the world that the earth was round, yet this was not new, for had not God created it in that shape? As space explorers delve into worlds unknown, they will blaze to the world the new discoveries, but we shall know that what they have found is new only to us and is a rediscovery of ancient truths and basic knowledge. When men have interplanetary travel, they will begin to approach what God showed a few of his favorite seers millennia before our modern science was born. (63-04)

Man's wisdom is nothing compared to God's. One young man resisted the counsel given by me on one occasion, saying, when I had assured him that a certain action was a wrong and a sinful one, "That's your opinion and this is mine."

And I rejoined, "... If it were your mind against mine—your logic against mine—your perception against my limited abilities, then I would retire and leave you to your deliberations and conclusions. But I'm expressing not my own opinion but the word of the Lord of heaven, and I am telling you God's truth—*that* act is sin. To compare your opinion with the Lord's proven truths might be like a grain of sand compared to the bulk and height of Mount Everest." (66-07)

Art

Create great art to communicate the truth. In our world, there have risen brilliant stars in drama, music, literature, sculpture, painting, science, and all the graces. For long years I have had a vision of the BYU greatly increasing its already strong position of excellence till the eyes of all the world will be upon us. . . .

It has been said that many of the great artists were perverts or moral degenerates. In spite of their immorality, they became great and celebrated artists. What could be the result if discovery were made of equal talent in men who were clean and free from the vices, and thus entitled to revelations? . . .

Oh, how our world needs statesmen! We have the raw material, we have the facilities, we can excel in training. We have the spiritual climate. We must train statesmen, not demagogues; men of integrity, not weaklings who for a mess of pottage will sell their birthright. We must develop these precious youth to know the art of statesmanship, to know people and conditions, to know situations and problems, but men who will be trained so thoroughly in the arts of their future work and in the basic honesties and integrities and spiritual concepts that there will be no compromise of principle.

For years I have been waiting for someone to do justice in recording in song and story and painting and sculpture the story of the Restoration, the reestablishment of the kingdom of God on earth, the struggles and frustrations; the apostasies and inner revolutions and counterrevolutions of those first decades; of the exodus; of the counterreactions; of the transitions; of the persecution days; of the plural marriage and the underground; of the miracle man, Joseph Smith, of whom we sing, "Oh, what rapture filled his bosom, for he saw the living God!"; and of the giant colonizer and builder, Brigham Young, by whom this university was organized and for whom it was named.

The story of Mormonism has never yet been written nor painted nor sculptured nor spoken. It remains for inspired hearts and talented fingers yet to reveal themselves. They must be faithful, inspired, active Church members to give life and feeling and true perspective to a subject so worthy. . . .

Our writers, our moving picture specialists, with the inspiration of heaven, should tomorrow be able to produce a masterpiece which would live forever. Our own talent, obsessed with dynamism from a cause, could put into such a story life and heartbeats and emotions and love and pathos, drama, suffering, love, fear, courage, and the great leader, the mighty modern Moses who led a people farther than from Egypt to Jericho, who knew miracles as great as the stream from the rock at Horeb. . . .

One of the rich rewards coming from doing great things is the capacity to do still greater things. (67-10)

The arts should build. We cannot give in to the ways of the world with regard to the realm of art. . . . Brigham Young said there is "no music in hell." Our art must be the kind which edifies man, which takes into account his immortal nature, and which prepares us for heaven, not hell. (75-51)

Down in New Zealand, I was the recipient of many courtesies while there. They sang and danced and rolled their eyes and stuck out their tongues. And so we applaud them, you know, and think it wonderful to encourage the continuation of that culture. But as it was interpreted to me, . . . they chant and sing battle hymns—not peace hymns. And so I said to some of the leaders: "With all your beautiful voices, your wonderful talent, why don't you develop some impressive songs on the themes surrounding the coming of Christ, about the restoration of the gospel, about lofty ideals, the latter-day exodus, the glories and good things which the gospel and the Church have brought us?" In all cultures, let us perpetuate not the mating dances, the sex stories, but the good and the beautiful and lofty as we sing and as we dance.

We should be perpetuating Mormonism and the gospel; the true way of life. That doesn't mean we need to bury all things of the past; but, if there is anything associated with paganism or sectarianism or sex, we eliminate. And so, we are building a great culture entirely different from that out there in the sectarian world. We are building a glorious culture of cleanliness and morality with high-minded, wonderful people. And, all the things the Church does—the singing of the songs, the speaking in public, the organization—the everything is devoted to this one thing: building a great spiritual culture that the Lord wants. (65-01)

Join forces with scholars who share our objectives. We can sometimes make concord with others, including scholars who have parallel purposes. By reaching out to the world of scholars, to thoughtful men and women everywhere who share our concerns and at least some of the items on our agendum of action, we can multiply our influence and give hope to others who may assume that they are alone.

In other instances, we must be willing to break with the educational establishment (not foolishly or cavalierly, but thoughtfully and for good reason) in order to find gospel ways to help mankind. Gospel methodology, concepts, and insights can help us to do what the world cannot do in its own frame of reference. (75-51)

Brigham Young University

BYU exists to build character and faith. This institution [BYU] has no justification for its existence unless it builds character, creates and develops faith, and makes men and women of strength and courage, fortitude, and service—men and women who will become stalwarts in the kingdom and bear witness of the restoration and the divinity of the gospel of Jesus Christ. It is not justified on an academic basis only, for your parents pay taxes to support state institutions to which you are eligible in every state of the union and most foreign countries. This institution has been established by a prophet of God for a very specific purpose: to combine spiritual and moral values and secular education. (78-23)

We do not want BYU ever to become an educational factory. It must concern itself with not only the dispensing of facts, but with the preparation of its students to take their place in society as thinking, thoughtful, and sensitive individuals who, in paraphrasing the motto of your centennial, come here dedicated to love of God, pursuit of truth, and service to mankind. (75-51)

Life at BYU is not just preparation. Sometimes people go to college to prepare to live. Not so at the BYU. We come here to begin our life. We live every phase of life. We have our studies, our good clean fun, our athletics. We do our courting, we marry, we have our families. We have the Church with all its quorum, ward, and stake activities. We have missionary work. The whole Church has moved in to be at our beck and call. We at BYU are living, not merely preparing to live. (58-10)

BYU students are guests of the Lord and his tithe-paying people. Beloved students, you are guests here—guests of the Lord, whose funds pay in large measure for your education. You are guests of the Lord, his Church, his leaders, his administration, his people. You and your parents make a smaller but necessary contribution.

In a faraway land to the south is an old man, somewhat crippled, untrained. The children, several, are ragged, the clothes are hand-me-downs, and winter or summer they trudge barefooted to a little primitive school. The home is tiny—two small rooms, one under the other with a ladder connecting. The little mother makes baskets and sells at the public market. The father makes chairs and tables out of the native jungle trees and, in his calloused, leathery bare feet, walks long distances, carrying his furniture those miles to market, hopefully. The middleman or the bargaining buyer leave him very little profit from his honest labor; but because he is a faithful member of the Church, he takes his tithing to his branch president and it finally reaches the treasury house and part of it is allocated to the Brigham Young University. And he, this dear old man, and she, this deprived little mother, and they, these gaunt little children, along with their fellow members and numerous others who are tithe payers, become host to you, the guests, and supply a goodly percentage of the wherewithal for land and buildings and equipment and instructions.

The boy working in the cornfield in India is your host, for he returns his 10 percent.

The rich man living in his luxury who pays his tithing is your host.

The widowed mother with several hungry children is your hostess.

The janitor of your meetinghouse is your host.

The Navajo on the desert following his little band of sheep trying to find enough grass—he is your host. His dollars are few, his tithing is meager, but his testimony of the gospel, his dreams for his children, and his love for his fellowmen and his Lord induce him to send in his little tithing. He also becomes a joint host for you. (68-06)

BYU is a proper place to seek a spouse. Frequently, we hear the threadbare quips referring to the Brigham Young University as a matrimonial bureau and facetiously dubbing it the "BY Woo." Some think it clever, others might repeat it to downgrade the school's high academic standard. I do not think it amusing. What coeducational university is not such a bureau? Have you ever visited a campus in the country where there were not occupied park benches, young couples sitting in the corner, and shy glances and formal courting? Is there any reason why there should not be a searching for life's companions at all colleges? Most young women marry between nineteen and twenty-three, the college years. This is the natural and proper time to develop the associations in preparation for the happy future and eternal companionships. The Brigham Young University is the greatest of all universities, not only because its scholarship is high and it furthers knowledge to subdue the world, but it gives the spiritual training and experiences necessary for the total rounded-out education of eternal laws and godliness. Of course there have been numerous happy marriages initiated here. Thank the Lord for that, and may there continue to be wonderfully happy marriages as the by-product of this and all other coed universities!

The university is designed to prepare its students for life, and certainly one's success in life depends in large measure on the companion one chooses and the support and harmony in that relationship. (63-05)

BYU dress and grooming standards serve important purposes. I assure you that all the standards, both those relating to moral conduct and those relating to dress and grooming, are the result of intense, prayerful consideration by those entrusted with the overseeing of this university. BYU is in the best sense of the word a showplace. You might be surprised at the great number of inquiries we get from people wanting to know more because of what they have seen of BYU, its students, its faculty, and its graduates. They see here the beautiful grounds and buildings, which you help to keep almost spotless; they see students who have mastered the skills and knowledge they came here to learn as well as learning self-discipline and hard work, and whom employers are eager to hire; they see men and women whose virtue makes them shine in a crowd; they see young adults whose clean-cut appearance demonstrates that they feel no need to follow after the pattern of the world, which often revels in filth and disorder and garish fads; they see young men and young women who look like men and women, who have not succumbed to the morally destructive trend toward a unisex appearance in dress and grooming; they see people living cheerful, orderly lives, devoted to improving their ability to serve God and their fellowmen. (79-17)

We would like you to feel comfortable about these rules and regulations, these codes of honor and discipline. They are part of what we hope to teach at the university. We would like you to see these standards as tools with which you can build a better self. But of course they must be respected as tools, and care should be exercised so you do not inflict unnecessary self-injury by abusing yourself against them. Many of you know the feeling of missing a nail and hitting your thumb with a hammer. Hammers were designed to drive nails, not to drive thumbs. These standards at BYU are designed to build character, to teach discipline, to symbolize propriety and restraint and honor among students, faculty, and the institution as a whole. We would hope you would not spend your time "banging your heads" against these regulations. They were not designed to create dissension or to make you unhappy or angry. Please respect them as you would any tool and use them for their intended purposes. We would be disappointed to think that they would cause you undue difficulty. As the Lord said of the Word of Wisdom, these regulations, too, are "adapted to the capacity of the weak and the weakest of all saints, who are or can be called saints." (D&C 89:3.) We believe everyone can live them without anxiety or hardship. (78-23)

Maintain a special character for BYU. I joy with you in this greatest university under the sun. Perhaps it is not the largest, though it is impressive in its size; perhaps not the most renowned, though it is known favorably and appreciated from ocean to ocean and pole to pole; perhaps not the most richly endowed, yet having a host who is at once generous, firm, secure, and financially adequate. But here is the institution with every proper advantage: a great, dedicated administrator; a loyal and highly trained faculty; a strong, devoted staff; with excellent facilities; and presided over generally by men and women of faith, character, devotion, and love; and a student body unexcelled—students with purpose, understanding, strength, and proper direction. What a great school and what a desirable place to be, and how grateful we should be!...

We are different. We are a peculiar people. We hope we shall always be unusual and peculiar. On this great campus, we need not dress as extremists do on other campuses. We need not follow the world in thought or action. We need not bow to pressures which restrain and limit and coerce. Our programs—music, drama, etc.—need not be the type that others produce. Our journalistic work need not follow the world. Our standards need not be set by men of selfish minds. We may live in the outskirts of the world yet be not of the world. Why must people ape in every field the stupid and silly actions and plans and programs of the world?...

Let us keep it an island of beauty and cleanness in an ocean of filth and destruction and disease. Let us keep it as a spring of pure, cool water though surrounded by sloughs and stagnant swamps of rebellion and corruption and worldliness outside.

Let us keep it a place of peace in a world of confusion, frustration, mental aberrations, and emotional disturbances. Let us keep it a place of safety in a world of violence where laws are ignored, criminals coddled, enforcement curtailed, buildings burned, stores looted, lives endangered.

May we keep this glorious place a home of friendships and of eternal commitments; a place of study and growth and improvement; a place where ambition is kindled and faith is nurtured and confidence strengthened; and where love for God and our fellowmen reaches its highest fulfillment. (68-06)

BYU must resist false ideas. In this university (that may to some of our critics seem unfree) there will be real individual freedom. Freedom from worldly ideologies and concepts unshackles man far more than he knows. It is the truth that sets men free. BYU, in its second century, must become the last remaining bastion of resistance to the invading ideologies that seek control of curriculum as well as classroom. We do not resist such ideas because we fear them, but because they are false. BYU, in its second century, must continue to resist false fashions in education, staying with those basic principles which have proved right and have guided good men and women and good universities over the centuries. This concept is not new, but in the second hundred years we must do it even better.

When the pressures mount for us to follow the false ways of the world, we hope in the years yet future that those who are part of this university and the Church Educational System will not attempt to counsel the Board of Trustees to follow false ways. We want, through your administration, to receive all your suggestions for making BYU even better. I hope none will presume on the prerogatives of the prophets of God to set the basic direction for this university. . . .

No one is more anxious than the Brethren who stand at the head of this Church to receive such guidance as the Lord would give them for the benefit of mankind and for the people of the Church. (75-51)

BYU must grow in excellence. That task will be persisted in. Members of the Church are willing to doubly tax themselves to support the Church Educational System, including this university, and we must not merely "ape the world." We must do special things that would justify the special financial outpouring that supports this university. . . .

I am both hopeful and expectant that out of this university and the Church Educational System there will rise brilliant stars in drama, literature, music, sculpture, painting, science, and in all the scholarly graces. This university can be the refining host for many such individuals who will touch men and women the world over long after they have left this campus.

We must be patient, however, in this effort, because just as the city of Enoch took decades to reach its pinnacle of performance in what the Lord described as occurring "in process of time" (Moses

7:21), so the quest for excellence at BYU must also occur "in process of time." . . .

Much more needs to be done, but you must "not run faster or labor more than you have strength and means provided." (D&C 10:4.) While the discovery of new knowledge must increase, there must always be a heavy and primary emphasis on transmitting knowledge—on the quality of teaching at BYU. Quality teaching is a tradition never to be abandoned. It includes a quality relationship between faculty and students. (75-51)

BYU passes on a double heritage. Your light must have a special glow, for while you will do many things in the programs of this university that are done elsewhere, these same things can and must be done better here than others do them. You will also do some special things here that are left undone by other institutions.

First among these unique features is the fact that education on this campus deliberately and persistently concerns itself with "education for eternity," not just for time. The faculty has a double heritage which they must pass along: the secular knowledge that history has washed to the feet of mankind with the new knowledge brought by scholarly research—but also the vital and revealed truths that have been sent to us from heaven. (75-51)

BYU faculty need scholarly and spiritual strength. Your double heritage and dual concerns with the secular and the spiritual require you to be "bilingual." As LDS scholars you must speak with authority and excellence to your professional colleagues in the language of scholarship, and you must also be literate in the language of spiritual things. (75-51)

BYU faculty should communicate spiritual attitudes. It would not be expected that all of the faculty should be categorically teaching religion constantly in their classes, but it is proper that every professor and teacher in this institution would keep his subject matter bathed in the light and color of the restored gospel, and have all his subject matter perfumed lightly with the spirit of the gospel. Always, there would be an essence and the student would feel the presence.

Every instructor should grasp the opportunity occasionally to bear formal testimony of the truth. Every student is entitled to know the attitude and feeling and spirit of his every teacher. (67-10)

BYU has great destiny. It ought to be obvious to you, as it is to me, that some of the things the Lord would have occur in the second century of the BYU are hidden from our immediate view. Until we have climbed the hill just before us, we are not apt to be given a glimpse of what lies beyond. The hills ahead are higher than we think. This means that accomplishments and further direction must occur in proper order, after we have done our part. We will not be transported from point A to point Z without having to pass through the developmental and demanding experiences of all the points of achievement and all the milestone markers that lie between! . . .

We must do more than ask the Lord for excellence. Perspiration must precede inspiration; there must be effort before there is excellence. We must do more than pray for these outcomes at BYU, though we must surely pray. We must take thought. We must make effort. We must be patient. We must be professional. We must be spiritual. Then, in the process of time, this will become the fully anointed university of the Lord about which so much has been spoken in the past. (75-51)

CHAPTER 15

Government and War

Working for Good Government

America's future depends on righteousness. This America is no
ordinary country. It is a choice land, "choice above all other lands."
(1 Nephi 2:20.) It has a tragic and bloody past, but a glorious and
peaceful future if its inhabitants really learn to serve their God.
(61-04)

God affects history. I have a firm conviction that the Lord led the
Pilgrims and the Puritans across the ocean, perhaps permitted the
persecutions that would bring them here, so that when they come to
the American shores with their righteous blood and their high ideals
and standards, they would form the basis of a nation which would
make possible the restoration of the gospel. I am sure that since there
was not religious liberty, not political liberty here, the Lord permitted
these few poorly armed and ill-clad men at Valley Forge and elsewhere to defeat a great army with its trained soldiery and its many
mercenaries, a few against the many, but the few had on their side the
Lord God of heaven, that gave them victory. And there came political liberty and religious liberty with it, all in preparation for the day
when a young boy would come forth and would seek and make
contact with the Lord and open the doors of heaven again. Following
that great manifestation to Joseph Smith came the opening of
Cumorah Hill and the speaking of the dead from the dust. (50-05)

Unrighteous government leads to revolution. [One who reads the Book of Mormon] will see people thriving in communal living, and taxed from 50 percent, and then to totalness, to slavery, and to bondage. He will see power-greedy, paternalistic, centralized governments move toward the inevitable revolution which finally impoverishes but frees the people to begin again from ashes. (63-02)

Pray for political leaders. Father, we are concerned with the political world of today, and that nations seem to need only the lighting of a match to bring war and desolation and destruction. Bless, we pray thee, the leaders of nations, that they may rule wisely and righteously and give thy people freedom to worship thee in truth and righteousness. Stay the powers, our Father, that would bring us to the brink of annihilation. (74-35)

Father, bless their deliberations that they may always obtain facts and consider them in proper perspective, and that as they ponder they shall have in mind the good of the people who elected them, and that as they make their final decisions they may have weighed every matter as to rightness rather than expediency, blessings to the masses rather than concessions to the cliques, and that their every desire may have proven proper motives rather than ulterior ones, and that they may always measure every issue by the yardstick of righteousness and weigh it by the scales of justice and ask themselves in every case, "How would my Lord and Master vote on this issue, were he a legislator here?" Father, there are many problems in our state which will challenge the sharpest minds and the cleanest hearts of conscientious men. Please bless and sustain them through the long, arduous hours of deliberation and planning. Inspire them, for here is a great need for power beyond the limited abilities of mortal man. Bless them with a rich portion of thy spirit, that the people of this beloved state of Utah may have a government with high moral standards and of great honor and integrity, that we may have ever-increasing freedom without invasion of devastating influences. Let this area be a haven of refuge for the oppressed, a place for the righteous pleasure of the fun-loving, a sanctuary of freedom and peace for all who choose to live here. (69-01)

Support constitutional principles of freedom. As members of Christ's true church we must stand firm today and always for human rights and the dignity of man, who is the literal offspring of God in the spirit. (79-03)

The Mormon people who are citizens of [the United States of] America today are intensely loyal to its Constitution and desire in every way to promote the God-given freedoms it was designed to protect. They have had experience with the tragedy that results when those freedoms are not protected, but this only feeds their determination to do all within their power to protect these freedoms, both for themselves and others, everywhere. (79-07)

Preservation of freedom requires effort. Now that Independence Day is here, let us glory in its blessings. It is a strange thing when you stop to think about it. The road to this land of the United States is pretty nearly a one-way street. Everyone wants to come here. Nobody wants to leave. You probably never knew anyone who wanted to give up his American citizenship.

Why is this so? Is it because we have more to eat? Better homes? Better living conditions? That cannot be, because people wanted to come here when this was a country of hardship.

No, it is not just dollars. The early pioneers could have told you what it was. It is freedom. It is personal liberty. It is all of the human rights that millions of Americans have died for.

The sad part of it is that a lot of us take our civil rights for granted. We were born in a free country. We think freedom could never end. But it could. It is ending today in many countries. We could lose it, too.

The only way we can keep our freedom is to work at it. Not some of us. All of us. Not some of the time, but all of the time.

So if you value your citizenship and want to keep it for yourself and your children and their children, give it your faith, your belief, and give it your active support in civic affairs. (76-30)

Sustain law actively. Not only shall we not steal, but we shall protect others' possessions. We employ law-enforcement officers, we cooperate with them and the judges; we help to develop a world where vice is unprofitable, uncomfortable, and disappointing. (MF 99)

Help select good officials. Furthermore, in order to implement our divine charge to seek for such "civil officers ... as will administer the law in equity and justice" (D&C 134:3), we urge Church members to attend the mass meetings of their respective political parties and there exercise their influence.

Every Latter-day Saint should sustain, honor, and obey the constitutional law of the land in which he lives. (74-02)

We urge you to study the platforms and acquaint yourself with the candidates. Then pray to the Lord for guidance, and go to the polls and vote. (74-30)

In political elections, people need in their representatives much more than talent and fluency and good looks, but power to make talent trusted. (67-02)

Avoid involving the Church in politics. To those of you who are citizens of the United States: I wish to urge you and your family members of voting age to go to the polls in large numbers and vote for the strongest, finest people who are certain to do the most to safeguard the rights and freedoms of this nation. We do not endorse any candidates, but we hope you will vote for good men and women of character, integrity, and ability. You are to be the judge. Further, we hope our Church buildings and our Church organizations will not be used to advance the candidacy or policies of any of the candidates. (80-33)

Uphold and sustain the law. Work within the law to be an influence for that which is good, as the Prophet Joseph Smith counseled us.

Please avoid, even by implication, involving the Church in political issues. It is so easy, if we are not careful, to project our personal preferences as the position of the Church on an issue. (76-26)

The First Presidency and the Twelve wish to reaffirm this important statement of 1968: We believe this is the wise course to pursue, wherein Church members are urged to do their duties as citizens. The Church of Jesus Christ of Latter-day Saints cannot be committed, as an institution, except on those issues which are determined by the First Presidency and Twelve to be of such a nature that the Church should take an official position concerning them.

We believe that to do otherwise would involve the Church, formally and officially, on a sufficient number of issues that the result would be to divert the Church from its basic mission of teaching the restored gospel of the Lord to the world.

We earnestly hope Church members will feel their individual responsibilities keenly and pursue them wisely.

We hope you Regional Representatives will counsel stake presidents and other local leaders in your respective areas to be careful about involving the Church as an institution in matters that are best pursued by Church members as individual citizens. We further hope you will help priesthood leaders and members to understand why the Church must decline many of their requests to involve the Church on a particular issue. The issue may be very deserving and the cause worthy, but for the reasons already indicated, appropriate involvement must come from Church members as individual citizens rather than from the Church as an institution. (78-04)

Avoid Political Extremes

Christ was not a political victor. The harbinger of peace was not accepted nor received by his people, for the brand of peace he offered was not the kind they had been expecting. Long centuries they had looked for a redeemer, but their interpretations of the numerous prophecies left them expecting a warrior to lead them victoriously against their political enemies and free them from Roman bondage. Wishful thinking and ambitious hopes had led them to look for a redeemer who would reign with the sword, as a political king, and put under his feet all kingdoms and dominions. . . .

Yet such a peace was never contemplated by the Lord, nor was such an one ever prophesied. But he did bring emancipation to a benighted world, to a people bound in the chains of superstition, lip service, and spiritual bondage. He came and organized his church, set up an eternal program, loosed the bands of death through his own death and resurrection, and outlined and lived before us a perfect plan by which all men might live eternally in joy and peace. (44-04)

Extreme political solutions are not compatible with gospel. Remember that the gospel of Jesus Christ is not compatible with radicalism or communism or any other of the "isms." There could be those among you who would profess to be your saviors. They could enslave you with their force or their so-called doctrines. If some of their leaders have motives that are selfish and questionable, you should have nothing to do with them. Perhaps some would even excite you to riot. Beware of them. Keep your feet on the ground and your heads high. (77-39)

Granted all this, that there is much bitterness, hatred, class and race distinction, inequalities, and suffering in the world, are you wise in your determination to attack the problems as you seem to have in mind? Granted that men should all be free, should be equal, should be secure, should be fed and clothed, are you going about it in the right way? Is not any revolutionary movement which you might join or lead only a means to an end? Is it the proper means? If I read the scriptures with understanding, I see the Creator of this world denouncing all the evils which you hate and which you would overcome, but attempting to solve the problems in a different way. Did not the same evils of hate and greed and selfishness and avarice, and inequality and oppression and slavery exist to an even greater degree perhaps when the Maker of the world walked the earth? The enlightened and scripture-reading Jews expected him to come as a revolutionary, as a politician, as a warrior who would rid them of their oppressors, and bring them peace and plenty. Because he chose to handle the situation in a different way, they rejected him and nailed him to a great timber. . . .

He saw the bitterness of race hatreds and forthwith went into hated Samaria. He sat at the well and conversed with the despised Samaritans against common custom, for as the woman said, "The Jews have no dealings with the Samaritans." And later revealed he to Peter that the Gentiles were as acceptable as the Jews. "What God hath cleansed, that call not thou common." His was a way of teaching equalities the slow, free-agency way rather than by revolutionary force.

He was grieved with the class distinction as shown by the priest and Levite toward the man rescued by the good Samaritan, and poured forth his indictments against the many groups who dealt in such hypocrisies, but instead of revolutionary tactics, he tried to shame them into a change of their way of life.

He deplored the accumulation of great wealth at the expense of the downtrodden. . . . He made no effort to organize political forces to take from the rich, but taught correct principles of welfare in which the poor would be provided for by the rich voluntarily. . . .

Aren't you becoming an extremist and losing your balance somewhat, and in that very radicalism will you not bring to yourself impotency in the very results which you would attain? Wouldn't you far better align yourself with all the constructive forces which attempt in a slower, more peaceful way to reach the same ends? With your great ability you might be able to go far in spreading the message of good will through Church media.

May I say again: when you include in the gospel plan of Christ the family, there is nothing else in all the world worth bothering with. Everything else is incidental only. Assume that you become the world leader of Socialism and in it have marked success, but through your devotion to it you fail to live the gospel. Where are you then? Is anything worthwhile which will estrange you from your friends, your Church membership, your family, your eternal promises, your faith? You might say that such estrangement is not necessarily a result of your political views, but truthfully hasn't your overpowering interest in your present views already started driving a wedge? (0/0/45)

Christ shunned revolutionary solutions. In his life the sword was ever present.... And yet he said that he who lived by the sword would perish by the sword. He would have nothing to do with it.... And though the world's ills were revolting to him, he sought to reform the world by teaching men correct principles and depending on them to properly govern themselves.

Today, many are becoming extremists and are losing balance and effectiveness and are missing the results which they would desire to attain. Wouldn't they be far better off to align themselves with the constructive forces and attempt a slower, more peaceful way to reach the same ends? (77-22)

Promoting Good Legislation

Limit evil by legislation and education. You heard Elder Hinckley talk about the flood of pornographic filth that nearly drowns us and the emphasis that is placed upon sex and violence. I liked the way he asked us to encourage the leaders—the legislature—to make the proper laws to control these situations—and when they do, to give them thanks and appreciation, and when they don't to give them a little nudging. (75-49)

Paul would understand us and our ceaseless battles against these powers of darkness and those of spiritual wickedness who use their political influence and their powers of office to harass the public and convince them an inch at a time to accept evil for good. There is little help from powers in high places to keep obscene written material out of the mails and away from our children. There is a constant pressure to legalize liquor, tobacco, gambling, and other evils because they are so heavily fortified with the spirits of evil which are not flesh-and-blood powers. They bring enticing arguments and deceive "even the very elect" if it were possible. They would have open immorality, prostitution, gambling, liquor, and everything that is evil....

Brethren, we must work with all other good agencies to protect our youth, so far as we can by legislation, and laws and the enforcement thereof. But we must concede that our only totally effective weapon against the wiles of the devil is proper and preventive education and preventive training. The hands of the devil cannot be handcuffed nor the barred gates of his prison cell be locked but by the righteousness of his intended victims. (66-07)

Law cannot create goodness. Men have tried through centuries to cure these evils and solve these problems and correct these crimes with police, courts, jails and penitentiaries. They have had blue laws to correct Sabbath breaking, obscenity, hedonism, immorality. They have tried wars to end wars. They have tried handouts and outright gifts to solve poverty, especially through taxation. They are trying numerous force and superficial ways to cure racism. They have used the law and the officers and the jails and systems of force to solve problems. Through the ages we have come to know we cannot legislate goodness. . . .

The world would legislate goodness and make men fear to do wrong. The gospel would cause men to do right because it makes them happy to do right. (71-17)

Legislation on family is often harmful. Whether from inadvertence, ignorance, or other causes, the efforts governments often make (ostensibly to help the family) sometimes only hurt the family more. There are those who would define the family in such a nontraditional way that they would define it out of existence. The more governments try in vain to take the place of the family, the less effective governments will be in performing the traditional and basic roles for which governments are formed in the first place. (80-32)

Exclusion of religion from school and government is unfortunate. It is a real travesty today when we hear the voices of the atheist, the godless, and the anti-Christ who would deny us the right of public expression of our worship of the Master. First they moved against the long-established institution of prayer in our public schools. They would remove any vestige of Christianity or worship of the Savior of mankind in our public gatherings; they would remove the long-established tradition of prayer in our Congress, remove the "In God

We Trust" insignia from our nation's emblems and seals and from our national coins.

The latest move of these anti-Christs would prohibit our own children from singing the beautiful and inspiring Christmas carols, relating to the Savior's birth or divinity, or "the heavenly angels singing" from our public schools. (78-43)

Prohibition of alcohol use would be desirable. The good people who would like to protect themselves and their families and their neighbors from all of the corruption that liquor brings instead of yielding to the opposition could start to move toward prohibition again. The Lord says the traffic is evil. Why will good people be tricked and deceived?

One cannot touch the liquor traffic without contamination. It is evil; it is prostituting the lives of men.

Should we not take the offensive, and move to eliminate the curse from our communities? Why stand always on the defensive while those who have ulterior motives campaign to make alcohol more readily available? Are we involved and beholden because of our rents, or holdings, or leases, or conventions, or tourists? Are dollars so important?

Why do we not close the bars and taverns? An aroused vote could put an end to loss and waste and annoyance and death and suffering from this source. If no one bought and consumed liquor, there would be no manufacture nor traffic in it. (67-13)

One of the saddest days in all of Utah's history was when the people, including the Latter-day Saints (for it could not have been done without them), rejected the counsel and urging of the Lord's prophet, Heber J. Grant, and repealed Prohibition long years ago— yet many of those voters had sung numerous times, "We Thank Thee, O God, for a Prophet." (68-06)

Support newspapers having good editorial policies. Bring to your home that newspaper which is most compatible with the teachings and standards of the Church.

Here in Salt Lake City, the world headquarters of the Church, we are also concerned. Certainly a powerful force in helping this city and state achieve its high standards has been the *Deseret News*. This newspaper has been a defender of our convictions relative to such moral issues as liquor, pornography, and abortion. It is vital to a safe, clean city and state, which are the heart of our growing, world-wide Church. (78-07)

The Sin of War

War curses victor and vanquished. When armies march and people fight, education suffers, art languishes, buildings crumble, forests are exploited, farms return to desert, and orchards to jungle. Fighting men build temporary bridges, forts, and towers instead of homes, public buildings, and observatories. There is neither time nor inclination to carve statues, paint landscapes, compose music, or record history. Communities on the march or in retreat have no schools nor teachers. Priceless records are destroyed with the buildings and cities which are burned and pillaged. Artists, scholars, writers, and clergy alike shoulder arms, stalking enemies, and laying seige to cities. Plunder replaces honest industry. Cattle, goats, and poultry are devoured by voracious soldiers. Calves, kids, and piglets are eaten, as are the seed-corn and the wheat. Fruit is devoured, and trees are burned for wood. Today's insatiable hunger swallows tomorrow's plenty. Armies carry movable tents and abandon homes and churches. Temples fall in ruins and are overgrown by vegetation. . . . Life becomes a sordid existence, bloody, with little purpose except to survive. . . .

Great cultures stagnate in war shadows and cease to survive when continuous wars make people migrants, when fields are abandoned, livestock appropriated for nonproducing soldiers, forests destroyed without replanting, and when farmers and builders become warriors, and businessmen shoulder arms and teachers mobilize. Men cannot plant, cultivate, and harvest when in camps, nor build when on the run. Long and bloody wars mean sacked, burned, ruined cities, confiscatory taxes, degenerated peoples, and decayed cultures.

Victory and defeat alike leave countries devastated and the conqueror and the conquered reduced. Wickedness brings war, and war vomits destruction and suffering, hate and bloodshed upon the guilty and the innocent.

This impressive book [the Book of Mormon] should convince all living souls of the futility of war and the hazards of unrighteousness. A few prophets, swimming in a sea of barbarism, find it difficult to prevent the crumbling and final collapse of corrupt peoples. (63-02)

Living the gospel is the road to peace. We do not favor war. We do not like the blood of war, the stench of war, the suffering of war, the deprivations of war, the cruelty of war, the degradation of war. We hate war but there are considerations that must be kept in mind. How can war be eliminated from the earth? The answer is simple but hard to realize. Let the people of this world live the gospel. Before peace can come to the world around us, it must come into our hearts. Greed is fostered by war and numerous profiteers come from it. Numerous communities would fade almost out of existence if war profits were to terminate. We cry war evils on one side of our mouths and cry for the profits of war on the other. Stocks and bonds would reduce. Many places have felt the squeeze of reduction in building. Chambers of commerce are alert always for new industries, many of which depend in large measure on war activities. (71-17)

Community change is accumulation of individual changes. It seems almost a hopeless undertaking to establish peace on earth and good will to men throughout the world, when at this very moment nations are in civil combat and are armed to the teeth; and yet, we may take comfort from the old adage that the "dripping water wears away the hardest stone." All great movements had their small beginnings, and as the acorn which falls into a crevice in the rock gradually and eventually splits the great stone wide open, so if we are persistent in our effort, certainly our dream of world peace will someday be realized. (36-01)

First we make ourselves humble. We change our own lives; that is the beginning. We all want to change the nation in a day. A nation is made up of individuals. We start and change our own lives, and then we help another life to get the same ideals—and then there are two lives. And all the other individuals around us do the same thing; and here we have a community, and there another community; and several communities make a state and several states make a nation. And we can do it. The Lord will protect us. He is not going to save a nation for one individual or community. But when the majority of the nation begins to get righteous there will not be wholesale destruction—make certain of that. And one reason why we haven't been destroyed in these two last great wars which we have suffered, is because there were some that the Lord was willing to save. (55-09)

No walls provide adequate security. The Great Wall of China with its fifteen hundred miles of unbreakable walls, with its twenty-five-feet-high impregnableness, with its innumerable watchman towers, was breached by the treachery of men.

The Maginot Line in France, these forts thought to be so strong and impassable, were violated as though they were not there. Strength is not in concrete and reinforcing steel. Protection is not in walls nor mountains nor cliffs, yet foolish men still lean on "the arm of flesh."

The walls of Babylon were too high to be scaled, too thick to be broken, too strong to be crumbled, but not too deep to be undermined when the human element failed. When the protectors sleep and the leaders are incapacitated with banqueting and drunkenness and immorality, an invading enemy can turn a river from its course and enter through a riverbed.

The precipitous walls on the high hills of Jerusalem deflected for a time the arrows and spears of enemies, the catapults and firebrands. But even then wickedness did not lessen, men did not learn lessons. Hunger scaled the walls; thirst broke down the gates; immorality, cannibalism, idolatry, godlessness stalked about till destruction came.

"Experience is a dear teacher but fools will learn by no other." But we continue on in our godlessness. While the iron curtains rise and thicken, we eat, drink, and make merry. While armies are marshalled and march and drill, and officers teach men how to kill, we continue to drink and carouse as usual. While bombs are detonated and tested, and fallout settles on the already sick world, we continue in idolatry and adultery. While corridors are threatened and concessions made, we live riotously and divorce and marry in cycles like the seasons. While leaders quarrel, and editors write, and authorities analyze and prognosticate, we break the Sabbath as though no command had ever been given. While enemies filter into our nation to subvert us and intimidate us and soften us, we continue with our destructive thinking: "It can't happen here."

Will we ever turn wholly to God? Fear envelops the world which could be at ease and peace. In God is protection, safety, peace. He has said, "I will fight your battles." But his commitment is on condition of our faithfulness. (61-04)

Men depend on armaments as on idols. O foolish men who think to protect the world with armaments, battleships, and space equipment, when only righteousness is needed!

The answer to all of our problems—personal, national, and international—has been given to us many times by many prophets, ancient and modern. Why must we grovel in the earth when we could be climbing toward heaven! The path is not obscure. Perhaps it is too simple for us to see. We look to foreign programs, summit conferences, land bases. We depend on fortifications, or gods of stone; upon ships and planes and projectiles, our gods of iron—gods which have no ears, no eyes, no hearts. We pray to them for deliverance and depend upon them for protection...like the gods of Baal. (60-06)

God will fight our battles if we honor him and serve him with all our hearts, might, mind, and strength....

The cause is not lost. If...integrity and worship reigned in the lives of men, the era of total peace would be ushered in. Fear would vanish, and enemies would be subdued.

Of course, a one-sided disarmament could be madness if worldliness and materialism continued, but a serious turn of the masses could forestall all military conquests, all tragedies of conflict. God is all-powerful. (61-04)

Warlike peoples pervert patriotism. We are a warlike people, easily distracted from our assignment of preparing for the coming of the Lord. When enemies rise up, we commit vast resources to the fabrication of gods of stone and steel—ships, planes, missiles, fortifications—and depend on them for protection and deliverance. When threatened, we become antienemy instead of pro-kingdom of God; we train a man in the art of war and call him a patriot, thus, in the manner of Satan's counterfeit of true patriotism, perverting the Savior's teaching:

"Love your enemies, bless them that curse you, do good to them that hate you, and pray for them which despitefully use you, and persecute you;

"That ye may be the children of your Father which is in heaven." (Matthew 5:44-45.)

We forget that if we are righteous the Lord will either not suffer our enemies to come upon us—and this is the special promise to the inhabitants of the land of the Americas—or he will fight our battles for us. . . .

What are we to fear when the Lord is with us? Can we not take the Lord at his word and exercise a particle of faith in him? (76-29)

After war we must help rebuild. There is but one race—humanity. We can hardly have a heaven in our own country and leave a hell outside. If we have peace now it must be a world peace. If we have economic security and individual liberty here we must export it to all other countries. The young men of other countries share also our desire for a better world with equal justice and liberty for all. (53-01)

Though food be scarce, and starvation stalks abroad, men will still share their portion, give succor to the afflicted, sympathy to the bereaved, and help to the unfortunate. Though cities be bombed, families separated, the meaning of sympathy and understanding and brotherhood will not change. Courage is not dead, ambition is not slain, love is not replaced. The bombed cities shall rise again, the grain that was burned shall be replanted, the fountain that evil has polluted shall flow pure again, the battered forests will shoot forth new foliage and the grass will spring forth anew to obliterate the traces of war. Even though a thousand times they shall afflict the earth, a thousand times will it come forth again and men will survive to plant the ground and build upon it. The conditions of life in this chaotic situation are changed, but the meaning of the fundamentals of life have not changed. (43-01)

Counsel to Soldiers

Killing in war is not murder. Men unfortunately must take others' lives in war. Some of our conscientious young men have been disturbed and concerned as they have been compelled to kill. There are mitigating circumstances, but certainly the blame and responsibility rests heavily upon the heads of those who brought about the war making necessary the taking of life. It is conceivable that even in war there may be many times when there is a legitimate choice, and enemy combatants could be taken prisoner rather than be killed.

Here is an excerpt from the message of the First Presidency dated April 6, 1942:

> The whole world is in the midst of a war that seems the worst of all time. The Church is a world-wide church. Its devoted members are in both camps. They are the innocent war instrumentalities of their warring sovereignties. On each side they believe they are fighting for home, country, and freedom. On each side, our brethren pray to the same God, in the same name, for victory. Both sides cannot be wholly right; perhaps neither is without wrong. God will work out in His own due time and in His own sovereign way the justice and right of the conflict but he will not hold the innocent instrumentalities of the war, our brethren in arms, responsible for the conflict. (MF 129)

Killing in war is tragic. If he [Heber C. Kimball] were here tonight [at this reunion] he would miss many intelligent young faces, and we would explain to him that these young sons are in uniform, fighting on far-flung battlefronts, in Italy, in Pacific waters, in Normandy. He would feel patriotic and willing for them to do their duty but would register in his kindly face deep sadness, knowing that perhaps as many as five hundred of his own flesh and blood were in hazardous zones, some of them prisoners of war, and still others in new graves. He would abhor the necessity of killing and might repeat to us what he said to his sons who were blessed by him as they went into the Black Hawk War. He promised them that they should not see an Indian while they were gone. And when they returned and told him his promise had been fulfilled, he said: "Didn't I tell you?" and then added: "I would rather have them kill you, than to have one of my sons shed their blood." (44-05)

Soldiers are not responsible for war. One Christmas during the World War, when no-man's-land between the trenches was white with snow, the troops in a certain "quiet sector" began to exchange holiday greetings by means of crudely painted signs. A few minutes later, men who spoke German and men who spoke English were climbing from their trenches without guns and meeting on neutral ground to shake hands and exchange souvenirs, unmindful of war. No venom, no meanness, no poisonous hatred between these men at war. Friends they were, not enemies, this Christmas Day. For the moment, blessed forgetfulness erased from their memory the masters who drove them into bloody conflict. . . .

Rather on the Lord's birthday they saw them [opposing soldiers] as fellowmen, men with homes they built, loved children who played about their knees, men who followed the same risen Lord and Master but who were tricked by the warlords and converted by leaders and propagandists that they should fight and kill. They understood each other now and liked each other.

It is ignorance that makes wars and most other differences possible. People believe the opposition capable of atrocious things, because they do not realize that human nature is very much alike, wherever you find it. (34-01)

Make good use of time in military service. [Some of you young men] are obligated to train for military service. Your time there need not be wasted. It can be a time for study, self-improvement, and service to others. Here you may learn to exercise authority gracefully so that you may have the enthusiastic cooperation from those you command rather than their insubordinate and sullen obedience. You may also learn to be a consistent follower, and how men work as teams in harmony, especially when lives depend on such unified cooperation. You will see men in their best and worst moods and learn how to judge them. Your ability to command respect from subordinates and superiors may well carry over into your business, professional, community, and ecclesiastical life.

In Bavaria, years ago, I attended the servicemen's conference. The wives of many of our American soldiers accompanied them. I found that some were profiting by their foreign assignment, while others were bored, hated the country, loathed the conditions and disliked the people and were annoyed at the language. To them I pleaded, "Here is your great opportunity. Learn the language. At home, you would pay tuition and spend years in college learning it. Enjoy and learn the customs, habits, ideals, and loves of these good people. Many folks spend thousands of dollars to tour these countries and get but a superficial acquaintance with all which you can so easily absorb now." (63-05)

True, there may be many bitter disappointments because of this holocaust. It may mean a termination of your schooling, a postponement in many cases of your marriage and family life.

It may be that a mission must be bypassed and careers forgotten for the present, but if you will it so, life may go on for you full, sweet, and abundant, for the worthwhile things do not change in times of trouble. Servicemen have written from all parts of the globe expressing their newly realized reliance upon the Lord, their appreciation for his Church and his gospel and his people. And so, hectic days seem to intensify our love of the real and the good. (44-06)

CHAPTER 16

Church History and Destiny

Christ's Church Has Been Restored

This is the only true church. Now, frequently, we have these requests. People who get careless; they don't want the home teachers to call on them; they are embarrassed by the Church; they have outgrown the Church, they think, and sometimes they don't want to have anything to do with it. Finally, if they are bothered too much, they will oftentimes send a letter in and say, "Take my name off the church records." They do not know what they are doing.

This is not *a* church. This is the Church of Jesus Christ. There are churches of men all over the land and they have great cathedrals, synagogues, and other houses of worship running into the hundreds of millions of dollars. They are the churches of men. They teach the doctrines of men, combined with the philosophies and ethics and other ideas and ideals that men have partly developed and partly found in sacred places and interpreted for themselves. But there is just one church which Jesus Christ, himself, organized by direct revelation; just one church that teaches *all* of his doctrines; just one church which has all of the keys and authorities which are necessary to carry on the work of Jesus Christ. And you would, of course, expect it to be the Church of Jesus Christ and not carry any other name. He says, "The church shall be called by my name. If it is somebody else's church, it will be called by their name." (See 3 Nephi 27:3-8.) So as you go down the roster, and find organizations named after everybody under the sun, every holy word in the scripture, every method and technique and program, it must be obvious that they aren't the Church of Jesus Christ. Surely there are good people— wonderful people in all of them; there are many people in leadership in those organizations who are sincere and devoted. That is not the thought we wish to convey. Many good people are deceived. The Lord restored his kingdom in these days, with all its gifts and powers and blessings. Any church that you know of may possibly be able to take you for a long ride, and bring you some degree of peace and happiness and blessing, and they can carry you to the veil, and there they drop you. The Church of Jesus Christ picks you up on this side of the veil and, if you live its commandments, carries you right through the veil as though it weren't there and on through the eternities to exaltation. (57-03)

We endeavor to convince the world that where the truths of man- made organizations end, the gospel of Jesus Christ continues. The truths they teach are largely ethical. We go forward from there with ethics and gospel that carries us through the mortal life and on past the heaven of their fondest dreams into worlds of progression and creative work which are to their religious concepts as the airplane to the bumblebee. (3/6/47)

The Church is based on new revelation. This Church has as its foundation the principle of revelation. There were many organiza- tions already in the world which had been organized by good men of understanding and spirituality—many churches planned by good men. The only justification for another church to come forth in 1830 was that the true church must be restored; a church that would come from the Lord Jesus Christ; it would have to be his church that would teach his doctrines by his authority and through revelation. (57-01)

The Great Apostasy

History describes repeated apostasies. The gospel came to Adam and his descendants. Apostates through the ages built their false doctrines on the basis of the truths. The barbarians, the primitives, the Indians, have distorted truths. Their ideas of God, and all the relationships between men and God, have had a truth from which to spring. There is no happenstance that the golden rule is found in some form in nearly every major religion. It was taught to Adam, and perverted peoples continued to carry that obvious truth through their wanderings. And so the Catholic church, an outgrowth of apostasy of a much later date, carries distorted truths in its program; and since the day of the Catholic church is far more recent than the beginnings of other major religions such as Buddhism, etc., the distortion is a little less.... God established the order of heaven. When revelation ceased, the usurpers placed upon every program a private interpretation and there came to be the genuine and the spurious in every line. (5/31/48)

This is not a continuous church, nor is it one that has been re-formed or redeemed. It has been restored after it was lost. It was lost—the gospel with its powers and blessings—sometime after the Savior's crucifixion and the loss of his apostles. The laws were changed, the ordinances were changed, and the everlasting covenant was broken that the Lord Jesus Christ gave to his people in those days. There was a long period of centuries when the gospel was not available to people on this earth, because it had been changed. (76-40)

From the beginning, people of the world have existed in alternating light and shadow, but most of the time in the greyness or darkness of the shadows, with relatively short periods of light.

The Lord is eager to see their first awakening desires and their beginning efforts to penetrate the darkness. Having granted freedom of decision, he must permit man to grope his way until he reaches for the light. But when men begin to hunger, when arms begin to reach, when knees begin to bend and voices become articulate, then and not until then does the Father push back the horizons, draw back the veil, and make it possible for men to emerge from dim, uncertain stumbling to sureness in the brilliance of the heavenly light.

Such a time was that when the noble Abraham broke the bands of idolatrous thralldom to let the clear light of heaven in and leave the earth illumined for many generations.

Also, after four centuries of Egyptian slavery and the consequent apostasy of the children of Israel, the spiritual sun went down and spiritual darkness covered "the earth, and gross darkness the people." (Isaiah 60:2.) A son of God found solitude in deserts and found companionship with dumb creatures; and while wandering to find grass and waterholes, he was searching the heavens, finally finding light in a burning bush. Amid lightnings and thunderings, he climbed the rugged Sinai and broke the stillness, opening the heavens. God was again revealing his secrets to his servants the prophets.

But unused gates sag and hinges rust and dust and weeds cover apertures. The spiritual wilderness encroaches and heaven's curtains are closed when men ignore and defy and lose this contact with their Lord. Communication was sporadic through those ages. For centuries the unheard and unheeded voices of the lone prophets were crying in the wilderness. But one day a new star blazed forth and the total light came into the world. Stars, moon, and sun bowed obeisance and total light shone forth and dark corners were penetrated. The Son of God, the light of the world, came and opened the curtains, and heaven and earth were again in communion. But when the light of that century went out, the darkness was impenetrable, the heavens were sealed, and the "dark ages" moved in. The thickness of this spiritual darkness was not unlike that physical darkness in Nephite history when "neither candles, neither torches; neither could there be fire kindled with their fine and exceedingly dry wood." (3 Nephi 8:21.) The spiritual vapor of darkness was impenetrable, and centuries were to pass with hardly the dim uncertain light of a candle to break its austere darkness.

Another day dawned, another soul with passionate yearning prayed for divine guidance. A spot of hidden solitude was found, knees were bended, hearts were humbled, pleadings were voiced, and a light brighter than the noonday sun illuminated the world—the curtain never to be closed again, the gate never again to be slammed, this light never again to be extinguished. A young lad of incomparable faith broke the spell, shattered the "heavens of iron" and reestablished communication. Heaven kissed the earth, light dissipated the darkness, and God again spake to man revealing "his secret unto his servants the prophets." (Amos 3:7.) A new prophet was in the land, and through him God set up his kingdom—a kingdom never to be destroyed nor left to another people—a kingdom that will stand forever. (60-09)

Men turned from truth. Lucifer turned men from the truth to fables. He changed men from revelation to human logic and mental gymnastics and convinced them that man was on his own, to make all his own determinations without the aid of God and his prophets and apostles. This earth, already much in darkness, slipped into the Dark Ages when the Holy Ghost was not available to men, when no prophets led the people, when men's minds were darkened, when few inventions came to benefit mankind. (75-19)

Philosophy replaced revelation. In the early centuries of the Christian era, the apostasy came not through persecution, but by relinquishment of faith caused by the superimposing of a man-made structure upon and over the divine program. Many men with no pretense nor claim to revelation, speaking without divine authority or revelation, depending only upon their own brilliant minds, but representing as they claim the congregations of the Christians and in long conference and erudite councils, sought the creation process to make a God which all could accept.

The brilliant minds with their philosopies, knowing much about the Christian traditions and the pagan philosophies, would combine all elements to please everybody. They replaced the simple ways and program of the Christ with spectacular rituals, colorful display, impressive pageantry, and limitless pomposity, and called it Christianity. They had replaced the glorious, divine plan of exaltation of Christ with an elaborate, colorful, man-made system. They seemed to have little idea of totally dethroning the Christ, nor terminating the life of God, as in our own day, but they put together an incomprehensible God idea.

They thus reached the point of muddled mysticism called "the mystery of mysteries," with contradictions that Gods are separate yet combined, substance yet without substance, anthropomorphic yet only spirit, the Son begotten yet unbegotten.

It took them years to develop this incomprehensible mysticism, and after many centuries the Christians are still mystified, and this has led in no small measure to the "Death of God" theorists, for as one modern thinker said: "It is easier to think of a dead God than one who is mystified, disembodied, inactivated, powerless, unimpressive." (66-05)

The Reformation reacted to apostasy. The apostles were killed and the saints were driven by the Roman emperors, and with the death of these important people, the authority went with them and authority was lost. . . .

About A.D. 300 Constantine, who was not a Christian, organized the great worldwide church.

Men with keen intelligence got together . . . [at] Nicea and created a God. They did not pray for wisdom or revelation. They claimed no revelation from the Lord. They made it just about like a political party would do, and out of their own mortal minds created a God which is still worshipped by the great majority of Christians. They took away all his physical properties, they took the Father and the Son and made them into one undefinable spirit, and they changed baptism to sprinkling, they changed other ordinances and doctrines, so by the time the great Luther came, there had been a great apostasy from the Church. Luther knew that. He did not expect to organize a new church. He just wanted to cleanse the old church, of which he was a priest. Now, we believe Luther was a great man. He was courageous. Yet, he did not claim revelation, as far as I have found; but he did a great service to mankind. He turned the key in the lock that opened the door of mental serfdom. For hundreds of years before Luther, there had been mental slavery. People did not read their Bibles, they listened only to the priest. They were in spiritual bondage. But beginning with this break of Martin Luther from the church of which he had been a member, freedom of thought and freedom of religion began to be a nearer reality. We know that Luther came as a servant of the Lord to open the way, just like Columbus discovered America in the part of the great program of our Heavenly Father, and just like the Puritans and Pilgrims who found their way to the new world.

Beginning with Martin Luther there came a flood of new re-formers, and hundreds of Protestant churches have grown up, and not one of them claimed a new revelation from God. They went their own ways. They interpreted the scriptures according to their own minds and, of course, there are marvelous people in all of those organizations, but God did not reveal those new organizations. (55-10)

Spiritual darkness was a desolation. We are pilgrims upon this earth, sent here with a mission to perform, a great work to do, for which we need guidance from the Lord. The fact that I was not born in the times of spiritual darkness in which the heavens were silent and the Spirit withdrawn fills my soul with gratitude. Truly, to be without the word of the Lord to direct us is to be as wanderers in a vast desert who can find no familiar landmarks, or in the dense darkness of a cavern with no light to show us the way to escape. (76-51)

Columbus was led by God. I'm sure that he inspired a little boy, Christopher Columbus, to stand on the quays in Genoa, Italy, and yearn for the sea. He was filled with the desire to sail the seas, and he fulfilled a great prophecy made long, long ago, that this land, chosen above all other lands, should be discovered. And so when he was mature, opportunity was granted to him to brave the unknown seas, to find this land which had been cut off from the rest of the world long centuries, and to open the door, as it were. (50-05)

America offered hope of freedom. With others, he [my ancestor Richard Kimball in 1634] left the comforts and ties and oppressions of Old England to find for himself and his children a home in the new world—their land of promise—a land of religious and political liberty—a land to which the eyes of liberty-loving, oppressed people were turning as did the children of Israel look to the land of Palestine, their promised land. As did the Israelites pass through the wilderness and through the deep waters of affliction to reach their haven of rest, so did these sturdy Puritans with their families, with undaunted hearts break loose from the ties of friendship where they left the graves of their forefathers, passed over the wilderness of waters, and reached the Canaan of their hopes. (71-07)

The Restoration of the Gospel

Joseph Smith's first vision restored knowledge of God. Of all the great events of the century, none compared with the first vision of Joseph Smith. (70-12)

Under special need, at special times, under proper circumstances, God reveals himself to men who are prepared for such manifestations. And since God is the same yesterday, today, and forever, the heavens cannot be closed except as men lock them against themselves with disbelief.

In our own dispensation came another similar grandiose experience. The need was imperative; an apostasy had covered the earth and gross darkness the people, and the minds of men were clouded, and light had been obscured in darkness. The time had come. Religious liberty would protect the seed until it could germinate and grow. And the individual was prepared in the person of a youth, clean and open-minded, who had such implicit faith in the response of God that the heavens could not remain as iron and the earth as brass as they had been for many centuries.

This budding prophet had no preconceived false notions and beliefs. He was not steeped in the traditions and legends and superstitions and fables of the centuries. He had nothing to unlearn. He prayed for knowledge and direction. The powers of darkness preceded the light. When he knelt in solitude in the silent forest, his earnest prayer brought on a battle royal which threatened his destruction. For centuries, Lucifer with unlimited dominion had fettered men's minds. He could ill-afford to lose his satanic hold. This threatened his unlimited dominion. Let Joseph Smith tell his own story:

> I was seized upon by some power which entirely overcame me . . . to bind my tongue. . . . Thick darkness gathered around me, and it seemed to me for a time as if I were doomed to sudden destruction.
>
> . . . at the very moment when I was ready to . . . abandon myself to destruction—not to an imaginary ruin, but to the power of some actual being from the unseen world . . . I saw a pillar of light exactly over my head, above the brightness of the sun.
>
> . . . I found myself delivered from the enemy which held me bound. When the light rested upon me I saw two Personages, whose brightness and glory defy all description, standing above me in the air. One of them spake unto me, calling me by name and said, pointing to the other—*This is My Beloved Son. Hear Him!* (Joseph Smith History: 15-17.) (64-03)

The heavens which had been closed in large measure for many centuries were now opened. The voices that had been still and subdued and unheard through many centuries now began to speak. The revelation that had been well-nigh obliterated and reasoned out of existence was again available. Prophets who had been eliminated for many generations were now there. They now began to spring up as a bulb in a new, rich soil in warm spring weather. And now a young man, named Joseph centuries ago, selected and foreordained before mortality, had an unsatisfied urge for the answer to questions and truth sprang from the earth. For this young boy, clean, free from all antagonistic and distorted ideas and with a sincere desire to find the truth, knelt in a secluded spot in a New York forest and poured out his soul to God, and with a faith the size of mountains he asked serious questions that none of the sects upon the earth had been able to fully answer.

A new truth, a concept not understood by the myriads of people on the earth, burst forth, and in that moment there was only one man on the face of the whole earth who knew with absolute assurance that God was a personal being, that the Father and Son were separate individuals with bodies of flesh and bones [and that he] had been created in their image. As the Son was in the image of his Father, the Father God was the same kind of image as the Son. (74-12)

Open vision was necessary. Nothing short of this total vision to Joseph could have served the purpose to clear away the mists of the centuries. Merely an impression, a hidden voice, a dream could [not] have dispelled the old vagaries and misconceptions. (65-03)

New revelation is always possible. Since that day the heavens have been open and to whomsoever was the ordained and acknowledged prophet have come the continued revelations of God to man. All men may have the benefit of the messages from God, but having given man his free agency, the Lord will not force anyone to listen or receive. Each determined soul who will not receive this truth may continue in his own mortal way without the glory of this new revelation. (73-05)

Joseph Smith joined the few who had seen God. The God of all these worlds and the Son of God, the Redeemer, our Savior, in person attended this boy. He saw the living God. He saw the living Christ. Few of all the man-creation had ever glimpsed such a vision—Peter, James, and John, yes, and Moses, Abraham, and Adam, but few others. Joseph now belonged to an elite group—the tried and trusted, and true. He was in a select society of persons whom Abraham describes as "noble and great ones" that were "good" and that were to become the Lord's rulers. (Abraham 3:22-23.) (70-12)

Joseph Smith's murder provided a martyr. "Mormonism will fail if we kill their prophet," they said a century ago as they murdered Joseph Smith in cold blood. Undoubtedly their fiendish grins of satisfaction at such a foul deed changed to perturbed grimaces when they came to realize that they had been but kicking against sharp points, injuring only themselves. Mormonism was not destroyed by the cruel martyrdom, but here was its vitality. The bullet-torn flesh fertilized the soil; the blood they shed moistened the seed; and the spirits they sent heavenward will testify against them throughout eternities. The cause persists and grows. (55-06)

Joseph Smith lived to organize the kingdom. Was there frustration in the martyrdom of Joseph Smith? Joseph was protected and his life saved in every instance of persecution until his work was finished and he had done his part in the restoration of the gospel and the priesthood and all other keys of the dispensation, and until the organization of the kingdom was effected. He could not be killed before that time, though all hell raged against him. (45-03)

Brigham Young and the pioneers demonstrated courage of faith. What great, stirring program could cause people to leave all that they had previously held dear—material possessions, family ties, friendships, and luxuries? Was there a pot of gold at the end of this newly found rainbow? A life of comfort, worldly acclaim, popularity, with wealth and affluence? Quite the contrary: There was to be hunger, and cold, and pain, and sorrow; there were insults, heartaches, despair, and privations. Only a great faith and an abiding testimony and assurance of divinity could lead men through such hardships....

Here was a generation of young men with stout hearts, strong minds, incomparable faith, grown old in wisdom by the countless experiences thrust rapidly upon them; young stalwarts, dependable in judgment because of the numerous problems they must constantly solve. Here were young elders, pure in heart because of their sufferings, and the implicit faith and childlike dependence of their followers; young heroes full of that superior courage which will admit no defeat. Here were youthful leaders with abiding faith, born of intimate association with the inspired Prophet of this dispensation and their close attunement with their Father in Heaven; here were men grown strong by constant and constructive use of their mental and physical powers; men grown tall by their ever reaching upward to God. Here were men like our great liberator, Lincoln, of whom Markham wrote: "Here is a man to hold against the world, a man to match the mountains and the sea." Brigham Young and his associates were just such men. Tall like the stately pines through which they [traveled] in the latter part of their journey, sun-crowned, dignified and stable as the granite in the everlasting hills of the

Wasatches. Men as persistent and determined as the changeless sea. Men of destiny. (44-06)

The Mormons found security in an untamed wilderness. Many had presented to the great leader, Brigham Young, the suggestion of other, kinder places to settle. There was Oregon with its many opportunities and resources; there was Texas with its vast expanse for settlement; there was California with its gold. But with the vision of a prophet, Brigham Young said of the desolate valley of the Salt Lake—"This is the right place." An isolated place, where a hard-working people could remain unmolested for time to build, was all he asked.

And so upon the unfriendly soil of a desert wilderness has come a mighty empire. Cities grace the land for hundreds of miles. Temple spires pierce the skies. School buildings are everywhere and happy homes of a God-fearing people are found surrounded with flowers, trees, and gardens. (47-05)

Following that first vanguard which reached Salt Lake country July 24, 1847, came numerous companies on horseback and on foot, in covered wagons and pushing handcarts. The trail was marked by the graves along the way. Eighty thousand people with their livestock and their world's goods went trudging across the interminable distance. Those who went in the spring found the streams swollen by melting snows were hard to cross, and deep water, quicksand, and steep banks increased the difficulties. Those who went in summer found in addition that the sands were hot and the way long. Those who were unlucky enough to travel in the early winter found to their sorrow that the winds were penetrating and the snows were deep and the way was hard. But faith is indomitable, and a great cause gave them their inspiration. There was no turning back. The story is told of one lady who heard the story of this incomparable trek for the first time, and in amazement she said: "How in the world could those people give up their comfortable homes and go forth to endure the hardships and dangers they had to face in making new homes in the wilderness?" "My good lady," replied the informer, "they thought that God was marching by their side." Then pausing a moment he said: "And I do not know but that they were right."

Some six thousand or more paid the supreme price and gave their lives for the cause. (47-05)

We should celebrate our pioneer heritage. I hope the day will never come when we will not celebrate, even out in the stakes that are far from Salt Lake. Always have some kind of a celebration to remember the devotion and sacrifices of our people. (74-16)

The Modern Church

This kingdom will last until the end. The Church of Jesus Christ of Latter-day Saints was restored in 1830 after numerous revelations from the divine source; and this is the kingdom, set up by the God of heaven, that would never be destroyed nor superseded, and the stone cut out of the mountain without hands that would become a great mountain and would fill the whole earth. (76-25)

Never again will the sun go down; never again will all men prove totally unworthy of communication with their Maker; never again will God be totally hidden from his children on earth. Revelation is here to remain. Prophets will follow each other in a never-ending succession, and the secrets of the Lord will be revealed without measure. (60-09)

Scriptures and the Church are witnesses for Christ. How marvelous it is, in a day of doubt concerning the divinity of Jesus Christ, that Jesus himself should once again guide and direct his people upon this planet. How significant it is, in a time of perplexity about the problems of mankind, that we should be given a second scriptural witness in the form of the Book of Mormon. The Book of Mormon supplements, but does not supplant, the Bible. The two books together declare the divinity of Jesus Christ and the importance of mankind's keeping the commandments of God, lest his judgments come upon them.

The Church of Jesus Christ of Latter-day Saints both bears the name and the form of Jesus Christ and is built upon the fullness of the gospel. It is a true and living Church—not a dying one nor a partially true church. (77-27)

Latter-day Saints are true Christians. We cannot understand how anyone could question our being Christians. It would certainly be a reflection upon anyone who would say such a thing, because if they attended even one session of any meeting of this church, they would come to realize that every prayer and every song and every sermon is centered in the Lord Jesus Christ. We are the true followers of Jesus Christ; and we hope the world will finally come to the conclusion that we are Christians, if there are any in the world. (76-43)

Primitive church offices have been restored. Not only the scientific atheists, but the Christian antagonists seem to be deeply at sea for want of a harbor, wandering around aimlessly but without direction or compass. They are lost in a wide ocean on rafts without engine, sail, or oar.

Paul, the apostle, gave them the answer. He would have an organization with apostles, prophets, evangelists, an organization with power to perfect the Saints and develop the ministry and to edify the people, and bringing a unity of the faith and a knowlege of the Son of God, and perfection of men until they should reach the stature of Christ. (66-05)

The Church has a crucial mission. One of the great central works entrusted to the Church is to bring the world to a knowledge of Jesus Christ. (74-01)

We are impressed that the mission of the Church is threefold:
—To proclaim the gospel of the Lord Jesus Christ to every nation, kindred, tongue, and people;
—To perfect the Saints by preparing them to receive the ordinances of the gospel and by instruction and discipline to gain exaltation;

—To redeem the dead by performing vicarious ordinances of the gospel for those who have lived on the earth.

All three are part of one work—to assist our Father in Heaven and his Son, Jesus Christ, in their grand and glorious mission "to bring to pass the immortality and eternal life of man." (Moses 1:39.) (81-05)

The gospel of Jesus Christ is a gospel for all the world and for all people. We proclaim the fatherhood of God and the brotherhood of all mankind. We proclaim the divine sonship of Jesus Christ and him crucified, that his divine sacrifice was a ransom for all mankind. We bear witness of his resurrection and that he lives today, standing at the right hand of God, to guide the affairs of his earthly kingdom. (76-25)

Church programs strengthen individuals and families. Our success, individually and as a church, will largely be determined by how faithfully we focus on living the gospel in the home. Only as we see clearly the responsibilities of each individual and the role of families and homes can we properly understand that priesthood quorums and auxiliary organizations, even wards and stakes, exist primarily to help members live the gospel in the home. Then we can understand that people are more important than programs, and that Church programs should always support and never detract from gospel-centered family activities. . . .

You will observe that all of these functions can best be accomplished through a strong home environment. Quorum leaders should ask themselves, how can we help our quorum members magnify their most important priesthood calling, that of husband and father in their own family? How can we help each priesthood bearer lead out in an environment of love and understanding, honoring his wife and consulting with her in her companion leadership role? Together with bishops and stake presidents they should ask, how can we help parents study the scriptures with their children and reap full blessings from regular and purposeful family home evenings together?

Relief Society leaders and teachers should ask, how can we help the wife and mother understand the dignity and worth of her role in the divine process of motherhood? How can we help her make her home a place of love and learning, a place of refuge and refinement? How can we strengthen her to assume an added family leadership role when her husband is away from the home, or in those homes without a father?

Auxiliary leaders and teachers of youth should ask, how can I help these young people to love and obey their parents, honor them, and be supportive of their family responsibilities? How can we schedule meetings, practices, and activities to avoid disrupting home relationships and responsibilities, and to allow time for family activities?

Our commitment to home-centered gospel living should become the clear message of every priesthood and auxiliary program, reducing, where necessary, some of the optional activities that may detract from proper focus on the family and the home.

We are mindful that many of our members live alone or with family members who do not share fully their commitment to gospel principles. We encourage them to join together in special home evening groups and to participate in local single adult activities to accomplish these same objectives, always striving to strengthen their family ties with parents, brothers and sisters, and other relatives.

As local Church leaders cautiously conserve the time that families can spend together, we say to both parents and children, "Come back home." Parents should spend less time in clubs, bowling alleys, banquets, and social gatherings, and more time with their children. Young men and women must balance their involvement in school and other social activities with supportive participation in family activities and appropriate time in the home.

All should work together to make home a place where we love to be, a place of listening and learning, a place where each member can find mutual love, support, appreciation, and encouragement.

I repeat that our success, individually and as a Church, will largely be determined by how faithfully we focus on living the gospel in the home. (78-04)

The gospel provides safety in time of distress. In 1946, a tremendous earthquake under the floor of the Pacific Ocean off the Aleutian Islands set in motion seismic waves which were forty feet high... racing unobserved toward the Hawaiian Islands. When the waves approached the islands, the water drained away from the shore, exposing the sea bottom far out from the coast, then with a cataclysmic roar, the gigantic wall of water smashed into Hilo and the Hamakua coast. One hundred and fifty-nine people lost their lives. ... One woman looked out toward the sea and saw a wave approaching, like a mountain. She and her husband grabbed up their baby and then ran for their lives up a hill. Two of their little girls were away from home playing near a clump of lauhala trees. When they saw the waves coming, they ran into the trees and held tight with their arms around the tree trunks. The first gigantic wave washed over them entirely, but they held on very strongly with their little arms until the first wave had begun to recede and their heads were above water. Then they ran for their lives up the hill. ...

We, too, are faced with powerful forces unleashed by the adversary. Waves of sin—they come with great power and speed, and they will catch us if we are unwary. But a warning is sounded for us. It behooves us to listen to the warning and to flee from evil for our eternal lives. We cannot stand against them unaided. It is not the brave man, but the fool, who stands against forces more powerful than he. We must flee to the safety of high ground, where the wave cannot reach us; or, if that is not possible, we must hold fast to that which can keep us from being swept away. Even if we are inundated, let us hold our breath and keep a firm grasp on that which can save us.

The tree to which we cling is the gospel of Jesus Christ. It is strong enough, flexible enough to protect us from whatever forces the evil one can muster.

"When the devil shall send forth his mighty winds, yea, his shafts in the whirlwind, yea, when all his hail and his mighty storm shall beat upon you, it shall have no power over you to drag you down to the gulf of misery and endless wo." (Helaman 5:12.) (78-22)

The Last Days

We are living in the last days, and they are precarious and frightening. The shadows are deepening, and the night creeps in to envelop us. (71-05)

The Church is under attack. The Church and its agencies and institutions constitute a little island in a great ocean. If we cannot hold the line and keep the floods of error and sin from entangling us and engulfing us, there is little hope for the world. Tidal waves of corruption, evil, deceit, and dishonor are pounding our shores constantly. Unless we can build breakwaters and solid walls to hold them back, the sea will engulf us and destroy us also. (66-07)

We are all very much aware, my brothers and sisters, that the world is in turmoil. We are continually being tried and tested as individuals and as a church. There are more trials yet to come, but be not discouraged nor dismayed. Always remember that if this were not the Lord's work, the adversary would not pay any attention to us. If this Church were merely a church of men and women, teaching only the doctrines of men, we would encounter little or no criticism or resistance—but because this is the Church of him whose name it bears, we must not be surprised when criticisms or difficulties arise. (81-03)

The Lord guides us through troubles. Now, my brothers and sisters, as you read of troubles in so many parts of the world, remember that the Lord knew these problems would come, and that even with these problems he has foreseen the growth of this Church and its people. Be of good cheer, for the Lord is guiding his church. (82-02)

The gathering of Israel now involves conversion. Now, we are concerned with the gathering of Israel. This gathering shall continue until the righteous are assembled in the congregations of the Saints in the nations of the world. This reminds us of the tenth article of faith, wherein the Prophet Joseph Smith said to his inquirer, "We believe in the literal gathering of Israel and in the restoration of the Ten Tribes; that Zion (the new Jerusalem) will be built upon the American continent; that Christ will reign personally upon the earth; and, that the earth will be renewed and receive its paradisiacal glory." . . .

Now, the gathering of Israel consists of joining the true church and their coming to a knowledge of the true God. . . . Any person, therefore, who has accepted the restored gospel, and who now seeks to worship the Lord in his own tongue and with the Saints in the nations where he lives, has complied with the law of the gathering of Israel and is heir to all of the blessings promised the Saints in these last days. (78-15)

The Saints are no longer to come to a single place. In 1955, Sister Kimball and I went to Europe. We spent six months touring all of the missions in Europe. The people were still laboring under the impression that they should come to America for the gathering process. The burden of our sermons to them was, "Stay where you are. You have received the gospel. The blessings will be brought to you. It will not be long until you have stakes, and the Brethren will come across the ocean to visit you. Eventually temples will come, and you will have all the blessings of Zion."

Now you folks of South America are in a different category: you have always lived in Zion. One of the Brethren said that Zion was all of America and that it is like a great bird with two wide wings: North America and South America. . . .

Many people have been holding their breath waiting to see the gathering of Israel. We are in Israel and are being gathered. (75-11)

Now, in the early days of the Church we used to preach for the people to come to Utah as the gathering process, largely because that was the only place in the whole world where there was a temple. Now we have sixteen temples, and two more that have been approved, scattered throughout the world. So it is no longer necessary that we bring the people all to Salt Lake City. Our missionaries preach

The Teachings of Spencer W. Kimball

baptism and confirmation. And then we come to you with conferences and to organize stakes. So we say again, stay in Korea. This is a beautiful land. In this land you can teach your children just as well as you could in Salt Lake City. Stay in Korea where you can teach the gospel to millions of people.

And so the gathering is taking place. Korea is the gathering place for Koreans, Australia for Australians, Brazil for Brazilians, England for the English. And so we move forward toward the confirmation of this great program the Lord has established for us. (75-43)

The First Presidency and the Twelve see great wisdom in the multiple Zions, many gathering places where the Saints within their own culture and nation can act as a leaven in the building of the kingdom—a kingdom which seeks no earthly rewards or treasures.

Sometimes, inadvertently, we have given artificial encouragement to individuals to leave their native land and culture and, too often, this has meant the loss of the leaven that is so badly needed, and the individuals involved have sometimes regretted their migrations.

I am hopeful that each of you will ponder carefully what it is the Lord would have you do with your lives, with the special skills, training, and testimonies you have. (74-06)

Tonga is Zion. When we sing the song, "Come to Zion, Come to Zion," we are not asking people to get in their boats and come back to the United States. We are asking them to get established in their own countries; to acquire property, build homes, and teach the young people truths of the world, as well as of the Church, through the schools that are developed. (76-12)

The Second Coming is near. Just as surely as Jesus was born in Bethlehem, just so surely will he come again, a resurrected, glorified being, and with him will come hosts, and there will be many spectacular changes. It will not be the end of the world in the sense of annihilation, but the end of its present relationships, and there will be many, many changes. Beginning with the bridegroom's coming will come the celestializing of this earth and tremendous changes which we can hardly think of or believe....

There are many people in the kingdom today who say, "Oh, they have been looking for the Savior ever since Peter and Paul, and he has not come yet." But he is coming, and the end of time is not too far away....

I suppose it depends considerably on what we are doing and the preparations we are making for the closing scene. The world has to hear the gospel; we must preach it. We are the only ones who can. There are things we must do before the end does come, and perhaps that controls it to some extent. At any rate, not anyone in this building knows when the end is coming or when the Christ will come, any more than did the ten virgins. But there were five who were wise, and they were prepared....

"But as the days of Noe were, so shall also the coming of the Son of man be." (Matthew 24:37.)...As it [the Flood] was a real drowning, there will be a real burning at this next great event when the end of the world comes, and the wicked will be burned. And, of course, we know that that is possible now. We did not know that when I was a child, that the earth could burn. We thought only material ordinarily considered combustible could be burned, but we find that everything can burn and melt. Since Hiroshima and Nagasaki we know that bombs can start a great conflagration, and other things can melt with fervent heat. And so the time is coming. I do not know when it will be. I only hope that when the examination is put on the blackboard, we will all be...able to answer the questions satisfactorily. (57-02)

The time of Christ's return is affected by our conduct. I've known people who have been promised in their patriarchal blessings that they would live to see the temple built and some of them are dying and haven't seen the temple built. Do you know why? In my estimation, the Lord's timetable is directed a good deal by us. We speed up the clock or we slow the hands down and we turn them back by *our* activities or our procrastinations. And do you know why I think people who are actually promised that they would live to see the temple built are dying before completion of the temple? Because we haven't converted Indians in large enough numbers; never shall we go to Jackson County until we have converted and brought into this Church great numbers of Lamanites. (63-10)

CHAPTER 17

Revelation and Church Leadership

The Principle of Continuing Revelation

Revelation is basic to the Restoration. The restored Church of Jesus Christ is founded upon the rock of revelation. Continuous revelation is indeed the very lifeblood of the gospel of the living Lord and Savior, Jesus Christ. . . .

How this confused world of today needs revelation from God! With war and pestilence and famine, with poverty, desolation, with more and more graft, dishonesty, and immorality, certainly the people of this world need revelation from God as never before. How absurd it would be to think that the Lord would give to a small handful of people in Palestine and the Old World his precious direction through revelation and now, in our extremity, close the heavens. . . .

If the Bible were "the end of the prophets," then it was through lack of faith and belief, and that is the reason the heavens at times were closed and locked and became as iron, and the earth as brass. . . .

I bear witness to the world today that more than a century and a half ago the iron ceiling was shattered; the heavens were once again opened, and since that time revelations have been continuous.

That new day dawned when another soul with passionate yearning prayed for divine guidance. A spot of hidden solitude was found, knees were bent, a heart was humbled, pleadings were voiced, and a light brighter than the noonday sun illuminated the world—the curtain never to be closed again. . . .

Never again will God be hidden from his children on the earth. Revelation is here to remain. (77-26)

God is eager to communicate. Someone said we live in a day in which God, if there be a God, chooses to be silent. The Church of Jesus Christ of Latter-day Saints proclaims to the world that the Father and the Son are not silent. They are vocal and reveal themselves with an eagerness to maintain communication with men. (66-05)

Every moment of every day, there are numerous programs on the air. We hear very few, relatively, for we are engrossed in our day's duties, but with powerful beaming broadcasting stations, we could hear any of the programs if we are tuned in.

For thousands of years there have been constant broadcasts from heaven of vital messages of guidance and timely warnings, and there has been a certain constancy in the broadcasts from the most powerful station. Throughout all those centuries there have been times when there were prophets who tuned in and rebroadcasted to the people. The messages have never ceased. (70-02)

Men's spirituality can be gauged by degree of communication. If revelations cease, either men are unresponsive and in the darkness of apostasy or God is dead. Since we know positively that God lives and is the same "yesterday, today and forever," we can gauge the faithfulness and spirituality of men by the degree of intensity of the communication between them and God. (65-03)

Revelation is communication through means beyond man's present knowledge. We live in a marvelous age with developments far beyond the most fantastic prognostications of a quarter century ago. Our communication lines have been extended from Pony Express to fast air service; transportation has been speeded from horse and buggy to globe-encircling jets for the masses, and speeds running into the thousands of miles each hour for the explorers. From the Vikings and Columbus, we come to [John] Glenn and the astronauts. Persistent scientists continue to explore land and sea, and now they are out in space. Much learning has been added, but astronauts and rocket riders and telegraphers can little realize how relatively elementary are their movements and discoveries and knowledge. Astronomers have sought knowledge through study, but prophets through faith. Astronomers have developed powerful telescopes through which they have seen much, but prophets and seers have had clearer vision at greater distances with precision instruments such as the Liahona and the Urim and Thummim, which have far exceeded the most advanced radar, radio, television, or telescopic equipment.

Is man earthbound? Largely so, and temporarily so, yet Enoch and his people were translated from the earth, and the living Christ and angels commuted.

Is there interplanetary conversation? Certainly. Man may speak to God and receive answers from him.

Is there association of interplanetary beings? There is no question.

Are planets out in space inhabited by intelligent creatures? Without doubt.

Will radioed messages ever come between planets across limitless space? Certainly, for there have already been coming for six thousand years, properly decoded, interpreted, and publicized messages of utmost importance to the inhabitants of this earth. Dreams and open vision, like perfected television programs, have come repeatedly. Personal representatives have brought warning messages too numerous times to mention, and it is our testimony to the world that God lives and abides in his heavenly home, and the earth is his footstool, and only one of his numerous creations; that Jesus Christ the Son of that living God is the Creator, Savior, and Redeemer of the people on this earth who will listen and obey; and that these interstellar messages—call them what you will, visions, revelations, television, radio—from the abode of God to man on this earth continue now to come to the living prophet of God among us this day. (62-07)

Revelation continues in the Church. From the prophet of the Restoration to the prophet of our own year, the communication line is unbroken, the authority is continuous, the light, brilliant and penetrating, continues to shine, the sound of the voice of the Lord is a continuous melody and a thundering appeal. For almost a century and a half there has been no interruption.

When a new temple is projected, when a new mission is organized, when stakes are divided and vital vacancies are filled, there is certainty and calm, tranquil assurance, and the peace of heaven settles over the hearts of true believers with a sureness. Even great and good men rise to new stature under the mantle of prime authority when keys of heaven are closed in their palms and then the voice of authority comes from their lips. (60-09)

Many revelations are not printed. Even all of the revelations that the Prophet Joseph Smith received are not recorded in this book of revelations. After years he went over the many revelations he had received and selected from them those which he seemed to feel would be applicable to the needs of the people. He apparently left out those revelations which had a very temporary need. So we do not have them all, not even all of his in the Doctrine and Covenants. In fact, the greatest revelation that ever came to this world, since Christ's advent at least, is not recorded here. I refer to the glorious vision when the Father and the Son, Elohim and Jehovah, appeared to the boy prophet, Joseph Smith, in New York State. (57-01)

Follow the living prophet. I had a young man recently about forty years of age who got into the cultist program. He studied the *Journal of Discourses* until he nearly knew them by heart. I confess that he knew them infinitely better than I did. However, he was depending wholly upon himself and his own interpretation of the program and was moving farther and farther away from the truth. He said, "I know more about the sermons of the brethren in the days of Joseph and Brigham and Heber C. than does the President of the Church, or any of the apostles, or any of the stake presidents or the bishops. Why should I go to them?" And, I tried to point out to him that we

have revelation these days as well as in the days of Joseph and
Brigham and Heber C., and that the present-day leaders have exactly
the same communication system and that it operates and is in effect.
He would not go to his pastors, apostles, and prophets but depended
upon himself. This young man became bold enough to say that President McKay may be a good man but that he was a false prophet.
(11/2/62)

He is a prophet. He does not just occupy a prophet's chair; he
does not just have a title of prophet, he is a real prophet and he is
responsible for . . . more revelations in his fifteen years of leadership
than are in all the Doctrine and Covenants. They are not in the
Doctrine and Covenants. We do not print them anymore like that.
We put them out in handbooks and by directives and by letters, and
our files and vaults are full of them. . . . I could take time to tell you
of these revelations—temples that have been appointed, people who
have been called, apostles who have been chosen, great new movements that have been established, great new eras, great new challenges as we have here today. They came by revelation. I want you to
know he is a prophet. Don't you question it. I do not know who will
be his successor, but whoever it is will be a great prophet, and you
need not ever worry. I had a man of great promise the other day in
my office and he said, "I wonder who would lead the Church when
President McKay dies?" I said, "I do not know. I do not even care to
know. It does not matter." But, I said to him, "Whoever it is, he will
be a real prophet of God." (66-12)

Recent Revelations

Plural marriage ended through revelation. We warn you against
the so-called polygamy cults which would lead you astray. Remember
the Lord brought an end to this program many decades ago through
a prophet who proclaimed the revelation to the world. People are
abroad who will deceive you and bring you much sorrow and
remorse. Have nothing to do with those who would lead you astray.

It is wrong and sinful to ignore the Lord when he speaks. He has spoken—strongly and conclusively. (74-30)

Vision of spirit world and calling of apostle came by revelation. Official revelations to the Church did not end with those relating to the 1890 Manifesto. Revelations have come constantly and often to the leaders of the Church before and since that day. In all ages when the recognized Church of the Lord has been on the earth, God has communicated with it and given it direction.

One outstanding example of revelation was the spectacular vision of the redemption of the dead received by President Joseph F. Smith in 1918, shortly before his death. . . .

President Heber J. Grant related an example of the revelations of the Lord to him. For twenty-two years he had felt the inspiration of the living God directing him in his labors. He wrote: "From the day that I chose a comparative stranger [Melvin J. Ballard] to be one of the apostles, instead of my lifelong and dearest living friend, I have known as I know that I live, that I am entitled to the light and the inspiration and the guidance of God in directing His work here upon the earth." (*Gospel Standards* [*Improvement Era,* 1941], pp. 196-97.) . . .

No, revelation has not ceased and will not cease. This kingdom of God has been set up for the rest of time, never to be torn down nor given to another people. It is a continuous program and will grow instead of diminish. Its doctrines are well established, but because of growth and expansion, improved ways are afforded to teach the gospel all over the world. Additional servants are called to the increasing work for a bigger world. Revelation and other miracles will never cease unless faith ceases. Where there is adequate faith, these things will continue. (71-03)

Priesthood limitation on blacks was changed by revelation. The things of God cannot be understood by the spirit of men. It is impossible to always measure and weigh all spiritual things by man's yardstick or scales. Admittedly, our direct and positive information is limited. I have wished the Lord had given us a little more clarity in the matter. But for me, it is enough. The prophets for 133 years of the existence of the Church have maintained the position of the prophet of the Restoration that the Negro could not hold the priesthood nor have the temple ordinances which are preparatory for exaltation. I believe in the living prophets as much or almost more than the dead ones. They are here to clarify and reaffirm. I have served with and under three of them. The doctrine or policy has not varied in my memory. I know it could. I know the Lord could change his policy and release the ban and forgive the possible error which brought about the deprivation. If the time comes, that he will do, I am sure. These smart members who would force the issue, and there are many of them, cheapen the issue and certainly bring into contempt the sacred principle of revelation and divine authority. (6/15/63)

Blacks and the priesthood: I am not sure that there will be a change, although there could be. We are under the dictates of our Heavenly Father, and this is not my policy or the Church's policy. It is the policy of the Lord who has established it, and I know of no change, although we are subject to revelations of the Lord in case he should ever wish to make a change. (73-11)

June 8, 1978
To all general and local priesthood officers of The Church of Jesus Christ of Latter-day Saints throughout the world:

Dear Brethren:
As we have witnessed the expansion of the work of the Lord over the earth, we have been grateful that people of many nations have responded to the message of the restored gospel, and have joined the Church in ever-increasing numbers. This, in turn, has inspired us with a desire to extend to every worthy member of the Church all of the privileges and blessings which the gospel affords.

Aware of the promises made by the prophets and presidents of the Church who have preceded us that at some time, in God's eternal plan, all of our brethren who are worthy may receive the priesthood,

and witnessing the faithfulness of those from whom the priesthood
has been withheld, we have pleaded long and earnestly in behalf of
these, our faithful brethren, spending many hours in the Upper
Room of the Temple supplicating the Lord for divine guidance.

He has heard our prayers, and by revelation has confirmed that
the long-promised day has come when every faithful, worthy man in
the Church may receive the holy priesthood, with power to exercise
its divine authority, and enjoy with his loved ones every blessing that
flows therefrom, including the blessings of the temple. Accordingly,
all worthy male members of the Church may be ordained to the
priesthood without regard for race or color. Priesthood leaders are
instructed to follow the policy of carefully interviewing all candidates
for ordination to either the Aaronic or the Melchizedeck Priesthood
to insure that they meet the established standards for worthiness.

We declare with soberness that the Lord has now made known his
will for the blessing of all his children throughout the earth who will
hearken to the voice of his authorized servants, and prepare themselves to receive every blessing of the gospel.

Sincerely yours,

Spencer W. Kimball
N. Eldon Tanner
Marion G. Romney

The First Presidency

(D&C—Official Declaration 2)

Now, there is one other thing I want to mention. You live in
South Africa. As you know, on the ninth of June a policy was
changed that affects great numbers of people throughout the world.
Millions and millions of people will be affected by the revelation
which came. I remember very vividly that day after day I walked to
the temple and ascended to the fourth floor where we have our
solemn assemblies and where we have our meetings of the Twelve and
the First Presidency. After everybody had gone out of the temple, I

knelt and prayed. I prayed with much fervency. I knew that something was before us that was extremely important to many of the children of God. I knew that we could receive the revelations of the Lord only by being worthy and ready for them and ready to accept them and put them into place. Day after day I went alone and with great solemnity and seriousness in the upper rooms of the temple, and there I offered my soul and offered my efforts to go forward with the program. I wanted to do what he wanted. I talked about it to him and said, "Lord, I want only what is right. We are not making any plans to be spectacularly moving. We want only the thing that thou dost want, and we want it when you want it and not until."

We met with the Council of the Twelve Apostles, time after time, in the holy room where there is a picture of the Savior in many different moods and also pictures of all the Presidents of the Church. Finally we had the feeling and the impression from the Lord, who made it very clear to us, that this was the thing to do to make the gospel universal to all worthy people. You will meet this situation undoubtedly as you bring the gospel to them on condition that their lives can be changed.

I anticipate the day when the gospel, that has come to you and your families and has transformed your lives, will begin to transform their lives and make new people out of them. They become people who will love the Lord and who will make the same sacrifices that you make. (78-30)

Until recently there was one group of people that had not been permitted to have the priesthood. But since June ninth of this year every boy that has ever been born is eligible for the priesthood if he will qualify. It matters not as to his color or his race. All boys have an equal chance to have these blessings.

One of the Brethren said yesterday that now has come one of the greatest changes and blessings that has ever been known. . . . Outside of a few people who always want to be contrary, the people of the world have accepted this change with their gratitude. . . . So we are very, very happy about this, especially for those who had been deprived of these blessings before. (78-21)

We had the glorious experience of having the Lord indicate clearly that the time had come when all worthy men and women everywhere can be fellow heirs and partakers of the full blessings of the gospel. I want you to know, as a special witness of the Savior, how close I have felt to him and to our Heavenly Father as I have made numerous visits to the upper rooms in the temple, going on some days several times by myself. The Lord made it very clear to me what was to be done. We do not expect the people of the world to understand such things, for they will always be quick to assign their own reasons or to discount the divine process of revelation. (79-02)

(FPM 21-46 describes many other modern revelations)

The Mode of Revelation

Church officers are called by inspiration. What about these bishops? . . . Were they called by the stake presidencies? Did the stake presidency just go into the room and look over the list and say, "Well, we'll take this man and we'll take that one"? No. I've been a stake president six years, I was a counselor in the stake presidency twelve years, and I was a stake clerk for twenty years, so I was very close to the stake presidency for a long while, and this isn't the way they do it.

Stake presidencies, like bishoprics and like General Authorities, are on their knees. They fast a little more than most people do. They pray a good deal more than most people do, and in general their lives conform to the gospel pretty closely. When they have prayed and fasted and thought and pondered and weighed and measured men for a long time, there come impressions to them, and finally the bishopric calls in a brother and asks him to be the superintendent of Sunday School, called of God through the bishopric, through the proper channels. The stake presidency finally brings to the high council the name of a man whom they recommend to be the bishop, and the high council, not knowing any reason why he shouldn't be made the bishop, they approve. A letter goes to the First Presidency and the Twelve, and every Thursday anywhere from eight to twenty-five or thirty of these bishops are approved by the Presidency and the Twelve. The name is approved, comes back. There is revelation all down the line there. When it comes back, the presidency of the stake then takes this bishop and installs him as bishop of the ward, subject, of course, to the vote of the people. Do you think it was the stake presidency who called him? Well, I don't think so. I think the Lord called him. Certainly he did if the presidency of the stake are close to the Lord as they should be. (56-09)

Individual revelations will harmonize with Church program. The one who receives revelation for any part of the Church, if his revelations are from God, will always be in the same direction as the general program the Lord has revealed to his prophets. In other words, the Lord will never reveal to a bishop a new program entirely contradictory to the program of the Church, even for his own ward. His revelations to the bishop, to the stake president, the mission president, will be more or less confirming and amplifying and giving further details. So each individual is entitled to the revelations of the Lord, call it inspiration if you want to, it's a matter of degree largely. (56-09)

Revelations come in one's area of responsibility. The father and mother of the family are entitled to revelation for the ruling of their family and all of their interests. The bishop is entitled to the revelations of God for his flock; the stake president for the stake, and the President of the Church, of course, is the only one that holds the keys actively and totally, and he will receive the revelations for the Church.

Whenever an individual gets out of his area and begins to tell the bishop of revelations he's received for the conduct of the ward, then he's wrong. His revelations are coming from the wrong source because God is not the author of confusion. (57-01)

Revelation responds to feelings of great need. When man begins to hunger, when arms begin to reach, when knees begin to bend and voices begin to articulate, then, and not until then, does the Lord make himself known. He pushes back the horizons, he breaks the curtain above us, and he makes it possible for us to come out of dim, uncertain stumbling into the sureness of the eternal light. (77-16)

Sometimes we don't recognize them when they come. We pray and pray and pray for wisdom and judgment and then we feel somewhat like we ought to go this particular direction. There was revelation there. The Lord answers these questions that you propose. (74-19)

Revelation comes to those who will hear. The Lord will not force himself upon people; and if they do not believe, they will receive no visitation. If they are content to depend upon their own limited calculations and interpretations, then, of course, the Lord will leave them to their chosen fate. . . .

The same revelations, visions, healings, and tongues are all available today as in any other day, providing there is the necessary faith.

The Almighty is with this people. We shall have all the revelations that we shall need if we will do our duty and keep the commandments of God. If men could just realize that there may be sound even though few ears hear it. There are revelations even though most minds be materialistic and most hearts impenetrable.

Remember that of all who traveled the "way to Damascus" that notable day, only Paul heard and recognized the face and voice of our Redeemer. And that of all the numerous professionals and court attachés in Babylon's court, only Daniel received the dream of Nebuchadnezzar and its interpretation; and while Belshazzar and others saw the handwriting on the wall, only the Prophet Daniel could give it meaning.

Remember:

If there be eyes to see, there will be visions to inspire.

If there be ears to hear, there will be revelations to experience.

If there be hearts which can understand, know this: that the exalting truths of Christ's gospel will no longer be hidden and mysterious, and all earnest seekers may know God and his program. (66-10)

Revelation can come to every good, faithful man who holds the priesthood of God, and to every good woman who is the matron in her home. The Lord will give you answer to your questions and to your prayers if you are listening. It doesn't have to all come through the prophet.... But all people, if they are worthy enough and close enough to the Lord, can have revelations. (78-32)

God communicates in various ways. You can in one sitting read everything that is recorded in the Holy Bible of the words of the Savior, and yet for three years constantly he was giving light and inspiration to the people of the world. The recorders got only part of it, and other parts have been lost. It is ridiculous to think that the words which Matthew, Mark, Luke and John have recorded are the only ones he said. It is absurd to think that all the revelations were recorded when these books were gathered together later by men who were not necessarily inspired totally. To think that that was all the revelations of God! If we progress, we need revelations, and we are receiving them, and they are continuous.

Some revelations come by dreams. Most of our dreams are flighty and have no meaning, but the Lord does use dreams for enlightening his people. I have mentioned Joseph of Nazareth. Nebuchadnezzar had a dream. (See Daniel 2.) It was a powerful one which he forgot, but Daniel came along and recalled to the king his dream and gave the interpretation. The Lord made it known to Daniel for a specific reason.

There was Peter's dream in which he saw a sheet come down from heaven filled with all kinds of animals and beasts, and it had a very specific meaning. (See Acts 10:9-35.)...

Paul in his great experience had the same kind of a revelation through a dream. "And a vision appeared to Paul in the night." And he received instructions that were necessary for him and for the kingdom. (Acts 16:9.)...

There are other spectacular revelations mentioned. There was the coming of Moroni, an individual, a resurrected being, to bring back the great record of the ancients of America and the restoration of the gospel....

Then came John the Baptist who had been beheaded by the king in a moment of weakness...[then] Peter, James and John now resurrected....So there came, step by step, a restoration of everything, and it all came by revelation, by vision, by dreams, or by deep impression.

Now, all of the revelations in the holy scriptures did not come by spectacular manifestations. As you read the Old Testament, you will find the Lord speaks. He spoke to Isaiah, to Jeremiah, and others, but those were not always personal appearances. It was much like Enos's experience, for as you read in the book of Enos in the Book of Mormon, he had been fasting and praying and was reaching and asking for information and for a forgiveness of his sins particularly: "And while I was thus struggling in the spirit, behold, the voice of the Lord came into my mind again, saying:..." (Enos 1:10.) In that manner, many, many of the revelations have come.

So revelation came: sometimes with actual personal appearance of heavenly beings....But most of the revelations of the Prophet Joseph Smith in this holy record, the Doctrine and Covenants, did not come in that manner. They came as deep impressions.

We have a paragraph written by Parley P. Pratt showing how those revelations came to the prophet:

> Each sentence was uttered slowly and very distinctly and with a pause between each, sufficiently long for it to be recorded by an ordinary writer in long hand. This was the manner in which all his written revelations were dictated and written. There was never any hesitation, reviewing or reading back, in order to keep the run of the subject; neither did any of these communications undergo revisions, interlinings or corrections. As he dictated them, so they stood, so far as I have witnessed; and I was present to witness the dictation of several communications of several pages each.

Now, many of the revelations, as I said, have come in ways not spectacular. There were instructions. One of them was a prayer. One of them was the blessing given by the angel when he restored the Aaronic Priesthood. Some are exhortations. Some are explanations of doctrines, but they are all the revelations of the Lord—received as deep impressions.

Now, someone asks, "Why do the revelations come in that manner? Why don't they come preceded by 'thus saith the Lord'? " They haven't always come that way, even in the days of old. When Wilford Woodruff gave us the revelations to him concerning the discontinuance of plural marriage, he explained then that "thus saith the Lord" was used very rarely by the latter prophets, just the same as we never use anymore in our writing the words "and it came to pass." He continued:

> I made some remarks last Sunday, upon the same revelations. Read the life of Brigham Young and you can hardly find a revelation that he had wherein he said "Thus saith the Lord," but the Holy Ghost was with him; he was taught by inspiration and by revelation, but with one exception he did not give those revelations in the form that Joseph did; for they were not written or given as revelations and commandments to the church in the words and the name of the Savior. Joseph said "Thus saith the Lord" almost every day of his life in laying the foundation of this work. But those who followed him have not deemed it always necessary to say "Thus saith the Lord," yet they have led the people by the power of the Holy Ghost. . . . I do not want the Latter-day Saints to understand that the Lord is not with us and that he is not giving revelations to us, for he is giving us revelation and will give us revelation until this scene is wound up. (Sermon of Wilford Woodruff, Logan, Utah, November 1, 1891.)

Revelations continue to come to this great kingdom all the time. I suppose there is never a week when there are not revelations received. (57-01)

For many it seems difficult to accept as revelation those numerous messages . . . which come to prophets as deep, unassailable impressions settling down on the prophet's mind and heart as dew from heaven or as the dawn displaces the darkness of night.

Many men seem to have no ear for spiritual messages nor comprehension of them when they come in common dress. . . .

Expecting the spectacular, one may not be fully alerted to the constant flow of revealed communication.

When in a Thursday temple meeting, after prayer and fasting, important decisions are made, new missions and new stakes are created, new patterns and policies initiated, the news is taken for granted and possibly thought of as mere human calculations. But to those who sit in the intimate circles and hear the prayers of the prophet and the testimony of the man of God; to those who see the astuteness of his deliberations and the sagacity of his decisions and pronouncements, to them he is verily a prophet. To hear him conclude important new developments with such solemn expressions as "the Lord is pleased"; "that move is right"; "our Heavenly Father has spoken," is to know positively. (73-05)

Not all revelations are from God. Certainly we should not be interested in signs. Signs are available and anyone, I believe, can have signs who wants them. I believe if one wants revelations enough to crave them beyond the rightness of it, that eventually he will get his revelations—but they may not come from God. I am sure that there can be many spectacular things performed, because the devil is very responsive. He is listening and he is eager to do it. And so he gives strange experiences. I think some actually do get unusual experiences and revelations.

I will tell you the way I have handled these situations. One woman, for example, claimed she was receiving revelations every day while putting up the lunches in the temple. The purported revelations were childish and silly and pertained to such little things as the Lord would never deign to control or guide. At first I said, "These are not from the Lord. He does not deal with these little things where we can make up our own minds, such as what clothes to wear or what to eat today." My observation to her did not do any good. Her "revelations" came all the more, and she knew they were from the Lord. Then I said to her, "Well, now, sister, *if* these come from the Lord, they are for you alone. Do not ever whisper them to a soul." When she quit telling about them, they ceased to come anymore. She was just glorying in her superiority over her fellow beings when she received them.... If one does receive revelations, which one may expect if he is worthy, they will always be in total alignment with the program of the Church; they will never be counter. And they will always be within his own jurisdiction and never beyond. (62-08)

Following Church Leaders

Following leaders is the path of safety. Every normal person may have a sure way of knowing what is right and what is wrong. He may learn the gospel and receive the Holy Spirit which will always guide him as to right and wrong. In addition to this, he has the leaders of the Lord's church. And the only sure, safe way is to follow that leadership—follow the Holy Spirit within you and follow the prophets, dead and living. (68-06)

No one in this Church will ever go far astray who ties himself securely to the authorities whom the Lord has placed in his Church. This Church will never go astray; the Quorum of the Twelve will never lead you into bypaths; it never has and never will. There could be individuals who would falter; there will never be a majority of the Council of the Twelve on the wrong side at any time. The Lord has chosen them; he has given them specific responsibilities. And those people who stand close to them will be safe. And, conversely, whenever one begins to go his own way in opposition to authority, he is in grave danger. I would not say that those leaders whom the Lord chooses are necessarily the most brilliant, nor the most highly trained, but they are the chosen, and when chosen of the Lord they are his recognized authority, and the people who stay close to them have safety. (51-03)

Personal failure of leaders should not affect testimony. Sometimes in the Church we have people who lose their faith because a bishop or a high councilor or a stake president goes astray. They fail to realize that all these people also are human, and while they have weaknesses they are striving to live better, but sometimes they succumb to the whirlpool of temptations about them. Sometimes in business transactions there are misunderstandings, and because one happens to be an official in the Church, the other becomes aggrieved at the Church rather than at the individual and seems to have difficulty in separating the individual from the Church. They fail to realize that if we waited until we could find absolutely perfect people to man the organizations in the Church, we would never have an organization, and that the best that can be found under the circumstances are generally chosen to give leadership; and that sometimes even those best ones fail. . . . This does not justify any other individual doing the wrong things; we merely recognize that people are human and that sometimes they fall and fail to live the commandments and therefore will fail to receive the blessing. (12/22/55)

Avoid criticism. The damage to one who becomes the critic and sets himself up as a judge is severe, especially if he finds fault with the leaders of the Church whom the Lord has appointed. Since the Crucifixion, there have been tens of thousands of men called by the Savior to fill positions of responsibility, not one of whom has been perfect, and yet all are called of the Lord and must be upheld and sustained by those who would be disciples of the Lord. That is the true spirit of the gospel. (MF 274)

How do you teach your children to love the authorities of the Church? If you are constantly saying good things about the branch presidency, the district presidency, the mission presidency, and the Presidency of the Church, your children will grow up to love the brethren. (52-07)

Nationality of leaders is irrelevant. Now, Brother McKay is the prophet of the Lord. There is only *one* in the world. He could be an Indian, he could be a Burmese, he could be a Japanese. He just happens to be an American. We have had Englishmen in the councils of the Church. Someday, we will have Mexicans; we will have Indians. (65-01)

Occupation of leaders is irrelevant. In the various countries, and especially in America, we are developing a great membership of professional and skilled men. However, we also have many good leaders and members who mine coal, and fire furnaces, and balance ledgers, and turn lathes, and pick cotton, and cultivate orchards, and heal the sick, and plant corn, all proudly and profitably. (76-27)

Church leaders are united. This boy finally said, "Is it true that the Brethren are divided?"

I said, "Yes, they are. Some of them are Democrats and some are Republicans. Some of them drive a Lincoln and some drive a Rambler. Some of them like red ties and some like blue ties.

"But I want to tell you, my boy, that when the Brethren approach anything that is important and vital—they are one! They *all* would die for the cause. They *all* know with absolute certainty that God lives. They *all* know that Jesus is really the Christ and that he is the Savior of the world and that he lives and reveals his program to the world. They *all* know...that David O. McKay is a prophet and that he succeeded several other real prophets whose declared and official word is equal to that of Joseph Smith or Moses or Abraham." (68-09)

New ideas must go through proper channels. Whenever the Lord turns over his program to the wisdom of men, there will come greater chaos than now. There is only one way: The Lord will always have leadership to whom he will reveal, and whom he will recognize. And that leadership must always be humble and in tune. And that is one of the reasons he cannot use the highly trained and brilliant; they are so built up in their own knowledge and brilliance that they will not listen to the voice of God. (5/31/48)

The membership of the Church will always be safe if they follow closely the instructions and admonitions and the leadership of the authorities of the Church. It must be obvious that if all brilliant and highly trained people in the Church were to teach all their multitudinous ideas as doctrines in the Church organizations, that only confusion and chaos would result. If the Church seems to move a bit slowly in accepting the ideas of men, perhaps in that very deliberateness and caution is great safety.

Any new program or doctrine, which comes to the Church, will come through the authorities of the Church and be approved by them. (4/28/48)

If it is a good idea, one can test it by going up the channel. We are always glad to hear good new ideas. Sometimes our ideas may be valuable—but we do not go out and put them into effect, but submit them up the proper channel. (65-01)

Apostasy often begins with criticism of current leaders. Apostasy usually begins with question and doubt and criticism. It is a retrograding and devolutionary process. The seeds of doubt are planted by unscrupulous or misguided people, and seldom directed against the doctrine at first, but more often against the leaders.

They who garnish the sepulchres of the dead prophets begin now by stoning the living ones. They return to the pronouncements of the dead leaders and interpret them to be incompatible with present programs. They convince themselves that there are discrepancies between the practices of the deceased and the leaders of the present. ... They allege love for the gospel and the Church but charge that leaders are a little "off the beam"! Soon they claim that the leaders are making changes and not following the original programs. Next they say that while the gospel and the Church are divine, the leaders are fallen. Up to this time it may be a passive thing, but now it becomes an active resistance, and frequently the blooming apostate begins to air his views and to crusade. He is likely now to join groups who are slipping away. He may become a student of the *Journal of Discourses* and is flattered by the evil one that he knows more about the scriptures and doctrines than the Church leaders who, he says, are now persecuting him. He generally wants all the blessings of the Church: membership, its priesthood, its temple privileges, and expects them from the leaders of the Church, though at the same time claiming that those same leaders have departed from the path. He now begins to expect persecution and adopts a martyr complex, and when finally excommunication comes he associates himself with other apostates to develop and strengthen cults. At this stage he is likely to claim revelation for himself, revelations from the Lord directing him in his interpretations and his actions. These manifestations are superior to anything from living leaders, he claims. He is now becoming quite independent....

History repeats itself. As the critics of the Redeemer still worshipped Abraham and the critics of Joseph Smith could see only the Savior and his apostles, and as the apostates of Brigham's day could see only the martyred Joseph, now there are those who quote only the dead leaders of the pioneer era. (59-06)

The President of the Church

Succession in Church Presidency is orderly. The work of the Lord is endless. Even when a powerful leader dies, not for a single instant is the Church without leadership, thanks to the kind Providence who gave his kingdom continuity and perpetuity. . . .

The moment life passes from a President of the Church, a body of men become the composite leader—these men already seasoned with experience and training. The appointments have long been made, the authority given, the keys delivered. . . . The kingdom moves forward under this already authorized council. No "running" for position, no electioneering, no stump speeches. What a divine plan! How wise our Lord, to organize so perfectly beyond the weakness of frail, grasping humans.

Then dawns the notable day . . . and fourteen serious men walk reverently into the temple of God—this, the Quorum of the Twelve Apostles, the governing body of The Church of Jesus Christ of Latter-day Saints, several of whom have experienced this solemn change before.

When these fourteen men emerge from the holy edifice later in the morning, a transcendently vital event has occurred—a short interregnum ends, and the government of the kingdom shifts back again from the Quorum of the Twelve Apostles to a new prophet, an individual leader, the Lord's earthly representative. (70-02)

Seniority established pattern of succession. It is reassuring to know that President Lee was not elected through committees and conventions with all their conflicts, criticisms, and by the vote of men, but was called of God and then sustained by the people. . . .

The pattern divine allows for no errors, no conflicts, no ambitions, no ulterior motives. The Lord has reserved for himself the calling of his leaders over his church. It is a study of great interest and importance. . . .

Full provision has been made by our Lord for changes. Today there are fourteen apostles holding the keys in suspension, the Twelve and the two counselors to the President, to be brought into use if and when circumstances allow, all ordained to leadership in their turn as they move forward in seniority.

There have been some eighty apostles so endowed since Joseph Smith, though only eleven have occupied the place of the President of the Church, death having intervened; and since the death of his servants is in the power and control of the Lord, he permits to come to the first place only the one who is destined to take that leadership. Death and life become the controlling factors. Each new apostle in turn is chosen by the Lord and revealed to the then living prophet who ordains him.

The matter of seniority is basic in the first quorums of the Church. All the apostles understand this perfectly, and all well-trained members of the Church are conversant with this perfect succession program.

Joseph Smith bestowed upon the Twelve Apostles all the keys and authority and power that he himself possessed and that he had received from the Lord. He gave unto them every endowment, every washing and anointing, and administered unto them the sealing ordinances. (72-10)

Recently a prominent doctor, knowing of my surgery and cancer treatments, exhibited a little surprise at my assuming the great responsibility of the Church Presidency. He was not a member of the Church and evidently had never known the pull and the pressure one feels when one has a positive assurance that the Lord is *not* playing games, but rather has a serious program for man and for his glory. The Lord knows what he is doing, and all his moves are appropriate and right. (76-57)

I know this is the right program, and the Lord has arranged so that I should be in this position. I am extremely humbled. (77-19)

A prophet must be virtuous and bold. We may expect the Church President will always be an older man; young men have action, vigor, initiative; older men, stability and strength and wisdom through experience and long communion with God....

The old patriarchs...were old in years, but from their accumulated experience came massive wisdom and security....

To be a prophet of the Lord, one does not need to "be everything to all men." He does not need to be youthful and athletic, an industrialist, a financier, nor an agriculturist; he does not need to be a musician, a poet, an entertainer, nor a banker, a physician, nor a college president, a military general, nor a scientist.

He does not need to be a linguist to speak French and Japanese, German and Spanish, but he must understand the divine language and be able to receive messages from heaven.

He need not be an orator, for God can make his own. The Lord can present his divine messages through weak men made strong. He substituted a strong voice for the quiet, timid one of Moses, and gave to the young man Enoch power which made men tremble in his presence, for Enoch walked with God as Moses walked with God....

What the world needs is a prophet-leader who gives example— clean, full of faith, godlike in his attitudes, with an untarnished name, a beloved husband, a true father.

A prophet needs to be more than a priest or a minister or an elder. His voice becomes the voice of God to reveal new programs, new truths, new solutions. I make no claim of infallibility for him, but he does need to be recognized of God, an authoritative person. He is no pretender as numerous are who presumptuously assume position without appointment and authority that is not given. He must speak like his Lord, "as one having authority, and not as the scribes." (Matthew 7:29.)

He must be bold enough to speak truth even against popular clamor for lessening restrictions. He must be certain of his divine appointment, of his celestial ordination, and his authority to call to service, to ordain, to pass keys which fit eternal locks. . . .

He need not be an architect to construct houses and schools and high-rise buildings, but he will be one who builds structures to span time and eternity and to bridge the gap between man and his Maker. (70-02)

No man comes to the demanding position of the Presidency of the Church except his heart and mind are constantly open to the impressions, insights, and revelations of God. (75-51)

By one means or another, the swiftest method of rejection of the holy prophets has been to find a pretext, however false or absurd, to dismiss the man so that his message could also be dismissed. Prophets who were not glib, but slow of speech, were esteemed as naught. Instead of responding to Paul's message, some saw his bodily presence as weak and regarded his speech as contemptible. Perhaps they judged Paul by the timbre of his voice or by his style of speech, not the truths uttered by him.

We wonder how often hearers first rejected the prophets because they despised them, and finally despised the prophets even more because they had rejected them. . . .

The trouble with using obscurity as a test of validity is that God has so often chosen to bring forth his work out of obscurity. . . .

The trouble with rejection because of personal familiarity with the prophets is that the prophets are always somebody's son or somebody's neighbor. They are chosen from among the people, not transported from another planet, dramatic as that would be! . . .

In multiple scriptures the Lord has indicated that he will perform his work through those whom the world regards as weak and despised. Of course, rejection of the holy prophets comes because the hearts of the people are hardened, as people are shaped by their society. . . .

Prophets have a way of jarring the carnal mind. Too often the holy prophets are wrongly perceived as harsh and as anxious to make a record in order to say, "I told you so." Those prophets I have known are the most loving of men. It is because of their love and integrity that they cannot modify the Lord's message merely to make people feel comfortable. They are too kind to be so cruel. I am so grateful that prophets do not crave popularity. (78-08)

Mantle of prophet enlarges men's capacity. President McKay had been a man among men, a great prophet and a great leader, and a counselor to two Church Presidents, but now after he was ordained and set apart as the President of the Church, I saw him rise to new pinnacles of power and authority and effectiveness. He began to speak with the voice of authority. The inspiration that came from him was contagious. His pronouncements were mature and all-encompassing. His leadership showed that unmistakably the mantle of his calling was upon him.

I saw the mantle pass again when on the day following the funeral of President David O. McKay, President Joseph Fielding Smith was elevated to the first place. When our hands were taken from his head and he now not only held all the keys and authorities and powers, but was set apart as the President of the Church, we seemed to feel almost an immediate growth. Although he was a very old man, very aged as judged by the world, he seemed to freshen and liven and throw off much of his years. His sermons were an inspiration. His sweet spirit was everywhere manifest. He was impressive to visitor and member alike.

Then more recently, the day after his funeral, in July 1972, there came to the Presidency of the Church, President Harold B. Lee, tried and true, educated in the program, spiritual, and above all, called of the Lord. The mantle changed its residence again. It fell on the newly ordained and set apart prophet and President, Harold B. Lee. We have seen this man, already trained and spiritual, grow and magnify his calling. As we see him make pronouncements and decisions, we recognize in them all the voice of the shepherd, the leader of men, a prophet of the Lord, the mantle bearer. (73-01)

The Apostles

Apostles are selected by inspiration. It is the President of the Church who calls the apostles, and he is the only one who calls them. However, what he may do is to ask the Council of the Twelve to submit some names of men we know to be of that stature. Then he may discard them all or he may select one of them.... When the individual is chosen, the prophet himself takes it to his counselors, the three of them take it to the Twelve, the [fourteen] of them decide on it all together, unified, never any discordant voice, they accept it, and then he is presented to the Church. He is ordained after he is presented and he is given all the keys that there are in the world—even the keys the President has, except that he holds them in a dormant condition, whereas the President of the Church has them active. (56-09)

God uses men in their weakness. For nearly forty years as a General Authority, I have watched Him guide this church. I marvel at how he can work to bring to pass his purposes by using us in our weaknesses, but he does! (82-02)

I know that those whom the Lord has called to give leadership to his children in this dispensation of time are recipients of divine inspiration. My grandfather sat in the first Quorum of the Twelve; my father served as mission president and stake president in a much smaller Church under five Presidents of the Church; I have served as a stake officer and General Authority for sixty-one years. Our three lives have spanned essentially the whole period of the restored Church; taken together, we have known with some intimacy almost all of the General Authorities since the Restoration. On that basis I tell you that those Church leaders were men whose great accomplishments have transcended even their substantial innate abilities, for the Lord has given them power to do his work. (79-17)

I know that the Lord called me to this position. I know that there are greater prophets, perhaps, than I, but I wish to do all I can to carry forward the work of the Lord as he wants it done. Every night and morning I kneel and pray with deep sincerity that the Lord will inspire me and reveal to me the direction I should go and what I should tell the people of this Church. (77-09)

There came to me the feeling, as I looked around the Church, that the intellectuals did not dominate the Church in numbers. The great men were few. There were many, many common people in the Church, untrained, unschooled, but with faith and good people, and maybe the Lord in getting this group needed one that was extremely common, and maybe that was the reason that I was called. It has given me a little comfort to feel that maybe there are people in the Church whom I can touch. (67-03)

Respect for leaders is largely for position. In a hotel in the Pocono mountains of Pennsylvania long years ago, I learned an important lesson when the president of the Rotary International said to the district governors in the assembly:

"Gentlemen: This has been a great year for you. The people have honored you, praised you, banqueted you, applauded you, and given you lavish gifts. If you ever get the mistaken idea that they were doing this for you personally, just try going back to the clubs next year when the mantle is on other shoulders."

This has kept me on my knees in my holy calling. Whenever I have been inclined to think the honors were coming to *me* as I go about the Church, then I remember that it is not to me, but to the *position* I hold that honors come. I am but a symbol. (58-12)

This time between stake conferences, I visited some areas that had never been touched by a General Authority out in the outskirts, way down in southern Chile and in little cities up in northern Argentina. To see these people come long distances at great expense to be there to greet us, I felt tremendously humble, like bowing my head as these people came in honor to one of our number here, and then I recognized again that I am but a symbol to them. They did not know me. They had never seen me. They came not to see me. They came to see the apostle and their reverence and their interest was to the Church, to its leadership, to the program, and I was but a symbol, and it makes me humble indeed. (66-13)

Long ago I learned that no one is indispensable and that the Lord's program will be little hampered or impeded by the loss of any one of us. The Church moves on—the gospel is preached and souls are coming to a knowledge of the truth. Even with the loss of Joseph Smith, the Church rolled on. The gospel is here forever now. No *one* or no *thing* can stop its onward movement. It "will never be taken from the earth nor given to another people." The Church moves forward—the only question is whether we as individuals will be moving along with it or whether we shall be drifting in the rear. (7/30/53)

Peter exemplifies faithful, fearless leadership. Some time ago a newspaper in a distant town carried an Easter Sunday religious editorial by a minister who stated that the presiding authority of the early-day church fell because of self-confidence, indecision, evil companions, failure to pray, lack of humility, and fear of man....

As I read this, ... my blood began to boil....

Then I opened my New Testament. I could find no such character as this modern minister described. Instead, I found a man who had grown perfect through his experiences and sufferings—a man with vision, a man of revelations, a man fully trusted by his Lord Jesus Christ....

When Christ chose this fisherman for his first and chief apostle, he was taking no chances. He picked a diamond in the rough—a diamond that would need to be cut, trimmed, and polished by correction, chastisement, and trials—but nevertheless a diamond of real quality. The Savior knew this apostle could be trusted to receive the keys of the kingdom, the sealing and the loosing power. Like other humans, Peter might make some errors in his developing process, but he would be solid, trustworthy, and dependable as a leader of the kingdom of God....

Much of the criticism of Simon Peter is centered in his denial of his acquaintance with the Master. This has been labeled "cowardice.'' Are we sure of his motive in that recorded denial? He had already given up his occupation and placed all worldly goods upon the altar for the cause. If we admit that he was cowardly and denied the Lord through timidity, we can still find a great lesson. Has anyone more completely overcome mortal selfishness and weakness? Has anyone repented more sincerely? Peter has been accused of being harsh, indiscreet, impetuous, and fearful. If all these were true, then we still ask, Has any man ever more completely triumphed over his weaknesses? . . .

Could he have felt that circumstances justified expediency? . . .

Could there still have been some lack of understanding concerning the total unfolding of the plan? . . .

Could it have been confusion and frustration that caused Peter's denial? . . .

The Savior had walked calmly from Gethsemane's garden, seemingly resigned to the inevitable sacrifice of himself. Simon had courageously manifested his willingness to alone fight the great mob to protect his Master. At the risk of death he had struck the contemptible Malchus and sliced off his ear. But this act of bravery and personal disregard was stopped by the Lord. . . . Could it be that in these last hours Peter realized that he should stop protecting his Lord, that the Crucifixion was inevitable, and that regardless of all his acts, the Lord was moving toward his destiny? I do not know. I only know that this apostle was brave and fearless. . . .

I do not pretend to know what Peter's mental reactions were nor what compelled him to say what he did that terrible night. But in light of his proven bravery, courage, great devotion, and limitless love for the Master, could we not give him the benefit of the doubt and at least forgive him as his Savior seems to have done so fully? Almost immediately Christ elevated him to the highest position in his church and endowed him with the complete keys of that kingdom. . . .

Peter was a man of faith. He healed the sick by their merely passing through his shadow. Prison walls could not hold him. Because of him, the dead came back to life. He walked upon the water. . . . Let him who would scoff at Peter's momentary wavering try such a feat himself. . . .

He accepted threats, beatings, and calumny. He defied those who condemned his Lord. . . .

When his work was done, his testimony borne, his witness delivered, his numbered days run out, Satan who had long desired him was now permitted to take him in martyrdom. His testimony came from his dying lips. . . .

The apostle lives. The weak things of the world confounded the wise. Millions have read his testimony. His powerful witness has stirred multitudes. Through the countless ages of eternity, he will live and extend his influence over the children of this earth. With his brethren, the Twelve, he will judge the nations. (71-12)

Regional, Stake, and Ward Church Assignments

Regional Representatives constitute new level of leadership. Brethren, this is a new experience for you and for us. This is a new day—new doors are opening, new keys are being used to unlock new doors; this is a new approach to meet an expanding church in an exploding world.

Never before has such responsibility been given to men who were not General Authorities. Perhaps you will be closer to the General Authorities than any group ever before has been in the history of the Church. This is a new day.

You will be representatives of the Twelve; you will speak for the Twelve; you will be set apart by the Presidency and the Twelve for this awe-inspiring responsibility. (67-11)

In the decade of the seventies, we have seen great strides in the growth of the Church. The Lord continues to bless his Church, and this growth will accelerate in the future. . . .

The Lord, through revelation, has made provision in the priesthood structure of the Church to accommodate for change and growth. (79-04)

Stake presidents lead by inspiration. In the perfect stake organization, the president uses counselors for counsel, but makes the primary decision and submits it to them for approval; and the high council is used in matters of stake business in like manner. They do not make major decisions, but may counsel and vote to sustain or reject the president's proposal.... An ideal stake will have a president who loves the word of God and is a student of the scriptures, who will know that true conversion comes first by knowing the will of God and, secondly, by living its principles carefully. He will be an unbiased judge, who will be governed by justice and never by any personal reasons. In his role as judge he will conduct interviews with stake leaders and members who will be placed in positions of trust and responsibility. He will want to be in tune with the Holy Spirit in order to best serve these people and to guide them and redirect them where necessary. Where cases of immorality are concerned, he will be anxious to see that justice is done and that penalties are paid in order that the dignity of the Church is maintained, the laws of God are followed, and the transgressor does proper suffering and is permitted to return later to the good life....

Such leaders will be kindly and understanding, but will be firm in handling every case according to its merits, remembering that to let some people "get by" with their sin is only to invite continual troubles; but when a leader is fair and just in every case, confidence will be strong in that leader.

A stake president's success will depend largely on his reliance on the Lord, on how much inspiration he can receive to perform his responsibilities. This involves bringing other members with special talents, gifts, and inspiration around him to help guide special facets of the work. This kind of leader must have a strong feeling of responsibility, moral courage, and a will to fulfill his responsibilities against all odds. He will need to develop good judgment and effective administration, always as guided by the Spirit. He recognizes and acknowledges the work and worth of others. He has a warm personal relationship with people and commands their respect by his treatment of them. He exerts influence with, rather than power over, his people. He listens attentively and sympathetically. He encourages and motivates others to be excited and responsive to their responsibilities. He encourages self-responsibility in others. He organizes his meetings well and keeps people posted on their work and responsibilities. He carefully and prayerfully calls and initiates people in their responsibilities so that they understand what the Lord expects of them in their callings. He has a systematic review of every system of the stake so that all facets and all programs are receiving the benefit of his stewardship and guidance. He recognizes that the stake presidency is to guard the people's morals, to look after their welfare, and to teach them the way of eternal life. He recognizes that a stake will be far from perfect whose leaders exercise unrighteous dominion, as carefully described and outlined by the Lord in Doctrine and Covenants section 121.

Goals are extremely important for every leader. It is well for him to set them himself for himself and induce his departments to set their own goals—goals that are realistic and can be reached but always greater than before, goals that are self-set and self-carried out; and the leader should have a feedback system, a continuing inflow of knowledge so that he may know how well it works.

This leader is totally loyal to the Lord, the prophet, the principles, and the people. (73-07)

The bishop's calling is one of spiritual power. A bishop is ordained with an everlasting endowment, and it is lost only through unworthiness which brings Church discipline, even to excommunication. He is set apart as bishop of a ward to provide it leadership. He becomes the judge, spiritual adviser, inspirer, counselor, discipliner. He becomes by ordination and setting apart the father of his people and should know them individually by name and nature and weakness and strength. He should foresee and forestall possible problems and, if some develop, be able and ready to help in their solution. His ward family should be his enlarged family and receive the same general interest as his own flesh and blood children....

By virtue of his call and ordination and setting apart, he also becomes a "judge in Israel" and has the responsibility of making many decisions which affect the progress and development of his people. He gives direction to their spiritual activities so that he can give them opportunities for growth, and judge their accomplishments. He decides as to their worthiness and eligibility for certain blessings and privileges. He holds the key to all temples in the world and it is he who must turn that key to open the doors thereof and that they may go through eternal marriage to life eternal.

He has the keys to the storehouses and must decide if one is eligible through need and worthiness to be given welfare assistance. . . .

Numerous suggestions have come from many sources in the years past that the bishops should be trained in social work to be able to meet the demands of the people in their numerous needs. But the Brethren have never felt that would be the answer. . . .

In the Church of Jesus Christ, the leaders have no formal academic training for their positions but gain experience through their lifetime, and they depend much upon the Spirit for guidance. . . .

It would be unrealistic and untrue to state that all these young men are perfect men or perfect bishops. They are mortals subject to the whims and weaknesses common to their fellows. They are not all as wise as Solomon. They are not all as personable as President McKay. They are not all as kind as President George Albert Smith was, but as I have known thousands of them personally through a half century and more, I am astounded at the power and strength and dignity and goodness and ability of these young men. . . .

Now, the bishop is a man of varied responsibilities and of many duties. He visits the "fatherless and the widows"; he blesses the sick; he buries the dead; he calls to responsibility; he appoints and releases; he conducts meetings and supervises all the numerous activities in the ward; he counsels, advises, calls to repentance, disciplines, and sometimes must handle people for their fellowship and membership. He is called of God and promised divine guidance and he will be led to make right decisions and follow proper courses as he is in total attunement with the Lord. (64-05)

Clerks hold important callings. Many revelations pertaining to this work have been given, and yet ward clerks and quorum clerks and secretaries are sometimes careless. I have been shocked many times as I have gone to conference week after week through thirteen years. I think I have never been to a stake conference when all the clerks who were invited were present in that Saturday night leadership meeting...they don't seem to think it is very important and so they absent themselves. They are doing something else. I want to tell you it is very important, so important that when the Lord, himself, came to the Nephites as recorded in 3 Nephi, he said to Nephi, who was the chief of the twelve disciples there, "Let me see your records."...

And I want every ward clerk and secretary of every organization to consider it a great privilege to be a recorder because he has a counterpart. There is an angel up there recording it too. Suppose you look at your records. Sometimes we find missing things—some very important prophecies that were made, some astute things that were said, some great exhortations that were given, in ward conference, in stake conference, sacrament meetings, and they didn't write them. They were sleeping on the job. (57-03)

Position is less significant than faithfulness. Oftentimes special notice is taken of the General Authorities—rightly so, since we are under responsibility to pray for them that they may be successful in their callings—but I know that the Lord is just as pleased with any soul on this earth who magnifies whatever calling the Lord has given him as he is with those whose lives and accomplishments are more visible. President J. Reuben Clark, Jr., said simply but eloquently, "In the service of the Lord, it is not where you serve but how. In The Church of Jesus Christ of Latter-day Saints, one takes the place to which one is duly called, which place one neither seeks nor declines." (79-17)

Calls to Church Positions

Church members have great leadership potential. You [student officers] are born leaders. Your patriarchal blessings will designate most of you as of Ephraim, the natural leaders. You must take your stance—you must assume your responsibility—you must measure up.

You have the leader potential. You have keen minds equal to the best of your contemporaries. You have strong bodies through generations of Word of Wisdom observance and plain, sensible living. You have the best blood of the age through generations of careful selectivity, and you have the basic knowledge which fits you for leadership . . . the knowledge of God and his purposes and his workings. (71-10)

Those likely to be called are humble, unassuming, and capable. The mighty and vain and noble and brilliant are not called because they are unteachable, sometimes. They feel they know so much that God cannot teach them. (46-03)

We could consistently say that power is safe only when it is possessed [by those] who are virtuous, selfless, and truly moral. (74-20)

We don't want you to be ambitious for position because so often we find that he who asks for a position in the Church is not worthy of it, and I know we do not call men to positions if they have shown desire for that position. The people we call, generally, are those who are reluctant to make demands because they are so humble and they feel their weakness so much that they stand back and wait for someone to select them. But they are people who have been living the gospel all these years. (47-11)

Frequently in calling men to high places in stakes, missions, and wards, they say they are willing but feel so inadequate. We usually say: "We are glad you feel inadequate. That means you will be humble and do all in your power to make yourself able. You will call upon the Lord, the source of power and strength." What a satisfaction it is to go finally again to the Lord for his benediction on one's efforts when he can honestly tell the Lord he has done all he could possibly do in preparation. (63-01)

The Lord made no mistake in his choice. The Lord knows that you and I are capable of doing the work to which he calls us. He makes no errors. But, if we fail to measure up in our responsibilities, sometimes it looks like the Lord might have made a mistake. (62-04)

Calls to Church positions involve definition of responsibilities.
The leader invites into his office the person selected for a position. As
he makes the call, he defines the position and its relationships;
second, he will interview, determining the willingness, availability,
and worthiness of the individual; third, he will give a job description,
indicating what is required—in some areas, this is called the charge.

There are situational calls and charges in which the demands of
the situation may go beyond the above criteria.

A certain man was recommended to be a bishop, not only to do
the regular work of a bishop but also to use his promotion abilities in
raising money and building a much-needed chapel structure. In the
call, this would be made clear and his success would be judged by his
achievement in all of the items mentioned in the call and interview.

There could be extra charges given to the individual, as in the call
of a high councilor who had been a very successful agriculturist and
who was asked to give special attention to a welfare farm or project.
(69-09)

Setting apart can lift officers to new power. The setting apart is an
established practice in the Church and men and women are "set
apart" to special responsibility, in ecclesiastical, quorum, and
auxiliary positions. All missionaries are set apart and it is remarkable
how many of them speak often of the authority who officiated and of
the blessings promised and their fulfillment.

To some folk the setting apart seems a perfunctory act while
others anticipate it eagerly, absorb every word of it, and let their lives
be lifted thereby.

The setting apart may be taken literally; it is a setting apart from
sin, apart from the carnal; apart from everything which is crude, low,
vicious, cheap, or vulgar; *set apart* from the world to a higher plane
of thought and activity. The blessing is conditional upon faithful
performance. . . .

In my experience there have been numerous people who like Saul
and David and Matthias, like Paul and Peter and Joshua, have,
through the setting apart, received "largeness of heart," extended
influence, increased wisdom, enlarged vision, and new powers. I have

seen many who have been given "a new heart" and who have been turned "into another man" and made into a "new creature." ...

Who has not watched the transformation of a person newly set apart to high responsibility? Who has not seen men already great rise to new plateaus of superior attainment braced with the authority, the keys, the mantle? And conversely, who has not seen the loss in stature, influence, and power after a great leader has relinquished the reigns of direction, and the mantle of authority diverted to other shoulders? It is not imaginary but very real. (59-12)

When the Lord has called a man He can perform miracles with him. I have seen it in the stakes. I have seen stake presidents installed and wondered, then a little later find them great and strong in power. I have seen other brethren come back and report stake reorganizations and they seemed somewhat dubious about the leaders, and then in a few months I have visited those stakes and find these men, with the mantle upon them, have risen to great heights. I have seen bishops, particularly, come from the ranks, and soon they are performing great service. I have been amazed, and then I realize the Lord can take a very humble thing and make it glorious. (52-01)

One should not resign from Church positions. If they are called of God, then they wouldn't want to presume to tell the Lord just how long they were going to serve him. So all the officers in the Church are all called on an indefinite tenure and at the discretion and the inspiration of those who preside over them. So a bishop may serve a year or twenty years. ... You have no right to resign any more than you have to call yourself to the work. (56-09)

It is well understood that conditions change and occupations sometimes require moves and occasionally health requires change. But dedicated men and women will accept the responsibility and serve in an MIA call as they would in an ecclesiastical call, from the time they are called of the Lord through proper leadership until they are released by the Lord by proper leadership. (69-06)

Service given grudgingly brings few rewards. But if you have accepted this position as a routine assignment that calls for so many hours a day or so many evenings a week or so many meetings a month—if you've accepted on that basis, I'm sorry for you. You are missing all the dessert. You are getting only the hard potatoes. (74-19)

Effective Leadership

Growing Church needs new leaders. We recognize our greatest problem is our rapid growth. Our increase in numbers is phenomenal, for the population has doubled in these past few years. . . . This unprecedented growth pleases us, but challenges us tremendously. We are interested in numbers only incidentally. We are obsessed first to see that all men obtain eternal life.

The monumental challenge in 1974, then, is to provide trained leadership for the fast-multiplying units of members and to help that membership to keep clean from that world in which they must live. (74-02)

Members need leadership training. An important part of missionary work is the creation of stakes, since new converts need further organization and activity to work out their exaltation. Much of the responsibility then falls upon the shoulders of the stake leaders, since, as has been pointed out, the number of General Authorities has increased very little since the Church had 20 stakes, and we now have 442.

Yesterday's tools and programs are outmoded today, and . . . more training and better training is necessary to meet the demands of today.

It is quite evident that our present methods are not sufficiently effective to handle the ever-increasing multitudes of members. We have reached plateaus in certain areas of our activity and now it is time that we pick up our load and start climbing to the higher peaks. . . .

Much of our ecclesiastical education must come through activity and on-the-job training. We must therefore employ a greater percentage of our fast-growing numbers in positions, giving opportunity for growth and training. We must then tell them how to do the work assigned and show them how to do it, and follow up to see that they do do it in the most approved way....

Two steps are being taken—sixty-eight Regional Representatives of the Twelve have been called to assist in the training procedures; and number two, stake presidents will have an increased responsibility. (67-01)

Jesus demonstrated exemplary leadership. Jesus knew who he was and why he was here on this planet. That meant he could lead from strength rather than from uncertainty or weakness.

Jesus operated from a base of fixed principles or truths rather than making up the rules as he went along. Thus, his leadership style was not only correct, but also constant. So many secular leaders today are like chameleons; they change their hues and views to fit the situation—which only tends to confuse associates and followers who cannot be certain what course is being pursued. Those who cling to power at the expense of principle often end up doing almost anything to perpetuate their power.

Jesus said several times, "Come, follow me." His was a program of "do what I do," rather than "do what I say." His innate brilliance would have permitted him to put on a dazzling display, but that would have left his followers far behind. He walked and worked with those he was to serve. His was not a long-distance leadership. He was not afraid of close friendships; he was not afraid that proximity to him would disappoint his followers. The leaven of true leadership cannot lift others unless we are with and serve those to be led....

Jesus was a listening leader. Because he loved others with a perfect love, he listened without being condescending....

Because Jesus loved his followers, he was able to level with them, to be candid and forthright with them. He reproved Peter at times because he loved him, and Peter, being a great man, was able to grow from this reproof....

Jesus saw sin as wrong but also was able to see sin as springing from deep and unmet needs on the part of the sinner. This permitted him to condemn the sin without condemning the individual. We can show forth our love for others even when we are called upon to correct them. We need to be able to look deeply enough into the lives of others to see the basic causes for their failures and short-comings. . . .

Jesus' leadership emphasized the importance of being discerning with regard to others, without seeking to control them. He cared about the freedom of his followers to choose. . . .

Jesus had perspective about problems and people. He was able to calculate carefully at long range the effect and impact of utterances, not only on those who were to hear them at the moment, but on those who would read them two thousand years later. So often, secular leaders rush in to solve problems by seeking to stop the present pain, and thereby create even greater difficulty and pain later on.

Jesus knew how to involve his disciples in the process of life. He gave them important and specific things to do for their development. Other leaders have sought to be so omnicompetent that they have tried to do everything themselves, which produces little growth in others. Jesus trusts his followers enough to share his work with them so that they can grow. . . .

Jesus was not afraid to make demands of those he led. His leadership was not condescending or soft. He had the courage to call Peter and others to leave their fishing nets and to follow him, not after the fishing season or after the next catch, but now! today! Jesus let people know that he believed in them and in their possibilities, and thus he was free to help them stretch their souls in fresh achievement. . . .

Jesus gave people truths and tasks that were matched to their capacity. He did not overwhelm them with more than they could manage, but gave them enough to stretch their souls. . . .

Jesus also taught us how important it is to use our time wisely. This does not mean there can never be any leisure, for there must be time for contemplation and for renewal, but there must be no waste of time. . . . Wise time management is really the wise management of ourselves. . . .

Those individuals whom we most love, admire, and respect as leaders of the human family are so regarded by us precisely because they embody, in many ways, the qualities that Jesus had in his life and in his leadership. . . .

We are not yet perfect as Jesus was, but unless those about us can see us striving and improving, they will not be able to look to us for example, and they will see us as less than fully serious about the things to be done.

Each of us has more opportunities to do good and to be good than we ever use. These opportunities lie all around us. . . .

We must remember that those mortals we meet in parking lots, offices, elevators, and elsewhere are that portion of mankind God has given us to love and to serve. It will do us little good to speak of the general brotherhood of mankind if we cannot regard those who are all around us as our brothers and sisters. (77-02)

Paul showed great leadership qualities. I have a great admiration and affection for our brother Paul, our fellow apostle. He was so dedicated, so humble, so straightforward. He was so eager, so interested, so consecrated. He must have been personable in spite of his problems, for the people hung onto him with great affection when he was about to leave them.

I love Paul, for he spoke the truth. He leveled with people. He was interested in them. I love Paul for his steadfastness, even unto death and martyrdom. I am always fascinated with his recounting of the perils through which he passed to teach the gospel to member and nonmember. (69-02)

Responsibilities of Leaders

Leaders must teach true principles. I realize I cannot convince you against your will, but I know I can help you if you will only listen and let me call to your attention some salient truths, and if you will listen with a prayer and a desire to know that what I say is true. I would not, even if I could, force your thinking, for free agency is the basic law of God and each one must assume the responsibility for his own response; but certainly each of us must do his part in influencing for good those who might need some assistance. (77-31)

We continue to warn the people and plead with them, for we are watchmen upon the towers, and in our hands we have a trumpet which we must blow loudly and sound the alarm....

Some may wonder why General Authorities speak of the same things from conference to conference....

Prophets say the same things because we face basically the same problems. Brothers and sisters, the solutions to these problems have not changed. It would be a poor lighthouse that gave off a different signal to guide every ship entering a harbor. It would be a poor mountain guide who, knowing the safe route up a mountainside, took his trusting charges up unpredictable and perilous paths from which no traveler returns. (75-47)

Leaders serve as examples. Long years ago when I was in the stake presidency in the St. Joseph Stake in Arizona, one Sabbath day I filled an assignment in the Eden Ward. The building was a small one, and most of the people were sitting close to us as we sat on the raised platform about a foot and a half above the floor of the building itself.

As the meeting proceeded, my eye was attracted to seven little boys on the front seat of the chapel. I was delighted with seven little boys in this ward conference. I made a mental note, then shifted my interest to other things. Soon my attention was focused on the seven little boys again.

It seemed strange to me that each of the seven little fellows raised his right leg and put it over the left knee, and then in a moment all would change at the same time and put the left leg over the right knee. I thought it was unusual, but I just ignored it.

In a moment or two, all in unison would brush their hair with their right hands, and then all seven little boys leaned lightly on their wrists and supported their faces by their hands, and then simultaneously they went back to the crossing of their legs again.

It all seemed so strange, and I wondered about it as I was trying to think of what I was going to say in the meeting. And then all at once it came to me like a bolt of lightning. These boys were mimicking me!

That day I learned the lesson of my life—that we who are in positions of authority must be careful indeed, because others watch us and find in us their examples. (74-32)

Lead by kindness, not by command. You are the men holding the priesthood and the leaders in your communities. From you we expect the real leadership. We hope you are going [to go] back to your homes and give better leadership to your homes and families, that you will teach and discipline your children, that you will be to your household as Christ is to the Church, that you will be kind to your wives and love your wives more than you love yourselves, and as you go back to your branches, that you will rule in kindness. There is no reason why anyone who holds the priesthood should become like Hitler. There is no place in this Church for masters or slaves. We are all equal, although we are deacons or apostles. We have callings and responsibilities, but we are all the sons of God and there is no reason for anyone to rise up in his majesty when he has a position of responsibility, and no place for any leader to lord it over others just because he has authority.

The Savior who was the head of the Church never ruled by force, but by kindness and long-suffering and love. So you branch presidents and you counselors go back and with greater love than ever before seek to give leadership to your branch as Christ does to the Church. (47-10)

Unlike the world, when we supervise, it should not be out of a need for status or need to control, but out of the desire to serve others and to help them in a way that increases their righteous capacity. (75-25)

Give training and supervision. Too often in the past we have called individuals, giving them little or no orientation and little or no supervision. We must begin to do otherwise, if we desire to lengthen our stride in the management of the kingdom at all levels of its operation. . . . This means each of us must be more willing to expend more of our time, talent, and means in providing leadership training in the broadest sense of that concept.... The Church is so organized that each of us has at least one supervisor, and we need to be helped by that supervisor in ways that really assist us in becoming more effective. Leaders often need to be directively helpful. (75-25)

Communicate expectations and enthusiasm. A prudent leader will not complain at the weakness or the inefficiency or the lack of interest of those with whom he works until he is certain that he has presented the program fully, concisely, thoroughly, and understandably, and that he has followed through to keep the matter fresh in their minds, being sure that they understand the program and go forward. He should evaluate his performance before he criticizes others in theirs. His success will be measured not by his brilliance, nor by how much he knows about the program, but by how well he can transmit the knowledge and enthusiasm to others. When one person speaks the people say, "How eloquent," but when another finishes speaking, they say, "Come, let us march." (67-15)

We who pretend leadership must set on fire those whom we would lead. (74-14)

Open new horizons. A man will remain a rag picker, as long as he has only the vision of a rag picker. So ambition is very, very essential. To be a leader, one must remember that he must excel in energy and power and mentality. (58-10)

A great leader will establish confidence in his men. They will see him accomplish the impossible and they will follow his example.

Simon Peter never would have attempted to walk on the sea without following the example of his leader. His faith sustained him for awhile until he began to think of the possibility of the water yielding to his weight and letting him into the boisterous sea. The Master caught him and lifted him and restored his faith sufficiently that they walked onto the ship and the wind ceased and the waves were calm. (76-37)

The problems of the world cannot possibly be solved by skeptics or cynics whose horizons are limited by the obvious realities. (74-29)

Counsel is given to new bishop and wife. Your call pleases me beyond expression and I wish for you a glorious administration. Do not ever permit yourself to become independent of your stake presidency; they are your file leaders. Never institute any new major procedures without their approval. Use your counselors. List the numerous duties to be performed by the members of the bishopric and then give the very heavy end of all of the matters which could be considered routine to your two counselors, retaining for yourself those things required of the bishop only: interviews, marital problems, morals problems, general supervision, your priests, the welfare—and you will still have more than the human being can do without a tremendous amount of help from the Lord. Stay close to your ward children through all their years and your youth as they grow. I am sure that your work should be mostly *prevention* and far less of *cure,* and that if you will delegate enough of your routine matters to your counselors you will have time to cultivate the faith and confidence of all your youth from the time they are ten or twelve so that they will love you so much and have such a degree of confidence in you they will accept your counsel and come to you for advice and will follow it.

Ruth, never in your life has an opportunity like this presented itself to you, and you can guarantee the success of your husband or nullify it. I know you will measure up fully. In large measure the wife of the bishop must sit and wait, and there will be much waiting and much sitting. It will take much patience, long-suffering. The wife and the family of the bishop can serve best by always being at their post of duty; always kind and thoughtful but never presumptuous in the slightest. Through one-sided telephone calls and words dropped here and there, the bishop's wife will be able to surmise much that is going on, but she will not display interest or draw conclusions or ever repeat. Her husband will never discuss with her the intimate matters of the bishopric and yet being smart she will almost intuitively sense much that is going on, but she will be wise and never reveal it. (11/19/58)

Use counselors. Mission presidents and stake presidents and ward bishops, do not ever say "I": "I will do this; I'm going to do this; I've decided this." The Lord gave you all two counselors, and it is always "We made this decision; we decided to do this." Recognize your counselors, give them opportunities also to develop, and if you ignore them, you are hardly worthy to be the executive. (75-11)

I was a counselor for twelve years and I wondered what the president of the stake was doing all the time. It seemed to me that I was doing all the work. When I became the president of the stake then I began to wonder, "Well, why don't my counselors do anything?" (74-17)

Delegate tasks. You cannot do both your own work and your subordinates' work. While the Church organization is perfect it can be greatly distorted. The president should ask himself constantly whenever confronted with a problem, "Is this something I must do or could it be done by others through one of my counselors?"... The bishop should realize that if he spends his precious time carrying water and hewing wood, telephoning, writing unnecessary letters, or doing any other duty that could be done by others under his direction, then he is in reality robbing his people of that precious time of his which belongs to them in the development of their spiritual life and welfare. (70-11)

Measure performance. One's performance is successful if he achieves what he has planned to accomplish....

Certainly, in the evaluating process, one must be purposeful. He must know where he is going. The Lord revealed: "Wherefore, now let every man learn his duty." Until he knows what is properly expected of him, how can he begin to judge his effectiveness?...

We ascertain and establish acceptable standards of excellence in a given field and measure our work accordingly. We should be less interested in excelling others but more concerned with excelling our own past records and using our established ideal standards and perfection as our goals and the measurement of our attainments and our degree of progress.

The criteria we can apply to ourselves grow out of several sources:

1. One criterion involves the formal requirements of the position as contained in handbooks or manuals.

2. There are the specific and general goals and duties given us in the scriptures that pertain to our callings.

3. An appraisal or evaluation may involve the element of time: How much of my time, myself, and my talent are being effectively used in my calling—adequate or too little? . . .

As for myself, I seem always to measure my own performance by the estimate and appraisal of people whose opinion of my service is paramount. For instance, in days gone by, nearly every sermon I gave in conference, nearly every decision I made, nearly every argument I advanced seemed always to be given with the thought, "What does Stephen L Richards think? How might he have appraised it? What are his expectations?" . . .

I find myself hungering and thirsting for just a word of appreciation or of honest evaluation from my superiors and my peers. I want no praise; I want no flattery; I am seeking only to know if what I gave was acceptable. (67-15)

We often complain at statistics and reports, but after all is said, we must have reports. Otherwise, how can we ourselves know what is going on, what progress is being made? How can the general and stake leaders appraise and evaluate and help unless they know the true status?

Granted, figures can lie, and statistics may be dry and boring, and reports are not always correct; but they do indicate trends and make us aware of the areas of need. Those of us who use these figures should first evaluate the report itself as to its correctness before criticizing any person or group.

Statistics are most impressive when they compare the unit with itself rather than with other units of different size and conditions. Statistics can be very helpful when they show the progress of the stake or ward or unit by comparing its own record in successive periods.

When I was stake clerk in the St. Joseph Stake, something was said in the stake presidency meeting about the noted progress of the stake in certain areas. I remarked that actually, we were not progressing in sacrament meeting attendance.

I was challenged. "Oh, you must be wrong. Don't you remember at Central Ward last week how they had to open the curtains into the cultural hall? And don't you remember how they had to carry in chairs in Layton Ward the week before?"

Yes, I remembered that, but I stated, "There are two factors that have distorted the picture. First, the stake president was in attendance, and that drew a crowd; and second, the communities have been growing, so there are more people. But the percentage of attendance is no greater."

Again I was challenged. I said nothing more but went to the vault and checked the records and found that in twenty-five years the stake had not moved a single percent. It was 25 percent a quarter century ago; it was 25 percent now. (67-15)

There need to be interim evaluations in which we are given help, assistance, and encouragement. Our Church procedures and organizations provide for these chances for improvement. So does our family life when we function properly. But too seldom does evaluation occur in a loving, helpful way, and this is one of the reasons many sincere members do not stride out confidently as they should. (75-25)

Interview carefully concerning worthiness. A bishop could go down the line and merely ask the conventional questions and listen only for the words of the answers. His effectiveness could be very poor. He might receive affirmative answers and yet the individual might be quite unworthy to go into the temple.

The bishop is entitled by revelation from the Lord to have discernment that would leave him uneasy about unworthy people, and thus he could prevent them from entering the sacred precincts of the temple. . . .

To be more specific, numerous leaders have asked in interviews, "Are you morally clean?" And the answer was, "Yes," when the individual actually was unclean. Perhaps in an occasion of this kind, the one being interviewed did not intend to lie, but the question was a general one, and he gave a general answer; and because they did not have a meeting of minds as to what was morally clean, the wrong answer was given. This has happened too many times to count. (67-15)

Handle transgressors justly. We are concerned that too many times the interviewing leader in his personal sympathies for the transgressor, and in his love perhaps for the family of the transgressor, is inclined to waive the discipline which that transgressor demands.

Too often a transgressor is forgiven and all penalties waived when that person should have been disfellowshipped or excommunicated. Too often a sinner is disfellowshipped when he or she should have been excommunicated.

Remember that President Taylor said you will have to carry that sin yourself. Are you willing to do it, brethren? . . .

It is so easy to let our sympathies carry us out of proportion; and when a man has committed sin, he must suffer. It is an absolute requirement—not by the bishop—but it is a requirement by nature and by the very part of a man. This discipline is especially applicable to adults and married people and more especially to those who have been to the temple. They must understand that they cannot tamper with the holy laws of God. (75-14)

Be concerned about individuals. Please be especially thoughtful of the sisters who are, through no fault of their own, not presently given the blessing of being sealed for all eternity to a worthy man, so they do not inadvertently feel left out as we rightfully focus on family life. (79-21)

Please, priesthood brethren, do not get so busy trying to manage Church programs that you forget these basic duties in what the apostle James described as "pure religion and undefiled." (James 1:27.) (78-25)

Be careful with time. Just as the bishop takes care that no more funds are expended from the ward budget than have been budgeted for each organization, so he should be the chief budget officer in monitoring local expenditure of the *time* of Church members. In both cases, he must always keep the budget in balance.

The measured flexibility we are giving you is to help you to use your time more effectively in serving the Saints. There is a difference between being "anxiously engaged" and busy work. (78-04)

Fathers and mothers, we must "come back home." We must sacrifice some of our other interests, and organize our Church programs better so that both parents and youth will not be away from the home so much of the time. We must get more people to work in the Church so that the burden will not fall so heavily on the few. Then we must organize and do the maximum possible in the minimum amount of time, so that there can be more proper home life. (MF 256)

We need at times to strive to focus on the basic purposes of our work so that mere busyness does not create the illusion that we are effective when we are not.

Merely attending meetings may be busyness, but to get something accomplished is the purpose of our call. (67-15)

Plan meetings for efficiency. In this connection, brethren, we hope you will be mindful of your own needs and preserve some of that precious time for your own wives and families. Be mindful, too, of your associates in the work of the Church, so that time is not taken unnecessarily from them and their families.

Avoid the tendency to crowd too many meetings in on the Sabbath day. When holding your regular meetings, make them as spiritual and effective as possible. Meetings need not be hurried nor rushed, for they can be planned in a manner that permits their sacred purposes to be accomplished without difficulty. (81-04)

Consolidated meetings leave time for family and service. You have seen an emphasis on simplification of Church programs....

Recently we established the new consolidated schedule which is aimed at enriching family life even further, together with greater opportunity for individual and family gospel scholarship and for more Christian service. We are trying to provide more time and emphasis on Christian service, so that our example can be more powerful in the world and so that those who are so worthy of attention might get more attention than they sometimes have in the past.

Please keep the spirit and purpose of these program adjustments before you. It would be a mistake simply to rush in to fill up the time with more meetings. It would be a mistake for families simply to pursue worldly activities on the Sabbath. It would be a mistake for us as a people to try to do so many different things at once that nothing gets done really well. (80-02)

Be concerned about economy. From time to time, we hear reports of unwarranted pressures which accompany the financial requests made of our Church members.

This is a matter of grave importance. In these days of inflation and emotional and political unrest, our people everywhere are being met with difficult and trying experiences on almost every hand. Prudence and wisdom not only suggest but dictate that we take some steps to retrench and husband our resources. We must not overburden our people.

Let us as individuals, as families, and as wards and stakes learn to live within our means. There is strength and salvation in this principle. Someone has said that we are rich in proportion to that with which we can do without. As families and as a Church, we can and should provide that which is *truly essential* for our people, but we must be careful not to extend beyond that which is essential or for purposes which are not directly related to our families' welfare and the basic mission of the Church. (81-04)

CHAPTER 18

Priesthood and Its Exercise

Priesthood in the Church

Priesthood is the means to exaltation. The priesthood is the power and authority of God delegated to man on earth to act in all things pertaining to the salvation of men. It is the means whereby the Lord acts through men to save souls. Without this priesthood power, men are lost. Only through this power does man "hold the keys of all the spiritual blessings of the church," enabling him to receive "the mysteries of the kingdom of heaven, to have the heavens opened" unto him (see D&C 107:18-19), enabling him to enter the new and everlasting covenant of marriage and to have his wife and children bound to him in an everlasting tie, enabling him to become a patriarch to his posterity forever, and enabling him to receive a fullness of the blessings of the Lord. (75-21)

Priesthood is only in the restored Church. There is no priesthood anywhere else today than in this restored Church. There is *priestcraft,* but no *priesthood.* (65-01)

Presumptuous and blasphemous are they who purport to baptize, bless, marry, or perform other sacraments in the name of the Lord while in fact lacking his specific authorization. And no one can obtain God's authority from reading the Bible or from just a desire to serve the Lord, no matter how pure his motives. (MF 55)

You cannot give the priesthood without having it. (74-14)

God extends the priesthood to many. The power of the priesthood is not with the General Authorities, with the apostles, with the stake presidents, or with the bishops alone. It is for every man who is given the Melchizedek Priesthood and made an elder. He is entitled, if he lives for it, to have these blessings. (76-33)

How privileged we are to hold this precious priesthood, which is greater than that held by kings and emperors. How wonderful it is for every boy to have this privilege with his brothers and father. (75-14)

No man can get the priesthood himself. You couldn't buy it if you had all the money in Scandinavia. You couldn't force it if you were a king. You just wait patiently and prove yourselves, and then the leader of the Church calls you to those positions. So we say to the bishops and stake presidents and the leaders of the missions and stakes, the responsibility is yours.

I attended a priesthood meeting at one time. There must have been thirty men and older boys in attendance. I said to them, "All the deacons stand," and the teachers and priests, and then the elders and seventies. When it came to the priests and to the elders there were very few that stood. I said to the president of the mission, "Why, are all these men inactive?" And he said, "They are not inactive; they are good, faithful men." I said, "Well, why aren't they given the responsibility in the priesthood?" He said, "They haven't been in the Church a full year yet." Now, there are some things that cause us to wait a year. After we are a member of the Church, we wait a year to go to the temple and be married in the temple. But there is no such ruling that I know of about the priesthood. I said, "I want you to get busy and get these men enjoying the priesthood benefits. We don't wait a year. We wait just a reasonable time to give them a chance to get themselves situated in their new calling." (76-45)

If a man is worthy to be baptized, he is worthy to be a deacon that day or that week or that month. With all your converts—do not let

them wait. If they are not worthy of that, then they are not worthy to
have been baptized; you have crowded them. (74-25)

Holders are responsible to magnify priesthood. Too many of us
just hold the priesthood; that is about all we do, but we must magnify
it. . . .

In a hotel I found, one time, a little glass attached to the regular
mirror. It was a magnifying glass. When I looked into that glass my
whiskers looked like forests alongside the Grand Canyon in Arizona,
because my whiskers and my wrinkles were all magnified.

Now, that is what you are going to do with the priesthood. You
are going to magnify it. You are going to make the small sticks seem
to be great forests. It is so big and so great and so wonderful that
in your whole life you will be blessed and made happy by it. (80-16)

This is not a plaything. The priesthood of God is the most serious
thing in the world. It was by the priesthood the world was created.
And it is by the priesthood that your world will be created; and if you
ever become a god in a world of your own, with your wife, your
family, it will be through the magnifying of this priesthood which you
hold. . . .

You are the sons of God. You are the elect of God, and you have
within your hands the possibility to become a god and pass by the
angels and the gods, who were set there, to your exaltation.

This should make us tremble, brethren; we should tremble as we
think of the responsibility that is on us. . . . Kings, and lords and earls
and dukes and emperors—they are men of the world. You are men
of heaven. You are men with all the potential. (74-25)

The faithful in the priesthood are those who fulfill the covenant
by "magnifying their calling" and living "by every word that pro-
ceedeth forth from the mouth of God." (D&C 84:33, 44.) Far more
seems to be implied in these requirements than token obedience—far
more is needed than mere attendance at a few meetings and token
fulfillment of assignments. The perfection of body and spirit are
implied, and that includes the kind of service that goes far beyond the

normal definition of duty. "Behold, there are many called, but few are chosen." (D&C 121:34.) (75-21)

One breaks the priesthood covenant by transgressing commandments—but also by leaving undone his duties. Accordingly, to break this covenant one needs only to do nothing. (MF 96)

Passing the sacrament is an honor. Now, there are many people who are joining the Church after they are adults. They should also be watched very carefully and should be given all of these privileges. These men should receive the various orders of the priesthood. After their baptisms, they should be ordained deacons, and they should know what it means to be humble enough to pass the sacrament, even with the boys that are only twelve years of age.

You remember that the Lord himself passed the sacrament to his Twelve Apostles. Practically every month we have a meeting in the temple in Salt Lake City for all of the General Authorities, and we have the sacrament. Who do you think are the ones who pass the sacrament? The Twelve Apostles, the Assistants to the Twelve, and the other General Authorities are given the opportunity to break the bread, to bless the bread and water, and to pass the sacrament to all of the Brethren. And so we hope that every man would want to pass the sacrament. (75-37)

For thirty years it's been my privilege to take part in the passing of the sacrament to hundreds and hundreds of men, the priesthood, in the temples, and I have always considered it a great blessing and a great honor to be one of those to pass the emblems of the Son of God. (74-09)

Boys grow through priesthood service. Young men do not usually become inactive in the Church because they are given too many significant things to do. No young man who has really witnessed for himself that the gospel works in the lives of the people will walk away from his duties in the kingdom and leave them undone....

As our young men learn quorum management, they are not only

blessing the Aaronic Priesthood youth in those quorums, but they are preparing themselves as future fathers and future leaders for the Melchizedek Priesthood quorums. They need some experience in leadership, some experience in service projects, some experience in speaking, some experience in conducting meetings, and some experience in how to build proper relationships with young women. (76-26)

Relief Society complements priesthood training. The Relief Society is the Lord's organization for women. It complements the priesthood training given to the brethren. There is a power in this organization that has not yet been fully exercised to strengthen the homes of Zion and build the kingdom of God—nor will it until both the sisters and the priesthood catch the vision of Relief Society.

What *is* our greatest potential? Is it not to achieve godhood ourselves? And what are the qualities we must develop to achieve such greatness? We might consider some:

First, intelligence, light and knowledge. What special opportunities do women have in this area? These qualities, you will remember, are part of the promise given to the sisters by the Prophet Joseph Smith. Since we learn best by teaching others, we think our Relief Society sisters see the fulfillment of that promise daily as they teach children at home, in Sunday School, and in Primary, in Relief Societies, in sacrament meetings, and in daily conversation. We urge our sisters who are called to teach to magnify their callings through study and prayer, recognizing the eternal values they are building for themselves, as well as for those they teach. We encourage all our sisters to take advantage of their opportunities to receive light and knowledge in school, in personal study, and in Relief Society. (76-23)

Priesthood Power and Miracles

Priesthood has great power. There is no limit to the power of the priesthood which you hold. The limit comes in you if you do not live in harmony with the Spirit of the Lord and you limit yourselves in the power you exert. (47-10)

The Lord was promulgating an eternal principle that where his priesthood is and where faith is found, there will be the signs of power—not for show, but for a blessing to the people. This eternal principle was understood by the disciples of the Lord in early days. (PKSO 71)

Not even Lucifer, the star of the morning, the archenemy of mankind, can withstand the power of the priesthood of God. (63-03)

I feel certain that all the knowledge that is available will not be enough to give the power to create the worlds without the priesthood and the power thereof.

When we shall have learned all about medicine, minerology, zoology, forestry, and biology, and all other ologies and all about the heavens, and all about the earth in all its moods, then if we also know and feel true theology perhaps we can then exercise our accumulated power to create an earth for our exalted family.

But of course marriage cannot wait for that accumulation of knowledge. We shall marry, have our families, teach and train them while we are learning other things and building toward creatorship. (73-06)

Miracles continue. A question often asked is: If miracles are a part of the gospel program, why do we not have such today?

The answer is a simple one: We do have miracles today—beyond imagination! If all the miracles of our own lifetime were recorded, it would take many library shelves to hold the books which would contain them.

What kinds of miracles do we have? All kinds—revelations, visions, tongues, healings, special guidance and direction, evil spirits cast out. Where are they recorded? In the records of the Church, in journals, in news and magazine articles and in the minds and memories of many people.

The rationalist continues: Many people are administered to and are not healed. That is true, as it has been in all times. . . . It was never intended that all should be healed or that all should be raised from the dead, else the whole program of mortality and death and resurrection and exaltation would be frustrated.

However, the Lord does make specific promises: Signs will *follow* them that believe. He makes no promise that signs will create belief nor save nor exalt. Signs are the product of faith. They are born in the soil of unwavering sureness. They will be prevalent in the Church in about the same degree to which the people have true faith. (59-07)

Miracles follow faith. Many would like to have the miracle to build their faith, but it is the result rather than the cause of faith. Rationalization can soon void and nullify a miracle if it has not a foundation of faith to precede it. Miracles of today can be argued and rationalized away at times as they could in days of old. Peter was able to perform a feat never done by any other man so far as I know. He actually walked on the water, as I have mentioned. So long as his faith was supreme, he was able to nullify gravity and walk on the crest, but when he came to himself, he could not sustain himself longer because his faith began to waver. (76-53)

Many miracles are small. As the history of the years was condensed, it would be expected that only the most spectacular of the healings would be chronicled, giving the impression that all miracles were spectacular ones and that all who asked were healed. (PKSO 78)

Miracles may involve rearrangement of natural phenomena. It is a miracle to force water uphill through a siphon, until we understand it. The lesser law of gravity is suspended while the air-pressure law is permitted to work.

The skeptic might say that the Red Sea episode of history was impossible, but people who have been to Egypt say that occasionally strong winds blow the water from the shallow portions of the sea, leaving it sufficiently dry for passage. Surely God could operate the natural laws in such a manner. Or the plagues of Egypt: A change in climatic conditions might foster the breeding of countless hordes of lice or flies or locusts and a lack of vegetation in other parts cause their migration to the rich valleys of the Nile at just the proper time to afflict Pharaoh and his people, and the very presence and filth of these pests would perhaps bring as a logical sequence the then-incurable epidemic to strike the members of every household in death and make possible the flight of the Israelites. Such a disease is not hard to imagine when we remember the death and misery in our own ranks brought about by the first epidemic of flu in 1918 and 1919. (63-03)

Ability to use power is limited. We've talked about the priesthood. This priesthood is the power of God delegated to men. You have the power of God. How would you feel if all at once the power of God were given to you? The power you have is somewhat limited by your lives, and your knowledge, and your power to do things. It would be unfortunate if you received the total power of God all at once if you were not wholly ready for it, because you might make many mistakes. You might make people well when they ought to pass away. You might make many, many errors if you had no limitations to your priesthood. So the Lord has very wisely given to you priesthood commensurate with your need and your ability to handle it.

It would be terrible, wouldn't it, if you put into the hands of little children live bombs or electric wires? That would be terrible, because they don't know how to control them nor how to protect themselves against it. That is the way it is with the priesthood.

But as fast as a man is worthy and able to handle it, the Lord will give him these powers. (75-06)

We tell you once more that to hold the priesthood is a powerful blessing. You can be a poor priesthood member, or a very wonderful one. You can, like your Savior, some day say, "Peace, be still" (Mark 4:39), and the storm will vanish. You can, like your Savior, some day say, "Bless this blind eye, this unhearing ear," and miracles will happen. Oh, brethren, our miracles are about as strong as we are. The power that you hold is limited only by you and your activities, and your purity of heart. So glory in your priesthood. (76-47)

I'm glad that I will not have unlimited priesthood power until I have enough judgment and wisdom and insight to use it. (61-02)

Ordinances and Blessings

Ordinances are basic to the gospel. Now, what is the gospel of which we speak? It is the power of God unto salvation; it is the code of laws and commandments which help us to become perfect, and the ordinances which constitute the entrance requirements.

The ordinances begin with baptism by immersion by proper authority for the remission of sins and for entrance into the earthly kingdom of God. It is followed by the reception of the Holy Ghost, which is promised to every person who qualifies. The priesthood is given, which opens further doors; the endowment is an indispensable feature in preparation for eternal life; and then, the sealing in the holy temple of a man and a woman for an eternal relationship. These are *indispensable!* No one can ever reach the heights of exaltation and eternal life without all of them. (62-01)

Now, the ordinances of the gospel are vital. Some day we must know all about them. We cannot imagine becoming gods ourselves until we know all things. A little child doesn't need to know all about the blessing. He may not fully comprehend all of the blessings of baptism when he is eight. One may not fully understand the full significance of the sacrament. And in like manner, one doesn't need to know all about electricity to enjoy its benefits. We encourage the gaining of knowledge, but keep in mind that it is the *doing* of the commandments that is the important thing.

The most important, of course, of all the ordinances are the sealing ones, and all the others lead up to them. We are blessed, we are baptized, we are confirmed, we are ordained, we are endowed, and we are finally sealed, without which no soul can ever be exalted. And this our youth need to have impressed upon their minds. The temple isn't just a nice place to go, a beautiful room in which to be married. It is not just the wish of our parents. Every boy and girl leaving your classes should know that the ordinance of sealing is an absolute. (62-08)

Church membership and priesthood are great treasures. The wreck of a plane, killing a hundred people; the sinking of a vessel, drowning a thousand; the killing of a million in a great world war would be nothing compared to your losing your membership, your priesthood, your blessings. They might never be restored to you. Men who die may live again, but when the spiritual death is total, it were better that a man were never born. (12/20/65)

I feel sometimes like severely lecturing men and women who enter into covenants without realizing the nature of the covenants they make, and who use little or no effort to fulfill them. (74-27)

President Brigham Young wrote a letter to President George A. Smith who was then in Washington, D.C.; this was in 1857, and he said, "The bread and cup we have withheld from the Saints for some months to afford them space and time for repentance, restitution and when ready for a renewal of their covenants." Suppose he should withhold from us our privileges—sacrament meetings, stake conferences, the sacrament itself, our assemblies. Suppose he would not permit us to open these temples. Sometimes we appreciate our blessings by our deprivations. When we hear excommunicants beg and plead for the return of privileges of partaking the bread and water, of wearing the garments, of attending their meetings, and of asking and answering questions, even, in the assemblies of the Saints, then we begin to realize, perhaps, the great blessings that we do enjoy. (65-05)

Ordinances serve as reminders. That is the real purpose of the sacrament, to keep us from forgetting, to help us to remember. I suppose there would never be an apostate, there would never be a crime, if people remembered, really remembered, the things they had covenanted at the water's edge or at the sacrament table and in the temple. I suppose that is the reason the Lord asked Adam to offer sacrifices, for no other reason than that he and his posterity would remember—remember the basic things that they had been taught. I guess we as humans are prone to forget. It is easy to forget. Our sorrows, our joys, our concerns, our great problems seem to wane to some extent as time goes on, and there are many lessons that we learn which have a tendency to slip from us. The Nephites forgot. They forgot the days when they felt good.

I remember a young Navajo boy returning from his mission who was supported largely by a seventies quorum in the Bonneville Stake. I happened to be present the day he made his report and as tears rolled down his face, he said, "Oh, if I could only remember always just how I feel now." (67-03)

Ordinances promise conditional blessings. Our very presence in this world is the result of a covenant we have made and a promise of and the result of faithfulness. Our baptism is a covenant in which the Lord promises us celestial life, if we live celestial laws. To fail to do so we are cheating both him and us, but more especially ourselves. This is true also of other ordinances. We receive the higher priesthood with an oath and a covenant with the Father, which covenant "He cannot break neither can it be moved," but we may break it and fail, and in so doing we break a vow and are dishonest with ourselves and him. Our free agency permits our doing what we wish to do, but it does not immunize us from the results of our failures.

The endowment in the holy temple is another contract of covenants which we solemnly make with our Heavenly Father. For faithfulness we are again promised unimaginable blessings. We may cheat, but the deprivations and sorrows and remorses will come to us who cheat. (58-07)

Patriarchal blessing is conditional prophecy. The patriarch is a prophet entitled to the revelations of the Lord to each individual on whose head he places his hands. He may indicate the lineage of the individual, but he may also pour out blessings that are prophetic to the individual for his life. We hope the people of this land will avail themselves of this great blessing. The blessings which he gives are conditional. They are promised, as are most other blessings that the Lord has promised to people, contingent upon their worthiness and fulfilling the obligations. There is no guarantee that the blessings will be fulfilled unless the individual subscribes to the program, but I bear my testimony to you that none of the blessings he pronounces will fail if the participant of the blessing fully subscribes. (75-42)

Patriarchal blessing offers guidance. The patriarchal blessing may not be necessary for salvation, but it is a guidepost; a white line down the middle of the road; a series of stakes around the mountain pass with reflector buttons in them so that whenever needed in the darkness and in the storm, they are available. The blessing can be reread like the reflectors that come up as the car approaches them on the turns. You would not urge patriarchal blessings for your students as you would urge a Boy Scout to pass his tests. They are never to be secondary or a means to an end. They are always first and basic. Every boy and girl may be encouraged to prepare for it, but never urged or forced to obtain their patriarchal blessings. Certainly these blessings should never be used to fill a requirement to achieve an award. It is a blessing for which young people should be adequately prepared, morally, mentally, and spiritually. (62-08)

In a real sense, your voice is to give utterance to the message of the Lord which he has in store for the individuals who come to you. You are not the source of the promises; you have no blessings for anyone; you are but the tube through which the blessing flows—the wire through which the promises are carried. You must be sure that you do not arrogate to yourselves any of these powers. One of the most important qualities for a patriarch to possess is that of *humility.* . . .

In each blessing, the patriarch will declare, under inspiration, the literal blood lineage of the person to be blessed and then, as moved upon by the Spirit, make a statement as to possibilities and the special spiritual gifts, cautions, instructions, admonitions, and warnings as the patriarch may be prompted to give. . . .

Patriarchal blessings are revelations to the recipients—a white line down the middle of the road to protect, inspire, motivate toward activity and righteousness. . . .

An inspired patriarchal blessing could light the way and lead the recipient on a path to fulfillment. It could lead him to become a new man and to have in his body a new heart. (69-07)

Patriarchs are to bless; recipients should come prepared. Everything reasonable should be done to keep the program dignified. Parents should teach their children the dignity and power of this program, which is unique in all the world.

The recipient may wish to fast in anticipation of the blessing and to especially pray for the patriarch that the blessing the Lord had in his heart would be received.

The children would not usually come in groups nor would a blessing be given to fill a requirement for other activities. It is never given to satisfy curiosity or cheap interests. It is of prime importance itself and should be surrounded with cautions and protections.

The patriarch will not solicit blessings, but the bishop and stake presidency may teach and stir the people to anticipate these great privileges. . . .

The prime duty of the patriarch is to give patriarchal blessings. He was ordained not as a consultant, an administrator, counselor, a financial adviser, or social worker in marital problems. People will be referred to their bishops in these matters. When a patriarch assists in administration of the sick, he does so as an elder and not as a patriarch. And, he does *not* have the right to forgive sins nor to adjust transgressions. This is the work of the ecclesiastical officers.

It becomes immediately apparent that a patriarch must be an example. He must be worthy, lovable, kind—and since he is the mouthpiece of the Lord in a very special sense, he will desire to live as nearly like the Lord as is possible. (69-07)

Fathers may bless family members. A child leaving to go away to school or on a mission, a wife suffering stress, a family member being married or desiring guidance in making an important decision—all these are situations in which the father, in exercise of his patriarchal responsibility, can bless his family. (74-31)

Children should ask for blessings. I hope you boys in this audience will keep that in mind. You have the best dad in the world, you know. He holds the priesthood; he would be delighted to give you a blessing. He would like you to indicate it, and we would like you fathers to remember that your boys are a little timid maybe. They know you are the best men in the world, but probably if you just made the advance, there would be some glorious moments for you. (74-04)

Healing the Sick

Rely on doctors for simple ailments. If they have ailments, I believe they should use judgment and refer their problems to men who are skilled in those fields, and then pray for the blessings of the Lord that their bodies will respond to treatments and that the experts will be skilled in their treatments. (74-20)

We should do all that we can for ourselves first: through proper diet, rest, and applying common sense, especially for minor trouble. Then we may send for the elders, the home teachers, or the neighbors or friends in whom we have confidence. Frequently this is all that is required, and numerous healings can be effected. In serious cases where the problem is not solved, we should turn to those who can help so wonderfully. (PKSO 84)

I hope we will use our priesthood. Use it frequently for the children when they are ill. Let their mother take care of the things she can do. If it is to rub a little something on their chest, that's fine; whatever she can do that seems proper, and then the priesthood follows. You do not need to go to the bishop and the stake president or even your home teachers; as long as you are worthy to administer through the priesthood, then it is proper. If you feel that you would like the faith of your home teachers, call them in, and they will gladly come and take care of this important ordinance. (76-33)

We may not recognize some miracles. Occasionally people become overly sentimental and fanatic, and ascribe as a miracle everything that happens. But for every person who is overzealous or who is overpsychic or fanatical, there are numerous persons who fail to see the miracle in numerous healings. "They would have recovered anyway," they say. I give one example: . . . Once when I was far away from home, after three days of quite intense suffering, I finally admitted to my companion, Brother Harold B. Lee, that I was in distress. He gave me a sleeping pill he had with him, then knelt by my bed and blessed me. Though I had gone through three nights in pain and almost without sleep (it was then three o'clock in the morning), I was fast asleep moments after the blessing. I am now ashamed to confess that the next morning when I awakened, my first thought was of the potency of the pill. Then, as hours passed and I knew the effect of the pill must have passed, the distress did not return, and I fell on my knees in remorse to ask forgiveness of the Lord for my having given credit to the medicine rather than to him. Months passed and still there was no return of pain or distress. I am ashamed, but I probably represent numerous people who have done likewise. (PKSO 82-83)

Blessing activates the body's own healing power. Instantaneous healings are numerous. They range into the areas of sight, hearing, lameness, internal organs, skin, bones, and all parts of the body. Incurable diseases have been healed. We are grateful beyond expression for the great skill and accumulated knowledge and patience and understanding possessed by our physicians. But it must be that numerous healings credited to doctors and hospitals have been the healing of the Lord through the priesthood and by prayer. We are generally too ready to give the credit to the physician when at best his was but a contribution, small or large.

It must be remembered that no physician can heal. He can only provide a satisfactory environment and situation so that the body may use its own God-given power of re-creation to build itself. Bones can be straightened, germs can be killed, sutures can close wounds, and skillful fingers can open and close bodies; but no man yet has found a way to actually heal. Man is the offspring of God and has within him the re-creating power that is God-given. And through the priesthood and through prayer, the body's healing processes can be speeded and encouraged. (PKSO 79)

Blessing the sick follows a pattern. Administration to the sick is an ordinance of two parts—the anointing and the sealing. An elder pours a small quantity of oil on the head of the one to be blessed, near the crown of the head if convenient, never on the other parts of the body, and in the name of the Lord and by the authority of the priesthood, he anoints the person for the restoration of health. The sealing is performed by two or more elders, one of whom, as mouth, seals the anointing and gives an appropriate blessing, also in the name of Jesus Christ and by authority of the priesthood.

Sometimes when oil is not available, or when two brethren are not present, or when the sick one has recently been anointed, a substitute program is followed whereby one or more elders give a blessing, likewise in the name of the Lord and by authority of the Melchizedek Priesthood. He will pronounce such blessings as seem appropriate and as the Spirit moves.

Anyone may pray for the sick; this is not a priesthood ordinance. Such a prayer of faith makes request to the Lord to heal, whereas the blessing or the administration is given by the power of the priesthood and in the name of Christ.

I feel that sometimes the holy ordinance is abused. One person I know left a standing order for the elders to administer to her every day for the several weeks she was in the hospital for a broken limb. Many feel that too frequent administrations may be an indication of lack of faith or of the ill person trying to pass the responsibility for faith development to the elders rather than self. . . .

Sometimes when one still feels the need of further blessing after having recently had an administration, a blessing without the anointing oil is given. (PKSO 73-75)

Many have authority to perform administrations. Because individuals have preferences, it is sometimes found that certain officials are besieged constantly to give blessings. When one is ill and weak and terrified, it is natural to want elders in whom he has much confidence because of their righteous living and their proven faith and devotion. It should be remembered, however, that not just the General Authorities or the stake or ward or mission authorities have the priesthood with power to heal. Numerous brethren throughout the Church, including home teachers, have the authority to bless; and their administration or blessing, combined with great faith from the blessed one, can bring about spectacular healings. This is evidenced by the numerous wonderful healings brought about through the ministrations of young, inexperienced missionaries. (PKSO 77)

Among the Latter-day Saint Indians, we do not have sings anymore. We honor the people who did; that was all they knew. We do not have sings for the healing of the sick, we administer with oil as the Lord prescribed. (65-01)

No pride should be taken in effecting a miracle. When the sick, through the administration by the elders, are healed, and especially if it approaches the miraculous, there is a temptation to the administering elders to tell of the matter and approach boasting about it. Their humility would be protected if they would always in the prayer, or otherwise, counsel the recipient not to mention the names of those who uttered the blessing but to give to the Lord all the praise and the honor and glory.

Occasionally we hear men boast, saying, "I have the gift of healing." What a hazardous thing to do! I would fear the Lord might hear me and reprove me like he did Moses, or he might take from me any gift I might have had. (63-01)

Faith of sick person is main factor in healing. The need for faith is often underestimated. The ill person and the family often seem to depend wholly on the power of the priesthood and the gift of healing that they hope the administering brethren may have, whereas the greater responsibility is with him who is blessed. There are persons who seem to have the gift to heal, as indicated in Doctrine and Covenants, section 46, and it is understandable why a sick one might desire a blessing at the hands of a person who seems to have great faith and proven power, and in whom the recipient has confidence, but the major element is the faith of the individual when that person is conscious and accountable. (PKSO 75)

The Lord said ... to the woman who had been suffering for twelve years, "Thy faith hath made thee whole." ... I have frequently said in blessings that I have given, "According to thy faith, be it unto you." If they have not any faith, then they have no right to demand a blessing. (76-53)

Healings are subject to God's overall plan. We are assured by the Lord that the sick will be healed if the ordinance is performed, if there is sufficient faith, and if the ill one is "not appointed unto death." (D&C 42:48.) Here are three factors. Many do not comply with the ordinances, and great numbers are unwilling or incapable of exercising sufficient faith. But there is the other factor which looms important: if they are not appointed unto death. Every act of God is purposeful. He sees the end from the beginning. He knows what will build us, or tear us down, and what will thwart the program and what will give us eventual triumph. (55-15)

When elders bless and recoveries do not follow, frequently there is not only disappointment but also sometimes a diminishing of faith, especially where there have also been many prayers and long fastings. The Lord has told us, "If they die they shall die unto me, and if they live they shall live unto me." (D&C 42:44.) (PKSO 80)

There often comes a time when it is imprudent to demand an extension of the Lord and most unsound to ask in an unqualified manner for an extension. Sometimes such could be a boomerang that would prolong, unwarrantedly, the time of suffering and deprivation and, in some cases, the burden upon the family. Consequently our prayers are properly offered and blessings pronounced if there is not an unqualified demand for restoration. Sometimes the body, under such circumstances, neither lives nor dies. (PKSO 82)

The power of the priesthood is limitless, but God has wisely placed upon each of us certain limitations. I may develop priesthood power as I perfect my life. I am grateful that even through the priesthood I cannot heal all the sick. I might heal people who should die. I might relieve people of suffering who should suffer. I fear I would frustrate the purposes of God.

Had I limitless power, and yet limited vision and understanding, I might have saved Abinadi from the flames of fire when he was burned at the stake, and in doing so I might have irreparably damaged him and limited him to a lower kingdom. He died a martyr and went to a martyr's reward—exaltation. He would have lived on the earth and could have lost his faith, his courage, even his virtue, and his exaltation.

I would likely have protected Paul against his woes if my power were boundless. I would surely have healed his "thorn in the flesh." And in doing so I might have foiled the program and relegated him to lower glories. Thrice he offered prayers, asking the Lord to remove the "thorn" from him, but the Lord did not so answer his prayers. Paul many times could have lost himself if he had been eloquent, well, handsome, and free from the things which made him humble.

I fear that had I been in Carthage Jail on June 27, 1844, I might have deflected the bullets which pierced the bodies of the Prophet and the Patriarch. I might have saved them from the sufferings and agony, but lost to them the martyr's death and reward. I am glad I did not have to make that decision.

With such uncontrolled power, I surely would have felt to protect Christ from the insults, the thorny crown, the indignities in the court, physical injuries. Perhaps I would have struck down his persecutors with shafts of lightning. When he hung on the cross I would have rescued him and would have administered to his wounds and healed them, giving him cooling water instead of vinegar. I might have saved him from death and lost to the world an atoning sacrifice and frustrated the whole program.

Would you dare to take the responsibility of bringing back to life your own loved ones? I, myself, would hesitate to do so. I am grateful that we may always pray: "Thy will be done in all things, for thou knowest what is best." (55-15)

We must not make demands on God. I had another experience when I first came to Salt Lake some thirty-four years ago. A young woman came to me who had been told by her physician that she could not have children. She was newly married, but she had a situation which made that impossible, he said. She said she wanted to be healed. The whole family and I joined with them in fasting. We fasted for a day and then came together and I administered to her and asked the Lord, myself being the mouth, if it was his will that he heal her. Well, time went on and on and on and she came into my office one day and she said, "Brother Kimball, I am only going to give the Lord this many more weeks to heal me." In other words, a demand. He has got to do it. He has got to do it. And I said, "My dear sister, what are you thinking of, making a demand of the Lord, telling him what to do, when he knows best, for he can see all the situations ahead and behind and now. That is a terrible thing. You had better go home and repent of your sins. That is a sin, to demand of the Lord something which you do not know anything about." (76-53)

Meetings and Teaching

The Objects of Sacrament Meeting

Sacrament meetings are for worship. We attend sacrament meetings to worship the Lord. If the meeting is conducted or if we attend with any other thought, we have missed the spirit of the occasion. Those who attend meeting only when the speaker is eloquent, the lecturer is noted, or the music is excellent, are far afield of the high purpose and loftiness of this meeting in the house of prayer. It should be worship from the first announcement to the final prayer, consisting of the singing of sacred songs, prayers of gratitude, the partaking of the sacrament with appropriate thoughts, and the expounding of the gospel and bearing testimony of its divinity. To attend in the spirit of worship is to *give.* To go to be entertained is to *get or draw out....*

And so can all come from their meetings a bit cleaner in mind and spirit, if they have had companionship with the spirits of their fellow members and with the Spirit of the Lord. Worship is an individual matter. The best choir, the best speaker, the most noted lecturer, cannot bring true worship into your soul. It must proceed from within, out of a deep sense of love and devotion and dependence and humility....

Because the speaker is local, or dry, is a poor excuse for not attending meetings, though it is often given. How very weak! If you sing and pray and partake of the sacrament worthily, you could sit through the next hour in worshipful contemplation with profit even if the speaker is poor. It is your responsibility to make the meeting worthwhile by your individual contribution. The average ward has in it many talented and forceful speakers. They should be used. They should be encouraged to fill their minds with useful knowledge so that their message and testimony will be of great value when they are called upon. The Lord has never agreed to bring finished sermons from empty minds and hearts, but he has covenanted that he will bring to your remembrance the things you have learned. (45-02)

One good but mistaken man I know claimed he could get more out of a good book on Sunday than he could get in attending church services, saying that the sermons were hardly up to his standards. But we do not go to Sabbath meetings to be entertained or even solely to be instructed. We go to worship the Lord. It is an individual responsibility, and regardless of what is said from the pulpit, if one wishes to worship the Lord in spirit and in truth, he may do so by attending his meetings, partaking of the sacrament, and contemplating the beauties of the gospel. If the service is a failure to you, you have failed. No one can worship for you; you must do your own waiting upon the Lord. (78-01)

Every service should be carefully appraised and to it should be applied the yardstick: will it build spirituality? (00-05)

We pray that this chapel may be protected and kept sacred; that here may be heard sweet music, subdued voices, inspired sermons, deep-seated testimonies, and that here may be received by thy people the sacred emblems of the sacrament of the Lord's Supper. Help thy people here to ever retain in this house the spirit of worship and a determination to serve thee and keep thy commandments. (51-05)

Meetings are occasion for acknowledgment of weaknesses. "Thou shalt offer thine oblations and thy sacraments unto the Most High, confessing thy sins unto thy brethren, and before the Lord."

(D&C 59:12.) This, of course, does not mean that the people must detail their major sins and crimes, but as has often been heard in testimonies, on fast day and otherwise, when people are speaking they say something like this: "I recognize my weaknesses and imperfections and I am striving constantly to overcome them and ask you, my brothers and sisters, to overlook my frailties and errors." (11/2/62)

Attendance at Meetings

Meeting attendance is not an end in itself. We are interested in all these statistics and attendances and activities only as they influence the spirituality of your people. The Lord has made it clear to us that all these activities are the means to the end of spirituality. In other words, he says we should attend the sacrament meeting not to get certain percentage, but that we may partake of the sacrament and worship, that we may "always have his Spirit to be with us." And all other activities, of course, are for that special reason. We are not interested in the *number* of young people who marry in the temple except that we know that the chances of happiness are increased. We are not interested in the *number* of missionaries who go into the field, only we know that not only will they bring many people into the Church but their own lives are enhanced and beautified and made more happy and glorious generally. (2/14/64)

Attendance at meetings can bring joy. There are many people in the world who think that to be religious, to attend meetings, is a burden, but, knowing the truth, we recognize that it brings to us deep joy and happiness. (74-09)

Children should go to meetings. We have many people who leave their children at home when they go to their meetings. They decide they will wait and let the child grow into the Church as he gets a little older. . . .

Some mothers rationalize: "My child could not get any good out of the meeting. Why take him? Let's leave him home."

No little child absorbs knowingly the sunlight; but unconsciously the light brings power to his little body. No child knows the value of his mother's milk nor of the food from opened cans which gives him nourishment. Yet, that is where he gets his strength and his power to grow and to become a man eventually. . . .

And every child, without realizing the full portent, can absorb much from a sacrament meeting. They will absorb something every time. (54-02)

My mother died when I was eleven years old. It was in October when she passed away. And up to that date, I had not missed a Sunday School or a sacrament meeting through that whole year, every week. And when she passed away, I was just a little boy, of course, and I wondered, "Should I miss Sunday School this week?" As I remember, her body was in Salt Lake and it had not reached home yet, so I think I went to Sunday School not only that day, but every week—every week to Sunday School, every week to sacrament meeting, every week to priesthood meeting. We do not just go and come as we might please. We have assumed a responsibility. (75-36)

Make a one-time decision to attend meetings. Wouldn't it be a loss of a great deal of time and effort if every Sunday morning we had to stop and say, "Shall I or shall I not go to priesthood meeting? Shall I or shall I not go to sacrament meeting today? Shall we or shall we not go?" What a lot of wasted effort. . . . Settle it once and for all. (74-16)

Improving Quality of Meetings

Speakers need enthusiasm. You can carry a great load with enthusiasm. You can speak a very mediocre sermon and do it with enthusiasm and people will think it was great. You can give a most profound sermon on a monotone basis and people may go to sleep, and they may say, that was the driest man I ever heard. Actually it was profound. . . . Give it with enthusiasm and make them know you believe it. (62-03)

Bishops should not use outside speakers to build attendance. I have noted with sympathy and appreciation the almost frantic efforts of bishops to obtain programs which will stimulate attendance at the ward sacrament meetings. While their motive is good, we must remember that prepared speeches on ethics and current events, or that travelogues, lectures, cantatas, concerts, and such, hardly fulfill the requirements of the Lord in his revelation. Such excellent programs have their place and time but are not in line with the spirit of the sacrament meeting. This meeting must increase faith in God and build testimony and measure up to the yardstick given by the Lord....

Wise bishops will use, largely, ward people to exhort and teach and preach and bear testimony, and will make other appeals to the people to attend the meetings rather than the artificial hypo administered by the announcement of a noted lecturer or traveler. The bishop will conduct his meetings in harmony with the revelations rather than succumb to the temptation to "tickle the ears" of those who would be enticed only by entertainment offered. (45-02)

Every congregation should have a choir. If you don't have a ward choir, you are not organized fully, any more than if you do not have a Relief Society. (70-03)

There are numerous branches and small wards...where the numbers are fewer and the talent less plentiful, but there surely could be no unit without sufficient singers and reasonably competent organists and directors to carry forward a splendid choir even though in some cases it may have fewer numbers. I once dedicated a chapel for a ward of eighty-two persons and they had a commendable choir of thirty voices.... A general announcement asking ward members to join and support the choir will not produce the best results. Prospective choir members should be invited individually in a dignified way. (68-01)

Enthusiastic singing enhances meetings. It is sad to me to see in the congregations many people standing silent when they could be singing "their hearts out." I wonder constantly if they would sing happily today if for twelve years they could only move their lips through thousands of songs and could make no sound? I wonder if the silent ones can even imagine what it is like to be unable to join fellow singers in praise to their Lord in music? . . .

If the conductor sings also, it will encourage the congregation and help them remember the words. . . . In every beat of the baton should be the pleading to the Saints of God: Sing. Sing. Sing from your hearts. (68-01)

Music and instruments should induce appropriate feelings. Musical sounds can be put together in such a way that they can express feelings—from the most profoundly exalted to the most abjectly vulgar. Or rather, these musical sounds induce in the listener feelings which he responds to, and the response he makes to these sounds has been called a "gesture of the spirit." Thus, music can act upon our senses to produce or induce feelings of reverence, humility, fervor, assurance, or other feelings attuned to the spirit of worship. When music is performed in Church which conveys a "gesture" other than that which is associated with worship, we are disturbed, upset, or shocked to the degree with which the musical "gesture" departs from or conflicts with the appropriate representation of feelings of worship. . . .

When people are invited to perform special numbers in sacred meetings, whether ward members or others, it is important to know in advance what numbers will be given and that they are devotional in character and in keeping with the spirit of worship. To be avoided are love songs, popular ballads, theatrical numbers, and songs with words not in harmony with the doctrines of the Church. Persons invited to perform should be specifically urged to remain throughout the service. (68-01)

Musicians hold a gift in trust. The responsibility for producing, selecting, and performing music for the Church requires discrimination, taste, knowledge, and the proper spirit; in short, it requires the best efforts that our best musicians can give inasmuch as we are using

gifts which the Lord has given us for the purpose of building up his
kingdom and as a demonstration of our faith and love for him. We
are in a position, as musicians, to touch the souls of those who listen.
(68-01)

Say "Amen." Brethren, a few of you said "Amen" when
Brother Simpson concluded his talk. . . . I know you'll all want to say
"Amen" when I conclude mine. Golden Kimball . . . got up to speak
one time as a General Authority, and when he sat down nobody said
anything. Nobody said "Amen." So he got right up again and he
said, "Well, I'll start again. You didn't want me to close so I'll just
go on and speak again." So he spoke for a little while, and then he
said "Amen." There were about a dozen or two people that remembered. He stood up again and tried it again. Now, that would be kind
of a pity, wouldn't it? Will you *always* say "Amen"? Never fail. That
means "so be it, what has been said is agreeable to me, that's what I
like." Of course if it's bad enough you might want to fail to say it.
(76-09)

I was glad to hear you say "Amen." Sometimes we forget to do
that and it is a very pleasing word to those who speak or pray or
preach, and we hope that that will always be very important in your
life and in your sacred services. That sounds better every time. Every
time that a sermon is concluded or a prayer is offered, every man,
woman, and child should say "Amen," loud enough so that the
person next to him or her can hear it. Again, I say, Amen. (79-11)

Church Conferences

Area conferences bring the Church to the people. Some few years
ago we established a new policy. As the Church grew large, populous,
and far-reaching, and realizing the cost of transportation from the far
reaches of the earth to this conference, realizing the limitation on the
facilities here even—for we had long since filled this building—we
determined to take the conferences to the people. . . .

We have been highly gratified with the reception. We have taken a group of the General Authorities and we have held for the local people a conference somewhat similar to this one. We have sustained the authorities of the Church; we have given to them the benefits that they might have received had they come to this conference.

We expect to continue this program and to go to different parts of the world and take the messages and keep in close touch with the great numbers of people who are congregating in the far ends of the Church. (75-15)

Area conferences . . . dramatize as nothing else could the truly international character of the Church, which now has formal Church organizations in sixty-five countries. (75-37)

Conferences are to strengthen members. We meet together often in the Church in conferences to worship the Lord, to feast upon the word of Christ, and to be built up in faith and testimony. (78-04)

You have come here seeking guidance. It is the purpose of your leaders to give that direction. As the Brethren speak, you will feel the inspiration of our Lord. (74-12)

The purpose of this conference is that we may refresh our faith, strengthen our testimonies, and learn the ways of the Lord from his duly appointed and authorized servants. May we take this opportunity, then, to remind each other of our covenants and promises and commitments. (75-13)

General Authorities offer guidance and inspiration. We are sent out to correct their errors, bolster their faith, show them how to overcome their problems, enlarge their visions of the work, and leave them with greater vision and warm hearts and with better ways and greater determination to build the kingdom than when we came.

Remember, the stake conferences are among the assignments which have priority. They must not be relegated to routine and commonplace. This one this week must not be a repetition of the one last week. Every conference is a special one with special needs—every leadership group is another body of dedicated people yearning for our help. Every congregation is another people hungering and thirsting for righteousness and our help and inspiration. (71-02)

Sermons are useful only if message is heard. You have heard many sermons in the past three days, many sermons that could be of great value to you. But it isn't so much what has been said that is important as it is what you have heard. (76-13)

Another historic conference became history. It will have been lost motion, a waste of time, energy, and money if its messages are not heeded. In the seven two-hour sessions and in the several satellite meetings truths were taught, doctrines expounded, exhortations given enough to save the world from all its ills—and I mean *all* its ills. A rather complete education in eternal verities was given to millions with a great hope that there were ears a-hearing and eyes a-seeing and hearts a-throbbing, convinced of truth. . . .

Let no conceited, self-assured, self-styled intellectual discard the truths taught and the testimonies borne. Let every one humble himself and accept the messages. (68-05)

We hope that the leaders and the members of the Church who have attended and listened to the conference have been inspired and uplifted. We hope you have made copious notes of the thoughts that have come to your mind as the Brethren have addressed you. Many suggestions have been given that will help you as leaders in the perfection of your work. Many helpful thoughts have been given for the perfection of our own lives, and that, of course, is the basic reason for our coming.

While sitting here, I have made up my mind that when I go home from this conference this night there are many, many areas in my life that I can perfect. I have made a mental list of them, and I expect to go to work as soon as we get through with conference. (75-49)

Now, brethren, you have heard so many good things tonight from all the Brethren. I hope you make copious notes. I wish you would get in the habit of making notes in every meeting you attend and prepare to speak every week. Elder Sill, one of the Seventies of the Church, told me that he never went to a meeting of any kind without preparing something to say in the event he was called. (77-21)

Talk about conference messages. As we return to our homes, brothers and sisters, I hope we will not close the door on the conference. Take it with us. Take it home with us. Tell our families about it, perhaps some to report in sacrament meetings of it. But take it to your families and give them the benefit of any inspiration that might have come to you, any determinations to change your lives and make them more acceptable to your Heavenly Father. (74-31)

Three men went to a sermon. One of them said, "That was a good sermon." The second man said, "That was a good sermon; I will tell some of my neighbors to live it." The third person said, "I will go straight home and put it all into my life." That, of course, is the proof. We hope that every family in Tahiti will gather together and discuss all the things that have happened this past week. (76-21)

Study conference messages. I hope you young people all heard the messages of the ages delivered last week. I hope you will get your copy of the *Improvement Era* and underline the pertinent thoughts and keep it with you for continual reference. No text nor volume outside of the standard works of the Church should have such a prominent place on your personal library shelves, not because of their rhetorical excellence, nor the eloquence of delivery, but for the content which points the way to eternal life. (68-05)

Teaching in the Church

Christ chose to be a teacher. It is highly significant to realize that the greatest intellect in human history—the most talented individual ever to grace this globe—chose to be a teacher! He chose this way of carrying out part of his awesome assignment. (67-14)

Effective teaching strengthens members. Stake presidents, bishops, and branch presidents, please take a particular interest in improving the quality of teaching in the Church. The Savior has told us to feed his sheep (see John 21:15-17). I fear that all too often many of our members come to church, sit through a class or meeting, and they then return home having been largely uninformed. It is especially unfortunate when this happens at a time when they may be entering a period of stress, temptation, or crisis. We all need to be touched and nurtured by the Spirit, and effective teaching is one of the most important ways this can happen. We often do vigorous enlistment work to get members to come to church but then do not adequately watch over what they receive when they do come. (80-33)

Home teaching program protects families. The priesthood home teaching program can become a huge umbrella under which all the people of the Church may huddle for protection from the storms of adversity, sin, crime, delinquency, carelessness in activity, and immorality; but, of course, like an ordinary umbrella, if it is leaky and is not whole, stretched silk will be little protection. (67-11)

When the home teachers go into every home and motivate parents, especially fathers, to teach their children by example and verbal teaching, can it be conceived that there will need to be penal institutions, divorce courts, special counseling service? Will there be need for reformatories, courts, and jails? . . .

When home teachers serve their few families as faithfully and as continuously as their bishops do their many families; when home teachers live the commandments near perfection; when they enter into every phase of the life of their charges; then will Satan be bound. . . .

Blessed will be the day when all home teachers, those working on the missionary, genealogical, and the welfare and all programs, become home teachers in every sense of the word, looking after every facet of the lives of their families—spiritual, temporal, financial, moral, marital. That will be the happy day! The great umbrella is available. It will protect no one from the storm, the tempest, the danger unless it is spread. (67-05)

Home teaching is a general priesthood responsibility. My two counselors, the two finest men in the world, President N. Eldon Tanner and President Marion G. Romney, are both home teachers. ... Stake presidents can do this, and bishops can do this, and Regional Representatives can do this. We never, not any of us, become too smart or too busy to go occasionally into the homes of the people and explain the gospel to them and warn them, and see if there is any fellowshipping needed. Fellowshipping is the answer. (76-35)

Visiting teaching is a great opportunity for service. To be successful, it seems to me that a visiting teacher would wish to have high purpose and remember it all the time, would want to have great vision, a terrific enthusiasm that cannot be worn down, a positive attitude, of course, and a great love....

You shall "teach the principles of [the] gospel, which are in the Bible and the Book of Mormon, in the which is the fulness of the gospel" (D&C 42:12)—not mere ethics—and you always have the liberty to turn to them, and to interpret them, and bring them to the point where your inspiration leads you to give it to that particular sister—a different message to every person, a different approach, a different conclusion, a different approach to testimony.

The teacher, of course, must be living all that she teaches. That goes without saying....

Don't let us be satisfied with just visits, with making friends; that, of course, has its place. With our missionary program, we constantly have that to consider. Sometimes a missionary gets it in his head that he has got to build a great bridge, and so he builds ten or twenty or thirty miles of approach to get over a quarter mile of bridge. He is worn out by the time he gets to the bridge, and then he has difficulty doing his job. Friendship, of course, is important, but how better can you make a friend than to teach somebody everlasting principles of life and salvation? ...

Your testimony is a terrific medium. As we tell missionaries, nobody can answer nor destroy your testimony. There are many smart people, just as we are, who know the scriptures just as well as we do, and who can debate, and probably quote the Bible even better than some of us. Many scripturalists spend all of their lives in studying the Bible, and they can know and debate the scriptures and turn to them better than many of us; but none of them can ever answer your testimony. It leaves them dumb—without rebuttal. You don't always have to bear it in the most formal manner; there are so many approaches. . . . Visiting teachers must excel and give leadership to the women into whose homes they go. They must excel in energy, and vision, and thoroughness—and in testimony, for above all things, their testimony is unanswerable. . . .

There are many sisters who are living in rags—spiritual rags. They are entitled to gorgeous robes, spiritual robes, as in the parable. It is your privilege more than your duty. We talk so much about duty, but it is your privilege to go into homes and exchange robes for rags. . . .

You cannot miss a home with impunity; you must not pass a sister by, even if she is a little uncomplimentary, or not too happy for your visit. . . .

For a [home] teacher or a visiting teacher to accept a responsibility of four, five, six, or seven homes, and leave them in their spiritual rags and tatters is without excuse; and when you go into the homes, there should be no vain babblings or swelling words. You are going to save souls, and who can tell but that many of the fine active people in the Church today are active because you were in their homes and gave them a new outlook, a new vision. You pulled back the curtain. You extended their horizons. You gave them something new. Maybe they will never tell you about it in all their lives, but you did the work just the same.

You see, you are not only saving these sisters, but perhaps also their husbands and their homes. . . .

"He which soweth sparingly," said Paul, "shall reap also sparingly; and he which soweth bountifully shall reap also bountifully." (2 Corinthians 9:6.) We don't get anywhere by just saying words. We have to put our heart in the words, and we have to plan and prepare our minds. I wonder if there are any sisters that ever fast, maybe the morning they are going visiting teaching. I don't know that it is required. There are a lot of things in the Church that are not required, a lot of things we would *like* to do. The one who goes just to visit homes, to knock on the doors, to pass the time of day, and then goes back to make the report, is a little bit like the one whom Paul speaks of who is fighting as one that beateth the air, and not making any progress, like one whose wheels are spinning on the ice. . . .

When you have a woman who won't open her door, and you know she is in the house; one who opens her door and does not want to; one who admits you and wishes you did not come; it would be well to follow the advice of the Lord, "Howbeit this kind goeth not out but by prayer and fasting."

You know the Lord has intangible methods and ways and means and forces that can touch hearts. . . .

It is easy to get discouraged. It is easy to quit, but you mustn't fail. You remember how Nephi went into an impossible situation and couldn't get the plates. His brothers couldn't. They couldn't buy them. They couldn't bribe them out of the hands of Laban. They couldn't force their way in, and their lives were hanging on a thread. In spite of all that, here comes one boy, unarmed, who walks into a city through a wall that was closed to him, through gates that couldn't be opened, into a garden that was impenetrable, into a vault that was locked, among soldiers that couldn't be bypassed, and comes out with his arms full of records to keep his posterity and others from perishing in unbelief. (See 1 Nephi 3-4.)

He did the impossible. But nothing is impossible to the Lord. Any time we have him on our side, when he has called us, given us a commandment, then, if our energy and our efforts and our planning and our prayers are equal to the size of the job, the job, of course, will be completed. . . .

You have to be humble. Our wealth, our affluence, our liberties, all that we possess must never make us feel above anyone. We must always keep in mind a deep sincerity, a great humility, and a total dependence upon the Lord. . . .

You can do that. Like the little vine, the little root, that can topple a wall or split a rock, you can touch hearts, and break them away from their moorings that are not good and bring them to total activity. It can be done! (58-11)

Seminary teachers have great influence. In my stake conference meetings with the bishoprics and stake presidencies and high councils, I have insisted that if they would see that the young people attended the seminaries and institutes, that you would almost guarantee their morality and worthiness, and that they would fill missions, marry in the temple, and live beautiful LDS lives. (64-05)

Responsibilities of Teachers

Seminary teachers should exemplify their teaching. "An ounce of prevention is worth a pound of cure," says the old adage. My experience would lead me to believe that the odds are greater. When I see the simple scraping of the upper arm and the application of a little vaccine in the prevention process, I compare it with what I suffered in my twenties with the dreaded smallpox when I could have died, remembering a couple of minutes for a vaccination against many days for the disease to run its course. And when I see one wince a little at the poke of a needle against typhoid fever, I contrast that moment with the many weeks of dizziness and distress and intense fever which nearly burned me out, followed by weeks of starvation and pain and hunger and weakness, trying to gain back my strength. Then I believe that our function is in prevention rather than or in addition to cure, with full assurance that as the one increases the other decreases. The less prevention, the more need of cure processes; and the more prevention, the less cure is needed. The more needles, the fewer hospital beds, psychiatrists' couches, and bishops' offices....

I hope you can guide them through their rebellious periods, for it seems that many youth reach a point of self-sufficiency which so many times is labeled rebellion. Perhaps when they come to know more than their parents, you are the ones who can still impress them, and what I ask for mine I wish for every other grandfather's posterity, who are as precious to them as mine are to me....

I hope that you will teach righteousness, pure and undefiled. I hope that if any of God's children are out in spiritual darkness, you will come to them with a lamp and light their way; if they are out in the cold of spiritual bleakness with its frigidity penetrating their bones, you will come to them with your coat and your cloak also; and when they need you to walk with them holding their hands a little way, you will walk miles and miles with them lifting them, strengthening them, encouraging them, and inspiring them. . . .

Knowing the tendency for most young people to be hero worshippers, I hope you will qualify for that admiration and almost adoration. May they have beautiful, abundant family lives patterned after the ideal image of an eternal family. This they can learn, a little from what you tell them but far more from what you show them. . . . This would lead me to expect from you and your successors honor, integrity, cleanliness, positiveness, and faith. I would expect you to appear before these young people well-dressed, well-groomed, positive, happy people from homes where peace and love have left a warm, vibrant influence as your day with them begins. I would want them to know by the feeling that you, their teacher, that very morning walked out of a loving home where peace reigned and love was enthroned. These students should know instinctively by your spirit that you were that morning on your knees at the breakfast table with your family and that there were soft words of pleading to your Heavenly Father for guidance, not only for your little family kneeling with you, but for your larger family also who were at this moment scurrying about in other homes to get ready for your classes. I'd like to hope that you were the perfect husband and father with proper control and relationships, and that they would see in you and your family the ideal after which to gear their lives. . . .

Above all, I hope you will teach them faith in the living God and in his Only Begotten Son—not a superficial, intellectual kind of acceptance, but a deep, spiritual, inner feeling of dependence and closeness; not a fear composed of panic and terror, but a fear of the Lord composed mostly of intense love and admiration and awesome nearness in a relationship of parent and offspring—father and son—father and daughter. (66-07)

Teachers must be creative. Your work is with the children. They are most important. You say, what are our tools? We will have to wait until they build us a meetinghouse. We will have to wait until we have some colored films to show them, and we will wait until we do this and that and the other. I want to say to you sisters, that you already have the tools if you have a heart full of love.

I found down on the reservation a young woman who was on a full-time mission who was sent out among the Indians and who has charge of Primary work, and she did not have anything to help her. She just was resourceful and went forward with a great heart to inspire children. She went to the store and got a common roll of ordinary wrapping paper and a bunch of crayons and she went to work. And she drew as she taught these children the story of the Book of Mormon. She drew the waves of the sea as the little barks went on their way across the ocean to the promised land. She drew a ship as best she could. She drew for these children the bow and arrow which the Lord had inspired Nephi to find and make so that he could provide food for the group. She drew the mountain from which the ore was taken, from which the plates were made. In a crude way she drew these pictures that taught the children the story of the Book of Mormon.... And so she put over her lessons.

Now, I would be very grateful if you had all the tools for which you might wish in your work among them, but if you do not have you can improvise them. (49-02)

Teachers learn through preparation and explanation. We learn to do by doing. If we study the gospel to teach it we have acquired knowledge, for where we carry the lantern to light the path of others we light our own way. As we analyze and arrange the scriptures to present an acceptable lesson to others, we have clarified our own minds. As we explain that which we already know there seems to come to us an unfolding of additional truths, and enlargement of our understandings, new connections and applications. (56-08)

Words are the tools of teachers. Words are means of communication, and faulty signals give wrong impressions. Disorder and misunderstandings are the result. Words underlie our whole life and are the tools of our business, the expressions of our affections, and the records of our progress. Words cause hearts to throb and tears to flow. Words can be sincere or hypocritical. Many of us are destitute of words and, consequently, clumsy with our speech, which sometimes becomes but babble. Paul said: "Except ye utter by the tongue words easy to be understood, how shall it be known what is spoken? for ye shall speak into the air." (1 Corinthians 14:9.)

Words should be kind and gentle or firm and bold, according to the need of the moment. So, in social life, and certainly in morals, there should be careful selection of the right word to express the thought. (65-02)

Teach children substantial principles. When the Lord spoke so earnestly to Peter, he did not say tend my sheep or watch my sheep, but *feed* my lambs and sheep. It is not enough to hold and entertain the children, but we must teach them and mold them and fortify them. Nothing will accomplish this like the basic doctrines of the gospel and the practices of the Church. The Sunday School has that responsibility more pointedly than the other organizations—to teach the gospel to *all* the people of the Church, *including* the little ones. (59-03)

The Sunday School of this generation and the next and the next must answer: Did you or did you not wield a powerful influence in the creating of kingdom builders for this life and for the eternities?...

The Sunday School must remember that it is not enough to teach ethics and good practices and common courtesies. It must teach exaltation through live faith in God. (00-05)

The sad, simple truth is that when we do not act preventively, we must, later on, act redemptively. (74-29)

Teachers should stay with basic principles. I have had many people ask me through the years, "When do you think we will get the balance of the Book of Mormon records?" And I have said, "How many in the congregation would like to read the sealed portion of the plates?" And almost always there is a 100-percent response. And then I ask the same congregation, "How many of you have read the part that has been opened to us?" And there are many who have not read the Book of Mormon, the unsealed portion. We are quite often looking for the spectacular, the unobtainable. I have found many people who want to live the higher laws when they do not live the lower laws.

I have in mind one man who came to talk with me about the united order. He had a long dissertation and many arguments why the Church had gone astray because it wasn't living the united order. Then I asked him, "Do you pay your tithes?" And he squirmed uneasily. He did not pay his tithes, but he wanted the Church to live the united order. Again, he wanted us to live the plural marriage law and he had much to say about it, but he did not attend his meetings—he did not even live the Word of Wisdom. But he *had* entered into the so-called plural marriage and had three or four women, who, he claimed, were wives and were, of course, with him in adultery. . . .

A teacher is doing a disservice to his students when he incites curiosity or encourages discussion about those things which are not a part of their lives or of their experience. . . . It would surely be wise for our teachers to leave these subjects alone and not worry about them nor worry students about them. The teachers should confine themselves to the practical, standard-living phases and not expound spectacular, strange, and exciting newnesses. (62-08)

We must admit that there are many mysteries of the kingdom. I am sure that the Lord will reveal them as fast as we are ready for them. We have enough to save and exalt us now. A small percentage of the people are living up to those teachings. The Brethren are united on all policies and programs, but when they go beyond the revealed word and they enter the field of conjecture, there will come differences of opinion. (5/31/48)

There are great numbers of unusually splendid and talented members of the Church all through the world who are intelligent and well-meaning, but I repeat again the statement I made in conference: That while they may think as they please, no one has the right to give his own private interpretations when he has been invited to teach in the organizations of the Church; he is a guest; he has been given an authoritative position and the stamp of approval is placed upon him, and those whom he teaches are justified in assuming that, having been chosen and sustained in the proper order, he represents the Church and the things which he teaches are approved by the Church. No matter how brilliant he may be and how many new truths he may think he has found, he has no right to go beyond the program of the Church. Certainly if any one or group of individuals have felt they have advanced inspiration or revelation, there is a way by which they can present it for approval. (4/28/48)

Teachers must remain orthodox. There are those today who seem to take pride in disagreeing with the orthodox teachings of the Church and who present their own opinions which are at variance with the revealed truth. Some may be partially innocent in the matter; others are feeding their own egotism; and some seem to be deliberate. Men may think as they please, but they have no right to impose upon others their unorthodox views. Such persons should realize that their own souls are in jeopardy.

And so we admonish the leaders in stakes, wards, and missions to be ever vigilant to see that no incorrect doctrines are promulgated in their classes or congregations. Wolves will come in sheep's clothing and will deceive the very elect, if that were possible. (48-02)

CHAPTER 20

Temple Work

The Temple Endowment

The temple is a holy place. The words "the Lord's house" appear on each of the temples. A temple *is* the Lord's house, and when we enter his house, we enter as his guests. Thus, we should do everything possible to keep the Lord's house holy, unpolluted, clean, and sweet. (77-01)

Every time a temple is dedicated to the Lord the darkness pushes farther back, prison doors are opened, and light comes into the world. (56-03)

As I awakened this morning and began to attain consciousness after the night, I saw the dawn advancing, and my thought first came to the holy temple which was to be dedicated this day. I thought, "No food today. Shoes must be shined, clothes pressed, and I must have a clean mind." All the way to Zollikofen I desired to say no word, and when I came into this room and sat by the president [McKay] and all he said was in sacred whispers, I knew then that I had been feeling some of the feeling he has felt. "Holiness to the Lord, Holiness becometh the Saints of the Lord." (55-12)

The house of the Lord is functional. Every element in the design, decoration, atmosphere, and program of the temple contributes to its function, which is to teach. The temple teaches of Christ. It teaches of his ordinances. It is filled with his Spirit. There is an aura of deity. (75-16)

The endowment teaches of man's journey. The temples are reserved for sacred ordinances pertaining to the living and the dead. Worthy members of the Church should go to the temples as often as possible to participate in this important work. One of the ordinances performed in the temple is that of the endowment, which comprises a course of instruction relating to the eternal journey of a man and woman from the pre-earthly existence through the earthly experience and on to the exaltation each may attain. (77-01)

The pioneers desired the endowment. My grandfather, Heber C. Kimball, wrote in his journal that during the last days of February 1846, groups were going through the Nauvoo Temple night and day, "way into the night and way into the day," he said. He indicated that Brother Brigham took a group through, Brother Willard took a group through, and he took a group through, and so on. The faithful Saints then were so anxious that they should receive the numerous blessings and ordinances which are given in the temple that they virtually lived in the temple those last few hours before they crossed the plains. Today we should begin to act with that same fervor and desire. (77-01)

All through Europe the past five months I have been encouraging the Saints to prepare their lives and put their houses in order and find the way to the holy temple. I told them in Germany the other day, "You can go to the temple." I knew their poverty and some of them, I know, would have difficulty going. And then I said to them, as they had a look of questioning in their faces, "You could walk to the holy temple." There was a little laughter. . . . And then I said, "I am not facetious. You could all walk to the holy temple and it wouldn't be nearly as far as many of our ancestors walked to go to a place where there was not a temple, but where there was a barren, desert ground on which a temple could be built, and then they worked forty years to build the temple so they might enjoy all these privileges." I am sure that they do not fully understand yet, nor can they until they have come and tasted of its sweet spirit. (55-13)

The endowment is for those mature in the gospel. Because of the sacred nature of the endowment and the other ordinances performed in the temple, those who go to the temple to receive them must be prepared and worthy. People who are converted to the Church often feel enthusiastic about going to the temple immediately after their baptism. But it takes time for them to adjust their thinking to things of an eternal nature, and it takes time for them to adjust their lives so that they are prepared and worthy when they do attend the temple. Thus, we have counseled stake presidents and bishops not to recommend people to go to the temple to receive their endowments until they are sufficiently mature in the gospel. We have established a policy that new converts should prepare themselves for *at least one year* after baptism before receiving these additional ordinances and blessings. (77-01)

It is not proper to go to the temple for the purpose of getting the strength to live righteously, but rather to acquire the strength and determination to live the commandments so that there can be total worthiness when you go to the temple. Certainly one will not want to go into the holy precincts and make any promises or covenants which he or she will not keep. It would be terrible to mock the Lord. It is well to gain control of appetites, passions, urges, desires first, then go into the temple to make them firm and to prepare for the eternities. (6/16/58)

Temple ordinances are futile without righteousness. But all these ordinances are futile unless with them there is a great righteousness. . . . So we go out into every field to perfect our lives. It is not enough to pay tithing and live the Word of Wisdom. We must be chaste in mind and in body. We must be neighborly, kind, and clean of heart. Sometimes people feel if they have complied with the more mechanical things that they are in line. And yet perhaps their hearts are not always pure. . . . With hearts that are absolutely purged and cleaned, and living the more mechanical things, we are prepared to come into the holy temple, . . . where perfection should be found. Here we receive extension of our glimpses we have had of the eternities. In our lives we have had little glimpses when the curtain has been moved a little. And here our vision will be extended until our knowledge and understanding will be greatly increased.

As we come here we will want to be sure that we are prepared for this great experience. Self-mastery is another name for the gospel of Jesus Christ. . . . When all of these ordinances are performed, then the self-mastery must accompany them. No one can be exalted in the kingdom of our Father without the ordinances. Neither can they be exalted without the righteousness; and sometimes people receive these ordinances unworthily, and at the least jeopardize their eternities. And then, as you know, in the world many people feel if they are just good they will receive all the blessings of eternity. Neither is complete in and of itself. They are joined together in one union which makes perfection; and to that end temples are built so that these final ordinances may be performed for the children of our Heavenly Father. (55-13)

Personal performance of ordinances is required of those warned. I talked to a man just a few days [ago] about this important thing. His wife had died. He was getting up in many years, and I said, "Your time is short; you're in your eighties now. You can't hope to live very much longer. Why don't you become active and do the things you need to do to get a temple recommend and go and do your own work in the temple while you're still alive to do it." "Oh," he said, "God is kind; he wouldn't take my wife away from me." And I said, "No, the Lord will never take your wife away from you, but you're the one who threw her away. You're the one that had the opportunity in your grasp. You could have been living the commandments all these days. You could have had her tied to you for all eternity, so that all the people in the world couldn't undo it. Nobody could; not even the devil with all his helpers could ever undo what you had done in that holy temple and with the accompanying faithfulness that followed it." "Oh," he said, "God is just; he wouldn't

take my wife away from me." And I repeated again, "No, the Lord
won't beat you or he won't curse you. He has just simply given us
laws, and if we won't follow the laws, then we pay the penalty, and it
is all charged against us, not the Lord." (74-05)

Temple participants must be worthy. Some of the ancient temples
were desecrated by the actions of outsiders. The temple of Solomon,
for example, was desecrated by those without authority who walked
into the temple, robbed it of its precious treasures, and took those
treasures to foreign lands for use in idolatrous practices. But the
possible actions of outsiders are not the only potential pollutants of
holy places.

Holy temples may also be defiled and desecrated by members of
the Church who go into the temple and make covenants unworthily
or which they are not prepared or willing to accept and carry forward. When people go to the temple and then make light of its sacred
principles, they are defiling it. When unrepentant people accept the
holy ordinances without full determination to prove worthy of them,
they are helping to violate the sacredness of the holy temple and they
are desecrating holy places.

When promises are made and covenants are entered into without
serious or pure intent to magnify them, pollutions may occur in the
holy temples. It is not only a matter of receiving a recommend to
enter the temples of the Lord, but it is also a matter of one having a
pure, sweet, and repentant spirit as well. (77-01)

When the bishop is ordained he becomes judge of his people. He
holds the keys to the temples and none of his ward members may
enter one without the turning of the key by the bishop. (MF 326)

This thought impressed itself upon me each time as we have gone
through this holy house, and I hoped that only men and women and
children who were clean in their lives would pass its portals and come
here to do the work. Far rather would I see the temple half filled with
worthy workers than to see the temple filled with those who were
unworthy. But it is my hope that this building will be used to its
capacity. (45-04)

Temples should be kept busy. In the book of Revelation, it speaks of serving the Lord "day and night in his temple." (Revelation 7:15.) So, I am looking forward to the day when a temple will not close. They won't have any holidays, ever, and there won't be any night or day. The temple will have its lights on all night long and will be going night and day and full all the time. When vacation times comes, they let people go on vacations but they don't let the temple go on vacation. (76-58)

Ordinance workers have human frailties. And the matter of proxy work is as old as the earth. It is in everyday life. And be too smart always, son, to confuse the mistakes of men with the program. Because some old man gets in a rut and repeats the temple ordinance prayers without feeling, you will be too wise and discerning to charge his failure to the program. (5/31/48)

Temple garments afford protection. I am sure one could go to extreme in worshipping the cloth of which the garment is made, but one could also go to the other extreme. Though generally I think our protection is a mental, spiritual, moral one, yet I am convinced that there could be and undoubtedly have been many cases where there has been, through faith, an actual physical protection, so we must not minimize that possibility. (5/31/48)

Changes in temples are made with authority. This holy temple will have changes, as has been stated this morning. I hope the people will realize that such changes as come are made by those who hold the keys that Peter held, that Joseph Smith held. I hope that all will be received with thanksgiving and gratitude and peace and joy. (55-13)

Ordinance work outside temples is exceptional. As a tentative and emergency situation, and by authority of the prophet of the Lord, we could be baptized [for the dead] in the Mississippi or in the ocean, or other places. We could be married for eternity in a faraway home or mountain top, properly approved and designed and set apart, but only in an emergency. The temple is necessary for these holy purposes. (75-16)

Temples will be built to meet the demand. It isn't a matter of just saying, "Well, we'll build one here, and one there," a geographical location. It's a matter of bringing temple work to the people that want it. (76-60)

Temple Ordinances for the Dead

The work for the dead is urgent. Recently I have felt impressed to share some thoughts about the work for the dead because I feel the same urgency for it that I do about the missionary work, since they are basically one and the same. Thus, I said to my Brethren of the General Authorities, "This work is constantly on my mind, for it must be carried forward."...

Missionary work is not limited to proclaiming the gospel to every nation, kindred, tongue, and people now living on the earth. Missionary work is also continuing beyond the veil among the millions and even billions of the children of our Heavenly Father who have died either without hearing the gospel or without accepting it while they lived on the earth. Our great part in this aspect of missionary work is to perform on this earth the ordinances required for those who accept the gospel over there. The spirit world is full of spirits who are anxiously awaiting the performance of these earthly ordinances for them. I hope to see us dissolve the artificial boundary line we so often place between missionary work and temple and genealogical work, because it is the same great redemptive work! (77-01)

There is an urgency to engage more fully in the redeeming of our kindred dead through more frequent temple attendance. All those who possess temple recommends should use them as often as possible to engage in baptisms, endowments, and sealings for the dead. Other members of the Church should concern themselves seriously with preparations to qualify for temple recommends that they, too, might enjoy these eternal blessings and also act as saviors on Mount Zion. There is an ever-increasing burden of temple work to be done by the Saints, and we should rise to meet this challenge. (78-27)

Many dead wait. One of the important phases of gospel living is to involve ourselves in temple and genealogical effort. We know full well that the spirit world is filled with the spirits of men and women who are waiting for you and me to get busy in their behalf. It is a grave responsibility that the Lord has placed upon our shoulders, one that we cannot avoid and for which we may stand in jeopardy if we fail to accomplish it. (78-04)

Some of us have had occasion to wait for someone or something for a minute, an hour, a day, a week, or even a year. Can you imagine how our progenitors must feel, some of whom have perhaps been waiting for decades and even centuries for the temple work to be done for them? I have tried, in my mind's eye, to envision our progenitors who are anxiously waiting for those of us who are their descendants and are members of the Church on the earth to do our duty toward them. I have also thought what a dreadful feeling it would be for us to see them in the hereafter and have to acknowledge that we had not been as faithful as we should have been here on earth in performing these ordinances in their behalf. (77-01)

The dead may accept or reject. Isn't it a beautiful program, a selfless program whereby we do work for those who cannot do it for themselves? Baptism is a human and mortal experience, and to receive the Holy Ghost is an experience of mortality, and the sealing in the temple is a mortal experience. All are designed to prepare us for that long eternity....

So the program is this: we do our own work in the temple, then we do the work for the dead. We do not know for sure what those spirits are thinking, whether they will receive it or not, but we will do the work and put it in the bank for them so that if they get ready for it, they can withdraw it. (75-43)

"God is not the God of the dead, but of the living." (Matthew 22:32.) There are no dead except those who have chosen to be dead as to the law, dead as to the benefits, dead as to the blessings, dead as to the eternal nature of the gift.

Temple sealings are for yours and my great-grandparents . . . back through the thousands of years, good people who could never find a temple, though they traversed the entire earth; good people who could not seal themselves up to eternal blessings, though they may have neared perfection in their lives. (73-06)

Vicarious work is for those who had no opportunity in life. Bill was not wedded. He had at this time no wife for eternity. However, as important and necessary as it is to be married in the celestial order here on earth in mortality, provisions will be made to take care of this matter for those who, through no fault of their own, failed in this sacred requirement. . . . They will not be deprived of any blessings which they might have received if they had lived up to all of the commandments with which they could comply. (52-04)

It must be remembered that vicarious work for the dead is for those who could not do the work for themselves. Men and women who live in mortality and who have heard the gospel here have had their day, their seventy years to put their lives in harmony, to perform the ordinances, to repent and to perfect their lives. (MF 314)

The righteous will be bound together. Through the priesthood's new and everlasting covenant of marriage, all the elect children of God who are gathered together out of the earth may be sealed together in family units into the lineage of Abraham, or, in other words, into the organized eternal family of God. (77-01)

Genealogical Research

Genealogical research is an "offering in righteousness." We have asked the members of the Church to further the work of turning the hearts of the children to the fathers by getting their sacred family records in order. These records, including especially the "book containing the records of our dead" (D&C 128:24), are a portion of the "offering in righteousness" referred to by Malachi (3:3), which we are to present in His holy temple, and without which we shall not abide the day of His coming. (77-01)

Now, my brothers and sisters, I rejoice with you in our temple-building activities and in the far-reaching program to glean the records and vital statistics from the world and bring them into our libraries where they are available to us. But we must never become complacent and satisfied with merely providing these beautiful edifices and wonderfully abundant research facilities. Full satisfaction can come only in their use to the utmost capacity for the searching after and redemption of our kindred dead. It is a responsibility which we cannot shirk, and we lie in jeopardy every hour that we leave this work and let it run. (77-29)

Research is aided from the spirit world. I am sure that the veil is thin. My grandfather, being one of a family, searched all his life to get together his genealogical records; and when he died, in 1868, he had been unsuccessful in establishing his line back more than the second generation beyond him. I am sure that most of my family members feel the same as I do—that there was a thin veil between him and the earth, after he had gone to the other side, and that which he was unable to do as a mortal he perhaps was able to do after he had gone into eternity. After he passed away, the spirit of research took hold of men—his family in the West and two distant relatives, not members of the Church, in the East. For seven years these two men—Morrison and Sharples—unknown to each other, and unknown to the members of the family in the West, were gathering genealogy. After seven years, they happened to meet and then for three years they worked together. The family feels definitely that the spirit of Elijah was at work on the other side and that our grandfather had been able to inspire men on this side to search out these records; and as a result, two large volumes are in our possession with about seventeen thousand names. (45-04)

CHAPTER 21

Spreading the Gospel

The Missionary Task

We must teach the world. We must teach the gospel. The duty of teaching the world is clearly that of the Church and especially that of the Twelve, and those sent by them. (68-06)

Evangelistic harvest is always urgent. The destiny of man and of nations is always being decided. Every generation is crucial; every generation is strategic.

We may not be responsible for past generations, but we cannot escape the full responsibility for this one, and we have our time and our generation and our missionaries and our great potential. (74-14)

Is it not time that we sent out a great army, not of uniformed men, but an army of missionaries to preach repentance to a world that is dying? (55-09)

Our objective as the Lord's army of missionaries is to (1) warn the world, (2) bring about conversions, (3) baptize people, (4) organize membership, (5) teach and train, and (6) develop activity toward (7) stake organizations. (68-08)

Your faith and knowledge of truth are the result of missionary work of days gone by, which you can repay only by giving to others the same opportunities. Hence it is well for every worthy and pre-pared young man, as he grows up, to desire mightily to fill a mission. Of course, there is no compulsion. Each person makes up his mind on this matter as he does in receiving the priesthood, paying his tithes, marrying in the temple, serving in the Church. He ought to do all these things, but has his free agency. (73-03)

We must warn the world. We are not interested in numbers. They are secondary. We are interested in warning the nations of the world. I believe we have not scratched the surface. We are like the person who said, "Pull up the ladder; I'm aboard." (74-29)

Our goal is nothing less than the penetration of the entire world. Our new office building is a world building with four giant maps, each showing a particular part of the globe. We are not promised that the whole world will believe. Evangelization of the world does not mean that all men will respond, but all men must be given the opportunity to respond as they are confronted with the Christ. (74-29)

We do not need to baptize all the world, but we do need to warn them and bring to their attention, in an effective manner, the bless-ings available to them, and the regrets and deprivations which will follow a rejection of the plan of salvation. (58-09)

The missionary task is huge. It is hard for us to conceive of the billions of souls who depend upon us to bring them the glorious message of the gospel.

Speaking of the untouched world, we have hardly scratched the surface. In the numerous countries where we have our missions, we have reached few people relatively and there are hundreds of millions more. . . .

We immediately become conscious of the several hundred million in the Soviet Union and its satellites; the half billion in China and Mongolia; the half billion in India; the hundred million in Pakistan and Burma; the thirty million in Turkey; and the other numerous millions in countries with fewer numbers but with great potential.

In the countries we already proselyte, there are many hundreds of cities with a hundred thousand people and without a missionary. (68-08)

Now is the moment in the timetable of the Lord to carry the gospel farther than it has ever been carried before—farther geographically, and farther in density of coverage. Many a person in this world is crying, knowingly and unknowingly, "Come over ... and help us." He might be your neighbor. She might be your friend. He might be a relative. She might be someone you met only yesterday. But we have what they need. Let us take new courage from our studies and pray, as did Peter, "And now, Lord, ... grant unto thy servants, that with all boldness they may speak thy word." (Acts 4:29.) (75-44)

Our gracious Father, we remember vividly the command of thy Son to "go ... into all the world, and preach the gospel to every creature." (Mark 16:15.)

Our Father, our efforts to fulfill this command seem small and infantile, not wholly rewarding. Give us, we pray, hearts of determination that we, thy people, may make such sacrifices as are necessary; that our sons may live righteously through their growing years and strive for spiritual excellence to be worthy to take the gospel to the nations of the world.

Our gracious Father, there are national gates which seemingly need to be unlocked and doors that need to be opened, and hearts of kings, presidents, emperors, and ministers which need to be softened, that they may permit the gospel to be taken to their people.

Our Father, bless the countless millions in the world, that they may receive thy truth, and bless the missionaries on whom the sun never sets, that nothing will prevail against them in their faithful presentation of thy gospel to the world, and bless especially, our Father, the children of thy people in overseas countries that they may devote their sons to this holy work. Wherein we have failed, help us to see our duties; wherein we have been prevented, open the doors, we pray, and swing the gates wide open and let thy servants cover the earth with their testimonies. (74-35)

Teaching the gospel is more important than other good deeds. You are in the greatest work in the world, and nothing in this world can compare to it. Building homes and bridges is nothing. Building worlds is nothing compared to the lives you are building. The saving of mortal lives isn't any important accomplishment as compared to what you are doing. You might go out here to one of these cemeteries and raise the dead, even a thousand or ten thousand of them, and you haven't done anything compared to what you are doing when you are saving people.

You may heal the sick, the blind may see by the power that you hold, but I want to say, brothers and sisters, you have done little in restoring sight to the blind as compared to that which you do when you bring the light of the gospel to the blind spiritually.

The Lord brought Lazarus from the tomb by the power of the priesthood. The man was dead, so dead "he stank," according to the words of his sister. The Lord brought him forth to life again and people marvelled, but that was little compared to the event when the Lord said just three words on the Sea of Galilee to Peter and Andrew.... The Redeemer said, "Come follow me," and two men followed him through three years of his life, and after the Savior ascended, Peter continued preaching the gospel and converting people by the thousands. He preached on the famed day of Pentecost and three thousand people came into the Church and later another five thousand. He took the gospel to the Gentiles. We have no doubts as to which was the more important occasion. (47-11)

Missionary work is not words as against actions, but is a set of inspired words which change lives and bring happiness and transform characters. And, of course, one should remember that when he has filled stomachs with food, fine as it is, the stomachs get hungry again, but when he has changed a soul to higher, more abundant living, he has probably done something that is lasting. I know, of course, that not all the people that are baptized are totally converted and changed, but again, that may be more fault than the missionary's fault. (10/14/70)

Responsibility for Full-time Missionary Work

Missionary work transcends this life. I spoke at the funeral service of a young student who died during World War II. There had been hundreds of thousands of young men rushed prematurely into eternity through the ravages of war, and I made the statement that I believed this righteous youth had been called to the spirit world to preach the gospel to these deprived souls.

In the "Vision of the Redemption of the Dead" by President Joseph F. Smith, he saw this very thing. He sat studying the scriptures on October 3, 1918, particularly the statements in Peter's epistle regarding the antediluvians. He writes:

"I beheld that the faithful elders of this dispensation, when they depart from mortal life, continue their labors in the preaching of the gospel of repentance and redemption...." (Joseph F. Smith, *Gospel Doctrine,* pp. 472-76.) [D&C 138:52]....

I would be happier to have my sons effective missionaries than to have them honored in high secular places, to be bishops in God's kingdom than kings on earthly thrones. For there is no greater work in which to be engaged, and the proselyting work does not end with death, but carries over into the life beyond. (55-15)

Missionary responsibility is urgent. My brothers and sisters, I must warn you this is not a new sermon. It is not a new subject, but our theme song, and maybe a few changed trinkets to add to the costume picture. For years we have been speaking of the life-giving blood on which we continue to grow, and our ever-present responsibility which we have barely touched as yet. There is urgency in our program. We are directed and commanded to convert the world. ... He has given us a time in which to accomplish his purposes. He gave to the Saints a time to build the temple. There is a time for all things. (74-14)

I fear sometimes lest some people, near and far, who are already partially converted will grow tired of waiting for us. I fear that sometimes we will wait too long to move, and miss certain golden opportunities to build the Church or to feed our Father in Heaven's children. We can be careful and yet move forward. It is better for something to be underway than under advisement. (78-25)

Though some good work has been done, it is almost as though we were removing the Wasatch Mountains with shovels.... There are hundreds of thousands waiting—honest souls who are waiting. It seems a formidable task, but with all the help and inspiration and inventions available to us, we can do it....

We have been baptizing the people of the world as individuals and families in dozens and scores. We must find ways to bring them into the kingdom by the thousands, and we must develop programs that will organize, teach, train, and educate these millions to take their part in the ever-expanding Church. (67-11)

Missionary responsibility belongs to members in all lands. We want you to know that this is really serious business. We're not merely inviting people to go on missions. We are saying, This is your work! The God of heaven, through his prophets, has called you to this service. (77-11)

This service has been rendered largely by missionaries from the U.S. and Canada. There was good reason for this in the beginning, but now we give out a bold and serious challenge to the Church world outside of upper North America to participate with corresponding faithfulness. Today, with the improvement in national economic conditions, the great increase of members, the excellent stake and mission organizations around the world, and available financial help, there seems to be no valid reason why the members in the headquarters part of the world should carry so nearly the whole load. There have been numerous sacrifices on the part of missionaries and their parents to do the monumental work that has been done largely by them the last 140 years. (70-05)

We need local missionaries. The Danish missionary and the Norwegian and the Swedish missionary could be more efficient because they know the people and they know the customs, and above all they know the language well. They are a part of the communities. Another good reason is that these young missionaries are getting a training for two years which helps to prepare them to become the bishops and the high councilors and the stake presidencies of these numerous stakes we are going to organize in these countries. Another good reason is the fact that we cannot send our American boys in the lands without a visa. At this moment there are some of the lands in which we have proselyted for years who have closed their doors, generally because of political reasons. And that makes us sad, indeed, when we cannot send any of our American boys to give the basis for the proselyting program. Therefore, we hope we will have enough well-trained, worthy local young men to carry on the work if, by chance, the doors be closed against the Americans. And, anyway, the responsibility is yours. (76-44)

Do you know of any reason why I should send my son but that you shouldn't send yours? All these leaders of the Church are sending their sons on missions. All three of my sons have gone on missions, and now my grandsons are going on their missions. I do not know how to make this emphatic enough. We hope from this day of warning that you will not need to be reminded, ever again.

This is a great nation and great people, and it is your responsibility to teach the gospel in these nations. When you have sent all the boys from this area on missions, we can send all the North American missionaries to India, or China, or Russia, or somewhere else. (75-11)

The basic missionary responsibility is on young men. While some young women will fill missions, the greater responsibility rests on the young men who bear the priesthood. Every normal boy in the Church should keep his life righteous so that he could fill a mission. (73-03)

Women missionaries receive special blessings. In addition, many young women have a desire to serve a full-time mission, and they are also welcome in the Lord's service. This responsibility is not on them as it is on the elders, but they will receive rich blessings for their unselfish sacrifice. The Lord is pleased at their willingness to bring souls to him. (PKSO 30)

Older people can contribute as missionaries. There are many people today who are being placed on retirement . . . far too early . . . and the rest of their life is almost valueless in many cases, because they need something to do. They need the experience that they could receive if they could go on a mission. (79-10)

We have rather forgotten, we older people, who have been retired and who have found an easy place to go with our camping outfit and with our other opportunities. We have found an easy way to satisfy our own thoughts and our own consciences that the work must go on—we will send our boys, we say.

All of us have this responsibility. Not all of us are able, but many, many of us are. Hundreds of thousands of Latter-day Saints are able to preach the gospel in a careful, splendid way. (79-06)

So let us make that the rule—that every boy *ought* to go on a mission. There may be some who can't, but they *ought* to go on a mission. Every boy, and many girls, and many couples. We could use hundreds of couples, older people like some of you folks, whose families are reared, who have retired in their business, who are able to go and spend their own money, to teach the gospel. We could use hundreds of couples. You just go and talk to your bishop—that is all you need to do. Tell him, "We are ready to go, if you can use us." I think you will probably get a call. (76-58)

Missionary Responsibility of All Members

Missionary activity is the responsibility of all members. My brothers and sisters, I call upon you to organize yourselves and your families and bring the gospel to your neighbors and your friends.

Remember the slogan President David O. McKay gave us, "Every member a missionary."

This is your privilege. This is your duty. This is a command from the presidency of the Church and from your Lord. Listen to the Lord's command:

"Behold, I sent you out to testify and warn the people, and it becometh every man [every man!] who hath been warned to warn his neighbor. Therefore, they are left without excuse, and their sins are upon their own heads." (D&C 88:81-82.) (74-22)

Each of us is responsible to bear witness of the gospel truths that we have been given. We all have relatives, neighbors, friends, and fellow workmen, and it is our responsibility to pass the truths of the gospel on to them, by example as well as by precept. (77-32)

We say to our friends of the world, we love and admire you. We are grateful for your resolve to be righteous in an increasingly wicked world. Bring all that you have that is good and wholesome with you, and let us add to all that you have, that which we have—the fullness of the gospel and the even greater blessings that can follow unto you through membership in The Church of Jesus Christ of Latter-day Saints! . . .

We believe that there are many good men and women in all the parties, in all the churches and denominations, who are kept from the truth by just not knowing where it is found. (77-27)

We would ask that you select a family, some family in your neighborhood, that you have considerable, high regard for, and then invite them to your home. Show them how to hold home evenings; teach them the gospel. There isn't anyone here that can't teach the gospel, and if there is, there are missionaries available. . . . If you can't think of anything else you can say, "I know that God lives." That's the greatest testimony in the world. And you don't need to have a thousand reasons for doing it. (76-20)

Member referrals greatly aid missionaries. We realize the conditions in all missions are not comparable, but having the Saints enthusiastic in their furnishing referrals is a mighty factor in getting conversions. (68-08)

Members should strive to refer entire families. The missionaries will teach single people, but they are sent out especially to bring entire families into the Church. A family will tend to remain stronger in the Church than individuals. Even one strong person in a family will help keep them all active and will help solve the occasional laxity of one or more members of the family. (77-32)

Every gospel teaching experience is a spiritual experience for all parties, regardless of whether it leads to baptism or not. Our goal should be to identify as soon as possible which of our Father's children are spiritually prepared to proceed all the way to baptism into the kingdom. One of the best ways to find out is to expose your friends, relatives, neighbors, and acquaintances to the full-time missionaries as soon as possible. Don't wait for long fellowshipping nor for the precise, perfect moment. What you need to do is find out if they are the elect. "[My] elect hear my voice and harden not their hearts." (D&C 29:7.) If they hear and have hearts open to the gospel, it will be evident immediately. If they won't listen and their hearts are hardened with skepticism or negative comments, they are not ready. In this case, keep loving them and fellowshipping them and wait for the next opportunity to find out if they are ready. You will not lose their friendship. They will still respect you.

Of course, there are discouragements, but nothing is ever lost. No one ever loses a friend just because he doesn't want to continue with the visits from the missionaries. The member can continue the association with no threat to his friendship or special relationship with that family. Sometimes it takes more time for some to come into the Church than for others. The member should continue to fellowship and try again at a later date for conversion. Don't be discouraged just because of a temporary lack of progress. There are hundreds of stories about the value of perseverance in missionary service.

In some areas of the world the members are having remarkable success. They are providing so many referrals, good referrals, ready to be taught in the member's home or in the family's home with the member present, that the missionaries are busy from morning until night just teaching and working with those families who are proceeding toward baptism.

The real goal for effective proselyting is that the members do the finding and the full-time missionaries do the teaching. This tends to solve many of the old missionary problems. When members do the finding they have a personal interest in fellowshipping, there are fewer investigators lost before baptism, and those who are baptized tend to remain active. Another by-product is that when a member is involved, even if only from a casual relationship, the investigator seems to sense much more quickly that Mormons have a special health code (the Word of Wisdom comes as no surprise), that Mormons spend Sunday in church and not fishing or playing golf (keeping the Sabbath Day holy comes as no surprise), and that Mormons contribute readily to the Church programs (tithing, fast offerings, budget, building fund, missionary funds, etc., are more readily understood). When there is little or no surprise, the reluctance to be baptized is more easily overcome.

Another old missionary dilemma is when the investigator says, "Yes, it's easy for you to be a Mormon because you haven't had to raise a family or change your life." The adult member or peer is the one who can effectively step in with his testimony to say, "I am no different than you are. I live the Mormon way of life. I'm happier and healthier and have more left over at the end of the month than if I didn't live the commandments. Besides, I know it is true." (77-32)

We should not worry because someone chides us a little for directing the missionaries to them. What a small price to pay for such a glorious blessing!

Sometimes we forget that it is better to risk a little ruffling in the relationship of a friend than it is to deprive them of eternal life by leaving them silent. Besides, our missionaries generally follow the counsel in the Book of Mormon: "Use boldness, but not overbearance." (Alma 38:12.) (74-26)

Members influence others by good example. The gospel is true. By studying and living its principles and seeking the help of the Holy Ghost, any earnest seeker can know for himself that it is true. But how much easier it is to understand and accept if the seeker after truth can also see the principles of the gospel at work in the lives of other believers. No greater service can be given to the missionary calling of this Church than to be exemplary in positive Christian virtues in our lives. (78-22)

Members should be open about discipleship. We could make a different mistake by too-brazen trumpeting of our motives for acting as we do, but most of us err on the other side. We fail to find some quiet way to let our colleagues at work and in social organizations and in our neighborhood know that we are first of all, and always, followers of Jesus Christ. (78-22)

Members must extend fellowship. As we lose numerous of our converts to apostasy and sin, we are prone to blame it on to the missionaries, who, we charge, failed to fully convert them. While there could be some laxness at times, the Saints in their organized capacity in missions and stakes must assume much of this responsibility. There is definitely and unquestionably a great loss through lack of fellowshipping and...lack of proper functioning of the organizations. (68-08)

Retaining present members is equally important. Remember that a soul at home kept warmed and fed and faithful is as valuable to the cause as is a new convert from the world, so that home service is equally important with foreign. (45-01)

Preparation for Missions

Prepare and send missionaries. I hope that if . . . at this conference I make no other point, I have made this one, that you send your boys on missions. The minute they come into your arms, you begin to teach them. . . .

I know that the Lord has asked this. The Lord is the one from whom it comes. The Lord is in heaven watching. He watches your efforts individually and collectively. He expects you to do this. If you don't do it, of course, you can answer to him when you get into the eternal world, because there we will stand before the judges and we will be required to tell why we were so reticent, if we were. (76-35)

Perhaps no mother ever says farewell to her son leaving for the mission field, but there are tears and loneliness, and yet that experience brings great blessings into that home. (55-05)

Develop mission-mindedness in children. In recent years nearly every time I see a little boy, I say, "You will make a great missionary, won't you?" You plant into his mind a seed. It is just like plants and other vegetation. It grows and grows, and if a father and a mother talk to their little boys, particularly, and their little girls, about going on a mission—when they are infants, almost—that little seed will grow and grow and they won't need to say anything about missionaries when they get a little older. The boys plan it. We have much evidence of that. (76-60)

We want *you* to never forget that every boy should be indoctrinated from the time he is born until he is nineteen that he should fill a mission. If he does not want to, that is up to him, but if he is not indoctrinated, then that is somebody else's fault. If the parents don't talk about it and pray about it, naturally the boys will make their other plans. But if they talk about the mission, they, of course, will be ready to go when the time comes. It is amazing now, as we go all around the world and shake hands with a lot of little boys. "Going on a mission?" "Yes, I have got so much money already saved." They are counting on it. They were not twenty years ago, not all of them. It is almost universal now. (76-58)

If you want your boys to go on missions, have them pray for the missionaries every time they pray. They will love the things they pray for. (76-49)

Establish a mission plan and fund early. I was in London. I was speaking to a big conference. I said, "All the boys that are twelve years old, please come up to the stand." When they were all lined up, I said to the first boy, "Where are you going when you are nineteen years old?" He said, "I don't know." I said, "Oh, yes, you do know. You're going on a mission." He said, "Am I?" I said, "Yes, when you are nineteen you are going on a mission. And here is a shilling to start you on your mission. Now you go back to your seat and tell your father and mother back there that you are going on a mission." To the second boy that came up the line, I said, "Where are you going when you are nineteen years of age?" He said, "I'm going on a mission." He learned quickly. And so will your boys learn quickly. If their older brother fills a mission, they will expect to fill a mission. (77-09)

Remind children often of mission plans. When your first son goes into the mission field, then it is easy to train all the others so that they will not fail to go. Another way to guarantee this matter is to start when they are little, tiny children to put in a little savings bank some pennies, nickles, and dimes. And every time that child receives a gift of money you say, "Well, what are you going to do with it now, Te'o? That would be good to go in your mission fund." As he grows up to maturity, his mission fund also grows and is available. Keep it before him all his life. Get a picture of the New Zealand Temple and a picture maybe of the Hawaiian Temple, and put them in his bedroom where he will see them every night when he goes to bed and every morning when he gets up. Then frequently remind him in home evenings, and at other times, of his obligation. These little boys are precious. And some day, some of them will be General Authorities of the Church, perhaps. They will be political leaders in your own communities. And they will bring you much joy and credit for all the effort you spend while they are little tiny fellows growing toward this. (76-04)

Young women should encourage missionary service. Do you young women realize how much power you have? If there was an army here telling them they had to go, it would not be as powerful as you would be. When one of these boys falls in love with you, you have the controls. You can just say what you want to say, but you could say, "Oh, let's wait until you get back from your mission." It is that important. (75-10)

Timely mission calls are most productive. Bishops have a "clock" by which to work. The child becomes eight and needs baptism. . . .

The chronological clock calls for a mission call for the young man at nineteen. If he is not prepared spiritually, financially, and according to his desires and moods about that time, the likelihood of his filling a mission at a later date is slim indeed. (69-09)

All should have an opportunity to serve a mission. Let the bishops understand it is not their right to stand off at a distance and decide whether a boy could go on a mission or should stay home and go to school or whether his mother could support him or whether his parents need his help, but let the boy make his own decisions, and the bishop will give every boy his opportunity. (74-29)

Missionary preparation includes worthiness, knowledge, and finances. His preparation consists largely of efforts in three areas:

1. Keeping his life clean and worthy and remaining free from all the sins of the world.

2. Preparing the mind and the spirit—to know the truth.

3. Preparing to finance his mission so it may be his own contribution, so far as possible.

1. As to his moral life, it is expected that everybody will have been taught from the cradle to his mission the fundamentals of the gospel and the need for the pure life. While total perfection is not expected, it is hoped that through family training, home evenings, father-son relationships, and other learning-training, he shall have resisted every temptation to do evil and shall have gone through these younger years totally free from the vices of the world—that every kind of moral vice shall have been bypassed and that he will have remained clean and pure and be able to look his bishop in the eye

many times during his growing-up years and tell the bishop truthfully that he has been the proper master of his desires, urges, and passions and is worthy to carry the sacred message of the Lord.

Should there have been incidents that would make him unworthy, there must be total and sustained repentance for a sufficient period to satisfy the bishop, stake president, and the General Authority that he is like Saul, "a new man" with "a new heart" and ready to honorably carry forward his duties. In the matter of forgiveness, every person who has transgressed seriously should seek earnestly to learn the real meaning of repentance—to learn that it means far more than mere desire to do better. . . .

There must be a deep consciousness of guilt before repentance gets under way, and in that real consciousness of guilt may come suffering of the mind, the spirit, and even the body sometimes. The constant teachings from infancy should leave every person to realize that he cannot commit sin without leaving himself unclean and scarred.

2. One should study, ponder, learn scriptures, and build his testimony so that he may be prepared to teach and train. The Lord has said, "If ye are prepared ye shall not fear" (D&C 38:30), and it is our hope that from infancy through all the years of maturing, the lessons taught in the auxiliaries, in the seminaries and institutes, in the home evenings, in the sacrament meetings, and elsewhere may bring every youth to a preparation that will eliminate fear. Every person approaching a mission should be schooled, trained, and indoctrinated for immediate and proper participation in proselyting. Gospel, doctrine, or organization illiteracy should never be found among our youth. Proper scriptures can be learned well and permanently by children; doctrines can be taught and absorbed by youth.

Why is it that some young folks are almost overly conscientious in their school work, even to neglecting their Church responsibilities, when the spiritual should have priority in the study time of every person if preference must be given? However, there is time for fulfilling every need.

To arrive at mission age and be illiterate, gospel-wise or otherwise, would be an unthinkable travesty. Certainly by the time a young man reaches his nineteenth birthday, he should be prepared to step from his conventional role at home into the important role of the missionary without a total reorganization of his life, his standards, or his training.

3. The financing of a mission should be undertaken, under parental guidance, when the male child is born. How wonderful it would be if each future missionary could have saved for his mission from birth. It would be ideal if the parents would establish for him a savings account or other investments and then remind the child every time money comes into his hands that part or all of it should go into his mission fund. This not only builds the mission fund but is psychologically firm. The boy is constantly reminded of his oncoming mission. This will encourage the boy to work. Side jobs and numerous services can be used to finance his mission. This could discourage the selfish growing up of many who have only their immediate desires in mind. If the child is permitted to spend his all on himself, that spirit of selfishness may continue with him to his grave.

How wonderful it would be if every boy could totally or largely finance his own mission and thereby receive most of the blessings coming from his missionary labors.

Of course if the boy is a convert in his teens, his years of saving are limited. If he lives in a country where the economic standards are low and opportunities are severely limited, he can still be governed by this policy and do the best he can.

Next to the contribution of the missionary comes that of his immediate family, and no missionary will receive a call who is totally supported outside of this program of family and self.

In countries where the pay for labor is much less or where the family has other serious financial problems that render their participation more difficult, then we have the quorums of priesthood in district, ward, branch, stake, and mission, one of whose principal functions is to raise funds for missionary purposes, and the Church has two funds that can be used in emergencies.

Every boy and many girls and couples should serve missions. Every prospective missionary should prepare morally, spiritually, mentally, and financially all of his life in order to serve faithfully, efficiently, and well in the great program of missionary work. (73-03)

Prospective missionaries must establish worthiness. We want to be sure our boys are going to be totally true to the covenants they have made when they go in the mission home. . . . [If] he admits that he has had sexual life with girl friends, would you just say, "Now, of course, it wouldn't be possible for you to go on a mission now, would it? Now, if you will just get really busy, if you are really repentant and can prove it to us that you are really repentant, maybe a little later we would give it consideration." I wouldn't ever promise them that in [any set period] . . . I'll let you go. Just say, when you have proved yourself then we will take a look at it again. . . .

As much as we need missionaries and as anxious as we are for them, he doesn't go on his mission unless he cleans up and convinces you that he has changed his life. You can easily tell if he has changed his life. If he doesn't pay his tithing while you are waiting, if he doesn't attend his meetings, if he has a bad attitude, if he goes with the wrong crowd, well, you could be fairly sure that he has not changed his life. He has got to change his whole life and his living, pay his tithing, and report to you as often as you think he should, and if you find out that he is worthy, then you send him on his mission. It is possible. It is possible. But you let him wait, and wait until *you* are sure, not when *he* is sure, but when you are sure that he is worthy and able to do it. (74-33)

At the beginning of the century we used to send young men on missions to reform them, but no longer. We shall not knowingly send any person out to reform him. (65-11)

Prepared missionaries anticipate service with joy. When I ask for more missionaries, I am not asking for more testimony-barren or un-worthy missionaries. I am asking that we start earlier and train our missionaries better in every branch and every ward in the world. That is another challenge—that the young people will understand that it is a great privilege to go on a mission and that they must be physically well, mentally well, spiritually well, and that "the Lord cannot look upon sin with the least degree of allowance." (D&C 1:31.)

I am asking for missionaries who have been carefully indoctrinated and trained through the family and the organizations of the Church, and who come to the mission with a great desire. I am asking for better interviews, more searching interviews, more sympathetic and understanding interviews, but especially that we train prospective missionaries much better, much earlier, much longer, so that each anticipates his mission with great joy. (74-01)

Prepared missionaries will be more effective. In that day of near-universal missions, young men having planned for nineteen years to fill a mission will be more fruitful, more effective, and more successful when they serve, and more people will come into the Church and will create more enthusiasm and there will be a chain reaction.…

Our timetable says now, now is the time to upgrade our missionary standards. (74-29)

Missionary Assignment and Supervision

Inspiration is sought in missionary assignments. In the assigning of missionaries there are numerous factors, the chief one being the inspiration received by the Missionary Executive Committee, who review carefully and prayerfully all of the recommendations sent to them by the stakes and missions. As this committee makes recommendations, it considers numerous factors: worthiness, age, experience, military status, home, finances, health, language ability, desires, quotas, limitations of countries, requests, nationality, general attitudes, and the needs of the various missions. When all these factors have been duly weighed, a sincere effort is made to ascertain where the person can make the greatest contribution; the inspiration of the Lord is sought earnestly. The tentative assignment is made subject to approval by the president of the Church, who then signs the call and has it mailed to the prospective missionary. (72-01)

Missionary assignments rely on divine direction. I am reading from section 32 where the Lord says:

> And now concerning my servant Parley P. Pratt, behold, I say unto him that as I live I will that he shall declare my gospel and learn of me, and be meek and lowly of heart.
>
> And that which I have appointed unto him is that he shall go with my servants, Oliver Cowdery and Peter Whitmer, Jun., into the wilderness among the Lamanites.
>
> And Ziba Peterson also shall go with them; and I myself will go with them and be in their midst; and I am their advocate with the Father, and nothing shall prevail against them. (D&C 32:1-3.)

There is probably no soul in this room but who accepts fully that that is a revelation. It was given through the Prophet Joseph Smith in 1830. We have no record of any appearance of an angel, or of a coming of the Father or the Son, or of any voice that was audible to the physical ear, or any handwriting on the wall that could be seen by the physical eye. We have no such record of that. But we accept it as revelation, don't we? Parley P. Pratt, Oliver Cowdery, Peter Whitmer, and Ziba Peterson were called on a mission to do nothing more than the hundreds that are sent to the Indians all the time in all of the missions of the Church, and to the other thousands who are sent to all the other missions of the Church. . . .

Those men who make those calls are in the temple every Thursday. They are as devout as they know how to be. They are asking constantly for the revelations of the Lord and, I am sure, in many cases receive very direct impressions as to where missionaries should go, and when they should go, or whether they shouldn't go. So I have the faith and confidence that every missionary is called of revelation. Therefore, I never feel too good when missionaries insist upon going to Hawaii, or to the Eastern States, or to Germany, or anywhere they might want to go. I am always happy when the missionary says, "I am in your hands, in the hands of the Lord, from this moment forward, and I want to go where he sends me." There's an indication if the boy or the missionary finds his own mission field that he hasn't total faith in the revelation that comes to the authorities of the Church. He thinks perhaps it's just a bunch of men up there who just arbitrarily say, "You take this one and I'll take that one." It isn't that way. (56-09)

Mission presidents are responsible for missionary effectiveness. You start with converts and then families and then branches and then districts and then stakes, and yours is a tremendously important work. You mission presidents are sent out, not to make new records primarily or to build statistical towers, but to fulfill the commandment of the Lord given on the Mount of Olives.

Now, you are going out on your mission not merely to make friends for the Church, though that is important, but to properly convert and baptize. You notice... "He that believeth and is baptized shall be saved" (Mark 16:16), not he that heareth, but he that believeth and is baptized.

Brethren, the spirit of this work is urgency, and we must imbue our missionaries and our Saints with the spirit of now, *now.* We are not just waiting for the natural, slow process of bringing people into the Church. We must move more rapidly....

Put your shoulders to the wheel, lengthen your stride, heighten your reach, increase your devotion and that of the missionaries so that we can begin to move the work along more rapidly....

It will be your responsibility to see that the missionaries are inspired, motivated, and indoctrinated. It will be your responsibility to see that the schedules are stimulating and productive. It will be your responsibility to see that your missionaries do not waste time and that you do not use the missionaries generally for errand boys or extra, unnecessary work. There must not be waste of manpower; there should not be six or eight or ten missionaries in the mission home doing the work there when three or four can do it. Missionaries should not be using mission vehicles or themselves to run errands and wait on the public generally. Missionaries in the office should also be proselyting missionaries in every mission. Sometimes the productive work of missionaries is diluted as would be a liquid poured into a sieve.

I asked one of the brethren once how he was getting along in a certain mission, and he said, "It's a wonderful mission, wonderful missionaries. They are doing everything but preaching the gospel.'' There are so many leaks of time and effort that the net product is greatly reduced. Each mission president should study prayerfully his own program and be sure that there are no leaks of energy or time, for in the end you are responsible for the two years that these wonderful missionaries give to the Lord. . . .

I am not convinced that mission presidents should ever set goals for missionaries. They may set goals for their mission if they like, and for themselves, but let the missionaries set goals for themselves and then the president will praise and give them adulation for succeeding in the goals which they set. (75-23)

You are not going to overwork your missionaries. There are few missionaries, if ever any, that have been destroyed by overwork. They have been destroyed by overworry and too little work and by immoralities and other things, but generally not by overwork. (75-23)

Converts need to learn participation. Of course, we realize that the new convert may have come from a church where the members only listened to the priest or minister. It is a far cry from that to the intensive activity in this, the true church. A part of their training and Church habits needs to be expanded, but that is part of their conversion. Before being baptized the new convert should understand that this Church is like a beehive, and that activity earns the rewards of heaven, and that just believing will not take one far in his quest toward exaltation. (73-07)

Mission presidents develop leaders. It is your responsibility to create great, strong, faithful, worthy leaders for the Church tomorrow, not only from among your missionaries, but also from the members who will come into the Church. (75-23)

Mission presidents should see the importance of their creating a great man out of each missionary who comes to them. One mission president wrote, "If I had known that he was going to marry my daughter, I'd have . . . trained him better." (74-29)

Correct abuses without overreaction. Some years ago, in what may have been a competitive enthusiasm, there was a great increase in baptisms. We believe that all would agree that there were abuses, and perhaps many who were not ready for baptism, and some who fell away from the Church, giving proof of the immaturity of their indoctrination.

We have always had a falling away. We have never retained all those who joined the Church—perhaps we never shall.

Undoubtedly, many who fell away were charged to immature indoctrination when they should have been charged to lack of fellowship.

Perhaps the most unfortunate thing which came out of it was the terrible reaction which set in. Missionaries began to talk about it; the Saints at home began to talk about it; everybody was condemning the mass baptisms; jokes were made about it; it spread around the world and missions far off caught the spirit of it; the pendulum swung back; baptisms all over the world reduced and it is our opinion that though there may have been errors in the big push, that perhaps far more people have suffered more by deprivation, by the reactionary movement or lack of movement. Certainly, we must learn to correct abuses without killing the program....

When the missionaries are making no baptisms, they are discouraged, have few harvests, and in turn lose their spirit, and therefore make fewer baptisms. (67-11)

Stake missions need continuity. Many stakes reorganize their missions too frequently, constantly making change, frequently releasing missionaries, and waiting for a propitious moment to reorganize. They are always preparing to get ready to train, to start to do missionary work. They are like a jet plane which stops every hundred miles—it hardly gets altitude until it is losing altitude for a stop....

Too many stake missions spend all their time in stringing and unstringing their violins, and they never get their music played. Do not spend all the time training missionaries—let them learn [through] "on-the-job training." (67-11)

Jews and Lamanites are not to be overlooked. I should like here to mention two groups of people sometimes overlooked—the Jewish people and the Lamanites. . . .

Now, presidents, we are not giving them special priority, but wherever they are found they should be given their opportunities to hear the gospel and they will be found in most of your missions in large or smaller numbers. . . . We urge that they not be bypassed. (75-23)

Lamanites are especially responsive. The Lord has a comprehensive plan, and I have a firm conviction that the blueprint he worked out many millennia ago will be carried out through the programs of the Church. Even now the Church is bringing to bear its resources to educate the Lamanites, to improve their living conditions and their health, to bring them to a knowledge of the gospel of their Redeemer. I have asked for increased effort in the missionary work among the Lamanites, and I have been most gratified by the response. The missions in the Lamanite areas are the most active and most productive of all, with many more converts per missionary than in any of the other missions. It is as in days of old: "And thus we see that the Lord began to pour out his Spirit upon the Lamanites, because of their easiness and willingness to believe in his words." (Helaman 6:36.) We have many Lamanite missionaries in the field now, and there will be many, many more, I am sure. . . .

The Lamanites must rise again in dignity and strength to fully join their brethren and sisters of the household of God in carrying forth his work in preparation for that day when the Lord Jesus Christ will return to lead his people, when the Millennium will be ushered in, when the earth will be renewed and receive its paradisiacal glory and its lands be united and become one land. (75-53)

Converts in poor countries need help. Of course, there are other challenges in so-called "third world" countries. Many of the congregations of interested black people are illiterate or poorly trained. We will need to help educate the youth of these congregations and teach them the principles of growth and development which will allow them to improve themselves economically and culturally as well as spiritually and intellectually.

But that is not so different from what we have had to do elsewhere in other times in our history. We have a great Church educational system, and a great program for welfare services, and a great priesthood department, a great system for training leaders and providing aids for teaching genealogy and doing missionary work and providing auxiliary programs for the children, the youth, and the women. We can do it, for the Lord has promised he would be our advocate with the Father and nothing should prevail against us. We have had many of our people at various times in those countries involved in their schools, their businesses, their political and economic life. It is a large continent. Roads are at a premium, and homes are usually far less than we are used to here. Poverty is widespread. Country after country has scarcely over $100 per year per person income for an economic base. But can we ask them to wait any longer? I believe that we cannot. We mention Ghana, but what of Nigeria, Libya, Ethiopia, the Ivory Coast, and the Sudan and others? These are names that must become as familiar to us as Japan, Venezuela, New Zealand, and Denmark have become. (78-25)

Church programs extend missionary effort. Now, to take the gospel to the whole world is a formidable undertaking. To even approach it, we must use every proper tool, device, and invention, and increase our effectiveness and our missionaries. . . .

May I suggest six ways we can approach our overwhelming task.

1. A more effective and intimate and friendly program of fellowshipping.

2. Every stake and mission overseas and those nearer home can carry forward vigorously the program of "Every member a missionary."

3. Overseas missions can have vigorous functioning district missions in many of their districts, which districts are in reality embryo stakes.

4. Overseas stakes can all have strong and functioning stake missions.

5. Missions and stakes overseas can send their proportion of the proselyters.

6. We can send more missionaries from the headquarter region of the Church. (68-08)

Effectiveness in Missionary Work

Bearing earnest testimony is basic to missionary success. We have something which no one else can have. The pope in Rome might be a good man. Some ministers and some priests may be righteous. Some might be as devoted and as sincere as we are. But there can be none, except in our church, of course, who have this controlling thing, the testimony of the truth, and that is the thing that brings people into the kingdom. It is not our logic. Some may be more adept than others, some may have more natural endowments and greater talents than others, and some may be able to give a better lesson. But that is not the controlling factor, though it helps. It is tremendously important that we do everything in our power to present it well, but the testimony is the sealing element. (62-02)

Humility is essential in missionary work. To convince people of the divinity of the work one must of necessity be humble. To be arrogant or "cocky" is to threaten to drive away the Holy Ghost who alone can convince and bring testimonies. (58-09)

Sometimes missionaries boast about the number of conversions they have made. It is the Holy Ghost who convinces men and bears witness to them of the truth of the gospel. Elders might properly tell how many baptisms they performed, for that is physical; but never would it be appropriate for one to claim to himself the conversion of others. (63-01)

The Holy Ghost converts, not missionary persuasion. Our role as

missionaries is not primarily to *convince* people of the truthfulness of
the gospel. If the Lord were primarily interested in *convincing* people
of the divine nature of this work, he could, and perhaps would,
demonstrate his powers in such a way that large numbers of people
could know the truth in a relatively brief period of time. He could
speak if he chose, and all the people on earth could hear in their own
language. Or he could emblazon his words in the sky, where all could
read or see them. But if those persons thus convinced did not really
change their lives for the better, repent of their sins, and turn to him
in righteousness, they would be worse off than before and would be
more insensitive to the whisperings of the Holy Spirit.

No, the Lord is not primarily interested in having his children
only *convinced* of his work. He would like them to be *converted* to
the gospel.

As missionaries, members are vital and necessary parts of the conversion process. Sometimes in our discussions of missionary work we
state that a missionary "converts" so many persons. Actually, the
missionary does not convert anyone: the Holy Ghost does the converting. The power of conversion is directly associated with the Holy
Ghost, for no person can be truly converted and know that Jesus is
the Christ save by the power of the Holy Ghost. (77-32)

Missionaries must go in faith. In the next room is a beautiful
mural—I had to stop and absorb it a little as I came in this morning.
It shows the Lord and his apostles. . . . He is giving the last instructions to his leaders who will carry on. Perhaps he is thinking: "Go
with a faith like that of Moses, that the impossible can happen—the
sea can open, the enemy pursuers can be stopped, the east wind can
be controlled and the children of Israel can be given a new world, a
new vision, a new opportunity." Perhaps he is thinking: "There are
bushes aflame with God in every desert; if one can see and hear and
understand, revelation is there." Perhaps he is saying: "There is a
smooth stone in every shepherd's pouch and a sling in every hand and
a faith in every heart, a true marksman David for every Goliath."
Maybe he is thinking: "There is a Brigham Young with perception
and faith and understanding for every wandering company of

pioneers—a leader who will see them through to their eternal destination." Perhaps he was seeing many Wilford Woodruffs hollowing out little ponds and baptizing thousands of followers. He is saying, "Go ye into all the world and preach the gospel to every creature." . . .

I repeat my witness that he will unlock doors, and his promises may be relied upon. I know he will stay the opposition. He will mellow hearts and he will pave the way if we have faith to pursue. (74-29)

A mission can be a lesson in sacrifice. Every boy ought to save his money. You should not have to send your boys on missions. They ought to go on missions and to pay their own way. Every once in a while when I was in charge of the Missionary Department we'd get the recommendation of a young men who would say he has $1900 saved towards his mission. This boy has $2000 saved towards his mission. This boy has $1500 saved towards his mission. He is going to spend every penny of it. We have had fathers who have said, "You put your money away. I will send you on your mission. You put your money away and have it when you come back." That is not a way to teach sacrifice. The gospel is to let them spend their money and make their sacrifice. Let them give it. Do not expect the father to give everything. Even though the father has a lot of money, he must not just splurge it on his son. Let the son learn sacrifice and to get along without. (74-33)

It is not a matter of going out into the mission field to develop myself, but to go out and see how much good I can do for others, how many people that I can bring into the kingdom of God. (78-02)

Missionaries should be bold and self-sacrificing. When I read Church history, I am amazed at the boldness of the early brethren as they went out into the world. They seemed to find a way. Even in persecution and hardship, they went and opened doors which evidently have been allowed to sag on their hinges and many of them to close. I remember that these fearless men were teaching the gospel in

Indian lands before the Church was even fully organized. As early as 1837 the Twelve were in England fighting Satan, in Tahiti in 1844, Australia in 1851, Iceland 1853, Italy 1850, and also in Switzerland, Germany, Tonga, Turkey, Mexico, Japan, Czechoslovakia, China, Samoa, New Zealand, South America, France, and Hawaii in 1850. When you look at the progress we have made in some countries, with no progress in many of their nearby countries, it makes us wonder. Much of this early proselyting was done while the leaders were climbing the Rockies and planting the sod and starting their homes. It is faith and super faith. (74-01)

We must begin to think about our obligation rather than our convenience. The time, I think, has come when sacrifice must be an important element again in the Church. Remember the story of how Brigham Young and Heber C. Kimball went on their missions. Remember, they were both ill. They were in poverty. Remember how Brigham Young fell down and couldn't get up, and Grandfather Heber C. Kimball went over and tried to lift him up but couldn't because he was so weak. So he called across the street to another brother and said, "Come on over here and help me get Brother Brigham up!" The next day, both of them were on their missions. But we ofttimes must have everything ideal and perfect! (68-09)

Missionaries should take initiative. Someone has said that initiative is doing the right thing at the right time without having to be told. What a thrilling thing it is to see an aggressive, resourceful, willing, untiring, well-directed, spiritual [stake] missionary who can do the right things on his own initiative and keep on doing them to the end. (67-11)

I remember when I started in my family life, we were raising alfalfa almost totally in the valley where I lived. Alfalfa was our main crop. We also had grain and such, but cotton came into the program, so we all plowed up our alfalfa fields and put them into cotton. We could get a great deal more per acre by raising cotton than we could alfalfa. We had to return to alfalfa once in a while because it enriched the soil and we needed the alfalfa once in a while to do that; but consistent with every good reason, we grew cotton because it brought us more money to take care of our family. That is the way it is in missionary work. There is always a better way to do it. Always something that will be more efficient to use, some plan, organization or otherwise, and that we continue to pray for. (78-30)

Missionary work benefits from enthusiasm. With such a noble work one should not find it too difficult to develop enthusiasm. Enthusiasm is real interest plus dedicated energy, and this combination provides the most dynamic of all human qualities. But anyone who does not have it naturally can cultivate it by applying autosuggestion. Merely deciding that a job is going to be interesting helps to make it so. (70-08)

You should always talk with a smile. Now, a smile goes a long way. If you can't do anything else, you can smile. The newest missionary can smile. And a smile just sweetens everything. You can smile when you sing and when you talk. Do you note that with some singers, there never is a smile. You can smile. That will increase your success, if you will....

Be positive and enthusiastic. You can be positive without being enthusiastic. Enthusiasm is an effective tool. If your voice is a monotone, train it and give it variety. Let your voice be flexible. You can improve your personalities, you can all improve your voices....

A missionary down in Texas told Brother Hunter, "My goodness, with all this new enthusiasm, I wish my mission were another year. I am sorry it is coming to an end." Brother Hunter said, "Well, how long do you have?" "I have two months. Only two months left." "How many baptisms will you have?" "I don't know. I'll do it as well as I can." "Well, then how many baptisms are you going to have? This is your mission. A two-months mission. Forget the other months when you did not do well. Make these two months your mission." He said, "Then I will baptize one every week. That is eight." He saw him again at the end of the period and asked, "How many did you baptize?" "I baptized ten," was the happy answer. (62-03)

Senior companions, remember it is wrong for the junior companion to go ahead of his senior. And it is wrong for you to hold back your junior. You are a millstone around his neck. When he comes fresh into the field he is filled with the Spirit of the Lord. He is enthusiastic and believes he can convert the whole world. The president puts him with an old companion who is, let's say, "relaxed." Some of you have experienced it and you know just what it does to you, and since you cannot go ahead of your companion, you figure it can't matter much and so you too "relax." (47-11)

Missionaries should work hard. We are asking you to jump clear to the farthest stars. Quit thinking about doing a little better. (61-03)

Nephi gave us the answer. "I will go and do what the Lord commanded me to do, for I know the Lord will not command us to do anything without preparing the way." (See 1 Nephi 3:7.) He commanded you to go out and proselyte and he commanded you to go out and baptize these people. He has not commanded you to do anything that cannot be done. When you are tired, just remember that the Lord has poured his Spirit out upon them. They will come in flocks. They will. I know it. (62-03)

Missionaries should be anxiously engaged in work. My brethren, I wonder if we are doing all we can. Are we complacent in our approach to teaching all the world? We have been proselyting now 144 years. Are we prepared to lengthen our stride? To enlarge our vision? (74-01)

The missionary has a tremendous responsibility, having covenanted to teach the nations. Less than full Church service time can hardly clean the blood from casual hands. Less than a great dedication will hardly free the missionary from blame. (58-09)

Therefore, it is expedient that missionaries go to with all their hearts, minds, mights, and strengths to meet as many of the proper people under the proper circumstances as possible and bring them to a knowledge of the truth. Constant effort should be made to reduce the fringe items of activity and press into consecrated fruitful hours that time saved from the less essential things.

And now, if missionaries will refrain from counting months and days and will zealously begin to count opportunities and move forward to see that every possible soul is fully warned and hears that powerful testimony which he has, "Then...the glory of the Lord shall be thy rereward. Then shalt thou call, and the Lord shall answer." (Isaiah 58:8-9.) (56-08)

In the Doctrine and Covenants the Lord said to the Prophet Joseph Smith that there was no reason why they should go rapidly up the Ohio River and forget all those people along the banks. "But verily I say unto you, that it is not needful for this whole company of mine elders to be moving swiftly upon the waters, whilst the inhabitants on either side are perishing in unbelief." (D&C 61:3.) We're doing that, you know, in our missions. We get on a bus and travel to our field of labor, but what of our neighbors—what of the people along the way? We are doing it every day, on trains, missing those "on either side." We travel from Salt Lake City and do not feel like missionaries until we get to our field of labor, and so we just go along waiting for our assignment. The president sends us out to work in some distant place and we're still just waiting for the "go" signal till we get located, taking sometimes days for that.

It is not an eight- or ten-hour-a-day job. Your whole time, energy, and soul should be turned to this work. It is more than ten or fifteen hours; it is a twenty-four-hour job, at any place that you might happen to be. You need sufficient sleep, not any more. You, of course, should eat good wholesome food and have what rest and relaxation are necessary, but the rest of the time belongs to this program to which you have consecrated your life; a little study, yes, but hours and hours of work. I hope that you are praying all day. As you come to each home, in your heart pray for the help of the Lord in your contacts that you might make the inspired approach in the right way. Ask him to help in finding the right people. Lose yourself in this work, and all who lose themselves will find themselves. Forget the things for pleasure and self, and consistent with good health, consecrate yourself and energies to the work, and you will find the magnificent obsession that what you want most to do is to touch souls. (47-11)

Time should be used efficiently. In the matter of compensation, how would you like it if the Lord changed his policy, and instead of the compensation already promised he would substitute dollars? Suppose he now said, "Missionary, from today on I pay you $5 an hour for your services, but for only those sacred hours of actual proselyting. And there will be a special bonus of $1,000 for each person whom you baptize who is thoroughly converted." Analyze your own reactions. Would you change your work habits? Would the fringe demands on your time increase or decrease? Would letter writing, toilet making, study, recreation, travel, be reduced? Would the day be planned more methodically and efficiently? Would the Saturdays and Sundays be clean-up days, and for what would holidays be used? Would you reorganize your day? (57-08)

It was nearly one o'clock in the afternoon, and when I knocked on the door, a missionary came rushing downstairs to answer it. He was not dressed for tracting. All the day he and his companion had spent in their rooms. They said they needed to study for a certain meeting that night. I realize you must study, but you do not need to study so much that you can't find time to tell it to the people. You already know ten times as much as you can tell to the people in your field. You already know faith, repentance, baptism, and the Holy Ghost, and that's what you are advised to tell them. You are to preach repentance but nothing about eternal worlds and way back beyond the time we were created. I say, "Teach repentance to a world that needs it." You don't need to be studying all the time. Don't misunderstand me. You must study some. You have study class periods. When you are walking you are learning the gospel and discussing it, and when you are riding buses you are studying. You are studying much of the time, but in order to study you must not stay away from the homes of these people who need your message. (47-11)

Timing is critical in missionary work. You have six lessons to give them. You won't take six weeks to give six lessons if you can help it, will you? You will take two or three weeks to give six lessons. If you hold a meeting Monday night with folks, and then you set another one for next Monday night, you have given the devil a whole week to marshal his forces. The first thing he does is to tell the relatives and neighbors and they begin working on them. They find fault and laugh at them and kid them about it and then they go to church and their minister already knows about it because somebody has told him. And so he attacks them and says, "You wouldn't be interested in anything like that." And he reiterates the old, ugly stories and gives them an anti-Mormon treatise. And so, by Monday night, they do not come.

When I was a little boy down in Thatcher, my father had a big orchard and I used to help plant the trees, and I got so as a little boy I could sight those trees just as straight as an arrow. We would get them all lined up this way, and that way. We would dig big holes. We had new fresh soil to cover the roots. We put these little treelets with the little new roots down in this soft soil and filled it with water. And then when we leave and the sun goes down and we look down the rows and say, that's marvelous, that's pretty good work even if I did it. The next morning, the trees are leaning in all directions. The earth didn't settle equally and the trees are out of line, but the roots haven't taken a strong foothold yet. So, we go back again and we straighten them out and we tamp the earth around them softly and gently and see that they are settled and then go on about our work and come again the next day and in a few days the soil is settled, the tree is straight and it stands up. No need to worry anymore.

A man was laying a cement apron for his garage. A little bird lighted on it and left his footprints in the concrete. A week later his cows get out and cross the same concrete and make no impression on it. The little bird did, when it was soft. If these contacts apostatize before you can convert them, that is not their fault. There have been too many breezes to tip over the trees. They are not solid yet. So we must get them many times that first week, before the minister sees them and before the friends know about it. After they have heard two or three of these lessons the concrete is firm. The ox can walk across and will not make any impression. But that first day or two, or three, those are the critical ones. Do not just say, "Well, that was a wonderful contact there. We will surely be happy to come back next week and see her again." Don't lose these people you have already invested much of your time and energy in. (62-03)

Numerous people have been converted to the gospel; then, because the converters did not follow through, other forces came in to discourage and dampen the ardor, and never again did the same individual come so near his baptism into the Church. "Strike while the iron is hot" is an old proverb used throughout our lives. While the enthusiasm is stirred and the interest is cultivated—this is the time to act! Since baptisms in the mission field have been speeded up and the training has been reduced to a few carefully planned lessons that cover the basic messages, there have been more baptisms—proper ones—than in years gone by. Certainly the impact is greater when there is quicker movement and time is of the essence.

Many people stirred in depth by a great sermon could that very day put it into their lives, as on Pentecost Day, but if the time element is ignored and the days and the weeks and the months pass, the lesson is forgotten and the good is not accomplished. The revivalists have learned this lesson, for after they have given a particularly moving sermon, they call for the volunteers to come to be "saved."

Again, this time angle has another face. In the priesthood advancement seminar, the participants must not be made to feel that it is now or never, for if they do not accept the program this month, certainly we will try again. However, when the iron is hot, the strike should be made. (67-15)

Procrastinating investigators may miss conversion. For more than a century the living gospel has been restored on the earth, and tens of thousands of missionaries have proclaimed to millions the true message. Their testimonies have touched many hearts that said, "Yes," but whose lips with human fears resisted their accepting the gospel toward their eternal welfare. They have trembled as the Holy Ghost whispered to their spirits, "It is true—embrace it," and yet poor excuses caused their postponing action. Numerous are those who all over the world have received the witness that the gospel is true, yet have postponed baptism. Great numbers have heard of the additional scripture, the Book of Mormon, which contains the fullness of the gospel, yet never have absorbed its truths. A million copies of it found their way in a million home libraries last year and other millions previously, yet procrastinating people have failed to complete their investigation and have remained estranged. "Tomorrow I will read it," they say; "another day I will invite the missionaries to teach me." But tomorrow is a sluggard and shifts along on leaden feet, and life goes on, and storms do come, and limbs are split, and trees do fall, and eternity approaches, and our sincere call goes unheeded. (66-03)

Missionary Conduct

Missionary conduct is noticed. You are known and recognized. You can't go into even a big town without being noticed. They see you in pairs and with books. They know you are ministers and they know you are Mormon missionaries and so the Church is what you show it to be. Someone may be watching you from a fourth-story window when you least expect it. And you are the Church to these people who know that you are members of it. (47-11)

Getting along with missionary companions teaches unselfishness. I find some difficulty between missionaries. Brothers and sisters, that's one of the tests for which you are here on the proving ground. If you can't get along with your companion, how can you get along with the person you choose to live with for the rest of your life? For your own sake, you must fit into your companion's life and adjust. Perhaps your homes are different. Grit your teeth and say, "I am going to give about 90 percent and I will only take 10 percent." You have to "give and take" in every phase of life. . . . How are you going to get along with a wife or husband? Just exactly the same way, a life of unselfishness and consideration for others. You must think of the other, love him more than your own self, and then you will have success. Marriage is not something which when you press a button you get happiness. You have to make happiness in marriage the same as in the mission field. . . . Instead of fighting for your own pleasure, you are fighting for the pleasure of the other. (47-11)

Missionaries are responsible for companions. Now I ask, nearly every time I interview a missionary, "Suppose you and your companion are in a distant town and he begins to flirt and break all the mission rules, where is your loyalty?" He is puzzled at first. He would like to be true to a fellow missionary. I know what is in his mind. I ask him where is his loyalty, to a lawbreaker or to the kingdom; to a companion who will not yield to the proper rules and regulations, or to your God in heaven? (58-10)

Breach of mission rules brings remorse. Last week, I had in my office two missionaries who were highly trusted and who had betrayed the trust and, having crossed the boundaries into another foreign country, had spent six days in touring. No sexual immorality was revealed, but these highly trusted young men had betrayed their trust. All the missionaries in the mission looked to them for high standards and impeccable, unimpeachable character. And I asked them, now that they were repentant, "Was it worth it?" And they admitted it was an inordinate price and they are suffering in remorse and anguish and sorrow. They betrayed their trust, causing their families embarrassment and losing respect for themselves. It was a fabulous price to pay for six days of unauthorized fun. (65-11)

Missionaries should not write General Authorities. Will you

please advise your missionaries not to write to the General Authorities on their personal problems and their doctrinal questions. That is
your responsibility; you are in a position to answer their questions. If
you need help, you can always write to us, of course, but we are
nearly submerged with letters from the field, from individual missionaries who are seeking answers to their particular questions. (75-23)

Missionaries need to solve or forget personal troubles. It grieves
me to know you are not getting as much as you should have from
your mission.

You are not there for your own comforts and conveniences and
desires. You did not go to see the world or get experiences. You went
to forget yourself into immortality, and while in total forgetfulness of
yourself, you would bring many to total conversion to the truth.

You have learned before now that there are all kinds of missionaries—good, poor, and indifferent—and that the mere call to a
mission does not transform a boy, but that it does provide an unusual
opportunity for him to improve himself and develop his powers and
spirit. . . .

Find the cause of your physical distress, then, first, treat and cure
it, if possible; and second, learn to live with it, if it cannot be cured.

Elder, everybody nearly has a cross, especially those a little older.
As you look around you—as you walk down the street—as you sit in
a meeting, nearly every soul has something, a bad heart, a broken
body, intense pain, a great sorrow, a terrific fear, or something, but
they cover their difficulty with a broad, deep smile till those about
them know nothing of the conflicts and agonies underneath which
are well-nigh intolerable.

Walk down Market Street in San Francisco. You think the hundreds you meet are carefree folks who do not have a headache like
you, or without a voice like me or with a heart which could stop any
minute like Brother Cowley, or a broken, sore, and aching body from
neck to toe like Brother Allen, or a son in the penitentiary like Mr.
Jones, or on the verge of losing home, car, furniture, and all earthly
possessions like Brother Blue who was in to see me this week, or like
Brother Black who is being sent to the mental hospital, likely for the

rest of his life; or the mother who this week had her four little children burned to death. My dear boy, we all have our crosses. If we can get rid of them we do, but if we can't we carry them and go about our life's work.... Maybe you need to sit down and "count your blessings, name them one by one, and it will surprise you what the Lord hath done."

I have much faith in you and am positive that you will emerge from this depression to climb high and lofty hills. I have confidence in you that when you have maturely analyzed your situation you will come out the strongest missionary, the most efficient leader of all. I hope you will take proper steps to get at the bottom of your trouble and cure it if possible; then move forward to forget yourself and remember the millions of good people about you who are perishing for want of what you can take to them. Forget time. You do not want to bargain with the Lord. You agreed to give him all your time for the two years, not six or eight or ten hours. Everything you do should be either proselyting or contributing thereto. Immerse yourself in your work, totally, and forget clocks. It is on the second mile where the honest in heart are often found. It is in the extra dozen homes which are contacted after the "time to quit" has come that the new leader converts generally live. (1/14/58)

The Fruits of Dedicated Effort

God will bless the work if we do our part. There are political barriers, time and space barriers, language and other barriers which in the past have kept us from reaching the ears of the millions of honest people. But iron curtains will crumble, bamboo curtains will fall, rice paddies will be crossed, mountain peaks will be scaled, and no power—human or otherwise—can hold the work back when we do our part. (67-11)

Don't you think that it is possible to convert whole congregations now as it was done one hundred years ago in England? Have we just baited the hook for the little fish, meaning of course in numbers and not the people, or are we going out with the net and bringing in so many that we will capsize our boats as did Peter. If you just completely accept this as an obsession and keep immersed in this work, giving yourself completely and forgetting yourself, you can contact so many people, and I am sure the time will come when ministers will come in with their congregations to join the Church.

I think when we put the zeal into this program that Paul had, we will see results. We have the ability, the wisdom, and we are far better trained than Paul, at least than Peter. Is there any reason why we can't do the work that they did? Sometimes we go out to put in eight hours a day. I want to tell you that the greatest miracle of the program is to touch every life that you can and leave every life sublimely better by that touch. (47-11)

God will open doors. By comparison with the widespread breakdown of morality and discipline in the western world, the Chinese are a disciplined, industrious, frugal, closely knit people. Their moral standards are very high by modern western standards. Honesty is assumed in China as a matter of course. Crime is rare. Drug abuse and prostitution have been virtually eliminated. Premarital sex is heavily censured and is rare. Homosexuality and lesbianism are virtually unknown. Family life is strong, with old family members still given great respect and care.

In contrast with many other emerging nations, neatness and order characterize the Chinese cities and countryside. One sees no trash or garbage, no wretched hovels, no beggars. People seem to take pride in their personal appearance and the appearance of their homes and surroundings. Flies have been virtually eliminated. Disease is controlled by a nationwide system of preventive medicine.

Unfortunately, there is in China little of the freedom that is so essential to the growth of the gospel.

But things are changing. China is planning to send more than ten thousand college-age students overseas during the next two years. The doors are opening gradually. The Spirit of the Lord is brooding over these nations under a new regime that is certainly more open and more receptive to western ideas than ever before. Such cultural and educational interchanges will offer opportunities for exposure to the gospel. We must be prepared. The Lord is doing his part and is wait-ing for us to open the doors. . . .

There are almost three billion people now living on the earth in nations where the gospel is not now being preached. If we could only make a small beginning in every nation, soon the converts among each kindred and tongue could step forth as lights to their own people and the gospel would thus be preached in all nations before the coming of the Lord. . . .

I believe the Lord can do anything he sets his mind to do.

But I can see no good reason why the Lord would open doors that we are not prepared to enter. Why should he break down the Iron Curtain or the Bamboo Curtain or any other curtain if we are still unprepared to enter? (78-25)

God will bless expanded effort to teach all nations. If we do all we can, and I accept my own part of that responsibility, I am sure the Lord will bring more discoveries to our use. He will bring a change of heart into kings and magistrates and emperors, or he will divert rivers or open seas or find ways to touch hearts. He will open the gates and make possible the proselyting. Of that, I have great faith. . . .

I am under no delusion, brethren, to think that this will be an easy matter without strain or that it can be done overnight, but I do have this faith that we can move forward and expand much faster than we now are.

As I see this almost impossible demand, I believe that you brethren, our representatives, can immediately accept the challenge and in your stakes and missions explain to the people how they must increase their missionaries, how they can finance their missionaries, how they can indoctrinate and train these additional missionaries, and how, through all the agencies of the Church, they can move ahead. Here is where you come in.

A year ago now I was in Japan and Korea, and as I saw the many handsome young men joining the Church and giving leadership to its organizations, I seemed to envision a great movement when there would be thousands of local men prepared and anxious and strong to go abroad. As I have been in Mexico since that time, I seemed to envision again Mexican youth and Latins from Central and South America in great numbers qualifying themselves for missionary service within their own country and then finally in other lands until the army of the Lord's missionaries would cover the earth as the waters cover the mighty deep.

I have stated the problem. I believe there is a solution. I think that if we are all of one mind and one heart and one purpose that we can move forward and change the image which seems to be that "We are doing pretty well. Let's not 'rock the boat.' "

It can be done.

We can change the image and approach the ideals set out by President McKay, "Every member a missionary." That was inspired!

I know this message is not new, and we have talked about it before, but I believe the time has come when we must shoulder arms. I think we must change our sights and raise our goals.

When we have increased the missionaries from the organized areas of the Church to a number close to their potential, that is, every able and worthy boy in the Church on a mission; when every stake and mission abroad is furnishing enough missionaries for that country; when we have used our qualified men to help the apostles to open these new fields of labor; when we have used the satellite and related discoveries to their greatest potential and all of the media—the papers, magazines, television, radio—all in their greatest power; when we have organized numerous other stakes which will be springboards; when we have recovered from inactivity the numerous young men who are now unordained and unmissioned and unmarried; then, and not until then, shall we approach the insistence of our Lord and Master to go into all the world and preach the gospel to every creature.

Brethren, I am positive that the blessings of the Lord will attend every country which opens its gates to the gospel of Christ. Their blessings will flow in education, and culture, and faith, and love, like Enoch's city of Zion which was translated, and also will become like the two hundred years of peaceful habitation in this country in

Nephite days. There will come prosperity to the nations, comfort and luxuries to the people, joy and peace to all recipients, and eternal life to those who accept and magnify it. (74-01)

Reaching the world requires preparation and prayer. We have hardly scratched the surface, though we have opened up a number of missions for proselyting and many, many good people have accepted the truth. We are sure the Lord is conscious, as we are, of the great world outspread before us which is without the gospel. Relatively small groups huddle in scattered areas in the world, and as we attempt to go into the new nations and cultures, we come to locked doors, but know of a surety that the Lord would never command us to do something for which he would not prepare the way....

With this in mind, we have launched a prayer campaign throughout the Church and hope that all people—parents, youth, children—will join in a serious, continuous petition to the Lord to open the gates of the nations and soften the hearts of the kings and the rulers to the end that missionaries may enter all the lands and teach the gospel in the approved way.

While it looks difficult, it is not impossible....

Perhaps the Lord is testing us to see if we can supply the missionaries. So our universal prayer should have the two requests: (1) that we may get all of the missionaries that are needed to cover the world as with a blanket, and (2) when we are prepared, the Lord will open the gates. "Is anything impossible for the Lord?" We shall do our part and know firmly that the Lord will do what he has promised when the time is ripe....

The Church has grown and now it is ready to put on its beautiful garments and go and preach the gospel, and we call upon all members of the Church, old and young, to accept the challenge and to assist in this great, prolonged, and relentless effort. (75-24)

We have already asked you, and we now repeat that request, that every family, every night and every morning, in family prayer and in secret prayers, too, pray to the Lord to open the doors of other nations so that their people, too, may have the gospel of Jesus Christ.

Until we get the permission of the political authorities, we are unable to go into these many countries and proselyte there. And so we are praying that the Lord will touch the hearts of the prime ministers, and queens, the emperors, the presidents, and the rulers of all the nations in the world, so that they will make it possible for our young missionaries to go into those fields. (80-10)

New Inventions Aid Missionary Work

Technology will help spread the gospel. We need to enlarge our field of operation. We will need to make a full, prayerful study of the nations of the world which do not have the gospel at this time, and then bring into play our strongest and most able men to assist the Twelve to move out into the world and to open the doors of every nation as fast as it is ready. I believe we have many men in the Church who can be helpful to us, who are naturally gifted diplomats. I believe we should bring them to our aid and, as stated before, I have faith that the Lord will open doors when we have done everything in our power....

I believe that the Lord is anxious to put into our hands inventions of which we laymen have hardly had a glimpse....

A significant revelation states: "For, verily, the sound must go forth from this place into all the world, and unto the uttermost parts of the earth—the gospel must be preached unto every creature." (D&C 58:64.)

I am confident that the only way we can reach most of these millions of our Father's children is through the spoken word over the airwaves, since so many are illiterate. We have proved the ability of our young men to learn other languages....

King Benjamin, that humble but mighty servant of the Lord, called together all the people in the land of Zarahemla, and the multitude was so great that King Benjamin "caused a tower to be erected, that thereby his people might hear the words which he should speak unto them." (Mosiah 2:7.)

Our Father in Heaven has now provided us mighty towers—radio and television towers with possibilities beyond comprehension—to help fulfill the words of the Lord that "the sound must go forth from this place unto all the world."

Even though there are millions of people throughout the world who cannot read or write, there is a chance to reach them through radio and television. The modern transistor radio can be mass-produced by the thousands in a size that is small and inexpensive. We can preach the gospel to eager ears and hearts. These should be carried by people in the marketplaces of South America, on the steppes of Russia, the vast mountains and plains of China, the sub-continent of India, and the desert sands of Arabia and Egypt. Some authorities claim that this tiny miracle will be recorded by future historians as an event even greater than the invention of the printing press. The transistor is an eloquent answer to the illiteracy and ignorance which reign supremely over the earth. The spoken voice will reach millions of hearers who can listen through a $3 or $4 transistor but could not read even an elementary treatise. . . . (74-01)

Our program must go to the illiterate. . . . We must give them the blessings and let the Church program bless them. They have hearts and minds and feelings and loves, and they could accept the gospel by the millions if we do our full duty, and then we will seek to educate and train them. . . . It cannot happen overnight, but is a long process, but remember, we must be about our Father's business. (74-14)

Technology must be augmented by missionaries. We shall use the inventions the Lord has given us to awaken interest and acquaint people of the world with the truths, to ease their prejudices and give them a general knowledge.

We shall need to answer specific questions, and perhaps that can be done by two-way radio and TV perfected to a point beyond our present imagination. . . .

President Lee has stirred our imaginations when he recently carried on from Salt Lake City a most successful two-way program with a large group of young people in Boston—a message was sent and questions were asked and answered.

It is conceivable that such a program greatly perfected could be multiplied ten thousand times in ten thousand tongues and dialects in ten thousand places far and near. . . .

Tens of thousands of young missionaries endowed with the power from on high will follow up the proselyting. The baptism of three thousand on the day of Pentecost by the ancients will be repeated in ten thousand places, and millions will come to Zion to further convince themselves of the truth of the incomparable message.

It is inconceivable that all people will accept the gospel, for Satan will deceive and hold his subjects in an iron vice to the bitter end, but in all lands are numerous peoples who are honest in heart. (70-05)

Benefits to the Missionary

Missionary service promises great rewards. And so we go and preach the gospel to one another all over the world. To take two years out of each man's life is nothing for what is received in return. (76-32)

What are you getting for your time and service? Well maybe nothing, maybe little, or maybe everything. That depends on you. What are you promised for devoted, efficient, humble labors? Everything. Exaltation. This is based on performance. . . .

In the early days of this dispensation two young . . . fellows were asking, pleading, praying for information. It came with thunderous power and with lightning sharpness: "The thing which will be of the most worth unto you will be to declare repentance unto this people, that you may bring souls unto me, that you may rest with them in the kingdom of my Father." (D&C 16:6.) (57-08)

I promise that when you get your release, if you have forgotten yourself these years, all will have come to you, the things that you might have wished for yourself, and you shall have them all, even though you did not anticipate and wait for them. You shall have obtained knowledge and the spirit of the gospel, and your testimony shall have increased. You shall be polished; you shall have a sublime and beautiful life. (47-11)

Our Father in Heaven, bless, we pray thee, thy great missionary program. To thy thousands of missionaries all over the globe, give thy rich assurance of the divinity of the work they teach. Help them to catch the vision of the work and cease not until all the nations of the earth are warned and taught the glories of thine exalted program. Protect the missionaries from sin and temptation; help them to live guileless lives, clean, dignified, and inspired; give to them the testimony of Peter and the quenchless fire of enthusiasm of Paul, that routine work may be replaced by conscientious, inspired proselyting and that while the world is being warned to repent, that exultation may come to the missionary, to his family, to his ward and stake, so that a resurgence of spirituality and activity may result in all of Zion. (47-12)

Missionaries mature into great leaders. Don't let any boy grow to maturity without having been interviewed for a mission. Now, some of them may not be worthy. Some of them may have been immoral. Some of them may not care, and maybe they will not repent. But most of your boys, if you start very young with them when they are just little boys, will stay clean. And they'll save their money. They'll be expecting a mission, they'll go on missions, and they'll bring into this Church millions of people through the years.

They'll do something else. While they are in the mission field they'll grow and develop like a blossoming plant. You've seen it and we've seen it. We've seen it with our boys. They grow and they prosper. They learn. They change lives. They become great leaders. Some of these young missionaries just thrill us. They just amaze us with the growth and the strength that comes to them while they have been in Brazil these two years. Now, that can happen to every one of your boys. (75-03)

A mission adds maturity. Two years make a tremendous difference in the life a young man. He goes out a boy and comes back a man. He goes out immature, he comes back mature and strong, gracious, and a worker and willing to serve. He goes back to college in most cases and there he will make higher grades than he ever made before, because he has purpose in his life. He is already enjoying purpose, and now he has a new purpose. (74-16)

Returned missionaries tend to continue active in the Church. As you know, of the young men who do fill honorable missions, there is a very high percentage of them who continue to live the gospel, who marry in the temple, and who become active heads of families. (74-29)

If our boys fill missions, they are going to catch the spirit in large measure. And if they catch the spirit of the gospel, they are going to live clean lives. And when they live clean lives and catch the responsibilities, they are going to give leadership to your people. (74-25)

Forgiveness of sins can come through faithful missionary service. Nothing will prevail against the missionary who with zeal, enthusiasm, and a great loving heart goes into the lives of other people with the gospel.

In our own day in several places in the Doctrine and Covenants the Lord has promised forgiveness of sins to those who preach the gospel and bear their testimony....

So here is a good chance for all of us to spread the gospel and thereby do good to others, and at the same time make another payment on our overdraft at the Lord's bank. (55-04)

Responsibilities of Returned Missionaries

Returned missionaries should retain language skills. As I spoke to these missionaries, I urged them to learn the languages well and for permanence to perfect their speech and their understanding, to retain their acquired facility when they came home and even teach them to their wives and children. Tomorrow we may need them, and their sons and daughters, to teach the gospel through radio, television, and other inventions. (70-05)

Returned missionaries should remain enthusiastic. If you will keep up this enthusiasm which you have here, you will be great leaders in the Church. When you see a missionary who goes home and says, "I have worked pretty hard, I shall now go home and relax," you see one on his way down. You aren't going home to relax. You are going home to raise the spirituality and activity in your wards. Someone may see you and say, "He just came back from his mission. He's radical or fanatic." Stay that way if they want to call it that. Don't let it wane or decrease. (47-11)

You are nineteen years old when you are called; maybe you will be seventy-nine when you die. In those sixty years, what a powerful influence you can bear. And you must do it! You must do it because it will be a wasted life, to a degree, if any one of you go home and let your hair grow and wear sloppy clothes and do ordinary things and break the Sabbath or any other of the laws of God.

You see, the Lord has put you out here in the world, both the foreign and the local missionaries, not only to give the lessons, not only to bear your testimony, but to take this body and this soul of yours and make something of it. And your decision is today, not at the conclusion of your mission. It is today and has already been made. That decision must be right, because when you get back into the swing of things the temptation will be greater. The Lord knew what he was doing when he impressed the Brethren to have you be neat and tidy and clean in the mission field. (77-11)

Returned missionaries should continue neat grooming. Sometimes we find a returned missionary who lets his hair grow long immediately. He is very anxious to become part of the world again. He has been free of the world for a couple of years, now he would like to taste that "sweet" world, if you can call it that. We find that some young men who return home from their missions put on their overalls the very first day they get home, and that old sweater that was ready to throw away before they left. They like to put on all those things. It always pleases me when I go to a community and I see the returned missionaries still well dressed, well groomed, and have their testimony and are eager to give the message that they had been teaching all those years. (78-30)

I want you to know it is hard for me to be disappointed, and I rejoice in the blessings of the Lord daily. But a few things disappoint me occasionally and one of them is the returned missionary who, after two years of taking great pride in how he looks and what he represents, returns to this campus or some other place to see how quickly he can let his hair grow, how fully he can develop a moustache and long sideburns and push to the very margins of appropriate grooming, how clumpy his shoes [can] get, how tattered his clothes, . . . how close to being grubby he can get without being refused admittance to the school. That, my young returned missionary brethren, is one of the great disappointments in my life.

I meet with prime ministers and presidents, with sovereigns and rulers, political and public figures all over the world and one of the things they inevitably say about us (and always with warmth and appreciation) is, "We have seen your missionaries. We've seen them all over the globe, in every state and every district of the union and in most countries of the world. Without exception, they look like young men ought to look. They are clean cut, neatly dressed, well groomed and most dignified." My, that makes me proud! I'm trying to do my own little part in missionary work and that kind of comment makes me *so very* proud of our 26,000 missionaries. Then sometimes these great leaders say, "Your missionaries look like just the kind of young man I would want to take in my business, or in my government, or in my embassy, or in my law firm." Sometimes they even say, "They look just like the young man I would like to have for a son-in-law." That makes me proudest of all.

Please, you returned missionaries and all young men who can understand my concern in this matter, please do not abandon in appearance or principle or habit the great experiences of the mission field when you were like Alma and the sons of Mosiah, as the very angels of God to the people you met and taught and baptized. We do not expect you to wear a tie, white shirt, and a dark blue suit every day now that you are back in school. But surely it is not too much to ask that your good grooming be maintained, that your personal habits reflect cleanliness and dignity and pride in the principles of the gospel you taught. We ask you for the good of the kingdom and all those who have done and yet do take pride in you. (78-23)

CHAPTER 22

Redemption of the Lamanites

Great Heritage of the Lamanites

God will redeem the Lamanites. Long ago, an elderly Navajo brother told me something that I have reflected upon many times in the years that have intervened. He said: "This gospel is something we have been trying all our lives to remember; now all at once it comes back. Our fathers used to be with your fathers in the long ago, but then we came to a division in the road with a great stone in the middle. We went one way and you went the other. We went around that big rock for a long time, but now we are back together and we will always walk together from now on."

There is great understanding in this view of the history of the Lord's dealings with his people.

Many times I have tried in my mind to span the long centuries that link us to our common fathers, this Lamanite brother and I, and my soul is stirred when I remember that in our veins flows the blood of the Lord's elect—the great patriarchs of the Old Testament, such as Adam, and Enoch, and Noah. I am humbled to know that our common father was Abraham, of whom it is said there were no greater ones and through whose seed the Lord has chosen to carry out his holy purposes on the earth. Isaac, one of the great prophets of all time, and Jacob, the father of all the house of Israel, are our ancestors. Joseph who was sold into Egypt, a man of constant virtue who was in his day a savior to his father's house, is also the father of most members of the Church today, including the descendants of Lehi, Ishmael, and Zoram.

I have thought of the parting of our ways, when our fathers began to take their separate paths around that great rock that has kept us apart these many centuries, when, through disobedience and rebellion, the words of Moses began to be fulfilled: "The Lord shall cause thee to be smitten before thine enemies...and [thou] shall be removed into all the kingdoms of the earth."...

Yet the Lord has not forgotten Israel, for though Israel was to be sifted among all nations, the Lord nevertheless said, "Yet shall not the least grain fall upon the earth" and be lost. (Amos 9:9.)...

And though we have seen the beginning only, yet shall the work of bringing Israel again to Zion expand to the uttermost parts of the earth....

Of immense importance to this work of gathering the scattered branches of the house of Israel is the work of carrying the blessings of the restored gospel of Jesus Christ to the Lamanites, for the Lord's work in these latter days can in no wise be complete until these children of great promise are brought back into the fold....

We are witnesses to these events; we ourselves, both Lamanite and Gentile, have seen the removal of the great stone of our separation....

Only the most brazen soul could fail to weep when contemplating the fall of this people, and yet it was the decree of the Lord that the Lamanites should be preserved in the land, that this remnant of Joseph should again come into their promised inheritance.

When I was a young man living among the Lamanites more than seventy years ago, the destruction of the Lamanites was a stark reality. It seemed impossible to me that this broken people could ever rise from the destruction and become a mighty people once more, as the Lord had promised....

Yet the Lord's promises with regard to the Lamanites began to be fulfilled with the coming forth of the Book of Mormon in this dispensation (see Ether 4:17), and I have lived to see them begin to flourish once more and to put on their beautiful garments....

Truly our paths have met once more—we a mixed remnant of Israel, principally Ephraim, even referred to as Gentiles, now come forth out of captivity (see, e.g., 1 Nephi 13:19, 39), a people with a long history of apostasy and darkness and persecution, now only through the grace of Almighty God restored to the blessings of the gospel, that we in turn might be a blessing to the nations of the earth; and the Lamanites, also a people of disobedience now returned to the fold, whose sufferings have been sore, and punishment severe, and humiliation complete, whose affliction these many centuries must certainly be fruit meet for repentance. And what should be the nature of our reunion? We are relatives. We are brothers and sisters under the skin. We should receive each other with great joy. (75-53)

Who are the Lamanites? The term *Lamanite* includes all Indians and Indian mixtures, such as the Polynesians, the Guatemalans, the Peruvians, as well as the Sioux, the Apache, the Mohawk, the Navajo, and others. It is a large group of great people. . . .

There are no blessings, of all the imaginable ones, to which you are not entitled—you, the Lamanites—when you are righteous. You are of royal blood, the children of Abraham, Isaac, Jacob, Joseph, and Lehi. (71-08)

Lamanites share a royal heritage. I should like to address my remarks to you, our kinsmen of the isles of the sea and the Americas. Millions of you have blood relatively unmixed with gentile nations. Columbus called you "Indians," thinking he had reached the East Indies. Millions of you are descendants of Spaniards and Indians, and are termed *mestizos,* and are called after your countries, for instance: Mexicans in Mexico; Guatemalans in Guatemala; Chilianos in Chile.

You Polynesians of the Pacific are called Samoan or Maori, Tahitian or Hawaiian, according to your islands. There are probably sixty million of you on the two continents and on the Pacific Islands, all related by blood ties.

The Lord calls you *Lamanites,* a name which has a pleasant ring, for many of the grandest people ever to live upon the earth were so called. In a limited sense, the name signifies the descendants of Laman and Lemuel, sons of your first American parent, Lehi; but you undoubtedly possess also the blood of the other sons, Sam, Nephi, and Jacob. And you likely have some Jewish blood from Mulek, son of Zedekiah, king of Judah. The name *Lamanite* distinguishes you from other peoples. It is not a name of derision or embarrassment, but one of which to be very proud.

You came from Jerusalem in its days of tribulation. You are of royal blood, a loved people of the Lord. In your veins flows the blood of prophets and statesmen; of emperors and kings; apostles and martyrs. Adam and Enoch sired you; Noah brought you through the flood; in the sandals of Abraham you walked from Ur of the Chaldees to your first "promised land"; you climbed in faith with Isaac to the holy mount of sacrifice; and you followed the path of hunger to Egypt with your father Jacob, and with Joseph you established, under the Pharaohs, the first great known welfare project.

You are the children of Ephraim and Manasseh, Joseph's sons, and of Judah his brother. Your fathers crossed the Jordan River with Joshua, and after centuries' absence you were again in your first "promised land."

The Genoese Italian boy, with his three ships from Spain, thought he had discovered a new world, but he was thousands of years late. Your people were on the shores to welcome Columbus and his men. Cortez, Pizarro, and their contemporaries, conquerors, exploiters found your "old people" already decadent intellectually, culturally, and spiritually, but populous in your wealth and poverty. Norwegian Vikings are said to have discovered this land before Columbus, but your people were already scattered from the Arctic to the Antarctic before there was a Norway or Vikings.

When your prophet Lehi led you out of Jerusalem about 600 years B.C., you brought with you the best of the culture of Egypt and Palestine and of the then known world; also the written language of your fathers and the holy scriptures from Adam down to your own time, these engraved upon brass plates. You brought with you an absolute knowledge of the God of Abraham, Isaac, and Jacob, and maintained for a long time thereafter open vision and clear, unobstructed lines of communication with your Lord.

In the new "promised land" the seeds you brought from Palestine multiplied and brought to you great prosperity on the extensive lands you farmed. In your explorations you found gold, silver, copper, and iron, and processed brass and steel. Your factories turned out machinery and tools for agriculture, architecture, and road building. And with those tools you builded cities, such as you knew in Egypt and Palestine, highways which would carry your traffic, and temples after the order of the world-famed Solomon's Temple.

Your culture was beyond the imagination of moderns. In your prosperity you wore "silks, scarlets, fine-twined linen, and precious clothing." (See Alma 1:29.) You bejeweled yourselves with ornaments of gold and silver and other metals, and with precious stones. You were fabulously wealthy in your day.

In the long years of prosperity and righteousness, your wealth graced temples and synagogues. You read, quoted, and lived by the teachings of the books of Moses and the inspired writings of the prophets. Your people knew faith such as has seldom been found upon the earth. There were years of conflict and wickedness, but also years of peace and unparalleled goodness.

You produced prophets of stature. There were your Lehis, Nephis, and Jacobs; your Almas, Abinadis, and Mormons. Your Lamanite prophet, Samuel, who prophesied of the Christ, had few peers and perhaps no superiors. (59-05)

Lehites are mixed with other peoples. Through the centuries of movements, discovery, exploration, settlement, and colonization of the people of this land, it is not impossible that there could have seeped across the Bering Strait a little Oriental blood, as claimed by some people, and possibly a little Norse blood may have crossed the North Atlantic. But, basically, these Lamanites, including the Indians, are the descendants of Lehi who left Jerusalem six hundred years before Christ. (67-07)

All through Book of Mormon history you will find that the Lamanites joined the Church and became Nephites and the Nephites fell away and became Lamanites. When you think of the Lamanites you could think that is this little group over here. As I read the Book of Mormon, it means *all* the children of Father Lehi, from his time to the present day, were Nephite-Lamanites. We are happy to use that name and we hope you are. If anyone ever makes any derogatory statements about Lamanites, you say, "Turn to the Book of Mormon, 3 Nephi, and read what the Savior said." (75-18)

Lamanites shared apostasy with all Israel. I have met some who are a little bit ashamed that they are Lamanites. How can it be? Some would rather define themselves as Nephites, or Zoramites, or Josephites, or something else. Surely there must be a misunderstanding. Would they separate themselves from the great blessings the Lord has promised to his covenant people? Would they cast off their birthright? For the Lord himself has chosen to call these people Lamanites —all the mixed descendants of Father Lehi, and Ishmael, and Zoram, and Mulek, and others of the Book of Mormon record; all of the literal seed of the Lamanites, "and also all that had become Lamanites because of their dissensions." (D&C 10:48.)

You who are Lamanites remember this: Your Lamanite ancestors were no more rebellious than any of the other branches of the house of Israel. All the seed of Israel fell into apostasy and suffered the long night of spiritual darkness, and only through the mercy of God have any of the branches been saved from utter destruction—the gentile-Ephraimite mixture first, and then the Lamanite remainder of Joseph, that the saying might be fulfilled, "the last shall be first, and the first last." (Matthew 20:16.) You who are Lamanites remember: In your past are men such as the Nephi and his brother Lehi who, cast into prison while in the service of the Lord as missionaries, were so righteous and full of faith that though they were encircled by fire they could not be burned; whose faces shone like that of Moses when he descended from the mount. (75-53)

"Lamanite" is an honorable name. This is an *honorable* name. It

was the Lord who so designated them, and every descendant of Lehi should proudly say, "I am a Lamanite, and I am proud of my heritage."

The Book of Mormon was written "to the Lamanites, who are a remnant of the house of Israel" for the express purpose of convincing "the Jew and Gentile that Jesus is the Christ, the Eternal God," and that the Lamanites might know their ancestors and the spectacular promises of the Lord to them. (See Book of Mormon title page.) (67-07)

I am wondering if some of the Indians are giving a connotation to the name that the Lord never intended, and this to their own disadvantage and discouragement....

I would be proud if I had Lamanite blood in me and would not hesitate to announce it. (2/27/63)

Indians take pride in their heritage. We often hear Indian youth bearing their testimonies, saying with considerable emotion: "I am *proud* that I am an Indian. And, I am *proud* that I am a Mormon Indian." Now that they are tasting the pride of accomplishment and feeling the spirit of acceptance, a new dignity has come to them and they are a proud, delightful people.

There are numerous white people who have Indian blood in their veins who now are beginning to point to it with pride, whereas in the old days it was a matter to be kept in the background. (65-08)

Indians are Saints first. Now, then, as proud as they are to be Indians, they are not Indians first. They are Latter-day Saints. I am not English first though my family came from England. I am a Latter-day Saint first. (65-01)

Gentiles and Lamanites alike are from Joseph. The Lamanite is a chosen child of God, but he is not the only chosen one. There are many other good people including the Anglos, the French, the German, and the English, who are also of Ephraim and Manasseh. They, with the Lamanites, are also chosen people, and they are a remnant of Jacob. The Lamanite is not wholly and exclusively the remnant of the Jacob which the Book of Mormon talks about. We are *all* of Israel! We are of Abraham and Isaac and Jacob and Joseph through Ephraim and Manasseh. We are *all of us* remnants of Jacob. (77-39)

Lamanites Scattered for Disobedience

The promised land was given on condition of righteousness. About twenty-five centuries ago, a hardy group left the comforts of a great city, crossed a desert, braved an ocean, and came to the shores of this, their promised land. There were two large families, those of Lehi and Ishmael, who in not many centuries numbered hundreds of millions of people on these two American continents. Their scriptures and records taught them of God. They had many blessings, and many promises. They were given, by the creator of this land, a clear title to the Americas—a certificate of title, free and clear of all encumbrance. There was, however, one condition: They must serve the Lord their God if they were to retain title to their property. Their wickedness brought on wars, which scattered and destroyed them and divided them into two factions, the Nephites and Lamanites, and finally they peopled the continents. The years went on apace; the Savior came to them after his resurrection. . . . The Savior so inspired them that for twice the period of our own Church history they were righteous and were devoted to their Heavenly Father. And then came prosperity and wealth. The sins of the world overtook them, and for about one hundred and seventy years both factions were wicked, very wicked indeed, until the great battle on Cumorah when the Nephites were literally destroyed. The prophet Mormon recounted sixty thousand people lying in their blood in death, and this because of their wickedness. Their enemies were permitted to come upon them. . . .

The penalty for their wickedness was that they were to be scattered and driven, cursed and scourged. They were to be "cut off from the presence of the Lord." Scales of darkness were to be their curse, and they were to become "as chaff is driven before the wind" or "a vessel is tossed about upon the waves without sail or anchor or anything wherewith to steer her." . . .

As the colonists came from Europe and settled along the Eastern seaboard, the great "push" continued. Mile by mile we crowded them back. When the Indians resisted our encroachments, we called them "murderous redskins" and continued our relentless aggression. When they killed us "whites," we called it massacre, but when we took their lives, we termed it a necessary riddance of a menace. We were fighting for their lands and rivers and forests and minerals, but they were fighting for their rights, their homeland, their families, their very lives.

I would not justify any evil that the Indians ever did, but can we not see that they were on the defensive, fighting for their liberty, for independence and to perpetuate their rights to the promised land to which they had title from the Creator?

But the laws had been broken. They had forfeited their rights because they had failed to keep the commands of God. The prophecies must be fulfilled, and the plan of God must now be consummated. It was necessary, for the ultimate good of the Indian himself, that the Gentiles must come from foreign shores to become "nursing fathers" to these benighted people; the Pilgrims and Puritans had come to settle this land; the Revolutionary War had to be fought and won so that peace and freedom and liberty could be established here, and so that the gospel could be restored, and this that the record of the ancestors of the Indians might come forth, and the gospel of Jesus Christ be made plain to them. (47-02)

War brought degradation. Your downfall came when your people walked the way to war. Revenge and hatreds made cold wars flame into hot shooting ones. Baptismal waters became rivers of blood. The parched earth policy was followed, and enemy armies surged back and forth across the land, tramping down crops, squandering livestock, and changing a stable people into nomads. . . .

In all this prolonged period of war and drivings, your immediate ancestors lost their written language, their high culture, and worst of all their knowledge of God and his work. Faith was replaced by fear, language by dialects, history by tradition, and a knowledge and understanding of God and his ways by idolatry, even to human sacrifice. Your priceless thousand years of history, laboriously engraved on plates of metal, and the brass plates of the Old Testament, were hidden by your inspired prophet-historian in the sacred hill in a stone box, to remain undisturbed until a wise Heavenly Father should bring them forth for you, their resting place known only in heaven.

In the business of killing human beings, there could be little inclination to face a Creator and a gospel of peace; the many-times restored gospel of Jesus Christ was lost; and spiritual darkness enveloped the whole world. (59-05)

Lamanites Suffered Persecution and Injustice

The Indians were victimized. I now speak of a people who went down from Jerusalem to America, and who after many days fell among thieves which stripped them of their raiment and wounded them and left them half dead—a people who were victimized by men considered by them to be gods, stripped of their gold and precious things, dispossessed of their cities, their homes, their soil; robbed of their liberty, enslaved, and branded as cattle—a people who fought their way down the bloody path of civil war into degradation, filth, idleness, idolatry, cannibalism—a people who were stripped of their homeland, their forests, their grazing lands, their game, and their fish, pushed by the invaders into ever-decreasing territory until they were imprisoned in reservations and exploited. (49-03)

The Cherokee "trail of tears" illustrates suffering. The expulsion and the exodus of the Cherokee Indians from the east—from the Carolinas and Georgia and Tennessee and that area—is a blood-curdling story and not less perhaps in sorrow and distress than the story of the exodus of the Mormons from Illinois to the valleys of the mountains. We lost on the trek six thousand out of sixty thousand, or about 10 percent of our people. The Cherokees lost four thousand out of sixteen thousand, or 25 percent, as they were herded—literally herded—moved from their homes and their lands which they had had from time immemorial. (58-08)

The Navajos were deprived of promised schools. Not till they [the Navajo] were starved out did they finally raise the flag of truce. We took them over into New Mexico on a reservation, and after four years of starvation and freezing and hopelessness for them we imposed upon them a treaty. They were to commit no more depredations and were to be given that vast area of territory of little value. They were to receive some small allowances. They were to require their children to go to the schools, and we were to furnish them a school and a teacher for every thirty children. If you could go with me to the reservation and hear those Navajo parents plead for schools for their children, you would realize how greatly we have failed to live up to our part of that treaty of 1868. There are more than twenty-four thousand children of school age, but with all the government schools, plus those schools operated by churches, only about 5,100 of the little folk can hope to get into a school. The nearly nineteen thousand children yearn in vain for schooling. In September, ambitious parents send these little ones long, rugged miles to a school building, only to find it locked for want of repair or a teacher. Back those long rugged miles, even longer now, they trudge home to wait another year, still hoping for better luck next time. There is a big backlog with many thousands of children and adults who have never had a day of school, and unless we change our policy, these defrauded people in the heart of this rich and educated nation will still be illiterate fifty years hence. The median school years for the Navajo is .9 of a year, as compared to 5.7 years for the average Indian and 8.4 years for our own children. (47-02)

Unhealthy living conditions prevailed. The health conditions are deplorable. They have but one full-time dentist for sixty-three thousand people and no field nurse or doctor, though they should have twenty-five or thirty of each to even approach rural standards. The birth rate is high, but the death rate is also very high, being sixteen per thousand as against 10.5 for the nation and 6.36 for the Church. The large family lives in the dirt hogan, being one small circular room with dirt floor, no windows, and with a stove or fire in the center. All members of the family sleep on sheep pelts on the floor. There is no privacy, practically no furniture or equipment. There are no sanitary conveniences inside or out. With a single towel, a common cup, no hot water nor disinfectants, it is easy to see why trachoma, impetigo, and other skin diseases run through the family, and why dysentery, venereal diseases, and tuberculosis run rampant. In a survey of thirty-one families it was found that three in each family had tuberculosis. In their scattered condition, and with such limited hospital facilities, many lie in their hogans, coughing in the air, spitting on the floor, to finally die on the ground floor without medical assistance. Their numerous superstitions bind them down. The use of peyote is increasing, and its demoralizing opiate effect is most destructive. The Indians have learned all the white man's vices, and liquor is "at flood stage" there. And thus they live without the power to raise themselves from the deplorable situation. They cannot lift themselves by their bootstraps. They must have help. (47-02)

Biased historians distorted Indian history. The historian has used the *white* ink to write his stories when he was emphasizing honor and integrity and honesty and glory and heroism; but when he was emphasizing terror and death and raids and scalpings and betrayals and broken covenants, always it was with bold *red* ink. (69-03)

The Indians suffer and need help. How I wish you could go with me through the Indian reservations and particularly Navajo lands and see the poverty, want, and wretchedness, and realize again that these are sons and daughters of God; that their miserable state is the result, not only of their centuries of wars and sins and godlessness, but is also attributable to us, their conquerors, who placed them on reservations with such limited resources and facilities, to starve and die of malnutrition and unsanitary conditions, while we become fat in the prosperity from the assets we took from them. Think of these things, my people, and then weep for the Indian, and with your tears, pray; then work for him. Only through us, the "nursing fathers and mothers," may they eventually enjoy a fulfillment of the many promises made to them. Assuming that we do our duty to them, the Indians and other sons of Lehi will yet rise in power and strength. The Lord will remember his covenant to them; his Church will be established among them; the Bible and other scriptures will be made available to them; they will enter into the holy temples for their endowments and do vicarious work; they will come to a knowledge of their fathers and to a perfect knowledge of their Redeemer Jesus Christ; they shall prosper in the land and will, with our help, build up a holy city, even the New Jerusalem, unto their God.

Only in our doing all in our power to restore these people to their heritage, can we even approach a justification for having taken their promised land. May the Lord assist us all to see our full duty respecting these people and give us the courage and determination to guarantee that they have the education, culture, security, and all other advantages and luxuries that we enjoy. (47-02)

Intolerance is hypocritical. Above all the problems the Indian has, his greatest one is the white man—the white man, who not only dispossessed him, but the white man who has never seemed to try to understand him—the white man who stands pharisaically above him—the white man who goes to the temple to pray and says, "Lord, I thank thee that I am not as other men are." The white man is his problem.

There are too many Pharisees among the white men, who are worried about unwashen hands; and too few Galileans who heal palsied hands and teach untutored minds and comfort broken hearts.

There are too many "superior" ones who call, "Unclean! Unclean!" as they pass by the deprived and who leave them to suffer, and too few who will humble themselves and ease the way and give opportunity. . . .

There are too many who pray on their knees for fulfillment of prophecy and too few who let their hearts be softened and become "nursing fathers and mothers" to the downtrodden.

There are too many willing that the Lamanites "blossom as the rose upon the mountains," but too few missionaries and proselyters and friends to assist.

There are too many who ascribe the degradation of the Indian as his just due, and too few willing to remove the curse and to forgive him.

There are too many priests who "pass by on the other side of the road," and too few Good Samaritans to "bind up the wounds and to pour in healing oil."

There are too many Levites who pull their robes about them and pass by with disdain, and too few who "take them to the inn" and give them tender treatment and care.

There are too many curiosity seekers, and too few laborers. We are constantly reminded of the eloquent scripture given to the Nephites: "Wherefore, a commandment I give unto you, which is the word of God, that ye revile no more against them because of the darkness of their skins; neither shall ye revile against them because of their filthiness; but ye shall remember your own filthiness." (Jacob 3:9.)

Again, there are too many who push down and tread under, and too few who lift, encourage, and help. (53-05)

Whites are not superior to Indians. Recently there came to my desk a letter, anonymously written. Generally the wastebasket receives all such messages, written by people who have not the courage to sign their statements. But this time I saved it. It reads in part as follows:

> I never dreamed I would live to see the day when the Church would invite an Indian buck to talk in the Salt Lake Tabernacle—an Indian buck appointed a bishop—an Indian squaw to talk in the Ogden Tabernacle—Indians to go through the Salt Lake Temple—
> The sacred places desecrated by the invasion of everything that is forced on the white race....

This letter now goes into the fire also, but it gives me the theme for the words I wish to say today.

If Mrs. Anonymous were the only one who felt that way! However, from many places and different directions I hear intolerant expressions. While there is an ever-increasing number of people who are kind and willing to accept the minority groups as they come into the Church, there are still many who speak in disparaging terms, who priestlike and Levite-like pass by on the other side of the street. . . .

In the letter quoted, there is the suggestion of a superior race! From the dawn of history we have seen so-called superior races go down from the heights to the depths in a long parade of exits. Among them were the Assyrians, the Egyptians, the Babylonians, the Persians, the Greeks, and the Romans. They, with more modern nations, have been defeated in battle, humiliated and crushed in economic life. Is the implication of Mrs. Anonymous justified, that the white race or the American people is superior? . . .

The Lord would have eliminated bigotry and class distinction. He talked to the Samaritan woman at the well, healed the centurion's kin, and blessed the child of the Canaanitish woman. And though he personally came to the "lost sheep of the house of Israel" and sent his apostles first to them rather than to the Samaritans and other Gentiles, yet he later sent Paul to bring the gospel to the Gentiles and revealed to Peter that the gospel was for all. The prejudices were deep-rooted in Peter, and it took a vision from heaven to help him to cast off his bias. The voice had commanded: "Rise, Peter; kill, and eat," when the vessel descended from heaven containing all manner of beasts, reptiles, and fowls. Punctilious Peter expressed his life-long prejudices and habits in saying, "Not so, Lord; for I have never eaten any thing that is common or unclean." Then the heavenly voice made clear that the program was for all. "What God hath cleansed," it said, "that call not thou common." Peter's long-sustained prejudices gave way finally under the power of the thrice repeated command. When the devout Gentile Cornelius immediately thereafter appealed to him for the gospel, the full meaning of the vision burst upon Peter and he exclaimed, "God hath shewed me that I should not call any man common or unclean." (See Acts 10:11-28.) . . .

And now, Mrs. Anonymous, when the Lord has made all flesh equal; when he has accepted both the Gentiles and Israel; when he finds no difference between them, who are we to find a difference and to exclude from the Church and its activities and blessings the lowly Indian? Have you read the scriptures, ancient and modern? Have you felt the magnanimity of the Savior, his kindness, his mercy, his love?

If the Lord were to acknowledge a superior race, would it not be Israel, the very people whom you would spurn and deprive? Do you carry in your veins as pure Israelitish blood as those whom you criticize? Do you find any scriptures, my critic, which would show that the Christ would exclude the Lamanite Israelites from the waters of baptism, from the priesthood, from the pulpit, or from the temple? Did not the Lord remove the Amalekites, Midianites, Canaanites to make place for the chosen Israel, and when centuries later he saw the impending destruction of Jerusalem and the temple, and when it was imminent that Judah and Israel were to be captured and exiled, did not the Lord send a righteous few, under Lehi, to find and colonize this American land, this choicest land under heaven? Did he not lead and teach and punish and forgive this same people through a thousand hectic years of varied experience, and did he not reiterate frequently his willingness to forgive and his eagerness to bless this very people? Did not the Lord show special and preferred interest in his Israel? Did he not reserve for them alone his personal visits and ministrations? ...

If Mrs. Anonymous would exclude the Indian from the temple, how could she justify the Lord's provision that they would assist in the building of the New Jerusalem with its temple?

O intolerance, thou art an ugly creature! What crimes have been committed under thy influence, what injustices under thy Satanic spell!

If it be so wrong for fraternization and brotherhood with minority groups and their filling Church positions and pews and pulpits of the Lord's Church, why did the Apostle Peter maintain so positively: "God ... put no difference between us and them." (Acts 15:8-9.)

And, "What God hath cleansed, that call not thou common." (Acts 11:9.)

"Of a truth I perceive that God is no respecter of persons: But in every nation he that feareth him, and worketh righteousness, is accepted with him." (Acts 10:34-35.) ...

It is most evident that all of the many prejudiced ones fail to catch the spirit of the gospel and the teachings of the Christ as they hiss and spurn and scoff and criticize. The Lord said in Matthew: "Judge not, that ye be not judged. For with what judgment ye judge, ye shall be judged." (Matthew 7:1-2.)...

I remember that the Lord was long-suffering with ancient Israel. For a long time he endured their pettiness, listened to their eternal complaining, revolted at their filthiness, groaned at their idolatries and their adulteries, and wept at their faithlessness; and yet finally forgave them and led the rising generation of them into the promised land. They had been the victims of four centuries of destructive background of servitude, but consistent now with their continued faithfulness, every door was opened to them toward immortality and eternal life.

Here he has the Indian or Lamanite, with a background of twenty-five centuries of superstition, degradation, idolatry, and indolence. He has loathed their wickedness, chastised them, brought the Gentiles to them for nursing fathers and mothers, and (it would seem) has finally forgiven them. Their sufferings have been sore, their humiliation complete, their punishment severe and long, their heartaches many, and their opportunities reduced. Has he not now forgiven them and accepted them? Can we not now forgive and accept them? Ancient Israel was given forty years. Can we not allow at least forty years of patient and intensive proselyting and organizing among modern Israel before we judge too harshly? (54-02)

We still find race prejudice and intolerance on the part of many non-Indians concerning the Lamanites. Often they are excluded from cafes, hotels, schools, and are made to feel unwelcome in church gatherings.

You have read of their weaknesses and sins and crimes. You have seen them languishing under their curse. They have suffered much and endlessly. But have you recalled their virtues, their strengths, and the promises and covenants made to them?

Have they not eaten husks long enough? Has not their day of restoration come? Can we not forgive their trespasses, that we might in turn be forgiven?

Intolerant people reproachfully indict these red men, saying: But they are illiterate! Yes. They are mostly illiterate, but when the conquerors fulfill solemn treaty obligations and give to the children of the conquered an education equal to that received by the children of the conquerors, illiteracy will be eliminated.

Prejudiced people who enjoy limitless luxuries say: But the Indian is economically a failure. Yes. His economic status is deplorable, but when his education and opportunity parallel our own, he will be independent and self-supporting.

A people surrounded by wealth, hospitals, doctors, and nurses say: But the red man is not sanitary—he lives in filth and disease! Yes. The solitary places given him in exchange for his rich and fertile America are barren, dry, and not conducive to good living. But give him accredited schooling in our own incomparable educational system, so that he may buy medical service, enjoy modern utilities, live in good homes, and he will not be diseased nor unclean.

People who have inherited the good things of an invaded land say of the victims: They are inferior! Yes. They do suffer from an inferiority complex that is well-nigh annihilating. Prisoners of war, slaves, and downtrodden people usually develop such a complex. But give them comparable education and opportunity with their non-Indian brother, acceptance and brotherly love by him, and they will emerge a rejuvenated people, the equal of the white man. (49-03)

Responsibility to Help Lamanites

Reservation Indian children need extra help. There should be discrimination [by you Seminary teachers] in their favor. Go to all lengths; go all out. Bring them in. Interview them, counsel them, help them find their way. Many Indians know little of how to take care of money. Many spend it as fast as they get it. . . . They can't be blamed too much. They are like children. They know little about budgeting, saving. They love each other devotedly, but they have many weaknesses. Many like to drink just like the white man does. White man has his liquor in his refrigerator and he drinks a little, and many of them, the social drinkers, never get drunk. But for the Indian, liquor has been against the law, so when he got some liquor he drank it all at once before the policeman saw him and threw him in jail. And so he got drunk and lay in the gutter, and so we hate him; but we don't hate the white man who carries his liquor a little more easily. . . .

These people are probably not more immoral than your own boys and girls. . . . The girls more often get pregnant and they marry or they have children out of wedlock more than your white girls. The white youth are more subtle in all the sin and transgression, and they don't get caught nearly so often. I don't think they are less moral than your white boys and girls. And I interview hundreds of our own boys and girls. But the Indians are crude about it, and it is less hidden, more obvious. . . . Get into their lives. Counsel and advise them. Warn them. Love them! Teach them chastity and honor and integrity. Protect them against themselves. (58-08)

The Indian needs opportunity. The chasm between what he is and what he will be is *opportunity.* It is ours to give.

Basically the Indian is intelligent, affectionate, responsive, honest, stable, and is of believing blood. There is every reason to be assured that the red man will remain loyal and true to the gospel and the Church, once he is brought into the fold. (49-03)

If there ever was a people in the world who needed friends— sympathetic, understanding friends—it is the Lamanites. They are trying now to pick themselves up by their bootstraps, but it's a rather difficult thing when they have neither straps nor boots. It isn't enough just to give them freedom to grow and develop; they need nursing fathers and mothers; they need friendly hearts; they need understanding. (53-05)

Integration is superior to segregation. The scriptures are filled with prophecies in connection with this people. Why, there are few subjects on which there is so much revealed. The prophecies must and will be fulfilled. They can be fulfilled only by our help. We must go out and do this work.

Now, we have tried segregation of the Indians in this nation for a hundred years. It did not work. Segregation has been almost a complete failure. Many of them are still "blanket" Indians, after a century of segregation. The program of the Church must be one of assimilation and integration. We must take them into our arms, into our hearts, into our Relief Societies, into our sacrament meetings, into our Sunday Schools, into our Primaries, into our Mutual, and into our hearts. (49-06)

Whites like Indians only at a distance. Too often too many of us love the Lamanites at a distance, as long as we don't have to wait on them or teach them or wash them or feed them. We like them as long as we can just read about them in the Book of Mormon or elsewhere, or if we can see them in their colorful costumes as a museum piece. (58-08)

Lamanites are like a glider needing a tow plane. The Lamanites have been carrying their burdens—mental, spiritual, physical burdens—since the great destruction, those hundreds of years ago. Is it not time that we must lift their burdens from their backs, their heads, their minds, their hearts? We, the Gentiles, from Puerto Montt to the Bering Strait, must help to bear their burdens; their poverty must be eased; their opportunities enlarged; their ignorance replaced with knowledge; their limitations reduced by opportunity. The gospel must be preached, for it is a catalyst which in its numerous manifestations will ease the loads. . . .

Sometimes I am sad when I see the lassitude and disregard and the ignoring by us of this important program of reclaiming the Lamanites. . . .

There are still many among us who hiss and spurn and do little to advance the cause of the Lamanite. . . .

A sail plane furnishes thrills and exhilarating experience to pilots in the great empty sky. . . .

But there is one thing the glider lacks. It has no engine; it cannot lift itself into the sky. An airplane tows it aloft some two or three thousand feet and the tow line is cut loose and the glider is then free to soar and to bank and to rise and to descend.

The sail plane is like the Lamanite; the tow plane, like the gospel and the Church; the tow line, like the programs of the Church.

The Lamanites may be well born—good blood, great ancestry, alert minds, fertile brains; but the tens of millions of them are bound by traditions, superstitions, and ignorance—these weighty elements. They cannot raise themselves by their bootstraps for they have no boots and no straps. They cannot soar aloft without a towing starting power.

The glider may be well built of piano wood, covered with expensive materials. It could even be painted with gold leaf and studded with diamonds, but unless there is a tow plane with a tow line to lift it, the glider would remain grounded until it rotted from age and weather. But given the lift, it can then cut loose from its parent unit and soar and bank and turn and fly to lofty elevations, to high altitudes, to unbelievable accomplishments.

The Lamanite must have initial help—a power beyond himself. The Church and its people can give this lift. The organizations of the Church and its individuals can tow them aloft. We shall not need to worry much about them after they are soaring in the clouds and have the feel of accomplishment and security. We find and develop for them the updrafts; we show them the instruments; we show them through shadow teaching and fly with them. Soon they can soar. Individuals like the hawks will find the thermals, and then they may fly and soar to their hearts' content.

The catalyst is the gospel of Jesus Christ—nothing else can tow them to high, lofty areas where they belong. (67-07)

Education is the key to progress. Education is the sure way. I believe the schools to which Indian children should go should be like in California where they attend state schools, not Indian schools where they associate only with other Indians. They will much quicker take their place in the community, state and nation. They learn the language better and faster. When well trained in the white culture the red man will be able to compete in employment, politics, leadership. To compete, the Indian must do so on the level of the dominant race. This country is dominated by the white man. The red man is limited yet in power, influence, and strength.

The many ignored treaties of the past furnish ample evidence that you must attack the problem in the white man's way, through the ballot and the courts and Congress. There must be representation in the law-making bodies. Universal education of the Indian is the answer. When the majority of Indians are voting; when they are prospering in the professions and in business and enjoying all the luxuries thereby; when they are prominent and influential in their cities, counties, states, and nations, perhaps then they can influence the honest fulfillment of past treaties if then they still feel the need of them. (51-04)

The LDS Indian student placement program is unselfish. I doubt that there is any single program of the gospel itself or any phase of the program of our Church which is more selfless or which can transform a deprived people more rapidly, more completely, more thoroughly, than the Indian student placement program. (68-10)

As we began to bring into the Church many faithful Indians, almost their first desire was that their children should have the schooling and church training which the non-Indian children enjoyed. Indian families working among us here in our beet, cotton, or potato fields saw the luxury enjoyed by white children who were well fed and well dressed, in comfortable homes, going to excellent schools daily. They saw their own little deprived fellows who must follow the family to the faraway fields so parents could earn money to feed them. Their dreams and yearnings finally forced the affectionate parents to become bold enough to approach a white employer: "Would you let our little girl stay with you and go to school after we have gone back to the reservation? She will be a good girl and cause you no trouble."

With the earnestness in their eyes and the pleading in their voices, who could resist? The experiment began. A few children were left in homes. They were happy and grateful. The foster parents were pleased, and neighbors wished also to participate. On the reservation, natural parents told their neighbors, who also wrote pleading letters for their own children. The number increased to twenty, sixty, eighty, and then last year to 253. It grew like Topsy. Arrangements at first were between natural parents on the reservation and willing foster parents in Utah; but when the Church determined to give it support, the plan was given legal status and brought under the Utah State Department of Public Welfare children's service, through the state license of the Relief Society. . . .

This is our adventure in good citizenship and righteous living, our experiment in human relationships carried on by this, The Church of Jesus Christ of Latter-day Saints. Knowing the origin and destiny of the red men and believing the promises of God as recorded in the Book of Mormon, our people are willing to sacrifice for the progress and development of these whose deprivations pyramided mountain high but whose curse is now being lifted. Hundreds more sacrificing Latter-day Saints may yet have the opportunity of providing temporary homes for Lehi's children to get an education and to learn the gospel and to become Church leaders.

This is not a proselyting program, for we bring from the reservations those Indian children who are already members of the Church and whose families generally are members. The program will make good young people, stalwart adults. It will fortify them against the evils of the world; it will train them to become self-sufficient; it will develop them into leaders prepared to return to their own people and bring to them the benefits which can come from education.

This program has many advantages: It has at once the multiple advantages of the boarding school, the day school, the home, the refining and cultural influences of an improved community.

The children are taught in superior schools, fully accredited, and among the best in the nation. They have sufficient companionship of their own race to retain their pride in and love for their own people, for in the same community and school are other Indian young people. They have the environment of the best communities where are found the least in the world's vices and the most of its culture and refinement. They retain their family ties with natural parents by correspondence, pictures, relayed reports, and also letters through the case workers, and they return to their homes for the summer months to keep bound their home and family loves and loyalties. They grow naturally into the culture of America at its best, attending with a minority of their own group and a majority of the non-Indian children, activities in school, community, church, and family. They are not institutionalized but individualized and become recognized members of the family where they are integrated and "counted in" for every family pleasure, adventure, or sacred experience.

Our program is unique. Here is no family of marginal income who must take in a boarder to supplement the family living. Here is no mercenary care. But here non-Indian families in a very real and lovable way absorb the Indian children as new members of the family. These families, give, give, and give as only dedicated people will give. There is no remuneration for them; but their total compensation for the food, clothes, shelter, care, and love they give is the satisfaction which comes in giving opportunity for an enriched life to one who could not otherwise have it.

We rejoice in the greatly accelerated schooling of Indian children by the government, the states, and other churches and agencies, but we present this program of training in home and school and community as the finest program conceived of man for the rapid and permanent advancement and progress of the Indian child so long deprived. Let them have one generation of this sustained program, and see a new Indian world of prosperity, culture, and happiness.

In conclusion we say: God bless these selfless hundreds of families who have become and are yet to become "nursing fathers and mothers" who will continue to carry the chosen children of the ancient prophet Lehi "in their arms and upon their shoulders." (56-12)

Progress in Improving Conditions of Indians

The placement program produces leaders. Both foster families and Indian families benefit from the experience. The placement program was inspired of the Lord. We have watched many of our Lamanite youth become strong leaders in the Church, and many have taken their place as leaders in their communities and in the world. (79-04)

Indians are growing in numbers. About the time some of us here were born, President Heber J. Grant said in Mesa, Arizona, at the temple dedication: "We beseech thee, Oh, Lord, that thou wouldst stay the hand of the destroyer from among the descendants of Lehi who reside in this land."

Until then the Indians were dying. It was a vanishing race. From about 1927, the Indians have changed the direction. Where there were sixty or seventy thousand Navajos then, today there are, I suppose, nearly twice that many. The government and other agencies have quit scattering the Indians. We are now gathering them. President Grant said: "And give unto them increasing virility and more abundance that they shall not perish as a people." They are growing in number, growing in strength. The mortality age has greatly bettered. Children are not often dying at birth. There is less hunger and thirst. There is less freezing. They are living more normal lives.

"That from this time forth," the president said, "they may increase in numbers and in strength and in influence."

That was yesterday that President Grant said this. Today is the fulfillment, that all the great and glorious promises made concerning the descendants of Lehi may be fulfilled in them. This is still coming with all the strength of a great new awakening day. (68-10)

Indians are improving economically. In the 1940s these [Navajo] people had an average income of about $81 a year. They lived upon land which to most of us seemed worthless, barren, and forbidding; but the desolate land is producing oil and gas and uranium and coal and lumber, and many millions of dollars are flowing into the tribal treasury. In early days it was each family for itself; today the Tribal Council is using wisely these vast sums to build highways and hospitals and schools and to give scholarships. What a strange paradox, that the land given to the Indians, desolate and unwanted, turns out to be the source of many blessings! Was not Providence smiling on these folks and looking toward this day?

Not only the southwest Indians, but Lamanites in general, are facing an open door to education, culture, refinement, progress, and the gospel of Jesus Christ. The Church has spent its millions in Hawaii and New Zealand and other islands to provide schools for the young Lehites. Surely, no descendants need go now without an education, and schools in Mexico will be followed by schools in other nations. Surely the number of deprived ones is being reduced, and opportunity is knocking at their door. Hundreds of Lamanites are serving in mission fields in both Americas and in the islands of the sea. Lamanites are exercising their priesthood and rearing their families in righteousness. A new world is open to them, and they are grasping the opportunities. God bless the Lamanites and hasten the day of their total emancipation from the thralldom of their yesterday. (60-10)

Lamanites are growing spiritually. We have come to the day of the Lamanite, and the work is going forward. We have come to the day when the Indians and other Lamanites are entering the Church by the tens of thousands, when they are being organized and taught leadership. We now have Lamanite bishops, high councilors, branch presidents, and numerous priesthood and auxiliary officers with faith and integrity. We find Indians who are paying their full tithing, their contributions toward the buildings and maintenance, and fast offering. Here is a young man who delayed his mission a few months to go back to the reservation to activate his family who had drifted. Here are groups of Indians who want no help, but only opportunity, who desire no welfare, want no coddling. The gathering is at hand. They are coming out of the dust. They are fast being restored to the knowledge of their fathers. (65-08)

Lamanites have a brilliant future. Yesterday you roamed the wilderness in feast or famine; today you are finding security in education and industry; and tomorrow your destiny will be brilliant in self-sufficiency, faith, fearlessness, and power. Like the Israelites released from Egyptian bondage, you have been promised deliverance from your foes of superstition, fear, illiteracy, and from the curses of want and disease and suffering.

Yesterday you traveled uncharted oceans, wandered over trackless deserts, lost your high culture, your written tongue, and your knowledge of the true and living God. Today you are arising from your long sleep and are stretching, yawning, and reaching. Tomorrow you will be highly trained, laying out highways, constructing bridges, developing cities, building temples, and joining in inspired leadership of the Church of your Redeemer. . . .

Your Lord has permitted you to walk through the dark chasms of your ancestors' making, but has patiently waited for your awakening, and now smiles on your florescence, and points the way to your glorious future as sons and daughters of God. You will arise from your bed of affliction and from your condition of deprivation if you will accept fully the Lord, Jesus Christ, and his total program. You will rise to former heights in culture and education, influence and power. You will blossom as the rose upon the mountains.

Together you and we shall build in the spectacular city of New Jerusalem the temple to which our Redeemer will come. Your hands with ours, also those of Jacob, will place the foundation stones, raise the walls, and roof the magnificent structure. Perhaps your artistic hands will paint the temple and decorate it with a master's touch, and together we shall dedicate to our Creator Lord the most beautiful of all temples ever built to his name. (59-05)

The Lamanites must rise in majesty and power. We must look forward to the day when they will be . . . sharing the freedoms and blessings which we enjoy; when they will have economic security, culture, refinement, and education; when they will be operating farms and businesses and industries and shall be occupied in the professions and in teaching; when they shall be organized into wards and stakes of Zion, furnishing much of their own leadership; when they shall build and occupy and fill the temples, and serving in them as are the natives now in the Hawaiian Temple where I found last year the entire service conducted by them and done perfectly. And in the day when their prophet shall come, one shall rise "mighty among them . . . being an instrument in the hands of God, with exceeding faith, to work mighty wonders." (2 Nephi 3:24.)

Brothers and sisters, the florescence of the Lamanites is in our hands. (47-06)

Sources

Listed below are more than 700 sermons and writings considered in selecting passages for inclusion in this book. They are listed in approximate chronological order. For sermons and articles the first two digits in the code indicate the year (00 means the year is unknown), and the last two digits identify items within each year. Citation to 66-04 would mean the fourth item in 1966. Insofar as information is available it is listed in this order: (1) title, (2) audience or occasion, (3) date, (4) place of publication, and (5) subject, if not suggested by the title. For general Church meetings held in Salt Lake City the place is not specified. Some sermons were used on more than one occasion, but usually only the first place is indicated; examples of such reused sermons are 49-01, 54-05, 57-02, 65-02, 65-03, 66-02, 71-12, 71-18, and 73-01. Where not otherwise specified, general conference and area conference sessions were general sessions.

A number of sermons have been separately published as small books: *Marriage* (Deseret Book, 1978) contains 49-01 and 76-52; *My Beloved Sisters* (Deseret Book, 1979) contains 78-24 and 79-19. Some have been widely distributed in pamphlet form, *e.g.,* "Tragedy or Destiny," "Hidden Wedges," and "Abraham: An Example to Fathers." Still others are included with sermons of other General Authorities in topical collections, such as *Youth of the Noble Birthright* (Deseret Book, 1960), *Prayer* (Deseret Book, 1977), *Women* (Deseret Book, 1979), and *Priesthood* (Deseret Book, 1981.)

Sermons and Articles

00-01	Dedicatory prayer, Yakima Branch
00-02	"Reverence in Our Chapels"
00-03	Commencement for Institute of Religion (service)
00-04	"The Spiritual Aspects of Body Preservation" (resurrection)
00-05	"Today and Tomorrow" (responsibility of Sunday School to build faith)
00-06	"Wait, Be Patient" (faith in skeptical environment)
25-01	"A Prophecy and Its Fulfillment," *Imp. Era* (1925), 1146 (H. C. Kimball prophecy)
30-01	"Spiritual Training in the School" (religion in public schools)
32-01	Commencement at Virden, NM, High School (5/20/32) (knowledge is power)
33-01	"'Great Treasures of Knowledge, Even Hidden Treasures,'" *Liahona* (1933), 392 (Henry Eyring)
33-02	"President Samuel O. Bennion," *R. S. Mag.* (June 1923), 327
34-01	St. Joseph Stake Primary (12/16/34) (Christmas)
35-01	"Friendships Through Community Service," Rotary Club (5/13/35)

35-02 Commencement at Eden, AZ, 8th grade and Ft. Thomas, AZ, High School (knowledge is power) (cf. 32-01)
36-01 43rd district of Rotary (July 1936) (spirit of Rotary is to do good)
38-01 "Prayer," address over KGLU, Safford, AZ (9/11/38)
38-02 Description of visit to Rome, 1937 (sufferings of early Christians)
39-01 "The Abundant Life," commencement at Safford, AZ, High School (money is not goal)
40-01 "I Travel the Greyhound Bus, a Soliloquy" (Arizona, about 1940)
41-01 "How Well Do Latter-day Saints Pay Their Obligations?" *Imp. Era* (1941), 206
42-01 Funeral of Terry Mortensen, AZ (5/23/42)
42-02 "The Duncan Flood," *Imp. Era* (June 1942), 364
42-03 Funeral of Virginia Curtis, Thatcher, AZ (11/9/42)
43-01 Funeral of Janie Pace, AZ
43-02 "Response to a Call," Gen. Conf., *Imp. Era* (Nov. 1943), 678; excerpted in *Instructor* (Aug. 1967), 302 (call to Twelve)
43-03 "What I Read as a Boy," *Children's Friend* (Nov. 1943) (Bible)
44-01 Talk on WWDC, in Washington, DC (3/4/44) (Church history)
44-02 "Book of Mormon," Craig, CO (March 1944)
44-03 "The Sabbath Day," Gen. Conf., *Imp. Era* (May 1944), 285; FPM 267
44-04 "The Peace Which Passeth Understanding," BYU (6/4/44) (Christ gives spiritual peace in world of hate)
44-05 "Heber C. Kimball: The Prophet, Peacemaker, Man of Destiny, Man of God," H. C. K. family reunion (6/14/44)
44-06 "'If for My Name's Sake,'" Pioneer Day sunrise service, SLC (7/24/44)
44-07 "Ye May Know the Truth," Gen. Conf., *Imp. Era* (Nov. 1944), 671; PKSO 18 (testimony)
45-01 "Your Responsibility Continues," *The Trumpeteer,* Central States Mission newsletter (March 1945) (missionary work)
45-02 Sacrament meeting, prepared for Gen. Conf. 4/6/45 but not delivered
45-03 "'Thy Son Liveth,'" Gen. Conf., *Imp. Era* (May 1945), 253 (death) (cf. 52-04; 55-15)
45-04 Dedication of Idaho Falls Temple (9/25/45) (genealogy, temple building)
45-05 "'In Mine Own Way,'" Gen. Conf., *Imp. Era* (Nov. 1945), 652 (righteous living)
45-06 "Foundations for Peace," NBC Church of the Air (10/7/45); *Imp. Era* (Nov. 1945), 660 (righteousness brings peace, America to be free)
46-01 Funeral of Joseph S. Peery (fall 1946)
46-02 "Family Prayer," *Children's Friend* (Jan. 1946), 30
46-03 "Spiritual Vision," BYU (3/19/46)
46-04 "The Pattern of Martyrdom," Gen. Conf., *Imp. Era* (May 1946), 286
46-05 Commencement at Safford, AZ, High School (5/16/46) (service)

46-06	"My Redeemer Lives Eternally," Gen. Conf., *Imp. Era* (Nov. 1946), 703; FPM 69 (Christ, restoration)
47-01	"Miracles," BYU (2/11/47)
47-02	"Weep, O World, for the Indian," Gen. Conf., *Imp. Era* (May 1947), 291 (wretched conditions)
47-03	Radio talk over CJOB, Grand Forks, ND (Indian problems)
47-04	"The Greatest Miracle," *R.S. Mag.* (April 1947), 219 (resurrection)
47-05	Talk over WCAZ, Carthage, IL (7/13/47) (pioneer trek)
47-06	"The Lamanites—'And They Shall Be Restored,'" Gen. Conf., *Imp. Era* (Nov. 1947), 717
47-07	"Elder Kimball Records Visit with the 'Most Unforgettable Character' Ever Met," *Church News* (11/1/47), 9
47-08	Lamanite Conf., Mesa, AZ (11/2/47) (courage and faith)
47-09	"Mis Queridos Hermanos y Hermanas," Lamanite Conf., Mesa, AZ (11/3/47); *Instructor* (Oct. 1952), 292 (bright future of Lamanites)
47-10	Lamanite Conf., priesthood meeting, Mesa, AZ (11/3/47) (lead by love)
47-11	Lamanite Conf., missionary report meeting, Mesa, AZ (11/4/47) (on being good missionaries)
47-12	Dedicatory prayer, 4th ward of Palmyra Stake, Spanish Fork, UT (11/23/47)
47-13	"U.S. Breaks Navajo Pact, Church Leader Charges," *Deseret News* (11/28/47)
47-14	"Deaf Ears Meet Appeal of Indians for Schools," *Deseret News* (11/29/47)
47-15	"Hope Sees a Star for the Sons of Lehi," *Church News* (12/20/47)
47-16	Dedicatory prayer, Hunter, UT, ward chapel (12/21/47)
48-01	"The Navajo—His Predicament," *Imp. Era* (Feb. & April 1948), 76 & 210 (government failure to educate and build roads)
48-02	"Build or Destroy," Gen. Conf., *Imp. Era* (May 1948), 282 (children's character)
48-03	Dedicatory prayer, Navajo-Zuni mission home (May 1948)
48-04	Funeral of Orley Glenn Stapley, Phoenix, AZ
49-01	"An Apostle Speaks About Marriage to John and Mary," *Imp. Era* (Feb. 1949), 74; FPM 125; *New Era* (June 1975), 2
49-02	Primary Conf. (4/1/49) (teaching Indian children)
49-03	"'Who Is My Neighbor?'" Gen. Conf., *Imp. Era* (May 1949), 277 (responsibility to Indians)
49-04	Dedication of Elberta Branch chapel, Santaquin-Tintic Stake, UT (4/24/49) (righteous living) (cf. 66-10; 71-18; FPM 259)
49-05	"When Is One Rich?" Salt Lake *Tribune-Telegram* (5/28/49) (attitude toward riches)
49-06	"'Unwashen' Hands vs. Hearts," R.S. Conf. (9/28/49), *R.S. Mag.* (Dec. 1949), 804 (working with Indians)

49-07   "'Except Ye Repent...'" Gen. Conf., *Imp. Era* (Nov. 1949), 712; FPM
          187 (forgiving)
49-08   Radio talk, Ft. Wayne, IN (Oct. 1949) (church and missionary program)
50-01   Funeral of Pearl Nelson Udall
50-02   "He Gave His Life" (March 1950) (Easter)
50-03   "Lamanites Attempt to Preserve Independence," Gen. Conf., *Imp. Era*
          (June 1950), 376
50-04   "Delbert Leon Stapley—An Apostle of the Lord," *Imp. Era* (Nov. 1950),
          873
50-05   "'The Work Among the Lamanites,'" Gen. Conf., *Imp. Era* (Dec. 1950),
          980 (Indian missionary work)
50-06   Dedicatory prayer, Meeteetse Branch, Big Horn Stake, WY
51-01   "A Style of Our Own," BYU (2/13/51); FPM 161 (modesty)
51-02   Funeral of President George Albert Smith (during Gen. Conf. April 1951)
          (work with Indians)
51-03   "Be Valiant," Gen. Conf., *Imp. Era* (June 1951), 432
51-04   League of Indian Nations Conf., Independence, MO (8/29/51) (Mormon
          interest in helping Indians)
51-05   Dedicatory prayer, Oklahoma City Branch, Central States Mission (Nov.
          1951)
51-06   Dedicatory prayer, East Wichita Branch, Central States Mission (Nov.
          1951)
51-07   Indian relations dept. of R.S. Conf. (10/3/51) (teach Indians of Christ)
51-08   "The Spirit Giveth Life," Gen. Conf., *Imp. Era* (Dec. 1951), 899 (living
          gospel)
52-01   Meeting of Council of the Twelve (1/9/52) (love for work)
52-02   "Whom Shall I Marry?" BYU (3/4/52)
52-03   "'Tis Not Vain to Serve the Lord,'" Gen. Conf., *Imp. Era* (June 1952),
          417; FPM 221 (rewards of obedience)
52-04   Funeral of William Layton, SLC (5/13/52) (death) (cf. 55-15)
52-05   "The Florescence of the Lamanites," R.S. Conf. (10/1/52), *R.S. Mag.*
          (Feb. 1953), 76 (service to Indians)
52-06   "Faith Precedes the Miracle," Gen. Conf., *Imp. Era* (Dec. 1952), 924;
          FPM 3
52-07   "Teach Children," Pachuca, Mexico, Stake (11/2/52)
52-08   Dedicating 7 Central American countries for missionary work, Guatemala
          City, Guatemala (11/16/52)
53-01   Rotary district conf., Flagstaff, AZ (fighting for liberty)
53-02   "With Songs in Their Souls," *Instructor* (March 1953), 68 (faithfulness of
          Lamanite Saints in Central America)
53-03   "Profane Not the Name of Thy God!" NBC Church of the Air (3/29/53);
          Imp. Era (May 1953), 320

53-04   "The Lamanites Are Progressing," Gen. Conf., *Imp. Era* (June 1953), 432 (Indian missionary work)

53-05   "The Lamanite," BYU (4/15/53); *Imp. Era* (April 1955), 226 (Book of Mormon promises, Indian education)

53-06   "Keep Your Money Clean," Gen. Conf., *Imp. Era* (Dec. 1953), 948

53-07   Dedicatory prayer at Institute of Religion, Los Angeles (12/11/53)

54-01   "Matthew Cowley, or The Man of Many Friends," *R.S. Mag.* (Feb. 1954), 78

54-02   "The Evil of Intolerance," Gen. Conf., *Imp. Era* (June 1954), 423; FPM 293

54-03   Funeral of Caroline Romney Eyring, Pima, AZ (died 4/23/54)

54-04   "Be Ye Clean! Five Steps to Repentance and Forgiveness," BYU (5/4/54); FPM 169

54-05   "What Manner of Men Ought Ye to Be," Jordan Seminary graduation, Sandy, UT (5/14/54) (cf. 72-05)

54-06   "Blind Obedience or Obedience of Faith," Gen. Conf., *Imp. Era* (Dec. 1954), 897

55-01   "A Picture and a Piece of Cloth" (interview by Howard B. Pearson about flannelboard use), *Instructor* (March 1955), 74

55-02   "The Fourth Article of Faith," *Instructor* (April 1955), 108 (gift of the Holy Ghost)

55-03   Ordination of Bishop Harold Turley

55-04   " 'That Ye May Bring Souls Unto Me,' " Primary Conf. (4/1/55) (Primary as missionary force)

55-05   Funeral of Edwin Marcellus Clark

55-06   " 'To Kick Against the Pricks,' " Gen. Conf., *Imp. Era* (June 1955), 425; FPM 305 (fighting against Church and God)

55-07   Heber C. Kimball family reunion (6/15/55) (H.C.K.)

55-08   Sheffield district, England (7/11/55) (testimony)

55-09   "I Will Fight Your Battles," Kidderminster, England (July 1955) (war)

55-10   "Revelation," Swedish mission (about June 1955)

55-11   Youth in Paris (Aug. 1955) (chastity)

55-12   Dedication of Swiss Temple (9/11/55) (temple work)

55-13   Dedication of Swiss Temple (9/15/55) (temple ordinances)

55-14   "Report on Europe," Gen. Conf., *Imp. Era* (Dec. 1955), 944 (faithfulness of European Saints, war)

55-15   "Tragedy or Destiny," BYU (12/6/55); *Imp. Era* (March 1966), 178; FPM 95 (death) (cf. 52-04)

56-01   "Church with a World-Wide Mission Field," *Millennial Star* (about 1956), 232

56-02   "Religion Is Life," U of AZ (Feb. 1956) (purpose of life)

56-03   "Temples—Hundreds of Them," dedication of Los Angeles Temple
         (3/12/56)
56-04   "The Resurrection Is Real," NBC Church of the Air (4/1/56)
56-05   "Bear False Witness," prepared for April 1956 Gen. Conf. but not
         delivered (gossip)
56-06   "Jesus the Christ," Gen. Conf., *Imp. Era* (June 1956), 436
56-07   "Dialogue Between Heber C. Kimball and His Posterity," H. C. K. family
         reunion (June 1956)
56-08   "Every Member a Missionary" (July 1956)
56-09   "Revelation in the Church Today," Portland Stake Conf. (9/9/56)
56-10   "Immodesty in Dress," Portland Stake Conf., MIA session (9/9/56)
56-11   "The Assistants to the Council of the Twelve Apostles," *Imp. Era* (Nov.
         1956), 790
56-12   "The Expanded Indian Program," Gen. Conf., *Imp. Era* (Dec. 1956), 937
         (student placement program)
56-13   Dedicatory prayer, Institute of Religion, Thatcher, AZ (12/9/56)
56-14   "A Birthday Gift for the Lord," Monument Park 2nd Ward, SLC
         (12/23/56); excerpted in *Instructor* (Dec. 1957), 360; *Instructor* (Oct. 1966),
         C4; and Era of Youth, *Imp. Era* (Dec. 1962), 988
57-01   BYU Stake Conf. (1/13/57) (welfare, revelation)
57-02   "The Oils of Righteousness," BYU Stake Conf. (1/13/57); FPM 249
         (diligence) (cf. 78-10; 78-21)
57-03   New York Stake Conf. (2/23/57) (true church, just deserts)
57-04   Council of Twelve (4/10/57) (throat operation, dream)
57-05   "The Spirit of Co-operation," *Imp. Era* (Sept. 1957), 632
57-06   10th anniversary of centennial trek group (7/22/57)
57-07   "One Silent Sleepless Night" (Sept. 1957) (reminiscences while recovering
         from operation on throat) (Bookcraft, 1975)
57-08   Letter to Eastern States missionaries (Sept. 1957) (missionary work)
58-01   "Women, Wonderful Women!" *R.S. Mag.* (Jan. 1958), 4 (influence of
         mothers on sons of Helaman)
58-02   "Relief Societies in Primitive Times?" *R.S. Mag.* (March 1958), 148
         (charitable works of women in scriptures)
58-03   "The Real Meaning of Easter," *Instructor* (April 1958), 100
58-04   "Are You a Modern Nicodemus?" Gen. Conf., *Imp. Era* (June 1958), 417;
         FPM 13 (skepticism)
58-05   " 'Knighted' in the Field: Henry Dixon Taylor, Assistant to the Twelve,"
         Imp. Era (June 1958), 397
58-06   "Heber C. Kimball's Message to His Posterity," H. C. K. family reunion
         (June 1958) (righteousness)
58-07   " 'Whatsoever Things Are Honest . . .' " BYU (June 1958)
58-08   "The Children of the First Covenant," seminary and institute teachers,
         BYU (6/27/58) (Indian sufferings and student placement)

58-09   Message for Houston Stake missionaries (Sept. 1958)

58-10   BYU student leadership conf., Sun Valley, ID (Sept. 1958) (leadership, dances, fraternities)

58-11   "Messengers of Faith and Charity," Monument Park Stake visiting teachers convention, SLC (9/16/58); *R.S. Mag.* (April 1959), 212; *Ensign* (June 1978), 24

58-12   "Search the Scriptures," Gen. Conf., *Imp. Era* (Dec. 1958), 940 (officers called by divine authority)

58-13   UT State U (11/25/58) (life likened to school)

58-14   "Christ and Alexander," Church employees Christmas program (12/18/58) (cf. 64-04)

59-01   "The Importance of Choosing a Proper Mate," California Mission Conf. (Jan. 1959)

59-02   "'Whom Say Ye...'" Gen. Conf., *Imp. Era* (June 1959), 440 (Christ)

59-03   "Those Previous, Early Years," stake junior Sunday School coordinators (4/5/59) (importance of children)

59-04   Dedication of Auwaiolimu Ward chapel, HA (8/25/59) (sacrifice)

59-05   "To You...Our Kinsmen," Gen. Conf., *Imp. Era* (Dec. 1959), 938 (Book of Mormon heritage of Lamanites)

59-06   "That You May Not Be Deceived," BYU (11/11/59) (apostasy)

59-07   "The Significance of Miracles in the Church Today," *Instructor* (Dec. 1959), 396 (faith)

60-01   Series of articles in *Church News,* 1960, under titles "Leader Asks Youth—What Is Your Norm?" "Perfection Is Our Goal," "Why the Hurry, Mother?" (early dating), "'Like All the Nations'" (following the world)

60-02   "Dance Pattern for Youth," closed circuit radio fireside for youth (Jan. 1960); in *Youth of the Noble Birthright* (Deseret Book, 1960), 73

60-03   "Youth and the Car," radio talk to youth (2/14/60); in *Youth of the Noble Birthright* (Deseret Book, 1960), 81

60-04   "Chastity, Its Price Above Rubies," radio talk to youth (Feb. 1960); in *Youth of the Noble Birthright* (Deseret Book, 1960), 91

60-05   Draft of address for Gen. Conf. missionary meeting (4/4/60) (stake missions)

60-06   "A Prophet Is Born," Gen. Conf., *Imp. Era* (June 1960), 426; *Instructor* (Dec. 1966), 474; FPM 323 (Joseph Smith)

60-07   Indians from southern Utah stakes, St. George, UT (April 1960) (do good, educate children)

60-08   Dedication of Heber C. Kimball home, Nauvoo, IL (7/3/60)

60-09   "'To His Servants the Prophets,'" *Instructor* (Aug. 1960), 256 (revelation) (cf. 73-05)

60-10   "The Day of the Lamanites," Gen. Conf., *Imp. Era* (Dec. 1960), 922 (faith of Indians, student placement program)

61-01　"The Unforgettable Holy Land," Gen. Conf., *Imp. Era* (June 1961), 422
61-02　Funeral of C. Rulon Harper, Pocatello, ID (April 1961)
61-03　Meeting on stake missionary work, East Los Angeles Stake center (4/23/61)
61-04　"Listen to the Prophet's Voice," Gen. Conf., *Imp. Era* (Dec. 1961), 936 (10 commandments)
61-05　"Prayer," BYU (10/11/61); excerpted in *New Era* (Mar. 1978), 14; *Instructor* (April 1966), 132; FPM 199
62-01　" 'Seek Ye First...,' " in *Life's Directions* (Deseret Book, 1962), 173 (getting spiritual knowledge)
62-02　Berlin Mission Conf. (1/15/62) (testimony)
62-03　Berlin Mission Conf. (1/15/62) (missionary work)
62-04　Hamburg Stake Conf. (1/21/62) (families, character, revelation)
62-05　Hamburg Stake Conf. (1/21/62) (righteousness)
62-06　"Delbert L. Stapley," *Imp. Era* (Feb. 1962), 90
62-07　"Spiritual Communication," Gen. Conf., *Imp. Era* (June 1962), 434; FPM 47 (revelation)
62-08　"The Ordinances of the Gospel," seminary and institute teachers, BYU (6/18/62)
62-09　" 'Spouses...and None Else,' " Gen. Conf., *Imp. Era* (Dec. 1962), 926; *Millennial Star* (April 1970), 2; FPM 141 (marital fidelity)
62-10　"Timing" (fall 1962) (early dating)
62-11　Monument Park 2nd Ward, SLC (12/16/62) (Christ, repentance)
63-01　"Humility," BYU (1/16/63); *Imp. Era* (Aug. 1963), 656
63-02　"The Book of Vital Messages," Gen. Conf., *Imp. Era* (June 1963), 490; FPM 329 (Book of Mormon)
63-03　Baccalaureate, Ft. Thomas, AZ, High School (5/14/63) (faith)
63-04　Baccalaureate, Eastern AZ College, Thatcher (May 1963) (existence of God)
63-05　BYU graduation (8/22/63) (advice to graduates)
63-06　"The Power of Books" (written with Camilla E. Kimball), *R.S. Mag.* (Oct. 1963), 724
63-07　"Keep Mothers in the Home," Gen. Conf., *Imp. Era* (Dec. 1963), 1071; FPM 115
63-08　LDS psychiatrists (Nov. 1963) (sex problems, repentance) (incorporated in 64-05)
63-09　Wells Stake, SLC (11/28/63) (gratitude) (68-12; 75-33)
63-10　Dedication of Southwest Indian Mission home, Holbrook, AZ (12/8/63) (Indian prospects)
64-01　"The Fourth Commandment," M Man-Gleaner Manual for 1963-64, 265 (Sabbath)

64-02   "Integrity," BYU (2/25/64); FPM 233
64-03   " 'For They Shall See God,' " Gen. Conf., *Imp. Era* (June 1964), 496; FPM 83 (prophets have seen God)
64-04   Dedication of Holbrook, AZ, Seminary (5/10/64) (Christ)
64-05   Seminary and institute teachers, BYU (7/16/64) (aiding transgressors, homosexuality) (cf. 63-08)
64-06   "So Long as You Both Shall Live," Gen. Conf., *Imp. Era* (Dec. 1964), 1054; excerpted in *Ensign* (Aug. 1974), 2 (temple marriage)
64-07   "The Ten Virgins," Monument Park 2nd Ward, SLC (12/22/64); FPM 249 (righteousness) (cf. 57-02)
65-01   Indian students, BYU (1/5/65) (intermarriage, Church for all)
65-02   "Love vs. Lust," BYU (1/5/65); Central Utah Stakes Young Adult devotional, Manti, UT (7/10/74); *Instructor* (April 1967), 138; FPM 151
65-03   "Revelation Is Continuous in the Lord's True Church," U of UT Institute (1/22/65); FPM 21
65-04   Organization of German ward, SLC (1/25/65) (learning English, holding positions)
65-05   " 'Accept, O Lord, Our Offering of This House,' " *Imp. Era* (Feb. 1965), 134 (dedication of Oakland Temple, follow prophet)
65-06   "Stone Without Hands," Gen. Conf., missionary meeting (4/2/65)
65-07   "Home Training—The Cure for Evil," Gen. Conf., *Imp. Era* (June 1965), 512
65-08   "Lamanite Prophecies Fulfilled," BYU (4/13/65)
65-09   "The Four Corners of the Earth," farewell of mission president W. Jay Eldredge, Jr. (summer 1965)
65-10   "Save the Youth of Zion," MIA June Conf. (1965); *Imp. Era* (Sept. 1965), 760 (chastity)
65-11   "Honor," Ricks College (9/27/65)
65-12   "A Changing World for the Barry Begays," Gen. Conf., *Imp. Era* (Dec. 1965), 1130; FPM 351 (bright future for Indians)
65-13   Dedication of Ecuador for teaching gospel, Quito (10/8/65)
65-14   Dinner honoring Ettie Lee, Los Angeles (11/6/65); *California Intermountain News* (12/2/65) (sacrifice)
66-01   "Edward C. Eyring, Our Grandfather," included in Caroline E. Miner, ed., *The Life Story of Edward Christian Eyring 1868-1957* (1966), 122
66-02   "Kings and Priests," BYU (2/15/66) (meeting challenge)
66-03   "Hidden Wedges," Gen. Conf., *Imp. Era* (June 1966), 523 (bad habits, procrastination)
66-04   Dedication of Colombia for preaching gospel, Bogota (5/11/66)
66-05   "God Is Not Dead," BYU (5/27/66); *Millennial Star* (Aug. 1966), 249; FPM 59

66-06   Beneficial Life convention, San Diego (1966) (honesty, hard work)

66-07   "What I Hope You Will Teach My Grandchildren," seminary and institute teachers, BYU (7/11/66) (honesty, chastity, faith)

66-08   Meeting of Council of Twelve (8/17/66) (faith of Abraham, sacrifice of Christ)

66-09   "I've Been in Heaven," dedication of Dillon, MT, chapel addition (9/11/66) (cf. 49-04; 71-18)

66-10   "Continuous Revelation," Gen. Conf., *Imp. Era* (Dec. 1966), 1105; similar talks to U of UT Institute (1/22/65) and UT State U Institute (3/24/65); FPM 21

66-11   "Stand by Your Guns," UT State U Institute (10/14/66); U of UT Institute (10/13/66); FPM 213 (protection against sin)

66-12   Missionary Conf., Cordoba, Argentina (11/17/66) (testimony)

66-13   Meeting of Council of Twelve (12/7/66) (gospel power)

67-01   Format for Quarterly Conference

67-02   "Honesty," LDS Businessmen's Association, San Francisco (3/6/67); FPM 233

67-03   Meeting of Council of Twelve (3/8/67) (remembering Christ)

67-04   "By Grace Are Ye Saved, by Works Exalted," prepared for April 1967 Gen. Conf. but not used

67-05   Seminar of representatives (April 1967) (home teaching)

67-06   "The Mistletoe," Gen. Conf., *Imp. Era* (June 1967), 60; FPM 225 (alcohol, tobacco, immorality)

67-07   "The Lamanites: Their Burden—Our Burden," BYU (4/25/67)

67-08   Dedication of Bolivia for preaching gospel, La Paz (6/1/67)

67-09   "Sewing Machines for the Pelotas Branch, Brazil," *R.S. Mag.* (July 1967), 504 (anonymous gift for Christ's birthday) (cf. 56-14)

67-10   "Education for Eternity," BYU faculty and staff (9/12/67); excerpted in *Ensign* (July 1977), 2 (religion in education)

67-11   "The Church Faces the Future in Missionary Work," Regional Representatives (9/25/67)

67-12   Format for Quarterly Conference, Regional Representatives

67-13   "Liquor: The Devil in Solution," Gen. Conf., *Imp. Era* (Dec. 1967), 52

67-14   "No Greater Call," Sunday School Conf. (10/1/67) (importance of teachers)

67-15   "How to Evaluate Your Performance," General Authorities (10/18/67); *Imp. Era* (Oct. & Nov. 1969), 12 & 22; (effectiveness in Church callings)

67-16   Meeting of Council of Twelve (12/17/67)

68-01   "How to Use Music More Effectively" (1/22/68)

68-02   "Indian Student Placement, Before and After," Gen. Conf., stake presidents meeting (4/5/68)

68-03   "Render Unto God That Which Is God's," Gen. Conf., *Imp. Era* (June 1968), 81; FPM 281 (tithing)

68-04   "Cancer and Its Fellows," UT Div. of Am. Cancer Soc. (4/13/68); *R.S. Mag.* (April 1969), 244 (control of diseases)

68-05   "Follow Leaders," U of UT Institute (4/14/68) (resurrection, righteousness, follow leaders)

68-06   "In the World But Not of It," BYU (5/14/68) (righteousness) (cf. 68-05)

68-07   Heber C. Kimball family reunion (6/16/68) (H. C. K.)

68-08   Seminar for new mission presidents (6/25/68) (mission work)

68-09   "Circles of Exaltation," seminary and institute teachers, BYU (6/28/68) (planning life)

68-10   Gen. Conf., stake presidents meeting (Oct. 1968) (Indian student placement)

68-11   "'Wisdom and Great Treasures of Knowledge, Even Hidden Treasures,'" Gen. Conf., *Imp. Era* (Dec. 1968), 99; FPM 273 (Word of Wisdom, testimony)

68-12   Thanksgiving, North Ogden Kiwanis Club, Ogden, UT (11/28/68) (63-09; 75-33)

69-01   Prayer at convening of Utah State House of Representatives (1/13/69)

69-02   "The Certainty of the Resurrection," Gen. Conf., *Imp. Era* (June 1969), 55

69-03   "The Lamanite and the Gospel," BYU (6/13/69); FPM 339 (responsibility to aid Indians)

69-04   "A Good Deal," Beneficial Life convention, Santa Barbara, CA (6/12/69) (insurance)

69-05   Seminar for new mission presidents (6/24/69)

69-06   "'I Know My Sheep and Am Known of Mine,'" MIA June Conf. (6/27/69)

69-07   Gen. Conf. meeting for patriarchs of the Church (10/3/69) (role of patriarch)

69-08   "Spiritual Reservoirs," Gen. Conf., *Imp. Era* (Dec. 1969), 47; FPM 109 (faithfulness, parental responsibility)

70-01   "Marriage," *Millennial Star* (April 1970), 2 (62-09)

70-02   "The Need for a Prophet," Gen. Conf., *Imp. Era* (June 1970), 92; FPM 313 (role of prophet)

70-03   "Goals," General Authorities workshop (4/8/70) (goal setting)

70-04   Funeral of James M. Smith (5/29/70) (Word of Wisdom)

70-05   Seminar for new mission presidents (6/23/70) (mission work)

70-06   "'God Hath Called Us to Peace,'" *Instructor* (July 1970), 233 (temple work)

70-07   "I Believe the Bible," *Millennial Star* (July 1970), 18 (revelation)

70-08   "Integrity in Insurance," Beneficial Life convention, Mexico City (7/9/70)

70-09   "The Years That the Locust Hath Eaten," Gen. Conf., *Imp. Era* (Dec. 1970), 73 (missed opportunities)

70-10   "The Church Expands," U of UT Institute (10/9/70)

70-11   "Leadership in the Stakes" (description of handling stake conferences)

70-12   UT State U Institute (12/13/70) (First Vision)
71-01   "I Learn the Law of Tithing," *Friend* (Jan. 1971), 34
71-02   General Authorities instruction (Jan. 1971) (handling stake conferences)
71-03   "Continuing Revelation," *Ensign* (Feb. 1971), 20
71-04   Meeting of Council of Twelve (spring 1971) (faithfulness, growth of Church)
71-05   "Decisions: Why It's Important to Make Some Now," *New Era* (April 1971), 2
71-06   "Voices of the Past, of the Present, of the Future," Gen. Conf., *Ensign* (June 1971), 16 (sexual sin)
71-07   Funeral of Michael David Maughan, SLC (4/24/71)
71-08   "Of Royal Blood," Lamanite Youth Conf. (4/24/71); *Ensign* (July 1971), 7 (Lamanites—race with great potential)
71-09   "A World Church," seminar for new mission presidents (6/21/71)
71-10   "The Royal Army," LDSSA and institute leaders at MIA June Conf. (6/27/71) (leadership)
71-11   "Near Enough," Beneficial Life convention (7/9/71) (service)
71-12   "Peter, My Brother," BYU (7/13/71) (greatness of Peter)
71-13   "Who Contendeth with the Almighty," prepared for Area Conference in Manchester, England, but not delivered (Aug. 1971)
71-14   "The Home and Love," draft of address prepared for Manchester, England (Aug. 1971)
71-15   Manchester, England, Area Conf. (8/28/71) (family training)
71-16   Manchester, England, Area Conf. (8/27/71) (missionary sacrifices)
71-17   "The Gospel Solves Problems of the World," BYU 10-stake fireside (9/26/71) (based on letter 10/14/70)
71-18   "Glimpses of Heaven," Gen. Conf., *Ensign* (Dec. 1971), 36; FPM 259 (righteousness) (cf. 49-04; 66-10)
71-19   "New Horizons for Homosexuals," pamphlet based on letter 0/0/66
72-01   "How Is the Missionary's Place of Assignment Determined?" *New Era* (Feb. 1972), 37
72-02   "Permissiveness," Ricks College (3/28/72) (abortion, sterilization, divorce)
72-03   "On Cheating Yourself," *New Era* (April 1972), 32 (wasted opportunities)
72-04   "What Manner of Men Ought Ye to Be," prepared for April 1972 Gen. Conf. but not used (Christ)
72-05   "Keep the Lines of Communication Strong," Gen. Conf., *Ensign* (July 1972), 37; FPM 137 (communication in marriage, prayer)
72-06   Ordination of Harold B. Lee as President of the Church (7/7/72)
72-07   "Integrity," Mexico Area Conf. (8/26/72)
72-08   Mexico Area Conf., young women's session, Mexico City (8/26/72) (chastity)
72-09   "How to Conduct Stake Conference," Regional Representatives (10/5/72)

72-10   "'We Thank Thee, O God, for a Prophet,'" Gen. Conf., *Ensign* (Jan. 1973), 33 (sustaining leaders)

72-11   "Church Growth and Lamanite Involvement," BYU (11/7/72)

72-12   "President Marion G. Romney: A Symbol of Righteousness," *Ensign* (Nov. 1972), 20

72-13   "From the Egg to Full Growth," Church College of Hawaii (12/1/72) (sin)

73-01   "The Mantle of the Prophet," Weber State College Institute (3/29/73) (divine authority)

73-02   "The Family Influence," Gen. Conf., *Ensign* (July 1973), 15 (child rearing)

73-03   "Advice to a Young Man: Now Is the Time to Prepare," *New Era* (June 1973), 8 (mission)

73-04   "Robert Louis Stevenson," Beneficial Life convention (6/5/73) (courage)

73-05   Munich Area Conf. (8/26/73) (revelation) (incorporates 60-09)

73-06   "The New and Everlasting Covenant," BYU 10-stake fireside (9/30/73) (marriage)

73-07   "The Image of a Stake," Regional Representatives (10/4/73)

73-08   "The Rewards, the Blessings, the Promises," Gen. Conf., *Ensign* (Jan. 1974), 14 (righteousness)

73-09   Rededication of South Africa to preaching gospel, Johannesburg (12/3/73)

73-10   "A Giant of a Man," funeral of Harold B. Lee (12/28/73); *Ensign* (Feb. 1974), 86

73-11   "President Spencer W. Kimball Ordained Twelfth President of the Church," report by David Mitchell, *Ensign* (Feb. 1974), 2 (press conference as new president [12/31/73])

74-00   Gen. Conf., welfare session (4/6/74), Conf. Report (April 1974), 184

74-01   "'When the World Will Be Converted,'" Regional Representatives (4/4/74); *Ensign* (Oct. 1974), 2 (missionary work)

74-02   "Guidelines to Carry Forth the Work of God in Cleanliness," Gen. Conf., *Ensign* (May 1974), 4 (sins of the world)

74-03   "What Do We Hear?" Gen. Conf., *Ensign* (May 1974), 45 (restoration)

74-04   "Planning for a Full and Abundant Life," Gen. Conf., priesthood session, *Ensign* (May 1974), 86

74-05   "The Cause Is Just and Worthy," Gen. Conf., *Ensign* (May 1974), 118 (Christ)

74-06   Commencement at Church College of Hawaii (4/13/74) (build home communities)

74-07   Dedication of Utah Granger North Stake (4/28/74) (sacrifice, missionary work)

74-08   Salt Lake Valley Young Adults fireside (4/28/74) (Christ)

74-09   Layton Region youth conference (5/5/74) (sin)

74-10   "What Is True Repentance?" *Ensign* (May 1974), 4

74-11   Commencement at Snow College (6/1/74) (improve world)

74-12   Meeting for investigators, Tempe, AZ (6/7/74) (Christ, restoration) (75-11)
74-13   "Small Acts of Service," MIA June Conf. (6/21/74); *Ensign* (Dec. 1974), 2; *New Era* (Sept. 1974), 4
74-14   Seminar for new mission presidents and Regional Representatives (6/27/74) (missionary work)
74-15   Sevier Stake Conf., Richfield, UT (7/7/74) (bad habits)
74-16   Devotional at Expo '74, Spokane (7/24/74) (missions, temple marriage)
74-17   Mormon Pioneer Day Festival, Expo '74, Spokane (7/24/74) (pioneer self-reliance)
74-18   "Stand by Your Guns," prepared for Expo '74, Spokane (7/24/74) but not used (moral pollution)
74-19   Dinner for stake presidencies, Spokane (7/24/74) (preparation for missions)
74-20   Beneficial Life convention, Snowmass, CO (Aug. 1974) (integrity)
74-21   "Marriage—the Proper Way," prepared for Stockholm Area Conf., youth meeting (8/17/74) but not used; *Ensign* (Feb. 1975), 2; *New Era* (Feb. 1976), 4
74-22   Stockholm Area Conf. (8/17/74) (missionary work, chastity, marriage)
74-23   "Home: the Place to Save Society," Stockholm Area Conf. (8/17/74); *Ensign* (Jan. 1975), 2
74-24   Stockholm Area Conf., youth meeting (8/17/74) (resist evil)
74-25   Stockholm Area Conf., priesthood session (8/18/74) (priesthood, missions, sacrifices)
74-26   Stockholm Area Conf. (8/18/74) (summary)
74-27   "Be Ye Therefore Perfect," BYU (9/17/74); U of UT Institute (1/10/75) (cf. 75-01)
74-28   Dedication of Bountiful 2nd and 21st Ward chapel (9/22/74) (sacrifices, missionary work)
74-29   "Lengthening Our Stride," Regional Representatives (10/3/74) (missionary work)
74-30   "God Will Not Be Mocked," Gen. Conf., *Ensign* (Nov. 1974), 4 (live commandments)
74-31   "Ocean Currents and Family Influences," Gen. Conf., *Ensign* (Nov. 1974), 110
74-32   "The Davids and the Goliaths," Gen. Conf., priesthood session, *Ensign* (Nov. 1974), 79 (temptation)
74-33   Priesthood leadership meeting, Holbrook, AZ (10/20/74) (chastity, missions)
74-34   Dedication of Sandy North Stake center, Sandy, UT (11/10/74) (strengths of Church)
74-35   Dedicatory prayer, Washington, D.C., Temple (11/19/74)
74-36   " 'What Think Ye of Christ?' " Church employees Christmas devotional (12/12/74)

74-37	"Integrity," Salt Lake Rotary Club (12/17/74)
74-38	Monument Park 2nd Ward, SLC (12/22/74) (life of Christ)
74-39	Special Interest fireside (12/29/74) (marriage, meeting difficulties)
75-01	"Eternal Vigilance—The Price of Victory and Perfection," U of UT Institute (1/10/75) (honesty) (cf. 74-27)
75-02	BYU (2/25/75) (Indian Book of Mormon heritage)
75-03	Sao Paulo Area Conf. (3/1/75)
75-04	Sao Paulo Area Conf., parents meeting (3/1/75)
75-05	Sao Paulo Area Conf., youth meeting (3/1/75)
75-06	Sao Paulo Area Conf., priesthood session (3/2/75)
75-07	Sao Paulo Area Conf. (3/2/75)
75-08	Buenos Aires Area Conf. (3/8/75)
75-09	Buenos Aires Area Conf., parents meeting (3/8/75)
75-10	Buenos Aires Area Conf., youth meeting (3/8/75)
75-11	Buenos Aires Area Conf., priesthood session (3/9/75)
75-12	Buenos Aires Area Conf. (3/9/75)
75-13	" 'Why Call Me Lord, Lord, and Do Not the Things Which I Say?' " Gen. Conf., *Ensign* (May 1975), 4 (live commandments)
75-14	"To Bear the Priesthood Worthily," Gen. Conf., priesthood session, *Ensign* (May 1975), 78 (transgressors, pride, youth, gossip)
75-15	"Why Do We Continue to Tolerate Sin?" Gen. Conf., *Ensign* (May 1975), 107 (temple, unchastity)
75-16	Dedication of remodeled Arizona Temple (4/15/75)
75-17	"Spiritual Aspects of Americanism," Dixie College (4/25/75)
75-18	Lamanite Conf., San Diego North Stake (5/3/75) (pride in being Lamanite, missions)
75-19	Meeting for investigators, San Diego (5/3/75) (preexistence, Christ, restoration) (74-12)
75-20	"Honesty," regional youth fireside, Safford, AZ (5/17/75)
75-21	"The Example of Abraham," *Ensign* (June 1975), 3 (magnifying priesthood)
75-22	Baccalaureate at UT State U (6/4/75) (spirituality, leadership)
75-23	Seminar for new mission presidents (6/20/75)
75-24	"The Lord's Plan for Men and Women," MIA June Conf. (6/27/75); *Ensign* (Oct. 1975), 2 (family)
75-25	MIA June Conf. (6/29/75) (righteousness)
75-26	Pioneer Day Town Meeting, Logan, UT (7/23/75) (pioneer sacrifices)
75-27	Public meeting, Chattanooga, TN (7/25/75) (Church growth, morality) (cf. 75-28; 65-02)
75-28	Youth conf., Murfreesboro, TN (7/26/75) (morality) (cf. 75-27; 65-02)
75-29	Dedication of Chattanooga 1st and 2nd Wards (7/26/75) (life pattern of faithful)
75-30	Tokyo Area Conf. (8/9/75) (temples)

75-31   Tokyo Area Conf. (8/9/75) (chastity)
75-32   Tokyo Area Conf., parents meeting (8/9/75) (family)
75-33   Tokyo Area Conf., priesthood session (8/10/75) (missions)
75-34   Tokyo Area Conf. (8/10/75) (temple work)
75-35   Manila, Philippines, Area Conf. (8/11/75) (righteousness, temple)
75-36   Manila, Philippines, Area Conf. (8/12/75) (priesthood, missions)
75-37   Hong Kong Area Conf. (8/13/75) (temples, missions)
75-38   Taipei, Taiwan, Area Conf. (8/14/75) (temples, missions)
75-39   Seoul, Korea, Area Conf. (8/16/75) (temples)
75-40   Seoul, Korea, Area Conf., youth meeting (8/16/75) (chastity)
75-41   Seoul, Korea, Area Conf., parents meeting (8/16/75) (family)
75-42   Seoul, Korea, Area Conf., priesthood session (8/17/75) (priesthood)
75-43   Seoul, Korea, Area Conf. (8/17/75) (temple work, missions)
75-44   "Always a Convert Church," *Ensign* (Sept. 1975), 2 (scriptures, fellowship)
75-45   "The Most Perfect Personage Was the Most Perfect Teacher," seminary and institute teachers, SLC (9/12/75) (teach with testimony, missions, morality)
75-46   "The Blessings and Responsibilities of Womanhood," R.S. Gen. Conf. (10/2/75); *Ensign* (March 1976), 70
75-47   "The Time to Labor Is Now," Gen. Conf., *Ensign* (Nov. 1975), 4 (clean up, Sabbath, missionary work, morality)
75-48   "The Privilege of Holding the Priesthood," Gen. Conf., priesthood session, *Ensign* (Nov. 1975), 77; *New Era* (Oct. 1978), 44 (Articles of Faith, becoming gods, Christ)
75-49   "Spoken from Their Hearts," Gen. Conf., *Ensign* (Nov. 1975), 111 (conference)
75-50   "There Is Still Much to Do," Gen. Conf., welfare session, *Ensign* (Nov. 1975), 128
75-51   "BYU's Second Century," BYU (10/10/75), *BYU Studies* (summer 1976), 445
75-52   "The Angels May Quote from It," *New Era* (Oct. 1975), 4 (journals)
75-53   "Our Paths Have Met Again," *Ensign* (Dec. 1975), 2 (restoration of Lamanites)
75-54   Holladay stakes, SLC (11/26/75) (gratitude) (63-09; 68-12)
75-55   Christmas interview (living the gospel)
76-01   "We Should Be a Reverent People," pamphlet published by Church 1976
76-02   Centennial, Parowan, UT (1/12/76) (town history)
76-03   "Revelation and the 89th Section," public meeting in Cleveland, OH (1/30/76) (restoration, Word of Wisdom)
76-04   Pago Pago, Samoa, Area Conf., special session (2/15/76)
76-05   Apia, Samoa, Area Conf. (2/17/76)
76-06   Apia, Samoa, Area Conf., priesthood session (2/17/76)

76-07   Apia, Samoa, Area Conf. (2/18/76)
76-08   Temple View, New Zealand, Area Conf. (2/21/76)
76-09   Temple View, New Zealand, Area Conf., priesthood session (2/21/76)
76-10   Temple View, New Zealand, Area Conf. (2/22/76)
76-11   Suva, Fiji, Area Conf. (2/23/76)
76-12   Nuku'alofa, Tonga, Area Conf. (2/24/76)
76-13   Nuku'alofa, Tonga, Area Conf. (2/25/76)
76-14   Nuku'alofa, Tonga, Area Conf., priesthood session (2/25/76)
76-15   Melbourne, Australia, Area Conf. (2/28/76)
76-16   Melbourne, Australia, Area Conf. (2/28/76)
76-17   Sydney, Australia, Area Conf., priesthood session (2/28/76)
76-18   Sydney, Australia, Area Conf. (2/29/76)
76-19   Brisbane, Australia, Area Conf. (2/29/76)
76-20   Brisbane, Australia, Area Conf. (3/1/76)
76-21   Papeete, Tahiti, Area Conf., priesthood session (3/2/76)
76-22   Papeete, Tahiti, Area Conf. (3/2/76)
76-23   "Relief Society: Its Promise and Potential," *Ensign* (Mar. 1976), 2 (service)
76-24   "Family Preparedness," Gen. Conf., welfare session, *Ensign* (May 1976), 124
76-25   "The Stone Cut Without Hands," Gen. Conf., *Ensign* (May 1976), 4 (work, pay debts, restoration)
76-26   "Boys Need Heroes Close By," Gen. Conf., priesthood session, *Ensign* (May 1976), 45; incorporated in *Priesthood* (Deseret Book, 1981), 1
76-27   "Seeking Eternal Riches," Gen. Conf., *Ensign* (May 1976), 107 (gospel living, testimony)
76-28   Easter, Scottsdale, AZ, Stake Conf. (4/18/76)
76-29   "The False Gods We Worship," *Ensign* (June 1976), 3
76-30   "The Winning of the West," Rotary Club, SLC (6/8/76) (pioneers, U.S. history)
76-31   Special conf., Rexburg, ID (6/13/76) (hardships from breaking of Teton Dam)
76-32   Manchester, England, Area Conf. (6/19/76)
76-33   Manchester, England, Area Conf., priesthood session (6/19/76)
76-34   London Area Conf. (6/20/76)
76-35   Glasgow, Scotland, Area Conf. (6/21/76)
76-36   Glasgow, Scotland, Area Conf., priesthood session (6/21/76)
76-37   "Jesus the Businessman," Beneficial Life convention, Sun Valley, ID (7/16/76) (Jesus as supervisor of salesmen for the gospel)
76-38   Paris Area Conf. (7/31/76)
76-39   Paris Area Conf., priesthood session (7/31/76)
76-40   Paris Area Conf. (8/1/76)
76-41   Helsinki Area Conf., priesthood session (8/2/76)

76-42   Helsinki Area Conf. (8/2/76)
76-43   Helsinki Area Conf. (8/3/76)
76-44   Copenhagen Area Conf. (8/4/76)
76-45   Copenhagen Area Conf., priesthood session (8/4/76)
76-46   Copenhagen Area Conf. (8/5/76)
76-47   Amsterdam Area Conf., priesthood session (8/7/76)
76-48   Amsterdam Area Conf., (8/7/76)
76-49   Dortmund, W. Germany, Area Conf. (8/8/76)
76-50   Dortmund, W. Germany, Area Conf. (8/8/76)
76-51   "How Rare a Possession—The Scriptures!" *Ensign* (Sept. 1976), 2
76-52   "Marriage and Divorce," BYU (9/7/76); excerpted in *Ensign* (Mar. 1977),
          3; published in *Marriage* (Deseret Book, 1978)
76-53   "The Priesthood," Monument Park Stake Conf., SLC, priesthood session
          (9/12/76)
76-54   "A Report and a Challenge," Gen. Conf., *Ensign* (Nov. 1976), 4
76-55   "Loving One Another," Gen. Conf., welfare session, *Ensign* (Nov. 1976),
          127 (care for aged, teaching children to work)
76-56   "Our Own Liahona," Gen. Conf., priesthood session, *Ensign* (Nov. 1976),
          77 (conscience)
76-57   "A Program for Man," Gen. Conf., *Ensign* (Nov. 1976), 110 (God is in
          charge)
76-58   Dedication of Fair Oaks Stake center, Fair Oaks, CA (10/9/76) (Church
          growth, missionary work)
76-59   "The Matter of Marriage," U of UT Institute (10/22/76); excerpted in
          Ensign (Oct. 1979), 3
76-60   Tangerine Bowl, Orlando, FL (12/18/76) (family)
76-61   Fireside in Orlando, FL (12/19/76) (missions, temple marriage)
77-01   "The Things of Eternity—Stand We in Jeopardy?" *Ensign* (Jan. 1977), 3
          (genealogy, temple)
77-02   "Jesus: The Perfect Leader," Young Presidents Organization, Sun Valley,
          ID (1/17/77); *Ensign* (Aug. 1979), 5
77-03   Mexico City Area Conf. (2/13/77)
77-04   Mexico City Area Conf. (2/13/77)
77-05   Monterrey, Mexico, Area Conf. (2/20/77)
77-06   Monterrey, Mexico, Area Conf. (2/20/77)
77-07   Monterrey, Mexico, Area Conf., priesthood session (2/20/77)
77-08   Guatemala City Area Conf. (2/22/77)
77-09   Guatemala City Area Conf., priesthood session (2/22/77)
77-10   San Jose, Costa Rica, Area Conf. (2/23/77)
77-11   San Jose, Costa Rica, Area Conf., priesthood session (2/23/77)
77-12   Lima, Peru, Area Conf. (2/26/77)
77-13   Lima, Peru, Area Conf., priesthood session (2/26/77)
77-14   Lima, Peru, Area Conf. (2/27/77)

77-15   Santiago, Chile, Area Conf. (3/1/77)
77-16   Santiago, Chile, Area Conf. (3/1/77)
77-17   Santiago, Chile, Area Conf., priesthood session (3/1/77)
77-18   La Paz, Bolivia, Area Conf., women's session (3/3/77)
77-19   La Paz, Bolivia, Area Conf., priesthood session (3/3/77)
77-20   Bogota, Colombia, Area Conf. (3/5/77)
77-21   Bogota, Colombia, Area Conf., priesthood session (3/5/77)
77-22   Bogota, Colombia, Area Conf. (3/6/77)
77-23   Drafted for Gen. Conf., welfare session (4/2/77), but not used
77-24   "The Lord Expects His Saints to Follow the Commandments," Gen. Conf., *Ensign* (May 1977), 4
77-25   "Our Great Potential," Gen. Conf., *Ensign* (May 1977), 49 (resurrection, godhood)
77-26   "Revelation: The Word of the Lord to His Prophets," Gen. Conf., *Ensign* (May 1977), 76
77-27   "The Family Is Forever," meeting for investigators, Baton Rouge, LA (5/15/77)
77-28   Message in Kimball Family News (June 1977) (journal keeping)
77-29   "Temple Work for the Dead as Urgent as Missionary Work," genealogy seminar, SLC (8/4/77)
77-30   Youth fireside of Woods Cross region, Bountiful, UT (8/28/77) (marriage, living righteously)
77-31   "Absolute Truth," BYU (9/6/77); *Ensign* (Sept. 1978), 3; based on letter 11/28/49
77-32   " 'It Becometh Every Man,' " *Ensign* (Oct. 1977), 3 (mission)
77-33   "Welfare Services: The Gospel in Action," Gen. Conf., welfare session, *Ensign* (Nov. 1977), 76
77-34   "The Foundations of Righteousness," Gen. Conf., *Ensign* (Nov. 1977), 4
77-35   "The Power of Forgiveness," Gen. Conf., priesthood session, *Ensign* (Nov. 1977), 45 (forgiving others)
77-36   "Jesus the Christ," Gen. Conf., *Ensign* (Nov. 1977), 73
77-37   "The Abundant Life," Weber State U (11/4/77), *Ensign* (July 1978), 3
77-38   Dedication of Utah Bountiful Stake tabernacle addition (11/6/77) (sacrifice)
77-39   Fireside, San Antonio (12/3/77) (family, Lamanites, church, Christ)
78-01   "The Sabbath—A Delight," *Ensign* (Jan. 1978), 2 (based on 44-03)
78-02   "Marriage and the College Student," Ricks College (2/5/78)
78-03   " 'Train Up a Child,' " *Ensign* (April 1978), 2
78-04   "Living the Gospel in the Home," Regional Representatives (3/31/78); *Ensign* (May 1978), 100
78-05   "Becoming the Pure in Heart," Gen. Conf., welfare session, *Ensign* (May 1978), 79 (self-reliance, unselfishness)
78-06   "The True Way of Life and Salvation," Gen. Conf., *Ensign* (May 1978), 4

78-07   "Strengthening the Family—The Basic Unit of the Church," Gen. Conf., priesthood session, *Ensign* (May 1978), 45 (media influences)

78-08   "Listen to the Prophets," Gen. Conf., *Ensign* (May 1978), 76 (morality)

78-09   "So Many Kinds of Voices," Long Beach, CA (4/9/78) (living together without marriage)

78-10   "The Ten Virgins," Las Vegas (4/16/78) (righteousness) (based on 57-02)

78-11   UT State U Institute (4/30/78) (permissiveness)

78-12   Missionary farewell for Richard Williams, Phoenix 25th Ward (5/14/78)

78-13   Special conf. of Hawaii Kauai Stake (6/11/78) (righteousness, missions)

78-14   "Sisters, Seek Everything That Is Good," dedication of Monument to Women, Nauvoo (6/28/78); *Ensign* (Mar. 1979), 2

78-15   "The Gathering of Israel," Honolulu Area Conf. (6/18/78) (Church growth, gathering)

78-16   "Do It!" Honolulu Area Conf. (6/18/78) (teach children, temples, prayer)

78-17   Beneficial Life convention, Tamarron, CO (7/13/78) (family, work)

78-18   Centennial, Snowflake, AZ (7/21/78) (pioneer accomplishments)

78-19   Young Adults, centennial, Snowflake, AZ (7/22/78) (neatness, live righteously)

78-20   Territorial Ball, SLC (7/22/78) (Mormon colonization)

78-21   10-stake fireside, Kansas City, MO (9/2/78) (righteousness) (cf. 57-02; 78-10)

78-22   Dedication of Independence, Missouri, Stake center (9/3/78) (based on 78-27) (live the gospel positively)

78-23   "On My Honor," BYU (9/12/78); excerpted in *Ensign* (April 1979), 2 (keeping promises) (cf. 79-17)

78-24   "Privileges and Responsibilities of Sisters," women's fireside (9/16/78); *Ensign* (Nov. 1978), 102; excerpted in *New Era* (Jan. 1979), 42

78-25   "'The Uttermost Parts of the Earth,'" Regional Representatives (9/29/78); *Ensign* (July 1979), 2 (missionary work)

78-26   "The Fruit of Our Welfare Services Labor," Gen. Conf., welfare session, *Ensign* (Nov. 1978), 74

78-27   "'Hold Fast to the Iron Rod,'" Gen. Conf., *Ensign* (Nov. 1978), 4 (do good) (cf. 78-22)

78-28   "Fundamental Principles to Ponder and Live," Gen. Conf., priesthood session, *Ensign* (Nov. 1978), 43 (honor womanhood, hunting, missionary work)

78-29   "An Eternal Hope in Christ," Gen. Conf., *Ensign* (Nov. 1978), 71

78-30   Johannesburg, South Africa, Area Conf., missionary meeting (10/23/78)

78-31   Johannesburg, South Africa, Area Conf. (10/24/78) (= FPM 305)

78-32   Johannesburg, South Africa, Area Conf. (10/24/78) (revelation)

78-33   Johannesburg, South Africa, Area Conf., priesthood session (10/24/78)

78-34   Montevideo, Uruguay, Area Conf. (10/27/78)

78-35 Montevideo, Uruguay, Area Conf. (10/27/78)

78-36 Montevideo, Uruguay, Area Conf., priesthood session (10/27/78)

78-37 Buenos Aires Area Conf. (10/29/78)

78-38 Buenos Aires Area Conf. (10/29/78)

78-39 Buenos Aires Area Conf., priesthood session (10/29/78)

78-40 Sao Paulo Area Conf. (11/4/78)

78-41 Sao Paulo Area Conf., priesthood session (11/4/78)

78-42 Sao Paulo Area Conf. (11/5/78)

78-43 "Putting Christ Back into Christmas," public meeting, San Diego (12/22/78)

78-44 "The Wondrous Gift," (pamphlet, Deseret Book, 1978) (Christmas gift to Savior) (cf. 58-14)

79-01 Hawaii Kahului Stake Conf. (2/11/79)

79-02 "The Savior: The Center of Our Lives," U of UT fireside (2/25/79); *New Era* (April 1980), 33

79-03 "Fortify Your Homes Against Evil," Gen. Conf., *Ensign* (May 1979), 4

79-04 "Applying the Principles of Welfare Services," Gen. Conf., welfare session, *Ensign* (May 1979), 98

79-05 "Preparing for Service in the Church," Gen. Conf., priesthood session, *Ensign* (May 1979), 47 (Wilford Woodruff)

79-06 "Let Us Move Forward and Upward," Gen. Conf., *Ensign* (May 1979), 82 (sin, missionary work)

79-07 "Images of the Past: The Mormon Pioneer Heritage," rededication of the Mormon Pioneer Memorial Bridge (4/21/79)

79-08 Kimball Family News (June 1979) (following Heber C. Kimball's example)

79-09 Houston Area Conf., women's session (6/23/79) (journals)

79-10 Houston Area Conf., priesthood session (6/23/79)

79-11 Houston Area Conf. (6/24/79)

79-12 Houston Area Conf. (6/24/79)

79-13 Toronto Area Conf., women's session (6/25/79)

79-14 Toronto Area Conf., priesthood session (6/25/79)

79-15 Toronto Area Conf. (6/26/79) (tithing)

79-16 Toronto Area Conf. (6/26/79)

79-17 "Integrity: The Spirit of BYU," BYU (9/4/79); excerpted in *Ensign* (Mar. 1980), 2 (cf. 78-23)

79-18 "The Importance of Celestial Marriage," *Ensign* (Oct. 1979), 3 (cf. 76-59; 78-02)

79-19 "The Role of Righteous Women," women's fireside (9/15/79); *Ensign* (Nov. 1979), 102

79-20 "We Need a Listening Ear," Gen. Conf., *Ensign* (Nov. 1979), 4

79-21 "Our Sisters in the Church," Gen. Conf., priesthood session, *Ensign* (Nov. 1979), 48; used in foreword to *Blueprints for Living* (BYU, 1980)

79-22   "Give Me This Mountain," Gen. Conf., *Ensign* (Nov. 1979), 78 (struggle to be worthy)

79-23   Dedication of Orson Hyde Memorial Garden, Jerusalem (10/24/79)

79-24   Auckland, New Zealand, Area Conf. (11/25/79) (growth of Church, missionary responsibility)

79-25   Sydney, Australia, Area Conf., priesthood session (12/1/79) (priesthood callings)

80-01   "Here and Now, Then and There," Young Women's fireside (3/22/80); *New Era* (July 1980), 9

80-02   "We Feel an Urgency," *Ensign* (Aug. 1980), 2; from talk to Regional Representatives (4/4/80)

80-03   "No Unhallowed Hand Can Stop the Work," Gen. Conf., *Ensign* (May 1980), 4

80-04   "Introduction to the Proclamation" and "Proclamation," Gen. Conf., *Ensign* (May 1980), 51 (restoration)

80-05   Dedication of the Fayette, New York, buildings, Gen. Conf., *Ensign* (May 1980), 54 (Christ lives)

80-06   "'Do Not Weary by the Way,'" Gen. Conf., *Ensign* (Nov. 1980), 76 (love)

80-07   "The Law of Tithing," Gen. Conf., welfare session, *Ensign* (Nov. 1980), 77

80-08   "A Deep Commitment to the Principles of Welfare Service," Gen. Conf., welfare session, *Ensign* (May 1980), 92

80-09   "'Let Us Not Weary in Well Doing,'" Gen. Conf., *Ensign* (May 1980), 80 (doing good)

80-10   Rochester Area Conf. (4/12/80)

80-11   Rochester Area Conf. (4/12/80)

80-12   Rochester Area Conf., priesthood session (4/12/80)

80-13   Jackson Area Conf., priesthood session (5/3/80)

80-14   Jackson Area Conf. (5/4/80)

80-15   Jackson Area Conf. (5/4/80)

80-16   Pasadena Area Conf., priesthood session (5/17/80)

80-17   Pasadena Area Conf. (5/18/80)

80-18   Pasadena Area Conf. (5/18/80)

80-19   St. Louis Area Conf., priesthood session (6/7/80)

80-20   St. Louis Area Conf. (6/8/80)

80-21   St. Louis Area Conf. (6/8/80)

80-22   Lakeland, FL, Area Conf., priesthood session (6/28/80)

80-23   Lakeland, FL, Area Conf. (6/29/80) (cf. MF 316)

80-24   Lakeland, FL, Area Conf. (6/29/80)

80-25   World Conference on Records, SLC (8/12/80) (family, record-keeping)

80-26   BYU graduation (8/15/80) (success)

80-27   "Acquiring Spiritual Literacy," BYU (9/30/80) (keep commitments, serve, marriage)

80-28	Ann Arbor, MI, Area Conf., priesthood session (9/20/80)
80-29	Ann Arbor, MI, Area Conf. (9/21/80)
80-30	Ann Arbor, MI, Area Conf. (9/21/80)
80-31	"Learn—Then Teach," Gen. R.S. meeting (9/27/80); *Ensign* (Nov. 1980), 102
80-32	"Families Can Be Eternal," Gen. Conf., *Ensign* (Nov. 1980), 4
80-33	"Ministering to the Needs of Members," Gen. Conf., priesthood session, *Ensign* (Nov. 1980), 45
80-34	"The Law of Tithing," Gen. Conf., welfare session, *Ensign* (Nov. 1980), 77
80-35	Manila, Philippines, Area Conf., women's session (10/18/80) (family)
80-36	Manila, Philippines, Area Conf., priesthood session (10/18/80) (priesthood)
80-37	Manila, Philippines, Area Conf. (10/19/80) (mission)
80-38	Manila, Philippines, Area Conf. (10/19/80) (restoration)
80-39	Hong Kong Area Conf., priesthood session (10/20/80) (priesthood)
80-40	Hong Kong Area Conf. (10/21/80) (mission)
80-41	Hong Kong Area Conf. (10/21/80) (restoration)
80-42	Taipei, Taiwan, Area Conf., priesthood session (10/22/80) (priesthood)
80-43	Taipei, Taiwan, Area Conf. (10/23/80) (mission)
80-44	Taipei, Taiwan, Area Conf. (10/23/80) (restoration)
80-45	Seoul, Korea, Area Conf., priesthood session (10/25/80) (priesthood)
80-46	Seoul, Korea, Area Conf. (10/26/80) (mission)
80-47	Seoul, Korea, Area Conf. (10/26/80) (restoration)
80-48	Tokyo Area Conf., priesthood session (10/30/80) (priesthood)
80-49	Tokyo Area Conf. (10/31/80) (mission)
80-50	Tokyo Area Conf. (10/31/80) (restoration)
80-51	Osaka Area Conf., priesthood session (11/1/80) (priesthood)
80-52	Osaka Area Conf. (11/1/80) (mission)
80-53	"President Kimball Speaks Out on Morality," *Ensign* (Nov. 1980), 94; *New Era* (Nov. 1980), 38; PKSO 1 (chastity)
80-54	"Jesus of Nazareth," *Ensign* (Dec. 1980), 3
81-01	"He Did It with All His Heart and Prospered," *Ensign* (Mar. 1981), 3 (tithing)
81-02	"Follow the Fundamentals," Gen. Conf., welfare session, *Ensign* (May 1981), 79 (share, live within means)
81-03	"We Are on the Lord's Errand," Gen. Conf., *Ensign* (May 1981), 78
81-04	"Rendering Service to Others," Gen. Conf., priesthood session, *Ensign* (May 1981), 45
81-05	"A Report of My Stewardship," Gen. Conf., *Ensign* (May 1981), 5
81-06	"President Kimball Speaks Out on Administration to the Sick," *New Era* (Oct. 1981), 44; PKSO 70
82-01	"'Therefore I Was Taught,'" *Ensign* (Jan. 1982), 3 (family, sabbath)

82-02   "Remember the Mission of the Church," Gen. Conf., *Ensign* (May 1982), 4
82-03   "The Lord Is at the Helm," Gen. Conf., *Ensign* (May 1982), 76
82-04   Gen. Conf. (10/2/82) (welfare of children, devotion)

Books

Books cited as sources are designated by initials, as follows:
MF   *The Miracle of Forgiveness* (Bookcraft, 1969), a treatise on sin and repentance.
FPM   *Faith Precedes the Miracle* (Deseret Book, 1972), 34 edited sermons.
PKSO   *President Kimball Speaks Out* (Deseret Book, 1981), nine articles appearing in the *New Era* (and in three instances in the *Ensign* as well) during 1980-81, drawn from earlier writings with minor additions.

Though not cited herein, other books by or concerning Spencer W. Kimball are:
Spencer W. Kimball, *One Silent Sleepless Night* (Bookcraft, 1975), childhood reminiscences.
Edward L. and Andrew E. Kimball, Jr., *Spencer W. Kimball* (Bookcraft, 1977), a biography.
A Noble Son: Spencer W. Kimball (Institute of Family Research, 1979), genealogy.
Caroline E. Miner and Edward L. Kimball, *Camilla* (Deseret Book, 1980), a biography of the wife of Spencer W. Kimball.

Letters

Letters listed as sources are identified by date, so far as known, and by subject matter. In nearly every case these are letters Spencer W. Kimball included in his collection of sermons because they had some broader interest than just to the addressee. Dates are unknown or uncertain for the first six letters listed.

1/0/00   Financial preparedness
2/0/00   Need for repentance
3/0/00   Worldliness
4/0/00   Interracial marriage
5/0/00   Interfaith marriage

0/0/45(?)	Political radicalism (cf. 77-22)
3/6/47	Testimony
10/29/47	Commitment to Church
1/9/48	Divine role of Christ
4/28/48	Orthodoxy, sustaining Church leaders
5/31/48	Chastity, missionary work, following leaders, ordinances, faith, suffering
2/11/49	Worldliness, service
11/28/49	Truth (cf. 71-31)
4/24/50	Sacrifice in mission
2/2/51	Repentance, missionary confrontation of sin
2/8/51	Limitations and deprivations as source of strength (S.W.K. personal experiences)
6/19/51	Divorce
7/30/53	Service to God first
12/22/55	Keeping commandments, diligence
0/0/56	Repentance, encouragement to missionary
12/17/56	Reactivation
9/6/57	Repentance
1/14/58	Encouragement to missionary
2/14/58a	Faith and testimony
2/14/58b	Tithing
2/20/58	Living up to potential
6/16/58	Temple, Word of Wisdom
11/19/58	Rewards of bishop's calling
12/30/58	Expectations of new members, apostasy, racism
0/0/59(?)	Interracial marriage
12/19/59	Gospel plan
1/5/60	Selfishness in marriage
10/19/62	Word of Wisdom
11/2/62	Intellectual vs. spiritual approach to learning
2/27/63	"Lamanite" not name to be resented
3/15/63	Covenants
5/2/63	Worthiness for partaking of sacrament
6/15/63	Patience in waiting on the Lord
8/28/63	Liquor and tobacco advertising
12/2/63	Part-member families
12/17/63	Apostasy, forgiving offenses
2/14/64	Encouragement to stake presidencies
2/20/64	Marriage, family, continued Church activity
8/13/64	Interfaith marriage
12/16/64	Suicide, adultery, sterilization

12/20/65	Homosexuality
0/0/66	Homosexuality (cf. 71-19)
2/28/66	Homosexuality
10/8/69	Tithing
10/10/69	Free agency, chastity
5/4/70	Homosexuality
10/14/70	Effectiveness of missionary work (cf. 71-17)

Index

clear, 156
searing, 87, 279
universal attribute, 113
Consecration, 155, 357, 364-65
Consolidated meeting schedule, 221, 493
Constantine, 426
Constitution, U.S., 405
Contemplation, 136
Contributions, generous, 211
"Contrite spirit," 88, 102
Conversion process, testimony-bearing, 138
Conversions, boasting of, 569
by Holy Ghost, 569-70
Converts, adjustment, 536
adult, 497
Church assignments, 259, 565
fellowshipping, 258-59, 555
minority, 260
poverty-stricken, 567-68
priesthood privilege, 495-96
prospective, 552
retention, 566
Cooperation, 363, 367, 420
Corruption, 171, 193
Cosmetics, 286-87
Council in heaven, 29-30
Council of the Twelve. See Quorum of the Twelve
Counseling, 475
Counselors, Church, 488
Courage, 14, 171, 431-32, 470-71
Courts, Church. See Church courts
Courtship, kissing, 281
on Sunday, 216
timing, 290
Covenants, fulfillment, 503
lightly taken, 195, 538
remembrance, 112, 226, 367, 503
Creatorship, 53, 499
Credit, 194
Criminality, 169
Criminals, 50
Critical members, 112
Criticism, of Church, 137, 182, 184, 240, 438, 460, 462
Cults, 462
Cultural arts, 384
Cursing. See Profanity
Customs duties, 197
Cynics, 487

—D—

Damnation, 110-11
Dancing parties, 290
Daniel, interpreted dream, 454
Dark ages, 424-25
Dating, 285-90
nonmembers, 300

Deacons, responsibilities, 145
Dead, the, 153, 541
Death, 15, 35
appointed unto, 511
character after, 41
free agency permits infliction of, 19
inevitable, 17, 37
meaning, 39, 45
"not taste of," 38
premature, 5, 39, 41
resurrection overcomes, 18
"tragic," 38
Deathbed repentance, 90
Debt, 14, 194, 196, 371, 373-74
Deception, 151-52, 204
Decision making, 25
Decisions, 164
Dedication prayers, 119
for homes, 339-40
Deformities, postmortal, 45
Degrees of glory. See Kingdoms of glory
Demands, on God, 512-13
Dependence, on God, 126
Depression (1929), 353
Deprivation, 98
Descendants, honorable, 156
Deseret News (newspaper), 413
Desires, 170-71, 276
Despondency, 106
Destiny, 27, 161
Detractors, in Church, 112
Developing areas, 567-68
Development, personal, 175-76
Devil. See Satan
Deviousness, 155
Devotion, 155
Lamanite, 178-79
Diet, 37
Difficulties, 254
Dignity, of man, 26, 405
Diligence, 173, 176-77
Diplomats, 587
Disarmament, 159
Disasters, 366
Discernment, 156
Disciples, 65
Discipleship, 176, 555
Discipline, for children, 340-41
inner, 170, 193
Discouragement, 91, 164
Discoveries, 392, 445
Discrimination, 236-40
Disfellowshipment, 98-100
Disfigurement, 37
Dishonesty, 148, 195, 197-98
Disillusionment, 128
Disobedience, 154-55
Distress, 168

priorities, 311
role, 316
selection, 303-4
student, 383
Women, development, 319-23
education, 383, 385-86
employment, 318
image, 25
life preparation, 295
opportunities, 328
respect, 317-18
scripture study, 129
service, 253
See also Single women; Wives; Mothers
Woodruff, Wilford, plural marriage, 457
Word of Wisdom, 41, 164, 201-5
Work, 359-62, 366, 369, 402
daily, 173
physical, 381-82
Sunday, 227-29
Works, and faith, 68, 71-72
judged according to, 70
World, conditions, 404, 408, 416-17, 438
evangelization, 545
physical, 171
spiritual, 24

World affairs, 257-58, 392
Worldliness, 236
Worry, 236
Worship, 2, 8, 30
Sabbath, 215, 219
spirit, 514-15
Worthiness, 29, 114
missionaries, 558-59, 561

—Y—

Young, Brigham, 42, 253, 378, 431-32
Youth, bishop's responsibility, 487
decisions, 165
family participation, 436, 492
rebelliousness, 528-29
scripture study, 129-30
social activities, 289-90

—Z—

Zest, for life, 186
Zion, 362-63
gathering to, 439-40